# THE MAKING OF
# URBAN AMERICA

# THE MAKING OF
# URBAN AMERICA

Raymond A. Mohl
Editor

Second Edition

A Scholarly Resources Inc. Imprint
Wilmington, Delaware

Scholarly Resources Inc.
104 Greenhill Avenue
Wilmington, DE  19805-1897

**Library of Congress Cataloging-in-Publication Data**

The making of urban America / Raymond A. Mohl, editor. — 2nd ed.
     p.     cm.
   Includes bibliographical references and index.
   ISBN 0-8420-2637-1 (cloth : alk. paper). — ISBN 0-8420-2639-8
(pbk. : alk. paper)
     1. Cities and towns—United States—History.  2. Urbanization—
United States—History.  I. Mohl, Raymond A.
HT123.M286    1997
307.76'0973—dc21                                                      97-2493
                                                                           CIP

⊗ The paper used in this publication meets the minimum requirements
of the American National Standard for permanence of paper for printed
library materials, Z39.48, 1984.

recycled paper

## About the Editor

RAYMOND A. MOHL is professor of history and chairman of the department at the University of Alabama at Birmingham. Previously he taught for twenty-six years at Florida Atlantic University. He graduated from Hamilton College, earned the M.A.T. at Yale University, and received his Ph.D. in history from New York University. He is the author, coauthor, or editor of ten books including *Poverty in New York, 1783–1825* (1971); *The Paradox of Progressive Education: The Gary Plan and Urban Schooling* (1979); *The New City: Urban America in the Industrial Age, 1860–1920* (1985); *Steel City: Urban and Ethnic Patterns in Gary, Indiana, 1906–1950* (1986); *Searching for the Sunbelt* (1990); *Urban Policy in Twentieth-Century America* (1993); and *The New African-American Urban History* (1996). He was the founding editor of the *Journal of Urban History* in 1974 and served as associate editor for book reviews from 1977 to 1995.

Professor Mohl has held Fulbright lectureships at Tel Aviv University, the University of Göttingen, and the University of Western Australia, as well as research fellowships from the National Endowment for the Humanities and the American Council of Learned Societies. He has won several teaching and writing prizes and in 1997 served as president of the Urban History Association. Currently he is completing a book on the history of race relations in the Miami metropolitan area.

# Contents

# Preface

Urban history has come a long way since the 1960s when scholars first began the systematic exploration of the American urban experience. Influenced by the new social history and by contemporary concerns about the "urban crisis," as it was then called, younger historians began delving into the history of the city. Over time, the subjects of urban history inquiry, the research strategies, the methodologies, and the interpretations have changed. But from the perspective of thirty years the results of this academic excursion into urban history have been impressive. We now have a much richer and fuller understanding of the American historical experience as a consequence of the research carried out by several generations of urban historians. It is a diverse body of research, reflecting the vast canvas of American urban life.

This second edition is designed to introduce students of urban history to recent interpretive literature in the field. Its goal is to provide a coherent framework for understanding the pattern of American urbanization, while at the same time offering specific examples of the work of historians in the field. The material presented in this book illustrates many of the important questions, issues, and interpretive ideas that American urban historians have been pursuing over the past decade. None of the essays presented here was published before 1985, and most are more recent than that. Only two of the essays from the first edition have been carried over into this second edition. Three of the pieces included are original essays published here for the first time. Taken together, and reflecting the nature of contemporary urban history research, the essays in this book emphasize the social and cultural history of the city, but political and economic dimensions are not completely ignored. As in the first edition, the essays are presented within a three-part chronological context covering the preindustrial city, the industrial city, and the twentieth-century city. Each section begins with a narrative introduction laying out the pattern of urban development during that period. These introductions have been revised and rewritten in part; they have been updated with new demographic and political data where necessary. Population tables have been added to the introductory section on the industrial city, and in Part Three the tables have been revised to include changes reported in the 1990 census. The bibliographical essay in Part Four has been extensively revised and expanded to reflect the outpouring of new work in the field since the first edition was published in 1988. Many urban historians who have used the first edition in their classes have provided useful evaluations of the book as a teaching tool. Their thoughtful suggestions have helped to shape the material included in this second edition.

*Raymond A. Mohl*

Part One

The Preindustrial City

# Introduction

Late twentieth-century Americans live in an urban age. The process by which a group of small colonial settlements in an untamed wilderness grew into a highly industrialized and urbanized nation is one of the central themes of American history. Over a period of almost 400 years, as the United States moved from colonial status to the modern era, Americans passed from a society characterized by small farms and villages to one dominated by huge central cities and massive sprawling suburbs. An understanding of the dynamic forces and values that nurtured, stimulated, and shaped American urban development is essential in comprehending the contours and the complexities of contemporary America.

Town, village, and urban life emerged quite early during the American colonial period. British and European settlers congregated in seaport towns and villages from the very beginning of the colonization effort. Many of the first colonists had been town or city dwellers in England or Europe, and they brought to the American wilderness urban values, attitudes, and aspirations. Although the populations of most colonial communities remained small throughout most of the prerevolutionary period, each colonial settlement, village, or town to some degree served traditional urban functions—that is, they became centers for the exchange of goods, services, and ideas. By the end of the seventeenth century, colonial Americans had created a fairly dynamic urban society. The larger seaport cities of Boston, Philadelphia, New York, Charleston, and Newport, all of which had populations ranging from about 2,000 to 6,700, exercised an influence throughout the colonies far out of proportion to their relatively small populations.

Several forces promoted colonial urban growth. In the early stages of settlement and on the colonial frontier, newcomers gathered together for security and mutual defense. Such primitive colonial communities were often surrounded by a wall or wooden stockade, as in Plymouth, Jamestown, and Savannah, while others were clustered around a fortress, as in New York, Charleston, St. Augustine, and Mobile. Most of these early defensive communities rapidly became agrarian towns. This pattern prevailed especially in New England, where a community-centered society required towns to regulate effectively social and religious life. Town building was also promoted by English or European merchant companies. Jamestown, Plymouth, New York, New Haven, and other colonial towns had such origins. English entrepreneurs and

investors viewed towns as necessary for successfully tapping the raw
materials and resources of the New World. Thus, they not only sponsored much of the early colonization effort but also provided the capital
and manpower needs required to sustain the new overseas outposts during the early difficult years of community building.

Many of the largest colonial towns grew because of their political
and administrative functions. British mercantilist policies required a
close supervision and regulation of colonial trade. Moreover, each colony
had its governing center: the residence of the colonial governor, the location of the administrative offices of government, and the meeting
place of the colonial assembly. The imperatives of mercantilism and
colonial government encouraged urban development, even in the southern colonies where geography and emerging agricultural and land distribution patterns militated against town life. As historical geographer
Carville V. Earle has suggested, "English colonizers everywhere regarded
towns as indispensable frontier cultural institutions. Colonization was
unthinkable without them."[1]

Above all, commercial activity in the colonies stimulated urbanization. During the seventeenth century, port towns such as Boston and
Philadelphia grew rapidly as a consequence of the economic demands
generated by new immigrant families. By the end of the seventeenth
century, colonial merchants and entrepreneurs had developed profitable
trading networks based on staple products derived from the New World
environment. Built primarily on the products of an extractive economy—
fish and furs, tobacco and rice, wheat and indigo, lumber and livestock,
naval stores and minerals—colonial trade with Britain, Europe, Africa,
and the West Indies expanded and prospered. Returning ships carried
new immigrants, slaves, sugar, manufactured goods, and products un-
obtainable in the New World. Intensive commerce of this kind promoted
the growth of seaport towns and cities up and down the Atlantic coast-
line.

Ultimately, these urban places became market cities where goods
changed hands. As some urban geographers have noted, the colonial
seaport cities served as an economic "hinge," as central points for the
collection of staple agricultural products for export and for the distribution of imported goods throughout the surrounding hinterland. In addition, the export-import function stimulated numerous supplementary
industries in the towns. Most ports became centers for flour milling,
shipbuilding, the processing of naval stores, and other simple manufacturing. Numbers of small shops produced rope, sails, barrels, and other
products, while a growing class of urban craftsmen serviced expanding
town and city populations. As a result of these advances in craft and
commerce, the colonial economy prospered at times. The gradual expansion of the domestic market strengthened the cities' economic role, thus
further intensifying the urbanizing trend.

The primacy of the colonial cities' economic functions contained the
seeds of future social and political change. As historian Gary B. Nash
has noted in *The Urban Crucible* (1979), the economically developing
colonial seaport cities experienced social and class distinctions at a very

early date. Although geographical mobility was always high, upward social and economic mobility was more limited in the cities than in other segments of colonial society. The continuous influx of new immigrants tended to keep wages down and economic opportunity circumscribed. More so than in agricultural and frontier regions, the colonial cities experienced a growing gap between the rich and the poor. In Boston, for instance, the class of propertyless laborers was increasing twice as rapidly as the population as a whole by the time of the American Revolution. In Philadelphia, the richest 5 percent of the population controlled equally as much wealth as the rest of the population combined. Thus, class lines were hardening by the mideighteenth century. At the same time, the colonial dependence on commerce meant that the New World settlements had become part of an intricate web of world trade, subject to economic fluctuations due to war, depression, inflation, currency declines, and falling crop prices. As a result, most of the colonial urban economies suffered periodic economic stagnation and often severe problems of unemployment, poverty, and poor relief.

These social and economic conditions influenced the development of urban political thinking and political action. From the beginning, colonial society had been strongly deferential in nature—that is, it was a society in which people knew their place and accepted it, in which the middle and lower classes generally yielded decision-making authority to the local political and economic elites. However, people at every level of society shared certain basic assumptions about the mutual obligations of classes and the need for social harmony, good government, and personal liberty. When the urban elites challenged or undermined or violated these assumptions, the middle and lower classes often abandoned deferential attitudes and asserted their collective power in the streets in the form of the mob or riot to protect the old values and restore the old order. By the mideighteenth century, moreover, the growth of the market economy, with the new emphasis on individual profit and the new reality of periodic depression, led to lower-class discontent, a decline of deference, and the rise of a popular and participatory politics in the seaport cities. As the artisans and the urban working classes developed an increasingly radical political consciousness, they began to take charge of their lives in new and dramatic ways. These changes, initiated in the colonial towns and cities, unleashed forces that hastened the coming of the American Revolution.

Indeed, the impact of the city on the coming of the Revolution cannot be overestimated. As urban historian Stanley K. Schultz has contended, "without urban grievances, the American Revolution never would have occurred."[2] During the revolutionary crisis, the colonial cities emerged as important centers of radical activity and propaganda. Based in the seaports, many colonial merchants saw urban prosperity and their own profits threatened by new British taxes and economic policies. The boycotts organized by the urban merchants and implemented in the port towns helped strike down the hated Stamp Act and the Townshend duties. The dissatisfaction and radicalism of urban workers, artisans, and sailors, stimulated by unemployment and the economic pressures of the

1760s, found frequent outlets in mobs and riots; the Sons of Liberty was primarily an urban group. For many patriots, mob actions against the British seemed a legitimate expression of popular sentiment. Pivotal events such as the Boston Massacre originated in the conflict between colonial urbanites and British troops stationed in the cities, while the Boston Tea Party reflected urban concerns about Parliamentary control of the economy. Such urban radical organizations as the Boston Committee of Correspondence, along with widely read city newspapers, filled the countryside with revolutionary propaganda and justifications for independence. The emergence in the cities by the mideighteenth century of a popular tavern culture provided a public arena for discussion, debate, and revolutionary propaganda. And, as historian Arthur M. Schlesinger suggested many years ago, the patterns of community life over the course of the colonial period offered a sort of "training in collective action" upon which patriot leaders drew during the intensifying revolutionary crisis.[3]

The urban dimension of American life during the colonial period, then, was significant and influential in several respects. The colonial towns and cities became the economic, political, and cultural centers of a sparsely populated agricultural hinterland. They provided the arena for the emerging market-oriented commercial economy, which in turn pulled the American colonies into the wider, more interdependent, and more fragile network of world trade. Social and economic stratification intensified as the urban populations grew, stimulating discontent, some class conflict, and a new emphasis on democratic and participatory urban politics. As deference declined in the cities, simultaneous movements began seeking both independence from Great Britain and social and democratic change in America. By the end of the revolutionary era, about 5 percent of the American population—some 200,000 people—lived in twenty-four urban places of 2,500 or more residents. The proportion of urbanites was relatively small, but the growing cities dominated their surrounding regions and stimulated social, economic, and political change.

In the years between the American Revolution and the Civil War, the United States was transformed by the emergence of a capitalist marketplace, involving the cotton kingdom in the South, an agrarian empire in the West, and the beginnings of industrialization in the East. The dramatic rise of an urban marketplace became indispensable to the progress of the national economy. The pace of urbanization accelerated considerably. New York emerged as a sort of "primate" city, a national metropolis dominating the economy of the entire country. A city of about 33,000 in 1790, New York increased in population by more than 50 percent each decade until 1860 (with the exception of the 1810 to 1820 period). By 1860 more than 800,000 people crowded the island of Manhattan. The other eastern seaports also grew into large commercial metropolises. Philadelphia's 28,000 people of 1790 had multiplied to more than 565,000 by the time of the Civil War. Brooklyn, a small suburb of less than 5,000 in 1790, had become the nation's third-largest city by 1860 with a population of over 265,000. Boston and Baltimore also increased their populations at substantial rates during the early nineteenth century. The east coast seaports constituted a regional system of cities. These marketplace cities each depended on overseas commerce for growth and prosperity while continuing to serve as regional marketing and distribution centers for expanding agricultural hinterlands.

Urbanization also spread into the interior of the continent during these preindustrial years. In the trans-Appalachian region, two new systems of cities spearheaded the westward movement and the settlement of the frontier. One group of cities sprouted along the Ohio and Mississippi rivers. Experiencing similar patterns of development, the cities of Pittsburgh, Louisville, Cincinnati, St. Louis, and New Orleans emerged as regional marketing and early processing or manufacturing centers. Spurred by transportation innovations, notably steam navigation and canal building, a second system of cities grew up along the shores of the Great Lakes—Buffalo, Cleveland, Detroit, Chicago, and Milwaukee. Although Cincinnati was being promoted as the "Queen City" of the West and had become the nation's third largest manufacturing center by the Civil War, it was clear that Chicago was rising quickly as the western metropolis. These ten western or interior cities, which by 1860 ranged in population from about 45,000 to nearly 170,000, gave an urban aspect to the westward movement and to American society generally.

The catalyst for western urbanization was the transportation revolution of the early nineteenth century. New York merchants and promoters were especially active in supporting new transportation innovations, which in large measure accounted for the great success of the eastern metropolis. Perhaps more than any other single accomplishment, the opening of the Erie Canal in 1825 assured the commercial primacy of New York City. The completion of the Erie route set off a wave of canal building and then railroad construction, as other eastern cities sought to compete with New York for the trade and produce of the Ohio Valley. This so-called urban imperialism not only hastened the completion of new transportation arteries but also fostered urbanization in the western regions and along the routes of the new canals and railroads. A whole string of cities grew up along the Erie Canal route between Albany and Buffalo.

Commerce and shipping, along with a host of supplementary trades and businesses, fueled the urban economy during most of this period. However, new technology as reflected in the steam engine and in textile machinery, the creation of the transportation network, and the growth of the domestic market in the midnineteenth century turned cities increasingly toward production for internal consumption. Factory production began in such industries as cotton textiles, woolen goods, finished clothing, boots and shoes, leather items, and iron products. Western cities, drawing on local resources and agricultural production, turned to flour milling, brewing, meat packing, mining, and lumbering. In New England, textiles and the footwear industry fostered the development of a number of smaller factory towns such as Lawrence, Lowell, Lynn, Haverhill, Fall River, New Bedford, and Manchester. A similar shift toward manufacturing was evident elsewhere, too, as cities ranging from Richmond and Lexington in the South to Newark, Paterson, Providence, Albany, and Troy in the North turned to factory production. By the 1850s the factory had become a recognizable feature of the urban landscape. Nevertheless, the commercial role of the cities remained predominant until the second half of the nineteenth century. By 1860, according to economic historian Eric Lampard, of the nation's fifteen largest cities, only five had more than 10 percent of their work force engaged in manufacturing. Thus, the industrial takeoff had not yet fully begun.

Like the growing factories, the social and political conditions of the preindustrial cities provided some hints about the shape of the urban future. European immigration, for instance, had begun to have a significant impact on the urban population. The immigrant tide began slowly at first in the early decades of the nineteenth century. During the 1830s, however, more than 490,000 newcomers arrived on American shores. Throughout the 1840s, European immigration to the United States surged to more than 1.4 million, and during the 1850s the seaborne influx almost doubled to over 2.6 million. Mostly Irish, English, and German, these newcomers received their first introduction to American life in the immigrant arrival ports of New York, Boston, Philadelphia, Baltimore, San Francisco, and New Orleans. Large numbers moved on to interior towns or settled in the midwestern farm belt. But many remained in the cities, where their influence was increasingly felt in politics, culture, and the workplace. By 1860 immigrants made up more than 50 percent of the populations of St. Louis, Chicago, Milwaukee, and San Francisco. Close behind were New York, Buffalo, Cincinnati, Cleveland, and Detroit, where the proportion of foreign-born ranged from 45 to 48 percent of the total city population.

Internal migration and geographical mobility also affected the growing cities. While newcomers from abroad flooded into urban America in unprecedented numbers, native-born migrants from the farm and from rural towns boosted city populations as well, especially at first in the Northeast and then in the Midwest. This pattern continued into the late nineteenth century, as new agricultural technology began to displace the rural peasantry of farm workers and hired hands. In addition, a substantial degree of population turnover within the cities contributed to the pace of urbanization and social change. Many early nineteenth-century observers noted the transiency and the migratory habits of the lower stratum of urban society. The working classes and the poor were often described as a "floating" population, or as being "constantly on the wing." Immigrants and natives alike passed in and out of the cities in search of jobs, better housing, or more opportunity. According to a study by urban historian Peter R. Knights, population turnover in Boston amounted to about 30 percent per year in the 1830s and 1840s and 40 percent per year in the 1850s.[4] This sort of intensive internal migration and mobility reflected the dynamic character of the urbanization process in the United States, even in the preindustrial period.

While immigration and internal migration altered the composition and character of the American urban population, the preindustrial cities changed in other ways as well. The larger cities, for instance, had begun to experience to a limited degree some of the problems that later plagued city people and municipal governments. Pre-Civil War urban growth was disorderly and unplanned, as the older cities outgrew the more regular street plans of the colonial era. Heavy population increases imposed pressure on limited housing resources; immigrants, workers, and the urban poor crowded into densely packed apartments, tenements, cellars, and shacks. Public health measures remained primitive, and most cities experienced periodic epidemics of typhoid, yellow fever, and cholera, often with devastating consequences. Poverty, unemployment, crime, and violence became common. A rage of urban riots afflicted most large cities in the 1830s and 1840s, reflecting social, economic, religious, racial, and ethnic tensions. As these and other problems developed, city governments seemed weak and ineffective. Municipal governments were slow in providing services to the citizenry, and they were generally unable to regulate the bigger, more populous, more heterogeneous, and more socially unstable city of the midnineteenth century.

By the 1850s, therefore, the transition from the preindustrial to the modern industrial city was nearly complete. The transitional process actually had been under way for some time. The colonial city was truly preindustrial in the sense described by sociologist Gideon Sjoberg in his classic study, *The Preindustrial City* (1960), in which he stated that the preindustrial city was characterized by the marketplace function and by patterns of handicraft and artisanal manufacturing. Animate sources of power—that is, human or animal power—were used in the system of production. Preindustrial urban workers labored in small shops with a few other craftsmen and apprentices. There was little specialization of work or division of labor. Using hand tools and individual skills, urban artisans created a finished product out of raw material. Skill was important and was transferred through the apprenticeship process.

The social organization of the preindustrial city was characterized by a relatively high degree of order and stability as well as by a shared sense of community. Social segregation was rather limited, and rich and poor lived close together, although they were not necessarily neighborly. Land uses were unspecialized, and very often living and working quarters were one and the same. Business and the household were intimately connected. Ethnic and religious homogeneity generally prevailed, although social diversity was on the rise by the revolutionary era. The social and political structure was dominated by a literate elite. In this hierarchical and deferential society, upward economic and social mobility was limited. Kinship ties were important, the extended family was more typical than not, and communication and personal contact were usually of the face-to-face variety. A sense of localism predominated, and change and innovation came slowly, if at all. All of these social and economic patterns prevailed in the American colonial town and city throughout most of the prerevolutionary period.

The first half of the nineteenth century, by contrast, was a period of substantial change—of transition and modernization. For example, the system of production began to undergo changes. The small shop pattern

of the colonial years increasingly gave way to factories by the 1830s and
1840s. New technology brought new machinery, especially in textiles,
supplanting the hand tools of the urban craftsman. The social organization of work was revolutionized in the factory setting. Skill became less
important, since machines rather than men were doing the job. Division
of labor and specialization of tasks rationalized the production process,
but the constant repetition of a single task meant a lifetime of mindless
monotony for the worker. New sources of inanimate power—first the
harnessing of waterpower to drive gears, shafts, and pulleys, and later
the application of the steam engine to operate factory machinery—replaced the human and animal power of earlier years. Communication
and transportation were speeded by the invention of the railroad and
the telegraph, thus contributing to a breakdown of localism and person-
alized human contacts.

    Similarly, the social order experienced changes during the early nine-
teenth century. By the 1830s increasingly heavy immigration and a substantial degree of rural-to-urban internal migration undermined social,
ethnic, and religious homogeneity. The shared sense of community of
the colonial town began to disappear, along with deferential attitudes
and adherence to generally accepted behavioral norms. A new working-
class political culture emerged by the 1820s and 1830s, accompanied by
an engaged rhetoric of "republicanism," as craftsmen responded to the
reorganization of work patterns and the beginnings of industrialization.
Mobility, at least of the geographical or residential sort, intensified—a
development reflecting a loosening of the ties binding the individual to
kin and community. Chances for upward economic mobility do not seem
to have been improved by the breakdown of traditional society, for the
loss of skill and the rise of the factory and commercial capitalism meant
that individuals had less control over their economic destiny. In the
modernizing city itself, various spatial changes were becoming recognizable. Land uses became more specialized and functional, as sections
of the growing cities were given over to residential, retail, and productive purposes. A more sharply defined class structure accompanied the
midnineteenth-century transformation of urban America. Social segregation increased as immigrants, workers, and the poor crowded older
housing in city centers, while the urban political and economic elites, as
well as the rising middle class, moved from the center toward the
periphery.

    Above all, change and innovation were becoming commonplace. The
fixed and timeless character of the preindustrial society was weakening
before the forces of nineteenth-century change. The patterns of the transitional city also set the stage for the tremendous surge of urbanization
and industrialization during the second half of the nineteenth century.

The essays in Part One demonstrate some of the interpretive
concerns of recent historians about the early American town and
city. GARY B. NASH's essay offers a new interpretive model for understanding the dynamics of urban social development in eighteenth-
century America. The colonial cities, Nash notes, were located at the

cutting edge of economic, social, and political change. His essay portrays urban change as an evolutionary process that reshaped community patterns, social networks, and group experience in the
preindustrial city. Drawing on the exciting research of a new generation of urban and social historians, Nash reveals the growing ethnic,
religious, and racial diversity of the early American city, a social pluralism that challenged and reshaped established ideas about community, conformity, and deference. New social realities were imposed
on the cities by the growing numbers of free urban blacks and by
a widening gap between rich and poor. The social geography of the
urban areas also began to change, and physical growth was accompanied by spatial segregation of social and economic groups. Nash
emphasizes the resilience of the human spirit—the ability of
urban people to cope and adapt, individually and collectively, to the
changing urban environment. In particular, the rise of a popular and
participatory politics, along with the emergence of voluntary associations, reflected the active role of city people in adjusting and adapting to change. The social forces underlying the American Revolution
carried into the early nineteenth century and formed the basis for
new conceptions of community, social institutions, and political
participation.

    TIMOTHY J. GILFOYLE uses that ubiquitous urban institution—prosti-
tution—as a prism through which to view the changing social character
of the early American city, especially new conceptions of gender and shifting patterns of rioting and collective action in New York City. Recent
European and American interpretations of mob and crowd behavior have
emphasized the organized and purposeful, but limited and symbolic,
nature of much early American rioting. When well-established traditions or deeply held values were violated by the seemingly arbitrary
actions of political or economic leaders, Americans often took their grievances to the streets. This "republican" tradition of crowd action continued well into the early nineteenth century. However, Gilfoyle has
uncovered a newer, more frequent, more spontaneous, and more unrestrained tradition of urban violence and rioting directed against prostitutes and brothels in the 1830s and 1840s. Especially notable in these
sprees of violence were gangs of drunken young men, part of an emerging male subculture in the rapidly growing city, a subculture freed from
familial restraints and bound together by new patterns of communal
drinking. To a certain extent, Gilfoyle attributes this new form of urban
collective behavior to changing gender roles, as working women asserted
a more public presence while a simultaneous "cult of domesticity" was
also developing. Violence against prostitutes thus reflected more widespread mysogynist attitudes toward women in public life: "gender became a sufficient cause for violence." But Gilfoyle also finds a political
dimension to these new forms of urban violence, as emerging political
machines used street gangs to regulate brothels and control the profits
of commercialized sex in the city. This essay, introducing issues of gender, sexuality, violence, and collective behavior, offers an entirely new
way of thinking about the social history of the early American city.

In his essay on the impact of European immigrants in pre-Civil War southern cities, RANDALL M. MILLER provides abundant evidence to contradict some well-established historical interpretations about the American South. Generally, the South has been portrayed as rural and agrarian, with little social or cultural distinction between countryside and city. More particularly, the traditional argument runs, European immigrants were attracted to northern cities and repelled by the idea of competing with slave labor, leaving the white populations of southern cities ethnically and culturally homogeneous. By contrast, and surprisingly, Miller's essay demonstrates not only the rapid urban growth in the South between 1820 and 1860 but also the high proportions of immigrants attracted to economic opportunities in southern port and river cities. By the time of the Civil War, most southern cities had developed a substantial white, ethnic working class that shared few of the cultural values of the Old South. These immigrant workers caused a restructuring of urban labor markets, disrupted established patterns of race relations, and altered the physical landscapes of southern cities. Assimilating slowly, if at all, these pre-Civil War immigrants to the urban South challenged mainstream regional cultural values and posed problems of social order and social control. Eventually, they asserted political influence through the vote and through domination of some types of city jobs—the Irish, for example, came to dominate the police forces in New Orleans, Memphis, Charleston, and Savannah. Immigrant influences on southern cities diminished greatly after the Civil War, but Miller's essay provides a persuasive antidote to established interpretations of antebellum urban life in the South.

In the final essay in this section, MARY RYAN illustrates new ways of conceptualizing an emerging urban popular culture in the early nineteenth century. Focusing on parades in New Orleans, San Francisco, and New York City, she offers a sophisticated interpretation built on the social theory of the German philosopher, Jürgen Habermas. According to Habermas, new forms of popular discourse and behavior developed in Europe and the United States by the end of the eighteenth century. These changes fostered a "public sphere" in which citizens assembled to express opinions or otherwise engage in collective action. The end of old regimes and the institution of protections for freedom of expression unshackled the press and opened avenues for public assembly and association. In postrevolutionary urban America, massive parades quickly assumed the role of great patriotic and civic ceremonies celebrating national holidays, important anniversaries, or other significant events. These parades initially were very inclusive, incorporating virtually all elements of the early American social order—merchants and businessmen, military groups, voluntary associations, artisans and craftsmen, unskilled laborers, and so on (although women were generally excluded)—all marching in hierarchical fashion in separate units or platoons. Ryan contends that these ritualized public performances, with their positive affirmations of the democratic spirit, served unifying functions in an urban society undergoing the strains of rapid growth and change. Over time, however, the social composition and the social purposes of the American parade changed. By the 1850s merchants, shop-keepers, and skilled artisans had dropped out of these civic ceremonies, leaving the parade mostly to the industrializing laboring classes, especially the immigrant Irish and Germans. Rising ethnicity challenged the social functions of the parade as an inclusive and unifying cultural event, while the wealthy and the native-born retreated to the private sphere of business and family. Other scholars, too, have explored the newly conceptualized public sphere, finding widespread use of city streets as an arena for varied forms of public expression. As Ryan and others point out, the streets of the early American city came to be invested with symbolic importance in the performance of public ritual, the display of collective action, and, ultimately, the quest for group power.

These four essays only begin to suggest the diversity and richness of recent historical interpretation on the preindustrial American city. They do, however, serve to introduce the reader to the historical imagination at work.

## NOTES

1. Carville V. Earle, *Geographical Inquiry and American Historical Problems* (Stanford, CA: Stanford University Press, 1992), 84.
2. Stanley K. Schultz, "The Growth of Urban America in War and Peace, 1740–1810," in *The American Revolution: Changing Perspectives*, ed. William M. Fowler, Jr., and Wallace Coyle (Boston: Northeastern University Press, 1981), 127.
3. Arthur M. Schlesinger, "The City in American History," *Mississippi Valley Historical Review* 27 (June 1940): 46.
4. Peter R. Knights, *The Plain People of Boston, 1830–1860: A Study in City Growth* (New York: Oxford University Press, 1971).

# The Social Evolution of Preindustrial American Cities, 1700–1820

*Gary B. Nash*

As the eighteenth century began, the population of Boston, the largest city in the English overseas world, stood at 7,000. New York City bustled with 5,000 inhabitants, while the villages of Philadelphia and Charleston, with only a few score buildings that had progressed beyond frame to brick structures, had about 2,000 people each. Four generations later, as the century ended, Boston had grown to 25,000, New York to 60,000, Philadelphia to 62,000, Charleston to 13,000, and Baltimore, a newcomer on the urban scene, to 27,000. Twenty-eight other towns exceeded 2,500 inhabitants, and just over 6 percent of the American population lived in urban centers of more than 2,500. Much greater growth lay just ahead, with Philadelphia and New York burgeoning to 118,000 and 131,000, respectively, by 1820. But even as Thomas Jefferson assumed the presidency, population increase and commercial development had reconfigured what had been an almost cityless landscape at the beginning of the century into one studded with urban places. Relative to England, probably the most urbanized country in the world in 1800, the United States lagged behind by half a century. Occupied after the Revolution in the business of expanding across the continent, land-hungry Americans remained largely a rural people for more than a century. Hence, not until 1840 would the United States be able to match the 15 cities over 20,000 in population that England boasted in 1800, and not until the 1880s would 30 percent of the population live in towns of 2,500 or more, as did this percentage of the English population in 1800.[1] Nor would the kind of industrial cities that grew so rapidly in the second half of the eighteenth century in England—cities such as Manchester, Liverpool, and Birmingham—be found in America at this time (Table 1). Yet like all modern nations, the United States was

*Gary B. Nash is professor of history at the University of California, Los Angeles. Reprinted from* Journal of Urban History *13 (February 1987): 115–45. Copyright 1987 by Sage Publications. Reprinted by permission of Sage Publications.*

launched on the historic course that would make it a nation of urban
rather than rural people.

### Table 1. Population of English and American Cities, 1700–1800

| 1700 | 1750 | 1800 |
|---|---|---|
| Norwich (30,000) | Norwich (36,000) | Manchester (90,000) |
| Bristol (20,000) | Bristol (25,000) | Liverpool (88,000) |
| Manchester (10,000) | Birmingham (24,000) | Birmingham (74,000) |
| BOSTON (7,000) | Liverpool (22,000) | Bristol (64,000) |
| Leeds (6,000) | Manchester (19,000) | PHILADELPHIA (62,000) |
| Birmingham (6,000) | BOSTON (16,000) | NEW YORK (61,000) |
| NEW YORK (5,000) | NEW YORK (13,000) | Leeds (53,000) |
| Liverpool (5,000) | PHILADELPHIA (13,000) | Norwich (37.000) |
| Portsmouth (5,000) | Sheffield (11,000) | Bath (34,000) |
|  | Portsmouth (10,000) | Portsmouth (33,000) |
|  | Leeds (10,000) | Sheffield (31,000) |
|  |  | BALTIMORE (27,000) |
|  |  | BOSTON (25,000) |

Sources: C. W. Chalkin, *The Provincial Towns of Georgian England* (London, 1974); B. R.
Mitchell, *European Historical Statistics, 1750–1820*, 2d ed. (New York, 1980); Gary B. Nash,
*The Urban Crucible: Social Change, Political Consciousness, and the Origins of the American
Revolution* (Cambridge, MA, 1979); U.S. Bureau of the Census, *Return of the Whole Number
of Persons within the Several Districts of the United States [1800]* (Washington City, 1802).

What did it mean for an urban center to increase from 5,000 to 60,000
over four generations? How did social relations, political life, and patterns of association change in the course of such development? Elsewhere I have argued that the seaboard cities were at the cutting edge of
change in early America. It was here that almost all the alterations associated with the advent of modern capitalist society first occurred, and
then slowly radiated outward to the small farming communities of the
hinterland. In the colonial cities, people first made the transition from
an oral to a literate culture, from a moral to a market economy, from an
ascriptive to a competitive social order, from a communal to an indi-
vidualistic orientation, from a hierarchical and deferential policy to a
participatory and contentious civic life. In the cities factory production
first began to replace small-scale artisanal production, and the first
steps were taken to organize work by clock time rather than by sidereal
cycles. These were, in fact, among the critical changes that Ferdinand
Tönnies identified as constituting the transition from *gemeinschaft* to
*gesellschaft*—a historic process that he identified as quintessentially an
urban phenomenon.[2]

How, amid such changes, did urban people experience life differently
and, most important, how did they confront these changes? Following
Thomas Bender's seminal suggestion, I propose that we reconsider the
*gemeinschaft* to *gesellschaft* formulation of change in which the vocabulary of analysis is composed of words like decay, decline, dissolution,
and disintegration of community. This analytic model is not without its
uses for urban historians. However, enough has been discovered about
the dynamics of urban social development in eighteenth-century towns
to keep us mindful that communities change at different rates of speed,

sometimes in different directions, not always in unilinear fashion, and rarely with all members of the community cleaving to the same values and responding identically to the same stimuli. Moreover, the organizing notion of decline and decay implicitly, if unintentionally, consigns to a passive role the city dwellers themselves, and especially those who were most adversely affected by change.[3]

The tendency has been almost irresistible to interpret the rise of materialistic, self-interested, contentious, class-oriented urban polity as a sign of social declension and shattered harmony. As in most things, we look backward to what we imagine were better days—a simpler time when mutuality, order, and a universal regard for the commonweal prevailed. Social cohesion and harmony, alas, were never so prevalent in the prerevolutionary cities as sometimes imagined, even if the richest and poorest inhabitants lived next door to each other, even if the poor were succored with familial forms of relief, even if journeymen lived with masters and worked with them under one roof. Moreover, the emerging urban social order of the late eighteenth century, while at many times difficult and hardly bearable, brought compensating advantages that offset some of the strains. Free black Americans, for example, were usually denied respect and equal access to jobs, education, and political rights when they migrated into these cities; but none of them would have traded their lot for their prior status as slaves, for freedom in the postrevolutionary cities, with all its disadvantages, was preferable to slavery, even in its mildest forms. Struggling shoemakers in the age of Jefferson no longer lived across the street from the mayor or worshiped in the same church as lofty merchants; but such socially integrating mechanisms had never guaranteed them employment in "the old days." Moreover, in their emerging working-class neighborhoods, where they frequented their own taverns, churches, and craft organizations, they found the opportunity to create a stronger culture of their own than had proven possible in the more class-mixed and socially mobile cities of the eighteenth century. Journeymen no longer lived with the master and ate at his table, but when it came time to vote, they were more likely to be found at the polls and went there more autonomously than before. *Gesellschaft*, in some of its forms, was in fact more likely to occur in cities where growing social stratification and social zoning occurred than in the less stratified and more socially integrated cities of the past.

Bender aptly asks: "Why cannot *gemeinschaft* and *gesellschaft* simultaneously shape social life," for both are "forms of human interaction that can act reciprocally on each other?"[4] Extending this, it may be asked whether homogeneity and smallness are the indispensable elements of community and viable social relations. In seeking to substitute new paradigms of social change for the overused *gemeinschaft* to *gesellschaft* model, it may be best to begin by observing life as close to the street level and the kitchen hearth as possible, searching for signs of how urban people struggled to create, adapt to, oppose, defend, or legitimize new circumstances. Rather than nostalgically tracing the *eclipse* of community, we need to trace the continuously evolving *process* of community. We need to look for the *different* meanings (rather than

the *less satisfactory* ones) that urban life took and the various strategies of living that people devised as their cities grew in size and complexity. In important ways, this article argues, the kinds of structural
changes occurring in the cities created conditions that encouraged—even
necessitated—the fabrication of communities within communities by
energized and mobilized groups that had previously often been politically and socially quiescent and detached from group activity, except in
churches.

E ven in their earliest years, the capitals of Massachusetts, Pennsylvania, New York, and South Carolina were not so ethnically and
religiously homogeneous as is sometimes supposed. But they were relatively unified by their settlers' common religious orientations and social
backgrounds, with East Anglican Puritans, Dutch Calvinists, English
Quakers, and West Indian Anglicans shaping the early social contours
of the four provincial capitals respectively. This religious homogeneity
broke down rapidly in Manhattan in the late seventeenth century and
in Philadelphia and Boston in the eighteenth, despite efforts to maintain it in Boston and because no one attempted to maintain it in Philadelphia. After the Peace of Utrecht in 1713, Philadelphia became the
port of entry for thousands of immigrants from Ulster, the Rhine, the
West Indies, and other points of the compass. In Boston, although as
late as 1718 five boatloads of Ulster immigrants would be hustled out of
town and directed to the New Hampshire frontier, the process eventually was much the same. Street signs would never be rendered both in
German and English in John Winthrop's Boston, as in William Penn's
Philadelphia, but the immigrants came, particularly after the Revolution, when the volume of immigration was heavier than previously believed according to recent estimates, to complete the process that the
early town fathers had so much feared—the diversifying of a community formerly composed of supposedly like-minded souls.[5]
    Urban historians still know very little about the exact patterns of
migration—from the rural hinterland, from other mainland colonies, and
from overseas—that spurred growth and turned American towns into
ethnic and religious bouillabaisses that in England had a counterpart
perhaps only in Liverpool and London. But while the timing and dynamics of this rapid diversifying of the urban populaces is murky, the
overall effects would have been obvious to any visitor strolling the streets
of the major seaport cities on a Sunday morning in 1800. In Philadelphia, for example, such a visitor would have witnessed people crowding
into thirty-five churches representing fourteen denominations and eight
ethnic groups, whereas a century before worshipers had attended only
the churches of four English denominations and one Swedish chapel.
Even in Boston, less than half the size of Philadelphia, nineteen churches
of eight denominations existed at the end of the eighteenth century.[6]
    Amid this growing cosmopolitanism, religious persecution, if not re-
ligious prejudice, faded. In the process, the early Boston meaning of
"community"—a collection of like-minded believers who extended to
"strangers" only the freedom "to be gone as fast as they can, the sooner

the better"—was eclipsed by the Philadelphia meaning of "community"—
a collection of believers, disbelievers, mystics, agnostics, and nihilists
who learned to see themselves linked to those around them by material
rewards and social necessities rather than by heavenly quests. In this
growing acceptance of the idea that diversity could be the cement rather
than the dissolvant of unity lay the roots of the pluralism that was to
become a mainstay of American society. That it set American cities off
from their English counterparts, London excepted, seems apparent from
the comments of English visitors, who often remarked on the
multichromatic and multilingual melanges in the American cities.

One immigrant group of a special character, largely absent in every
English town except London, figured importantly in the urban landscape.
At the beginning of the century the cities contained only small numbers
of America's involuntary immigrants—the sons and daughters of Africa.
But their proportion of the population grew rapidly between 1720 and
1760, spurred by the demand for labor in the growing towns and, during
the Seven Years' War, by the nearly complete stoppage of the indentured servant trade. Boston's slave population grew from about 300 to
1,544 between 1710 and 1752; slaves in New York City increased so rapidly in the same era that by 1746 half the white households held slaves.
In Philadelphia, where those investing in bound labor had chosen Irish
and German indentured servants more often than African slaves in the
first half of the century, merchants and artisans alike purchased record
numbers of Africans during the Seven Years' War, multiplying the black
population to above 1,400 by war's end. In Charleston, capital of the
colony with the highest proportion of slaves in British North America,
54 percent of the city's 11,000 residents were slaves by 1770.[7]

In the last third of the century, however, this rapid growth of black
laborers underwent two enormous changes. First, slave imports to the
growing cities came to an abrupt halt except in Charleston. The depression that followed the Seven Years' War convinced many urban capitalists of the advantages of free laborers, whom they could hire and fire as
economic cycles dictated. The growth of abolitionism in the cities and
their occupation by the British during the Revolution put the finishing
touches on slave imports. All over the northeastern seaboard the black
slave populations in the cities plummeted in the revolutionary era, as
dying slaves went unreplaced by new recruits from Africa and as younger
slaves fled to the British when they occupied the towns.

The second change was the dramatic rise of the free black populations in the postrevolutionary cities, including those in the South such
as Norfolk, Baltimore, Savannah, and Charleston. In the northern cities, just as quickly as the black slave population had diminished between 1765 and 1780, the free black population rose from 1780 to 1800.
Philadelphia, the southernmost of the northern cities, was especially
notable. Its free black population of perhaps 250 on the eve of independence approached 10,000 by 1810. Almost every northern seaport exerted a powerful magnetic force upon freed blacks, for the city
represented a place to make a living (which was very difficult in the
countryside for those lacking capital to invest in land and equipment), a

place to find marriage partners and compatriots, a place, in short, to start a community within a community.[8] In the southern cities, the free black population also grew rapidly, far outstripping increases in the white and slave populations. In Baltimore, where only a handful of free blacks resided at the end of the Revolution, nearly 6,000 free blacks congregated by 1810. Richmond and Petersburg, Virginia, and Charleston, South Carolina, all had free black communities exceeding 1,000 by 1810 (Table 2).[9]

America's northern city dwellers, in an average person's lifetime, witnessed the rapid growth of slavery, a sudden black depopulation during the war, the dismantling of urban slavery, and then a swift repopulation of the cities by free blacks, many of them streaming in from the hinterland and the upper South. New York lingered half a generation behind in this manumission process, and the southern cities represented a different case altogether, but in all the cities the urban character of modern Afro-American life was taking shape. When Cato, Cudgo, and Betty, who had formerly lived *in* the houses of merchants and artisans as lifelong servants, became Cato Freeman, William Thomas, and Elizabeth Anderson, who lived *down the street* as free persons who controlled their own destinies, white and black urbanites both had to make psychological adjustments. Some could not, and consequently the black emancipation process was fraught with difficulties. Nonetheless, growing black populations smithied out the elements of modern Afro-American life and culture on the anvil of urban coexistence with those who had formerly been their masters. In the southern cities (and in New York City until about 1820), free blacks lived precariously among blacks still enslaved. They too, albeit under more difficult circumstances, formed neighborhoods, established families, and organized churches, schools, and benevolent societies.[10] One important urban group had made the transition from individuals whose collective action was strictly prohibited to persons who eagerly formed religious and social groups and acted collectively in a number of other ways.

### Table 2. Urban Free Black Population, 1790–1810

|  | Free Black Popul. | | Percent Change, 1790–1810 | | |
|  | 1790 | 1810 | Free Blacks | Whites | Slaves |
| --- | --- | --- | --- | --- | --- |
| Boston | 761 | 1,484 | +95 | +90 | NA |
| Providence | 427 | 865 | +103 | +56 | -88 |
| New York | 1,101 | 8,137 | +639 | +192 | -29 |
| Philadelphia | 2,078 | 9.653 | +365 | +17 | -99 |
| Baltimore | 323 | 5,671 | +1,656 | +204 | +272 |
| Richmond | 265 | 1,189 | +349 | +138 | +153 |
| Petersburg | 310 | 1,089 | +251 | +92 | +72 |
| Charleston | 951 | 1,472 | +55 | +31 | +29 |

**Sources**: U.S. Bureau of the Census, *Heads of Families at the First Census of the United States Taken in the Year 1790: Pennsylvania* (Washington, DC, 1908); *Aggregate Number of Persons within the United States in the Year 1810* (Washington, DC, 1811).

Blacks emerging from the house of bondage in the late eighteenth-century cities sought opportunity as other poor immigrants had done for decades. The parallel was closest with those who had arrived as indentured servants and worked off their labor contract. However, manumitted blacks at the end of the eighteenth century (along with newly arriving immigrants) were entering an economy that differed markedly from that which humble aspirants had found before the Revolution. The early eighteenth-century towns were filled with men who had risen to modest wealth from artisan backgrounds, mostly through the mechanism of urban land speculation or military subcontracting in time of war. Still young and fluid, the cities were arenas of opportunity for the industrious and bold. Benjamin Franklin was everyone's model of the plucky, shrewd, and frugal leather-apron man who might advance rapidly from apprentice to journeyman to master. Many, like Franklin, watched their wives replace the pewter spoon and earthen porringer at the breakfast table with a silver spoon and china bowl, symbolizing the ascent beyond a "decent competency" that was the artisan's self-proclaimed goal in the preindustrial city. Of course, only a handful rose so rapidly and stylishly as Poor Richard in the early years; yet few ever imagined that their families would go hungry or that they might awaken one morning inside an almshouse. More and more that fate awaited those who entered urban life at the bottom of the social ladder in the last third of the century.

Even those who faithfully followed Poor Richard's precepts of industry and frugality sometimes fell into poverty in the prerevolutionary generation. Boston suffered earlier and more intensively than other towns, its economy wracked after the 1720s by war-induced inflation and heavy taxes and its coffers strained from supporting hundreds of war widows and their fatherless children. By midcentury, New England's commercial center was the widow capital of the Western world, with one of every three married women heading a husbandless household. By the early 1750s Boston officialdom was describing the abodes of the poor where "scenes of Distress we do often behold! Numbers of Wretches hungry and naked shivering with Cold, and, perhaps, languishing with Disease."[11] Although it has been axiomatic among historians that poverty corroded the lives of ordinary people to a far greater extent in English than in American towns, the selectmen, in this same year, ventured to claim that poverty was so widespread that they were obliged to expend relief monies double those of any town of equal size "upon the face of the whole Earth."[12]

In all the cities poverty spread during the deep recession following the Seven Years' War. Nobody in the cities of Cotton Mather, Robert Hunter, and James Logan could have imagined a report such as came from the Philadelphia almshouse managers, who wrote, as the Continental Congress was conducting its epic debate over independence a few blocks away, that "of the 147 Men, 178 Women, and 85 Children [admitted to the almshouse during the previous year] most of them [are] naked, helpless and emaciated with Poverty and Disease to such a

Degree, that some have died in a few Days after their Admission."[13] To control the strolling poor, whose support drove up poor taxes and whose very appearance threatened social disorder, town leaders tightened residency requirements, systematically examined and expelled nonresidents, and built workhouses and almshouses with harsh daily regimens to control those who qualified for relief.[14]

Research conducted by a second wave of those who have followed in the wake of the pioneering work done on tax lists a generation ago by Robert E. Brown and Jackson T. Main has led to the discovery that urban poverty on the eve of the Revolution was far more extensive than ever imagined. We now know that the tax lists that once were regarded as snapshots of the entire community do not include a very large group of urban adult males. In Providence and Newport, Rhode Island, for example, about 30 and 45 percent of all adult males were too poor to be included on the assessors' lists on the eve of the Revolution.[15] In Philadelphia, at least one fifth of the population, mostly people who lived as roomers in boardinghouses or rented back buildings, sheds, and crude apartments in alleys, courtyards, and side streets, is missing from the assessors' rolls.[16] This large floating population, associated conceptually with a society in which opportunities are restricted and in which geographical rather than social mobility gives rise to the term "strolling poor," lends an entirely new look to the contours of urban society on the eve of the Revolution. It was into this altered urban scene that newly emancipated blacks would stride during and after the war.

The postwar reconstruction of the American cities, most of which were physically ravished during the British occupation, by no means eliminated urban poverty. In fact, it grew as the cities suffered through several severe trade depressions in the decade after the Peace of Paris. Struggling to absorb new waves of immigrants, particularly poor Irish sojourners who often could not find work, urban people were also scourged repeatedly by yellow fever at the end of the century. In the worst microbic attack ever to afflict American cities, the fever struck unremittingly from New York to New Orleans in the 1790s, especially striking down laboring families who could not afford to flee to the countryside, as did their social superiors. In several cities yellow fever claimed nearly 10 percent of the population in a single year (which amounts to something like 15 percent of the working classes) and strained poor relief resources in every municipality.[17]

The urban centers of the new American republic, while busy centers of growing overseas trade and early manufacturing, also became the centers of the highest mortality, criminality, and poverty rates ever known on the eastern seaboard. What a visiting committee of the Methodist Hospitable Society found in Philadelphia in 1803 was by no means unusual. Prowling the back alleys and the laboring-class neighborhoods on the edge of the city, the Methodists described scores of families living "in rooms with shattered furniture, in tenements almost in ruins, [some] laying on straw with a few rags to cover them."[18] This kind of urban immiseration, primarily associated by historians with European cities or with the industrializing, immigrant-filled American cities of the midnineteenth century, was, in fact, much in evidence by the time of Jefferson's presidency.

Alongside urban poverty rose urban elegance, architecturally visible in the handsome Georgian mansions that rose in the cities in the last third of the century; and evident in the cobbled streets—twisted in Boston, curved in New York, and straight in Philadelphia—as a growing battalion of four-wheeled carriages rolled by. One of the by-products of this new urban wealth, which also produced a broader middle class than existed earlier, was the growth of a consumer ethos. The sheer range of articles available for purchase in the cities grew enormously in the eighteenth century, as can be traced in newspaper advertisements, in urban occupational specialization, and in inventories of wealth in the probate records.[19]

A revolution fought for liberty and equality, but also for property and the right to acquire it as plentifully and competitively as people knew how, did nothing to retard the polarization of wealth and the growing material appetites of middle- and upper-class urbanites. The Revolution, in fact, removed several obstacles to the quest for wealth. Among the casualties of the victory over England was the concept of the commonweal and of a corporate economy in which the guarantee of the right to eat outweighed private pursuit of gain. Such a traditional ideology, with roots deep in the medieval past, had been losing ground steadily in the eighteenth century, even among master craftsmen. However, it had a revival amid the millennial fervor of the early years of revolution, when many men hoped the conflict would achieve a double victory: independence from corrupt and oppressive England and self-purification through a restoration of civic virtue, Spartan living, and disdain for worldly things. The yearning of an urbanite like Samuel Adams for a return to ancestral virtue and communal attachment quickly dissipated, however, even before the war's end. The *novus ordo seclorum* that large numbers of city dwellers sought was not Adams's "Christian Sparta" but an unfettered stage on which a drama composed by Adam Smith could be played out by actors who spoke not of the fair wage and the just price but of the laws of supply and demand and the greater benefits to the community of unbridled competition and consumer choice freed from the restraining hand of government.

The changes wrought in the second half of the eighteenth century, during a protracted period of war, economic volatility, and commercial expansion, were systematically recorded in the tax lists and the probate records of the period. These records, although understating the case because they do not include large numbers of the poorest city dwellers, confirm what was evident architecturally in the cities—that a substantial redistribution of wealth occurred, particularly, it appears, in the period from 1740 to 1765 when a number of large fortunes, based on overseas trade and urban land speculation, created America's first truly wealthy urban elite (Table 3). More important than the shifting proportion of wealth held by each stratum of urban society was the fact that the concentration of the community's resources in the hands of the elite was accompanied by a hefty increase in the proportion of propertyless and indigent urban dwellers. This growing economic inequality might have continued for some time without objections if middle- and lower-class city dwellers had not seen the amassing of great fortunes as one of the main causes of the growing poverty and indigency that afflicted every city in the second half of the eighteenth century.[20] From the revolutionary era to the early nineteenth century, the distribution of urban wealth seems to have changed less rapidly. Then, during a period of early industrialization from about 1820 to 1850, a second major period of wealth redistribution further widened the gap between the top and bottom of urban society and left in the purses of the bottom half of society little more than 10 percent of the community's assets—about half as much as they had possessed a century before.[21]

### Table 3. Wealth Held by Richest Ten Percent of Urban Population

|                   | Late 17th Century | Mid-18th Century | Late 18th Century |
|-------------------|-------------------|------------------|-------------------|
| Boston (t)        | 46                | 64               | 65                |
| Boston (i)        | 41                | 60               | 56                |
| New York (t)      | 45                | 46               | 61                |
| Philadelphia (t)  | 45                | 66               | 61                |
| Philadelphia (i)  | 36                | 60               | 72                |

Sources: Nash, *Urban Crucible*, 395–98, Tables 3, 5; Allen Kulikoff, "The Growth of Inequality in Postrevolutionary Boston," *William and Mary Quarterly*, 28 (1971), 381; Billy G. Smith, "Inequality in Late Colonial Philadelphia: A Note on Its Nature and Growth," Ibid., 41 (1984), 629–45; Gloria Main, "Inequality in Early America: The Evidence from Probate Records of Massachusetts and Maryland," *Journal of Interdisciplinary History*, 7 (1977), 559–81; Bruce Martin Wilkenfeld, *The Social and Economic Structure of New York City, 1695–1796* (New York, 1978), pp. 161–62.

Note: t = based on tax assessment; i = based on probated inventories of wealth.

It has been suggested that these changes in the division of economic resources stemmed primarily from the increasing youthfulness of eighteenth-century American society and that propertylessness was primarily a function of "social age." The propertyless, according to this argument, were mostly younger sons waiting for their landed inheritance. Because they were increasing as a proportion of the population, it appears that wealth became less equally divided when, in reality, it was age inequality that had spread.[22] This argument may hold for rural communities where ownership of land was the rule and sons waited far beyond the taxable age of eighteen to acquire their fathers' estates. However, in the cities, where propertylessness was becoming the rule at the lower ranks of society, changes in the age structure of the population, according to the one empirical study available, do not account for the widening disparity between rich and poor.[23]

In urban centers, enhanced opportunities for amassing great wealth among those positioned advantageously increased the relative wealth of those at the top of the social pyramid. Meanwhile, depressed real wages (partly caused after the Revolution by the increase in immigrant labor available in the cities), cyclical economic buffetings that struck hardest at those with the thinnest margin of security, and the vengeful yellow fever of the 1790s, which was America's first class disease, appear to have been the main factors bearing on the deepening social inequalities. Benjamin Franklin Bache, a Philadelphia newspaper editor, understood the growing disparity of wealth in much this way. "Is it not heart rending," he wrote in 1797 "that the laboring poor should almost exclusively be the victims of the disease introduced by that commerce, which, in prosperous times, is a source of misery to them, by the inequality of wealth which it produces?"[24]

Although comparable data for provincial towns in England are not available, it seems possible, because the old English provincial towns were exporting their dispossessed while American seaboard towns were absorbing them, that by the end of the eighteenth century the American cities harbored as many or possibly more transient poor than their English counterparts. By 1790, if one can generalize from one case study of Philadelphia, more than a third of the population was too poor to pay even the most modest tax—and this ratio would increase to more than half by 1830.[25] The smokestack towns that were already growing rapidly in Manchester, Liverpool, and Birmingham were still a generation away in America as the eighteenth century closed, so the proper comparison is between the American cities and the older provincial towns such as Norwich, Bath, and Bristol. The unflattering comments of almost all Americans who traveled in England notwithstanding, American towns may have differed in their social structure from their English counterparts primarily in that the English urban poor were indigenous and white (and therefore noticed) whereas in America the poor were immigrant and black (and therefore overlooked).

While a century of urban growth increased the gap between gentry and common folk, it also transformed the spatial patterns of working and living, and, perforce, social relations. Much of the changing social geography stemmed from the rapid rise of urban land values in the old cores of the seaport towns. Before the Revolution, except in the stagnant town of Boston, land values multiplied many times, making real estate investment a greater source of wealth than trade. After the Revolution, land values again soared. In Manhattan, they climbed 750 percent between 1785 and 1815 alone, and a similar trend prevailed in other cities.[26] In Philadelphia, "A Friend to Equal Justice" complained bitterly in 1793 that rents (which reflected the market value of land) had doubled, trebled, and even quadrupled after Congress moved to Philadelphia from New York in 1789.[27]

The century-long rise of land values and rents, because it far outstripped advances in the wages of artisans and laborers, led to two historic changes in the social geography of the cities. First, property ownership became more concentrated in the hands of merchants, professionals, shopkeepers, and speculative builders. As the price of urban land spiraled upward, leather-apron men found that a building lot cost four or five years' wages, rather than the four or five months' pay it had cost their grandfathers earlier in the century. Hence, tenancy rates climbed from about 30 percent of all heads of household at the beginning of the eighteenth century to about 80 percent one hundred years later.[28] In Baltimore, a young town where the entire process of social formation lagged several generations behind that of the older cities, the proportion of lower artisans without real property increased from about 48 percent to 69 percent in a single decade after 1804.[29]

Second, facing the urban real estate market with wages that increased only slowly in the second half of the eighteenth century, working people were obliged to seek cheaper land and rental housing on the periphery of the city. This, in turn, led to another change—the separation of the place of residence from the place of production. Thus emerged the pattern of concentric residential zones that became common to all growing urban centers of the Atlantic basin. Towns whose neighborhoods had previously been integrated by occupation and class now began to develop a core dominated by the wealthy, a surrounding belt containing primarily the middle class, and a periphery populated by the laboring poor. This "social zoning," as Peter Clark has termed it, has been traced in several cities where inspection of the tax lists revealed median assessments in the core from four to ten times as great as on the outlying edges.[30]

Overlapping this increasing class segregation, which was still in the early stages at the beginning of the nineteenth century, was a growing racial clustering that occurred when free blacks establishing their own residences replaced slaves living with masters throughout the cities. The modern term "segregation," connoting a racial separation imposed by the dominant group, is not entirely appropriate in the early nineteenth-century American context because the concentration of black families in certain neighborhoods, as they worked their way free of the residual effects of bondage after the Revolution in the northern cities, or made their way thence from the upper South, was partly the result of their own desire to live near the independent black churches they built, near the schools associated with these churches, and near relatives, friends, and associates.[31] Nonetheless, the physical separation of blacks and whites, if we can generalize from the Philadelphia example, increased rapidly, with the index of dissimilarity growing from .149 in 1790 to .514 in 1820.[32]

As well as reflecting rising land values and rents, the social geography of the cities changed with the reorganization of work. Early in the century, apprentices and journeymen, working within a household mode of production, had usually lived with the master artisan in a familial setting in which residence and work location were merged. By the end of the century, a larger scale production led many masters to relocate their shops away from their place of residence, journeymen usually lived independently of the master, typically in rented rooms or in that new urban phenomenon of the late eighteenth century—the boardinghouse. Moreover, journeymen increasingly found themselves in an antagonistic relationship with their masters, for by the early nineteenth century the traditional pathway that led from apprentice to master craftsman was becoming severely clogged.[33] In Boston, for example, where as late as 1790 a majority of journeymen carpenters could expect to become masters, only one in five achieved that goal in the decades after 1810.[34]

By the early nineteenth century, artisans who formerly would have expected to achieve the status of master were increasingly obliged to depend on others for wage work. "The time before long will come," decried one craftsman, "when we shall tread in the steps of Old England."[35] The term "walking cities" still applied at the end of the eighteenth century because urban geographical spread was still not very great, and people of many stations lived within hailing distance of each other. But while the geographical proximity of urban social classes remained relatively close, the social distance grew between employers and employees, rich and poor, black and white.

For urban women somewhat different changes in the social environment of work were taking place, particularly in the late eighteenth and early nineteenth centuries. First, the gradual transfer of male productive labor from the household to a commercial place of business "reduced the transmission of business and craft knowledge within the family" and thus decreased the likelihood that widows would continue their husbands' enterprises after their death.[36] A trend away from female proprietorships, noted in the case of Boston many years ago by Elisabeth Dexter on the basis of newspaper advertisements, has been statistically demonstrated for Philadelphia in a study of women's occupations listed in city directories. As late as the 1790s the probability remained high that widows would manage their deceased husbands' businesses—including the widows of ironmongers, pewterers, printers, coopers, turners, and tallow chandlers. However, by the antebellum era, the likelihood of this had been much reduced, and midwivery, although for different reasons, was also being taken out of women's hands.[37] In these areas of work, women of middling rank were pushed out of the public realm and into the private sphere.

At the same time the middle-class female proprietorships were decreasing, lower-class female household production in one important area—textiles—grew rapidly after the middle of the eighteenth century. The first attempts to utilize the labor of poor urban women—and increasingly their children—came in Boston, the capital of impoverished widowhood in America. But women balked at the separation of domestic responsibilities and income-producing work, and this resistance played a large part in the failure of the linen manufactory that merchants opened in 1750. However, women adapted readily to the putting-out system under which they spun thread in their homes while simultaneously discharging familial responsibilities.[38] In most of the cities after the Revolution, merchant-entrepreneurs established large putting-out networks for the domestic spinning of cotton yarn. Where immigrant labor was available, as in Philadelphia, the system soaked up the labor of poor urban women until as late as the 1830s, thus maintaining the home as a workplace.[39] In other cities, such as Boston and Pawtucket, the mechanization of cotton spinning drew large numbers of women and children out of their homes and into textile factories as early as the 1790s, in imitation of the much more developed practice in English industrial towns.[40] Thus began a long history of urban women and children of the lower orders in textile work—a chapter of urban history that would take

another turn in the antebellum years with the movement of poor women
and their children into the needle trades.[41]

In the last generation, historians have discovered much more about
structural changes in eighteenth-century urban society than they have
about how people responded to these alterations. The utilization of quan-
tifiable sources, such as deeds, tax and probate documents, and poor
relief records, has advanced our knowledge of what Tönnies called "gemeinschaft of locality"—the physical life of the community—more than
our comprehension of what he termed "gemeinschaft of mind"—the mental life of the community. Hence, any agenda of research in eighteenth-
and early nineteenth-century urban history ought to be headed by topics relating to the individual and collective strategies of urban people as
they sought to cope with their changing environment.

Insofar as they have inquired into the mental and behavioral responses of urban people to the passage of their locales from seaport villages to commercial and protoindustrial cities between 1690 and 1820,
historians have looked primarily to the realm of politics. Some of them
have argued that while the chasm between rich and poor grew and movement between the tiers of society decreased, conditions associated with
the transition from *gemeinschaft* to *gesellschaft*, the reverse was happening in the political arena. The urban upper class in the American
cities, as in England, had long believed in a system of political relations
defined by gentle domination from above and willing subordination from
below—a contractual arrangement that historians call deference politics. However, deference eroded markedly in the eighteenth-century cities, especially during critical periods when unemployment and declining
real wages impoverished many working people and threatened the security of many more, thus sharpening their consciousness of inequalities of wealth and status. When artisans (and even laborers and
mariners) mobilized politically, no longer believing that the elite managed affairs in the interest of the whole community, then the traditional
rules of genteel politics began to change.

Long before the Revolution the instrumentalities of popular politics
appeared in the cities—outdoor political rallies, vitriolic campaign literature, petition drives, club and caucus activity, and attacks on the
wealthy as subverters rather than protectors of the community's welfare. During the Revolution this transformation of mechanic consciousness ushered in a new era of politics in which laboring people began to
think of themselves as a distinct political entity. This led in turn to campaigns for transforming the political process through annual elections,
secret balloting, universal male suffrage, rotation of office holding, inclusion of artisans as candidates for municipal offices, formation of ex-
tralegal committees for enforcing trade restrictions, self-convened
outdoor political assemblages, and the opening of legislative debates to
the public.[42] In the drawing rooms of polite society, men sputtered that
"the Mechanics have no Right to *Speak* or *Think* for themselves," and
should not presume to "intermeddle in state affairs."[43] The genie was
out of the bottle, however, and would never be imprisoned again.

The political self-empowerment that was occurring in the revolutionary cities is often seen as a breakdown of an older social system in which interclass relations were marked by harmony, trust, mutual respect, and a sense of partnership within hierarchy. To some extent this notion of a prior social equilibrium is a convenient fiction created by historians who wish to chart change from a golden age. But the *relative* social equilibrium that had prevailed in the cities before the 1760s *was* in disarray because the conditions necessary for its survival were crumbling—an economy in which laboring people could fulfill their goals of earning a "decent competency," achieving an independent status, and obtaining respect in their communities.

Yet the overturning of the old system of political management partially mitigated the social disequilibrium because it offered the possibility that through a democratic political system each interest group in the urban polity could contend equally for its particular advantages. In time, the new system would be celebrated as uniquely American, although many urban nabobs could never accept the active participation in the political process of the "mere mechanics," the "rabble," the "unthinking multitude." This popularization of politics continued after the Revolution, despite a conservative reaction in the last decade of the century. While economic development, population growth, and the differential effects of war on urban society had led to a widening chasm between the top and bottom of urban society, in politics the increasingly distinct social ranks were forced into a common political process in which it was entirely legitimate for the lower orders to raise their voices, take to the streets, and formulate demands arising from their understanding of how the social system was changing. For those panjandrums who sat at the pinnacle of the more sharply defined social pyramid, popular politics carried the horrifying ring of anarchy, especially after the outbreak of the French Revolution. Beneficiaries of the advancing social exclusiveness, they were obliged to tolerate a growing political inclusiveness. Their discomfort was made all the more acute by the popular attacks mounted against them in the postrevolutionary era—fusillades that increased in intensity by the end of the century and escalated further as merchant capitalists organized banks, built factories, and penetrated such crafts as shoemaking and house building.[44]

Eventually finding a home in the Democratic-Republican party that formed in the 1790s, urban workingmen, often led by small merchants, professionals, and master artisans turned manufacturers, pressed hard for a more democratic system of politics and for specific changes in the way power was distributed in such varied aspects of urban life as the availability of credit, schooling, taxation, militia duty, and indebtedness laws. Strains of the old corporatist ethic remained alive in artisan republicanism, although the upward movement of many master craftsmen into the ranks of manufacturers carried them into a realm where Madisonian political economy was particularly congenial.[45]

Meanwhile, within the lower orders the egalitarian ideology enunciated during the Revolution was refurbished from about 1790 to 1830 and adapted to the new conditions of labor taking hold in the first third

of the nineteenth century. Running deeply through this thought of the
radical urban democracy was a deep suspicion of wealth and of the concentrated power that lower-class and many middle-class city residents
believed was its handmaiden. The belief grew that republican "simplic-
ity and equality of manners essential to equal rights" was being undermined by a parasitic class of merchant capitalists—nonproducers whose
unrestrained acquisitiveness and lack of concern for the community led,
eventually, to the degradation of productive labor. As William Duane,
the fiery immigrant editor of the Philadelphia *Aurora* expressed it in
1806 (in the context of the conviction of striking journeymen shoemakers for conspiring to restrain trade), "the doors of industry are to be
closed so that a breed of *white slaves* may be nursed up in poverty to
take the place of the *blacks* upon their emancipation."[46]

This is not to argue that the lower orders were able to use their
newly gained political voice to transform the conditions under which
they lived and worked in urban society. Far from it. There emerged in
the postrevolutionary era no crystallization of artisan consciousness or
all-craft solidarity, and short-term working-class victories were outweighed by long-range defeats. Despite structural changes in shoemaking, tailoring, printing, and other trades that were separating journeymen from masters, it proved difficult for working people to unite in
a society in which the ideology of laissez-faire had penetrated deeply. In
New York, it took until 1804 for those who did not own property—a growing proportion of the laboring population—even to obtain the vote in
municipal elections, and thereafter they were able to accomplish much
less than they hoped for at the ballot box. In Philadelphia, prosperous
mechanics, allied with professionals and some merchants, even formed
their own wing of the Jeffersonian party in the early nineteenth century, adopting positions on economic and fiscal issues that made them
hardly distinguishable from the Federalists. Such men did not share
the radical social perspective that inspired the periodic insurgency of
the lower artisans, mariners, and laborers, who imbibed a small producers' ideology stressing egalitarianism and communitarianism—and
who were less than a generation away from embracing socialism and
from founding workingmen's parties in all the major cities.[47]

In spite of the effects of westward movement and political cooptation
in dissipating political radicalism in the seaboard cities, the revolutionary and postrevolutionary experience heightened artisan consciousness
and brought working people into the political arena as never before.
Once in that arena, they did not unify completely or act collectively at
all moments. But the realization spread that the changes overcoming
urban society could not be addressed by autonomous individuals who
singly exercised their political rights but only by collective actions and
intertrade alliances. The advent of a "gemeinschaft of mind" was hastened, moreover, by the residential class clustering that was emerging.
For the first time in the history of American cities, political alignments
became closely connected with neighborhoods and wards and were reflected not simply in national and state political parties but also in the

subcommunities that gathered themselves in trade associations, militia companies, and mutual aid societies.[48]

Much remains to be done on urban politics, especially in the neglected period between the end of the Revolution and the beginning of the Jacksonian era. Preoccupation with the emerging national party system has obscured the dynamics of local politics, which seem, to judge by a few recent studies, to have been far more clamorous and less cleansed of mob activity than is usually supposed (although there is no gainsaying the fact that public authorities became less tolerant of mob activity and moved ruthlessly to suppress it after the Revolution). There may be much more continuity between the revolutionary period and the 1820s than meets the eye. By the latter decade, the democratic strivings inherited from the revolutionary era were bursting through the boundaries of conventional Jacksonian party politics in most of the cities. An extraordinary set of characters—Paineite free thinkers, Jacobin feminists, Owenite visionaries, radical political economists, and early socialists—were mobilizing the lower orders and sometimes middle-class people with their various formulas for reforming a republic that they believed had turned its back on the revolutionary promise of freedom, equality, and the elimination of corruption and exploitation. The work of Sean Wilentz and Paul Gilje on New York's plebian politics after the 1780s and Susan Davis's fruitful explorations of the rise of the folk street drama "as a mode of political communication" in early nineteenth-century Philadelphia are just three of the new pioneering works that are illuminating the neglected period in the history of the early republic in ways that suggest the responses outside the formal realm of politics devised by urban people who saw themselves contending with threatening new situations.[49]

A brief look at voluntary organizations in the postrevolutionary cities provides evidence of one important way in which urban people knit themselves together in subcommunities in order to cope with the forces of social change that were rending the larger community. Three decades into the nineteenth century, Alexis de Tocqueville would marvel at the fervor of Americans to join local voluntary groups. "Americans of all ages, all conditions, and all dispositions," he wrote, "constantly form associations. They have not only commercial and manufacturing companies . . . but associations of a thousand other kinds, religious, moral, serious, futile, general or restricted, enormous or diminutive."[50] What the French observer described had its roots, in fact, in the postrevolutionary seaboard cities where a phenomenal growth of voluntary associations occurred.

For Tönnies, voluntary associations were characteristic of a system of *gesellschaft* because they were special interest groups directed at particular, not universal, ends and were based on contractual agreements among their members, whose principal aim was to advance their own wealth. In a *gesellschaftlich* society, "which presupposes every individual person with separate spheres of rational will," Tönnies argued, these associations provided "the only possible type of interrelationship." Yet, after witnessing the rise of producer and consumer cooperatives among the laboring poor of Germany in the early twentieth century, Tönnies discerned in these associations the revival of "a principle of gemeinschaft economy" that might lead to the resuscitation of "other forms of gemeinschaft."[51]

The potential of voluntary associations in the postrevolutionary era to act as antipodal centers of urban group activity deserves much more attention from historians. Voluntary societies were not new to the postrevolutionary cities, of course. Charitable societies and fire companies had existed since the early eighteenth century, and journeymen's societies were not far behind. The latter, established to buffer aspiring craftsmen against the economic cycles that could undermine the security of those living close to the margin, served first as mutual aid associations but almost as importantly as nodal points of social and political organization.

After 1760, urban voluntary associations multiplied rapidly, if we are to judge by the cases of New York and Boston, the two cities that have been most closely examined in this regard.[52] Volunteer fire companies, reform-minded benevolent organizations, volunteer militia companies, and literary, artistic, and scientific groups mushroomed, attracting thousands of city dwellers to endeavors that provided them with the satisfactions of sociability as well as service. Composed only of men before the Revolution, such associations began forming among urban women as well by the late 1780s, bringing into collective activity the social group that had been traditionally most restricted to functioning within the family and whose options in the economic sphere were beginning to narrow at this time. By 1800, at least seventy-eight voluntary organizations were meeting in Boston, whereas only fifteen had existed in 1760.[53] Parallel growth, as yet charted only imperfectly, seems to have occurred in other cities as well. Among urban women, the 1790s and the first decade of the nineteenth century witnessed a spectacular growth of such groups, which far more than their male counterparts were devoted to religion, reform, and supporting the marginal people of the growing cities—the poor and sick, the orphaned and insane, and criminals and prostitutes.[54]

Why did this movement that made America a nation of joiners blossom in the late eighteenth-century cities? To some extent the new concept of citizenship ushered in by the Revolution, which enjoined the active involvement of citizens, nourished the desire to enlist in order to improve and perfect the new republic. Apathy, the revolutionary generation learned, was the enemy of a virtuous, improving people. A number of voluntary associations in the cities, founded out of educational, artistic, and reformist motives, fit this explanation. But a larger number of voluntary groups seem to have originated as mechanisms for buffering people against the forces of change or as a means of promoting or resisting change. Some organizations were explicitly meant to advance or defend the interest of a group, such as the journeymen's societies that grew rapidly between 1780 and 1820. Others were purposefully exclusionary, offering members a "surrogate community of harmony" in a world that had thrown off the patriarchal ideal and, in its political ideology, had abandoned hierarchy.[55] The best example here is the Masonic lodges, which grew at a dizzy pace in the late eighteenth-century cities. Modeling their organization to recapture the world as they thought it used to be, the Masons instituted an elaborate hierarchy, maintained strict deference between ranks, and prized harmony and stability.[56] Their fraternity was, in fact, a surrogate family, although by drawing heavily on the leisure time and emotional resources of their male members, they may have simultaneously weakened traditional family life.

More research is needed on urban voluntary associations to determine the composition and motives of their members and their meaning to those who joined. Tentatively, it appears that they were of many kinds and purposes; but all of them served particular segments of much enlarged and diversified urban populations by creating communities within communities. Facilitating interpersonal contact, providing small-scale arenas for self-improvement and mutual reinforcement, and training ordinary people in organizational skills, they helped to stitch together urban centers that sometimes seem, in historical perspective, to have been coming apart at the seams. Often engaging in highly ritualized public display, such associations sharpened their members' group consciousness and impressed upon their fellow urbanites the extent to which various groups regarded themselves as distinct. Yet the marching of Masons through the streets, or the procession of artisans under emblems of their trade, also made visible how extensively urban life involved group as against individual activity.[57]

The eighteenth-century cities, in sum, while places of rapid change, were also places of continuous readjustment. Urban people had to be resilient, for they were regularly buffeted by serious blows from economic and natural sources. Bostonians, for example, suffered major fires on ten occasions between 1653 and 1760 that wiped out as much as a tenth of the town's buildings with each conflagration. They withstood eight raging smallpox epidemics between 1640 and 1730, sustained military casualties proportionate to World War II death tolls four times from 1690 to 1780, and twice between 1740 and 1780 experienced hyperinflation that nearly wiped out the value of currency. Nevertheless, Boston, like other cities, survived, recovered, and grew. To a considerable extent this was possible because city people became adept at creating viable subcommunities, ranging from neighborhoods to voluntary associations, and they learned to use them to defend their interests, perpetuate sociability, and cope with (and sometimes counteract) structural changes affecting urban life.

NOTES

1. P. J. Corfield, *The Impact of English Towns, 1700–1800* (Oxford, 1982), 7–8; the population data for American towns are drawn from the published decade censuses.

2. Gary B. Nash, *The Urban Crucible: Social Change, Political Consciousness, and the Origins of the American Revolution* (Cambridge, 1979), passim; Ferdinand Tönnies, *Community and Society*, translated and ed. by Charles P. Loomis (East Lansing, MI, 1957).

3. Thomas Bender, *Community and Social Change in America* (New Brunswick, NJ, 1978), ch. 1–2.

4. Ibid., 31, 33. In attenuated form this had been Tönnies's original formulation. See *Community and Society*, 227.

5. Henry A. Gemery, "European Emigration to North America, 1700–1820: Numbers and Quasi-Numbers," *Perspectives in American History*, New Series, 1 (1984), 283–342.

6. The churches are listed in the Boston and Philadelphia city directories for 1800.

7. Statistics on urban slave populations are taken from Nash, *Urban Crucible*, passim, and, for Charleston, from Evarts B. Greene and Virginia S. Harrington, *American Population Before the Census of 1790* (New York, 1932), 178. On the absence of blacks in all English towns except London, see James Walvin, *Black and White: The Negro and English Society, 1555–1945* (London, 1973), ch. 4.

8. Gary B. Nash, "Forging Freedom: The Emancipation Experience in the Northern Seaport Towns, 1775–1820," in Ira Berlin and Ronald Hoffman, eds., *Slavery and Freedom in the Age of the American Revolution* (Charlottesville, VA, 1983), 3–48.

9. Ira Berlin, *Slaves Without Masters: The Free Negro in the Antebellum South* (New York, 1974), ch. 2.

10. Among the new community studies of free blacks are Jay Coughtry, *Creative Survival: The Providence Black Community in the 19th Century* (Providence, RI, 1982); Robert J. Cottrol, *The Afro-Yankees: Providence's Black Community in the Antebellum Era* (Westport, CT, 1982); Leroy Graham, *Baltimore: The Nineteenth Century Black Capital* (Washington, DC, 1982); Susanne Lebsock, *The Free Women of Petersburg: Status and Culture in a Southern Town, 1784–1860* (New York, 1984).

11. *Industry and Frugality Proposed as the Surest Means to Make Us a Rich and Flourishing People. . .* (Boston, 1753), 8–10.

12. *Reports of the Record Commissioners of the City of Boston* (39 vols., Boston, 1876–1908), XIV, 222, 240.

13. "Report of the Contributors to the Relief and Employment of the Poor," in *Pennsylvania Gazette*, May 29, 1776.

14. John Alexander, *Render Them Submissive: Responses to Poverty in Philadelphia, 1760–1800* (Amherst, MA, 1980); Raymond A. Mohl, *Poverty in New York, 1783–1825* (New York, 1971); Douglas Jones, "The Transformation of the Law of Poverty in Eighteenth-Century Massachusetts," *Publications of the Colonial Society of Massachusetts*, 62 (1984), 153–190; Lynn Withey, *Urban Growth in Colonial Rhode Island: Newport and Providence in the Eighteenth Century* (Albany, 1984), ch. 4.

15. Withey, *Urban Growth in Colonial Rhode Island*, 123.

16. Sharon V. Salinger and Charles Wetherell, "A Note on the Population of Prerevolutionary Philadelphia," *Pennsylvania Magazine of History and Biography*, 109 (1985), 369–386.

17. J. H. Powell, *Bring Out Your Dead: The Great Plague of Yellow Fever in Philadelphia in 1793* (Philadelphia, 1949); John Duffy, *A History of Public Health in New York City, 1625–1866* (New York, 1968).

18. *The Nature and Design of the Hospitable Society* (Philadelphia, 1803), quoted in Ronald Douglas Schultz, "Thoughts Among the People: Popular Thought, Radical Politics, and the Making of Philadelphia's Working Class" (Ph.D. dissertation, University of California, Los Angeles, 1985), 322.

19. Among the occupations listed on the 1789 Philadelphia tax assessor's list that indicate the specialization occurring within the luxury trades were bucklemaker, combmaker, muffmaker, looking glass maker, fan maker, and piano maker. On the rise of a consumer ethos, see Carole Shammas, *The Pre-industrial Consumer in England and America* (Oxford, Eng., 1990).

20. The causal connection that many urban commentators perceived between the simultaneous rise of great wealth and dire poverty was expressed repeatedly from the 1760s onward. See Nash, *The Urban Crucible*, passim.

21. Peter H. Lindert and Jeffrey Williamson, *Inequality in America: A Macroeconomic History* (New York, 1980); James A. Henretta, "Wealth and Social Structure," in Jack P. Greene, and J. R. Pole, eds., *Colonial British America: Essays in the New History of the Early Modern Era* (Baltimore, 1984), 276.

22. John J. Waters, "Patrimony, Succession, and Social Stability: Guilford, Connecticut in the Eighteenth Century," *Perspectives in American History*, 10 (1976), 156; Jackson Turner Main, "The Distribution of Property in Colonial Connecticut," in James Kirby Martin, ed., *The Human Dimensions of Nation Making: Essays on Colonial and Revolutionary America* (Madison, WI, 1976); and James A. Henretta, "Families and Farms: *Mentalité* in Pre-Industrial America," *William and Mary Quarterly*, 35 (1978), 6–8.

23. Billy G. Smith, "Inequality in Late Eighteenth-Century Philadelphia: A Note on Its Nature and Growth," *William and Mary Quarterly*, 41 (1984), 629–645.

24. Quoted in James Douglas Tagg, "Benjamin Franklin Bache and the Philadelphia 'Aurora'" (Ph.D. dissertation, Wayne State University, 1973), 155.

25. Tom W. Smith, "The Dawn of the Urban-Industrial Age: The Social Structure of Philadelphia, 1790–1830" (Ph.D. dissertation, University of Chicago, 1980), 151. The exclusion of a large percentage of free black householders from the assessment lists is not usually noted by historians; when this omission is corrected, the percentage of unassessed in the urban population by the early nineteenth century grows to about 50–60 percent.

26. Betsy Blackmar, "Rewalking the 'Walking City': Housing and Property Relations in New York City, 1780–1840," *Radical History Review*, no. 21 (1980), 131–148; Arthur L. Jensen, *The Maritime Commerce of Colonial Philadelphia* (Madison, WI, 1963), 126–27.

27. *Federal Gazette*, April 27, 1793.

28. Blackmar, "Walking City," 132–139; Smith, "Dawn of the Urban-Industrial Age," 151, Table 60; Sharon V. Salinger and Charles Wetherell, "Wealth and Renting in Prerevolutionary Philadelphia," *Journal of American History*, 71 (1985), 829.

29. Charles G. Steffen, *The Mechanics of Baltimore: Workers and Politics in the Age of Revolution, 1763–1812* (Urbana, IL, 1984), 40; Smith, "Inequality in Late Colonial Philadelphia," 633, Table 1. Peter Clark, ed., *The Transformation of English Provincial Towns, 1600–1800* (London, 1984); Allan Kulikoff, "The Progress of Inequality in Revolutionary Boston," *William and Mary Quarterly*, 28 (1971), 375–412; Smith, "Dawn of the Urban-Industrial Age," 278–279; Carl Abbott, "The Neighborhoods of New York, 1760–1775," *New York History*, 55 (1974), 35–54.

30. Peter Clark, ed., *The Transformation of English Provincial Towns, 1600–1800* (London, 1984); Allan Kulikoff, "The Progress of Inequality in Revolutionary Boston," *William and Mary Quarterly*, 28 (1971), 375–412; Smith, "Dawn of the Urban-Industrial Age," 278–279; Carl Abbott, "The Neighborhoods of New York, 1760–1775," *New York History*, 55 (1974), 35–54.

31. Nash, "Forging Freedom," 40–43; Leonard P. Curry, *The Free Black in Urban America, 1800–1850: The Shadow of the Dream* (Chicago, 1981), ch. 4.

32. Smith, "Dawn of the Urban-Industrial Age," 278, Table 89.

33. Steffen, *Mechanics of Baltimore*, ch. 2, 5; Sean Wilentz, *Chants Democratic: New York City and the Rise of the American Working Class, 1788–1850* (New York, 1984), ch. 1–2, passim; Bruce Laurie, *Working People of Philadelphia, 1800–1850* (Philadelphia, 1980), ch. 1–2, passim.

34. Lisa Lubow, "Journeymen and Masters: The Changing Relations of Artisan Labor [in Boston]" (dissertation in progress, University of California, Los Angeles).

35. *1820 Census of Manufactures, National Archives, Return of Robert Wellford [Philadelphia]*, quoted in Schultz, "Thoughts Among the People," 320.

36. Claudia Golden, "The Changing Status of Women in the Economy of the Early Republic: Quantitative Evidence" (paper delivered at the Social Science History Association Conference on Quantitative Methods in History, California Institute of Technology, March, 1983), 13.

37. Ibid., 13–18. Golden's findings largely confirm what Mary Beard argued four decades ago in *Women as Force in History: A Study in Traditions and Realities* (New York, 1946).

38. Gary B. Nash, "The Failure of Female Factory Labor in Colonial Boston," *Labor History*, 20 (1979), 165–188.

39. Cynthia Shelton, "The Role of Labor in Early Industrialization: Philadelphia, 1787–1837," *Journal of the Early Republic*, 4 (1984), 365–394.

40. Kulikoff, "Progress of Inequality," 379; Gary Kulik, "Pawtucket Village and the Strike of 1824: The Origins of Class Conflict in Rhode Island," *Radical History Review*, no. 17 (1978), 5–37; Barbara M. Tucker, *Samuel Slater and the Origins of the American Textile Industry, 1790–1860* (Ithaca, NY, 1984).

41. Christine Stansell, "The Origins of the Sweatshop: Women and Early Industrialization in New York City," in Michael H. Frisch and Daniel J. Walkowitz, eds., *Working-Class America: Essays on Labor, Community, and American Society* (Urbana, IL, 1983), 78–103.

42. Edward Countryman, *A People in Revolution: The American Revolution and Political Society in New York, 1760–1790* (Baltimore, 1981); Gary B. Nash, "Artisans and Politics in Eighteenth-Century Philadelphia," in Margaret Jacob and James Jacob, eds., *The Origins of Anglo-American Radicalism* (London, 1984), 162–182; Steven Rosswurm, "'As a Lyen out of His Den': Philadelphia's Popular Movement, 1776–1780," in ibid., 300–323; Richard Walsh, *Charleston's Sons of Liberty: A Study of the Artisans, 1763–1789* (Columbia, SC, 1959). For a contrasting view of prerevolutionary urban politics and the tension between capitalist development and the structure of urban values see Christine Leigh Heyrman, *Commerce and Culture: The Maritime Communities of Colonial Massachusetts, 1690–1750* (New York, 1984). Heyrman's study stops on the eve of the Seven Years' War and therefore is not altogether comparable to the studies cited above.

43. *Pennsylvania Gazette* September 27, 1770.

44. Alfred F. Young, *The Democratic-Republicans of New York: The Origins, 1763–1797* (Chapel Hill, NC, 1967), passim; William Bruce Wheeler, "Politics in Nature's Republic: The Development of Political Parties in the Seaport Cities in the Federalist Era" (Ph.D. dissertation, University of Virginia, 1967); Schultz, "Thoughts Among the People," ch. 4–5;

Steffen, *Mechanics of Baltimore*; Howard B. Rock, *Artisans of the New Republic: The Trades-men of New York City in the Age of Jefferson* (New York, 1979).

45. Drew R. McCoy, *The Elusive Republic: Political Economy in Jeffersonian America* (Chapel Hill, NC, 1980); Schultz, "Thoughts Among the People"; Wilentz, *Chants Democratic*; Rock, *Artisans of the New Republic*; Steffen, *Mechanics of Baltimore*.

46. Philadelphia *Aurora*, January 14, 1807; November 28, 1805, quoted in Schultz, "Thoughts Among the People," 296, 303.

47. Schultz, "Thoughts Among the People," and Wheeler, "Politics in Nature's Republic" are the two best studies to consult.

48. Rock, *Artisans of the New Republic*; Steffen, *Mechanics of Baltimore*; Schultz, "Thoughts Among the People."

49. Wilentz, *Chants Democratic*; Thomas Slaughter, "Mobs and Crowds, Riots and Brawls: The History of Early American Political Violence" (unpublished), 18–22, 47; Paul A. Gilje, "Mobocracy: Popular Disturbances in Post-Revolutionary New York City, 1783–1829" (Ph.D. dissertation, Brown University, 1980); Susan G. Davis, *Parades and Power: Street Theatre in Nineteenth-Century Philadelphia* (Philadelphia, 1986); Amy Bridges, *A City in the Republic: Antebellum New York and the Origin of Machine Politics* (Cambridge, 1984).

50. Alexis de Tocqueville, *Democracy in America*, quoted in Richard D. Brown, "The Emergence of Voluntary Associations in Massachusetts, 1760–1830," *Journal of Voluntary Action Research*, 2 (1973), 64.

51. Tönnies, *Community and Society*.

52. Brown, "Voluntary Associations in Massachusetts," 64–73; Jacquetta Mae Haely, "Voluntary Organizations in Pre-Revolutionary New York City, 1750–1776" (Ph.D. dissertation, SUNY, Binghamton, 1976); Anne M. Boylan, "Women in Groups: An Analysis of Women's Benevolent Organizations in New York and Boston, 1797–1840," *Journal of American History*, 71 (1984), 497–523.

53. Brown, "Voluntary Associations in Massachusetts."

54. Boylan, "Women in Groups," passim.

55. Brown, "Voluntary Associations in Massachusetts," 71.

56. Dorothy Ann Lipson, *Freemasonry in Federalist Connecticut* (Princeton, NJ, 1977), ch. 2.

57. Davis, *Parades and Power*, passim.

# Strumpets and Misogynists: Brothel "Riots" and the Transformation of Prostitution in Antebellum New York City

*Timothy J. Gilfoyle*

In the past three decades, historians have produced an impressive volume of work examining the composition, form and motives behind the riotous behavior of early American crowds and mobs. Nineteenth-century examinations of crowds, notably those of Gustave Le Bon and Hippolyte Taine in Europe and Joel T. Headley in New York, depicted collective violence as the behavior of bloodthirsty, irrational men seeking the destruction of civilized society. Inspired by the pathbreaking revisionist work of George Rudé, Eric Hobsbawm, and E. P. Thompson, most American historians now view crowd behavior, especially in the Revolutionary and preindustrial eras, as a beacon for raw, unfettered social equality and political fairness, a reaction against the arbitrary distribution of justice, and a vindication of time-honored traditions. When perceived rights were ignored or violated, especially by agents of the state, rioting to redress grievances was a common resort.[1]

Historians of the early American republic concur that the tradition of "republican" violence continued into the early decades of the nineteenth century. For example, Leonard L. Richards found Rudé's model appropriate for antiabolition mobs. Most were "destructive," "discriminating," and "purposeful," and some included respectable, middle-class citizens. Similarly, Sean Wilentz concluded that such violence-prone groups followed the "rules of classic 'preindustrial' urban mobs by choosing their targets with care, attacking property, but not persons, and by taking advantage of every symbolic opportunity." Indeed, from handloom weavers in Philadelphia to day laborers in the building trades to antiabolitionist crowds in New York City, artisans and unskilled workingmen violently defended their occupations from industrial technology, changing market relationships, and racial or ethnic competition.[2]

*Timothy J. Gilfoyle is associate professor of history at Loyola University of Chicago. Reprinted from* New York History 68 (January 1987): 45–65. *Reprinted by permission of the New York State Historical Association and Timothy J. Gilfoyle.*

In their efforts to understand early industrialization and class formation in the United States, historians have neglected important exceptions to this model of reactive, limited collective violence. With at least one social group, such violence exceeded traditional restraints and frequently evolved into terror. From 1825 to 1857, at least fifty New York City brothels, "female boarding houses," and their residents were violently attacked. Especially during the 1830s, recurrent attacks upon females waxed into a popular sport, and public women became victims of terror. Violent acts transformed the behavior of prostitutes, the power of madams, and the role of prostitution in New York society. And in a larger sense, brothel riots reflected dramatic changes in urban politics, gender roles and male sexual aggression. Some attacks on prostitutes were personal, private vendettas; others were public, with large numbers of participants. Their unprecedented frequency and visibility evidenced increasing male resentment and misogyny against sexually independent women and a desire to control them.[3] Outside the domestic sphere, *gender* was a justification for violence.

Historians have only scratched the surface in delineating patterns of violence against prostitutes. Europeanists like Lawrence Stone discovered seventeenth-century London apprentices plundering bawdy houses on Shrove Tuesday, ostensibly to remove temptation during Lent. Nancy Tomes has argued that nineteenth-century London prostitutes were "considered fair game for violence by working-class men." In antebellum Detroit, John C. Schneider found that violent incidents against the city's brothels centered around racial tensions between black prostitutes and German immigrants and a desire by the latter for increased residential space. The most extensive examination, however, remains Jacques Rossiaud's study of fifteenth-century French towns. Rossiaud attributed the rise in sexual violence to sudden changes in gender relations. Once a woman was violated by one man, others were entitled to the same. Women were either pure or whores. Thus, rape and attacks on public women became a means to acquire the privileges of manhood.[4]

Brothel attacks in New York City were not unique to the antebellum period. In Revolutionary New York, soldiers mistreated by "ladies of pleasure" sacked several whorehouses. In 1793, Philip Hone witnessed a remarkable attack on a house of ill-fame that included the dispersal "of 'Mother Carey's chickens,' the destruction of mahogany tables and looking glasses." Soon the "air was filled with feathers, and the street with rags and fragments," according to Dr. Alexander Anderson. The mob's excesses did not desist with "this Mother Damnable," and men "continued their riotous proceedings several successive nights, and many houses of ill-fame in other parts of the city were demolished and their miserable inmates driven naked and houseless into the streets." In 1799, a crowd of nearly one thousand gathered to destroy a Murray Street brothel but was thwarted by the timely intervention of the mayor and local magistrates. Two years later, a large assemblage of Haitians attacked Madame Volunbrun's reputed house of sin. Similarly, the disorderly house of William and Catharine Mackline on George Street was besieged by four men in 1807. Five years later, several hundred rioters tried to pull down a brothel on James Street.[5]

These incidents of mob action against prostitutes were sporadic, uncommon, and infrequent. In each instance, the mob sought to close a brothel and put it out of business. Rare was the personal assault or homicide. Such onslaughts originated from particular circumstances unrelated to prostitution itself—the castration and murder of a soldier, the seduction of the daughter of a popular ship pilot, or the murder of a fellow seaman in a whorehouse. These preindustrial attacks resembled the spontaneous "extrainstitutional," retributive actions described by Pauline Maier during the Revolutionary era. They were a recourse to justice when civil authority failed. To Philip Hone, perched in a tree over Madame Carey's house, they even had the quality of a spectator sport. Violence was inflicted only upon property, not upon individuals. As reactions to specific events, brothel attacks in the colonial and early republican eras were limited, isolated forays against the private property of misbehaving citizens. To paraphrase Bernard Bailyn, heads did not roll in brothel riots; mobs did not turn to butchery.[6]

After 1820, physical violence against prostitutes increased dramatically. As the ideology of "separate spheres" for the sexes grew in popularity, collective violence played an increasing role in intergroup relations.[7] Previously tolerated behavior by women was subjected to a new misogynist offensive. By inflicting pain upon individual prostitutes, certain males crossed a threshold and redefined the place of prostitution and thereby the boundaries of public sexuality in the antebellum city.

Assaults upon prostitutes appeared in three different forms during the mid-nineteenth century. Some attacks were vigilante acts by an individual or group perpetuating the traditional focus upon the brothel as an institution. The spontaneous individual attack was a second type. Short, quick, and angry, such violence frequently resulted from a prostitute's refusal to submit to unusual sexual demands. Finally, the most significant variety of sexual assault was the "spree" or "row," a form of destructive, group male behavior, emblematic of the changing nature of antebellum violence.[8] These latter two varieties of aggression, shifting from institutional to individual objects of attack, reflected increasing male resentment against independent, autonomous women who refused to conform to the emerging "cult of domesticity."

Group vigilante action against prostitution—premeditated, well-designed, and organized—continued the colonial tradition of extrainstitutional violence. The men (and in one case, a woman) who instigated these attacks had clear plans of how to enter the house and specific intentions once inside. Repeated attacks by certain individuals, the circumspect behavior inside the brothel, the "respectable" backgrounds of some offenders, and the accusation by prostitutes that city officials encouraged certain assaults, suggest premeditation and calculation. The prostitute's property, not her person, took the beating. The tools of a prostitute's craft—her bed, furniture, glassware and crockery—were destroyed.

Several examples reveal the vigilantes' limited goals. Early one morning in 1842, Jane Williams's house was stoned and then forcibly entered by three men who simply destroyed her furniture.[9] May Wall admitted five potential customers to her house after they arrived in a hack one evening in 1833. After sitting down, they requested a drink and inquired about her glasses and decanters. Then, "one of them grabbed a fire shovel and commenced breaking . . . all most [sic] everything on the sideboard. . . ." Likewise, the four men who entered Mary Ann Davis's house on Centre Street "behaved in a very noisy and disorderly manner, breaking tumblers, cursing and swearing and when they were going away they took one of her decanters." Isaac Roberts celebrated Christmas in 1851 by leading forty men to Catherine Cauldwell's brothel on Lispenard Street, "to give a benefit." Once inside, Roberts gave orders to "ribbon everything," and his accomplices put tumblers in their pockets, broke a sofa and destroyed a piano stool. Before departing, they heaved stones through the front window.[10]

Such riotous assaults were well-planned. George Gale was indicted in four brothel attacks during a two-week period in 1831. In three of them, he was accompanied by his friend Bentley Curran. Forcibly entering Elizabeth Baker's establishment on several different occasions, they broke her windows, destroyed her stoop, and committed "many outrages of an . . . offensive nature." Enoch Carter joined Gale at Phoebe Doty's brothel on Church Street one evening, when they began "cursing and swearing, kicking the furniture and taking lamps down, spilling the oil and threaten[ing] to knock her down . . ."[11]

Individual assaults marked a second form of misogynist violence. Drunken, disorderly, and delerious males often exploded when a prostitute or madame denied them their heart's desire. John Evans, for example, was arrested for throwing stones at the house of Eliza Vincent after she "refused him admittance." One January evening in 1834, William Green traversed Church Street, hopping from groggery to brothel, his drunken enchantment terminating only after he broke the window of a house of ill-fame.[12] The rash, impulsive character of these attacks reveals that they were not directed at institutions, but at individuals.

Even personal acquaintance afforded little protection for vulnerable prostitutes. Murdered on 11 April 1836, Ellen Jewett was beautiful and popular, "the goddess of a large race of merchants, dealers, clerks and their instruments," and lived in Rosina Townsend's "City Hotel" brothel. No one was ever convicted of the bloody deed, but most contemporaries were convinced that her paramour, Richard Robinson, was guilty.[13] Jewett's murder was not an isolated act of violence by a prostitute's acquaintance. Early one summer morning in 1844, for example, Hannah Fuller was awakened by William Ford. After kicking in her door, he removed his boots and pants, carried her to the bed, and attempted "to ravish and . . . carnally know her." Only the last-minute intervention by the watch prevented the rape. Fuller later dropped the charges because Ford was an "old friend."[14]

Women had even less protection on the street. Mary Smith, a Leonard Street prostitute, was walking home in 1832 after an evening at the

Park Theatre when William Nosworthy seized the spritely grisette "in a grossly rude and indecent manner and raised her clothes so as to expose her nakedness to the passers by."[15] Such occasions, which became more frequent as mid-century approached, indicate that prostitutes were fair game for the aggression of frustrated males.

The final and most significant form of assault was the spree or row. Sprees were violent, illegal acts by young males, hoping, in part, to earn respect within their male subculture. These violent outbursts reflected deindividualization—the loss of inhibition and sense of individual accountability when part of a large group. Fueled by male camaraderie and substantial quantities of liquor, the spree, as Edgar Allan Poe aptly described it, was "the mad excess of a counterfeit hilarity—the joint offspring of liberty and of rum."[16]

Gangs of drunks on a rampage often moved from one saloon or brothel to another, becoming increasingly obnoxious and violent at every stop along a trail of bacchanalian indulgence. The arbitrary, unplanned, and unstructured behavior revealed a predilection for intoxicated conviviality, not prudish outrage at the existence of prostitution. Some attacks, for instance, stopped just short of personal assault. In 1834, John Lawrence, Henry Flender and a dozen others attempted to break into several Chapel Street brothels, but settled instead for spattering the front doors with mud. On another occasion, Samuel Anderson, Charles Dykes, and their chums failed to break into a brothel on Anthony Street, retreating to the street and launching stones through the front windows. Finally, William Weed brought eight to ten accomplices "to take possession" of Eliza Swinson's Chapel Street brothel, but only stoned her "castle" after she locked them out.[17]

Many sprees, however, evolved into scenes of sadistic terror. The three rioters who stoned Amanda Smith's house on Franklin Street also "destroyed her furniture, knocked her down, beat her on the face and head so as to blind her entirely, and after having knocked her down, kicked her." The invaders then beat her crippled son William "in a most shameful and outrageous manner." Witnesses testified that the same men forced their way into two other Orange Street brothels, "making a great noise and disturbance, breaking the furniture." Likewise, John Golding led four other men into Elizabeth Rinnell's Crosby Street house and demanded food, drink, money, and entertainment. After their drunken orgy, Golding assaulted and beat Miss Rinnell. On another occasion, Jane Williams refused to open her brothel door to a dozen men. Two then forced their way through a window, punched Williams in the head, went to the front door, admitted the remainder, and then stampeded about the house. Similarly, when John Williams entered an Anthony Street brothel, he threw oil of vitriol in Mary Ann Duffy's face, severely scarring her. In 1836, seven men, upon entering Mary Gambel's Crosby Street brothel, "fell upon her with their fists." Their violence culminated when one attacker "drew a sword and stabbed her in the nose . . . and left her face most shockingly cut and injured."[18]

The threat of rape was common in many brothel riots. Five men broke into Eliza Logue's Thomas Street house when she refused them admittance. After breaking the crockery and throwing a lamp at the head of a prostitute, they strangled Logue and "threw her across the foot of a bed and endeavored by force and violence to have connection with her. . . ." A nearby watch heard the commotion and prevented consummation of the act. In another instance, more than ten laborers from the Eleventh Ward broke into Eliza Ann Potter's Suffolk Street house, violently assaulted her and "threatened to pickle" and rape her before hastily departing.[19]

Since most sexually related crimes go unreported, the brothel riots described above (most of which appeared in the prosecution papers of the district attorney) surely represented but a small portion of a widespread phenomenon.[20] Undoubtedly, numerous repeated assaults upon prostitutes produced significant changes in the structural development of nineteenth-century commercial sex. Specifically, prostitutes attuned to the increasing misogynist resentment resorted to three sources of protection: self-defense, the municipal government, and the "pimp." Several examples illustrate how working-class women, particularly prostitutes, employed physical violence to assert and protect their autonomy. For instance, the calendar of the Court of General Sessions in 1828 disclosed an unprecedented seventy cases of assault and battery by women.[21] In 1843, one angry prostitute stabbed a client in his chest on the steps of the Astor House. Only a deflection by his rib prevented the knife from piercing his heart. On another occasion, when John Briggs became uncontrollably drunk and disorderly in Phoebe Doty's and Moll Stephens's brothel, one prostitute tried to shoot him with a pistol. Similarly, Mary Gambel, upon being stabbed in the nose, scratched her assailant's face so badly that nearly a month later she was convinced that "he must [still] carry the marks with him."[22]

Antebellum prostitutes also used the law to protect themselves. By initiating legal proceedings against their aggressors, prostitutes utilized the machinery of the state to defend their interests and property rights, firmly entrenching their profession in the social fabric of the metropolis. Even streetwalkers sought legal redress when threatened or attacked. When a drunken male approached and kissed a prostitute promenading on Broadway, she objected to his uninvited sexual advances and prosecuted him.[23] On another occasion, Jane Williams charged Jim Waters with assault after he struck her when she abandoned him on the street for another client. Unapologetic, Waters justified his actions: "I had no notion of letting her off," he insisted. "She wanted to go away with another fellow cause [sic] he was dressed a little better than I was."[24] Williams, unsatisfied, fully prosecuted her assailant. Instead of retreating to the domestic hearth, Williams and her sagacious compatriots asserted themselves through every means at their disposal.

Prostitutes were undoubtedly an exploited and marginal group in antebellum New York City. Historians Judith Walkowitz and Christine Stansell have nevertheless demonstrated how prostitution became an increasingly viable alternative for working women affected by the industrialization process during the nineteenth century. Such women did not necessarily become outcasts from their laboring counterparts. Rather, their prostitution was often understood to be a temporary means of survival and adaptation.[25] Just as the extreme behavior of men in brothel attacks revealed a transformation in attitudes toward prostitution and the nature of male violence in antebellum society, the use of the legal system by prostitutes to defend themselves was equally important. These prostitutes did not see themselves as "fallen women." They publicly defended their personal integrity and private property instead of succumbing to violent intimidation, and they refused to act as fugitives from justice. They rejected a defensive, reticent posture when subjected to violent terror. By asserting their rights, they forswore surrender.

Forcing the resolution of these conflicts into a public forum, prostitutes turned the municipal government into their agent and protector. For example, they summoned the watch when attacked and prosecuted violators upon arrest. Some rioters even considered the watch a protector of the brothel. When Marshal Joseph L. Hays tried to arrest three men in the process of destroying Miss Robins's house of ill-fame, the culprits temporarily took him hostage too. Another time, Charles Taylor and Charles Jennings berated the watch who removed them from Adeline Miller's house, "saying it was a damned shame that watchmen should receive pay for protecting whore houses. . . ."[26] In court, prostitutes were outraged by the destruction of their property.[27] Rioters were thus compelled to repair the damage even when the judge knew about the illicit carnal activities of the plaintiff. Although the records of the district attorney provide no clue as to the final decisions in most cases, on at least eleven occasions the courts convicted the riotous defendants.[28] In other cases, men eluded conviction only because the prostitute dropped the charge.[29]

In this ironic fashion, the state both defended and protected prostitution. Unlike later forms of legal intervention which sought to regulate, control, and hinder the independence of prostitutes, governmental power was invoked for their benefit.[30] When prostitutes exercised their property rights, the municipality was compelled to defend prostitution and prosecute its more violent enemies. Since antebellum government was primarily devoted to protecting the interests of taxpayers and private property, a bewildered municipality faced an unappealing, imperfect choice: suppress sexual deviancy, punish prostitutes and thereby violate their (and ultimately others') property rights, or punish their male aggressors and tolerate the existence of prostitution. In the end, the state chose to defend property, and thus prostitution, at the expense of other laws and the puritanical sensibilities of many New Yorkers.

What sort of men were these "brothel bullies"? Ordinary laborers constituted 71 percent of those charged. Of the remainder, 9 percent were semiskilled laborers, 15 percent skilled artisans, and 5 percent white-collar professionals.[31] Most rioters lived in the same or adjacent ward as the prostitutes they attacked. Less than a quarter lived in more distant areas of the city.[32] While most were working-class laborers, brothel rioters crossed class lines. In 1831, for example, attorney James Lozier joined his neighbor, grocer Charles Taylor, and two others in attacking Adeline Miller's Elm Street brothel.[33] The instigators of these

assaults, therefore, were not simply disenchanted "rabble," parts of unruly mobs, professional criminals, or clearly defined deviants, but "respectable" elements of society as well. Indeed, their behavior was
tolerated and sometimes condoned by neighbors and the municipality.

These brothel riots depart in several ways from the earlier forms of
pre-industrial collective violence described by Rudé and others. First,
much violence was inflicted on the persons, not simply on the property.
Second, while some assaults were planned and had political motives,
many were virtually spontaneous forms of terror. Third, unlike those
who attacked such agents of the state as soldiers, tax collectors or government officials, who often fought back with greater ferocity than the
mob, brothel bullies faced little physical opposition from a protective
authority defending their victims. Finally, since prostitution always existed in New York, preservation of it as an institution was an unlikely
motive behind their behavior.[34]

Why, then, did men choose to act with such violence toward prostitutes? Historians Christine Stansell and Amy Gilman Srebnick have
shown how antebellum society grew increasingly restless over the public activities and accessibility of working women in general.[35] Contemporaries feared that women in public places risked destructive physical
harrassment. "There are strange things said of attacks upon females in
the streets of New York, . . . if alone," reported *Niles' Register* in 1831.
Philip Hone bemoaned that some outrage occurred nightly by "young
ruffians who prowl the streets insulting females." Even George Templeton
Strong was selective in his remorse. When nineteenth-century feminists
encouraged women to wear bloomers and speak before public audiences,
Strong confessed he was "glad to see them respectfully pumped upon by
a crowd of self-appointed conservators of manners and morals." In his
opinion, the "strumpets of Leonard and Church streets are not *much*
further below the ideal of womanhood than these loathsome dealers in
clack, who seek to change women into garrulous men without virility."[36]
For women, the message was clear—get off the streets, stay in the home.

The increasingly prominent role played by prostitutes in urban social life was a second factor. Outside the home, prostitutes were among
the most visible women in the industrializing antebellum city. After 1820,
the geographic expansion of prostitution and the appearance of at least
four red-light districts reflected the rise of a new sexuality and the commercialization of sex.[37] One newspaper complained that "a new code of
ethics" had emerged by 1836 glamorizing the prostitute with her gold
watch, splendid earrings and embroidered stockings, at the expense of
"a poor hardworking man, who sticks to one woman, . . . his wife." Indeed, by 1825 madams like Maria Williamson were successful enough to
own several brothels and actively engage in New York's lucrative real
estate market. Others like Rosina Townsend, Adeline Miller, and Julia
Brown were public figures appearing on the front pages of the penny
press, in the diaries of the city's gentry, and in guidebooks sold at corner
newstands.[38] The *Herald* asked when "was there ever found an instance
of the open and shameless defence [*sic*] of the character of a public prostitute?" Why, indeed, had leading prostitutes become models "of truth

and virtue"?[39] At a time when gender roles were in the initial stage of redefinition and the "cult of domesticity" was gaining ground, the behavior of some prostitutes was a vivid counterpoise.

From 1820 to 1840, women had greater control and influence over prostitution than at any other time. Low wages in the factory and the household made prostitutes the best-paid women workers in the nineteenth-century city. And the willingness of many prostitutes to prosecute their violators in the public arena illustrated their personal faith and confidence in their own individual rights. The sporadic, infrequent attacks prior to 1830, the sharp decline after 1840, and the sudden and unprecedented rise in violent abuse between 1832 and 1838 make those years a watershed in the transformation of attitudes regarding prostitution, sexuality, and women. Clearly, some men found the increased economic and social power of prostitutes threatening. And others intended to shape and control commercialized sex, resorting to terror when necessary.

Simultaneously with the sudden rise in brothel riots, America experienced an increase in male communal drinking. According to W. J. Rorabaugh, such group forms of intoxication were commonplace after 1820 and endowed the participants with feelings of liberty and independence while inducing a sense of equality. The group drinking binge was an ideological inebriation; to be drunk was to be free. Liquor, therefore, increased the American male's sense of autonomy.[40] Brothel sprees were an extension of such drunken displays of egalitarianism. Participants unleashed pent-up male frustration by attacking a visibly independent, autonomous, and sometimes materially successful woman. Whereas a vigilante attack on a house of prostitution was a public protest, a spree was a source of fun. As mock-heroic skirmishes of pride and violation, such attacks were an aggressive form of misogynist, masculine recreation, a means to assert male perogative and supremacy at the expense of a hapless, unprotected, vulnerable prostitute. The spree was an illusion of power for powerless men.[41]

Political control over the profits of prostitution was a final motivating force in some brothel attacks. In 1836, John Chichester and his politically connected gang attacked at least three bordellos. Entering Jane Ann Jackson's Chapel Street brothel with bats, they destroyed windows and shutters, and threatened to cut Miss Jackson's throat. Chichester's consorts then broke into Eliza Ludlow's house and forced her to serve brandy, and concluded their guzzling by tossing the glasses in the fire. Then they "abused the inmates of the house," burnt a rug, broke a bench by hurling it at a prostitute, and threatened to toss one woman out the window.[42] Similarly, Thomas Hyer's gang raided at least four brothels from 1836 to 1838. Upon breaking into Ellen Holly's house in 1836, they grabbed one inmate, and "by the most forcible and violent means," gang raped her. Despite conviction for the deed, a year later Hyer led the same culprits into Mary Banta's house, destroyed her tableware, and knocked an inmate unconscious. Within the next two decades, Hyer's pugilistic habits were rewarded with the American heavyweight boxing championship, political alliances with Nativist Bill Poole, Democrat Mike

Walsh, and Republican William Seward, and control of the prostitution, saloons and gambling dens along Mercer Street.[43]

While motives were less evident in other attacks, the participants had significant political connections. For example, rioters who destroyed Jane Wetson's, Sarah Ferguson's, and Adeline Miller's belongings were white-collar workers and skilled laborers, allegedly acting on orders from Justice Bloodgood and Street Inspector Daniel McGrath.[44] In 1834, Phoebe Doty accused William H. Tuttle, a clerk for the mayor, and John L. Martin, a tavernkeeper, of attacking her bawdy house, during which they "commenced a work of outrageous and disorderly conduct . . . by squirting upon them . . . dirty water . . ." On a separate occasion, Andrew R. Jackman, a City Hall officer and future city assessor and common school trustee, and seven other skilled workers broke into Mary Adams's Thirteenth Ward establishment. While inside, they accosted an inmate, wrapped her up in a straw mat, and rolled her down the stairs.[45]

In antebellum New York, gangs like those led by Hyer, Chichester and others played critical roles in the distribution of power and early formation of the political machine. As Amy Bridges argues, wealthy elites in New York concentrated on national and state issues. Local concerns and grass-roots organization were left to a new political animal—the career politician, who employed gangs to keep opponents away from the polls, guard ballot boxes and enforce political conformity. Hyer, for example, was allied to the Nativist "Bowery B'hoys" who, according to Alvin Harlow, were not as vicious as rival Five Points gangs and had a tendency "toward the political rather than the purely savage or criminal."[46]

While the ward-based, career politician controlled votes, he lacked money. In order to establish a secure financial base, ward politicians resorted to bribery and extortion of neighborhood proprietors of saloons, gambling dens, and houses of prostitution in return for ignoring laws outlawing or regulating such activities. As prostitution became a significant revenue source for the local political boss, gangs were probably used as a means to control and police brothel keepers and their inmates. Employing terror, politically organized gangs restructured prostitution into a male-controlled institution and established a financial foundation for the political machine for the remainder of the century. After 1880, it was commonplace for one-time gang leaders and political allies like "The Allen," "Big Tim" Sullivan and Martin Engel to dominate important institutions of commercial sex.[47]

This mixture of violence and politics gave rise to a new participant in commercial sex—the "pimp." American historians have erroneously attributed the appearance of pimps and male control of prostitution to greater police harassment after 1890. But as brothels were attacked with increasing frequency during the 1830s, men for the first time were hired to provide protection. Both brothel keepers and prostitutes admitted that men lived in their houses of prostitution to provide physical protection or perform services such as buying groceries, repairing the house, or serving the guests. Even streetwalkers were not exempt from this trend. By the 1850s, a visible, well-established system of pimps existed in New York. When Mayor Fernando Wood instigated a campaign against streetwalkers in 1855, pimps appeared with them in court. Commonly referred to as "Broadway Statues," pimps and their associates stood in front of the "monster" hotels along New York's best-known avenue. These "scamps have the audacity to address [women] without ceremony," complained one reporter, "and if their advances are received with indignation, . . . the wretches apologize and plead mistake." The corner of Broadway and Broome Street was a notorious hangout for pimps waiting for prostitutes to hand over their earnings before returning to work.[48] By the mid-nineteenth century, pimps were a standard feature of New York prostitution. They remain so today.

For the nineteenth-century female, prostitution was the quintessential symbol of male sexual coercion. By 1840, such coercion had escalated to dangerous levels of physical abuse and intimidation. If assumptions about women were expressed within structures of feeling rather than in bodies of well-defined ideas, as Christine Stansell argues, then antebellum brothel riots were most emblematic of a new misogynist attitude toward prostitutes and women in public life. Bypassing older, traditional limits of collective protest and crowd behavior, antebellum males resorted to terror. Gender became a sufficient cause for violence.[49] On one level, individual antebellum males believed they had the right to control, if not physically coerce, prostitutes and other public women. Efforts to extend male power over autonomous and sexually independent women, however, met with defiance. Through self-defense and utilization of the legal system to defend their property, prostitutes protected themselves. Ultimately, the final victor in this struggle was the local ward politician. As Tammany Hall emerged as the political reckoning force of Gotham, violent gangs allied to neighborhood machine representatives used force and terror to restructure commercial sex and insure male control over the profits of prostitution.

NOTES

1. Joel T. Headley, *Great Riots of New York, 1712–1871* (New York, 1873), 66–110; George Rudé, *The Crowd in History* (New York, 1964, revised edition 1981); idem., *Paris and London in the Eighteenth Century: Studies in Popular Protest* (New York, 1970); idem., *Ideology and Popular Protest* (New York, 1980); Eric Hobsbawm, *Primitive Rebels: Studies in Archaic Forms of Social Movement in the Nineteenth and Twentieth Centuries* (New York, 1959); E. P. Thompson, "The Moral Economy of the English Crowd in the Eighteenth Century," *Past and Present* 50 (1971), 76–136. For American examinations, see Dirk Hoerder, *Crowd Action in Revolutionary Massachusetts, 1765–1780* (New York, 1977); Edward Countryman, *A People in Revolution: The American Revolution and Political Society in New York, 1760–1790* (Baltimore, 1981), 36–71; idem., "The Problem of the Early American Crowd," *Journal of American Studies* 7 (1973), 77–90; Pauline Maier, *From Resistance to Revolution: Colonial Radicals and the Development of American Opposition to Britain, 1765–1776* (New York, 1972), chapter 1; Gary B. Nash, *The Urban Crucible: Social Change, Political Consciousness, and the Origins of the American Revolution* (Cambridge, Mass., 1979), chapter 11; Rhys Issac, "Dramatizing the Ideoogy of Revolution: Popular Mobilization in Virginia, 1774–1776," *William and Mary Quarterly* 33 (1976); Gordon S. Wood, "A Note on Mobs in the American Revolution," *William and Mary Quarterly* 23 (1966), 635–42; Arthur M. Schlesinger, "Political Mobs and the American Revolution, 1765–1776," *Proceedings of the American Philosophical Society* 99 (1955), 244–50.

2. Leonard L. Richards, *"Gentlemen of Property and Standing": Anti-Abolition Mobs in Jacksonian America* (New York, 1970); Sean Wilentz, *Chants Democratic: New York City and the Rise of the American Working Class, 1788–1850* (New York, 1984), 264–65, 168–70. Examining Jacksonian era riots in Philadelphia, Michael Feldberg says that Pauline Maier's model applies because "action was motivated . . . by appeals of natural justice, constitutional rights, and the notion that community interests superseded private rights." See "Urbanization as a Cause of Violence: Philadelphia as a Test Case," in Allen F. Davis and Mark H. Haller, eds., *The Peoples of Philadelphia: A History of Ethnic Groups and Lower Class Life, 1790–1940* (Philadelphia, 1973), 53–70; idem., "The Crowd in Philadelphia History: A Comparative Perspective," *Labor History* 15 (1974), 323–36; idem., *The Philadelphia Riot of 1844: A Study in Ethnic Conflict* (Westport, Conn., 1975); idem., *The Turbulent Era: Riot and Disorder in Jacksonian America* (New York, 1980). David Grimsted argues that during the Jacksonian period rioting "regained its eighteenth century status as a frequent and tacitly accepted if not approved mode of behavior." See "Rioting in Its Jacksonian Setting," *American Historical Review* 77 (1972), 364. For other New York examples, see Ray Allen Billington, *The Protestant Crusade, 1800–1860* (New York, 1938), chapters 3, 4, 9; Linda K. Kerber, "Abolitionists and Amalgamators: The New York City Race Riots of 1834," *New York History* 48 (1967), 28–39; Paul O. Weinbaum, *Mobs and Demagogues: The New York Response to Collective Violence in the Early Nineteenth Century* (Ann Arbor, 1979); Amy Bridges, *A City in the Republic: Antebellum New York and the Origin of Machine Politics* (Cambridge, England, 1984), 72.

3. Records of brothel attacks are in the New York City District Attorney Indictment Papers, Court of General Sessions, New York City Municipal Archives and Records Center (hereafter DAP), and the New York *Sun*. In the former, the defendant was usually charged with "rioting" and not simply assault and battery. The indictment did not always describe the dwelling under attack as a house of prostitution, but in most cases, the individual proprietor appeared in other indictments for operating a disorderly house. Furthermore, the physical description of the attack, the interior arrangement of the house, and the behavior of the men and women involved frequently indicated that it was a house of prostitution.

On the transformation of antebellum work and class relations, see especially Wilentz, *Chants Democratic*; and Christine Stansell, "The Origins of the Sweatshop: Women and Early Industrialization in New York City," in Michael H. Frisch and Daniel J. Walkowitz, eds., *Working-Class America: Essays on Labor, Community, and American Society* (Urbana, Ill., 1983), 78–103. For a description and analysis of the spread of prostitution in antebellum New York City, see Timothy J. Gilfoyle, "The Urban Geography of Commercial Sex: Prostitution in New York City, 1790–1860," *Journal of Urban History* 13 (May, 1987).

4. Lawrence Stone, *The Family, Sex, and Marriage in England, 1500–1800* (New York, 1977), 616; Nancy Tomes, "'A Torrent of Abuse': Crimes of Violence Between Working-Class Men and Women in London, 1840–1875," *Journal of Social History* 11 (1978), 337; John C. Schneider, *Detroit and the Problem of Order* (Lincoln, Nebraska, 1980), 20–31, 121; Jacques Rossiaud, "Prostitution, Youth, and Society in the Towns of Southeastern France in the Fifteenth Century," in Robert Forster and Orest Ranum, eds., *Deviants and the Abandoned in French Society: Selections from the Annales* (Baltimore, 1978), 1–31. Despite his compelling argument and innovative use of sources, Rossiaud sometimes confuses fact and hypothesis, never conclusively showing that males attacked females for these reasons. In her essay, Tomes admits that she found very few attacks on prostitutes in her sampling of crimes. Finally, Marcia Carlisle, in "Prostitutes and Their Reformers in Nineteenth Century Philadelphia" (Ph.D. dissertation, Rutgers University, 1982), 31, argues that the absence of attacks on prostitutes from 1800 to 1840 was a reflection of their general acceptance and respectability. Yet, she admits factory girls and others were often mistaken for prostitutes and abused. More importantly, the failure to find a record of attacks may be the result not of social toleration, but of the lack of acceptance, and fear by prostitutes to publicly prosecute their violent opponents. If so, the dearth of violence in the public record may show *greater* disrespect and unacceptability of prostitution.

5. Countryman, *A People in Revolution*, 41; Edward Bangs, ed., *Journal of Lt. Isaac Bangs, 1776* (Cambridge, Mass., 1890), 29–30; Allan Nevins, ed., *The Diary of Philip Hone* (New York, 1927), 339; Dr. Alexander Anderson Diary, October 14, 15, 1793, Columbia University; I. N. Phelps Stokes, *The Iconography of Manhattan Island, 1498–1910* (New York, 1912), V, 1301, 1370, 1550; DAP, Case of Jeanne Matharine Dronillan Volunbrun, October 9, 1801; People v. Perry, October 10, 1807. For other attacks, see DAP, People v. Varian, et al., April 11, 1812; People v. Rioters, July 9, 1814.

6. Bernard Bailyn, ed., *Pamphlets of the American Revolution, 1750–1776* (Cambridge, Mass., 1965), I, 581–84; Maier, *From Resistance to Revolution*, chapter 1; Schlesinger, "Political Mobs." Maier mentions similar attacks on brothels during the colonial period. For other examples of antiprostitution violence in the antebellum period, see Schneider, "Public Order and the Ge-

ography of the City: Crime, Violence, and the Police in Detroit, 1845–1875," *Journal of Urban History* 4 (1978), 193.

7. The literature on "the cult of domesticity" is voluminous. I have been most influenced by Nancy Cott, *Bonds of Womanhood: Woman's Sphere in New England, 1780–1835* (New Haven, 1977); Barbara Welter, "The Cult of True Womanhood," *American Quarterly* 18 (1966), 151–75; and Suzanne Lebsock, *The Free Women of Petersburg: Status and Culture in a Southern Town, 1784–1860* (New York, 1984).

8. Brothel "mobs" differ from the two types of anti-abolition mobs identified in Richards, *"Gentlemen of Property and Standing,"* 84–85, 112, 129. Unlike anti-abolition mobs, the size of the crowd and number of participants varied in both planned and unplanned attacks on houses of prostitution. Furthermore, planned assaults occurred without the support of local government officials. Finally, brothel riots were greater in number and continued over a longer period of time.

9. DAP, People v. Ford, September 28, 1842. The accused included William Ford (bootcrimper, 22 Watts Street), John McCloster, and George Remus. See *Longworth's City Directory* (New York, 1842).

10. DAP, People v. Valentine, March 11, 1833; People v. Kelso, et al., September 10, 1829; People v. Isaacs, March 19, 1852. A year later, Cauldwell still resided at the same address. See People v. Roberts, September 15, 1853.

11. DAP, People v. Gale, June 14, 1831.

12. *Sun*, September 3, 1833, January 22, February 11, 1834. Roberts was probably a prostitute because in other breaking and entering cases the newspaper coverage describes the victim as living in a "respectable" house or family. See *Sun*, February 12, 1834. This part of Anthony Street was also a major zone of prostitution from 1820 to 1850.

13. *Herald*, April 13, 15, 25, 28, 30, June 7, 9, 1836; George W. Walling, *Recollections of a New York Police Chief* (New York, 1887), 25; Nevins, *Diary of Hone*, 213; *National Police Gazette*, 26 August 1882.

14. DAP, People v. Ford, August 10, 1844. Ford, however, was convicted of assaults on three police officers who arrested him.

15. DAP, People v. Nosworthy, March 12, 1832. Nosworthy was a leader in an unrelated attack on Mary Bowen's Leonard Street brothel.

16. Edgar Allan Poe, "The Mystery of Marie Roget," in *The Complete Tales and Poems of Edgar Allan Poe* (New York, 1938), 197; Allan Nevins and Milton Halsey Thomas, eds., *The Diary of George Templeton Strong* 5 vols. (New York, 1952), I, 22–24, 62, 84. See also W. J. Rorabaugh, *The Alcoholic Republic: An American Tradition* (New York, 1979), 150–61.

17. *Sun*, February 4, March 11, 1834; Police Court Papers, New York City Municipal Archives and Records Center (hereafter PCP), Box 7445, Stewart v. Anderson and Dykes, January 2, 1833.

18. Most of these cases are in the DAP. See People v. Samis, February 20, 1837; People v. Golding, February 11, 1842; People v. Mott, October 20, 1842; People v. Small, January 16, 1829; People v. Dikeman, et al., December 14, 1836.

19. DAP, People v. Timpson, April 11, 1842; People v. Henrietta, April 8, 1836; *Herald*, January 9, 1836.

20. Sociology of crime studies show that only 20 to 25 percent of sexual crimes are reported. See Rossiaud, "Prostitution, Youth, and Society," 6.

21. *Niles' Register*, July 19, 1828.

22. *National Police Gazette*, January 2, 1847; DAP, People v. Dikeman, et al., December 14, 1836; DAP, People v. Norman, November 23, 1843. Most interestingly, the prostitute in the Astor House stabbing, Lydia Brown, alias Amelia Norman, was acquitted of her crime.

23. *Sun*, May 5, 1834. She later dropped the charge when he apologized.

24. *Sun*, May 17, 1834.

25. Christine Stansell, *City of Women: Sex and Class in New York 1789–1860* (New York, 1986), 169–92; Judith R. Walkowitz, *Prostitution and Victorian Society: Woman, Class and the State* (Cambridge, Eng., 1980), 14–20.

26. DAP, People v. Anderson, et al., January 12, 1829; People v. Lozier, et al., June 14, 1831. For corruption as early as 1815, see Ebenezer Burling to Humane Society (circa 1815), Society for the Suppression of Vice and Immorality Manuscripts, Reel 3, John Jay Papers, New York Historical Society.

27. DAP, People v. Small, et al., January 16, 1829; People v. Gale, June 14, 1831; People v. Nosworthy, March 12, 1832; People v. Tuttle, January 15, 1834; People v. Graham and Cole, December 14, 1836; People v. Hyer, et al., December 17, 19, 1836.

28. *Sun*, March 11, 1834; DAP, People v. Small, January 16, 1829; People v. Chichester, May 11, 1836; People v. Hyer, December 13, 1836; People v. Thorp, et al., February 13, 1841; People v. Golding, February 11, 1842; People v. Timpson, April 11, 1842; People v. Isaacs, December 25, 1851; People v. Moody, et al., January 15, 1852.

29. DAP, People v. Samis, February 20, 1837; People v. Pearsall, December 6, 1832; People v. Ford, August 10, 1844. Marcia Carlisle and John C. Schneider found that antebellum Philadelphia and Detroit prostitutes also resorted to the legal system to defend their rights and property. See Carlisle, "Prostitutes and Their Reformers in Nineteenth Century Philadelphia," 36–40; Schneider, *Detroit and the Problem of Order*, 20–21.

30. Walkowitz, *Prostitution and Victorian Society*. On American efforts to regulate prostitution, see David C. Pivar, *Purity Crusade: Sexual Morality and Social Control, 1868–1900* (Westport, Conn., 1973), 51–71.

31. The term "brothel bullies" was used by George Templeton Strong. See Nevins, *Diary of Strong*, IV, 113. In the 50 known or suspected attacks on disorderly houses from 1825 to 1857, 132 individuals were indicted (a much larger number were arrested, but not recorded). At least 16 of these defendants were repeat offenders involved in two or more attacks. In identifying rioters, I used the city directory. If the individual was unlisted, I followed those occupations given in the indictment. The ward numbers and occupations recorded on the standard indictment form, however, tended to be inconsistent and unreliable. In many cases, the ward listed was *where* the crime occurred and contradicted other information on the indictment. Even when skilled occupations were given in the defendant's testimony, the indictment frequently listed him as "laborer." See DAP, People v. Tuttle, January 15, 1834; People v. Chichester, April 8, May 11, 1836; People v. Graham, et al., December 13, 14, 1836. The breakdown for 12 semiskilled workers was: grocers and saloon keepers - 7, boardinghouse keepers - 2, cartmen - 1, female dressmaker - 1, stable keeper - 1; for skilled workers: butchers - 5, river pilot - 1, ship carver - 1, baker - 1, tailor - 1, masons - 3, printer - 1, binder - 1, bootmaker - 1, bootcrimper - 1, caulker - 1. (Three others had several listed for the same name, but all were either skilled or professional occupations); and for 7 white collar or professional workers: clerks - 2, engineer - 1, attorney - 1, City Hall or mayor's official - 3.

32. The wards and addresses of the rioters were based, firstly, on city directories, and secondly, on the ward given in the standard indictment. The breakdown was: 113 total defendants with a known address or ward, 39 from the same ward, 47 from an adjacent ward, and 27 from another part of the city.

33. DAP, People v. Lozier, et al., June 14, 1831. The occupations and addresses for the participants were: James Lozier, attorney, 65 Division Street; Charles Taylor, grocer, 64–66 Division Street; Jeremiah Dodge, ship carver, 264 Rivington Street; Charles B. Jennings, unknown. See *Longworth's City Directory* (New York, 1831).

34. For a convenient classification scheme on pre-industrial riots, see Rudé, *Paris and London*, 18–23.

35. Stansell, "Women, Children, and the Uses of the Streets: Class and Gender Conflict in New York City, 1850–1860," *Feminist Studies* 8 (1982), 309–35; Amy Gilman Srebnick, "The Murder of Mary Rogers: Identity, Sex and Class in Mid-Nineteenth Century New York City" (paper delivered to the American Historical Association Annual Meeting, New York City, December 29, 1985).

36. *Niles' Register*, January 8, 1831; *Diary of Hone*, 435, 451. For examples of attacks on women, see *Tribune*, March 13, 1844, March 27, May 1, 1846; Nevins, *Diary of Strong*, II, 129–30.

37. Gilfoyle, "The Urban Geography of Commercial Sex."

38. *Herald*, 23 June 1836. For front page stories, see the *Herald* and *Sun*, April 13–30, 1836, June 7–20, 1836, and *The Whip*, July 9, 1842, copy in DAP, People v. Wooldridge, July 14, 1842. Maria Williamson appears in New York City Land Title Registrations, Pre-1917 Conveyance Records, Office of City Register, liber 137, page 25, May 15, 1819; and Record of Assessments, Fifth Ward, 1820–1825, New York City Municipal Archives and Records Center. On the popular attention given to prostitutes, see Nevins, *Diary of Strong*, I, 114, 133; II, 270; Robert Taylor Diary, February 14, April 4, 17, November 17, 18, 20, 21, 22, 23, December 5, 6, 17, 1846, January 6, 1847, New York Public Library.

39. *Herald*, June 26, 1836.

40. W. J. Rorabaugh, *The Alcoholic Republic: An American Tradition* (New York, 1979), 150–52, 161.

41. David Grimsted similarly argues that Jacksonian rioters attacked groups less powerful and influential than they were. Their victims tended to be "the oppressed, the unpopular, and the unprotected." See "Rioting in Its Jacksonian Setting," 392–93.

42. People v. Chichester, May 8, 11, 1836. One of Chichester's accomplices, John Boyd, only four years earlier broke into Mary Bowen's Leonard Street domicile with a gang of fourteen males and destroyed her furniture. See PCP, Box 7445, People v. Boyd, et al., December 18, 1832. The Chichester gang is mentioned in Samuel Prime, *Life in New York* (New York, 1847), 180; *Herald*, April 15, 25, 1836; Herbert Asbury, *The Gangs of New York* (New York, 1927), 29; Weinbaum, *Mobs and Demagogues*, 151, 155. Their headquarters was at 44 Bowery.

43. DAP, People v. Hyer, December 17, 1836; People v. Roberts, et al., January 10, 1838. Among Hyer's accomplices was Abraham Vanderzee, who earned a position on the police force when it was created in 1844. See D. T. Valentine, *Manual of the Corporation of the City of New York* (New York, 1846), 59. Hyer's gang operated out of saloons at 42 and 50 Bowery. On Hyer and Poole, see *Tribune*, March 10, 12, 1855; Asbury, *Gangs*, 87–100; Frank Moss, *The American Metropolis* (New York, 1897), II, 397. On Hyer's alliances with Walsh and Seward (whom he supported at the 1860 Republican convention), see Wilentz, *Chants Democratic*, 328; Alvin F. Harlow, *Old Bowery Days: The Chronicles of a Famous Street* (New York, 1931), 301, 306.

44. DAP, People v. Graham, December 13, 14, 1836. The five arrested included: James Graham, age 21, clerk, 53 Lumber Street; William C. Rider, age 19, bartender, 505 Pearl Street; Henry Bertholf, age 25, mason, 76 Amos Street; James Cole, age 19, engineer, 38 Hubert Street; George Mayne, age 21, printer, 29 Madison Street. McGrath was listed as a street inspector in *Longworth's City Directory* (New York, 1835), 47.

45. DAP, People v. Tuttle, January 15, 1834; People v. Ryerson, et al., December 10, 1834. *Longworth's City Directory* (New York, 1834) lists the following occupations and addresses for the accused: John K. Ryerson, tailor, 28 Ludlow Street; Joseph B. Smith, butcher, 64 North (Houston) Street; Samuel Hill, butcher, 51 1st Street; James Johnson, butcher, 86 Delancey Street; Andrew Jackman, City Hall officer, 101 Elizabeth Street; Jacob Vogle, butcher, 50 1st Street. Charles Kemp and Henry Avis were not listed. Jackman was listed as an Eleventh Ward Common School trustee in 1843 and a city assessor in 1846. See D. T. Valentine, *Manual of the Corporation of the City of New York, 1842–43* (New York, 1843), 75; idem., *Manual* (New York, 1846), 47.

46. Bridges, *A City in the Republic*, 73–77, 126–36, 152–53; Harlow, *Old Bowery Days*, 188, 205, 296–301.

47. On the gang associations and involvement of "The Allen" in prostitution, see *National Police Gazette*, 28 August 1880. On Sullivan, see Harlow, *Old Bowery Days*, 505–22.

48. *National Police Gazette*, December 8, 1866, June 8, 1867; *Tribune*, 28, 29 March 1855. *McDowall's Journal* reported that boarding houses acting as fronts for parlor houses usually employed one man for such purposes. See *McDowall's Journal*, May 1833; PCP, Box 7448, Bennett v. Pearce, November 9, 1835; DAP, People v. Shannon, April 19, 1836; People v. Smith, July 25, 1840; James MacCabe, *The Secrets of the Great City* (Philadelphia, 1868), 290. This evidence contradicts Christine Stansell's and Ruth Rosen's thesis that pimps and male dominance of commercialized prostitution did not appear until after 1890 and greater police harassment. See Rosen, *The Lost Sisterhood: Prostitution in the Progressive Era, 1900–1918* (Baltimore, 1982), 33, 40; Stansell, *City of Women*, chapter 9. Jacques Rossiaud found prostitutes with pimps in fifteenth-century France. See "Prostitution, Youth and Society," 18.

49. Ellen Carol DuBois and Linda Gordon, "Seeking Ecstasy on the Battlefield: Danger and Pleasure in Nineteenth-Century Feminist Sexual Thought," *Feminist Studies* 9 (1983), 7–25.

# The Enemy Within: Some Effects of Foreign Immigrants on Antebellum Southern Cities

*Randall M. Miller*

Among American historical perennials, few have persisted so long as the concept of Southern distinctiveness. However much historians differ on the exact configuration, they do agree that the Old South was unique. Historians trace the roots of Southern distinctiveness to the pervasive influences of evangelical Protestantism, plantation agriculture, and black slavery, all of which nourished a common folk culture among whites regardless of class or condition. In such a Southern gemeinschaft society, cities appear largely as extensions of the countryside, performing commercial and financial functions to sustain an agricultural economy and remaining subservient to the values of a planter-dominated world. The rootless, impersonal, diverse cities of modern society have no place in this portrait of Southern distinctiveness.[1]

Antebellum Southern society was never so tidy. In the late antebellum period Southern cities tugged in two directions—toward continued support of the traditional, rural interests that service to the region's plantation economy demanded and toward increasing commercialization and social diversity that urban growth encouraged. Neither force was quite yet capable of overcoming the other, but the tensions the contrary pulls created threatened to reshape Southern urban society in several ways. Cities played vital social and political roles in Southern life, in addition to their economic functions. They also diverged in important ways from prevailing Southern social and political norms as the Old South veered toward secession. From the 1830s through the 1850s the expansion of urban economies and the attendant growth of urban populations fundamentally altered the urban landscape. New city dwellers, a majority of whom were foreign-born, created new social conditions to accommodate their needs, as they also fostered values at war with the countryside. By recasting the conceptual framework of Southern life to

*Randall M. Miller is professor of history at Saint Joseph's University. Reprinted from* Southern Studies: An Interdisciplinary Journal of the South *24, no. 1 (Spring 1985): 30–53. Reprinted by permission of* Southern Studies.

include immigrant and working-class culture in cities, it is possible to
see the extent of urban-rural divergence in the late antebellum era. It is
also possible to get new angles from which to view Southern society
generally.

In the rural world the slaveholders made, social order hinged on the
informal bonds of family and race. Proslavery apologists, among others,
preached the social unity of a Herrenvolk democracy, a concept of white
supremacy that obscured any class or cultural differences among whites,
and they reminded white Southerners of all classes that as white men
stood together to protect slavery, they also preserved order. In defending the region's peculiar institution, and thereby Southern culture itself, Southerners developed a philosophy of social stasis that derived
from the strong sense of cultural and social unity in the Old South. Slavery and the Southern brand of evangelical Protestantism, which infused so much of the region's life, bred among white Southerners a
conservative social temperament distrustful of government and fatalis-
tic toward human suffering. Then, too, the region had enjoyed a remarkably high level of ethnic homogeneity, having a significantly smaller
proportion of new immigrants in its total population than did the North.
The cultural and racial consensus among whites allowed political participation to expand in the 1840s and 1850s without the dissensions and
disruptions that marked Northern political life.[2]

The philosophy of social stasis praised agrarianism and traditional-
ism while it simultaneously, if sometimes only implicitly, fostered mis-
trust of modern cities where poverty, class tension, and ethnic division
brought on social disorder. Southerners increasingly drew invidious distinctions between their ruralism and Northern urbanism during the late
antebellum era. In doing so, they fastened on the instability and social
turmoil they saw in Northern cities as evidence of the dangers of mod-
ernism. It was highly significant for them that so many immigrants in
the 1840s and 1850s congregated in the North, as it was equally significant that so many fewer immigrants went South. More than anything
else, the growing number of poor, unassimilated, working-class urban
dwellers and the crime and violence in Northern cities provided grist
for the Southern proslavery mill.

Although Southern diatribes against Northern ills contributed to the
defense of slavery, they also falsely reassured Southerners that diversity and disorder were not great problems for their section. By exagger-
ating the contrast between urban North and pastoral South, Southerners
were able to submerge their own fears about potential trouble at home.
It was, however, a case of denying painful reality, for even as the South
basked in its self-proclaimed rural superiority, its cities were becoming
seedbeds of modern social and economic change, and it was surely a
portent of danger that Southern cities too were filling up with poor,
unassimilated, working-class immigrants.[3]

Southern cities grew at a rapid rate between 1830 and 1860. The
vast majority of newcomers to Southern cities were foreigners, some traveling southward from New York or Philadelphia and others entering
Southern ports directly, particularly through New Orleans. Southern

urban populations doubled and even tripled in some instances in the thirty years before the Civil War as a result of the large immigrant influx and, to a lesser extent, the movement of Northern-born migrants and Southern-born blacks and whites. However transient their intentions, many immigrants remained long enough in Southern cities to burden charities, transform labor relations, and create a new social order.[4]

The heavy immigration of the 1840s and 1850s made its chief impact on the size, composition, and character of the working classes of the urban South. By 1860 foreign-born workers comprised the principal source of free labor in all important Southern river and port cities. Indeed, the proportion of foreign-born persons in the whole adult male population of the South's ten largest cities was higher than in almost every Northern city. Because immigrants to Southern cities were disproportionately male, they comprised a higher percentage of the urban work force, which tended to be male-oriented in its job categories, than their numbers in the whole urban population might suggest. Adding the Northern-born migrants to the foreign-born population reveals even more clearly the non-Southern character of the late antebellum Southern urban working class. In Savannah, a representative case, the arrival of immigrants and Northern-born workers accounted for over 60 percent of the increase in the whole free population during the 1850s, a decade when the city's population tripled. According to the 1860 federal census, approximately 70 percent of Mobile's free adult males came from outside the South.[5]

During the 1850s Southern cities developed a large white working class in which the typical worker likely shared few values of the Old South. The growth of this labor force in no way represented an extension of the countryside into the city, for very few nonslaveholding whites left the rural South for work or residence in Southern cities. In the 1850s, in many Southern cities, European immigrants, Northern-born migrants, and blacks made up more than 90 percent of the entire working class, and most of that working class was free and foreign-born. The immigrant infusion whitened up the Southern work force generally and even restored white numerical majorities in Charleston and New Orleans.

The arrival of Irish and German workers in large numbers in the 1840s and 1850s injected a new and somewhat dangerous dynamic into the urban workplace. The new workers displaced local white and black labor in several occupations—a process already under way in the Lower South by the 1840s where significant immigration had occurred in the 1830s, but only beginning in the late 1840s in the Upper South, which received its foreign immigration later than did most Southern seaboard cities. Probably the most affected by the significant immigrant competition were Southern-born white workers who all but vanished from the urban workplace. They survived only in such select trades as printing and building, where their native origins might have given them some advantage, and where their self-imposed insulation from the bulk of the working classes by means of closed shops, unions, and clubs allowed them to avoid debasement by association with blacks and immigrants.

Virtually everywhere in the urban South by the 1850s immigrants had come to dominate most artisan work, except in Charleston where free black and slave artisans thrived through the Civil War. In the unskilled occupations Southern-born whites hardly existed by the 1850s. Immigrants and blacks alone competed for manual labor and unskilled positions—work that white Southerners increasingly deemed unworthy and degrading.[6]

Across the urban South immigrant workers elbowed free black competitors aside in skilled and unskilled occupations and eroded the already precarious economic and social conditions of many free blacks. Using numerical strength and incipient organizations, throughout the 1850s immigrant workers forced municipal authorities to acknowledge the old, but often unenforced, legal restrictions on black employment in many different trades. Even small cities did not escape such pressures. In 1858 in Little Rock, Arkansas, for example, a German blacksmith led a protest meeting to remove free blacks, as well as slaves and convicts, from the crafts.[7]

Licensing fees and other legal impediments, pressure on white employers, and violence were the "public" means of proscription, but, more than anything else, it was the immigrants' initial willingness to underbid local labor for any and all work that drove free blacks into despair and poverty. Immigrants ignored local taboos about "nigger work" and crashed into free black monopolies everywhere, from drayage to barbering. Immigrant women also participated in this process, entering into domestic service, particularly in the Upper South where they were often preferred to blacks, and competing with free black women as washerwomen, seamstresses, and prostitutes.[8]

The history of immigrant versus black competition in Norfolk, Virginia, illustrates the changing dynamics in Southern cities. Until the 1850s blacks dominated the wharves and shipping-related occupations as common laborers or mechanics—carpenters, cordwainers, plasterers, caulkers, coopers, riggers, blacksmiths, stonecutters, pilots. They also controlled domestic service. Widespread hiring of free black domestics contributed to the stability of free black households by providing women with incomes to supplement or, in some instances, to sustain their men's contributions. Because so many blacks relied on those occupations, any competition threatened their survival and autonomy as a community. Black females were especially vulnerable because they had only domestic service or prostitution available as important sources of employment.[9]

By 1860 immigrant Irish girls had begun to displace black women in domestic service. Black males also suffered from new competition. The number of black carpenters, shoemakers, shopkeepers, among several occupations, declined in the face of immigrant rivals. Even drayage, which contemporaries commonly assumed was impervious to white encroachment, attracted immigrants in the 1850s. By 1860 the skilled trades in Norfolk had passed from black to white hands. The increasing number of immigrants entering Norfolk and becoming naturalized citizens there—that is, committing themselves to settlement—largely accounted for the shift. A carpenter from Spain, a shoemaker from Ger-

*Replaced the immigrant work force for blacks*

many, a tailor from England, a stonecutter from England, a weaver from Ireland, a baker from Germany, and so on, were among the 648 naturalized citizens in Norfolk in 1860 who found urban employment in trades once ruled by free blacks.

Increased competition between white and black workers led the former to try to circumscribe black workers altogether. Angry white laborers and artisans demanded that employers justify any hiring of blacks. Although protests often proved unsuccessful, immigrant opposition to black hiring apparently discouraged some preference for blacks and introduced a new voice into Norfolk's labor and social relations.

The fluctuations of urban market economies in the 1840s and 1850s, however, interrupted or slowed the decline of the free blacks' position, as a free market in labor operated everywhere but in the realm of municipal employment, where whites held political advantage. In New Orleans yellow fever and cholera epidemics combined with spasmodic economic growth to create periodic shortages of skilled and unskilled labor and to raise wage rates considerably. When the epidemics ended or the economy flagged, black and white job competition intensified in the city, but during periods of economic prosperity the seeming need for an enlarged labor pool convinced many white employers and local authorities to ignore restrictions on free black employment, and slave hiring too for that matter, thereby preserving black places in the economy. Irish and German immigrants had pushed blacks out of drayage, taxi service, and hotel employment in the 1850s, but dockwork and the river trades remained open to blacks. The militancy of dissident Irish workers who demanded improved wages and working conditions on the docks and riverboats, once they became firmly established there, induced several white employers to support a free black labor reserve. Also, some employers recruited blacks in efforts to drive down wage rates in unskilled occupations and to disrupt any sense of class commonality among working people generally.[10]

In Charleston free blacks staved off complete displacement by immigrants. Charleston's employers simply preferred free blacks in several skilled trades, thereby undermining the immigrants' efforts to penetrate all areas of employment. The seasonal nature of much of the Irish immigration before the 1850s also favored the native Charleston working population in moving into and controlling skilled trades. Failing to get state legislative support in their campaigns to restrict black employment in skilled occupations, the immigrants turned to city government for relief. Only a few upwardly mobile immigrants, particularly Germans, won places in skilled trades, but many did receive municipal employment. The Irish especially benefitted from government largess.[11]

The truculence and unpredictability of foreign workers dissatisfied employers and helped to keep slaves and free blacks employed. The Irish, once they had gained their bearings in the new land, seemed to be particularly intractable. Disgruntled workers abandoned employers at a moment's notice, refused to work beyond their contractual times, and spoke out against abuses—actions few slaves or free blacks could safely take. Irish laborers at Fort Jackson, outside New Orleans, rebelled in

1849 when their employer tried to keep them at work amid rumors of a cholera outbreak. The laborers ceased work and threatened to tar and feather their work boss. In 1856 the Irish longshoremen in Savannah, who had a history of work stoppages, exasperated local merchants by calling a strike. The merchants pledged to "dispense altogether" with immigrant labor and to employ black labor instead. Complaints about the lack of deference, sloppy work, and excessive demands by Irish workers echoed throughout the urban South.[12]

The erratic work performances of immigrants, the preference of some whites to be served by blacks, and the movement of free blacks and runaway slaves into the interstices of urban economies allowed "free" blacks to survive in the late antebellum period, but the immigrant advance into the workplace was inexorable. Most white employers were indifferent to the fate of free blacks. Others no doubt thought that the destruction of free black autonomy was a good thing in a slave society. Besides, newly arrived immigrants often came cheap.

The immigrants' relationship with urban slave labor was more complex and somewhat contradictory. The size of the urban slave population fluctuated in response to several factors, including the price of slaves, the character and vigor of the local economy, the labor demands of the surrounding countryside, and the rate of foreign immigration. Slavery declined in some cities while it grew, even prospered, in others amid the floodtide of immigration in the 1850s. Between 1820 and 1860 the slave population's share of the total population fell in the ten largest cities, but it rose in the ten second largest cities. Numbers, however, do not reveal the social dynamics at work. As an institution, slavery resisted immigrant competition, but slaveholders, and surely slaves too, recognized changes in the assumptions about slavery's place in a changing city once immigrants arrived to build a working-class world of their own.[13]

Slaves continued to work in virtually every field of manual labor throughout the 1850s, and in some cities, especially Charleston, they clung tenaciously to several artisanal occupations. But the presence of immigrant workers, when combined with the transfer of many slave artisans into the agricultural sector in the 1850s, severely limited slave participation in the crafts and the petit bourgeois urban economy, and so crippled slave leadership in the cities. Urban slaves became increasingly concentrated in a few trades, such as carpentry, or they moved into such industries as tobacco and iron manufactures. Many slaves remained as domestics or day laborers. Meanwhile, German immigrants gravitated toward the mechanical arts and retailing, while, by 1860, Irish immigrants predominated in the semi- and unskilled occupations.

Immigrants wanted jobs and resented hired slaves jostling them for places. Unskilled workers relied on their strong backs to drive slaves from the labor market. Failing that, they used their fists. Skilled workers sought legislative remedies for their problems, but they enjoyed only minor successes. Planter-dominated legislatures balked at any attempt to deny slaves access to the urban economy. Urban slave ownership and the need to hire slaves remained sufficiently widespread in the 1840s and 1850s to insure that city councils would respect slavery's interest in

urban employment, although city authorities found it increasingly difficult to ignore demands for stricter enforcement of slave codes limiting
slave hiring. The elasticity of labor demand in Southern cities relieved
some of the pressures, for as rural demand for slave labor in the 1850s
siphoned off slaves from cities, immigrants moved in to fill the gaps.
The rising costs of hiring slaves in the cities—due to high demands for
labor generally, high slave prices, and the slaves' greater control over
their arrangements through the regularization of bonus payments and
other accommodations hirers had to make to attract slaves—also enhanced immigrants' employability by making the actual cost of hiring a
slave more than the cost of hiring a white person in many instances.
Still, an inherent conflict between immigrant workers and slavery remained built into the Southern urban economy, and slaveholders knew
it. When attempts to reserve places for slaves broke down because immigrants demanded not only the most menial jobs, but also the most
lucrative ones, slaveholders became assertive everywhere in holding on
to their slave-hiring prerogatives.[14]

Immigrants' willingness to engage in work that Southern whites
considered fit only for slaves blurred distinctions between white and
black, free and slave. Economic necessity and cultural preference led
Irish girls to ignore the strong Southern prejudice against domestic service, which whites identified with blacks. Gangs of immigrant Irish and
German men dug ditches, repaired levees, built roads, and loaded and
unloaded cargoes, just as blacks did. The immigrant workers' mean diet,
wretched shelter, onerous labor, and poor health degraded them in Southern eyes. Indeed, the parallels between black slavery and the gang labor of the ditchers and others did not escape contemporaries, who thought
that such immigrants reeked of servitude.[15]

If the immigrants' work debased them, it also threatened to elevate
the blacks. The *Richmond Enquirer* spoke for many Southerners in 1857
when it warned against blacks and whites competing in any menial occupation, for "slaves or negroes may be inclined to consider themselves
on a par of equality with white servants." Some proslavery apologists
insisted that slaves should do all work and that all workers should be
slaves, but slaveholders' rhapsodies about white solidarity made little
sense to immigrant workers pitted against blacks in the labor market.[16]

Skilled mechanics complained about the degradation they felt because of competition with slaves. By permitting slaves to compete with
whites, slaveholders dragged the whites down to the level of the blacks,
thereby breeding "discontent and hatred" against slavery. Rather, as
one master mechanic in Charleston wrote in 1860, slaveholders should
relegate blacks to their "true position" of subordination "under a master
workman" to effect "a closer bond of union" among the white classes of
the city. Of course, enlarging opportunities in skilled trades for whites
meant increasing competition among blacks and whites in the unskilled
ones.[17]

Satisfying the demands of all white workingmen required the removal of slaves from the urban economy, something slaveholders were
not willing or able to do even to achieve white unity. Thus, on the eve of

secession, white workers and slaveholders did not necessarily stand together. As long as white immigrants performed tasks identified with
bondage and competed for work with slaves, the natural affinity of race
and property that bound slaveholder and nonslaveholder together in
the countryside suffered strains in the city.

The economic growth of Southern cities, which brought immigrants
into competition with slavery, also altered the physical environment of
the city, making Southern cities similar to Northern ones in many ways
and, also, transforming the social dynamics governing black and white,
foreign-born and native-born, worker and employer, poor and rich. Warehouses, manufacturing establishments, and tenements consumed open
spaces, foliage, and grass, particularly along the waterfront and on the
peripheries of cities. The older, rural features of urban life—parks, trees,
gardens, and yards—survived almost solely in areas occupied by the
upper classes. The appearance of distinct areas within cities, differentiated by physical landscape, revealed the breakdown of urban community into subdivisions based on economic function, class, and culture.
The proliferation of city directories in the 1850s, which has allowed us
to map the physical and social terrain of urban change, further attested
to the shift from an organic, small-town, even rural, sense of community as a direct and personal experience to one that was increasingly
impersonal, abstract, fragmented, and formal.

Such unsettling effects were new to Southern experience. During
the 1830s Irish and German immigrants in Southern cities had generally dispersed within each city, although they occupied places around or
close to the central business area. Before efficient local transportation
or the centralization of urban employment, workers sought residences
within short walks to work to compensate for the long hours on the job.
Unskilled occupations offered irregular and short-term employment at
best so that laborers needed easy access to the main wharves, warehouses, and business district where employment was available and daily
hiring took place. As long as the labor pool remained small or grew mod-
erately, the walking cities accommodated newcomers without undue
stress on housing or dramatic changes in the cityscape. The physical
proximity and integration of all classes facilitated communication and
interaction, retarding class or cultural exclusiveness and preserving the
rhythms of small-town life.[18]

The dispersal of small immigrant populations in geographically confined cities made possible their incorporation into traditional Southern
social and political communities. In Charleston, gentlemen of property
and standing early became acutely self-conscious about their racial and
social vulnerability in a city where blacks outnumbered whites and where
wealth was concentrated in few hands. Consequently, they fostered a
familial, paternalistic urban ethos and appealed to immigrants and
native-born white workers on the basis of common racial interest. Any
ethnic division among whites threatened white solidarity. In Northern
cities associational life increasingly reflected neighborhood, ethnic, or
class exclusiveness, but Charleston's clubs and social organizations were
"broadly inclusive" and assimilative in practice, open to whites regard-

less of national background or religion. In turn, by the 1830s all the important ethnic societies, such as the Hibernian Society and the German Friendly Society, had adopted the Charleston way, ending membership restrictions based on ethnic identity. In the 1840s such organizations were electing to office persons who had no ethnic ties to the original membership, and throughout the 1850s they were honoring Southern statesmen and supporting Southern rights. By that time the organizations had little connection with the new Irish and German immigrants who were streaming into Charleston.[19]

The process of assimilating outsiders into Southern interests remained incomplete even in the 1830s. New, poor Irish arrivals did not participate in Charleston's older associations, although the Hibernian Society did provide relief to the very needy among them. Irish Catholics preferred their own organizations or none at all, cutting them off from the Protestant-dominated Hibernian Society. The party preferences of association members reveal other fissures within ethnic groups. The leaders of the Hibernian Society supported the Nullifiers in the 1830s, but the rank and file remained heavily Unionist in sentiment. Insomuch as leaders of ethnic organizations function as connectors, binding disparate elements within the group together through newspapers, petitions, and public service in dealing with the host society, the Charleston "leaders" were sending false signals to the larger Southern community. They did not speak for their groups, which were changing rapidly anyway. Neither cohesion nor consensus fully occurred in the 1830s and 1840s, before the great crunch of new immigrants in the 1850s shattered any illusions of unity.[20]

During the 1850s the sheer volume of immigrants coming into Southern cities combined with the economic expansion of those same cities to prevent older assumptions about social community from operating. Between 1850 and 1860 residential patterns revealed that urban dwellers were dividing along lines of class, race, culture, and wealth. Free blacks and Irish immigrants tended to be the most residentially segregated in virtually every city in which they lived in significant numbers. Their poverty condemned them to the least desirable locations. Even Germans, who had a wider range of skills and wealth and religious divisions among Protestant, Catholic, and Jew, clustered together into definite "German blocks" within neighborhoods. The rise of a commercial middle class of clerks, professionals, and managers—drawn largely from Northern-born or second generation immigrants and native Southerners—further bifurcated the cities. Separate associations sprang up around each clustering of function, class, residence, race, or whatever, thereby solidifying separate identities.[21]

In Charleston, Irish immigrants crowded into the low, dirty streets along the Cooper River, north and east of the city's warehouses and wharves. Frederick Law Olmsted thought the "packing filth, and squalor" there equal to the worst he had seen in any comparable Northern town. Savannah's working-class immigrants, who were largely Irish, jockeyed with blacks for space in the "low, dingy, squalid, cheerless negro huts" along the city's fringes, wherever rents were cheapest. Even small inland cities like Augusta had ethnic/working-class neighborhoods. In Augusta the Irish employees of the Georgia Railroad shared "Dublin" with a small black community.[22]

Richmond's topography of hills and waterways created natural enclosures that allowed different classes and groups to isolate themselves from one another. Isolation bred strong neighborhood identities. So, too, did the segregation of economic functions into distinct areas. The working classes composed of blacks, Irish, and Germans massed along Shockoe Creek and the James River, near the factories and wharves; as that area filled up, they settled on the outskirts of the city.[23]

Immigrants spread throughout New Orleans, but they concentrated in the lower and upper reaches of the waterfront, close to their work. In the Third Municipality, where most immigrants entered the city, numerous immigrant shanties cropped up. Other immigrants swarmed into the Second Municipality and, by the 1850s, also controlled the suburbs of Lafayette and Carrollton. Neighborhoods with such names as "Little Saxony" and the "Irish Channel" staked off ethnic and class boundaries within the city. They also corresponded with the poorest and least healthy sections, which, as one observer remarked in 1853, had "as many destitute poor crowded together" as any city in Europe. Contemporaries measured the class, and by implication the ethnic, differences in New Orleans according to the "declivity of the soil." Anyone living below the water line belonged to the lower class. Grog shops, groceries, and brothels flourished in the poor districts, giving an unsavory, sordid reputation to the neighborhoods—and their denizens.[24]

Crammed into low-lying areas along waterways, debilitated by travel and work, and undernourished, poor immigrants became easy prey for diseases, but their suffering evoked more contempt than compassion from native-born Southerners in the 1850s. The high mortality among immigrants during the epidemics became a source of animus toward them. That immigrants burdened hospitals and poor houses was problem enough in a society that regarded poverty as a personal failing. That they shared those facilities with blacks was cause for further disgust. That the unacclimated immigrants proved unusually susceptible to the regional plagues of cholera and yellow fever convinced many Southerners that immigrants would never fit into Southern society and that they posed an immediate danger to it.

In the antebellum period most Americans equated disease with moral failure. Disease and social disorder both emanated from violations of natural law. To prevent or cure such ills, society had to inculcate proper values in its members, and individuals had to practice good hygiene. Although some Southern medical doctors urged sewerage and drainage improvements in cities to stave off epidemics, most educated persons continued to believe that "disease was a judgment." Dr. E. H. Barton of the New Orleans Board of Health confessed as much in 1849, when he blamed the victims of cholera for their affliction: "The liability being individual, the municipal power can only aid by cleanliness and ventilation." The presence of immigrants, others added, actually imperiled Southern cities because their vicious habits and improvidence invited disease, and the epidemics they "caused" discouraged more responsible persons, capital, and trade from entering Southern cities. The immigrants were pariahs.[25]

In surveying the ethnic/working-class districts, too many Southerners missed the internal diversity among the lower classes and saw only disease and disorder. They lumped the lower classes into one alien mass, irrespective of differences in color, caste, or condition. Southerners regarded the lower classes collectively as "the worst elements" and treated them accordingly. In Savannah, in 1855, the police chief believed the worlds of the "quieter" people and lower-class "disturbers of the peace" were so incompatible in values and interest that he urged the city to build two police stations as a barrier to safeguard life and property in the respectable sections from the disruptive elements surrounding them. Southerners expected the working-class immigrants to cause trouble. When a series of fires broke out in Mobile during a yellow fever epidemic, Mobile authorities initially charged that "the low Irish populations about the harbor" committed the arson to plunder a prostrate city. Only the confessions of several runaway slaves shifted blame away from the immigrants.[26]

City authorities across the South sought control over an alien population of immigrants and blacks. Police practice seemed to operate on the assumption that immigrants, especially the "fighting Irish," and blacks made up a criminal class needful of close, constant supervision. Municipal arrest and court records reveal that the Irish and blacks comprised the overwhelming majority of persons charged with criminal or antisocial behavior, including vagrancy, disorderly conduct, drunkenness, petit larceny, and brawling. In New Orleans immigrants were uniquely prone to arrest for being "dangerous and suspicious characters," even when they had broken no law. Throughout the arrest proceedings the city authorities identified the immigrant by his foreignness. He was Irish, "a stranger," or whatever. Like blacks, the new immigrants did not quite belong among the respectable classes and bore watching. The disportionately high percentage of foreign-born in Southern prisons further confirmed the Southern "guardians" worst suspicions about the aliens among them, and about the social disorder in their own changing cities. Where once, in the 1830s, Charleston authorities assigning work and charity for poor people on relief refused "to break down any of the distinctions" between black and white poor "by subjecting them to a common mode of punishment" or work, by the 1850s the immigrant poor came in for rougher handling. All the residents of the poor districts required discipline.[27]

By the 1850s the immigrant workers represented more than just potential criminal types: they were social disruption personified. Southerners feared workers who spent much time in grog shops, groceries, saloons—all those places and activities where the host society's control was weakest, and where, too, slaves mingled easily with free blacks and lower-class whites. Thrown together in the workplace and lower-class neighborhoods, and often practicing the same trades, immigrants and blacks did not just fight one another. Immigrant tradesmen kept up an illegal traffic with country slaves bringing produce into the city, dispensed liquor to blacks with complete disregard for city ordinances and social custom, and, on occasion, assisted slave runaways. Immigrants violated the etiquette of race relations and disgusted Southerners by living, trading, drinking, and even sleeping with blacks, slave and free. More than anything else, slaveholders feared a world in which blacks were elevated above whites. In the poor districts white prostitutes took money from black men for sexual services, and white workers sometimes worked for black employers. Blacks in cities had the experience of seeing whites under them in several ways.[28]

Antebellum Southern cities, unlike their Northern counterparts, lacked many formal means of imposing order. The factory system did not exist to regiment life, nor did most people toil in large-scale workplaces where they came under a common discipline. Southern cities failed to establish enough public schools capable of inculcating a shared set of values in children of all classes. German-born Christopher G. Memminger, among others, argued that Charleston could reverse economic stagnation and alleviate class tensions by building a common school system. Its principal purpose, he contended, would be to battle the disaffection and lack of "public spirit" among lower-class whites, especially immigrants, and so achieve the unity of purpose and white solidarity necessary to preserve Southern institutions. In 1849 the commissioners of the free schools of St. Philip's and St. Michael's warned that, unless immigrants were brought into common schools, they would "always be an easy prey to political seduction, and trouble, under the excitement of general elections or the promptings of an unprincipled leader, to break out into excesses," and to defy the law. In cities, they continued, the "ignorant and uneducated" poor were the first to engage "in outrage and violence" and to oppose Southern institutions. During the 1850s, New Orleans followed Charleston in building a public school system to provide a common language and experience in an otherwise culturally and socially divided city. But the Charleston and New Orleans cases were exceptional, and even in those cities most lower-class whites did not attend schools regularly or for very long, if at all.[29]

Religion, a powerful matrix of Southern civilization, also failed to generate much centripetal force in Southern cities. Most of the new immigrants were Catholics for whom the dominant evangelical Protestantism of the region meant little, except perhaps as a source of oppression, and Protestant churches made few efforts to bring immigrants under the Southern religious canopy. Methodists did, for example, support a mission among Germans in Mobile in the 1840s, and various ministers attempted to effect death-bed conversions of individual immigrants in hospitals, but too many evangelicals recognized the immigrants only to condemn them. Even the Catholic church, whose leaders shared Southern values regarding slavery and a conservative social order, failed to provide unity among the newer immigrants. As in the North, ethnic divisions within the church, grafted onto longstanding disputes between the laity and the hierarchy over church finances and control of pastors, wracked the universal church and kept it weak and defensive.[30]

Responding to public fears about a breakdown of law and order amid increasing population density and diversity, city authorities, like their Northern counterparts, established uniformed police forces. Along with the creation or extension of poor houses, sewer systems, waterworks, health boards, and the like, the introduction of a professional police force promised to restore discipline and harmony by enforcing common standards of morality and private behavior. But immigrants intruded in the process by making police work their own. While native-born Southerners and second-generation immigrants commanded the better paying positions of constables, marshals, detectives, and captains and lieutenants, immigrant Irish and German laborers filled the ranks of the police on the beats or in patrols. The Irish were especially overrepresented in the New Orleans, Memphis, Charleston, and Savannah police forces, although a reform administration in Charleston and Know Nothing administrations in Memphis and New Orleans in the late 1850s reduced the size of the Irish presence in their police departments. Without marketable skills, lower-class immigrants found police work attractive. Despite low pay and unpleasant duties, it afforded them regular work or, frequently, a second income and the possibility of upward mobility in municipal employment. Poor pay and their affinity to the lower-class persons they were supposed to control led to graft, abuses, and countless infractions of police regulations. The police were not fit or able to impose Southern order on the cities. Control of police departments also became a major political issue in local elections, and it encouraged increased immigrant involvement in urban politics.[31]

The entrance of immigrants into city politics further threatened social control. As long as "respectable" people served as policemen, magistrates, and jurors, Southerners thought they could maintain discipline over the lower classes. By the 1850s the native-born Southerners' political hegemony in several cities had been so eroded that they had to resort to ethnic politics just to stay in power. Charleston patricians symbolically conceded as much when they added Irish and German candidates (acceptable to them) to their tickets in municipal elections. In Savannah the issues of police harassment of immigrant shopkeepers specifically and police department reform generally (which meant closer surveillance of and interference in lower-class activities) defined political categories from 1854 to the Civil War. Democrats there appealed openly for immigrant support, declaiming on the party's love of laborers and, more importantly, providing patronage jobs in city government or on public projects and winking at immigrants who violated laws regarding the sale of liquor to blacks.[32]

Democrats, who tended to align with immigrant voting blocs, were themselves never wholly comfortable with the new politics. Political leaders still tried to preserve some of the older political style, based on assumptions of an organic and natural relation among all whites, by using race as a weapon, but immigrant workers' insistence on issues related to their interest made such appeals increasingly anachronistic in a divided metropolis. The experience of Thomas Avery, running for Congress in 1848, illustrates the uneasy adjustment of the Democrats to their own politics. Avery ventured into "Pinch," the rough Irish working-class neighborhood of north Memphis, to attend a social gathering put on by an Irish workingmen's union. Avery brought his three young sisters to the affair, and the boys of Pinch danced all night with the Southern belles. After the meeting Avery thanked his sister Elizabeth for her sacrifice on his behalf: "You have done splendidly. *I* know how you feel, but luckily I don't think those fellows know. You made them think you were having the time of your life. It will make them feel kindly toward me." A natural affinity among whites of all classes was nowhere apparent in Avery's confession. Going among the immigrants was strictly business, or politics.[33]

Immigrants flexed their political muscles to win places in city governments, which, in turn, made those governments less an instrument of social control. Native-born Southerners joined businessmen, many of whom were Northern-born or second generation immigrants, in crusades to clean out the vice and corruption of the poor districts. Out-of-power, such persons formed vigilante groups to drive out the ruffians and evildoers in their midst. Whitecaps in Atlanta in 1851 and vigilantes in New Orleans in 1859 bracketed a decade of extra-legal "justice." Nativism also functioned as a weapon of control. Election day riots by the Irish in several Southern cities in the 1850s inflamed public opinion against immigrants, while businessmen and slaveholders fanned the controversies by reminding Southerners about the immigrant working classes' contributions to disorder. Know Nothing leaders in New Orleans ran on promises to crack down on corruption and vice, especially prostitution, in the poor districts. The South's most cosmopolitan city escaped a class war only because the Know Nothings failed to deliver on their pledges once in power, becoming preoccupied with building railroads and improving the city's business climate.[34]

The anti-immigrant, antiworking-class movement reached its apogee in the late 1850s when planters enlisted businessmen and manufacturers in the campaign to reopen the African slave trade. As Governor James Adams of South Carolina explained, the South demanded a subordinate, unenfranchised labor force, for the influx of unassimilated but enfranchised immigrant workers into Southern cities invited conflicts between capital and labor. The South, Adams concluded, needed more slaves and fewer white workers if it was going to retain its liberty. During the secession proceedings in Virginia, Alexander Stuart, among other conservative businessmen, urged his state to use the opportunity of secession to reassert control over the immigrants and working classes already in the South. He suggested that Virginians revise the state constitution so that propertyless whites would lose the suffrage. Other Southern statesmen shared Stuart's concern about the loyalties of the urban working class and expressed their dire forebodings about internal chaos erupting at home during the secession crisis, unless slaveholders acted to curb the working-classes' political power.[35]

The fears were real, and in some ways justified, but the Civil War did not bring civil war to Southern cities. Many working-class immigrants fled the cities to escape Confederate service; others signed oaths swearing that they never intended to become citizens, thereby making them ineligible for the draft; and some openly taunted the Confederacy by falling in with federal forces or rallying with Southern unionists. For reasons of pride, profit, or personality, however, enough immigrants joined the Confederate armies to dispel fears of white chaos from within the South. After the war the dangers from immigrant workers seemed to fade. Foreign immigration to Southern cities virtually ended, and blacks, newly freed from bondage and poor, now flooded Southern cities. Many immigrants and their children who survived the war edged up the economic and social order in Southern cities. Where great gaps of wealth and culture had separated the upper class from the working class in Charleston in the 1850s, and elsewhere to a lesser extent, race now became the index of class. The poor were black. They did the "nigger work" and left the "respectable" trades, management, and property to whites of all national backgrounds. Although ethnic and class differences did not disappear completely from politics and social relations, these differences receded in the face of the new racial demographics of Southern cities. Southerners lapsed back into their philosophy of social stasis as whites. In the countryside and city alike they united to resist Reconstruction. The end of significant urban immigration from abroad and the rise of a black unskilled working class in Southern cities reversed the divergence between countryside and city. Ruralism, racism, and regionalism again governed the whole South.[36]

On the eve of secession, immigration, cultural diversity, urban disorder, and class conflict all posed real threats to the slaveholding way of life, but the Southern philosophy of stasis denied their very existence. Ironically, when external forces besieged the Old South, it was that philosophy's mythical homogeneity that somehow prevailed. Created to describe a present that did not actually exist, the myth became instead a self-fulfilling prophecy that shaped the South's postwar future. Thanks in part to its belated accuracy, it has also informed historical treatments of the antebellum past, obscuring the impact of immigration on midnineteenth-century Southern society.

## NOTES

1. The literature on Southern character and distinctiveness is enormous and still growing. A good recent statement, which includes references to other important works, is James M. McPherson, "Antebellum Southern Exceptionalism: A New Look at an Old Question," *Civil War History* 29 (September 1983): 230–44. But see also Bertram Wyatt-Brown, *Southern Honor: Ethics and Behavior in the Old South* (New York, 1982); Carl Degler, *Place Over Time: The Continuity of Southern Distinctiveness* (Baton Rouge, 1977); and David Potter, *The South and the Sectional Conflict* (Baton Rouge, 1968). A recent attempt to deny Southern distinctiveness is Edward Pessen, "How Different from Each Other Were the Antebellum North and South?" *American Historical Review* 85 (December 1980): 1119–49, which also has many useful references; but see also the reactions to Pessen's arguments by Thomas Alexander, Stanley L. Engerman, and Forrest McDonald and Grady McWhiney, and Pessen's reply, in *"AHR Forum*—Antebellum North and South in Comparative Perspective: A Discussion," ibid., 1150–66.

2. On Herrenvolk democracy, see especially George M. Fredrickson, *The Black Image in the White Mind: The Debate on Afro-American Character and Destiny, 1817–1914* (New York, 1971), 61ff. On the unity imposed by religion, see Samuel S. Hill, Jr., *The South and the*

*North in American Religion* (Athens, Ga., 1981), 46–89; Anne C. Loveland, *Southern Evangelicals and the Social Order, 1800–1860* (Baton Rouge, 1980); and Donald G. Mathews, *Religion in the Old South* (Chicago, 1977), chapters 3 and 4. On the increased political participation among all classes of white Southerners, see especially William J. Cooper, Jr., *Liberty and Slavery: Southern Politics to 1860* (New York, 1983), 184–87 and passim. Cooper focuses almost exclusively on the rural South.

3. The most recent, and best, overview of the proslavery argument is Drew Gilpin Faust's excellent introduction in Faust, ed., *The Ideology of Slavery: Proslavery Thought in the Antebellum South, 1830–1860* (Baton Rouge, 1981), 1–20. See also William S. Jenkins, *Proslavery Thought in the Old South* (Chapel Hill, 1935), 285–308; and Eugene Genovese, *The Political Economy of Slavery: Studies in the Economy & Society of the Slave South* (New York, 1965), 28–36.

4. An excellent discussion of the changing urban workplace in the Old South is Ira Berlin and Herbert Gutman, "Natives and Immigrants, Free Men and Slaves: Urban Workingmen in the Antebellum American South," *American Historical Review* 88 (December 1983): 1175–1200. No full survey of foreign immigration in the South exists. Several useful overviews are Ella Lonn, *Foreigners in the Confederacy* (Chapel Hill, 1940), 1–32; Randall M. Miller, "Immigrants in the Old South," *Immigration History Newsletter* 10 (November 1978): 8–14; and Herbert Weaver, "Foreigners in Ante-Bellum Towns of the Lower South," *Journal of Southern History* 13 (1947): 62–73. The best studies of immigrants in particular cities are Edward L. Ayers, *Vengeance and Justice: Crime and Punishment in the Nineteenth-Century South* (New York, 1984), chapter 3 (on Savannah principally); Kathleen C. Berkeley, " 'Like a Plague of Locusts': Immigration and Social Change in Memphis, Tennessee, 1850–1880" (Ph.D. diss., University of California, Los Angeles, 1980); Christopher Silver, "A New Look at Old South Urbanization: The Irish Worker in Charleston, South Carolina, 1840–1860," in Samuel M. Hines and George W. Hopkins, eds., *South Atlantic Urban Studies* (Columbia, S.C., 1979), 141–72; and Fredrick M. Spletstoser, "Back Door to the Land of Plenty: New Orleans as an Immigrant Port, 1820–1860," 2 vols. (Ph.D. diss., Louisiana State University, 1978). On Southern cities, with some discussion of foreign-born immigration, see Clement Eaton, *The Growth of Southern Civilization* (New York, 1961), chapter 11; and especially David R. Goldfield, *Cotton Fields and Skyscrapers: Southern City and Region, 1607–1980* (Baton Rouge, 1982), chapter 2, who makes a strong case for continuity between countryside and city throughout Southern history.

5. Based on the Seventh Census of the United States, 1850, Population and Industrial Schedules; and Eighth Census of the United States, 1860, Population and Industrial Schedules (National Archives) for the various cities under review: Augusta, Atlanta, Charleston, Louisville, Memphis, Mobile, Nashville, New Orleans, Norfolk, Richmond, Savannah. For aggregate data, see U.S. Bureau of Census, *The Seventh Census of the United States, 1850* (Washington, 1853); J. D. B. DeBow, *Statistical View of the United States* (Washington, 1854); and U.S. Bureau of Census, *Population of the United States in 1860* (Washington, 1864). Some of this data is conveniently tabulated by Berlin and Gutman, "Natives and Immigrants," 1176–84; Dennis Rousey, "Town Versus Country in the Antebellum South: Presidential Balloting, 1836–1860" (paper read at the Southern Historical Association meeting, November 1983); Lonn, *Foreigners*, pp. 2–9, 29–32; and Weaver, "Foreigners," 66–67. Some representative figures are: In New Orleans between 1850 and 1860 foreign-born males (eighteen years or older) constituted 70 percent of the entire white, adult male population of the city. In Charleston they numbered between 45 percent (1850) and 49 percent (1860); in Savannah their share rose from 37 percent (1850) to 51 percent (1860); and in Memphis it grew from 35 percent (1850) to 49 percent (1860). Except for Atlanta, Georgia, and Montgomery, Alabama, all sizable inland cities also experienced a significant increase in the percentage of foreign-born persons in the white, adult male population. The proportion of foreign-born in Augusta's white, adult male population went from roughly 21 percent in 1850 to 35 percent in 1860; Nashville's from 22 to 38 percent; and Richmond's from 25 to 34 percent, to cite three examples. Immigrant populations in Southern cities were probably higher, but their transiency no doubt caused census takers to miss many of them in their canvasses.

6. On the effects of immigrant competition, see Berlin and Gutman, "Natives and Immigrants," 1175–1200, for a convenient summary of the data.

7. On immigrant competition with free blacks, see Ira Berlin, *Slaves Without Masters: The Free Negro in the Antebellum South* (New York, 1974), 230–33; and Leonard P. Curry, *The Free Black in Urban America, 1800–1850* (Chicago, 1981), 29. Curry underestimates the influence of immigrants in the South largely because he ends his discussion with 1850. On the Arkansas example, see Orville Taylor, *Negro Slavery in Arkansas* (Durham, N.C., 1958), 111–12.

8. See, for example, Spletstoser, "Back Door to the Land of Poverty," 383–85; Joseph Holt Ingraham, *The Sunny South; or, The Southerner at Home, Embracing Five Years' Experience*

of a Northern Governess in the Land of the Sugar and the Cotton (Philadelphia, 1860), 504; Amelia Murray, Letters from the United States, Cuba and Canada (New York, 1856), 212; Narrative of Tom Eikel, "Irish Channel Narratives—Unpublished" [1941], Louisiana Federal Writers' Project Narratives (Northwestern State University of Louisiana, Natchitoches); Commissioners' Minutes, 7 January 1836, Charleston Orphan House Records (South Carolina Historical Society); Berlin, Slaves Without Masters, pp. 231–32. For an early example, see Martha Richardson to James P. Screven, 25 February 1821, Arnold-Screven Papers (Southern Historical Collection, University of North Carolina at Chapel Hill). See also the federal census schedules for 1850 and 1860 to identify immigrant employment in Southern cities.

9. The paragraphs on Norfolk are based on the Eighth Census of the United States, 1860, Population Schedule, Norfolk, Virginia (National Archives); and Tommy L. Bogger, "The Slave and Free Black Community in Norfolk, 1775–1865" (Ph.D. diss., University of Virginia, 1976), 163–67, 174–79.

10. In New Orleans many workers in the 1850s earned two dollars per day for manual labor: Spletstoser, "Back Door to the Land of Poverty," pp. 377–79. On employment patterns in New Orleans, see Richard R. Tansey, "Economic Expansion and Urban Disorder in Antebellum New Orleans" (Ph.D. diss., University of Texas at Austin, 1981), 94–97, 103; H. A. Murray, Lands of the Slave and the Free, or Cuba, the United States, and Canada, 2 vols. (London, 1855), II: 25; Frederick Law Olmsted, A Journey in the Seaboard Slave States (New York, 1856), 589; John S. C. Abbott, South and North: or Impressions Received During a Trip to Cuba and the South (New York, 1860), 112–13. New Orleans' laws discouraged boat captains from hiring blacks so that blacks did not necessarily benefit from employers' dissatisfaction with white workers or upswings in the local economy. In Mobile police protected black stevedores and dockworkers when they were attacked by tough "Dagoes" in 1852, and at least one newspaper supported the move because blacks were law-abiding and spent their money in the city: Mobile Advertiser, 23 December 1852.

11. Silver, "A New Look at Old South Urbanization," pp. 157–59; Eighth Census of the United States, 1860, Population Schedule, Charleston, South Carolina (National Archives).

12. Octavia Smith to Richard Smith, 29 June 1839, Richard Smith Correspondence (Louisiana State University); Walter H. Stevens to W. S. Rosecrans, 2 January 1849, William S. Rosecrans Papers (University of California, Los Angeles); New Orleans Picayune, 11 December 1856; Sara Lawton to Mrs. A. L. Alexander, 6 March 1847, Alexander-Hillhouse Papers (Southern Historical Collection, University of North Carolina at Chapel Hill). For an example of the bounding from job to job by an Irish immigrant, follow the course of John Abbott, who worked on board a brig sailing between Charleston and Havanna, as a servant in the Mills House in Charleston, and as a policeman, among other jobs within a span of less than three years; Report of the Committee on Health and Drainage, on the Origin and Diffusion of Yellow Fever in Charleston in the Autumn of 1856 ([Charleston], n.d.), 3, 14; and Report on Yellow Fever (n.p., n.d.), 6–7, 9.

13. The viability of slave labor in cities has occasioned a hot debate among historians. The debate is framed by Richard Wade, Slavery in the Cities: The South, 1820–1860 (New York, 1964), who argues that the social arrangements of urban life, combined with economic factors, threatened slavery's existence; and by Claudia Goldin, Urban Slavery in the American South, 1820–1860: A Quantitative History (Chicago, 1976), who argues that increasing rural demand for slaves, rather than any imminent decline in the institution's economic health in cities, drew off slaves. Only Goldin addresses the place of immigrants in this process; she suggests that immigrant labor in cities contributed to the elasticity of the Southern labor system.

14. Goldin, Urban Slavery, pp. 28–33; Wade, Slavery in the Cities, pp. 50–51; Ronald T. Takaki, Iron Cages: Race and Culture in Nineteenth-Century America (Seattle, 1982ed.), 123.

15. Roger W. Shugg, Origins of Class Struggle in Louisiana: A Social History of White Farmers and Laborers During Slavery and After, 1840–1875 (Baton Rouge, 1972ed.), 93–94; Harper's Magazine 7 (1853): 755; Frederick Law Olmsted, The Cotton Kingdom, Arthur M. Schlesinger, ed. (New York, 1953), 70. On Irish girls' preference for domestic service, see Hasia R. Diner, Erin's Daughters in America: Irish Immigrant Women in the Nineteenth Century (Baltimore, 1983), 74–84.

16. Richmond Enquirer, 27 August 1857. The previous year the Enquirer had welcomed the arrival of immigrant workers: ibid., 17 October 1856.

17. Charleston Courier, 7 December 1860. The connection between wage slavery and chattel slavery was well developed in the British Isles and may have been known by Irish immigrants. Irish abolitionists tried to mobilize the working classes against slavery on that basis. On these points, see Marcus Cunliffe, Chattel Slavery and Wage Slavery: The Anglo-American Context, 1830–1860 (Athens, Ga., 1979), chapters 1 and 2, for the general view; and Douglas Riach, "Blacks and Blackface on the Irish Stage, 1830–60," Journal of American Studies 7 (1973): 241.

18. On urban residence patterns generally, see David Ward, *Cities and Immigrants: A Geography of Change in Nineteenth-Century America* (New York, 1971), 105–7.

19. Jane H. Pease and William H. Pease, "Social Structure and the Potential for Urban Change: Boston and Charleston in the 1830s," *Journal of Urban History* 8 (1982): 173–75, 177–79; Frederic Cople Jaher, *The Urban Establishment: Upper Strata in Boston, New York, Charleston, Chicago, and Los Angeles* (Urbana, 1982), 332–34, 375, 393–95; Hibernian Society, *Constitution and Rules . . . revised . . . 1838* (Charleston, 1838), 21–30; George J. Gongaware, *The History of the German Friendly Society of Charleston, South Carolina, 1766–1916* (Richmond, Va., 1935), 206–17; German Friendly Society, Charleston, Minutes, VIII (12 February 1840), IX (24 April 1850), IX (30 April 1851), German Friendly Society Papers (South Caroliniana Library, University of South Carolina).

20. Jane H. Pease and William H. Pease, "The Economics and Politics of Charleston's Nullification Crisis," *Journal of Southern History* 47 (1981): 346–47. On the function of ethnic leaders, see John Higham, ed., *Ethnic Leadership in America* (Baltimore, 1978), 8 and passim.

21. My conclusions are based on my mapping of the various groups, compiled from city directories and the federal census for 1850 and 1860 in Charleston, Memphis, Mobile, New Orleans, Richmond, and Savannah. Good summaries of ethnic concentrations include Berkeley, " 'Like a Plague of Locusts,' " pp. 29–30, 39–57; Victor Hugh Treat, "Migration into Louisiana, 1834–1880" (Ph.D. diss., University of Texas at Austin, 1967), 260–77, 288–98; Alan S. Thompson, "Mobile, Alabama, 1850–1861: Economic, Political, Physical, and Population Characteristics" (Ph.D. diss., University of Alabama, 1979), 200–13. On the relationship between geographical proximity and intensity of ethnic identity and associational life, see especially Kathleen Neils Conzen, "Immigrants, Immigrant Neighborhoods, and Ethnic Identity: Historical Issues," *Journal of American History* 66 (1979): 603–15. The rise of modern retailing and the general expansion of financial and commercial activity also broke down older conceptions of ties between the artisan and shopkeeper. A new "middle class" of salaried workers emerged in the 1840s and 1850s with few ties to the craftsmen. This class also tended to live apart from the artisans. For the process of change in Charleston, see Stuart Blumin, "Black Coats to White Collars: Economic Change, Nonmanual Work, and the Social Structure of Industrializing America," in Stuart Bruchey, ed., *Small Business in American Life* (New York, 1980), 105–06 and passim. For the emerging pattern wherever large amounts of goods had to be moved and sold, see also Grigsby H. Wooton, Jr., "New City of the South: Atlanta, 1843–1873" (Ph.D. diss., Johns Hopkins University, 1973), 52–55; Thompson, "Mobile, Alabama," pp. 250, 255, 279–80; Richard H. Haunton, "Savannah in the 1850s" (Ph.D. diss., Emory University, 1968), 50–51; Robert C. Reinders, "A Social History of New Orleans, 1850–1860" (Ph.D. diss., University of Texas at Austin, 1957), part I, 159–63. That some of this class were foreign-born, and many second generation immigrants, suggests that upward mobility was occurring in Southern cities.

22. Olmsted, *Journey in the Seabord Slave States*, p. 404; Charles G. Parsons, *Inside View of Slavery: or a Tour Among the Planters* (Boston, 1855), p. 23; *Savannah Daily Journal and Courier*, 23 March 1855; *Savannah Evening Journal*, 22 March 1853; *Directory for the City of Augusta and Business Advertiser for 1859* (Augusta, Ga., 1859).

23. Michael B. Chesson, *Richmond After the War, 1865–1890* (Richmond, Va., 1981), 121–23.

24. Treat, "Migration into Louisiana," pp. 260–77; Spletstoser, "Back Door to the Land of Plenty," pp. 366–69; J. Henno Deiler, *Geshichte der New Orleanser Deutschen Presse* (New Orleans, 1901), 9–11; John F. Nau, *The German People of New Orleans, 1850–1900* (Leiden, 1958), 17; Shugg, *Origins of Class Struggle*, p. 40; [Edward Henry Durell], *New Orleans As I Found It* (New York, 1845), 17–18; Samuel Cartwright, "On the Prevention of Yellow Fever," *New Orleans Medical and Surgical Journal* 10 (1853–54): 315 (quote); and New Orleans *Daily Picayune*, 19 May 1849 (quote). Earl F. Niehaus, *The Irish in New Orleans, 1800–1860* (Baton Rouge, 1965), 28–34, argues that the Irish were not concentrated in any one district; rather, he places them throughout the city. My research in the federal census, local business directories, and hospital and poor house records leads me to think otherwise. Although the Irish dispersed, newer and poor immigrants in the 1840s and 1850s settled in identifiable "Irish districts." Most contemporaries thought so.

25. On attitudes toward health generally, see William B. Walker, "The Health Reform Movement in the United States, 1830–1870" (Ph.D. diss., Johns Hopkins University, 1955); John B. Blake, "Health Reform," in Edwin Gaustad, ed., *The Rise of Adventism: Religion and Society in Mid-Nineteenth Century America* (New York, 1974), 30–49; Charles S. Rosenberg, *The Cholera Years: The United States in 1832, 1849, and 1866* (Chicago, 1962), 142–50. For Southern examples, see Shugg, *Origins of Class Struggle*, pp. 53–55, who describes the "medical Know Nothingism" of the day; John Duffy, *Sword of Pestilence: The New Orleans Yellow Fever Epidemic of 1853* (Baton Rouge, 1966); New Orleans *Daily Delta*, 31 July, 31 August 1853; Cartwright, "On the Prevention of Yellow Fever," 305–6, 312–16; I. H. Charles to John Liddell,

18 November 1847, Isaac H. Charles Letters (Louisiana State University); E. H. Barton, "Annual Report of the New Orleans Board of Health," *Southern Medical Reports* 1 (1849): 83 (quote). For an opposing view, see J. C. Simonds, "On the Sanitary Condition of New Orleans, as Illustrated by Its Mortality Statistics," ibid., 2 (1850): 207. The disease environment of Southern cities, which discouraged many immigrants from settling there, raises the counterfactual question of how Southern cities might have developed if they had compared more favorably with Northern cities.

26. *Savannah Republican*, 24 March 1855; *Savannah Daily Journal and Courier*, 25 March 1855; George Lewis, *Impressions of America and American Churches* (Edinburgh, Scotland, 1845), 173.

27. Herbert Weaver, "Foreigners in Ante-Bellum Savannah," *Georgia Historical Quarterly* 37 (1953): 8; Ayers, *Vengeance and Justice*, pp. 72–106, 319–20; Chatham County Superior Court Minutes, 1850–1861 (Georgia Department of Archives and History); Record Book of Arrests Charges, Penalties, Charleston Police Records, 1855–1856 (Charleston Library Society); Charleston Police Morning Reports, Lower Wards, 1861–1863 (Charleston Library Society); Vagrant Record Books (1859–61, 1861–62), Recorder's Office, Third District, New Orleans (City Archives, New Orleans Public Library); Reports of Arrests (1852–61), Department of Police, Recorder's Court Records, Third District, New Orleans (City Archives, New Orleans Public Library); "Station House Register, 1858–1860," Memphis Police Department Records (Memphis and Shelby County Archives, Old Cossitt Library, Memphis Public Library); Reinders, "A Social History of New Orleans," part I, 219–31; *Report of the Board of Control of the Louisiana Penitentiary . . . 1859* (Baton Rouge, 1859), 45–57; Charleston Alms House Records, vol. 1834–40, p. 298 (South Carolina Historical Society); Board of Commissioners of Charleston Poor House Minutes, Record Book 1852–58, pp. 54–56, and Record Book 1858–66, pp. 38–39 (City Archives, Charleston); Minute Book, Board of Managers, Savannah Poor House and Hospital, 1836–76, 16, 17 September 1839, 6 February 1844, Savannah Hospital Papers (Georgia Historical Society); Roper Hospital Case Book, number 2, 1859–62 (Waring Historical Library, Medical University of South Carolina).

28. Weaver, "Foreigners in Ante-Bellum Savannah," 7; Haunton, "Savannah in the 1850s," p. 18; Richard H. Shryock, ed., *Letters of Richard D. Arnold, M.D., 1808–1876* (Durham, N.C., 1929), 39, 44; Wade, *Slavery in the Cities*, pp. 149–60, for a general view; J. Milton Mackie, *From Cape Cod to Dixie and the Tropics* (New York, 1864), 162; Olmsted, *Journey in the Seaboard Slave States*, p. 589; David Kaser, "Nashville's Women of Pleasure in 1860," *Tennessee Historical Quarterly* 23 (1964): 379–82; William Still, *The Underground Railroad, . . .* (Chicago, rpt. 1970), 251; Grand Jury Presentment, May 1851, Grand Jury Presentments, Charleston District, 1790–1865 (South Carolina Department of Archives, Columbia).

29. Memminger quoted in Laylon Wayne Jordan, "Education for Community: C. G. Memminger and the Origination of Common Schools in Antebellum Charleston," *South Carolina Historical Magazine* 83 (1982): 110; Memminger to J. H. Hammond, 28 April 1849, James H. Hammond Papers (Library of Congress); Minutes of Commissioners of Free Schools—St. Philip's and St. Michael's [Charleston], January 1844—January 1855 [1858], 11 November 1846, pp. 34–35, 20 November 1854, p. 121 (quote) (City Archives, Charleston). See also Jaher, *Urban Establishment*, 380–82. On New Orleans, see *Annual Report of the Superintendent of Public Schools, Fourth District, New Orleans, May 12, 1855* (New Orleans, 1855), 7–8. More typical was the divided nature of "public" education in Mobile in which the Catholics created their own system because they were excluded from public support. No sense of the organic whole operated there to bring Catholic children, many of them immigrants, and Protestant children together. See Thompson, "Mobile, Alabama," pp. 164–66.

30. On the German mission, see *Mobile Register*, 24 January 1844. On the failure of the Catholic church to impose cultural unity, see Randall M. Miller, "A Church in Cultural Captivity: Some Speculations on Catholic Identity in the Old South," in Randall M. Miller and Jon L. Wakelyn, eds. *Catholics in the Old South: Essays on Church and Culture* (Macon, Ga., 1983), especially pp. 20–37.

31. Laylon Wayne Jordan, "Police Power and Public Safety in Antebellum Charleston: The Emergence of a New Police, 1800–1860," in Hines and Hopkins, eds., *South Atlantic Urban Studies*, pp. 122–40; Dennis C. Rousey, "'Hibernian Leatherheads': Irish Cops in New Orleans, 1830–1880," *Journal of Urban History* 10 (November 1983): 61–84; Ayers, *Vengeance and Justice*, pp. 82–91. For a study of the cries for public order and the ineffectiveness of the new police even to impose order on its immigrant recruits in one city, see *Charleston Courier*, 6 February, 1 May 1854, 25 October 1855, 15 January 1856; *Charleston Mercury*, 2 September 1835 (for early criticisms of foreigners on the city guard), 7 January 1856; *Statement of Receipts and Expenditures of the City Council of Charleston, 1849–1850* (Charleston, 1850); *Mayor's Report on City Affairs . . . 1857* (Charleston, 1857), 17–18; Records of Arrests, Charges, Penalties . . . Charleston Police Records, 1855–1856 (on officers' neglect of duty and other infractions). In New Orleans the police department became a patronage nest, ruining its

credibility and effectiveness. See Reinders, "Social History of New Orleans," part I, 216–218; Board of Police Minutes, 1854–56 (City Archives, New Orleans Public Library); Record of Police Oaths, New Orleans, 1856–61 (City Archives, New Orleans Public Library); and Mayor's Office, Personnel Records of the Police Department, 1852–1868 (City Archives, New Orleans Public Library). The Southern ethic of honor, with its attendant distrust of government, relied on private justice to control society. In the countryside where an organic relationship among whites operated communal pressures worked well enough, but in the diverse and commercially-oriented cities citizens turned to formal means of control, which demanded deference to law as an abstract principle. For some good insights into the process whereby a society moves away from organic or formal conceptions of law, see David T. Konig, *Law and Society in Puritan Massachusetts: Essex County, 1629–1692* (Chapel Hill, 1979). On Southern honor and communal control, see Wyatt-Brown, *Southern Honor*, pp. 71–72, 365–66; Michael Hindus, *Prison and Plantation: Crime, Justice, and Authority in Massachusetts and South Carolina, 1767–1878* (Chapel Hill, 1980); Dickson Bruce, *Violence and Culture in the Antebellum South* (Austin, Texas, 1979). For some perceptive observations on the differences between city and countryside, see Ayers, *Vengeance and Justice*, chapters 3 and 4.

32. Robert N. Olsberg, "A Government of Class and Race: William Henry Trescot and the South Carolina Chivalry, 1860–1865" (Ph.D. diss., University of South Carolina, 1972), 81–84; Shryock, ed., *Letters of Richard D. Arnold*, pp. 39, 44–46, 47, 55; *Savannah Republican*, 20 November 1852, 26 July 1854, 1 December 1855; Weaver, "Foreigners in Ante-Bellum Savannah," 8–11.

33. Elizabeth Avery Meriwether, *Recollections of Ninety-Two Years, 1824–1916* (Nashville, 1958), 40–41. The organization of workingmen's clubs and unions, like the one that hosted Avery, became common in the 1850s. Many such associations were exclusive, allowing only members of a particular ethnic, social, or occupational group to join. See, for example, Nau, *German People of New Orleans*, p. 57; J. Henno Deiler, *Geschichte der Deutschen Gesellschaft von New Orleans mit einer Einlectung . . .* (New Orleans, 1897), 54–84; Shugg, *Origins of Class Struggle*, pp. 114–15; Spletstoser, "Back Door to the Land of Plenty," pp. 380–81, Proceedings of the Charleston Typographical Union, number 43, September 1859 (South Caroliniana Library, University of South Carolina). Indicative of the ethnic links to workingmen's groups, Gerald Stith, organizer of the heavily native-born Southerner New Orleans Typographical Society, used his Southern working-class ties to combat both immigrants and blacks in mayoral campaigns of the 1850s: Leon Soulé, *The Know-Nothing Party in New Orleans: A Reappraisal* (Baton Rouge, 1961), 94. The old-style personal politics generally made little sense in the 1850s, not only because of ethnic and party differences, but also because differences based on occupation became more pronounced. See n. 21 above. More importantly, great gaps in wealth increasingly separated the white classes. By 1860 in Charleston "most whites had in common with blacks a very low level of wealth," Michael P. Johnson, "Wealth and Class in Charleston in 1860," in Walter J. Fraser, Jr., and Winfred B. Moore, Jr., eds., *From the Old South to the New: Essays on the Transitional South* (Westport, Conn., 1981), 71.

34. For examples of ruffianism, crowd activity, and immigrant and native-born clashes, see C. E. Taylor to father, 11 September 1854, C. E. Taylor Letters (Tulane University); Gustave A. Breaux Diaries, 2, 16 September, 11 October 1859 (Tulane University); George D. Armstrong, *The Summer of Pestilence: A History of the Yellow Fever in Norfolk, Virginia, A.D., 1855* (Philadelphia, 1856), 45–47; and W. Darrell Overdyke, *The Know-Nothing Party in the South* (Baton Rouge, 1950), 240–60, for a general treatment. On the New Orleans law-and-order appeals of the Know Nothing party, see Tansey, "Economic Expansion," chapter 2.

35. Theodore Jervey, *The Slave Trade* (Columbia, S.C., 1925), 114; for Stuart and a perceptive analysis of developments elsewhere, see Fred Siegel, "Artisans and Immigrants in the Politics of Late Antebellum Georgia," *Civil War History* 27 (1981): 221–30. See also Michael P. Johnson, *Toward a Patriarchal Republic: The Secession of Georgia* (Baton Rouge, 1977), 100–1. The threatened clash between native-born and foreign-born whites compelled some city leaders to oppose nativism, reminding their fellow Southerners of the need to maintain a white consensus above all else. See Samuel Mordecai, *Richmond in By-Gone Days* (Richmond, Va., 1856), 246.

36. Berlin and Gutman, "Natives and Immigrants," 1199–1200; Peter Jay Rachleff, "Black, White, and Gray: Working-Class Activism in Richmond, Virginia, 1865–1890" (Ph.D. diss., University of Pittsburgh, 1981), 5, 14–16, and passim; Shugg, *Origins of Class Struggle*, pp. 54–55, 107–12; Berkeley, " 'Like a Plague of Locusts,' " chapter 6. On the postbellum developments, see especially Howard N. Rabinowitz, *Race Relations in the Urban South, 1865–1890* (New York, 1978); and Goldfield, *Cotton Fields and Skyscrapers*, chapter 3.

# The American Parade:
# Representations of the
# Nineteenth-Century Social Order

*Mary Ryan*

The *San Francisco Morning Call* began its report on the July Fourth celebration of 1864 with this perfunctory comment: "The chief feature of the day was the great Procession of course." By midmorning, the editor went on, "the streets began to be thronged with platoons, companies and regiments of soldiers, benevolent associations etc., swarming from every point of the compass and marching with music and banners toward the general rendezvous like the gathering hosts of a mighty army." An hour later these contingents of citizens had formed into a linear sequence and proceeded to file through the principal streets of the city "rank after rank, column after column, in seemingly countless numbers."[1] Having traversed much of the city, the marchers quietly disbanded. Not even the editor stayed on to observe the songs and orations that concluded the public commemoration of the nation's birthday.

Accounts like this were commonplace between 1825 and 1880 in the press of the three cities I have investigated: San Francisco, New York, and New Orleans. They indicate that Americans had devised a distinctive and curious mode of public celebration, in which a sizable portion of the urban population organized into "platoons," "companies," "regiments," "ranks and columns," and paraded through the public thoroughfares. This particular type of celebratory performance seems to have been an American invention. In the *Oxford English Dictionary*, the first listing for the modern meaning of the word *parade*, an adaptation of the term for military muster to encompass civic and ceremonial purposes, includes the phrase "especially in the United States."

The parade stands out in the chronicles of American public life as the characteristic genre of nineteenth-century civic ceremony. A grand

*Mary Ryan is professor of history and director of the Women's Studies Program at the University of California at Berkeley. Reprinted from Lynn Hunt, ed.,* The New Cultural History *(University of California Press, 1989), 131–53. Reprinted by permission of the Regents of the University of California and the University of California Press.*

procession of citizens was "of course" the central event in the cyclical patriotic rite, the Fourth of July celebration, and to a lesser extent of Washington's Birthday. It was also the focal point of local holidays: Evacuation Day in New York, Admission Day in San Francisco, and the anniversary of the Battle of New Orleans. When it came time to celebrate civic improvements—the Erie Canal, the Atlantic cable, the transcontinental railroad—or the erection of any number of new monuments in public squares, a parade was again in order. The parade was called into ceremonial service on somber occasions as well. The procession that accompanied Lincoln's casket through the streets of New York was, in structure and organization if not in mood, like a classic American parade.

The parade presents historians with a kind of cultural performance from which anthropologists have extracted rich meaning. Milton Sanger tells us that these ceremonies "encapsulate a culture." Clifford Geertz finds a more intimate revelation in such public events: they are the "stories a people tell about themselves." And according to John Skorupski, "Ceremony says, 'look, this is how things should be, this is the proper, ideal pattern of social life.' "[2]

Translated into the more modest language of historians, the reports of parades are simply very resonant documents. First, the parade offers a well-rounded documentation of past culture; it conjured up an emotional power and aesthetic expressiveness that the simple literary formulation of ideas or values lacked. Second, accounts of parades record the actions as well as the words of the past. In a parade, an organized body, usually of men, marched into the public streets to spell out a common social identity. Third, whatever insights can be drawn from parades offer a very high level of generality. This public performance occurred before a massive audience and engaged a large number of participants—in the extreme case a single parade would find fifty thousand on the line of march and three-quarters of a million more observing on the sidelines. Finally, many parades, including those spotlighted in this analysis, were predicated on some level of public consensus: they were funded and arranged by democratically elected public officials, who designed these pageants to attract and satisfy the city as a whole. By focusing on this variety of celebration, rather than on the holiday festivities that engaged only select groups in the population or processions of a more militant sort, I hope to reconstruct the most general and broadly public picture that American cities presented of themselves.

The appropriate procedures for analyzing such documents might seem comparable to those of literary analysis, for the parade is like a text in its susceptibility to multiple interpretations. But the parade is a peculiar text, intricately entangled with its social and historical context. It has multiple authors: the thousands of marchers who carried their own chosen symbols into one composite ceremony. If there is any overarching meaning, any capsule summary of a culture embedded in this text, it was not the design of an *auteur* but the creation of specific individuals and distinct groups who operated within the social constraints and political possibilities of their time. The parade, then, can tell us something of the historical process whereby cultural meaning is created. The multiple architects of such cultural creations, furthermore, did not simply inscribe meaning onto some preordained literary genre; rather, they devised ceremonial forms specific to their own times, needs, and possibilities.

Thus, before extracting substantive meaning from these documents, it is necessary to specify some of the characteristics of the parade as a form of cultural performance. The term *parade* refers to that ritualized, collective movement through the streets that took a distinctive form in nineteenth-century American cities. It had several essential features. First, the parade was clearly organized into separate marching units, each representing a preestablished social identity. The filing by of these constituent parts of the society, sometimes termed a *desfile*, was the basic action and structure of the American parade.[3] Second, an American parade—unlike, for example, an eighteenth-century French procession, which, according to Robert Darnton, "ended at a relatively elevated point in the hierarchy of local officials"—enrolled a large portion of the local population.[4] A New Orleans newspaper editor said of the line of march in 1849, "All will find a place who wish to join the celebration."[5] Of course, some exclusionary clauses restricted the invitation to parade, based chiefly on race and gender. Still, the line of march was quite open, and rarely was any group who bothered to apply to the committee of arrangements denied admission. The third identifying characteristic of the American parade was its seeming aimlessness, or lack of plot, so to speak. The marchers did not set off single-mindedly for an established civic center, there to place an offering to a patron saint, profess fealty to a leader, or enact a civic pageant. This was not a march of governors or priests who conferred some legitimizing or sanctifying power on the places they passed. The typical parade simply wove its serpentine way through all the principal streets of the city, allowing the participants to present themselves to throngs of citizens gathered all along the way. Marching units therefore invested great effort and money adorning their persons with ribbons, sashes, and bright uniforms. In sum, then, the American parade seemed to be a march for the sake of marching, as well as for the display of the ordinary citizens who marched.

The parade is, of course, a species of procession, with ancient and geographically widespread antecedents. The first notable procession mounted in the United States harked back at least to the Renaissance in its form and imagery. This mobile pageant was conducted in Philadelphia in 1788, to celebrate the ratification of the Constitution. It was draped in classic symbolism and surrounded by public drama and communal festivity. Tradesmen plied their crafts along the route; other marchers impersonated archetypal figures like Christopher Columbus; still others carried sacred icons such as mementos of George Washington; and all proceeded to a definite destination where the participants celebrated their communal bonds by feasting, thousands strong, from a common public larder.[6] In the early Republic, then, the procession had not yet acquired the streamlined characteristics of the parade, nor did it occupy the center of ceremonial time and space. It was not yet a parade.

The civic ceremony that begins my analysis, organized in New York in 1825 to pay proud homage to the completion of the Erie Canal, gave greater definition to the genre of parading. There were many festivities on that day, including a public dinner for three thousand citizens and the ritualized mingling of the waters of Lake Erie and the Atlantic, but the center of public attention and the focal point of civic participation was a procession on land. This long march, a mobile display of a wide spectrum of the corporate groups of the city, supplied the basic form of parading for many years to follow. After 1825, and at an accelerated pace during the 1840s and 1850s, public processions became increasingly commonplace on city streets, and they occupied center stage on such holidays as the Fourth of July, Washington's Birthday, and local anniversaries. Through most of the antebellum period these full-scale, publicly constituted processions shared the streets and the calendar with a panoply of more specialized and spontaneous processions—walks to serenade a nominee for political office, journeys to Sunday school picnics, torchlight drills of the local militia, and public displays of new fire engines.

In the 1850s and through the Civil War, use of the streets grew more restricted as ceremonial energies came to be focused on a few tightly organized parades and circumscribed by elaborate police arrangements. In these decades, the ceremonial form of the parade expanded to incorporate more and more marching units, organized into an ever increasing number and variety of divisions. After mid century, even as the parade form seemed most solid and elaborate, its claim to dominance of public ceremonial life was placed in jeopardy as civic processions began to ravel along cleavages in the urban community. Yet even as late as 1876, a full, hearty, and classic American parade was assembled in all three of my study cities, that is, in the North, South, and West of the United States, to celebrate the centennial of the Declaration of Independence.

The invention of the classic American parade and its installation at the center of public ceremony were, in sum, the product of a distinct, if imprecise, historical period that lasted roughly from 1825 to 1850. Several features of urban history set the context for this cultural creation. First, this was a period of extraordinary demographic growth in each city: New York's population grew sevenfold between 1825 and 1880, when the city harbored 1.2 million residents; the population of New Orleans tripled during the same period; and the wilderness by San Francisco Bay was transformed as an instant city of fifty thousand arose after the Gold Rush and mushroomed to a population of a quarter-million by the closing date of this study. The population of each city diversified as it grew, taking in the foreign-born by the thousands and grudgingly accommodating racial minorities. Each local economy took the critical steps toward industrialization during this same period, as merchants, capitalists, shopkeepers, artisans, industrial workers, and day laborers pursued their conflicting interests in a mixed urban economy. These groups took their clashing interests into the political arena, where fierce contests of popular political parties supplanted the stewardship of older elites. Concurrently, each city was the site of major riots, with scores in

New York alone, as well as total breakdowns of political legitimacy—vigilantism in San Francisco, and the military occupation of New Orleans during Reconstruction. A simple cultural functionalism would suggest that the necessity of fostering order in such diverse, turbulent, and contentious populations might lead to the invention of some unifying public rituals.

Yet the antebellum city placed certain constraints on such ceremonial practices, especially physical ones. The dense built environment provided few open spaces large enough for the entire population to enact their communal dramas. A swift march through the public arteries would seem to be the ceremonial path of least resistance, for social as well as spatial reasons. The genius of the parade was that it allowed the many contending constituencies of the city to line up and move through the streets without ever encountering one another face to face, much less stopping to play specified roles in one coordinated pageant. The parade was much like the social world in which it germinated—mobile, voluntaristic, laissez-faire, and open. Like a civic omnibus, the parade offered admission to almost any group with sufficient energy, determination, organizational ability, and internal coherence to board it.

The parade was something more, however, than an automatic, reflexive expression of American pluralism. It was also a positive assertion of democracy. The parade evolved as a civic ceremony at a time when many groups resorted to processions in order to assert their civic rights. Neophyte political parties took to parading when such popular democratic action was still suspect. Tradesmen "turned out" in procession to protest against their bosses. Groups of immigrants, especially the Catholic Irish, marched through the streets to demand the full rights of citizenship in defiance of rampant nativism. These processions—what we might today call demonstrations—were quite properly seen in the 1830s, 1840s and 1850s as insurgent public actions. The multiple architects of the antebellum parade incorporated these gestures of a militant democracy into public ceremony.

The parade can also be seen as a kind of cultural equivalent of what Hanna Pitkin calls "descriptive representation."[7] In the classic parades of the midnineteenth century, constituent groups in the polity actually presented themselves, rather than abstract symbols, for public view. The parade represented the urban population, forming a detailed descriptive portrait of urban social structure. The thousands who made the effort to march in these antebellum parades acted out an implicit political theory, asserting their prerogative to participate actively and in their own right in the creation of urban culture.

Finally, the emergence of the parade was predicated on an open, public political process in which popular forces acted in tandem with constituted authorities. Most civic ceremonies were funded by the city government and organized by a committee of arrangements appointed by elected officials. Private citizens often initiated the original proposal for a celebration, and sometimes called a public meeting to promote it. While the appointed committee arranged certain portions of the day's program—the firing of arms at daybreak, the fireworks in the evening—

the organization of the parade was an exercise in popular sovereignty. The first act of the committee of arrangements was to publish an open invitation to a public meeting where any group could apply for a place along the line of march. Despite evidence of contention at some of these meetings and repeated incidents of conflict along the line of the march, antebellum political institutions both tolerated and actively promoted this democratic procedure for creating public culture.[8]

In an ad hoc, experimental way, these institutions gave shape to the parade as the characteristic genre of American celebration. That genre was something like a street railway on which a panoply of different social groups mounted and occupied a string of cars, with each car embodying cultural and historical meaning and giving ceremonial definition to some component of the urban social structure. Filing neatly by in a parade, the parade participants presented a compact documentation of how "society takes cognizance of itself, its major classifications and categories."[9] Because this ceremony permitted countless Americans to write their identities on the streets in full public view, the parade can posit answers to basic questions of concern to social and cultural historians. It reveals, in a particularly powerful, publicly sanctioned way, how contemporaries construed, displayed, and saw the urban social order.

To historians, then, the parade constitutes the public, ceremonial language whereby nineteenth-century Americans made order out of an urban universe that teemed with diversity and change. By choosing to join the march in specific contingents, paraders acted out a social vocabulary, impressing their group identities on the minds of countless bystanders. Their words were also strung into sentences—the order of the line of march—that adumbrated social ranks and relationships among the contingents. In the composition and order of the parade, historians can read both the vocabulary and the syntax by which social and cultural order was created out of urban multiplicity.

Although the basic cultural performance—the public display of especially salient constituent groups of the community—remained the same between 1825 and 1880, its composition changed in significant ways as the most prevalent contingents were replaced, replenished, and rearranged over time. The following account of this metamorphosis highlights three different principles of parade formation and social classification, based respectively on class, ethnicity, and gender. This progression is roughly chronological as well as topical, reflecting changes in the principles according to which urban culture organized itself on ceremonial occasions.

In the formative years of parading, the ceremonial structure was filled by groups that loosely resembled classes. The marching units based their common identity in their occupations and prominently displayed their contributions to the local economy. The Erie Canal procession on 5 November 1825 set the pattern: nearly every marching unit grouped men together according to their occupations, from journeymen tailors to members of the Medical Society. The symbols that these groups carried into the parade identified position within the urban economy as the primary principle of group formation. This was especially true of the artisans, who played such a prominent role in the Erie Canal parade. Some, like the hatters, carried banners honoring the patron of their trade, St. Clement; others, like the butchers, enacted their workaday role, towing along the parade route animals ready for the slaughter.[10] Although the artisans were best represented and most ebullient in New York processions, occupation was the basic principle of the line of march in the merchant economy of New Orleans as well. Bodies representing an array of occupations participated in the New Orleans Fourth of July procession of 1837, from the Chamber of Commerce to the Mechanics Society.[11] In New Orleans, be it July Fourth, January Eighth, or Washington's Birthday, the rank order of occupations proceeded from the civic officials and elite occupations on through the tradesmen who took up the rear of the procession. Whereas in New York tradesmen led the procession, some semblance of occupational hierarchy was maintained there as well. The more elite, nonmanual workers—doctors, lawyers, clergymen, and the faculty and students of Columbia University—were all clustered together at the end of the line of march, with the city officials and most honored guests, the Canal commissioners.

In New Orleans this form of parade, which reconstructed society as an inclusive and hierarchical arrangement of corporate groups based primarily on occupation, endured with only minor additions and changes right up to the Civil War. Parades in New York, in contrast, as well as in the stripling town of San Francisco, expressed class in new and more varied ways. First the higher ranks of the social structure dropped out of the line of march. The *New York Herald* noted this striking absence in its description of the parade celebrating the opening of the Croton Aqueduct in 1842. In the division where the bar, the judges, the Chamber of Commerce, and the students and faculty of Columbia were to appear, "none of them were to be seen." Only at a moment of extraordinary national unity, in the funeral procession of President Lincoln, would these more prestigious members of the community parade again. (Even the New-York Historical Society marched that year.)[12]

The aristocrats of labor—skilled craftsmen—soon followed the professionals and merchants in withdrawing from the line of march. Although these groups still made a prominent appearance in 1842 in New York, and although a few butchers still carried symbols of their skills in parades of San Francisco even in the 1860s, they never were represented as fully as in the parade of 1825. As artisans exited the parade, however, their positions were taken up by workers of lesser skill. The common laborers of New York, San Francisco, and New Orleans—longshoremen, quarrymen, cartmen, draymen—became regulars in the line of march after mid century. These workers sometimes organized on a new basis, calling themselves either benevolent associations or outright unions. During Lincoln's funeral procession, for example, the largest single contingent was the Workingmen's Union, assembled in twenty-six branches. In San Francisco, trade unions were powerful enough to attempt a wholesale usurpation of public ceremonies. In 1869, much to the chagrin of the local press, the Fourth of July procession was dominated by some twenty-four unions organized into the eight-hour movement.[13] Yet at other times industrial workers put another kind of consciousness on public display. In both New York and San Francisco some workers paraded docilely behind their bosses, carrying the name of an industrial firm rather than an example of their craft into the line of march.

Thus, although signs of economic status had not disappeared from the line of march at midcentury, they had certainly become more various and difficult to read. Alongside old craft values and corporate occupational groupings could be found class-conscious industrial workers, compliant employees, and the invisible factor of the more prestigious occupations who disappeared from the line of march entirely. There were even a few attempts, in both New York and San Francisco, to replace the old symbols of production with emblems of a consumer economy. Occasionally after mid century, wagons draped with the manufacturers' names of such commodities as beer, pianos, and sewing machines made brief but colorful appearances in parades. Yet this innovation, a blatant form of advertising, never acquired full legitimacy, and after a brief experiment in San Francisco, advertising cars were barred from the parade.[14] Despite this amorphous conceptualization of class, Americans were not yet ready to place an ethic of consumption in the proud place where craftsmen once carried the icons of skilled production.

However defined, emblems suggestive of class lost their privileged ceremonial position around 1850. For the next few decades the line of march was swollen with new contingents whose variety and heterogeneity defied categorization. Throughout this robust yet transitional and anomalous period groups of workers were far outnumbered by contingents composed of the members of voluntary societies. When San Francisco began officially to sponsor Fourth of July processions in the 1850s, it adhered to the new principles of parade composition that had become typical in New York and New Orleans as well. Scattered in the line of march were a few occupational groups: the clergy, the Chamber of Commerce, printers, and stevedores. These contingents were outnumbered, however, by voluntary organizations of four sorts: fraternal orders, militia companies, temperance associations, and ethnic benefit societies.[15] By midcentury in each city, the press had devised a shorthand for describing the line of march, dividing these myriad groups into two categories: the military and the civic societies. Such a simple schema could not hide a radical resorting of the cells of the ceremonial community— public group identity was now a matter of voluntary choice between such alternatives as national origins, fraternal associations, and even allegiances to a particular personal code such as temperance. The military contingents were not drafted into service, but made their public appearance as members of volunteer militia companies. Notoriously ill trained in the martial arts, these ubiquitous antebellum associations were devoted above all else to the sport of parading.

To confuse things further, most members of these marching units, whatever the banners they carried into the parade, actually had multiple identities in common. Whatever allegiances they displayed most prominently—martial skills, temperance reform, or fraternal conviviality—most units were bound by ethnic and class ties as well. The military units were generally homogeneous in both class and ethnicity. In New York, for example, the Seventh Regiment was composed of gentlemen, as was the Continental Guard in New Orleans and the Washington Guard in San Francisco. Given the expense involved in outfitting oneself for a parade, few militia companies enrolled anyone below the middling economic ranks. The ethnic makeup of the militia companies was common knowledge—New York's Seventh Regiment was composed of the native-born; the Sixty-ninth was Irish; and behind the banner of the Empire Hussars marched a band of young Jewish men. The story was much the same in the other cities. In New Orleans, the elite Washington Artillery acknowledged its ethnicity by officially changing its name to the Native Americans.[16] Ethnicity and temperance were also closely, if not predictably, allied. During Lincoln's funeral procession, for example, the fifth division was identified as a contingent of temperance societies in one column of the *New York Herald*, and a collection of Irish societies in another. In fact the two were probably the same, for Irishmen often marched behind the banners of temperance. For example, eighteen Roman Catholic Total Abstinence Societies, each associated with a different parish, marched in New York's centennial parade.[17] In sum, the individual units that came to dominate parades after 1850 often had dual or even quadruple identities, based in this instance in temperate habits, ethnic roots, religious practice, and neighborhood proximity.

The committee of arrangements was hard pressed to create a logical linear arrangement of all these multifarious marching units. Aside from the convention of leading off with a contingent of the military, the arrangement of marchers into divisions seemed somewhat arbitrary. The program for Lincoln's funeral procession was particularly anomalous, reflecting no doubt the difficulty of the task faced by the committee of arrangements, which had hastily to assemble an unprecedented number of marching units into a rational order. In this moment of national sorrow, the organizers of the parade fell back on old principles of social hierarchy—at least in the front ranks of the procession, where the elite assembled in groups such as the Chamber of Commerce and the Union Club, followed immediately by state and local officials. The remainder and bulk of the procession, however, was grouped into divisions that defied comparison and rank ordering: "Fourth: Masonic and Other Orders"; "Fifth: Various Temperance Organizations"; "Sixth: Trades, Societies, Clubs and Associations." Although these categories seemed to encode ethnic differences (with the third and fourth largely native-born, the fifth Irish, and the seventh heavily German), this logic was neither perfect nor explicitly stated.[18] The midnineteenth century had introduced a whole new ceremonial vocabulary—denoting new voluntary units of the community—but had not devised a new syntax to connect these terms in any logical whole.

When New York City celebrated 4 July 1876, much of this confusion was still visible. Take the seventh division of the centennial parade, for example, which contained old craft workers, including blacksmiths and bricklayers, along with the William Cullen Bryant Club and a

contingent of the Cadets of Temperance. Young teetotalers would seem
unlikely, and not particularly flattering, companions to the old aristocrats of labor. Within this heterogeneous ceremonial mixture, however,
the dominance of one principle of social organization had become more
obvious, and that was ethnicity. In New York, two divisions were purely
Irish, two were purely German, and another, while primarily Italian,
contained explicit subdivisions for Cubans and Swedes. A colored division marched behind the Grand Army of the Republic. Because elite occupations did not join the line of march at all in 1876, and since the first
division was given over to a full ethnically mixed assemblage of the military, no stigma of rank applied to any position within the line of march.
The parades that celebrated the centennial in both San Francisco and
New York were a mosaic of the two cities' ethnic makeup. Of the sixteen
divisions in the San Francisco parade, for instance, six were ethnically
homogeneous bands: one Scotch, one German, one Italian, and three
Irish; Austrians, Scandinavians, and Swiss and Portuguese shared two
other divisions; and the native sons took up a position near the end of
the procession along with the children of the public schools. By this date
in New Orleans elite occupations had withdrawn, allowing ethnic societies, French and Portuguese as well as Irish and German, to assume
dominance.[19]

By 1876, then, the American parade had apparently become an ethnic festival. The *New York Tribune* fumbled for words to characterize
the multiethnic pageant that celebrated the centennial, choosing the
adjectives "incongruous" and "cosmopolitan" to describe how "German
singing bands followed the American militia; German Schutzen corps
and Irish temperance societies were in adjacent divisions; trade unions,
civic associations and secret societies moved in one body; the Ancient
Order of Hibernians and the post of the Army of the Republic were a
close company; while Spanish, Swiss, French, and Italian associations
were combined in the same division."[20] If the *Tribune* were speaking of
San Francisco, or to a lesser extent New Orleans, this idyllic picture of
ethnic harmony might accurately reflect the ceremonial life of the city
as a whole. The actual relationship between ethnicity and public ceremony, however, especially in New York City, is far more complicated
and bears further scrutiny.

Well before 1876, ethnicity had begun to erode the public and inclu-
sive character of parading. As the editor of the *Tribune* knew full well,
New York parades had fractured along ethnic lines long before and now
were reassembled only on special occasions, such as that of 4 July 1876.
In 1870 the *Herald* had reported that the closest approximation to
an old-fashioned parade was a procession of forty thousand Irish on 17
March, a separate holiday that was not accorded official sponsorship.[21]
By contrast, the annual Fourth of July parade in New York had degen-
erated into a short military procession. The festive Irish parade every
St. Patrick's Day did not win the approval of the city press, or of their
middle-class readers; on the contrary, it brought annual complaints about
disruption of business. In 1871, moreover, the Irish proclivity for marching precipitated one of the bloodiest police confrontations in the city's

history when the Orange Irish paraded to celebrate the anniversary of the Battle of the Boyne.[22] On St. Patrick's Day two years later, the *New York Times* expressed equal disdain for the Irish and the ritual of the parade. Commenting on the procession of some twenty-five thousand marchers, it opined: "It is difficult in the extreme for the American Mind to understand."[23] Parading, if we are to believe the *Times*, had become an ethnic rather than a civic ritual, and the peculiar avocation of the Irish.

The withdrawal from parades of the ethnic groups that the *Times* called "American" had taken some time to accomplish. Before 1850, parades, whether flush with artisans, freemasons, or temperance reformers, were composed principally of native-born Anglo-Saxons. The native born did not immediately cede this public ceremonial territory to the new arrivals from famine-torn Ireland. On 4 July 1850, the press congratulated the city on the polite reception it gave militia companies representing many different nationalities.[24] At the funeral procession for Zachary Taylor just a few weeks later, however, the *Herald* quietly noted that contingents of Catholic Irish scuffled briefly with a division of the nativist organization, the United Americans.[25] For the next decade the Irish marched defiantly through the most virulent seasons of nativism, and by the late 1850s they seemed to have won out over all ethnic opposition. In 1858 the *New York Herald* commented that parading had become almost synonymous with the ethnic label Irish-American.

On 1 September of that year, however, native-born Protestants took the offensive by converting the celebration of the completion of the Atlantic cable into an undisguised assertion of Anglo-Saxon culture. A bevy of Protestant associations—the St. Nicholas, St. George, St. Andrew, St. David, and Scotch societies—paraded through the streets decorated with anti-Irish taunts. Indeed, the Irish immigrant and virulent opponent of all things English might well take exception to such slogans as "There is no word as fail for Saxon Blood" or "Severed July 4, 1776, united August 12, 1858."[26] As it turned out, this would be the last time that Anglo-Saxons would play such a prominent role in parades. Furthermore, middle-class associations—the medical society, the bar, mechanics' associations, literary societies—retired from public display at the same time, preferring to spend civic holidays quietly at home or journeying up the Hudson to rural retreats. Class and ethnicity were simultaneously converging and unraveling at this critical juncture in the history of the parade.

The retreat of the native born is an early sign of the decline of parading as a fully public rite, capable of enrolling a wide spectrum of social groups. Ethnicity seemed, furthermore, to provide the umbrella under which the middle and upper classes, including the artisans who flocked into nativist associations, departed from the parade. This process whereby the American parade began to unravel cannot be understood without considering a third social category. The category is gender, and it operated largely to define parading as a male prerogative, offering women only a shadowy position in the line of march.

The parades of the nineteenth century were almost exclusively male affairs. The exceptions to this rule, however, are revealing. Although

the evidence is too scanty to sustain a full argument, interesting speculations may be proffered. For example, a few women appeared in the
Erie Canal celebration—not in the prosaic parade, but in a procession of
boats that sailed to Long Island Sound to ceremonially mingle the waters of the Atlantic and Lake Erie. These choice women were wives of
the city elite who traveled in barges with names like the "Lady Clinton"
and the "Lady Van Rensselaer." After disembarking, the ladies walked
in a body from the Battery to Bowling Green, thus enacting a brief and
rare women's parade. This ritual gesture seemed a throwback to a by-
gone era, best exemplified perhaps by the processions of Renaissance
Italy, and still appropriate to aristocratic circles of the early American
Republic, in which marital and family alliances were so critical to social
standing that female ties were publicly honored.

The common man who marched through the streets in the age of
Jackson was unencumbered by such bonds. The classic American parade celebrated Republican manhood, an individual identity exercised
through voting, breadwinning, and marching. Nearly every contingent
of the parade reflected a male social role, that of the citizen, the public
official, the worker, the college student, or the soldier. All participants
assumed the masculine posture, stepping high, chest expanded, as they
marched into the public ceremony. There were, however, a few references to female contingents in antebellum parades. Two of the many
temperance units that marched in New York during the 1840s had suggestive titles: "Happy Wife" and "Lady Franklin." Although these contingents in the parade were probably composed entirely of men, the
temperance societies gave at least nominal recognition to the second
sex, whom they routinely included in their private, indoor ceremonies.
From San Francisco comes another, more definite, notice of women, eight
of whom marched as auxiliaries of the Masons. In both these instances,
and in other cities as well, those rare women who appeared in marching
units were in the company of native-born Protestant males, the contingents most likely to withdraw from parades before the Civil War.[27]

Before they surrendered this public ceremonial space to the foreign
born of lowlier economic status, however, these same groups introduced
women into their parades in yet another ominous way. A temperance
parade on 4 July 1842, composed largely of the native born and middle
class, contained this novel contingent: a wagon carrying thirteen young
girls representing the thirteen states of the Union—a role that early in
the century small boys had played. The middle-class congregation of
Whigs who commemorated the erection of a statue of Washington in
Union Square in 1847 actually admitted an adult woman to the line of
march, where she impersonated the Goddess of Liberty. This classic female symbol appeared once again on a nativist banner in 1850: the Goddess of Liberty was depicted passing the torch of freedom from
Washington to the chief official of the United Americans. Women had
won at least a symbolic place in the parades of the native born and middle
class. Yet by the middle of the century these classes had largely withdrawn from public ceremonial life. In a sense, then, these female sym-

bols portended the ultimate retreat of the middle class and native born into a privatized Victorian culture.

These same symbols continued, however, to be incorporated into the parades of others during and after the Civil War. The Irish, by the 1860s in New York and in San Francisco, had adapted and elaborated the role of women as living symbols. Comely young ladies, sometimes in carriages, sometimes on horseback, were given prominent places in St. Patrick's Day parades, playing the roles of both the Goddess of Liberty and the Maid of Erin. When the Fourth of July was still celebrated with a parade, as in San Francisco in the 1870s, emblems of gender differences headed the line of march. In 1877, the parade began with two divisions of the military, followed by a Goddess of Liberty and thirty-eight young women representing the states of the Union. After the Civil War those military contingents conveyed a new meaning. No longer dashing citizen-soldiers, they were veterans of a bloody war or members of the National Guard, ordered to parade by their commanding general. During the waning days of parading, symbols of sexual dimorphism, of male power and female gentleness, loomed over the city on the Fourth of July. The American eagle and the Goddess of Liberty were favorite images in the fireworks that had become a prominent part of Independence Day celebrations in all three cities. These icons spoke symbolically and vaguely of but two social groups: the male and the female.

The Goddess of Liberty was obviously just an allegorical figure whose presence in the parade did not reflect the actual composition of the procession, which was decidedly male. Throughout the Jacksonian era, indeed, male marchers simply represented themselves, enacting a kind of cultural equivalent of descriptive representation. By contrast, the Goddess of Liberty, the Maid of Erin, and the female embodiment of the thirty-odd states of the Union evoked some abstract concept far removed from the women themselves—an overt expression, perhaps, of their cultural utility. The female symbols were serviceable in a variety of ways. Their status as the quintessential "other" within a male-defined cultural universe made them perfect vehicles for representing the remote notions of national unity and local harmony. Similarly, as nonvoters they could evoke the ideal of a nation or a city freed of partisan divisions. As supposedly domestic creatures, they could stand above the class conflicts generated in the workplace. Defined by their roles as wives and mothers, women provided excellent symbols for ethnic solidarity: through marriage and childbirth they knit the bonds of ethnic communities. Finally, when the Civil War magnified the power of the state, the female allegory of the Goddess of Liberty evoked the soothing, humanizing imagery of maternity and nurturance. These complementary symbols were drawn together explicitly in San Francisco's Fourth of July parade in 1872. The ornamented wagon that carried thirteen fair young women was called the "Ship of State."

The rise of female symbolism represents a mode of civic ritual fundamentally at odds with the parade genre. Instead of displaying the constituent elements of the urban social order, albeit imperfectly and incompletely, these symbols transcended such mundane realities and washed out the actual social differences within the polity. To use Hanna Pitkin's terminology, gender imagery invoked symbolic rather than descriptive representation. The public presentation of civic groups was replaced by signs—goddesses, eagles, and flags—whose imprecise but evocative references manipulated the diffuse feelings of the audience rather than representing the body social and political.

The central but illusive role of gender in this transition can only be alluded to here. At issue is a complex political and cultural history that commenced with those masculinist assumptions of the early Republic which placed women outside the arena of public deliberation and discourse, thereby creating a feminine, depoliticized cultural field for the abstract symbols around which the republic could seek ideological unity. Accordingly, by the early nineteenth century both France and the United States had constructed female allegories to legitimize their fragile new republics.[28] In the Jacksonian era, however, and in its characteristic ceremony, the parade, these classic female allegories receded from public view, eclipsed by the ceremonial display of the distinct components of the democracy. When, after mid century, that constituency became too contentious, female symbols acquired new currency. By then popular literary culture had invested female symbols with a domestic meaning, proffering a reassuring imagery of purity, passivity, and hence social harmony. At the same time, the association of femininity and privacy lodged a challenge to the cultural authority of public ceremonies in the parade itself. In intricate, still poorly understood ways this serpentine history of gender contributed to the decline of parading as the characteristic genre of American ceremony.

Thus when, as in New York in 1883, it came time again to commemorate an epochal event in the history of civic improvement, the parade was only a small part of the ceremony. The procession that opened the Brooklyn Bridge on 24 May was hardly a parade at all. Only the president of the United States, a long line of municipal officials, and the Seventh Regiment of the National Guard marched across the span of steel and masonry. The rest of the society assembled as a largely undifferentiated mass of spectators. The reporter for the *New York Tribune* found only two sources of relief from the visual monotony of the crowd: the glitter of the soldiers' muskets and the billowing white of the ladies' handkerchiefs. Similarly, the end of Reconstruction in New Orleans was commemorated in a spectacle of gender and power. While the White Leagues, triumphant soldiers who had once ousted the radical Republicans from office, marched through the streets, women in white waved their handkerchiefs in approval. That abstract and dualistic image replaced the complex language of social structure once inscribed in the parade.

Left behind, however, is valuable evidence for historians. The parade offers some answers to the questions about group formation and group identity that have preoccupied historians of nineteenth-century America. The parades of 1825 to 1880 document the development of such concepts as class, ethnicity, and gender, all in forms that were legible to contemporaries. This public ceremonial language was both complex and highly mutable. Any witness to a parade could see that the American city was an intricate mixture of nationalities, occupations, and allegiances. In a lifetime that spanned those fifty years, a spectator along the parade route could see those differences sorted first along lines of occupation, then fragmented into a kaleidoscopic array of voluntary associations, and finally reordered according to ethnicity. In the third quarter of the nineteenth century, the public itself resolved the historian's persistent question about the relative importance of class and ethnic consciousness, in favor of the latter. As symbols of gender became more prominent in these public displays, the syntax as well as the vocabulary of civic celebration began to change. Cultural unity no longer inhered in the representation of the diverse components of the social order but was woven in abstractions that hovered in an imaginary sphere above the line of march.

In its heyday, the parade provided a public lexicon that organized the diverse population of the city into manageable categories. It performed this cultural and social service during times of major social transformation. These buoyant festivals were mounted amid the most inauspicious historical circumstances, as cities grew at an extraordinary rate, took in a diverse array of new immigrants, and incorporated whole new social classes and modes of economic organization. Parading spanned the harrowing transition from urban village to industrial city and survived seasons of rioting, fierce partisan battles, and even a civil war. On parade days, all this confusion was sorted into neat categories and dressed in its Sunday best. The disorder and cacophony that reigned most of the year was ordered into reassuring, visually and audibly pleasing patterns.

The parade was an exercise in self-discipline as well as social discipline. Especially after 1840, its participants, whether organized into actual militia companies or simply mimicking such regimented bodies, all accepted the responsibility to maintain an exacting order in their ranks. Irish benefit societies, for example, exacted a one-dollar fine from any member who smoked, left ranks without permission, or otherwise behaved "improperly" during a parade.[29] Under the pretense of play, thousands of men marched at specified times, in rigid postures, in straight ranks, in uniform clothing. Thousands of newcomers to the city, many of them scarcely rehabilitated peasants, practiced the etiquette of urban living in public.

The paraders were not only agents of social order, but also parties to the creation of urban culture. The Irish, in a particularly obstinate way, forced Anglo-Saxon Protestants to acknowledge them as members of American culture as well as citizens. They actively demonstrated that an ethnic parade, not a melting pot, would be the most fitting symbol of a multiethnic society. Although this ethnic fragmentation ultimately undermined the parade as a citywide celebration, ethnic affirmation kept the form alive. The St. Patrick's Day parade was the first of many examples of independent parading whereby distinctive social groups imprinted their identity on the public mind. Blacks would use parading in a similar fashion in Reconstruction New Orleans. Workingmen would write themselves into ceremonial and social history during the great Labor Day parades of the 1880s. And finally, in the second decade of this century, suffragists took to the streets in processions and won for women a representative rather than a symbolic place in public ceremony.

Parades continue to this day, providing a ceremonial method of forging and asserting the diverse social identities that compose American culture. These groups take to the streets on Martin Luther King Day, Cinco de Mayo, Gay Pride Day, and many other occasions. Seldom, however, does a wide array of different social groups send contingents to a common public ceremony. The celebration of the centennial of the Statue of Liberty, for example, gave center stage to the commander in chief, assorted Hollywood celebrities, corporate executives, and mass-marketed commodities. The pageantry was choreographed by public relations experts and advertisers, not hammered out in public meetings. Still, those sporadic isolated parades recall a past, and perhaps inspire a future, in which diverse social groups could come together both to display themselves and to acknowledge one another.

NOTES

1. *San Francisco Morning Call*, 6 July 1864.
2. John J. MacAloon, ed., *Rite, Drama, Festival, Spectacle: Rehearsals Toward a Theory of Cultural Performance* (Philadelphia, 1984); and John Skorupski, *Symbol and Theory: A Philosophical Study of Theories of Religion in Social Anthropology* (Cambridge, 1976), p. 84. See Susan G. Davis, *Parades and Power: Street Theatre in Nineteenth-Century Philadelphia* (Philadelphia, 1986), for an excellent account of a variety of processional forms in one city, and an interpretation that differs from my own.
3. Robert Da Matta, "Carnival in Multiple Planes," in *Rite, Drama, Festival, Spectacle*, ed. MacAloon, pp. 208–40.
4. Robert Darnton, *The Great Cat Massacre and Other Episodes in French Cultural History* (New York, 1984), pp. 116–24.
5. *New Orleans Picayune*, 4 July 1849.
6. William L. Stone, *History of New York City from Discovery to the Present Day* (New York, 1872), pp. 280–90.
7. Hanna Fenichel Pitkin, *The Concept of Representation* (Berkeley and Los Angeles, 1967).
8. *New York Tribune*, 18 March 1850.
9. Barbara Babcock, "Clay Voices: Invoking, Mocking, Celebrating," in *Celebration: Studies in Festivity and Ritual*, ed. Victor Turner (Washington, D.C., 1982), p. 24.
10. Martha Lamb, *History of the City of New York: Its Origin, Rise, and Progress* (New York, 1880), pp. 696–730; *New York Evening Post*, 3, 5 November 1825.
11. *New Orleans Picayune*, 4 July 1837.
12. *New York Herald*, 15 October 1842; 25 April 1865.
13. *San Francisco Chronicle*, 4 July 1869.
14. *Daily Alta California*, 4 July 1868; *New York Tribune*, 31 May 1877.
15. *Daily Alta California*, 6 July 1853.
16. Marcus Cunliffe, *Soldiers and Civilians: The Martial Spirit in America, 1775–1865* (Boston, 1968), p. 223–30.
17. *New York Herald*, 25 April 1865; 2 July 1876.
18. *New York Herald*, 25 April 1865.
19. *New York Herald*, 2 July 1875; *San Francisco Chronicle*, 4 July 1876; *New Orleans Picayune*, 4 July 1876.
20. *New York Tribune*, 4 July 1876.
21. *New York Herald*, 18 March 1869; 18 March 1870.
22. See extensive accounts of the Orangemen riots in the *Herald*, *Times*, and *Tribune* for 13 July 1870, and 13 July 1871.
23. *New York Times*, 18 March 1873.

24. *New York Tribune*, 4, 5 July 1850; *New York Herald*, 6 July 1850.

25 *New York Herald*, 23 July 1850.

26. *New York Tribune*, 1 September 1858; *New York Herald*, 1 September 1858.

27. *New York Tribune*, 21, 22 October 1847; *San Francisco Chronicle*, 22, 23 February 1872; Davis, *Parades and Power*, p. 42; and Jean Gould Hales, "'Co-Laborers in the Cause': The Women in the Ante-Bellum Nativist Movement," *Civil War History* 25 (1979): 119–38.

28. Lynn Hunt, *Politics, Culture, and Class in the French Revolution* (Berkeley and Los Angeles, 1984), pp. 61–66; and Maurice Agulhon, *Marianne into Battle* (Cambridge, 1981).

29. "Articles of Incorporation, Constitution, By-Laws and Rules of Order of the Irish American Benevolent Society" (San Francisco, 1871), p. 29.

*Part Two*

# *The Industrial City*

# Introduction

By the time of the Civil War the United States was poised on the threshold of the industrial era. In the years between 1860 and 1920 the face of urban America was reshaped and restructured by technology, transportation, economic development, demographic shifts, and the rise of corporations and other large bureaucratic organizations. Powerful and dynamic forces such as capitalism, competition, individualism, and consumerism triggered economic and social changes. Driven by the profit motive, the process of modernizing change did not always have pleasant results. The large American industrial city—for the most part ugly, congested, noisy, smelly, smoky, unhealthy, and ill governed—emerged during this period. At the same time, city people tried to understand, manage, and overcome the new forces and conditions reshaping the cities. Politicians, reformers, businessmen, engineers, educators, and experts of various sorts sought to govern, build, and reform the industrial city. Heterogeneous groups of immigrants and rural migrants, unaccustomed to urban life and work, struggled to adjust to new conditions. As the cities grew to enormous size, they also became more socially divided, segmented, and disorderly.

One of the most noticeable differences between the industrial city of the late nineteenth century and the commercial metropolis of the pre-Civil War period was population size. New York, with less than one million people in 1860, exceeded 5.5 million by 1920. Chicago, which had a little over 100,000 in 1860, neared the three million mark in 1920 (see table). Most of the older eastern and midwestern cities grew at a startling pace. In addition, explosive urban growth occurred in a number of smaller cities in the South, the trans-Mississippi West, and the Pacific Coast region, as evidenced by Omaha, Kansas City, Minneapolis, Denver, Seattle, Portland, San Francisco, Oakland, Los Angeles, and Atlanta. Amazingly, the Great Lakes city of Duluth, Minnesota, grew tenfold in the 1880s, from 3,300 to over 33,000; even more amazing was that Duluth's annual shipping tonnage eventually exceeded that of New York City, mostly because of the enormous bulk of the wheat, timber, and iron ore shipped out of the dynamically growing lake port. In the South, Birmingham, Alabama, grew from 3,000 to over 26,000 in the 1880s, the result of new industrial development during the decade. By 1920 the U.S. census revealed that more than 50 percent of all Americans lived in urban places, a vast jump from the less than 20 percent who lived in cities in 1860. "We cannot all live in cities," New York editor Horace

Greeley wrote in 1867, "yet nearly all seem determined to do so."[1]
Greeley's analysis was not far off the mark, for the nation had become
truly "citified" by the early twentieth century.

The rapid urban population growth of the period was the consequence
of a great release of rural population, both in the United States and in
Europe. A rising birth rate, a falling death rate, and annexation by cities of surrounding areas accounted for some of the increase, but most of
the new urbanites came from rural America and peasant villages in
Europe. Agricultural depressions and the hardships of farm life forced
American farmers and their families off the land and into the cities in
search of economic opportunity. Many young people from the farms were
also lured to the city by its more active social, cultural, and recreational
life.

Simultaneously, millions of European peasant farmers and villagers
cast their lot with the cities in migrating to the "land of opportunity."
During the century after 1820, about 34 million immigrants arrived in
the United States. The first wave consisted primarily of Irish, German,
British, and Scandinavian newcomers. By the 1880s, southern and eastern Europeans began arriving at the immigrant ports, as well. In the
twentieth century the European influx to the cities was swelled by the
migration of rural southern blacks to cities in the North, West, and South.
And by the 1920s, migrants from rural Mexico had joined the movement
to the American city, not only in California and the Southwest but as far
as Chicago, Minneapolis, and Detroit.

These demographic shifts contributed to the reshaping of the modern American city. The presence of such large numbers of rural newcomers, unaccustomed to city ways and industrial labor, drastically altered
the fabric of urban life. Ethnic, religious, and racial diversity became
common in almost every city. The foreign-born presence was especially
pervasive. By 1910 more than 70 percent of the populations of New York,
Chicago, Boston, Cleveland, Detroit, Buffalo, and Milwaukee was composed of immigrants or their American-born children. The percentage of
foreign stock ranged between 50 and 70 percent in such other major
cities as St. Louis, Philadelphia, Cincinnati, Pittsburgh, Newark, and
San Francisco. Even as late as 1920, the foreign-born proportion of industrial city populations remained enormous (see table). Swelling the
inner districts of the cities where housing was cheap and jobs were available, the immigrants made the city look, sound, and feel different.

Strangers in their new surroundings, the immigrants sought identity in common with their fellows. They could not recreate the village
society of peasant Europe, but old institutions such as family and church
remained strong; and they established new community agencies such as
newspapers, benevolent societies, unions, even saloons, that helped
maintain their group identities. At the same time, through the public
school, the political system, and the workplace, the assimilation process
began. Industrial cities of the late nineteenth century, then, served as
huge centers for social interaction and cultural change. In the process
of community building, farmers and peasant folk became city people,
shepherds and fruit growers became factory workers, Sicilians and

**Population and Composition of 25 Largest Cities, 1860–1920**

### 1860

| Rank | City | Population | Percent Black | Percent Foreign Born |
|------|------|-----------|---------------|----------------------|
| 1 | New York | 813,669 | 1.50 | 47.60 |
| 2 | Philadelphia | 565,529 | 3.90 | 28.90 |
| 3 | Brooklyn | 266,661 | 1.60 | 39.20 |
| 4 | Baltimore | 212,418 | 13.10 | 24.70 |
| 5 | Boston | 177,840 | 1.30 | 35.90 |
| 6 | New Orleans | 168,675 | 14.30 | 38.30 |
| 7 | Cincinnati | 161,044 | 2.30 | 45.70 |
| 8 | St. Louis | 160,773 | 2.10 | 59.80 |
| 9 | Chicago | 109,260 | 0.90 | 50.00 |
| 10 | Buffalo | 81,129 | 1.00 | 46.40 |
| 11 | Newark | 71,941 | 1.80 | 37.00 |
| 12 | Louisville | 68,033 | 10.00 | 33.70 |
| 13 | Albany | 62,367 | 1.00 | 34.70 |
| 14 | Washington | 61,122 | 18.00 | 17.60 |
| 15 | San Francisco | 56,802 | 2.10 | 50.10 |
| 16 | Providence | 50,666 | 3.00 | 24.80 |
| 17 | Pittsburgh | 49,221 | 2.30 | 36.70 |
| 18 | Rochester | 48,204 | 0.90 | 39.20 |
| 19 | Detroit | 45,619 | 3.10 | 46.80 |
| 20 | Milwaukee | 45,246 | 0.20 | 50.50 |
| 21 | Cleveland | 43,417 | 1.80 | 44.80 |
| 22 | Charleston | 40,522 | 42.30 | 15.60 |
| 23 | New Haven | 39,267 | 3.80 | 27.10 |
| 24 | Troy | 39,235 | 1.60 | 34.30 |
| 25 | Richmond | 37,910 | 37.70 | 13.10 |

### 1920

| Rank | City | Population | Percent Black | Percent Foreign Born |
|------|------|-----------|---------------|----------------------|
| 1 | New York | 5,620,048 | 2.70 | 36.10 |
| 2 | Chicago | 2,701,705 | 4.10 | 29.90 |
| 3 | Philadelphia | 1,823,779 | 7.40 | 22.00 |
| 4 | Detroit | 993,678 | 4.10 | 29.30 |
| 5 | Cleveland | 796,841 | 4.30 | 30.10 |
| 6 | St. Louis | 772,897 | 9.00 | 13.40 |
| 7 | Boston | 748,060 | 2.20 | 32.40 |
| 8 | Baltimore | 733,826 | 14.80 | 11.60 |
| 9 | Pittsburgh | 588,343 | 6.40 | 20.50 |
| 10 | Los Angeles | 576,673 | 2.70 | 21.20 |
| 11 | Buffalo | 506,775 | 0.90 | 24.00 |
| 12 | San Francisco | 506,676 | 0.60 | 29.40 |
| 13 | Milwaukee | 457,147 | 1.30 | 24.10 |
| 14 | Washington | 437,571 | 25.10 | 6.70 |
| 15 | Newark | 414,524 | 4.10 | 28.40 |
| 16 | Cincinnati | 401,247 | 7.50 | 10.70 |
| 17 | New Orleans | 387,219 | 26.10 | 7.10 |
| 18 | Minneapolis | 380,582 | 0.90 | 23.20 |
| 19 | Kansas City | 324,410 | 9.50 | 8.50 |
| 20 | Seattle | 315,312 | 0.90 | 25.70 |
| 21 | Indianapolis | 314,194 | 11.00 | 5.40 |
| 22 | Jersey City | 298,103 | 2.70 | 25.60 |
| 23 | Rochester | 295,750 | 0.80 | 24.10 |
| 24 | Portland | 258,288 | 0.50 | 19.30 |
| 25 | Denver | 256,491 | 2.50 | 14.90 |

**Sources**: U.S. Census, 1860 and 1920

Calabrians became Italians, and foreigners became Americans. These changes were occurring simultaneously at different levels and at different rates. Moreover, change of this kind was a constant feature of life in the city because new immigrants continued to arrive until the restrictive immigration legislation of the 1920s. If anything, the industrial city was a place of continual social and cultural change.

If population changes dramatically affected urban life during this period, so also did new transportation technology that did away with the "walking city." Beginning with the horse-drawn omnibus in the 1830s, a series of transportation innovations revolutionized life in the city by the late nineteenth century. These innovations—the commuter railroad, the horsecar, the electric trolley, the cable car, and finally the subway and the elevated railroad—brought structural and spatial change to the city. New transportation opened up distant peripheral areas to development and permitted the physical expansion of the city. New housing sprouted along streetcar, trolley, and subway lines. Wealthy and middle-class residents moved from the central districts to the outer fringes and suburbs, as city workers and immigrants began occupying older housing vacated in the center.

The transportation lines focused on the city center, driving up land prices, creating downtown shopping districts, and bringing workers to centrally located businesses and factories. Land uses became much more differentiated and specialized. Functionally, urban regions split between the center (comprising older, low-income housing and industrial, commercial, and business establishments) and the outlying ring of expanding suburbs; often separating the two was a "zone of emergence," working-class sections on the inner edges of the central district. By the end of this period, the motor truck and the automobile had begun to have an impact, intensifying some of the earlier patterns of physical development but creating new ones as well.

New methods of urban transit had other long-range results. Physical growth of the city promoted social fragmentation, as community life tended to segregate by class, ethnicity, and race. The personal and face-to-face contacts that characterized the walking city were replaced by looser and more impersonal human relationships. The sense of community that had prevailed in earlier years eroded in the industrial city; the common value structure of a prior era had little impact on a heterogeneous population composed of numerous ethnic, religious, and racial subcultures. Similar patterns prevailed in the streetcar suburbs, which most new residents conceived of only as an escape from the city and where, according to some interpretations, community life seemed to be less centered than in the older urban neighborhoods.

Transportation innovations between cities also had a powerful effect on urban life and economic development. Railroad mileage increased from 30,000 miles in 1860 to 190,000 miles in 1900, reflecting the completion of an integrated national railroad network by the end of the nineteenth century. During these years, smaller rail lines were consolidated into large railroad empires, while the transcontinental railroads pushed out across the Great Plains and the Rocky Mountains to Pacific Coast cities. These developments, linking far-flung cities and fostering the growth of new ones, brought a national market within reach of manufacturers and businessmen and helped make an industrial revolution possible after the Civil War.

By the late nineteenth century the stage was set for the rise of the large, sprawling industrial city. Population growth had created a large internal market, and transportation innovations offered a means of gathering raw materials and distributing finished products and consumer goods. The rural migrants and new immigrants pouring into the cities provided a ready pool of cheap labor. Technology supplied the skills and machinery needed for industrial output and mass production, and new sources of energy such as steam, oil, and electricity supplied the necessary power. The emergence of finance capitalism, as opposed to the older and more localized merchant capitalism, made investment funds readily available for new industrial endeavors. New and consolidated forms of business organization, especially the corporation, tended to cut competition, facilitate economies in production, and spur large-scale economic activity. And, finally, in a variety of ways government promoted economic growth as a desirable end. The unregulated, laissez-faire atmosphere of the era enabled the new corporations to flourish without much governmental intervention. The concatenation of these developments brought an industrial revolution to the American city.

As a result of this revolution, American cities had become massive centers for manufacturing and related economic enterprises. The cities of the period differed markedly from the mercantile and commercial cities of the pre-Civil War years. The largest urban centers in the Northeast and the Midwest all developed highly diversified economies, while smaller ones often gained reputations for specialized manufacturing. Most big cities also served regional financial and marketing functions, as subsidiary industries and businesses emerged.

The growth of the urban market also encouraged a consumer revolution. The new downtown shopping districts boasted newly popular department stores and chain stores, all stocking standardized products, while promotional advertising helped to create a mass consumer market. The new mail-order houses of Sears, Roebuck and Montgomery Ward, centered in Chicago and relying on widely distributed catalogs, typified the businessman's new approach to capturing the consumer dollar. Even in the midst of the industrial era, the growth of a mass consumer society was causing a shift of the work force toward a variety of service occupations. The giant corporations, for example, developed huge bureaucracies of managers and office workers, and mass marketing required tens of thousands of service workers to move the product to the consumer.

Technology, capitalism, and the widespread American faith in competition, consumerism, and economic growth propelled the United States into the industrial era. By the end of the nineteenth century, the value of American industrial output surpassed the combined totals for Britain, France, and Germany, the world's industrial leaders in 1860. Emerging in the late nineteenth century, the American industrial city became an economic center with wide-reaching functions. It was a center for manufacturing, wholesaling, and retailing; it was the point of concentration for financial and corporate decision making; and it was the place of work for millions of new urbanites. Clearly, the changes introduced by transportation, economic growth, and industrialization had important and long-lasting impacts on life in the American city.

Changes of this kind can be perceived in urban political developments during the industrial era. City politics provided an arena for conflicting interest groups. Not surprisingly, municipal politics reflected the emerging residential pattern that encouraged the creation of urban neighborhoods and communities according to class, ethnicity, and race. These groups vied for city council positions, school board seats, municipal patronage, and a share of power in the allocation of funds for urban physical development. As individuals sought economic gains in the competitive society, so also did special interest groups compete for city jobs for relatives and friends, better parks and streets in their neighborhoods, or governmental favoritism of one kind or another.

Holding these fragmented political communities together was the political machine and the city boss. Numerous recent studies have demonstrated that the urban bosses did more than simply rob the public treasuries. As sociologist Robert K. Merton has noted, the machine had a number of "latent functions"—services beyond those provided by the official government.[2] Such services could take the form of a municipal job, a Christmas turkey, winter fuel for the poor, a utility or transit franchise for the businessman, or a free hand to gamblers, saloonkeepers, and prostitutes. The machine, however, exacted something in return, such as votes, graft, kickbacks, and protection money. The link between machine politicians and such popular sports as baseball, boxing, and horse racing also suggests the complex ways in which the bosses played to a varied constituency.

It also appears now that most of the classic urban bosses—Tweed in New York, Shepherd in Washington, Cox in Cincinnati, the Pendergasts in Kansas City—supported and promoted urban physical development. They lavishly spent municipal funds for new streets and docks, public buildings, schools, parks, transit facilities, public utilities, and other services. Important sectors of the business community such as real estate interests, banking, building and construction concerns, and transit and power companies often found an ally in the boss, who provided cheap municipal land, bank deposits of municipal funds, construction contracts, tax exemptions, franchises, and other payoffs. The costs were high and the political corruption reprehensible, but, according to recent interpretations, the bosses mastered the fragmented metropolises, brought order out of chaos, and provided a kind of positive government. At the same time, the boss was something of a philanthropist and social reformer, promoting the interests and serving the needs of a large immigrant and working-class constituency.

The strong prodevelopment position of most urban bosses stands in marked contrast to the policies advocated by the so-called municipal reformers. As some historians have suggested, these middle-class, good-government advocates were often "structural" reformers who promoted changes in the constitutional structure of city government.[3] They sought city charter changes granting home rule, creating stronger mayors and smaller councils, consolidating school boards, and in general centralizing authority. They advocated a streamlined government administered by experts, an objective thought achievable through the city manager or commission form of municipal government. Their goals included greater efficiency, more honest government, less extravagance, and lower taxes. Thus, these structural reformers usually took an antidevelopment stance, and they opposed huge expenditures for urban physical development.

Drawn from the professions and the bureaucracy of the new corporate structure and often residents of the periphery and the suburbs, the middle-class reformers fought the bosses and the machines for control of urban government. In one sense, as historian Bruce M. Stave has suggested, it was a struggle "between the center-as-residence (for the bosses and their immigrant following) and the center-as-place-of-business (for the reformers)."[4] The reformers represented the forces of centralization, while the machines sought to preserve the decentralized structure held together by the ward heeler, the precinct captain, and the boss. When elected, the reformers found it difficult to retain the support of the voters who wanted services and patronage and the business groups that thrived on urban development. Thus, although reformers were periodically swept into office on a wave of revulsion against corruption and the machine, the bosses were just as regularly put back into power by a constituency fed up with efficiency experts, moral preaching, the merit system, reduced social programs, and rigorous law enforcement in the immigrant neighborhoods. In short, over the long span of American urban history, machine politics has demonstrated a surprising strength and resiliency. It was a political system that fit remarkably well with the business values of the industrial era.

Machine politics is not the only legacy of the industrial city. The competitive spirit carried over into other areas of urban life, as well. For example, the physical and spatial configurations of American cities have been determined largely by entrepreneurial values. Urban land in the United States has been conceived of as a private resource; city land owners sought to use their land in the most profitable ways, without much regard for public convenience or human welfare or physical consequences. The resulting mixed patterns of land use left much to be desired. Valuable business property in downtown areas was gobbled up for factories, railroad yards, and office and storage buildings. Entire neighborhoods were uprooted in the interests of business and industrial groups, and the impact upon the urban environment was ignored. When zoning ordinances and city planning commissions were introduced in the early twentieth century, these tools generally served the interests of the business leaders and affluent property owners who controlled the urban economy. In southern cities, zoning was used to impose rigorous patterns of racial segregation as well.

The city planning profession that emerged in the industrial era reinforced such patterns. The planners usually worked for the real estate

developers or for municipal governments dominated by business interests. The widespread adoption of the rectangular, gridiron street pattern typified the orientation of the planners; the gridiron brought a
monotonous sameness to American cities, but it was the most efficient
and profitable method of dividing up urban land for business purposes
and for speculation. There were some creative planners, such as Daniel
Burnham in Chicago, Horace Cleveland in Minneapolis and St. Paul,
and Frederick Law Olmsted in New York. But those with wealth and
power and political influence generally determined the planning and
physical development of the city. Entrepreneurial values and business purposes predominated in the planning and building of American
cities.

These values also affected many other aspects of American urban
life in the industrial era. In the competitive society the business ethic
prevailed; economic success and individual achievement were valued
over human welfare and the idea of community. In a wide range of
areas—housing, sanitation, public health, education, working conditions,
wages—the bulk of urban residents and workers suffered abominably.
The overcrowded tenement house came to typify living conditions in large
metropolises such as New York City, while unsightly two- and three-
family structures characterized Boston, Chicago, and St. Louis, and dingy
bungalows were the norm in working-class districts in smaller industrial cities such as Detroit, Buffalo, and Milwaukee. By the twentieth
century, new technology had only begun to bring improvements in municipal sewage systems, sanitation, and public health. Public schooling
for most city children encompassed only the elementary years, and thousands of children were annually thrown into the labor market and forced
into dead-end jobs. Factory, mine, and mill jobs were dangerous, and
industrial accidents common. Social services for sick, injured, unemployed, or otherwise dependent persons were inadequate. Incredibly,
during the long depressions from the 1870s to the 1880s, public relief
was abolished in many big cities.

For those who could not compete, there were few rewards. But even
for many who did compete by selling their labor for wages, the rewards
were differential—that is, they were distributed in inequitable ways.
Industrial laborers were buffeted by the periodic depressions of the industrial era; unprotected by unions, they worked long hours at subsis-
tence or even below-subsistence wages. Women and children slaved away
in garment sweatshops or in the factories, mines, and mills of America.

Conditions were even worse for black Americans in the city. Rural
southern blacks envisioned northern cities as a kind of "promised land"
in the post-Civil War years. Over the entire period from 1870 to 1920,
about 1,100,000 southern blacks became northern urban dwellers. The
movement was especially strong after 1900 because of the promise of
economic opportunity. The jobs were there, but white workers faced with
competition for work and housing responded with discrimination and
racism and violence. Tension often resulted in bitter racial conflicts by
the end of the period. The race riots in East St. Louis in 1917 and in
Chicago in 1919 exemplified these patterns of response and reaction.

The racial ghettoes so common in midtwentieth-century America were first created during the industrial era.

The urban society that emerged during the industrial era, then, contained the seeds of the contemporary American city. Population changes, transportation and other technological innovations, and economic advances all combined to thrust the city into the industrial revolution. The competitive drive for entrepreneurial success, a phenomenon most apparent in the cities, moved the United States into the front ranks of the modern industrial nations. But the same kinds of values—individualism, consumerism, competition, and economic achievement—made acceptable the appalling kinds of social and working conditions that prevailed in the city. Neighborhoods and communities often were divided by class, race, and ethnicity. Cities were fragmented functionally and politically. Bosses and businessmen, both driven by the dollar, controlled urban destinies. Economic growth and urban expansion were unplanned and unregulated. Most Americans conceived of such growth in positive ways, but social and environmental costs were ignored in the process. In many of its physical aspects, the city represented the triumph of expedience and profit over aesthetic and environmental considerations.

The city had its problems, to be sure. But there was a positive side to the urban pattern, especially as reflected in the ways in which the human spirit not only survived but also thrived in the urban centers. Indeed, it has been argued that man's best achievements have been encouraged by urban life, particularly in cultural, artistic, and intellectual endeavors. Recent historians, moreover, have emphasized the persistence of old communal and cultural values in the modern industrial city. Despite the pressures for adaptation and conformity to American and urban ways, newcomers from the farm and from across the seas often maintained their old life ways to a remarkable degree. The family structure, religious patterns, and group life remained strong, and the sense of community among the new urbanites could not be extinguished.

T he essays that follow illustrate some of the significant patterns of urban life and change in the industrializing city to about 1920. CLAY MCSHANE and JOEL A. TARR, historians of urban technology, provide a new street-level perspective on urban life in their study of the horse in the American city. From the vantage point of the late twentieth century, it is difficult to imagine that the modernizing city of the industrial era was so heavily dependent on animal power for much of its economy and virtually all of its local transportation. But in the "horse-powered society" of the late nineteenth century, urbanites relied on over 3 million horses (in 1900) to provide power in many industries, to haul freight, to make local deliveries, and to pull omnibuses and horsecars. Feeding and stabling tens of thousands of horses was a major business in every large city. Entire industries employing thousands of workers emerged to build carriages, wagons, and all manner of accoutrements such as harnesses, whips, and horseshoes for the horse-centered economy. Modern-day automobile traffic jams had their late nineteenth-century counterparts as thousands of horses crowded city streets and caused incredible numbers of traffic accidents. And most significantly, horses created serious environmental problems and health hazards, largely because of the ubiquitous manure that made every city smell much like a barnyard. However, until the arrival of electric streetcars in the 1890s, and eventually automobiles, buses, and trucks, the horse was an essential element in the urban economy. Compared to these new technological innovations, the inefficiencies of the horse-powered society become clear. As the authors suggest, the horse played a vital role in the emerging technological networks of the industrial city—one that persisted well into the twentieth century.

Traditional interpretations of urban politics in the industrial era have emphasized the conflicts between the political bosses and the municipal reformers. DANIEL CZITROM takes a new look at this subject in his essay on "Big Tim" Sullivan, an important cog in New York City's notorious Tammany Hall political machine. What he finds suggests the complexity of the subject. A state assemblyman representing a densely populated Irish immigrant slum neighborhood, and later a state senator and U.S. congressman, Sullivan mastered not only traditional forms of patronage and constituent service but also new methods of appealing to urban voters with massive summer outings and extensive programs for providing food and clothing to needy New Yorkers. Opponents charged that "Big Tim" lived off the profits of commercialized vice, but in reality the Tammany leader was in the forefront of efforts to bring organized modern leisure and entertainment to the city. Along with political and business partners, Sullivan helped legalize boxing and horse racing, built neighborhood burlesque and vaudeville theaters, developed a national chain of vaudeville theaters, and later brought the nascent movie industry to New York City. By the early years of the twentieth century, he also helped steer Tammany toward support of a variety of social reforms, especially at the state level. These reforms included protections for women workers, factory safety legislation, women's suffrage, even gun control. The many sides of "Big Tim" Sullivan's career—as a powerful Tammany boss, as a social reformer, and as a businessman facilitating New Yorkers' access to new forms of mass culture and entertainment —all suggest the inadequacy of the more traditional boss-reformer dichotomy.

Few working-class and immigrant neighborhoods in the industrializing city were without their saloons. In her article on "The 'Poor Man's Friend,' " MADELON POWERS elaborates on the significant role of the saloon and the saloonkeeper in the urban community and in working-class culture. According to Powers's analysis, a popular code of reciprocity characterized late nineteenth-century drinking rituals—a code that had many varied implications. On one level, the reciprocal code seemed simple enough, as saloon customers treated one another and the barkeeper to drinks and expected to be treated in return. But there were deeper dimensions to the symbolic code of reciprocity. As an important operative in the urban political machine, the saloonkeeper treated customers to food and drink but was expected to deliver the "saloon vote" on Election

Day. Bar drinkers voted for machine candidates not only because it was expected but also because they derived practical benefits from doing so. Similarly, saloons provided free lunches, cashed workers' paychecks, and offered rooms for club and union meetings, but a lot of beer was sold at lunch, on paydays, and during meetings. The social functions of the saloon, with their mutually beneficial practices, extended throughout the urban neighborhood over many decades during the industrial era. However, several important forces for change after 1900 gradually undermined the role of the saloon as the "poor man's club." First, the increasing control of the saloons by the large breweries diminished the force of the reciprocal code in favor of greater profits. Second, other forms of mass entertainment and culture such as movie theaters and spectator sports arose as alternative leisure-time activities for the working class. Finally, the now more powerful antisaloon forces, with help from some in the labor movement, successfully pushed for temperance and then prohibition, which was achieved by passage of the Eighteenth Amendment to the U.S. Constitution in 1919. Nevertheless, few social institutions in the industrializing city played such an important role in working-class life as the saloon.

The corner saloon rarely opened its doors to women, but working-class girls and women were developing their own leisure-time culture. In her essay, KATHY PEISS illustrates the social impact of changing work patterns in the industrializing city. As late as 1880, most working women in the city labored in domestic service or other home-based occupations. A dramatic transformation in the social organization of work by 1900 created new opportunities for working-class women. Increasingly, by the twentieth century, women worked in a factory setting, especially in the garment trades. The centralization of retailing and corporate activities in the city also opened up jobs for them as sales clerks in department stores and as secretaries, typists, and telephone operators in business offices. For a variety of reasons the workday was shortened as well, leaving more time for female recreation and leisure. Peiss contends that a distinctive women's work culture developed during this era, one through which women collectively gained some degree of control over the workplace and over their pleasure-oriented, leisure-time activities. Peiss's essay neatly blends new urban approaches to labor history, women's history, and cultural history.

DOMINIC A. PACYGA's essay on the Chicago race riot of 1919 gives a powerful example of how social tension and violence stemmed from new configurations of race and ethnicity, and of class and neighborhood, in the industrial city. As blacks moved out of the South during the World War I years, they encountered new social realities in big immigrant cities such as Chicago, where they competed with other groups for jobs, housing, schooling, and recreational space. A violent confrontation at a Lake Michigan beach ignited the spark for Chicago's 1919 racial conflagration, but underlying the triggering incident were several layers of ethnic, racial, and class conflict. Pacyga places the 1919 riot in the context of Chicago's South Side neighborhoods, whose settlers were mostly Irish, Polish, and African American. His analysis provides a startling

degree of specificity by demonstrating why the upwardly mobile, more
Americanized, lower middle-class Irish, whose Catholic neighborhoods
were physically adjacent to the expanding black community, actively
participated in the prolonged race riot. The role of the Irish athletic
clubs and youth gangs in pursuing organized violence was especially
important. By contrast, the Polish community was more distant from
black neighborhoods, had not yet fully accommodated to the racism of
American society, seemed more sensitive to the plight of Chicago's newly
arrived black migrants (the Poles were relatively recent arrivals as well),
and actually sought to build alliances with black workers in the packinghouse union. Pacyga gives considerable evidence to support his analysis of the riot—both of the underlying conditions and of the actual
instigation. Unfortunately, the outcome of the 1919 race riot was to intensify racial barriers on Chicago's South Side, as the Poles and other
East European immigrants discovered race to be a more important self-
identifier than class in the process of Americanization.

These essays suggest some of the exciting and innovative research
currently being pursued by urban and social historians. Each offers important interpretive perspectives on urban America during the industrial era.

NOTES

1. Quoted in Charles N. Glaab and A. Theodore Brown, *A History of Urban America* (New
York: Macmillan, 1967), 136.
2. Robert K. Merton, *Social Theory and Social Structure*, rev. ed. (Glencoe, IL: Free Press,
1957), 71–82.
3. See, for example, Samuel P. Hays, "The Politics of Reform in Municipal Government in
the Progressive Era," *Pacific Northwest Quarterly* 55 (October 1964): 157–69; Melvin G. Holli,
*Reform in Detroit: Hazen S. Pingree and Urban Politics* (New York: Oxford University Press,
1969); Kenneth Fox, *Better City Government: Innovation in American Urban Politics, 1850–
1937* (Philadelphia: Temple University Press, 1977); Martin J. Schiesl, *The Politics of Efficiency: Municipal Administration and Reform in America, 1880–1920* (Berkeley: University
of California Press, 1977); and Bradley R. Rice, *Progressive Cities: The Commission Government Movement in America, 1901–1920* (Austin: University of Texas Press, 1977).
4. Bruce M. Stave, "Urban Bosses and Reform," in Raymond A. Mohl and James F.
Richardson, eds., *The Urban Experience: Themes in American History* (Belmont, CA:
Wadsworth Publishing Company, 1973), 188.

# The Centrality of the Horse in the Nineteenth-Century American City

*Clay McShane and Joel A. Tarr**

O n November 9, 1872, most of downtown Boston caught fire. The flames burned unchecked for thirty-five hours, destroying 776 buildings valued at more than $73.5 million. The fire killed only fourteen people, but thousands of others saw their jobs go up in smoke. The flames were so intense that iron columns twisted and granite building stones turned to dust. While not as severe as Chicago's fire of the previous year, the disaster devastated Boston's economy.

What had transformed what normally would have been a localized blaze into a conflagration? The answer was an "epizootic"—a severe episode or epidemic of an equine or horse disease. Boston was proud of being a "modern" metropolis, equipped with water and sewer systems, a fire-alarm telegraph system (the first constructed in the nation when it was installed in 1852), and a flourishing downtown office district, but the city still depended upon horses to pull its steam-powered pumps to fires. During that week of November 1872, almost every horse in Boston was dead or sick from the infamous "Great Epizootic," probably the most extensive equine "flu" epidemic to strike the nation's horse population in the nineteenth century. The epizootic caused fits of sneezing and coughing, lung infections, and general debility. Veterinarians ordered complete rest, and horses working in defiance of their orders frequently developed pneumonia and died. In a desperate attempt to ensure that fire equipment would get to fires, the municipality had hired day laborers to pull the steam-powered pumpers, but they were too slow. Unable to deploy its pumpers, the fire department actually resorted to blowing up buildings to stop the onrushing flames. For want of horses, half of the Boston central business district burned to the ground![1]

The destruction caused in Boston because of the lack of healthy horses to pull its fire engines provides an insight into the extent to which the

*Clay McShane is professor of history at Northeastern University. Joel A. Tarr is Richard S. Caliguiri Professor of Urban and Environmental History and Policy at Carnegie Mellon University. Original essay printed by permission of authors.*

nineteenth-century city was dependent upon the equine beast. But horses did far more than just pull fire engines; the entire internal city circulatory system depended upon them for a multitude of transportation-related services such as freight delivery, passenger transportation, food distribution, and police and ambulance services. Furthermore, horses supplied energy for factories, their manure served as fertilizer for crops, and their carcasses and hides were made into a variety of useful products.

*functions of horses*

Because of their centrality to the movement of people and goods, cities staggered under the massive disruption of business that an epizootic caused. The Great Epizootic had started in Toronto, spread to Buffalo, and then to Rochester, New York City, and Boston, all of which experienced literal business standstills. While New York did not undergo Boston's catastrophe, business nearly halted.[2] The intrepid diarist, George Templeton Strong, wrote that "the horse disease spreads. Aspect of the streets is wholly changed. Hacks, omnibuses, and horsecars are reduced by more than half."[3] Panic occurred in the marketplace, as deliveries in and out were foiled. Fish shipments rotted at the Fulton Fish Market for lack of cart horses. Some millers tried to use wheelbarrows to carry flour to neighborhood bakers, an expensive expedient. Beer prices soared in neighborhood saloons because deliveries ran out. Coal dealers doubled prices as supplies from outside the city slowed to a trickle. A lack of horses to pull boats along the Erie Canal, or to pull the wagons of vegetable hawkers along city streets, caused a shortage of produce.

Approximately 5 percent of the horses in cities in the northeastern United States, Quebec, and Ontario died, the rest recovering from the epizootic in about two weeks. All cities in the region underwent the same economic problems as New York, if not the devastation of Boston. The tragedy and panic they experienced demonstrated the dependence of nineteenth-century cities on animal power as well as the limitations of that power source.[4] As the editors of the *Nation* commented, "the present epidemic has brought us face to face with the startling fact that the sudden loss of horse labor would totally disorganize our industry and commerce."[5]

How many horses were there in the United States and in the nation's cities in the late nineteenth and early twentieth centuries? In 1870 the U.S. census enumerated 8,690,219 horses in the United States, including 1,547,370 "Not on farms."[6] By 1900 the census counted over 24,148,530 horses, with just under 3 million in cities. In that year, for instance, New York City, the largest in the nation, had 130,000; Chicago, the second-largest, had 74,000; and Philadelphia, the third-largest, had 51,000. From the perspective of horses per humans, however, the order is somewhat different. Kansas City, at 7.4 humans per horse led the list, followed by Los Angeles at 12.7, Indianapolis at 14, and Denver at 14.7. The big cities with the highest horse populations had somewhat smaller densities. By 1910 the total number of urban horses stood at 3.1 million (23 million total) and by 1920 had dropped to 1.7 million (21.4 million total).

We believe, however, that the census understates the number of urban horses, and that other data suggest much larger increases. Separate calculations, for instance, show that the horse population was urbanizing at a rate 50 percent higher than the human population, a sign of increasing urban dependency on horses (see table). In the ten largest cities in the United States in the late nineteenth century, for instance, human populations doubled, while the number of teamsters tripled.[7] The number of horses likely increased proportionately. On Fifth Avenue, New York City, for example, traffic counts showed that 5,460 horse-pulled vehicles traveled past Madison Square daily in 1885, with this number increasing to 6,300 in 1896 and 12,608 in 1904, a 120 percent increase over the nineteen years.[8] While the street railways, undoubtedly the owners of the largest urban herds, replaced their horses with electric motors in the 1890s, the number of horses and teamsters grew as the volume of freight traffic obviously outpaced this loss of passenger traffic.[9]

## Human and Horse Populations in Urban Counties, 1870-1900

|  | *1870* | *1900* | *Growth* |
|---|---|---|---|
| Number of counties with 100,000 people | 25 | 62 | 37 (148%) |
| Human population of United States | 39,818,449 | 75,994,575 | 36,176,126 (90.8%) |
| Human population of urban counties | 6,012,910 | 19,227,818 | 13,214,908 (219%) |
| Percentage of humans in urban counties | 15.1% | 25.3% | — |
| Horse population of United States | 7,145,379 | 24,148,530 | 17,003,151 (238%) |
| Horse population of urban counties | 166,509 | 783,527 | 617,018 (371%) |

Source: U.S. Bureau of the Census. Urban counties are counties with more than 100,000 population (all counties of this size did include a major urban center). We use it as the unit of analysis because the 1870 census only collected horse data by county. In a few heavily urban counties (notably New York and San Francisco), there seems to be a severe undercount in the central city in 1870, since the census instructed some enumerators to ignore urban horses. In a few cases, the census separately listed county and central city horse populations, but we combined them for consistency's sake.

Ironically, the most critical factor in the transportation revolution of the nineteenth century—the immense growth of steam railroads—dramatically increased the demand for urban horses.[10] As the *Nation* noted in 1872, the society's dependence on the horse had "grown almost *pari passu* with our dependence on steam."[11] In America, steam railroads increased their freight shipments from nearly 327 million tons in 1880 to more than 640 million tons in 1890. Almost every single ton required local delivery by horse or transfer from railroad siding to factory. Urban growth increased the length of deliveries and of commuting. Building contractors relied upon horses to carry building materials from freight terminals to construction sites and to haul dirt away from them. Any

*[handwritten margin note: effects of steam railroads on use of horses]*

factory not located on a waterway or railroad required wagons to ship goods.

This essay will consider the importance of the horse to the nineteenth- and early twentieth-century American city in five areas: manufacturing, freight and passenger transportation, the character of the built environment, food and product consumption, and effects on the urban environment. It will conclude by examining the final, but still relatively slow, replacement of the horse by the automobile and the motor truck in the first half of the twentieth century.

## Horses as a Manufacturing Power Source

Although almost forgotten as a source of power to drive machinery, for centuries horses played an important role in this regard. Animal-powered machines predated the industrial revolution and were in wide use in Europe and America before the development of the steam engine; some persisted long after steam engines were widely in use. Essentially, animal-powered machines converted the effort of animals (or men) to rotary power, usually through the use of gears.[12] While several different types of animals, such as oxen and mules as well as horses, powered machinery, horses were probably the most common.

Horsepower was used for gristmills, sawmills, and tanneries in small eighteenth- and nineteenth-century American communities that lacked millstreams.[13] In cities, manufacturers relied on horse-powered machines in construction, shipbuilding, cotton mills, breweries, sawmills, foundries, and machine shops. In Pittsburgh in 1814, for instance, a horse-powered sweepmill constructed to build machinery for a Fulton steamboat drove "a perpendicular shaft, wheels, and drums to turn the lathes and drills."[14] Horsepower was also found extensively in the brewing industry until the late nineteenth century, not only for deliveries but also to grind the malt and to power the water pumps.[15]

Horse- or animal-powered machines usually fell into two classifications—vertical and horizontal—with the horizontal most commonly used. *Appletons' Cyclopaedia of Applied Mechanics* (1895 edition) illustrates and describes three machines that utilize the strength of a horse in a machine. *Appletons'* first examined a technology it called the "well-known Bogardus machine," a device in which the animal moved in a circle about a central pivot, and the rotary motion was transmitted by belts and gearing. The second type of apparatus consisted of a treadmill that utilized the weight of the horse as well as its muscular power. The horse walked on wooden stepboards arranged in an endless belt supported by a series of small rollers. An "apron" connected to the rollers rotated a drum attached to gearing that transmitted the power by belting.[16] The third type of horse-powered machine described was called an "impulsoria." This relatively rare device drove a horse on a treadmill to power a "locomotive" pulling a railway car.

The use of horses for power offered an advantage in terms of their flexibility and their cheapness. Manufacturers could easily add or subtract horses as needed or supplement other forms of power.[17] While evidence of types of horse-powered machines in cities is scarce, state censuses do provide the number of firms using horsepower. In 1850, for instance, the Massachusetts State Census reported that 10 percent of the state's manufacturing firms operated horse-powered machines, as compared to 24 percent with steam power and 66 percent with water power. The firms using horsepower were concentrated in the wood and metal products areas. One can assume that horsepower was even more heavily in use before that date. Kentucky had the highest percentage of horsepower in manufacturing at 20 percent, but much of this was probably rural. By 1860, however, in both Massachusetts and Kentucky, the percentage of firms using horsepower had shrunk to 5 percent, with steam power the fastest growing replacement.[18] It is a reasonable assumption that horse-powered machines in manufacturing continued to decline throughout the century, but it is also reasonable to assume that, as a cheap supply of power, horses continued to be found in low-power industries such as wool carding, bagging, and rope works.[19] As Jennifer Tann notes, horsepower made it possible for men with small capital resources to enter a mechanized field, "being the bridge between human muscle and steam power for men of moderate or larger capital."[20] Eventually, however, cheap electric and internal combustion engines, both available in the 1880s, totally eliminated the use of the urban horse in manufacturing.

## The Horse as a Source of Transportation

The urban horse served primarily to move freight or common carriers such as omnibuses (the forerunner of modern buses) and streetcars. While urban residents might esteem horseback riding in the new parks and parkways of the late nineteenth century as a leisurely pastime, evoking noble images of a rural past, few horseback riders can be observed in photographs of nineteenth-century urban downtowns. Traffic counts in downtown areas of twelve major cities in 1886 did not find a single rider on horseback, although some western cities undoubtedly were familiar with the single rider.[21] Horseback was not an acceptable commuting mode, since one would arrive at the office smelling of exercise and of horses. Controlling accident-prone horses in urban traffic demanded a high level of skill. Once at work, they required stabling and care and could not just be parked at the curb. Even if thieves did not steal them or they did not run away, they might bite or kick passersby. Mounted police officers, on the other hand, rode horses for purposes of crowd control and to patrol parks, and were familiar urban figures.

Cities in the late nineteenth century also experienced an increase in recreational riding by elites in the new parks and parkways.[22] A few wealthy individuals commuted by carriage, but their numbers were small. Private carriages were for the leisurely display of wealth, not everyday travel. The expense of keeping horses in densely populated cities was extremely high. One contemporary writer estimated an initial minimum layout for horse and carriage of $1,300, but costs could rise to $27,000 for a custom-designed vehicle and team of prize horses; annual expenses ranged from $3,229 to $7,216. Storing the carriage and horse required high-priced urban land; horses also needed grooms to care for and feed them, muck out the stables, and repair and clean harnesses and carriages. Competent coachmen required as much as three years of training to drive safely, and those skills were in high demand. Carriage-riding was the province of the extremely rich. A 1921 stable management manual, for instance, suggested that cars were safer, less expensive to operate, and easier to drive.[23]

## OMNIBUSES

The first horse-powered common carriers for intracity passenger transportation appeared shortly after 1800, having first been introduced in Paris. Initially these taxilike common carriers were hackney coaches (hacks) or later cabriolet and hansom carriages (cabs). They plied for hire along city streets or stood in wait for customers at public places such as docks or inns. Their designers patterned them after private carriages and stagecoaches. High fares limited ridership and thus the number of vehicles. Customers had to haggle over fares, which ran about twenty-five cents per mile. Throughout the nineteenth century, wealthy urbanites continued to ride in hacks when they desired higher speeds or privacy in their travel, even after the appearance of trolley cars.

Abraham Brower's horses pulled the first omnibus (forerunner of the modern bus) on Broadway, New York City, in 1829. Entrepreneurs initiated service in most large cities shortly thereafter, mostly the outgrowth of early hackney coach or intercity stagecoach routes. These twenty-seat vehicles operated on fixed routes at scheduled intervals, picking up anyone who flagged them down and dropping off passengers where they chose. Their drivers typically charged a rider four or five bits (a bit was a twelve-and-one-half-cent coin). Where hills, heavy ridership, or poor pavements demanded an extra horse, fares were higher. The number of omnibuses in New York grew from seventy in 1830 to 350 by 1849, with a peak of 683 in 1854. They carried up to 120,000 passengers daily. By 1858, Philadelphia had 322 omnibuses. In 1859, St. Louis had ten different bus routes with headways as low as ten minutes. There were fewer buses in smaller, western cities. Milwaukee and Pittsburgh, for example, had only four short omnibus routes before the Civil War.[24]

The omnibus had severe limits as a transit mode. The rough cobblestone streets of the time held these vehicles' speed to three or four miles per hour, not much faster than walking, and provided a bumpy ride. Thus, they barely expanded the commuting radius. They operated sporadically during the winter since cities did not remove snow from the streets, although a few owners substituted sleighs. For most city dwellers, fares were prohibitively high, and riders complained about their lack of comfort. Omnibuses could pose dangers since drivers could not control their horses easily or rapidly brake the top-heavy vehicles on a rough surface, especially when competing drivers raced each other to pick up a passenger. In New York in 1865 omnibuses caused fatal accidents, mostly to pedestrians, at six times the rate per vehicle as the new street railways.[25]

Omnibuses, like cabs, retained a role in the late nineteenth century. They shuttled between transportation terminals to serve passengers who could not carry baggage on a streetcar. Some hotels operated omnibus services to draw customers from these terminals. Passengers rode them extensively on Fifth Avenue in New York where residents, for status purposes, had managed to have the city ban less-expensive rail-operated common carriers, although urban elites also complained about the experience of riding on omnibuses crowded with poor and ill-smelling immigrants.[26] Omnibus fares remained expensive, typically twenty-five or fifty cents per passenger for relatively short rides. Washington had more omnibuses and cabs for its size than any other city, largely because its relatively good paving lowered the speed differential between horsecars and street-running vehicles.[27]

## HORSECARS

Cities prohibited steam railroads from running with mechanical power downtown, fearing pollution, dangerously high speeds, and boiler explosions.[28] As early as 1832, the New York Central Railroad was uncoupling its locomotives outside the city center and using horses to pull its passenger cars downtown, a forerunner of the true urban horsecar. Other cities soon followed this example. These downtown routes developed considerable local ridership, but railroads were slow to understand the innovation that they had produced. It was not until 1852 that New York chartered the first horsecar lines independent of steam railroad connection. By 1860, New York and Brooklyn already had franchised 143 miles of horsecar lines. In 1856, after the successful operation of a Boston-Cambridge street railway, other cities began to adopt the system. Most major cities chartered their first lines in the late 1850s, and the idea spread as far west as St. Louis and Milwaukee and as far south as New Orleans before the Civil War.[29]

Because iron rails allowed horses to pull twice the load at twice the speed of omnibuses, horsecars revolutionized urban travel, becoming the first mass transit systems. They could profit with only a five-cent fare, one-fifth of what an omnibus charged. Horsecars increased the possible half-hour commuting distance on city streets from about two miles to three miles, expanding the potential residential area of a city from 12.6 to 28.3 square miles under ideal geographic conditions. In Boston, the proportion of people who commuted, as listed in the city directory, increased from 6 percent in 1846 to 18 percent in 1860. Horse railways also made downtown more accessible to suburban women, who had been reluctant to walk long distances on public streets.[30] The greater speeds allowed Americans to fulfill the new dream of the middle class, a detached home with a yard on the outskirts of a city.

*benefits of horse car 1st mass transit*

The number of horsecar riders in New York City (and probably else-where) tripled in the 1860s. By 1870, New Yorkers, on the average, took 100 rides per year, a measure of the innovation's popularity. Many of the city's more affluent citizens were probably commuting daily, with others making frequent shopping trips, although most residents could not afford to ride, except on special occasions. Lower East Side residents, for example, might take a Sunday outing to distant Central Park. Not surprisingly, suburban realtors built most of the new horsecar lines, since downtown access boomed their subdivision's values. By 1890, probably the peak year for horsecar transportation, 32,505,000 passengers rode along 5,783 miles of streetcar track operated by 789 companies. Of the total trackage, 4,062 miles were animal-powered, with the rest divided among electric (914 miles) and cable (283 miles). Approximately 84,000 horses and mules pulled the animal-powered streetcars. The national figure for annual rides per inhabitant in large cities (over 100,000) in 1890 was 172, with New York having the highest total at 297 rides per inhabitant, followed closely by Kansas City with 286, San Francisco at 270, and Boston at 225.[31]

*problems w/ horsecars*

The horses and mules that powered the new transit system also were the new technology's greatest limitation. Roans were the preferred breed, but even they were occasionally hard to control, caused frequent accidents, and deposited large amounts of manure and urine along their routes. Nature limited the pulling power of a horse as well as its life span. On the average, street railways had to replace horses every four years. In the summer, they rotated teams frequently, since overworked horses often dropped from heat stroke. They also stationed extra teams at steep hills to help pull up the horsecars. Snowstorms also required extra teams. Horses sometimes died or collapsed en route, delaying both the cars they pulled and those on the line behind them.[32]

In very large cities, horsepower reached its travel limits by 1885. Complaints about the speed and range of the horses were commonplace.[33] While the cars could be made larger, the strength of horses placed limits on size and speed. Improvements in horses, such as the introduction of Percherons, a new breed, in the 1870s, only helped a little. By the mid-1890s, however, the electric streetcar had eliminated most horses, although they persisted on a few lines up until the 1920s.

## HORSES AND FREIGHT

*freight horses*

The largest number of urban horses pulled wagons carrying freight, merchandise deliveries, and personal possessions. In the early decades of the nineteenth century, one-horse, two-wheeled carts dominated freight movement. In New York City, for instance, "cartmen," the haulers of commodities, held a privileged and licensed position, controlling intracity transportation until the midnineteenth century. As historian Graham R. Hodges observes, the cartmen, "dressed in a uniform of a white frock, trousers, boots, farmer's hat and long-stemmed pipe, were all-purpose carriers of the city's merchandise and possessions."[34] In 1824,

New York City had 2,500 carters, a number that had grown to 3,400 by 1840.[35]

City regulations controlled much of the cartmen's operations, dictating that they could own just one horse and cart, and it had to be free and clear of debt. They could only hire employees by the day and could not expand their operations. Regulations also controlled the size of wagons in order to protect New Yorkers against short-weighing, with strong penalties for violations. Furthermore, the city tried to force the cartmen to walk their horses and to travel at no more than a "leisurely pace," but this regulation was often violated. In 1807 the *Evening Post* complained that the cartmen drove in a manner that was "a public nuisance. . . . It is a prime ambition to possess the fastest pacers and the public streets are the race tracks."[36] As the number of carters grew, their driving behavior became increasingly unacceptable, and in 1825 the city council appointed a superintendent of carts with the responsibility to ensure that all carts were licensed, were in good working condition, and followed city driving rules. In spite of these regulations, the cartmen continued to act in a manner prejudicial to the public order, racing their carts dangerously through the streets, charging exorbitant rates, and insulting citizens. In 1850, as new types of wagons made the carts outmoded, the municipality took away the cartmen's privileged position, permitting companies to hire their own teamsters and to operate in a manner similar to the modern capitalist trucking corporation.[37]

While carters may have been the largest single group of urban horse owners in New York City until midcentury, increasingly large organizations, such as street railways, that owned hundreds and even thousands of horses came to dominate intraurban horse transportation. After street railways, the largest urban horse owners likely were railroads (for local delivery, a function often contracted to express companies such as Wells Fargo or American Express), brewers and millers (for daily, timely deliveries to neighborhoods), coal companies (who often delivered ice in the summer), and construction firms (both to deliver materials and remove earth). These firms kept their livestock in huge, multistory stables. Increasingly, in the late nineteenth century, commercial bakeries, dairies, and groceries delivered goods to customers by way of light wagons, usually drawn by a single horse. Often horse-drawn delivery routes would be developed when the makers of a commodity, such as baked goods, were consolidated into a single large firm. These routes were usually limited to a maximum of ten miles per day.[38] Minor owners (doctors, peddlers, florists, undertakers, cabbies, and others) might have one or two horses, which they boarded in a livery stable, or, if they lived in a neighborhood with a low enough population density, in a backyard shed.[39]

To meet growing freight delivery needs, by 1900 breeders had increased the size and weight of urban horses by 25 percent since the start of the century. Wagon size and type increased also. In 1894 a New York wagon maker produced a thirty-two-foot, seven-ton vehicle to move heavy machinery, the largest wagon ever built. It required fifty horses to pull it when fully loaded.[40] More commonly used by industry were dead-axle drays, which had no springs and which were usually fourteen feet long and fifty inches wide. Special dead-axle drays and city-teaming gear were constructed to haul loads of pipe, poles, and newsprint rolls. In heavy manufacturing cities such as Pittsburgh, large wagons hauled iron and steel beams and ingots through the streets. Also found on city streets were express wagons; milk and beer wagons; merchant, drygoods, and grocery delivery wagons; bakers' and butchers' wagons; lunch wagons; garbage wagons; and ice, coal, and pie wagons.[41] These vehicles increasingly clogged the city's streets. In Chicago in 1907, for instance, the Department of Public Works counted 39,936 one-horse, 21,005 two-horse, 417 three-horse, and 34 four-horse vehicles.[42] Improvements in harnesses allowed larger loads, with a maximum of two tons carried on two-wheeled carts, but up to eight tons on four-wheeled wagons.

The larger owners considered horses almost entirely from an accounting viewpoint. "The horse is looked on as a machine, for sentiment pays no dividend."[43] Typically, major urban horse owners bought draft horses at the age of four or five after farmers had raised them to full maturity, broken them to the harness, and gelded them.[44] Rapid price fluctuations made buying more complex. Consider this price series for urban horses: 1880: $54.75, 1889: $72.00, 1894: $48.00, 1895: $31.00, 1900: $49.00.[45] Horses over the age of five did not have a long-enough working life expectancy to justify purchase, and younger horses would break down or catch diseases more commonly in cities.[46] Those already broken in on the farm still required a two-month apprenticeship to urban conditions, while gelding supposedly made them easier to manage.[47] There were a few mares in big cities, primarily on cabs or light delivery vehicles. Police officers refused to ride mares, considering them "unmanly."

While mules outnumbered horses as the most numerous American draft animals, southern farmers most commonly employed them. Except in a few warm-weather cities, urban teamsters avoided them because they were weaker than horses, rarely reaching fourteen hands. (A hand, the standard unit of horse height, is four inches, measured from the ground to the withers, or shoulders.) Their truculence was legendary and likely worse in heavy traffic.[48] American breeders imported large numbers of European draft animals after midcentury. Percherons, the most common breed and a French import, could be seventeen hands high and weigh 2,500 pounds. Belgian horses, which worked more slowly, were the second most common. Teaming companies had to buy horses matched in size and strength, since an unbalanced team often wound up overworking or laming one of the horses.[49]

Buying and scheduling horses was very complex, especially since strength varied from horse to horse. One writer reported on a brewery horse, chronically lame when pulling four tons, that gave excellent service when pulling only 3.5 tons.[50] Horses with certain personalities worked better if matched to humans with kindred sensibilities. Some worked best when whipped, while others responded to whistles and songs. Some were smarter than others and knew when to stop without being pulled up, or they could return drunk, passed-out drivers home unaided.

In general, stable operation manuals advised avoiding cruel treatment, which they believed would shorten life expectancies and make horses difficult in traffic. However, there were numerous public complaints about cruel teamsters. At least one stable manual suggested starting horses by lighting fires under them.[51] *cruelty*

Urban teaming firms paid special attention to questions of fatigue. A "properly harnessed horse" could produce a pulling force of one-tenth of its weight on a good surface, but on poor surfaces the pulling force was greatly reduced. Over a longer period of time, such as an eight- or ten-hour day, the horse's power output was reduced. The horses of teamsters and railway and canal contractors worked up to twelve hours per day, but at slower speeds.[52] Street railway operating manuals suggested only four-hour shifts, one-third of what humans worked, since constant starts and stops caused the greatest wear on horses. Horses employed in industry (turning treadmills and the like) only worked three-hour shifts.[53] Cart horses could work for seven to eight hours per day because their loads were light and they rarely traveled faster than three miles per hour.[54] Cab horses worked fourteen-hour days, pulling light loads and making fewer stops. Brewery, coal company, and railroad delivery horses apparently worked twelve-hour days. While they carried heavy loads, they made relatively few stops and lost freight with each delivery. About half the time they pulled no load since they returned empty to their starting points. Few owners worked their horses on the Sabbath.[55] Since horses spent the day off confined to a stall, not grazing, they tended to experience stiffness and sluggishness on Monday. All hauling businesses got rid of their horses soon after the age of ten, selling them for the plow, for lighter vehicles like cabs, or perhaps to a "knacker" or a rendering plant for slaughter and reprocessing in other forms.

The same steel technology that made railroads possible also allowed the springs and steel bodies that made modern wagons possible.[56] By the 1890s wagon makers were building all-steel garbage trucks, tank trucks, and even tree transplanters capable of carrying up to fourteen tons.[57] Studebaker even produced an aluminum wagon for the 1893 Columbian Exposition in Chicago. In 1904 more than a fifth of urban wagons weighed over three tons, with heavier weights requiring long, hard-to-manage multiple horse teams.[58] Improved elliptical springs and rubber tires also allowed new delivery services for fragile goods such as bottled beer. By the 1880s undertakers and florists displayed their wares in glass-sided vehicles.[59] Harnesses contained over fifty parts, more in multiple horse teams.[60] They also improved, notably after the adoption in the 1870s of the whippletree to equalize the pull of different horses.[61] This allowed less precision in matching and eliminated the ancient practice of in-line teaming.[62] All of these technical refinements could not keep up with the increased demand. By the mid-1890s freight rates per ton mile in big cities were increasing far more rapidly than intercity costs, as the efficiency of steam railway operations greatly increased. As with horsecars ten years earlier, it looked as if horse-towed freight had reached its maximum effectiveness.

Horses filled needs for display as well as for pure haulage. Breweries employed especially expensive horses—Clydesdales imported from Scotland—to deliver their products. While the Clydesdales were less suitable to American conditions than Percherons, breweries adopted the huge horses for public relations purposes because they looked and walked in a manner that people found attractive.[63] Firms often placed advertisements on platforms pulled by horses, and no business that promoted itself in this manner or put advertisements on its delivery trucks wanted them hauled by sorry-looking nags. Livery stables had to offer their elite customers who were renting rigs for a Sunday afternoon drive perfectly matched bay horses, preferably with braided manes and docked (cut-short) tails. Customers expected undertakers to have totally black horses pull their hearses, and the demand for such horse-drawn hearses persisted into the 1930s.

## Horses and the Built Environment

### STREETS

The reliance of the city on horses for transportation and hauling strongly impacted the built environment, especially in regard to street pavements and stables. American cities used cobblestones for their first street paving, but after 1850 they largely adopted rectangular granite block pavements on heavily traveled streets. The shoes worn by urban horses had cleats, called caulks, that could grip the grooves in block pavements for extra traction. The quality of urban paving in the United States was poor compared to Europe, in part because Americans more extensively used horsecar lines. The smooth rails allowed fast common carrier travel and reduced the need for good pavements elsewhere. Even teamsters, when possible, tried to drive along the tracks for a smoother surface. Asphalt paving was first used in American cities in 1876, when engineer Edward J. de Smedt laid a model asphalt pavement on Pennsylvania Avenue in Washington for the centennial celebration. Asphalt pavements spread rapidly to other cities, becoming the dominant paving material by 1900. Asphalt cost more than granite blocks and provided less traction for horseshoes. Still, urban teamsters sought out asphalt streets because their smooth surface allowed wheels to roll more easily, and fewer horses went lame because of its relative softness. The new pavement also allowed mechanical street sweeping, a major cost saving for cities.[64]

### STABLES

The housing of horses was a major issue for crowded cities, although horse density per stable varied greatly from locale to locale. In 1900 the census recorded 1,454,000 stables in the twenty-three leading American cities. Boston had the most horses per stable in the nation, at 7.8, with New York close behind at 6.7,[65] and Pittsburgh and San Francisco tied for third at 4.8. Those with the smallest number of horses per stable were largely in the Midwest or the Far West, with Cleveland, Detroit, Denver, Indianapolis, and Los Angeles all having under 3 horses per stable. The largest stables, undoubtedly, were those for major horse users, such as the streetcar companies, which needed to be large not only because they housed more horses but also because they had to accommodate hay and grain storage as well as provide shoeing and harness repair facilities and manure bins.[66] Average stable size almost doubled in many cities by 1910; and although data are lacking for the pre-1900 period, stable size had also probably increased in the decades before the turn of the century because of rising densities and land costs.

A good example of the different types of big city stables and the conditions found there is described in the 1866 *Report upon the Sanitary Condition of the City,* issued by the New York Council of Hygiene and Public Health of the Citizens' Association. This report provided a careful district-by-district examination of the factors affecting the city's public health as understood from the perspective of the 1860s, including extended discussions of the prevalence and condition of stables as major public health factors.

Stables, according to the report, were ubiquitous in New York City; they came in all shapes and sizes and were constructed of both wood and brick. Some, like the "well-known Bull's Head stables" on 23d Street between Lexington and Second Avenues, were quite large, containing 35 stables with 1,000 stalls. Other districts had a mix of small and medium-sized stables. The city's Third Sanitary District, located in the lower part of Manhattan, had 108 stables that housed 585 horses. Of the 108 stables, 68 contained less than 5 horses (202 in total), while 40 contained 5 or more horses (383) in total. The inspector for this district reported that owners kept larger stables clean, but that smaller ones were often crowded together and "their surroundings . . . frequently neglected and uncleanly."[67] He maintained that these stables were the source of outbreaks of diseases such as scarlatina and diphtheria. The inspector in the Sixth Sanitary District made similar judgments. He noted that the district's 43 stables, some located in the basement of "tenant-houses," others situated between the front and rear of tenant houses, were "prolific sources of disease."[68] The Twelfth Sanitary District, the healthiest one in the city, housed both rich and poor people as well as a number of industries. Twenty-nine livery stables were listed in the district as well as 161 private stables and stalls, most "neat and most carefully kept," with some above and others below ground.[69]

Livery stables were usually the best kept and increased in number as cities grew between 1870 and 1900.[70] Detailed descriptions, if somewhat exaggerated (usually advertisements), of their features can be found in various city guidebooks and business directories, giving insight into stable conditions and also the varied uses of horses. In Chicago, for instance, Isaac Shillington advertised a Livery and Boarding Stable on 210–212 Indiana Street with "fine horses and carriages available" for "shopping or driving at reasonable rates." S. E. Cleveland and Sons had a livery and boarding stable on West Madison Street that could board 125 horses and, according to one guidebook, had the "best" stock of horses to be found in the city for "balls, parties, funerals and pleasure driving." The Gunderson and Lindberg Livery and Boarding Stables on East Superior Street boasted that it had twelve assistants supervised by the owner who cared for the horses boarded.[71] Of course, Chicago also had rundown and overcrowded stables similar to those in New York.

### TRAFFIC CONDITIONS

Unfortunately, few measures of late nineteenth-century urban traffic exist. The earliest recorded urban traffic jam involved carriage-riding New Yorkers traveling to the famous match race between Eclipse and Sir Henry in 1823, the best attended equestrian event in the city's history. The traffic led to a chain reaction accident, during which many horses drove their traces through the rear panel of the preceding vehicle.[72] By 1866, after the Civil War, traffic greatly increased. Nine hundred streetcars and 6,125 other vehicles, all horse-drawn, passed the corner of Third and Market Streets in Philadelphia in one ten-hour February day.[73] Isolated traffic counts suggest that traffic at least doubled between 1885 and 1905. Broadway, New York's main north-south artery, had daily traffic jams by the mid-1890s, a precursor of modern urban life. The city stationed a traffic officer on each Broadway intersection to keep traffic flowing. In 1907, Chicago had over 61,000 horse-drawn vehicles, most of which were one- or two-horse, although 451 were drawn by three or four horses. Sharing the city streets were 3,665 automobiles and 68 trucks.[74] By this time New York and other cities were also experiencing jams around bridges, passenger terminals, and even theater districts near curtain time. The situation was clearly becoming worse.

A sign of growing traffic was an increase in accidents. A 1900 report calculated that horses were causing some 750,000 accidents per year.[75] Between 1890 and 1896, New York's fatality rate attributed to wagons and carriages doubled. In 1900 horse-pulled vehicles killed nearly 200 New York residents, mostly children, a higher fatality rate than that caused by cars today. Runaways or speeders were responsible for some of these accidents, but horses kicking passersby or children playing in the street caused more accidents. Chicago actually had a higher fatality rate than New York, although other cities lagged far behind.[76]

## The Horse as Consumer

Just as a vast industry of manufacturers, showrooms, repair shops, garages, petroleum refineries, gasoline stations, and automobile-related decorations has grown up to serve the needs of the automobile, a similar situation existed in regard to the horse. The horse-drawn society required coach, carriage, and wagon makers; manufacturers of blankets and other "horse clothing"; saddles, harnesses, and whips; and horseshoers and wheelwrights. Between 1870 and 1900, as society became more dependent on the horse, the amount of capital invested and the number of workers employed in industries such as carriage-making and repair, saddlery and harnesses, and whip manufacture vastly increased. Boston's wheelwrights, for instance, doubled from 15 in 1870 to 30 in 1900, blacksmiths and horseshoers increased from 126 to 238, and carriage dealers and builders from 62 to 105. Striking is the surge in express companies from 38 to 826 and veterinarians from 11 to 62, due to the increasing division of labor in the industrial city and the rise of veterinary medicine as a profession.[77]

On a national basis, the number of support industries and establishments needed to maintain the horse-powered society was extensive and varied. In terms of employment and capital invested, the carriage and wagon industry was most important, with many models and specialized firms. By 1876 over 11,000 patents had been taken out for carriages and 2,543 for harnesses. In the 1890s nearly 700 manufacturers were members of the Carriage Builders National Association. The total number of firms, however, many relatively small and specialized, was much larger. In 1904, 5,588 establishments manufactured carriages and wagons, employing over 90,000 workers.

The products of this industry were sold throughout the world as well as in the United States, with large firms having distribution agencies in different cities. The Abbot Downing Company of Concord, New Hampshire, for instance, manufactured mail, stage, and hotel coaches, buggies of various sorts, road wagons, express and delivery wagons, heavy and light trucks, and sprinklers as well as the famous Concord Wagon, and by the 1870s it had showrooms in Boston, New York, Chicago, and San Francisco. The Elkhart Carriage & Harness Manufacturing Company, with two large factories in Elkhart, Indiana, boasted that it was the largest mail-order manufacturer of vehicles and harnesses selling directly to customers. The largest manufacturer of horse-drawn vehicles, however, was Studebaker, founded in 1852 by the Studebaker brothers in South Bend, Indiana. By 1874 the firm was building over 11,000 vehicles per year; and by 1895 yearly production had advanced to over 75,000 vehicles, with fifty-four different styles. In the 1880s, Studebaker opened a number of urban dealerships to sell regular carriages and wagons and specialized vehicles such as sprinklers, flushers, sweepers, and dumpers. In addition to the manufacture and sale of new vehicles, some firms also dealt in used carriages.[78]

As late as 1909, thirty-three establishments employing 1,830 workers manufactured horse clothing, while fifty-seven firms employing 1,946 workers manufactured whips. The whip industry, which had originally been organized in small craft shops, had been consolidated and mechanized. The various materials that went into the whip were "subjected to the operation of the most delicate and complicated machinery, and to various other skillful processes before the work is complete."[79] The making of horseshoes, which had for many years been the province of blacksmiths, had now become an activity of large iron foundries even though blacksmiths still fitted and installed the shoes.

Hay, oats, straw, and occasionally beans were the principal diet of the urban horse. Oats were also grown on northern farms, over one-half of the crop originating in New York, Pennsylvania, Ohio, and Illinois. One study calculates that horses consumed, on the average, 2.4 tons of hay per year and 1.4 tons of oats, although, of course, actual feeding practices varied among different horses, horsekeepers, and workloads.[80] If one assumes an urban horse population of approximately 3 million in 1900, then 7,200,000 tons of hay and 4,200,000 tons of oats were consumed by city horses per year. To grow this amount of fodder may have required as many as 15,000,000 acres.[81] Feeding horses was expensive, and the bill for streetcar companies often exceeded wages by nearly one-half. According to transportation historian John H. White, Jr., the "care and feeding of horses made up 40 to 50 percent of operating costs and about 40 percent of total investment."[82]

Until the midnineteenth century, because of its bulk, hay could not be transported very far. As a result, a belt of farms relatively close (up to thirty miles) to the city specialized in hay production for the urban market, cultivating hay as a cash crop. The ground required fertilizers, and horse manure provided one of the best. A reciprocal recycling relationship therefore developed in several regions, whereby hay was grown on farms in order to feed urban horses, and, in return, farmers gathered manure from stables and city streets to enrich their soil. Long Island farmers, for instance, fertilized their sandy soil by importing vast amounts of manure from New York City, a "veritable manure factory."[83] Recycling systems similar to that which existed in the New York region also were found in other areas close to growing cities such as Baltimore, Boston, and Philadelphia.[84]

Canals and railroads lowered the cost of hay transportation, but it was seldom moved more than fifty to seventy-five miles.[85] In the 1830s and 1840s, however, machines to compress the hay were invented, and it became a much less bulky and less costly commodity to ship. The development of the mower and the horse-drawn rake and tender in the 1840s and 1850s made possible large increases in the amount of hay produced.[86] The rate of technological innovation in agriculture increased during and after the Civil War, a time when a growing military horse population required more feed. Among these innovations were the revolving horse-drawn hayrack (1864), the spring-tooth rake, the harpoon hay fork (1864), and perfection of the continuous baling press (1866). Mechanization reduced prices and baling lowered transportation volume, a major cost savings.[87] Within the city itself, hay and oats were distributed from large hay markets that often sold meat, fruits, and vegetables as well as other goods.[88]

## The Horse and the Urban Environment

While the nineteenth-century American city faced many forms of environmental pollution, none was as all encompassing as that produced by the horse.[89] The most severe problem was that caused by horses defecating and urinating in the streets, but dead animals and noise pollution also were serious annoyances and even health problems. The ordinary city horse produced between fifteen and thirty-five pounds of manure per day and about a quart of urine, usually distributed along the course of its route or deposited in the stable. While cities made sporadic attempts to keep the streets clean, the manure was everywhere—along the roadway, heaped in piles or next to stables, or ground up by the traffic and blown about by the wind. In 1818, in an attempt to control the manure nuisance, the New York City Council required that those who gathered and hauled manure, so-called dirt carting, be licensed, and it restricted aliens to this type of carting activity.[90] Thousands of loads were gathered in special "manure-yards" to undergo a process of "rotting," and "gangs" of men were employed to turn over the manure and expose it to weathering. In 1866 the Citizens' Association's *Report upon the Sanitary Condition of the City* observed that "the stench arising from these accumulations of filth is intolerable."[91]

Nineteenth-century urbanites considered the stench or miasmas coming from the manure piles a serious health hazard, but street cleaning was sporadic at best. These manure piles also attracted huge numbers of flies, in reality a much more serious vector for infectious diseases, such as typhoid fever, than odors. By the turn of the century public health officials had largely accepted the bacterial theory of disease and had identified the "queen of the dung-heap," or fly, as a major source. Inventors and city officials devised improved methods of street cleaning, and street sweeping became a major urban expense. Increasingly, however, it became obvious that the most effective way to eliminate the "typhoid fly" (so named by L. O. Howard, chief of the Bureau of Entomology of the Department of Agriculture and a leader in the campaign against flies) was to eliminate the horse.

Because of the manure on the streets, especially when rain created a quagmire, "crossing sweepers" (like those in London) were employed to help ladies and gentlemen wade through the liquid mess. Citizens frequently complained about the "pulverized horse dung" that blew into their faces and windows and that covered outdoor displays of merchants.[92] The paving of streets accelerated the problem, as wheels and hoofs ground the manure against the hard surfaces and raised dust. Writing in *Appletons' Magazine* in 1908, Harold Bolce argued that most of the modern city's sanitary and economic problems were caused by the horse. Bolce charged that each year 20,000 New Yorkers died from "maladies that fly in the dust, created mainly by horse manure."[93]

Although not as serious a problem as the manure, the noise created by horses' iron shoes and the iron-tired wheels of cars and wagons on cobblestone streets was a constant annoyance. Benjamin Franklin had complained in the late eighteenth century of the "thundering of coaches, chariots, chaises, wagons, drays and the whole fraternity of noise" that assailed the ears of Philadelphians. Boston and New York both passed ordinances banning traffic from certain streets to protect hospitals and legislative chambers from the noise. As late as the 1890s a *Scientific American* writer noted that the sounds of traffic on busy New York streets made conversation nearly impossible, while William Dean Howells complained that "the sharp clatter of the horses' iron shoes" on the pavement tormented his ear.[94]

If the horse created many problems for the city, it was also true that city life was extremely hard on the horse. The average streetcar horse had a life expectancy of about four years, and it was common to see drivers and teamsters whip and abuse their animals to spur them to pull heavy loads. Overworked and mistreated horses often died on the city streets. In 1866 the *Atlantic Monthly* described Broadway as clogged with "dead horses and vehicular entanglements," and in that year the mistreatment of the urban horse stimulated Henry Bergh to found the American Society for the Prevention of Cruelty to Animals.[95] Streets paved with cobblestones or asphalt were slipperier than dirt roads, and a horse that broke a leg would have to be destroyed. Veterinarians recommended that city draft horses be shod with rubber-covered horseshoes, but few owners followed this advice.[96] In 1880, New York City removed 15,000 dead horses from its streets, and as late as 1916 Chicago carted away 9,202 carcasses.[97] Special trucks were devised to remove dead horses; since the average weight of a carcass was 1,300 pounds, one text on municipal refuse advised that "trucks for the removal of dead horses should be hung low, to avoid an excessive lift."[98]

Because of their size and numbers, the disposal of dead horses presented a special problem. In New York City, for instance, horse carcasses, as well as those of other animals, were sometimes dumped with garbage into the bays or the rivers, often floating there or washing up on the shoreline.[99] Dead animals, however, had some value, and they were frequently collected and processed by fat, offal, and bone-boiling firms. In the late 1860s an "offal dock" stood at the foot of West 38th Street in New York. From there, the carcasses of horses as well as other dead animals and offal from the city's slaughterhouses were either dumped in the bay or sent to a rendering plant outside the city.[100] Any animal parts that had a special value were removed beforehand to be made into various products such as gelatin, glue, and fertilizer. By 1880 most large cities contracted with a specific rendering house to take all its dead animals. Because rendering firms were considered an extreme nuisance, cities attempted to keep them outside their borders (at least ten miles from downtown), but often without success.[101]

Since horses were a key element in the urban economy, cities applied public health rules to them to avoid a recurrence of the disruptions caused by the Great Epizootic. City boards of health, originally created in the 1850s and 1860s because of epidemics of cholera and yellow fever that threatened human health, now began regularly to inspect stables. They could, and did, destroy diseased animals, with no compensation to owners for such losses.[102] Horses were, and are, subject to some of the same contagious diseases as humans. Veterinarians, like doctors (in fact, some individuals filled both roles), mostly practiced environmental medicine in the nineteenth century. They focused on cleanliness, healthy food, and pure water. As with humans, this "sanitary" approach reduced mortality considerably, although it often obscured the real causes of disease, as when most veterinarians insisted that bad weather and filthy stable environments spread the Great Epizootic, very likely a contagious influenza.[103] The disease of the horse's frog (hoof) called "thrush" was also blamed on "filthy" stable conditions as well as on muddy streets and roads. Farcy (a leg infection) and glanders (an infection of the mucus membranes) were probably the leading killers of horses. They were highly contagious and spread rapidly through crowded stables, city streets, and public watering troughs.[104] Better sanitation did lead to health improvements, and stable mortality evidently decreased considerably in the last twenty years of the nineteenth century.

## Conclusion: The Decline of the Horse in the Twentieth Century

Horses did not just disappear from cities overnight; rather, they went function by function. It has already been noted that while horse-powered machines persisted in manufacturing until about 1850, they were largely replaced by other energy sources in the following decade. The next use of urban horses to disappear was in pulling streetcars. Their demise was very rapid, since between 1888 and 1892 almost every street railway in the United States was electrified. A few small companies kept horses for about another decade because they could not obtain permission to electrify, but they were a minor element in the industry. The rapidity of the change is explained primarily by the incredible technological advantage of electric traction in terms of speed in spite of its capital intensiveness. Another benefit was that the pollution from streetcars was reduced and moved from a nonpoint mobile source (the horse) to a fixed-point source, the coal-burning, electricity-generating plant. In addition, cities no longer had to worry about removing dead traction horses from their streets.

The coming of the automobile dealt another heavy blow to the use of horses. Experimental motor cars had been around for a long time, but cities had always banned them. The crisis of the 1890s and early twentieth century involving public health fears about pollution, traffic jams, and rising prices for hay, oats, and urban land made municipal governments and urban residents much more ready to switch to autos. A number of articles in popular magazines repeated the argument by a writer in *Munsey's Magazine* that "the horse has become unprofitable. He is too costly to buy and too costly to keep."[105] The process of substitution went faster in the United States than in Europe because American incomes were higher, cars and fuel cost less, and distances were greater. Leisure drivers came first, since the early car was purely a luxury vehicle. (When Woodrow Wilson rode in a carriage to his 1917 inaugural, the last president to do so, he marked the end of the horse as a status object.) By 1907 urban doctors and some members of footloose occupations, such as salesmen and construction engineers, had adopted cars. Mechanized cabs became commonplace around the same date. In 1906 motor buses replaced horse-drawn omnibuses on New York's Fifth

Avenue, likely the last omnibus service left. In 1912, New York, London, and Paris traffic counts all showed more cars than horses for the first time. The drop in Model T prices that followed after Henry Ford opened the first assembly-line plant in 1913 led to the adoption of cars by commuters. Most cities experienced their first daily traffic jams throughout the central business district in 1914.

Perhaps the last horse-powered function in the city to disappear was that involving freight and deliveries. Even though some city firms, such as Altman's Department Store in New York, adopted light trucks for package delivery as early as 1907, truck substitution for horse-drawn wagons was slower than automobile adoption and considerably slower than the replacement of streetcar horses by electric traction.[106] Trucks did not really replace wagons until in the 1920s, when commercial manufacturers adopted the Liberty truck developed during World War I. Two million American horses went to France during the war; many were purchased by the British army, but very few returned.[107] Cities began to eliminate watering troughs for horses, to demand that wagons carry taillights, and even to give the traffic right of way to cars. In 1925 both Washington and Los Angeles banned horses from downtown. A few horse-use specialties remained. Horse-drawn bakery wagons still accounted for approximately 70 percent of home deliveries as late as 1926 and persisted long after that date.[108] Suburban dairies delivered milk by horse into the 1950s, as did a few itinerant fruit and vegetable peddlers and rag merchants. There was some revival of urban horses during World War I gas rationing. Today, many cities still provide livery stables and bridle paths in large, Olmsted-era parks. It is still a mark of status and romance to rent a carriage for an afternoon's drive in Central Park. New York's and other police departments have trained horses for riot control and park patrol.

Evaluating the significance of the horse for the nineteenth-century city requires a long perspective. Horses were invaluable for both passenger transportation by omnibus and streetcar and for freight transfer for much of the century. Rather than displacing the horse, steam railways, important for connecting cities and for linking suburbs with the central city, actually stimulated demand because of the need to move freight from railway cars to their destination. Just like the automobile and motor truck that eventually replaced them, horses provided the flexibility that tracked vehicles lacked.

However, because of certain problems—manure and urine, hard-to-dispose-of carcasses, and noise—as well as their limited pulling power and the cost of feeding and housing them, horses became less and less functional. Late nineteenth-century cities were increasingly characterized by modern technological systems—electric and gas utilities, telegraphs, telephones, piped-in water, and sewerage, and especially by electric traction, automobiles, and motor trucks—and the inefficiencies of the horse became more obvious. It was becoming an anomaly, "one of the last stands of animal strength over science."[109]

In a somewhat different sense, the city in the nineteenth century can be viewed as an emerging technological and networked system in which the horse was a critical and interactive element.[110] In fact, it is useful to view the horse not necessarily as an animal but rather as a technology that had played a vital role in the urban system—but a technology that grew increasingly inefficient as the networked city developed around it. Thus, the horse became what historian of technology Thomas Parke Hughes calls a *reverse salient*, or a lagging element in a technological system that held back the development of the whole network as different sectors became increasingly mechanized.[111] As a reverse salient, the eventual demise of the horse could have been predicted, although its use persisted well into the twentieth century, especially in commercial trucking, where operating and capital costs and flexibility and versatility had to be carefully estimated.[112] It is exactly in those areas that cannot be easily mechanized or networked—horse racing, pleasure riding, and local police work—that the horse still survives.

## Notes

*The authors would like to thank Columbia University Press for permission to use material from Clay McShane, *Down the Asphalt Path: American Cities and the Automobile* (New York: Columbia University Press, 1995), and American Heritage to use material from Joel A. Tarr, "Urban Pollution Many Long Years Ago," *American Heritage* 22 (October 1971): 65–69.

1. Christine M. Rosen, *The Limits of Power: Great Fires and the Process of City Growth in America* (New York: Cambridge University Press, 1986), 176–79. Boston, like many cities, had banned steam-powered vehicles, fearing boiler explosions; hence, the irony of horses pulling steam engines to fires. See Clay McShane, *Down the Asphalt Path: American Cities and the Automobile* (New York: Columbia University Press, 1995), chap. 5. For a discussion of fire horses in general, see Arthur Vernon, *The History and Romance of the Horse* (Garden City, NY: Halcyon House, 1939), 372–80.

2. In New York, 3.7 percent or 1,416 of the city's 38,272 horses died. Many others, however, were sick but recovered. See Adoniram B. Judson, "History and Course of the Epizootic among Horses upon the North American Continent in 1872–3," *American Public Health Association Reports and Papers* 1 (1873): 95.

3. Allan Nevins and Milton H. Thomas, eds., *The Diary of George Templeton Strong: Post-War Years, 1865–1875* (New York: Macmillan Company, 1952), 448.

4. *New York Times*, October 10, 1872; October 23–30, 1872.

5. "The Position of the Horse in Modern Society," *The Nation* 383 (October 31, 1872): 277–78.

6. Bureau of the Census, Interior Department, "Remarks upon the Statistics of Agriculture," *Ninth Census* (1870): 75–76.

7. Census Office, Interior Department, *Statistics of Population in the United States: Ninth Census* (June 1, 1870) (Washington, DC: Government Printing Office, 1872), 775–804; Census Office, Interior Department, *Statistics of Population of the United States at the Tenth Census* (June 1, 1880) (Washington, DC: Government Printing Office, 1887), 860–909; Census Office, Department of the Interior, *Report on the Population of the United States at the Eleventh Census: 1890* (Washington, DC: Government Printing Office, 1897), 544, 630–743; Bureau of the Census, Department of Commerce and Labor, *Occupations at the Twelfth Census* (Washington, DC: Government Printing Office, 1901), 428–79; Bureau of the Census, Department of Commerce, *Thirteenth Census of the United States, Taken in the Year 1910, Agriculture* (Washington, DC: Government Printing Office, 1913), 441–46.

8. Clifford Richardson, "Street Traffic in New York City, 1885–1904," *American Society of Civil Engineers Proceedings* 32 (May 1906): 384. There were very few autos in 1904.

9. Some cities appear to have had a greater dependency on horses than others. In general, lower-density western cities had relatively larger herds. The average trip was probably longer in such low-density places. The generally lower level of land prices must have reduced stabling costs, and western locations were also closer to the source of food. Kansas City seems to have been the most important center of the national trade in draft horses. More horses resided in New York City than any rural county in the United States. The question of why some cities relied more than others on horses requires further investigation.

10. F. M. L. Thompson, "Nineteenth–Century Horse Sense," *Economic History Review* 5, no. 29 (1976): 64–67. The Thompson article provides an evaluation of the importance of the horse to nineteenth-century British society, especially in London.

11. "The Position of the Horse in Modern Society," 277–78.

12. J. Kenneth Major, *Animal-Powered Machines* (Princes Risborough, Aylesbury: Shire Publications, 1985), 3.

13. Louis C. Hunter, *A History of Industrial Power in the United States, 1780–1930,* vol. 1, *Waterpower in the Century of the Steam Engine* (Charlottesville: University Press of Virginia, 1979), 13, 25–28, 29, 181.

14. Ibid., 432.

15. Thomas C. Cochran, *The Pabst Brewing Company: The History of an American Business* (New York: New York University Press, 1948), 25–26; Harold L. Platt, " 'A Veritable City within a City': Energy Systems, Technological Innovation, and the Transformation of the American Brewing Industry," unpublished paper presented to the 19th International Congress of History of Science, Zaragoza, Spain, August 25, 1993.

16. Seje Park Benjamin, ed., *Appletons' Cyclopaedia of Applied Mechanics* (New York: D. Appleton and Company, 1895, revised and improved ed.), 60; Major, *Animal-Powered Machines,* 3–4.

17. Jennifer Tann, "Horse Power, 1780–1880," in F. M. L. Thompson, ed., *Horses in European Economic History: A Preliminary Canter* (Reading, England: British Agricultural History Society, 1983), 29–30.

18. Hunter, *A History of Industrial Power in the United States, 1780–1930,* vol. 2, *Steam Power* (Charlottesville: University Press of Virginia, 1985), 109–11. Unfortunately, Hunter only supplies percentages and does not record total number of establishments. The 1855 report of Joseph Whitworth to the House of Commons on the New York Industrial Exhibition illustrates the manner in which horses were used to supply power in the wood products industry. Whitworth noted that in "no branch of manufacture does the application of labour-saving machinery produce . . . more important results than in the working of wood." In the process of woodworking, portable sawing machines, "driven by horse-power," were commonly used to saw up logs. These were particularly useful at various railroad stations where logs were prepared as locomotive fuel. The "horse-power machine," as described by Whitworth, consisted of a moving frame or treadmill where the horse's motion moved the platform, thus causing chain wheels to revolve and the power to be conveyed to a "circular saw or other machine." Occasionally these machines used one horse, at other times two horses. See Nathan Rosenberg, ed., *The American System of Manufactures* (Edinburgh: Edinburgh University Press, 1969), 344.

19. Hunter, *Steam Power,* 111.

20. Tann, "Horsepower, 1780–1880," 26–27. According to Tann, British breweries were using horses to grind malt and pump wort as late as the 1870s.

21. Francis V. Greene, "An Account of Some Observations of Street Traffic," *American Society of Civil Engineers Transactions* 15 (1886): 123–38.

22. McShane, *Down the Asphalt Path,* chap. 2, describes the evolution of Olmsted-style parks as "driving parks."

23. Reginald S. Timmis, *Modern Horse Management* (Toronto and New York: Cassel and Company, 1915), 66. Timmis complained that too many stable owners lacked "horse sense" and were better off relying on professional care for their horses; Robert West Howard, *The Horse in America* (New York: Follett Publishing, 1965), 138; John W. Boettjer, "Street Railways in the District of Columbia" (master's thesis, George Washington University, 1965), 9–10; George Rogers Taylor, "Beginnings of Mass Transportation in Urban America, Part 1," *Smithsonian Journal of History* 1 (Summer 1966), 41; Albert C. Rose, "The Highway from the Railroad to the Automobile," in Jean Labatut and Wharton J. Lane, eds., *Highways in Our National Life* (Princeton: Princeton University Press, 1950), 81.

24. Glen E. Holt, "The Changing Perception of Urban Pathology: An Essay on the Development of Mass Transit in the United States," in Stanley K. Schultz and Kenneth T. Jackson, eds., *Cities in American History* (New York: Alfred A. Knopf, 1972), 324–35; Taylor, "Beginnings of Mass Transportation, Part 1," 41–47; Frederick W. Speirs, *The Street Railway System of Philadelphia, Its History and Present Condition* (Baltimore: Johns Hopkins University Press, 1897), 10–11; Boettjer, "Street Railways in the District of Columbia," 9–10; John Noble and Co., *Facts Respecting Street Railways: The Substance of a Series of Official Reports from the Cities of New York, Brooklyn, Boston, Philadelphia, Baltimore, Providence, Newark, Chicago, Quebec, Montreal, and Toronto* (London: P. S. King, 1866), 15–18; St. Louis Board of Public Service, *Report on Rapid Transit for St. Louis* (St. Louis, 1926), 34; *New York Times,* June 10, 1866; Joel A. Tarr, *Transportation Innovation and Spatial Change in Pittsburgh, 1850–1934* (Chicago: Public Works Historical Society, 1978), 4–5; Kenneth T. Jackson, *Crab-

*grass Frontier: The Suburbanization of the United States* (New York: Oxford University Press, 1984), 33.

25. John Noble and Co., *Facts Respecting Street Railways*, 17.

26. Holt, "The Changing Perception of Urban Pathology," 324–43.

27. Greene, "Construction and Care of Streets," 197; "Growth of City Traffic," *Engineering News* 18 (October 15, 1887): 273; Richardson, "Street Traffic in New York City," 385.

28. McShane, *Down the Asphalt Path*, chap. 5.

29. See Taylor, "Beginnings of Mass Transportation in Urban America, Part 1," *Smithsonian Journal of History* 1 (Summer, Fall 1966), pts. 1, 2:35–50, 31–54; Tarr, *Transportation Innovation*, 6–13; and John H. White, Jr., "Horse Power," *American Heritage of Invention and Technology* 8 (Summer 1992): 44.

30. George Hilton, *The Cable Car in America* (Berkeley, CA: Howell-North Books, 1971), 14–15; St. Louis Board of Public Service, *Report on Rapid Transit*, 34; Boettjer, "Street Railways in the District of Columbia," 13–23; Henry Binford, *The First Suburbs: Residential Communities on the Boston Periphery, 1815–1860* (Chicago: University of Chicago Press, 1985), 130, 141–42.

31. U.S. Bureau of the Census, *Report on the Transportation Business in the United States, Eleventh Census*, vol. 18, pt. 1 (Washington, DC: Government Printing Office, 1895), 682, 684, 714–20.

32. U.S. Bureau of the Census, *Street and Electric Railways, 1902* (Washington, DC: Government Printing Office, 1905), 191–92.

33. Many urban elites complained about the experience of riding on omnibuses and streetcars crowded with poor and ill-smelling immigrants.

34. Graham R. Hodges, *New York City Cartmen, 1667–1850* (New York: New York University Press, 1986), 2.

35. Ibid., 35, 111, 136, 144, 157.

36. Ibid., 116.

37. Ibid., 139–40, 145, 150–52, 162–65. The carters were both nativist and racist. In 1850, however, the city council also permitted aliens to enter the trade.

38. William G. Panschar, *Baking in America: Economic Development*, vol. 1 (Evanston, IL: Northwestern University Press, 1956), 73–74, 130, 134.

39. See the range of types of horse-drawn wagons illustrated in Jack D. Rittenhouse, *American Horse-Drawn Vehicles* (New York: Bonanza Books, 1948), esp. 54–97; and Francis Haines, *Horses in America* (New York: Crowell, 1971), 175–79,

40. Don H. Berkebile, ed., *Horse-Drawn Commercial Vehicles: 255 Illustrations of Nineteenth-Century Stagecoaches, Delivery Wagons, Fire Engines, etc.* (New York: Dover Publications, 1989), 11.

41. Rittenhouse, *American Horse-Drawn Vehicles*, 70–97.

42. Chicago Department of Public Works, "Number of Vehicles in City by Wards," *Annual Report* (1907), 404.

43. W. J. Gordon, *The Horse World of London* (London: The Religious Tract Society, 1893), 16. Here and elsewhere, we have relied on a number of British sources. We don't think this distorts much, since all the British works were in American libraries. Quite clearly, information about draft horses, and indeed horses themselves, moved back and forth across the ocean with little obstacle. To be sure, there were some national preferences, and these have been labeled as such.

44. Herman Bidell et al., *Heavy Horses: Breeds and Management* (London: Vinton & Co., 1919), 155; Charles Wharton, *Handbook on the Treatment of the Horse in the Stable and on the Road* (Philadelphia: J. B. Lippincott & Co., 1873), 14.

45. T. C. Barker "Delayed Decline of the Horse in the Twentieth Century," in Thompson, *Horses in European Economic History*, 105. The major decline in prices came after the electrification of street railways diminished demand.

46. Gordon, *The Horse World of London*, 50.

47. James A. Garland, *The Private Stable: Its Establishment, Maintenance and Appointments* (Boston: Little, Brown, 1903), 118; Bidell et al., *Heavy Horses*, 153.

48. Richard Mason, M.D., *The Gentleman's New Pocket Farrier, Comprising a General Description of the Noble and Useful Animal, the Horse* (Philadelphia: Grigg and Elliot, 1846), 160–85. It is a measure of the low level of professionalism for both physicians and veterinarians that a physician would write what was, in large part, a veterinary text.

49. See, for instance, the discussion of "The Working Horse," in Elwyn Hartley Edwards, *The Encyclopedia of the Horse* (Markham, Ontario: Reed Books Canada, 1994), 246–311.

50. Keith Chivers, *The Shire Horse: A History of the Breed, the Society, and the Men* (London: J. A. Allen, 1976), 92.

51. Timmis, *Modern Horse Management*, 12.

52. Dorian Gerhold, *Road Transport before the Railways: Russell's London Flying Waggons* (New York: Cambridge University Press, 1993), 59. In the late eighteenth century, James Watt calculated the standard horsepower measure based on a three-quarter-ton horse traveling at 3.7 kilometers per hour for a short distance and capable of pulling a cart with a tractive force of one-tenth of its weight. One British engineer calculated in the 1840s that the optimum speed for a horse working eight hours per day was approximately 2 5/8 miles per hour (covering 23 1/3 miles per day), compared to about 2 1/3 miles per hour with a ten-hour day (covering 21 miles per day).

53. Tann, "Horsepower, 1780–1880," 26–27.

54. John Stewart, *Stable Economy: A Treatise on the Management of Horses* (New York: D. Appleton, 1845), 359.

55. Timmis, *Modern Horse Management*, 43. If they worked their horses on the Sabbath, they provided another day of rest.

56. Howard, *The Horse in America*, 179.

57. Berkebile, *Horse-Drawn Commercial Vehicles*, 54, 93, 96.

58. Richardson, "Street Traffic in New York City," 384.

59. Berkebile, *Horse-Drawn Commercial Vehicles*, passim.

60. Maurice Tellen, *The Draft Horse Primer* (Emmaus, PA: Rodale Press, 1977), 7.

61. Ibid., 245.

62. Ibid., 64–65.

63. Clydesdales often went lame on hard American streets, and their feathered fetlocks (furry legs) tended to become infected when slush got in the hair and froze in the winter. Freezing conditions were more common in most U.S. cities than in Scotch cities.

64. Sanitation workers had to scrape the grooves between granite blocks by hand. On pavements, see Clay McShane, "Transforming the Use of Urban Space: A Look at the Revolution in Street Pavements, 1880–1924," *Journal of Urban History* 5 (May 1979): 279–307. Horses pulled street sweepers with rotating brooms.

65. A census taken by the New York City Board of Health in 1896 counted 4,649 stables and 73,746 horses, or an average of approximately 16 horses per stable. This is actually much higher than the figures provided by the census and very likely more accurate. See John Duffy, *A History of Public Health in New York City, 1866–1966* (New York: Russell Sage Foundation, 1974), 109.

66. White, "Horse Power," 44.

67. Citizens' Association of New York, *Report . . . upon the Sanitary Condition of the City* (New York: D. Appleton and Co., 1866; 2d ed., reprinted by Arno Press, 1970), 27.

68. Ibid., 81.

69. Ibid., 133, 138.

70. In Boston, for instance, the number of livery stables increased from 71 to 175. Boston, *City Directories*, 1870, 1900.

71. Elmer E. Barton, *Business Tour of Chicago* (Chicago: E. E. Barton, 1887), 62, 66, 108–9, 125, 128; [no author], *Chicago's First Half-Century* (Chicago: Inter-Ocean Publishing, 1883), 30–31. The authors are grateful to Harold Platt for supplying references on Chicago.

72. John Gilmer Speed, *The Horse in America: A Practical Treatise on the Various Types Common in the United States with Something of Their History and Varying Characteristics* (New York: McClure, Phillips & Co., 1905), 46.

73. Noble, *Facts Respecting Street Railways*, 39.

74. Chicago Department of Public Works, *Annual Report 1907* (Chicago, 1907), 404. However, compare these data with the much higher automobile counts shown in a survey of Chicago boulevard traffic, taken by the South Park Commissioners. See "Chicago Counts Its Boulevard Traffic," *Motor Age* 16 (September 30, 1909): 9.

75. M. G. Lay, *Ways of the World: A History of the World's Roads and of the Vehicles that Used Them* (New Brunswick: Rutgers University Press, 1992), 132.

76. McShane, *Down the Asphalt Path*, 49.

77. Data from Boston, *City Directories*, 1870–1900.

78. Stephen Longstreet, *A Century on Wheels: The Story of Studebaker* (New York: Henry Holt and Co., 1952), 20, 49, 54–61. See Berkebile, 89, 142–44, 166, for descriptions of carriage and wagon manufacturers in the 1870s; and Rittenhouse, *American Horse-Drawn Vehicles*, passim, and G. & D. Cook & Co., *Illustrated Catalogue of Carriages and Special Business Advertiser* (New York: Dover Publications, 1970; originally published in 1860). For interesting correspondence relating to the purchase of carriages, see Elkhart Carriage & Harness Mfg. Co. to J. N. Pew, April 19, 1900; Pew Family Papers, Hagley Museum and Library, Wilmington, Delaware.

79. Glenn Porter, ed., *Asher & Adams Pictorial Album of American Industry, 1876* (New York: Routledge Books, 1976), 43–44.

80. Thompson, "Horses and Hay in Britain, 1830–1918," in Thompson, *Horses in European Economic History*, 60. Using actual stable records, Dorian Gerhold reports that in the 1820s "Hard-working waggon horses" consumed a little over 8 tons of oats, beans, and hay per year, or the produce of about 9 acres. Gerhold, *Road Transport*, 130–31.

81. Barker, "The Delayed Decline of the Horse," 102–3.

82. White, "Horse Power," 43.

83. The 1866 Citizens' Association *Report upon the Sanitary Condition of the City* noted Liebig's theory about using urban wastes to fertilize the land. See note on p. cxxviii.

84. Joel A. Tarr, "From City to Farm: Urban Wastes and the American Farmer," *Agricultural History Review* 49 (October 1975): 602–5; Richard A. Wines, *Fertilizer in America: From Waste Recycling to Resource Exploitation* (Philadelphia: Temple University Press, 1985), 8–20.

85. Wines, *Fertilizer in America*, 63–70.

86. Paul W. Gates, *The Farmer's Age, 1815–1860*, Vol. III: *The Economic History of the United States* (New York: Holt, Rinehart and Winston, 1960), 172–73, 249–55.

87. Fred A. Shannon, *The Farmer's Last Frontier: Agriculture, 1860–1897* (New York: Rinehart and Co., 1959), 133–34.

88. See the description of Boston's Brighton Market, in David C. Smith and Anne E. Bridges, "The Brighton Market: Feeding Nineteenth-Century Boston," *Agricultural History Review* 56 (October 1982): 9–10. The authors note that while horses and hay were sold in the Brighton Market, teamster horses were apparently not. "The horse markets," they comment, "involved more trading and demanded special knowledge."

89. Joel A. Tarr, "Urban Pollution Many Long Years Ago," *American Heritage* 22 (October 1971): 65–69.

90. Hodges, *New York City Cartmen*, 133–36; Duffy, *A History of Public Health in New York*, 23, 63, 127.

91. Duffy, *History of Public Health*, 264.

92. See Citizens' Association of New York, *Report . . . upon the Sanitary Condition*, passim; John S. Billings, "Municipal Sanitation in New York and Brooklyn," *The Forum* 16 (November 1893): 352; George E. Waring, Jr., "Disposal of a City's Waste," *The North American Review* 161 (July 1895): 52; and [no author], "The Prevention of Dust on City and Suburban Roads," *The American City* 7 (1912): 435.

93. Harold Bolce, "The Horse vs. Health," *The Review of Reviews* 47 (May 1908): 623–24.

94. Carl and Jessica Bridenbaugh, *Rebels and Gentlemen: Philadelphia in the Age of Franklin* (New York: Galaxy, 1965), 12; Carl Bridenbaugh, *Cities in Revolt* (New York: Capricorn, 1964), 35; Bayrd Still, *Mirror for Gotham* (New York: New York University Press 1956), 183; "The Horseless Carriage and Public Health," *Scientific American* 80 (February 18, 1899): 93; and William Dean Howells, "Letters of an Altrurian Traveller," IV, *Cosmopolitan* 16 (1893–1894): 46.

95. "The Position of the Horse in Modern Society," 277–78; "Use of Steam Carriages on the Street Railways and Common Roads," *Engineering News* 3 (April 22, 1876): 131; and "The Treatment of the City's Horses," *New York Times*, July 18, 1906.

96. Howard, *The Horse in America*, 237–38.

97. "Through Broadway," *Atlantic Monthly* 18 (December 1866): 717; George E. Waring, Jr., comp., *Report on the Social Statistics of Cities*, Pt. II, *The New England and the Middle States* (Washington, DC: Government Printing Office, 1887), 591; "Clean Streets and Motor Traffic," *The Literary Digest* 49 (September 5, 1914): 413; and Chicago Department of Health, *Annual Reports, 1911–1918* (Chicago, 1919), 398. Long-term contracts and competitive bidding produced a profit for Chicago from its dead animal removal service.

98. Rudolph Hering and Samuel A. Greeley, *Collection and Disposal of Municipal Refuse* (New York: McGraw-Hill, 1921), 413,

99. For a graphic picture of dead horses being disposed of in New York harbor at night, see "How Disease Is Generated in New York," *Frank Leslie's Illustrated Newspaper* (August 20, 1870), 354, 359.

100. Citizens' Association of New York, *Report . . . upon the Sanitary Commission*, 264.

101. Waring, *Social Statistics of Cities*, passim. In the late nineteenth century, for instance, the New York Rendering Company had a contract with the city to remove all offal and dead animals beyond the city limits but continued to render the material within the city. When the board of health closed down their plant, the firm dumped the offal and carcasses into the bay, only to have the material float back to the shore. See Duffy, *History of Public Health in New York City*, 24–25, 61, 117–18, 131–32. In London, those who collected and processed dead horses were called "knackers."

102. For example, see *New York Times*, July 18, 1873.

103. Ibid., October 22–24, 1872; and D. E. Salmon, ed., *Special Report on Diseases of the Horse*, U.S. Department of Agriculture, Bureau of Animal Industry (Washington, DC: Government Printing Office, 1896), 491–92.

104. Salmon, *Special Report on Diseases of the Horse*, 391, 533–34.

105. Herbert N. Casson, "The Horse Cost of Living," *Munsey's Magazine* 48 (March 1913): 997; "The Horse as an 'Economic Anachronism,'" *The Literary Digest* 47 (July 26, 1912): 140, 142.

106. Leon N. Moses and Harold F. Williamson, Jr., "The Location of Economic Activity in Cities," *American Economic Review* 57 (May 1967): 211–22.

107. The mortality rate was high. One estimate is that over 500,000 horses were killed on the Western Front and in Mesopotamia, while 15,000 drowned in torpedoed ships. The military found it cheaper to sell them in Europe than bring them home. American horse owners used the profits generated by the high wartime prices on horses to mechanize.

108. Panschar, *Baking in America*, 134.

109. Bolce, "The Horse vs. Health," 623–24.

110. See Joel A. Tarr and Gabriel Dupuy, eds., *Technology and the Rise of the Networked City in Europe and America, 1850–1930* (Philadelphia: Temple University Press, 1987).

111. Thomas Parke Hughes, *Networks of Power: Electrification in Western Society, 1880–1930* (Baltimore: Johns Hopkins University Press, 1983), 14–15; Thomas P. Hughes, "The Evolution of Large Technological Systems," in W. E. Bijker, T. P. Hughes, and T. J. Pinch, eds., *The Social Construction of Technological Systems: New Directions in the Sociology and History of Technology* (Cambridge: MIT Press, 1987), 51–82; and Svante Lindqvist, "Changes in the Technological Landscape: The Temporal Dimension in the Growth and Decline of Large Technological Systems," in Ove Granstrand, ed., *Economics of Technology* (Amsterdam: North-Holland, 1994), 280–84.

112. Lindquist, "Changes in the Technological Landscape," 280–82; Barker, "The Delayed Decline of the Horse," 105–12; and Thompson, "Nineteeth-Century Horse Sense," 64.

I believe in liberality. I am a thorough New
Yorker and have no narrow prejudices. I
never ask a hungry man about his past; I
feed him, not because he is good, but because he needs food. Help your neighbor,
but keep your nose out of his affairs. . . . I
never sued a man in my life and no man
was ever arrested on my complaint. I am
square with my friends, and all I ask is a
square deal in return. But even if I don't
get that, I am still with my friends.

—TIMOTHY D. ("Big Tim") SULLIVAN, 1907

# Underworlds and Underdogs: Big Tim Sullivan and Metropolitan Politics in New York, 1889–1913

*Daniel Czitrom*

O n April 17, 1889, members of the New York State Assembly crowded
around an obscure young colleague as he angrily and tearfully defended himself against charges that he was the boon companion of
thieves, burglars, and murderers. Timothy D. Sullivan had first been
elected to represent the Five Points slum district of New York City in
1886, at the age of twenty-three. His accuser was the formidable
Thomas F. Byrnes, chief inspector of the New York police department,
hero of a popular series of mystery novels, and the most famous detective in the nation. Sullivan had angered the inspector by opposing a bill
that would have given city police the power to jail on sight any person
who had ever been arrested. After learning that his two saloons had
been suddenly "pulled" for excise law violations and after reading
Byrnes's denunciations of him in the New York press, Sullivan disregarded the advice of friends, rose on the assembly floor, and made what
everyone agreed was an extraordinary response. "The speech," reported
the *New York Herald*, "was given in the peculiar tone and language of a
genuine Fourth Warder, and while it was interesting in that respect to
the countrymen, its tone was so manly that Tim gained much sympathy.
If the Inspector's bill had come up today it would have been beaten out
of sight."[1]

Sullivan's defense consisted of an autobiographical sketch stressing his impoverished and fatherless childhood, the saintly influence of
his mother, the necessity that he go to work at age seven, and his steady

*Daniel Czitrom is professor of history at Mount Holyoke College. Reprinted
from* Journal of American History 78 (September 1991): 536–58. *Reprinted
by permission of the Organization of American Historians.*

131

progress from bootblack and newsboy to wholesale news dealer. He had
known some thieves in school and on the street, as there were a good
many in his district. But Sullivan, in rejecting Byrnes's guilt-by-
association charge, proudly detailed his own commitment to honest
work "and outlined such a busy, struggling life that, when, at the conclusion, he asked if he had any time or money to spend with thieves,
there was a 'No' on nearly every member's lips."[2]

This story already contained the key elements of the "honest Bowery boy" narrative at the core of Tim Sullivan's enormous personal popularity and political power in New York. For the next twenty-five years,
Sullivan effectively cultivated a public persona, the character of Big Tim,
on the way to creating a new metropolitan political style. That style was
rooted in a deep knowledge of city street life, particularly as experienced by the city's immigrant and tenement populations. It ingeniously
fused traditional machine politics, the techniques (and profits) of commercialized entertainment, and influence within New York's underworld.
Sullivan and his circle used it to accumulate enormous political and
cultural power. Significantly, Sullivan consistently celebrated the strong
guiding hand of women in his own personal development. That celebration translated into a social feminism combining support for woman
suffrage and protective welfare legislation with the promotion of a
heterosocial popular culture.

Hotly contested by politicos, journalists, business partners, and constituents, the public character of Big Tim had many sides. Sullivan himself left no private papers or diaries and only a few brief letters.
Historians attempting to reconstruct the life and thought of the private
man are utterly dependent on journalistic accounts, what others said
about him, and attention to Sullivan's own construction of a persona.
The battles over Big Tim's true meaning and significance illuminate the
complex connections among machine politics, the urban underworld,
commercial entertainment, and the emerging welfare state. As a
Tammany boss, Sullivan ruled the political districts below Fourteenth
Street when that area had the highest population density and percentage of immigrants in the city. As an entrepreneur of vaudeville, amusement parks, and motion pictures, Sullivan amassed a personal fortune
by consciously pleasing his public in entertainment as well as in politics. As a political protector of certain figures in the city's flourishing
vice economy, he left himself open to charges from middle-class reformers that he was "King of the Underworld."

Over the years Sullivan countered those charges with an ethnic- and
class-inflected rhetoric and restatements of his own personal honesty
and probity. At the same time, he effectively socialized portions of the
vice economy, particularly gambling and the alcohol trade, to support
welfare activities in his district. Sullivan understood that the term *underworld*, popularized in the 1890s, was ambiguous, evincing contradictory meanings in the cosmopolis.[3] The underworld was simultaneously
a zone of pleasure for visiting businessmen, tourists, and slummers; raw
material for journalists and guidebook writers; a potent political weapon
for upstate politicians; an economic and organizational resource for

Tammany Hall and the police department; and a space associated with the commercial amusements of the city. Sullivan understood, too, that enormous political and economic power could be created by exploiting the structural fact of transience so central to metropolitan life.

Sullivan was born on July 23, 1863, at 125 Greenwich Street, in a neighborhood and city still smoldering from the most violent and destructive civil rebellion in the nation's history. The racial, class, and political hatreds that had exploded in the draft riots only a week before, between Irish immigrants and blacks, tenement house dwellers and the uptown elite, and working poor and the Metropolitan police, would haunt the city's collective memory for decades to come. Sullivan's parents, Daniel O. and Catherine Connelly Sullivan, had been part of the great Irish migration into the city during the 1840s. Like many New York families of their class and background, the Sullivans moved frequently from tenement to tenement within the neighborhood near the lower Hudson River docks. For them, as for the vast majority of the half-million people packed into the roughly two-square-mile area south of Fourteenth Street, housing and health conditions were abominable.[4]

Daniel Sullivan died around 1867, leaving his twenty-six-year-old widow, Catherine, with four small children. She remarried soon after and moved, with her new husband, Lawrence Mulligan, an Irish immigrant laborer three years younger than herself, to the Five Points district in lower Manhattan. As the geographical center of the city's burgeoning Irish community, the Points had been notorious for decades as the worst slum in the nation. It was very likely the most thoroughly chronicled neighborhood in the United States, a favorite subject for city journalists, foreign visitors like Charles Dickens, and popular novelists. The 1870 manuscript census shows the Mulligan/Sullivan household of ten, including five children and three boarders, living in a packed wooden tenement at 25 Baxter Street. Dysentery, consumption, and heart disease had killed 3 of the building's 51 residents in the previous year alone. In the surrounding election district, 99 people had died out of a total population of 3,680, for an annual death rate of about 1 in 37.[5]

If the less empathic sanitary inspectors of the day routinely labeled portions of the downtown population as ignorant and depraved, some also tried to distinguish the "very poor, yet respectable, hard-working persons," or "the laboring classes," from the "vicious, intemperate, and degraded." Such distinctions must have been especially important within a family not only struggling to get a living but also warring against itself. Tim Sullivan's stepfather, Lawrence Mulligan, was a violent alcoholic who beat his wife and children. His behavior led to Tim's early decision never to drink alcohol. In reminiscences about his life, Sullivan carefully excluded any mention of Mulligan's role or presence, an act of willful amnesia. The public construction of his childhood, so important to his political identity, would always emphasize the powerful presence of his mother, who took in neighborhood laundry to make ends meet, and his older sister, who went to work in a garment sweatshop when she was fourteen.[6]

At age seven Sullivan started working on Manhattan's Newspaper Row, bundling papers for delivery at $1.50 per week. He also worked as a bootblack in the Fourth Precinct police station house on Oak Street. He completed his course at the Elm Street grammar school at age eleven and was eligible to attend the free high school on Twenty-third Street, but as he later recalled, "as free as it was, it was not free enough for me to go there." Sullivan gained his real education as he progressed to wholesale news dealer. He won a local reputation as a leader and patron of poor newsboys. "He not only furnished my working capital," recalled the Bowery writer Owen Kildare, "but also taught me a few tricks of the trade and advised me to invest my five pennies in just one, the best selling paper of the period." By age eighteen he was working for five different papers, establishing connections with news dealers all over the city, and serving as manager for a large circulation agency. His job took him as far north as Fifty-ninth Street and gave him an intimate knowledge of the city's geography in a time when most Fourth Warders might spend their entire lives without ever venturing above Fourteenth Street.[7]

Sullivan, grown to over six feet tall and weighing two hundred pounds, with a round handsome face, bright smile, and piercing blue eyes, had an imposing physical presence that was an important asset in a day when local political careers frequently began as extensions of masculine prowess or athletic skill. The widely repeated story of how he won the Second District Democratic nomination for the state assembly in 1886, at age twenty-three, may well be apocryphal, but its persistent retelling reinforces this point. Sullivan, so the tale went, encountered a local prizefighter beating up a woman in front of the Tombs, the city prison on Centre Street. He intervened, conquered the rough in a fair fight, and thereby won a great reputation among the male youth of the district.[8]

Sullivan's 1889 fight with Inspector Byrnes attracted publicity from the city press and the attention of the Tammany leadership. It gave him a double-edged celebrity that would define the basic tension in his political persona; in future campaigns he would proudly recall how Byrnes's attacks "made a man of me." The *New York Times*, for example, supported Byrnes and attacked Sullivan for "attracting attention to himself and the criminal resorts which he keeps." A reporter assigned to visit Sullivan's small saloon on Doyers Street, right off the Bowery, cast himself as an explorer in a dangerous foreign land: "It is safe to say that there are not a hundred people in this city who live above Canal street who know where Doyers street is, and if they did they would shun it as the plague. . . . It is narrow and dirty, and in the day time is repulsive enough to keep anybody from trying to penetrate its mysteries, but at night, in addition to its ugliness, it looks dangerous."[9]

Such newspaper attacks served only to increase Sullivan's standing with downtown voters and Richard Croker, the shrewd, taciturn, and menacing leader of Tammany Hall. After the electoral triumph of 1892, in which Tammany swept city offices and helped return Grover Cleveland to the White House, Croker made Sullivan the leader for the new

Third Assembly District, a populous, polyglot area bisected by the Bowery, and not previously a Tammany stronghold. Sullivan sold off his saloons, won election to the state senate in 1893, and concentrated on creating the powerful fiefdom that would dominate the political life of lower Manhattan. A tightly knit group of literal and figurative kin ran this machine within the machine: first cousin Timothy P. ("Little Tim") Sullivan, a canny lawyer and political power in his own right; half brother Lawrence ("Larry") Mulligan; and three other Sullivan "cousins," the brothers Florence, Christopher, and Dennis Sullivan. By 1895, the *Tammany Times* hailed Big Tim as "the political ruler of down-town New York" and "the most popular man on the East Side." Tammany's enemies grudgingly acknowledged his district to be "the most perfectly organized and the strongest in New York."[10]

Big Tim's election to the state senate in 1893 solidified the Sullivan machine's control of the Bowery district. This was a sprawling, multiethnic area of some three hundred thousand people, crowded into the tenement-lined streets surrounding Manhattan's busiest boulevard. The mile-long Bowery was the shopping and commercial center for a vast, largely foreign-born, and poor population. Workers with irregular hours (railroad men, streetcar drivers, printers, and restaurant employees), as well as transients and the unemployed, found shelter in Bowery lodging houses. These were jammed alongside theaters, concert saloons, lager beer gardens, dime museums, restaurants, oyster bars, pawnshops, clothing stores, and jewelry shops. At night the Bowery was "probably the most brilliantly lighted thoroughfare on this planet," a magnet for tourists, sailors, slummers, and others in search of a good time or a cheap place to spend the night. Late nineteenth-century observers had long noted the distinctly German flavor of Bowery life, but other languages, increasingly heard in the theaters, tenements, and shops, reflected the new immigration to Manhattan's Lower East Side: Yiddish, Italian, Chinese, Greek. Tammany Hall as an institution remained, of course, distinctly Irish, as reflected in the overwhelming number of Irish district leaders and patronage appointees. How to organize new immigrant voters and to make them regular Democrats in the face of strong Republican and Socialist appeals was the central political task facing the Sullivan machine.[11]

Operating out of his modest three-story clubhouse, Sullivan hitched electoral politics to the commercial flash of the Bowery. Huge, carnivalesque summer chowders gave tenement dwellers a much appreciated escape to the country. Although these summer excursions were by no means invented by Sullivan, he developed them into a new sort of extravaganza, remembered by Al Smith and others as always the biggest Tammany affairs of the year. As many as ten thousand five-dollar tickets might be sold; but the great majority of those who came did not pay, obtaining their tickets from saloonkeepers, businessmen, and others who bought them in large bunches as campaign contributions.

The chowder began with Tim himself leading a street parade to an East River dock where steamboats ferried the eager picnickers up to Harlem River Park or out to College Point, Long Island. The all-day celebration typically included a clam fritter breakfast, amateur track and field competition, fish and chicken dinner, beer, band music and dancing, and a late night return with torchlight parade and fireworks. Sideshow entertainments ran the gamut from impromptu prize fights to pickup baseball games to pie-eating contests to the awarding of a barrel of flour to the couple with the largest family. Gambling was ubiquitous, with stakes ranging from pennies to thousands of dollars. The assortment of games reflected the ethnic mixture of the crowds who eagerly played Italian *saginetto*, Jewish *stuss*, and Chinese *fan-tan*, alongside the less exotic poker, craps, and monte. Speechmaking was held to a minimum, but scores of politicians from all over the city paid their respects and mingled.[12]

Sullivan's friendship with two older, Tammany-connected New York theatrical producers helps explain the enormous success of his chowders. Henry C. Miner, prosperous owner of five vaudeville theaters, preceded Sullivan as district leader in the Third and donated the clubhouse at 207 Bowery, next door to his thriving People's Theatre. After relinquishing the post to devote more time to his business and to run for Congress, Miner took the much younger Sullivan under his wing, introducing him to theatrical society in New York and Saratoga. An even closer ally was George J. Kraus, proprietor of two Bowery and Tenderloin concert saloons. Kraus's experience as a musician, caterer, bookkeeper, law clerk, and theater manager made him the perfect producer for these events. Sullivan and Kraus formed a partnership in 1896 that eventually managed several burlesque houses and music halls.[13]

With his own origins in the crowded, life-threatening tenements of the Five Points, Sullivan understood the deep significance of democratizing public and commercial recreational space in the city. Tenement dwellers especially appreciated greater opportunities to get out of the house and enjoy themselves. As a state senator in the 1890s, Sullivan first grasped the possibilities for using state power to improve the living conditions of his constituents through his intimate involvement with the creation, sale, and regulation of commercial leisure. Sullivan championed a liberal policy of state licensing for leisure activities associated with the bachelor male subculture of the city, such as boxing and horse racing. In Albany, he led the movement to legalize and regulate professional boxing, and he had a commercial interest in several city athletic clubs that sponsored matches. After the turn of the century, he became more identified with protecting (and investing in) heterosocial popular amusements such as vaudeville, motion pictures, and Coney Island's Dreamland.[14]

In the depression winter of 1894, Sullivan also started the tradition of feeding thousands of poor people a free Christmas dinner. Under the direction of Kraus, the suppers were served in relays to all comers by election district captains and other local politicians at Sullivan's Bowery headquarters, which could seat about 250 at a time. Enough turkey, ham, stuffing, potatoes, bread, beer, pie, and coffee were provided for as many as 5,000 hungry diners, most of them single men from the neighborhood lodging houses. Local vaudeville singers and musicians entertained at these feasts, once described by the senator as "the best Christmas meal ever gotten up with the object of making people forget they are poor."[15]

In 1903 Sullivan began giving away shoes and wool socks every February to as many as six thousand people who lined up for blocks around the Bowery clubhouse. The inspiration for this practice was a kindly female schoolteacher who had arranged to get the impoverished young Tim a free pair of shoes during one of the brutal winters of his childhood. Sullivan's charity was not, of course, the only brand available on the Bowery. But it was famous for its total lack of conditions—no distinctions made between the deserving and the undeserving, no home investigations, no questions asked. "Help your neighbor, but keep your nose out of his affairs," Sullivan said in 1907, explaining his creed. "I stand with the poet of my people, John Boyle O'Reilly, against the charity that only helps when you surrender the pride of self-respect: 'Organized charity, scrimped and iced,/In the name of a cautious, statistical Christ.' " The innovative food and clothing giveaways and the popular summer chowders were widely covered in the press. They became simultaneously the most tangible and the most symbolic expressions of the Sullivan base of support among lower Manhattan's tenement and floating population—those New Yorkers most vulnerable to the worst economic and social insecurities of metropolitan life.[16]

The Sullivan machine was not all bread and circuses. It carefully organized the Bowery neighborhood using scores of loyal election district captains, each of whom might be responsible for an area containing several thousand people. A large number of the captains were Germans, Jews, and Italians; many were attorneys, liquor dealers, merchants, or other community influentials. Big Tim himself often led groups of workers in early morning treks to uptown public works, making sure the men got the employment he had promised them. He also regularly visited the city prison and local police courts, offering bail money, the promise of a job, or simple encouragement to petty thieves, vagrants, and others down on their luck.[17]

In an era when the New York State vote frequently determined the outcome of presidential elections, Sullivan's controversial efforts to mobilize the Bowery's large, semitransient population had national implications. He employed street-level, physical intimidation at the ballot box both to control and to expand the suffrage. It was the latter that most troubled Sullivan's critics, as in 1893 when, during his state senate campaign, the *New York Herald* routinely stigmatized Sullivan's supporters as "bullet headed, short haired, small eyed, smooth shaven, and crafty looking, with heavy, vicious features, which speak of dissipation and brutality, ready to fight at a moment's notice." The *New York Tribune* appeared most disturbed by Sullivan's success with the lodging house men, as an editorial noted uneasily that district registration exceeded that for 1892, a presidential election year. During an 1894 state senate investigation into police corruption and election fraud, Big Tim and Florence Sullivan were among those prominently accused of interfering with patrolmen assigned to maintain order at polling places and of physically beating Republican poll watchers who challenged voters' credentials. But none of the Sullivans were called to testify, perhaps because the Republican-dominated committee recognized that both parties were deeply implicated in the practices of machine politics.[18]

Court records show that Big Tim himself personally bailed out men arrested on election law violations, putting up thousands of dollars in cash or pledging his own property as security. He also arranged for legal counsel from the pool of politically ambitious lawyers at the machine's disposal. The defendants were mostly Italians and Jews, often ex-cons, petty criminals, or aggressive district captains, eager to please their leaders by stretching the ambiguous registration and naturalization laws as far as possible. The Sullivan machine occasionally employed rival gangs for strong-arm support at election time, especially during the rare but bruising intra-Tammany primary fights. The largest and most notorious of these were the Jewish Monk Eastman gang and the Italian Paul Kelly Association, whose bitter feuding sometimes exploded into gunfire on Lower East Side streets.[19]

The Sullivan machine's self-conception of its strength rested on a political version of the American work ethic and a notion of service that ironically inverted the ideals of genteel reformers. The Sullivans were nothing if not dedicated businessmen, political entrepreneurs as fiercely proud of their enterprise and as eager to chalk up success to individual initiative as any captain of industry. "All this talk about psychological power and personal magnetism over man is fine business for pretty writing," Big Tim observed in 1909, "but when you get down to brass tacks it's the work that does the business. . . . It's just plenty of work, keep your temper or throw it away, be on the level, and don't put on any airs, because God and the people hate a chesty man." The Tammany leader was successful precisely because he was working at his business on the Fourth of July and Christmas, tending all year round to the personal obligations that translated into votes on election day.[20]

Charges that the "King of the Bowery" was in reality "King of the Underworld" rang loudest at the turn of the century when Tim Sullivan emerged as the preeminent symbol of Tammany's connections with the carnal pleasures of gambling, drinking, prostitution, and commercial entertainments. With the creation of Greater New York, a vast metropolis of three hundred square miles and over three million people, the political stakes had never been higher. Charges that the city ran "wide open" became a regular, election-time rallying cry for Tammany's opponents. A crucial tactic for Sullivan's enemies was the elision of any differences between his interest in burlesque houses and his alleged profits from prostitution and "white slavery," or between his support for Sunday drinking and Sunday vaudeville and his supposed role as head of a secret "vice commission" that controlled all of New York's gambling.[21]

For example, Sullivan and his partner George Kraus remodeled the Volks Garden Music Hall on East Fourteenth Street, previously a church, and reopened it in September 1898 as the fourteen-hundred-seat Dewey Theatre, named for the hero of Manila. Sullivan's political clout ensured lenient treatment from municipal departments responsible for fire safety and building permits and the continuation of a concert saloon license. The Dewey, with a novel policy of changing its program every week and presenting matinee and evening performances each day, quickly became one of the most popular theaters in the Union Square district. A typical program might include turns by singers, dialect comedians, performing monkeys, Irish clog dancers, chorus girls, acrobats, and pantomimists. Shows usually concluded with one-act musical burlesques with titles such as "King of the Hobo Ring," "A Wild Night in Washington," and "The Divorce Court." The black minstrel team of Bert Williams and George Walker appeared there regularly. Profits from the Dewey alone netted Sullivan around $25,000 a year, enabling him to purchase title to the property that first year for a reported $167,000 mortgage.[22]

Sullivan's new burlesque and vaudeville house became an issue in the very close 1898 gubernatorial campaign in which Theodore Roosevelt narrowly defeated Tammany's Augustus Van Wyck, brother of Robert Van Wyck, mayor of New York City. To Frank Moss, prominent Republican attorney, counsel for the Society for the Prevention of Crime, and former city police commissioner, Sullivan's theatrical venture epitomized the wide-open city. "What shall we say today," he asked a Cooper Union election rally, "about the Dewey Theatre, openly run with a city license, under police surveillance, patronized by men, women, and children, upon whose stage have been given those shows which have kindled unquenchable flames of passion in the breasts of hundreds of its patrons—a theatre boasting the Tammany cause, displaying the Tammany emblems, right opposite Tammany Hall." It was like all those "horrible concert halls and gardens besprinkling the Bowery and other streets in the city, running under license, which, while being by law under constant police observation, are patronized by men, women, and children, who see dances so immoral that the imported oriental dance of 'Little Egypt' would be a Sunday school lesson to their participants."[23]

In fact, the accusations that echoed throughout the city press had all been aired the previous year in the course of the state assembly's Mazet committee investigation into city corruption under Tammany rule. Moss had served as the chief counsel for that strictly partisan, highly selective inquiry, an effort by the state Republican machine to embarrass Tammany. But the Mazet hearings resulted in no indictments or resignations and produced no political earthquake. The notion of a secret, highly centralized, perfectly controlled "Gambling Commission," attractive as it was to Tammany's opponents and the newspapers, was nonetheless impossible to prove. It was all untrue, claimed Sullivan. "I was here during the whole session of the Mazet committee. Why didn't they subpoena me? They know they have nothing against me. They make a lot of talk, but they haven't a particle of proof."[24]

The most explosive and potentially damaging charge against Sullivan alleged that he directly profited from the growing prostitution trade on the Lower East Side. In the fall of 1900, an Episcopal bishop, Henry C. Potter, began to speak out publicly on the issue in response to complaints of open soliciting by prostitutes, pimps, and their runners on the streets and in the tenements. This was a sensitive point, too, for members of the expanding Jewish community, disturbed to see so many of their daughters and sisters forced by poverty into at least casual prostitution. An angry Richard Croker warned that any Tammany leader accepting vice tribute must resign, and he heatedly denied any personal involvement, declaring to his district chiefs, "Some people think that you leaders walk down to me every little while with handfuls of money collected from these people. I am not talking for political effect." Sullivan and his close ally, East Side district leader Martin Engel, had difficult private meetings with Croker, who announced creation of Tammany's own antivice committee for the purpose of investigating the moral conditions of the city. Skeptical reporters wondered out loud "how Martin Engel and Tim Sullivan make a living."[25]

Sullivan became a special target of the fusion campaign that ousted Tammany in the vitriolic elections of 1901. William Travers Jerome styled his candidacy for district attorney "a movement against the protection of vice and crime," a strategy that helped sway many East Side Jewish voters from the Democrats. Jerome repeatedly attacked Sullivan, reviving and embellishing the old charges made by Inspector Byrnes in 1889. On his home turf, at Miner's Bowery Theatre, Sullivan dismissed Jerome as "a liar, a four carat lawyer, a collegiate." He ridiculed Jerome's threat to invade the East Side with outside poll watchers: "If Jerome brings down a lot of football playing, hair-mattressed college athletes to run the polls by force, I will say now that there won't be enough ambulances in New York to carry them away."[26]

Did Sullivan and Engel, in fact, control and grow rich from the mushrooming East Side underworld, its prostitution, gambling, and related criminal activity? That is a difficult question to answer. Engel, one of the first Jews to achieve power within Tammany, no doubt had enormous authority within the increasingly Jewish red-light district centered on Allen Street. His brother Max owned 102 Allen, one of the most notorious fifty-cent houses in the neighborhood. But he manifested his real influence as a bail bondsman and fixer in the crowded halls of the nearby Essex Market Courthouse, the local police court. After making a fortune in the wholesale poultry business, Engel had begun to make himself useful to Tammany by regularly putting up various properties, worth around two hundred thousand dollars, as surety for accused criminals. By the mid-1890s Engel had come to dominate the day-to-day business of the Essex Market court, which, as the place where accused criminals directly confronted the police power of the state, was a critical site of political pull on the Lower East Side.[27]

Some of Sullivan's loyal lieutenants on the Lower East Side undoubtedly had a direct involvement with prostitution, and they enjoyed some political and legal protection in exchange for financial contributions. For his part, Tim Sullivan always vehemently denied any personal connection to the prostitution flourishing below Fourteenth Street. "Nobody who knows me well," he declared in 1901, "will believe that I would take a penny from any woman, much less from the poor creatures who are more to be pitied than any other human beings on earth. I'd be afraid to take a cent from a poor woman of the streets for fear my old mother would see it. I'd a good deal rather break into a bank and rob the safe. That would be a more manly and decent way of getting money." No solid evidence ever emerged linking him to prostitution or white slavery. Nonetheless, shortly after the 1901 election, partly in response to all the unfavorable publicity, both Sullivan and Engel resigned their district leaderships. Their replacements were Little Tim Sullivan and Florence Sullivan. The latter quickly acted to deflect the vice charges against the Sullivan clan by personally leading invasions of East Side brothels, throwing furniture out on the street and roughing up neighborhood pimps.[28]

Sullivan's main connection with the city's vice economy was gambling, not prostitution. He was himself a chronic, flamboyant, and, by all accounts, poor gambler, losing heavily at horse racing and cards all his life. He always tried to turn his habit to economic and political advantage by investing in gambling enterprises and insisting on a democratic approach to betting. Sullivan helped organize the Metropolitan Jockey Club and became a principal investor in its Jamaica racetrack. He offered protection to the scores of small pool rooms, policy joints, and *stuss* houses that dotted the East Side in exchange for using them as all-purpose hiring halls. Gamblers were expected to make five-dollar-per-day payments known as "CODs" to Big Tim's friends and supporters, usually for doing nothing. Private social clubs throughout the East Side brought professional gamblers and professional politicians together across ethnic lines. The Hesper Club on Second Avenue, founded around 1900 and dominated by the Sullivan clan, was the most prestigious of these, a place where Irish and Jewish Democrats came together for fund raisers, poker parties, annual balls, and outings.[29]

The 1901 election of Seth Low as mayor and the overall fusion sweep portended drastic changes for both Sullivan and Tammany as a whole. In 1902, after sixteen years as Tammany's leader, Croker, now a multimillionaire largely through real estate investments, finally retired to breed racehorses at his English estate. Sullivan himself could have replaced Croker, but he preferred to maintain his semi-independent power base and, instead, threw his considerable influence behind Charles F. Murphy, who ruled Tammany until his death in 1924. With Murphy's ascendancy, Sullivan began to withdraw from direct involvement in city politics, preferring to stay in the background and concentrate on expanding his business interests.[30]

He was elected to Congress in 1902 and 1904, but the House, dominated by Republicans, bored him. He missed the Bowery and declared that in Washington "they don't think any more of a Congressman than they would of a wooden Indian in front of a cigar store. Why, they hitch horses to Congressmen whenever they want to use them." His stay in Washington, however brief, made him less of a provincial Tammany figure and opened his eyes to the commercial potential of national theatrical circuits. In 1904 he put up $5,000 to help John W. Considine, an ambitious theater manager in Seattle, purchase four small-time vaudeville houses in the Pacific Northwest. Considine had begun his career in the dance halls and honky-tonks of the Alaska gold rush, and with further financial assistance from Sullivan, he began mining the more lucrative Klondike of nationally organized vaudeville.[31]

By 1907 the Sullivan-Considine firm controlled or owned about forty midsized theaters, mostly west of Chicago, as well as a very profitable booking agency. Some of the biggest names in early twentieth-century show business, including Charlie Chaplin and Will Rogers, got their start touring the circuit's popularly priced "ten-twent-thirt" houses, run by Considine with industrial precision. Sullivan's half interest in the company brought him as much as $20,000 a month, or around $200,000 each year. When the company sold its assets in 1914 to Loew Theatrical Enterprises (which added feature motion pictures to the live acts), the Sullivan estate's share of the stock was estimated to be worth at least $750,000.[32]

Sullivan's involvement with the early New York movie industry brought a steady stream of income from another popular yet somewhat disreputable form of leisure. By 1908, Manhattan alone had some two hundred vaudeville houses, storefront nickelodeons, and penny arcades projecting motion pictures to audiences. Nearly one-third of these were concentrated on the Lower East Side, and although no official records of Sullivan's interest in this trade survive, both he and cousin Little Tim evidently received several thousand dollars each month from direct nickelodeon investments and the granting of informal licenses to operate in their territory.[33]

As movies became a booming feature of the commercial amusement scene, the Sullivans made a political and business alliance with William Fox, the archetypal Jewish immigrant movie mogul. Fox pioneered the so-called small-time vaudeville that combined the cheap admission and movie program of the nickelodeon with live performances and a more "high-class" environment. In 1908 Fox paid $100,000 for a one-year lease on two Sullivan vaudeville theaters in prime locations, the Dewey on Fourteenth Street and the Gotham on One Hundred and Twenty-fifth Street. The trade press soon called the Dewey "the best run and most profitable" movie house in New York. Fox's relatively clean, comfortable theaters mixed seven or eight vaudeville acts with movies, attracting a more middle-class patronage, and anticipated the gaudy movie palaces of the teens.[34]

Fox became a leader, too, in organizing New York City motion picture exhibitors in response to continual wrangling over city licenses and suits brought for violations of the Sunday blue laws. The key spokesman for Fox's interests and ultimately the Moving Picture Exhibitors Association was Gustavus A. Rogers, a Jewish attorney from the Lower East Side and longtime lieutenant for Florence Sullivan. Simultaneously, as Tammany leader on the Board of Alderman, Little Tim Sullivan led the fight for city ordinances allowing Sunday vaudeville and movies. Big Tim claimed in 1907 that "the best way to ruin a large cosmopolitan city like ours, which virtually lives off our visiting strangers, is to enforce or keep on the statute books such blue laws which don't belong to our age."[35]

Sullivan had become a wealthy man and generosity with money was an important part of the mystique. His geniality about it perhaps reflected a keen personal satisfaction at having traveled so far from the desperate insecurity of his childhood. But the political charity may have also substituted for the home life Sullivan lacked as an adult. He married Nellie Fitzgerald in 1886, but they became estranged and had no children. An illegitimate daughter, born in 1896, surfaced publicly only after his death, during the fight over his estate. He had no real home, dividing his time between an apartment in the Bowery's Occidental Hotel, a house on East Fourth Street, Albany hotels, and long vacations to Europe and Hot Springs, Arkansas. Sullivan could have retired comfortably, but in 1908 he decided to return to the New York State Senate. Sullivan refocused his political attention on legislative work in Albany as he withdrew from city politics and the internal affairs of Tammany Hall.[36]

In the final stage of his life Sullivan embodied and contributed to an important shift in Tammany and the Democratic Party—an expansion from a personal, service-based politics to one more centered on legislative achievements in social welfare. In the 1890s, as Robert F. Wesser has argued, Democrats stood basically for "personal liberty, negative government, and local autonomy." By the end of World War I, they had become identified with an economic and social liberalism stressing "labor and social reform as well as a broad advocacy and defense of the interests and values of immigrant groups and ethnic minorities." Sullivan's last years in Albany both exemplified and furthered this change.[37]

Sullivan had always publicly identified himself with the city's working class. Over the years he had quietly and effectively intervened in labor disputes and had persuaded large caterers and music hall proprietors to employ unionized waiters, bartenders, and musicians exclusively. While running for Congress in 1902 he had told supporters, "I never sat a day in the Senate without bein' glad as I wasn't on the front end of a motor car or on the rear, as a conductor." But in his final years in Albany he began translating his longtime rhetorical identification with working-class voters into important legislative achievements. A key collaborator in this last phase of his life was the young Frances Perkins.[38]

In 1911, in response to massive, socialist-led organizing drives in New York City's garment district and in the aftermath of the disastrous Triangle Shirtwaist fire, Democrats in Albany set up the Factory Investigating Commission (FIC) to survey working conditions throughout the state. For nearly four years, under the leadership of Senator Robert F. Wagner and Assemblyman Al Smith, the FIC conducted an unprecedented series of public hearings and on-site inspections that ultimately produced laws that dramatically improved state industrial conditions. Both Wagner and Smith were deeply affected by what they saw in the canneries, textile shops, and candy factories they visited. They were also changed by their collaboration with social Progressives such as Frances Perkins. Eventually appointed the first secretary of labor under Franklin D. Roosevelt, at the time Perkins was a lobbyist for the National Consumers' League and already an expert on comparative wage and hour rates around the state. Her first real political triumph, and the fight that brought her to public attention, was the passage in the final moments of the 1912 legislative session of the fifty-four-hour law limiting the hours of labor for about four hundred thousand women in New York factories.[39]

In both published and private versions of that battle, Perkins portrayed Tim Sullivan as her first political mentor. Unlike Wagner, Smith, Charles F. Murphy, or the haughty young state senator Franklin Roosevelt, Sullivan impressed her as the only politician who accepted the principle of the bill and was willing to guide it through the rough shoals of the legislature. As Perkins recalled in interviews with an oral historian: " 'Well,' he said, 'me sister was a poor girl and she went out to work when she was young. I feel kinda sorry for them poor girls that work the way you say they work. I'd like to do them a good turn. I'd like to do you a good turn. You don't know much about this parliamentary stuff, do you?' " With Sullivan's aid in the senate, she outwitted opposition to the measure by accepting an amended assembly version that exempted about ten thousand cannery workers—a compromise that neither manufacturers nor reluctant Democrats believed she would accept.[40]

After a tumultuous, last-minute vote in which two waverers switched and voted no, the bill's supporters called for a reconsideration. Perkins frantically telephoned the boat dock where Big Tim and his cousin, Sen. Christy Sullivan, were just about to leave Albany for New York City, believing the bill had safely passed. They rushed back to the capitol, running up the steep hill, "one red-faced and puffing, one white-faced and gasping," and dramatically burst into the senate chamber. Their hands were upraised, and they were yelling to be recorded in the affirmative. The bill passed, and as Perkins recalled the scene, "The Senate and galleries broke into roars of applause. . . . The Sullivans were heroes. I got some of it."[41]

Sullivan tied his views on labor to an outspoken support for woman suffrage. "Years ago," he noted in a 1910 campaign speech, "if you stood on a corner most anywhere down here early in the morning you would see twenty men to one woman going to work. But it's different now. Now, there's about as many women going past the corner to work every morning as there are men. They break about even. If women are going to be the toilers I'm going to give them all the protection I can." As one of the first prominent Tammany men to support the vote for women, Sullivan became a close ally of Harriot Stanton Blatch, leader of the Equality League of Self-Supporting Women. The two shared a basic understanding of the connections between women's economic status and their political rights. Blatch, daughter of Elizabeth Cady Stanton, was part of a new generation of women leaders making a labor-based appeal for suffrage. "It is with woman as a worker that the suffrage has to do," she argued. "It is because she is the worker the state should have the value of her thought." Blatch combined militant street demonstrations with backroom political lobbying. She and Sullivan struck up a friendship during her regular trips to Albany to testify before legislative committees and press for suffrage bills. He told her that workingmen who came to Albany were listened to far more respectfully than working women. "And," Blatch wrote in 1912, "he has declared again and again that he wants to give women the same advantage as men enjoy in dealing with the legislators who incline a listening ear to the voters of their district." Sullivan made his argument repeatedly before the senate and also became a popular speaker before women's groups around the state.[42]

Sullivan's views dovetailed with his defense of the broadest possible franchise, a politics of inclusion when it came to voting. Always sensitive about defending the voting rights of recent immigrants, casual laborers, the very poor, and transients in his district, he made an explicit analogy between women and blacks. Independent of the question of women's economic status, he told the senate in 1911, they deserved the suffrage. "Just recollect that less than fifty years ago you would not let a man vote on account of his color; because his color was not right he could not vote. . . . It's going to come and you can't stop it." But opposition and fence straddling by Tammany powers like Murphy and Smith continued to help defeat woman suffrage measures in New York until 1917 when, four years after Sullivan's death, the urban immigrant vote provided the margin of victory in a statewide referendum.[43]

Big Tim's political career came full circle with passage of the so-called Sullivan Law. The politician whose public identity had for years been routinely associated with the city's underworld authored the state's first gun control legislation, making it a felony to carry a concealed weapon and requiring the licensing and registration of small firearms. Sullivan introduced the measure partly in response to a marked increase in highly publicized violent street crime below Fourteenth Street. "The gun toter and the tough man—I don't want his vote," he insisted in his 1910 election campaign. "There are a lot of good, law-abiding people in the lower east side. They do not like to have the red badge of shame waved over that part of the city. They have no sympathy with the tough men, the men who tote guns and use them far too frequently."[44]

Yet Sullivan remained a favorite target for sensational and nativist exposés. Writing in *McClure's* in 1909, George Kibbe Turner dredged up the twenty-year-old charges of Inspector Byrnes, portrayed Sullivan as a white slaver, and held him responsible for positioning Tammany to control the city primarily through its alliance with professional criminals. In an emotional campaign speech, made to a packed house at Miner's Bowery Theatre, Sullivan responded by denying any involvement with prostitution and noting that he had made money from his theatrical interests. He paid special tribute to his mother and then moved the crowd with the melodramatic story of how a kindly female schoolteacher had arranged for him to get a free pair of shoes during a hard winter, thus inspiring his own brand of charity.[45]

Sullivan's end was both bizarre and pathetic. He had decided to return to Congress in 1912, anticipating a national Democratic victory that could give him the influence in Washington previously denied him under Republican rule. He never took his seat. In July 1912 he began to suffer from severe mental disorders that included bouts of manic depression, delusions of food poisoning, violent hallucinations, and threats of suicide. In September 1912, after the funeral of his wife, from whom he had been separated for many years, Sullivan had a complete nervous breakdown. Desperate family members had him committed to a private sanitarium in Yonkers. In January 1913, a sheriff's jury declared him "a lunatic and incapable of managing himself or his affairs" and implied that his illness was caused by tertiary syphilis—although this point did not make it into most press accounts. One doctor described Sullivan as "absolutely dominated by delusions of terrifying apprehension, fear, conspiracy, plot, attempts of poisoning, and efforts to do him bodily harm in every conceivable direction. . . . He had an expression which was consistent with his mental trait. It was one of terror and depression, and it was impossible to divert his attention or to engage him in conversation in any subject whatever apart from the terrifying delusions and hallucinations." A court-appointed committee of family and close friends took charge of his business and personal affairs and shuttled Sullivan between sanitariums, trips to mineral baths in Germany, and private home care.[46]

He lived out his last few months in the seclusion of his brother Patrick's country house in Eastchester, in the Bronx. He had virtually no contact with the press or his friends; the few who saw him found a haggard, thin, and melancholy man who occasionally brightened when talk turned to old Bowery days. Publicly, the family held out hope for recovery. He ran away a few times to the city by catching rides on freight trains, but he would inevitably call to be picked up. On August 31, 1913, during an all-night card game that had put his male nurses to sleep, Tim disappeared for the last time. For two weeks the city's press was filled with conflicting rumors and stories about his whereabouts. Old cronies swore to reporters that they had seen and talked with him on the Bowery, or Fourteenth Street, or Fifth Avenue. Others feared suicide. Finally, on September 13, a patrolman assigned to the Bellevue Morgue recognized an unmarked, mangled body as that of Big Tim, just before it was to be shipped off for a pauper's burial in Potter's Field. Sullivan, it turned out, had been run over by a train on the night he slipped away, perhaps as he tried to hop a freight. The body of one of New York's best-known citizens had lain unidentified in the Fordham and Bellevue morgues for thirteen days before being sent downtown for final disposal.[47]

As many as seventy-five thousand people lined the Bowery for a funeral procession described as one of the largest in New York history and remarkable for its class and ethnic diversity. "There were statesmen and prizefighters," the *New York Sun* reported, "judges, actors, men of affairs, police officials, women splendidly gowned and scrubwomen, panhandlers and philanthropists—never was there a more strangely heterogeneous gathering." Even his oldest enemies now recognized that he could not be dismissed as merely the chum of criminals. As the *New York World* put it, "he welcomed the title of 'King of the Underworld' in the sense that he had won his kingship through his friendship for the underdog."[48]

His career and fortune were rooted in the merger of politics and show business. Sullivan thus helped shape a key feature of modern American life. His power had rested upon an uncanny and shrewd melding of job patronage and legal services, charity and poor relief, urban carnival, protection of gambling and the saloon trade, and tolerance for a broad range of commercial entertainments. He supported the vote for women and their full inclusion in the newly emerging world of mass culture. Sullivan's sensitivity to women's issues no doubt reflected his own female-centered upbringing. But in a deeper sense, the evolution of Sullivan's metropolitan style suggests that an explicit ideology of gender informed the political and legislative agenda of the emerging welfare state.[49] Above all, as a pure product of life among the city's poorest tenement Irish, Big Tim saw as no one else before him the political and cultural power latent in an urban underclass too easily dismissed as inherently criminal, depraved, and vicious.

## NOTES

1. *New York Herald*, April 18, 1889, p. 7. No verbatim account of Timothy D. Sullivan's speech appeared in contemporary press accounts, but for the most complete coverage, see *New York Sun*, April 18, 1889, p. 5. Thomas F. Byrnes had recently gained national prominence as the author of a book on criminals and as the hero of a series of five popular detective novels based on his diaries, ghostwritten by Julian Hawthorne, son of Nathaniel, and published in 1887 and 1888. Thomas F. Byrnes, *Professional Criminals of America* (New York, 1886).

2. *New York Herald*, April 18, 1889, p. 7.

3. The term *underworld* was first popularized by Josiah Flynt, who made a journalistic career writing first-person accounts of his experiences with tramps and professional criminals. See Josiah Flynt and Francis Walton, *Powers That Prey* (New York, 1900); and Josiah Flynt, *The World of Graft* (New York, 1901). Both of these books were originally published in serial form in *McClure's Magazine*.

4. There are no official birth records for Sullivan in Municipal Archives and Record Center, New York, N.Y. I have based the birth information on an account he gave during his 1902 congressional campaign. See *New York Times*, Oct. 16, 1902, p. 3; and *New York Herald*, Oct. 16, 1902, p. 5. Adrian Cook, *The Armies of the Streets: The New York City Draft Riots of 1863* (Lexington, Ky., 1974), 2–17; Iver Bernstein, *The New York City Draft Riots: Their Significance for American Society and Politics in the Age of the Civil War* (New York, 1990).

5. Schedule 1, "Inhabitants in 6th District, 6th Ward, in the County of New York," p. 11, "Census, New York City, 1870, 6th Ward" (New York County Clerk's Office, Surrogate Court Building, New York City); Schedule 2, "Persons who Died during the Year ending 1st June, 1870 in Sixth Elect. Dist., 6th Ward," pp. 1–3, *ibid.* My thanks to Joseph Van Nostrand for making these records available to me. "Riots and Their Prevention," *American Medical Times*, July 25, 1863, pp. 41–42; Albon P. Man, Jr., "The Irish in New York in the Early 1860s," *Irish Historical Studies*, 7 (Sept. 1950), 81–108.

6. Citizens Association of New York, *Report of the Council of Hygiene and Public Health Upon the Sanitary Condition of the City* (New York, 1865), 77. For information on Lawrence Mulligan, I am grateful to Patricia Sullivan, granddaughter of Sullivan's brother Patrick. The baptismal records of the Transfiguration Church, 29 Mott Street, show that Catherine Connelly bore at least four more children to Mulligan between 1870 and 1881.

7. *New York Times*, Oct. 16, 1902, p. 3; Owen Kildare, *My Mamie Rose: The Story of My Regeneration* (New York, 1903), 51. See also James L. Ford, *Forty Odd Years in the Literary Shop* (New York, 1921), 169–70.

8. *New York Herald*, May 19, 1907, magazine section, pt. 1, p. 2.

9. *New York Times*, April 17, 1889, p. 4; *ibid.*, April 22, 1889, p. 5. See also *New York Sun*, April 16, 1889, p. 1; *ibid.*, April 17, 1889, p. 1; *New York World*, April 17, 1889, p. 3; and *ibid.*,

April 18, 1889, p. 3. Byrnes had given a statement to reporters in which he named nine notorious criminals as Sullivan's companions or patrons. Part of the controversy involved the arrest of two of Sullivan's bartenders for excise law violations, allegedly in retaliation for his opposition to Byrnes's bill in Albany.

10. On Richard Croker and his leadership of Tammany, see Martin Shefter, "The Emergence of the Political Machine: An Alternative View," in *Theoretical Perspectives on Urban Politics*, ed. Willis D. Hawley et al. (Englewood Cliffs, 1976), 14–44; and David C. Hammack, *Power and Society: Greater New York at the Turn of the Century* (New York, 1982), 158–81. *Tammany Times*, Nov. 4, 1895, p. 3; Hartley Davis, "Tammany Hall, The Most Perfect Political Organization in the World," *Munsey's*, 24 (Oct. 1900), 67. For a recent, comparative study that stresses Irish ethnicity as the key factor in the construction, maintenance, and limits of political machines, see Stephen P. Erie, *Rainbow's End: Irish-Americans and the Dilemmas of Urban Machine Politics, 1840–1985* (Berkeley, 1988). See also Thomas Henderson, *Tammany Hall and the New Immigrants: The Progressive Years* (New York, 1976), 1–15.

11. Julian Ralph, "The Bowery," *Century*, 43 (Dec. 1891), 234. For other contemporary descriptions of the Bowery, see H. C. Bunner, "The Bowery and Bohemia," *Scribner's*, 15 (April 1894), 452–60; Arthur Montefiore, "New York and New Yorkers," *Temple Bar*, 84 (Nov. 1888), 343–57; and Helen Campbell et al., *Darkness and Daylight; or, Lights and Shadows of New York Life* (Hartford, 1897), 459–75. On the early development of the Bowery as a distinctive cultural milieu, see Christine Stansell, *City of Women: Sex and Class in New York, 1789–1860* (New York, 1986), 89–101; and Peter G. Buckley, "Culture, Class, and Place in Antebellum New York," in *Power, Culture, and Place: Essays on New York City*, ed. John Hull Mollenkopf (New York, 1988), 25–52.

12. On the chowders, which seem to have begun in 1892, see *Tammany Times*, Aug. 6, 1893, p. 5; *ibid.*, Aug. 4, 1894, p. 4; *ibid.*, Sept. 19, 1898, p. 5; *ibid.*, Sept. 13, 1902, p. 11; *New York Times*, Aug. 2, 1892, p. 2; *ibid.*, Aug. 2, 1893, p. 5; *ibid.*, Sept. 14, 1897, p. 4; *ibid.*, Sept. 13, 1898, p. 7; *ibid.*, Sept. 11, 1900, p. 14; *ibid.*, Sept. 15, 1903, p. 2; *New York Tribune*, Aug. 2, 1893, p. 5; and Al Smith, *Up to Now: An Autobiography* (New York, 1929), 31–32. In the early years, press accounts included detailed results of the amateur track and field events.

13. On Henry C. Miner, see *Tammany Times*, Aug. 4, 1894, p. 4; *ibid.*, Nov. 3, 1894, p. 4; *New York Times*, Feb. 23, 1900, p. 1; Henry C. Miner Clipping File (Theatre Collection, Performing Arts Research Center, New York Public Library, Lincoln Center, New York, N.Y.); and *Harry Miner's American Dramatic Directory* (New York, 1884). On George J. Kraus, see *Tammany Times*, Aug. 20, 1893, p. 11; *ibid.*, Oct. 28, 1893, p. 7; *New York Times*, June 3, 1914, p. 13; *ibid.*, June 16, 1914, p. 10.

14. Steven A. Riess, "In the Ring and Out: Professional Boxing in New York, 1896–1920," in *Sport in America: New Historical Perspectives*, ed. Donald Spivey (Westport, 1985), 95–128; Steven A. Riess, "Sports and Machine Politics in New York City, 1870–1920," in *The Making of Urban America*, ed. Raymond A. Mohl (Wilmington, 1988), 99–121. On the shift from homosocial to heterosocial popular culture, see Kathy Peiss, *Cheap Amusements: Working Women and Leisure in Turn of the Century New York* (Philadelphia, 1986), 6–33.

15. *New York Times*, Dec. 24, 1897, p. 7. See also *ibid.*, Dec. 25, 1897, p. 2; *ibid.*, Dec. 26, 1898, p. 3; *ibid.*, Dec. 26, 1899, p. 12; and *Tammany Times*, Dec. 25, 1899, p. 7.

16. *New York Herald*, May 19, 1907, magazine section, pt. 1, p. 2. For descriptions of the shoe giveaways, see the interviews conducted in 1955 by Dean Albertson, *The Reminiscences of Frances Perkins*, Columbia University Oral History Collection, pt. 3, no. 182 (microfiche, Glen Rock, N.J., 1977), transcript, 225–26; *New York Tribune*, Feb. 7, 1905, p. 8; *ibid.*, Feb. 7, 1908, p. 4; *New York Times*, Feb. 7, 1909, p. 8. For a competing notion of scientific charity, see, for example, Mrs. C. R. Lowell, "The Unemployed in New York City, 1893–94," *Journal of Social Science*, 32 (Nov. 1894), 19–23.

17. *New York Herald*, Oct. 22, 1893, sec. 3, pp. 2–3; Davis, "Tammany Hall," 66–67; Henderson, *Tammany Hall and the New Immigrants*, 135–36.

18. *New York Herald*, Oct. 22, 1893, sec. 3, p. 2; *New York Tribune*, Oct. 24, 1893, p. 6; New York, State Senate, *Report and Proceedings of the Senate Committee Appointed to Investigate the Police Department of the City of New York* (5 vols., Albany, 1895), III, 191–253. The best discussion of the city's election process in these years is still William Mills Ivins, *Machine Politics and Money in Elections in New York City* (New York, 1887). See also C. K. Yearley, *The Money Machines: The Breakdown and Reform of Governmental and Party Finance in the North, 1860–1920* (Albany, 1970), 97–118. For a persuasive overview showing how election fraud was endemic to the political system of the day, see Peter H. Argersinger, "New Perspectives on Election Fraud in the Gilded Age," *Political Science Quarterly*, 100 (Winter 1985–1986), 669–87.

19. Lower court justices friendly to Tammany dismissed nearly all of these cases due to "insufficient evidence." District Attorney's Book of Cases, 1900–1902 (Municipal Archives and Record Center, New York, N.Y.). See, for example, *People v. Charles Kramer* (1900), Court

of General Sessions of the County of New York, *ibid.*; and *People v. Sonny Smith* (1900–1902), *ibid.* See also *New York Times*, Nov. 11, 1898, p. 1; *ibid.*, Oct. 17, 1902, p. 1; and *ibid.*, Nov. 5, 1902, p. 3. On Monk Eastman, a very shadowy historical figure, see *People v. William Delaney* (1904), Court of General Sessions of the County of New York. Paul Kelly was born Paolo Vaccarrelli and later became vice-president of the International Longshoreman's Association. On street violence between the Eastman and Kelly gangs, see *New York Times*, Sept. 17, 1903, p. 8; and *ibid.*, Sept. 20, 1903, p. 1. On the Kelly and Eastman gangs as training grounds for a later generation of crime figures, including Al Capone and Charles ("Lucky") Luciano, see Humbert S. Nelli, *The Business of Crime: Italian and Syndicate Crime in the United States* (New York, 1976), 101–40.

20. "Big Tim Sullivan, the Rain Maker," *Current Literature*, 47 (Dec. 1909), 623–24.

21. See, for example, "Editorial," *Harper's Weekly*, Oct. 30, 1897, p. 1030; and Franklin Matthews, "'Wide Open' New York," *ibid.*, Oct. 22, 1898, p. 1046.

22. On the Dewey Theatre, see *Tammany Times*, Oct. 24, 1898, p. 12; *ibid.*, Oct. 31, 1898, p. 20; *New York Tribune*, Oct. 4, 1898, p. 2; and New York, State Assembly, *Report of the Special Committee of the Assembly Appointed to Investigate the Public Offices of the City of New York* (5 vols., Albany, 1900), II, 1364–69. For a review of a typical Dewey show, see *Tenderloin*, Nov. 12, 1898, p. 8.

23. *New York Herald*, Nov. 1, 1898, p. 7. Examples of extremely nativist views abound in Frank Moss, *The American Metropolis* (3 vols., New York, 1897), II, 399–410, III, 28–55. For continued attacks on the Dewey and unsuccessful attempts by the New York Sabbath Committee to get its license revoked for violation of the Sunday laws, see *New York Tribune*, June 7, 1899, pt. 2, p. 2; *New York Times*, April 28, 1900, p. 2; *ibid.*, May 2, 1900, p. 9; and *ibid.*, Jan. 27, 1901, p. 8.

24. *New York World*, March 10, 1900, p. 2. See also *New York Times*, March 9, 1900, p. 1; and *New York Herald*, March 10, 1900, p. 4.

25. *New York Times*, Nov. 16, 1900, p. 2; *New York Tribune*, Nov. 17, 1900, p. 2. For Henry C. Potter's open letter to the mayor, see *New York Times*, Nov. 17, 1900, p. 1. On the report of the Tammany antivice committee, see *ibid.*, March 12, 1901, p. 1.

26. *New York Times*, Oct. 25, 1901, p. 2; *ibid.*, Nov. 4, 1901, p. 2; *New York Tribune*, Oct. 25, 1901, p. 2. For William Travers Jerome's revival of Byrnes's old charges and Sullivan's reply, see *New York Times*, Oct. 29, 1901, p. 2; and *ibid.*, Oct. 30, 1901, p. 2.

27. On Engel, see *Tammany Times*, Sept. 7, 1895, p. 9; *New York Times*, May 4, 1901, p. 16; and Edward J. Bristow, *Prostitution and Prejudice: The Jewish Fight against White Slavery, 1870–1939* (New York, 1982), 146–68. On the Essex Market gang, see New York, State Senate, *Report and Proceedings of the Senate Committee Appointed to Investigate the Police Department of the City of New York*, III, 2975–3021, IV, 4719–4905.

28. *Tammany Times*, Jan. 21, 1901, p. 5. On Little Tim and Florence Sullivan as district leaders, see *ibid.*, Feb. 3, 1902, p. 13; and *ibid.*, April 18, 1903, p. 10. For confirmation of Florence's reputation for breaking up brothels, see Jonah J. Goldstein interview by Arthur A. Goren, Oct. 24, 1965, transcript, p. 32 (American Jewish Committee Archives, New York, N.Y.).

29. *Tammany Times*, Dec. 23, 1901, p. 9. On Sullivan's relations with East Side gamblers, see the confidential reports made by Abe Shoenfeld for the New York *Kehillah* in 1912 and 1913, "Case histories of criminals," stories 1–53, SP/126, reel 2434, Correspondence and Reports, New York, N.Y., 1912–1919, Judah L. Magnes Papers (American Jewish Archives, Cincinnati, Ohio). The original papers are housed in Central Archives for the History of the Jewish People, Jerusalem, Israel.

30. On Sullivan's role in Charles F. Murphy's succession, see *New York Times*, Sept. 20, 1902, p. 1; *Tammany Times*, Sept. 27, 1902, p. 1; and Alfred Connable and Edward Silberfarb, *Tigers of Tammany: Nine Men Who Ran New York* (New York, 1967), 238–40. On Murphy, see Nancy Joan Weiss, *Charles Francis Murphy, 1858–1924: Respectability and Responsibility in Tammany Politics* (Northampton, 1968).

31. *New York Times*, March 21, 1905, p. 1. On the origins and growth of the Sullivan-Considine circuit, see *Variety*, Dec. 14, 1907, p. 10. Sullivan endorsed notes for up to $30,000 after the initial $5,000 investment. *Ibid.*, Sept. 19, 1913, p. 7.

32. After Sullivan's death the circuit was bought out by Marcus Loew and his associates for an estimated $1.5 million. See *Variety*, March 13, 1914, p. 5; *ibid.*, March 27, 1914, p. 5; and *ibid.*, April 3, 1914, p. 1. *New York Times*, Feb. 13, 1943, p. 11; David Robinson, *Chaplin: His Life and Art* (New York, 1985), 92–98; Groucho Marx, *Groucho and Me* (New York, 1959), 133–35.

33. For the high concentration of movie shows on the Lower East Side, see Joseph McCoy, "Moving Picture House Census," July 28, 1908, Motion Picture Patents Company Papers (Edison National Historic Site, West Orange, N.J.). See also Robert C. Allen, "Motion Picture Exhibition in Manhattan, 1906–1912," *Cinema Journal*, 18 (Spring 1979), 2–15.

34. On the relationship between small-time vaudeville and the evolution of the movie business, see Robert C. Allen, *Vaudeville and Film, 1895–1915: A Study in Media Interaction* (New York, 1980), 218–44, 310–34. On William Fox and the Sullivans, see *Variety*, July 4, 1908, p. 7; *Moving Picture World*, Dec. 28, 1907, pp. 699–700; Glendon Allvine, *The Greatest Fox of Them All* (New York, 1969), 37–53; and the William Fox Clipping File and City Theatre Clipping File (Theatre Collection, Performing Arts Research Center).

35. On Gustavus A. Rogers, see *Tammany Times*, Dec. 26, 1903, p. 8; *Moving Picture World*, Jan. 4, 1908, p. 7; and *New York Times*, March 20, 1944, p. 19. On Little Tim and Sunday blue laws, see *Moving Picture World*, Dec. 21, 1907, p. 684; *New York Times*, Dec. 11, 1907, p. 1; and *ibid.*, Dec. 18, 1907, p. 1. *New York World*, Dec. 9, 1907, p. 2.

36. On Sullivan's free spending and political charity, see accounts collected in Newspaper Clippings, vol. 1, Sept. 1911–March 1913, Edwin P. Kilroe Papers (Rare Book and Manuscript Library, Butler Library, Columbia University, New York, N.Y.); "The Reminiscences of John T. Hettrick: Interview Conducted by Dean Albertson," 1949, pp. 48, 191 (Oral History Research Office, Butler Library); Roy Crandall, "Tim Sullivan's Power," *Harper's Weekly*, Oct. 18, 1913, 14–15; and Oliver Simmons, "Passing of the Sullivan Dynasty," *Munsey's*, 50 (Dec. 1913), 407–16. Sullivan's illegitimate daughter, Margaret Catherine, was born in 1896 to Margaret A. Holland. She was granted a fifty-thousand-dollar life insurance policy from his estate. See *New York World*, Dec. 10, 1913, p. 1; and *New York Tribune*, Dec. 10, 1913, p. 5.

37. Robert F. Wesser, *A Response to Progressivism: The Democratic Party and New York Politics, 1902–1918* (New York, 1986), 218–19. See also J. Joseph Huthmacher, "Urban Liberalism and the Age of Reform," *Mississippi Valley Historical Review*, 49 (Sept. 1962), 231–41; and John D. Buenker, *Urban Liberalism and Progressive Reform* (New York, 1973). The journalistic tradition in historical writing thoroughly ignored this side of Sullivan's career. See, for example, Alvin F. Harlow, *Old Bowery Days: The Chronicles of a Famous Street* (New York, 1931), 487–528; M. R. Werner, *Tammany Hall* (Garden City, 1928), 497–510.

38. *New York Tribune*, Nov. 3, 1902, p. 2. On Sullivan's interventions in labor disputes at Donnelly's Grove on College Point, Long Island, site of the annual summer chowders, and at Schley's Music Hall on West Thirty-fourth Street, see *Tammany Times*, April 9, 1900, p. 6.

39. Frances Perkins, *The Roosevelt I Knew* (New York, 1946), 12–14. For a contemporary account, see Leroy Scott, "Behind the Rail: Being the Story of a Woman Lobbyist," *Metropolitan Magazine*, 36 (July 1912), 19–20, 52. George Martin, *Madame Secretary: Frances Perkins* (Boston, 1976), 90–100; Wesser, *Response to Progressivism*, 70–75.

40. *Reminiscences of Frances Perkins*, 110.

41. *Ibid.*, 114.

42. *New York Times*, Nov. 7, 1910, p. 4; Nancy F. Cott, *The Grounding of Modern Feminism* (New Haven, 1987), 24; *New York Times*, March 25, 1912, p. 10. Harriot Stanton Blatch recounted Sullivan's support for suffrage legislation in Harriot Stanton Blatch and Alma Lutz, *Challenging Years: The Memoirs of Harriot Stanton Blatch* (New York, 1940), 151–70. On Blatch's contribution to the cause, see Ellen Carol DuBois, "Working Women, Class Relations, and Suffrage Militance: Harriot Stanton Blatch and the New York Woman Suffrage Movement, 1894–1909," *Journal of American History*, 74 (June 1987), 34–58.

43. Blatch and Lutz, *Challenging Years*, 152; Doris Daniels, "Building a Winning Coalition: The Suffrage Fight in New York State," *New York History*, 60 (Jan. 1979), 59–80; John D. Buenker, "The Urban Political Machine and Woman Suffrage," *Historian*, 33 (Feb. 1971), 264–79.

44. *New York Times*, Nov. 7, 1910, p. 4; *ibid.*, Dec. 4, 1910, pt. 5, p. 3. For the debate over the Sullivan Law, which had a diverse coalition behind it, see *ibid.*, May 11, 1911, p. 3; *ibid.*, May 30, 1911, p. 1; and *ibid.*, Sept. 7, 1911, p. 5. On Sullivan's other legislative activity, see *New York Legislative Index, 1909–1912* (New York State Library, Albany).

45. *New York World*, Nov. 1, 1909, p. 4; *New York Times*, Nov. 1, 1909, p. 3; *New York Tribune*, Nov. 1, 1909, p. 4; George Kibbe Turner, "Tammany's Control of New York by Professional Criminals," *McClure's*, 33 (June 1909), 117–34; George Kibbe Turner, "The Daughters of the Poor," *ibid.*, 34 (Nov. 1909), 45–61.

46. New York Supreme Court, County of New York, "In the Matter of the Application for the Appointment of a Committee of the Person and Property of Timothy D. Sullivan," Jan. 24, 1913 (in Timothy P. Sullivan's possession); Dr. William B. Pritchard, Stenographer's Minutes, Sheriff's Jury, Jan. 22, 1913, *ibid.*, Timothy P. Sullivan is the grandson of Little Tim Sullivan and currently deputy clerk of New York County. See also Newspaper Clippings, vol. 2, 1913–1914, Kilroe Papers.

47. *New York Times*, Sept. 10, 1913, p. 1; *ibid.*, Sept. 11, 1913, p. 4; *ibid.*, Sept. 14, 1913, p. 1; *New York World*, Sept. 10, 1913, p. 3; *ibid.*, Sept. 11, 1913, p. 2; *ibid.*, Sept. 14, 1913, p. 1. Despite rumors of foul play, even murder, a coroner's jury ruled Sullivan's death an accident. *New York Times*, Sept. 30, 1913, p. 2.

48. *New York Sun*, Sept. 16, 1913, p. 4; *New York World*, Sept. 14, 1913, p. 2.

49. See Seth Koven and Sonya Michel, "Womanly Duties: Maternalist Politics and the Origins of Welfare States in France, Germany, Great Britain, and the United States, 1880–1920," *American Historical Review*, 95 (Oct. 1990), 1076–1108; and Linda Gordon, "The New Feminist Scholarship on the Welfare State," in *Women, the State, and Welfare*, ed. Linda Gordon (Madison, 1990), 9–35.

Saloonkeepers are notoriously good fellows. On an average they perform vastly greater generosities than do business men. When I simply had to have ten dollars, desperate, with no place to turn, I went to Johnny Heinhold. . . . And yet—and here is the point, the custom, and the code—in the days of my prosperity . . . I have gone out of my way by many a long block to spend across Johnny Heinhold's bar. . . . Not that [he] asked me to do it or expected me to do it. I did it, as I have said, in obedience to the code.

—JACK LONDON[1]

# The "Poor Man's Friend": Saloonkeepers, Workers, and the Code of Reciprocity in U.S. Barrooms, 1870–1920

*Madelon Powers*

The unwritten barroom "code" of which Jack London wrote in 1913 was the code of reciprocity, a centuries-old feature of tavern society that took on an extraordinary new significance in the hands of U.S. saloonkeepers during the turbulent industrializing years between 1870 and 1920. According to this code, men who did each other the honor of drinking together also were expected to celebrate and reinforce their special bond through the swapping of drinks, favors, small loans, and other gestures of mutual assistance and friendship. The saloonkeeper, too, was expected to participate in these rites of reciprocity, treating his regular customers to free drinks and offering other tokens of goodwill, just as tavern proprietors had been doing since colonial times.

*Code of reciprocity*

Yet, the U.S. saloonkeeper after 1870 had one great advantage over his predecessors: The pivotal position he occupied between vote-seeking machine politicians and their liquor-industry allies on the one hand, and the nascent working class with its need for municipal services and assistance on the other. By brokering the interests of these groups in his own little corner of the urban scene, the proprietor of a local saloon could become a key figure in the social, political, and economic affairs of his community. Saloonkeepers, of course, were a varied lot. Some preferred to keep their operations small, informal, and neighborly; others

*position of saloonkeeper*

*Madelon Powers is assistant professor of history at the University of New Orleans. Reprinted from* International Labor and Working-Class History *45 (Spring 1994): 1–15. Reprinted by permission of* International Labor and Working-Class History.

turned their establishments into veritable "reciprocity machines" in which drinks, favors, jobs, and votes were routinely and openly swapped. It was this latter group that particularly outraged the Anti-Saloon League and other temperance advocates, whose campaign against the liquor trade ultimately resulted in the implementation of nationwide prohibition in 1920. In their view, such favor-swapping saloonkeepers were not only peddling the poison of drink, but also perverting the political process and thereby imperiling the very survival of the republic. To workers in great need of small favors, however, the reciprocal arrangement between themselves and their bartenders—rooted in long-standing and venerable barroom tradition—seemed both legitimate and indispensable.[2]

A major reason for the strength of the reciprocal code between saloonkeepers and their customers was their similarity in occupational status, ethnic heritage, and gender identification. As the alcohol industry grew and consolidated in the late 1800s and early 1900s, the majority of urban saloonkeepers changed from being independent proprietors to dependent employees of one of the major breweries such as Pabst, Schlitz, Anheuser-Busch, and Miller. Through what was called the "tied-house" arrangement, the brewery industry gradually gained control of most saloons either through outright ownership or exclusive distributorship rights. Thus, many urban barkeepers by the early 1900s were essentially hired hands, as subject to the directives of their brewery bosses as their wage-earning customers were to their employers. It is true that, once hired, an ambitious barkeeper might cultivate political allies and parlay his plebian post into a position of considerable community influence. In class origin, income, and occupational status, however, most saloonkeepers were not far removed from the circumstances of their customers.[3]

Saloonkeepers often shared the ethnic background of their patrons as well. European immigrants who arrived by the millions in this era usually sought out barrooms which were run and patronized by their fellow countrymen. The man behind the bar who shared the ethnic heritage of his immigrant clientele was able to inspire considerable customer loyalty. Recognizing this fact, both breweries and independent bar owners who did not share the ethnic backgrounds of their clienteles often hired bartenders who did. Settlement worker Robert Woods observed, for example, that while several saloons in Boston's North End were owned by Jews, "Irish and Scandinavian bartenders are employed in them to draw in the trade of the Irish and Scandinavians." Similarly, native-born whites and blacks, especially those migrating from rural areas to northern industrial cities, were drawn to establishments where the clientele, bartender, and social atmosphere were familiar and supportive. This was particularly true of African Americans, who faced severe discrimination from whites in this period. The black saloonkeeper often had influential business and political contacts in the black community, so regular customers in search of advice or favors could turn to him just as immigrants turned to their saloonkeepers in times of need.[4]

A third reason for the affinity between saloonkeepers and their customers was that most were males participating in the predominantly masculine drinking culture of the saloon. The copious drinking, raucous talk, and sometimes obstreperous behavior of male customers, combined with the presence of nude female portraits on the walls, spittoons, mustache towels, and other indelicate bar accessories, meant that the barroom proper was anything but a proper social venue for most respectable working-class women. There were some family-style saloons, though most of these had moved to the suburban districts by the 1890s. In urban areas, some women did enter by the side or "ladies" entrance to proceed to the saloon's back room, where they could consume the "free lunch" (a hearty meal available for the price of a five-cent drink) or accompany their dates to the parties and modest vaudeville shows that were occasionally held there. Others used this same inconspicuous entrance to purchase carry-out beer by the pailful. Sometimes prostitutes might even ply their trade in the back room, though their haunts were usually the low saloons and dives of the worst slum districts.[5]

With these few exceptions, however, the world of the urban working-class saloon was primarily a masculine domain. It was a place where the workingman spent his time "in purely masculine ways . . . untroubled by skirts or domesticity" and received "a hearty recognition of his merits as a man," according to journalists Hutchins Hapgood and George Ade. Furthermore, the saloonkeeper was careful to supply his customers with the amenities of a men's social club. As settlement worker E. C. Moore observed,

> It is the workingman's club. . . . In it he finds more of the things which approximate to luxury than he finds at home, almost more than he finds in any other place in the ward. In winter the saloon is warm, in summer it is cool, at night it is brightly lighted. . . . More than that there are chairs and tables and papers and cards and lunch, and in many cases pool and billiards. . . . What more does the workingman want for his club?[6]

Female saloonkeepers were also a rarity, particularly by the 1890s when commercial, brewery-backed saloons and tougher licensing policies had all but crowded out the informal, unlicensed "kitchen saloons" which immigrant women (often widows) had formerly run in their tenement flats. Nevertheless, there were some women in the late nineteenth and early twentieth centuries who ran barrooms, either by themselves or as part of a mom-and-pop family business. Those in business for themselves often seem to have been very colorful characters indeed, running places with such unforgettable names as "Peckerhead Kate's" in South Chicago, "Indian Sadie's" in Green Bay, and "Big Tit Irene's" in Ashtabula. More commonly, though, saloonkeeping was a male occupation, and both bartenders and bar-goers appear to have zealously supported male-only exclusivity of the barroom proper.[7] Thus, identifying with one another in terms of gender, ethnicity, and economic background, barkeepers and

their regulars developed a sense of commonality and fellowship that
formed the foundation for the reciprocal code of the barroom.

To understand how the code of reciprocity among barkeepers and
customers operated, it is useful to begin with the custom of the treat,
one of the oldest and most widespread features of American drinking
lore.[8] Jack London described how his mastery of treating won him acceptance and cooperation in dozens of workingmen's saloons in the 1890s
and early 1900s. Upon entering a saloon for the first time, London would
approach the bar counter—the center of barroom conviviality—and immediately treat himself to a drink, thereby establishing himself as a
paying customer who understood the drink-buying imperative in every
bar. He then made the strategic move of offering to treat the bartender,
an overture that not only cultivated a valuable ally but also encouraged
the keeper to warm to his time-honored role as public-house host. Next,
London made what he called his "opening query," often a request for
travel information, though the subject of inquiry could have been almost anything. Since colonial times, taverns had traditionally servd as
clearinghouses for all kinds of information, be it local lore and gossip,
political news, job opportunities, sporting-event updates, or any other
topic of current interest. Counting on this as well as the barkeeper's
treat-induced good will, London posed his question and waited. Then,
as the motivated bartender fielded the question among regulars in the
know, London knew his chance was at hand to gain full welcome to the
club. He offered to treat those who offered to help him. And, unless they
were hopeless barroom boors, he knew that they would feel inclined—
indeed, obligated—to return the favor through the friendly exchange of
more information and reciprocal treating. In this way, London was able
to employ the treating ritual as a social catalyst that seldom failed him.
In his words, "I was no longer a stranger in any town the moment I had
entered a saloon."[9]

As London's example indicates, the first rule of barroom treating
was that the recipient was expected to reciprocate, in drinks or favors
or some other mutually acceptable manner. The term "treat" is somewhat misleading in this regard, for it tends to imply a one-way favor,
and language purists might wish that saloon-goers had used the more
precise term "reciprocal treat." But bar folk well knew the point of honor
involved in accepting a treat, according to London. As he remarked of
another drinking episode involving a friend and some regulars in the
National Saloon in Oakland, California, "They treated, and we drank.
Then, according to the code of drinking, we had to treat."[10]

Treating the bartender at first glance might appear a peculiar custom, since he had easy access to the bar stock and could presumably
help himself to free drinks whenever he chose. For many barkeepers,
however, their "first rule of conduct was not to do any nipping while 'on
watch,'" according to George Ade. This claim was corroborated by George
Washington Plunkitt, a powerful Tammany machine politician in New
York who often dealt with bar owners in organizing the saloon vote. In
Plunkitt's words, "The most successful saloonkeepers don't drink them-

selves and they understand that my temperance is a business proposition, just like their own." Furthermore, many bar owners strictly forbade their employees to imbibe on the job, under threat of immediate dismissal.[11] Oddly enough, then, the bartender, who was seemingly in the best position to drink freely and for free, was oftentimes the one person not drinking at all—not unless, that is, he was offered a treat.

For the bartender, just as for any other barroom denizen, a treat was an offer he could not refuse. This lesson was learned the hard way by Rumanian immigrant M. E. Ravage when he began tending bar for one Mr. Weiss in New York in the early 1900s. "From him I first learned . . . that bar-men never drink," Ravage stated, "except at a customers' invitation, which is another story and is governed by a special ethical rule." Yet, though the young bartender had been told to accept customer's treats, he was reluctant to comply. He disliked beer and detested whiskey, the two drinks most commonly consumed in saloons and most often involved in treating. To resolve his dilemma, he suggested to one of his customers that the man simply give him the money for the treat instead. In terms of drinking tradition, however, Ravage had refused a treat, a grave personal affront to the customer. In addition, he had had the audacity to suggest money in place of drink, an action that struck both his customer and his boss as a baldly mercenary, unsociable solicitation for personal gain. Moreover, because the treat was supposed to be rung up on the cash register like any other sale, he had in effect proposed robbing the proprietor of his drink-selling revenue. Ravage might have lost his job over this egregious violation of the "special ethnical rule" that governed bartenders and treating, except that Mrs. Weiss intervened on his behalf. Thereafter, however, "My employer constantly impressed it upon me that it was my duty to his firm to accept every treat that was offered me," Ravage reported. "It pleased the customer, he explained, and it increased the sales."[12] Thus, the bartender, who often was forbidden to drink on his own during business hours, could accept a drink—indeed, was obligated to accept—when a customer invoked the ritual of the treat.

Had Ravage but known, there were some diplomatic dodges that the saloonkeeper could employ to give the appearance of accepting a treat without actually imbibing large quantities of alcohol. He might take a cigar instead, which was acceptable because it cost the same as beer (generally five cents), and because treating with tobacco was regarded as a sociable and roughly comparable gesture to treating with alcohol. Otherwise, if a customer insisted the bartender drink with him, he might use a special glass called a "snit," which according to Ade was "about the size of an eyecup and the supposed drink was all foam." Snits and cigars enabled the bartender to fulfill the requirements of treating tradition without incapacitating himself or insulting his customer. Such ruses point up the highly symbolic nature of barroom treating. The customer could make the offer, the bartender could pretend to accept, and both were satisfied as long as the spirit, if not actually the letter, of treating law was observed.[13]

It also was customary for the bartender to treat big spenders and particularly his regulars from time to time, to cultivate goodwill and to reciprocate treats offered him. "Once in so often, if a group of enthusiastic buyers had been pushing important money across the moist mahogany," observed Ade, the barkeeper "was expected to announce, smilingly and suavely, 'Gents, this one is on the house,' thereby establishing himself as one of nature's noblemen." A bartender might also treat his customers on special occasions, such as St. Patrick's Day. As Arizona saloonkeeper George Hand remarked in his diary entry for March 17, 1875, "Treated all the boys. Everyone drunk. . . . Got tight myself." Another Arizona bartender, M. E. Joyce of the Oriental Saloon in Tombstone, made a daily ritual of treating and storytelling. First he treated his morning customers to a round and a joke; after that, he reciprocated each customer's offer to treat with another anecdote, and so on all day until well past midnight.[14]

Temperance advocates complained that such treating by bartenders was simply a ploy to entice and obligate customers to spend extravagantly, particularly when business was bad. As reformer Robert Bagnell asserted, "often when the sales lag the saloon keeper himself treats to start business going again."[15] In some cases the saloonkeeper's treating may have been done for the sole purpose of promoting sales, but the congenial relationship that usually obtained between him and his regulars makes the bald profit motive an unlikely sole explanation. Rather, such treating was just as often motivated by the same code of reciprocity that obtained among the regulars.

In addition to social and economic motives, the saloonkeeper often had strong political motives for treating his clientele to drinks and other favors. In New York, Chicago, San Francisco, and many other urban areas, saloonkeepers depended on the goodwill of voters to elect sympathetic machine politicians, who in turn would fight temperance advocates attempting to restrict or shut down saloonkeepers. Politicians, once in office, depended on saloonkeepers (and the powerful liquor industry behind them) to contribute to their campaign coffers and to help deliver the saloon vote at election time. Saloon-going voters, meanwhile, depended on ward politicians to secure them jobs and licenses, to bail them out of jail when necessary, and to perform various other favors, as well as to keep saloonkeepers in business by blocking passage and enforcement of temperance legislation.[16]

Saloons and politics were so thoroughly intertwined that many saloonkeepers themselves became machine politicians, such as Michael "Hinky Dink" Kenna, who ran a Chicago barroom significantly called the "Workingmen's Exchange" and, with his partner, "Bathhouse John" Coughlin, ran much of Chicago as well from the 1890s to the late 1930s.[17] Many other political machines utilized saloons as their headquarters, including the Tammany organization in New York and Christopher "The Blind Boss" Buckley of San Francisco, whose Alhambra Saloon back room was dubbed "Buckley's City Hall." In cities nationwide, then, the saloon was a principal arena of local politics, with the saloonkeeper serving as

liaison and power broker between the machine politicians and the barroom voters. As Raymond Calkins observed, "By his position he is a
leader. He is the man to whom the politicians must go before the realization of his schemes. If there is any bribery, it concerns the saloonkeeper, who is asked to treat 'the boys' in return. Such are the varied
functions of the barkeeper; such is his social position; such is his
influence."[18]

Reformers charged that the politically motivated treat was a bribe
and that workers were being tricked and manipulated in a gross perver-
sion of the American political process. In the context of drinking tradition and symbolism, however, the barkeeper's treat was more accurately
a bid for fellowship and favor swapping, something that bar-goers did
among themselves all the time. Workers did not regard this use of treating as dishonorable or perverse, nor did it seem that they were being
defrauded or duped. On the contrary, the treat sealed a pact between
political leader and constituent that each would contribute and derive
something of value from the arrangement. It was not subversion or trick-
ery at all, but rather a very practical and mutually beneficial implementation of the barroom ideal of reciprocity.[19]

The unwritten code of reciprocity also governed workers' use of the
saloonkeepers' celebrated free lunch. While the notion of serving food
in drinking establishments was by no means new in the saloon period,
the idea of serving it on a massive scale using the latest marketing
and distribution techniques was most definitely an innovation of late-
nineteenth-century industrial capitalism. In what amounted to one of
the most successful public relations schemes of the era, the powerful
liquor industry used its resources and connections to supply barkeepers
with vast quantities of food at extremely low prices. As a result, in barrooms from San Francisco to New York, any poor man who bought at
least one five-cent beer could then help himself to whatever "free" edibles
the proprietor had to offer. By deftly combining age-old tavern tradition
with modern marketing techniques, the saloon trade was able to provide an almost gratis repast that swiftly became the chief daytime food
source for much of the working class of America.[20]

Though the liquor trade performed an essential role in procuring
cheap, plentiful footstuffs, the resounding success of the free-lunch idea
ultimately depended on the workingman's voluntary cooperation and
sense of fair play. In fact, most bar-going folk appear to have observed
an unwritten code of honor when it came to buying the requisite drink
and monitoring how much food they consumed for their nickel. The
saloonkeeper trusted his regulars not to take unfair advantage, in return for which they expected him to let them eat in peace. So pervasive
was this atmosphere of mutual trust that even gourmands were usually
persuaded to exercise some restraint. "It is only the man who comes
seldom or evidently comes for the lunch alone who need fear the eye of
the bartender," as Raymond Calkins explained. "However, there is a kind
of etiquette about the use of the free lunch which acts as a corrective to
the greed of some patrons."[21]

Temperance advocates, who in the 1880s had themselves demanded that barrooms offer food to counteract the intoxicating effects of alcohol, understandably were bewildered and appalled when the liquor industry responded by creating the tremendously popular free lunch. Some tried to discredit the custom by pointing out the mercenary motives of saloonkeepers who required the poor and hungry to buy drinks for the privilege of eating. Ironically, however, this policy of offering the free lunch primarily as a business proposition was probably one of its most appealing features to working people too proud to countenance outright charity. They knew a nickel was obviously just a token amount to pay for such bounty, and yet because it did cost them something, the deadly stigma of the handout was avoided. As Royal Melendy remarked of the saloon free lunch, "The general appearance of abundance, so lacking in their homes or in the cheap restaurants, and the absence of any sense of charity, so distasteful to the self-respecting man, add to the attractiveness of the place."[22]

To promote the loyalty of local residents toward his barroom, the saloonkeeper often extended special financial privileges to the steadiest members of his neighborhood clientele. A great many workingmen relied on saloonkeepers to cash their paychecks, with the understanding that they would purchase a drink or two to repay the favor. For example, a manufacturer in Joliet, Illinois, stated in 1908 that of the 3,600 paychecks his firm issued on one payday, 3,599 came back with a saloonkeeper's endorsement (the last one having been cashed in a grocery store selling liquor). It is probably true that this check-cashing custom was the cause of much unconscionable extravagance in saloons on payday. Yet, it is also important to note that banks were usually located miles from the factory districts and that many workers, especially first-generation immigrants, found the stiff institutionalism of banks confusing and intimidating. As Peter Roberts noted in his 1904 study of coal-mining communities in Pennsylvania, the company "pays the laborer and the saloon serves a useful purpose by accommodating these men with change." Thus, the saloon acted as the poor man's bank. Moreover, some workers exercised greater restraint than temperance advocates often gave them credit for. From reports on workers' household budgets in South Chicago, New York City, and Homestead, Pennsylvania, for example, it appears that a customary practice among many married men was to cash their paychecks in the saloon, go home and turn over the majority to their wives, and then return to the saloon with a moderate drinking allowance.[23]

Saloonkeepers also frequently permitted regulars to establish a credit account or "tick" (short for "ticket"), an account which they were honorbound to pay down as soon as they were able. In one Pennsylvania coal-mining town, for instance, Roberts asked a local proprietor what he did to encourage steady patronage. "His answer was, 'I keep good stuff, give good measure, keep a clean place and sell on tick.'" In saloon parlance, the privilege of drinking on credit was known as "getting trusted," a significant thing in the lives of the working poor. Furthermore, a man temporarily short of cash could always treat his neighbors to a friendly round and thereby maintain his status in the community. In the eyes of many reformers, this credit arrangement constituted an insidious trap to encourage extravagance and indebtedness, but to the bar-going worker, the fact that "the saloonkeeper trusts him for drinks" represented both a privilege and "a debt of honor," as E. C. Moore observed.[24]

*bar credit*

Not only credit accounts, but small loans were a method by which the saloonkeeper courted and rewarded the loyalty of his neighborhood customers. For example, when Jack London was flat broke, he often turned to Johnny Heinhold, the proprietor of the Last Chance Saloon in Oakland, California, for loans "without interest, without security, without buying a drink." This was in sharp contrast to the only other place London knew to borrow money, his neighborhood barber shop, where he was charged five percent interest every month until the loan was repaid. Royal Melendy noted a similar philosophy underlying the loans extended to neighborhood customers in Chicago saloons in 1900. "No questions are asked about the 'deserving poor'; no 'work test' is applied; and again and again relief is given in the shape of money, 'loaned expecting no return.' " But, of course, there was a return: the future patronage of a grateful customer.[25]

*small loans*

Saloonkeepers, particularly those with political ambitions, sometimes extended outright charity to needy families in the neighborhood even if the recipients were not regular patrons of their saloons. In 1897, for example, Moody Morton, a printer by trade, learned that the family of an ailing workman in his neighborhood was in desperate need of assistance, and so Morton suggested to his wife and a family friend that they solicit help from the Associated Charities. The friend contended, however, that from the charity organizations they would receive "nothing but red tape and blanks and tracts and references," and instead said, "I'd rather call on a few saloon keepers. They'll do more and do it quick." Deciding to try both avenues, Mrs. Morton and her friend went to the Associated Charities while Mr. Morton approached several local merchants, including saloonkeepers. "So we separate, and the ladies have just the experience predicted," reported Morton, "while I secure . . . a sack of flour from one grocer, bacon and coffee from another, and money from several liquor dealers." This duty of saloonkeepers to act as the "poor man's friend" in their districts was confirmed by a New York proprietor in 1909. "Whenever a case of distress became known in my neighborhood, it was to my place that the first appeal was made." Through such charitable gestures, the barkeeper earned the goodwill of his community and increased the loyalty of his regular customers.[26]

*charity*

In addition to performing favors for individuals and families, saloonkeepers assisted workers' organizations through the offer of their back rooms as meeting space. Many places had at least one such room, and a few featured several that might also be located behind, beside, above, or in the basement below the barroom. Sometimes customers used the back room for gathering informally in order to chat, play games, consume the free lunch, or attend parties or shows. More often,

*union organizing*

however, this space was utilized by more formally organized groups that required a gathering space with more privacy than was possible in the barroom. As Raymond Calkins observed,

> A serious difficulty which confronts all the clubs of the working people is the lack of suitable club-rooms. . . . It is just here that the saloon makes its appeal. . . . Here groups are naturally formed from among those habitually meeting in the same place. Hither groups already formed come to meet because they have no other shelter. The saloon has been quick to see its advantage and to make the most of it. The process by which its hold is increased through the club instinct which it fosters and satisfies is an interesting study.[27]

With few other affordable facilities available to them, working-class groups of all varieties and persuasions depended on the saloon premises to accommodate them. According to Melendy, the back rooms of thousands of Chicago saloons hosted such groups as trade unions, fraternal organizations, political clubs, and even wedding parties. "It is, in very truth, a part of the life of the people of this district," he concluded. Similarly, Calkins noted that the Casino Saloon in New York City hosted twenty-eight groups each week in its back room, supplying mailboxes for their correspondence and encouraging them to display members' photographs on the walls. Thomas I. Kidd, secretary of the Amalgamated Wood Workers in 1900, summed up the place of saloons in workers' lives as follows:

> This institution is looked upon by the vast majority of workingmen as their club. When out of employment the workingman can get a free lunch and meet a congenial soul to cheer him in the saloon when there is nothing but discouragement for him elsewhere. Probably seventy-five per cent of our unions meet in halls in the rear or over saloons.[28]

Still, the saloonkeeper was a businessman, and his back room, a valuable commodity, was not to be had for free. According to an unwritten but widely honored rule, each member of a workers' group was duty-bound to contribute a minimum of five cents—though more commonly ten to twenty cents—toward the purchase of alcohol, usually beer, for consumption during the meeting. By this scheme, the saloonkeeper was assured of compensation by his profit on beer sales, while the workers were assured of meeting space. "For example," noted Melendy in Chicago in 1900, "a certain German musical society, occupying one of these rooms, fully compensates the saloonkeeper with the money that passes over the bar as the members go in and out of the club-room." Calkins reported in 1901 that the secretary of a 250-member trade union estimated "that probably on an average the members would drink two glasses of beer per meeting," amounting to sales of about twenty-five dollars per week for the saloonkeeper. Even more lucrative were the revenues from clubs associated with the socialist labor movement. "They gather each evening and on Sunday by the hundred," reported Calkins, "Their meeting-place, like that of all the other clubs of which we have spoken, is often in or over the saloon, where they are expected to 'drop' fifteen or twenty cents a night per member." Sometimes the proprietor also charged a small rental fee for the room, but the custom of club members "dropping" some change in the saloon that hosted them was always the centerpiece of the arrangement.[29]

How powerful the pressure was on club members to uphold their share of the group's drink-buying obligation was illustrated by the remarks of a Chicago labor leader, himself an abstainer, interviewed by Melendy in 1901:

> Mr. Thomas J. Morgan, speaking of the early days of the Socialist Labor Party, said that for years they met in the back room of a saloon, the churches and schoolhouses being closed against them, and that he felt a sensation akin to shame coming over him as night after night he passed the bar without paying his 5 cents for a drink.[30]

And shame he should have felt, for in the context of barroom society, he was a freeloader and a welsher on a deal. The saloon clubroom was "free" only in the sense that the free lunch was free: A customer who honored the barroom imperative of drink buying was welcome to enjoy the facilities. The same rule applied to organized groups, and each member knew that it was a matter of honor to uphold the code of reciprocity by paying his share to his brothers' keeper.

Though the relationship between saloonkeepers and their working-class customers was mutually beneficial in many respects, it was not without problems. Some of the difficulties were related to changes in the saloon trade at the turn of the twentieth century. As the breweries continued to seize control of saloons, they hired a legion of inexperienced bartenders who often had neither respect nor flair for the art of saloonkeeping. Meanwhile, the higher licensing fees and taxes demanded by antisaloon groups had the result of pushing many older, more respectable proprietors to the brink of desperation and bankruptcy. "We rented the rooms up-stairs to women, and have gambling wheels, and sell all the liquor we can to anybody who wants it, just to keep from going broke," one harried saloonkeeper admitted. "Don't think we're doing all those things because we like it. I wish to God we didn't have to do them."[31] As competition rose and competence and respectability fell, both the role and character of the typical saloonkeeper began to deteriorate.

Equally important was the growing self-sufficiency of the working class itself in the early 1900s. As marriage rates rose, housing improved, and new entertainments like movie theaters and ballparks proliferated, workers were less dependent on the saloon as a refuge from the raw urban-industrial environment. An increasing number of lodges and social clubs offered an alternative source of financial help in the form of insurance and mutual aid benefits.[32] Perhaps most important, the labor movement was beginning to distance itself from the saloon, the saloonkeeper, and his political cronies. The barman who used his political and business contacts to provide jobs and other favors to customers had performed a valuable service when workers were disorganized and desperate. As the union movement grew, however, workers became better able to deal directly and collectively with employers, thereby lessening the need for a bartending middleman whose powerful friends might not always have labor's best interests at heart. Indeed, as more labor candidates ran for municipal office, they began criticizing entrenched machine politicians for caring more for corrupt business schemes than for the welfare of workers. As the twentieth century began, the graft, fraud, and bribery trials of such saloon-connected politicians as Boss Abraham Ruef of the Union Labor party in San Francisco tended to bear out the labor candidates' accusations.[33]

After 1900, an increasing number of labor leaders, such as Samuel Gompers of the American Federation of Labor, supported the idea of worker temperance (though not necessarily abstinence or prohibition) and believed that organized laborers needed more clear heads, steady hands, and sober surroundings to achieve their goals. Many workers apparently agreed, for a growing number of unions began establishing their own independent headquarters, a trend also observable among some fraternal organizations and other workers' groups.[34] For the saloon-keeper, the loss of liquor sales was problematic, but even more serious was the loss of influence and prestige when he could no longer depend on playing host to the workingman's club life. He might still have his loyal circle of customers, but his formerly powerful role in the working-class community was diminishing.

Before nationwide prohibition took effect in 1920, however, the barkeeper had managed to uphold the code of reciprocity and serve the many needs of his working-class constituency remarkably well. "He has often been called the 'poor man's friend,' and his place the 'poor man's club,' and I must say there is a kernel of truth in this," as one proprietor remarked in 1909.[35] It is important to keep in mind that the barman was first and foremost a businessman selling liquor for profit. That he also provided a wide array of comforts and services that for decades were not readily available to workers elsewhere is a revealing commentary on the condition of American society in its industrializing phase. To be sure, many criticisms could be made of the saloonkeeper's makeshift efforts to provide a workingman's employment bureau, union headquarters, political action center, immigrant way station, banking and credit agency, and neighborhood charity dispensary. Imperfect as his efforts were, though, the "poor man's friend" filled a void in workers' lives until better solutions could be devised.

NOTES

1. Jack London, *John Barleycorn: Alcoholic Memoirs* (1913; reprint, Santa Cruz, Calif., 1981), 206–7.

2. Scholarly studies of the workingmen's saloon in the late nineteenth and early twentieth centuries include Madelon Mae Powers, "Faces Along the Bar: Lore and Order in the Workingman's Saloon, 1870–1920" (Ph.D. diss., University of California, Berkeley, 1991); Perry R. Duis, *The Saloon: Public Drinking in Chicago and Boston, 1880–1920* (Urbana, 1983); Roy Rosenzweig, *Eight Hours for What We Will: Workers and Leisure in an Industrial City, 1870–1920* (New York, 1983); Thomas J. Noel, *The City and the Saloon: Denver, 1858–1916* (Lincoln, Nebr., 1982); and Elliott West, *The Saloon on the Rocky Mountain Mining Frontier* (Lincoln, Nebr., 1979). Detailed accounts of saloons by men who witnessed them firsthand include George Ade, *The Old-Time Saloon: Not Wet—Not Dry, Just History* (New York, 1931);

Raymond Calkins, ed., *Substitutes for the Saloon* (Boston, 1901); and London, *John Barleycorn*. Regarding the temperance movement during the saloon period, some of the most useful studies include Jack S. Blocker, Jr., *American Temperance Movements: Cycles of Reform* (Boston, 1989); Harry Gene Levine, "The Discovery of Addiction: Changing Conceptions of Habitual Drunkenness in America," *Journal of Studies on Alcohol* 39 (January 1978): 143–74; Norman H. Clark, *Deliver Us from Evil: An Interpretation of American Prohibition* (New York, 1976); James H. Timberlake, *Prohibition and the Progressive Movement, 1900–1920* (New York, 1970); Joseph R. Gusfield, *Symbolic Crusade: Status Politics and the American Temperance Movement* (Urbana, 1963); and Peter H. Odegard, *Pressure Politics: The Story of the Anti-Saloon League* (New York, 1928).

3. By 1909, the major brewing companies owned or controlled approximately 70 percent of the saloons nationwide, according to Timberlake, *Prohibition and the Progressive Movement*, 104–6. The impact of the tied-house system on the occupation of saloonkeeping is analyzed in Duis, *The Saloon*, 15–45. The working-class origin and orientation of most barkeepers is discussed in Rosenzweig, *Eight Hours for What We Will*, 52–53.

4. Robert A. Woods, *Americans in Process: A Settlement Study* (Boston, 1902), 201. For more discussion of immigrants and urban saloons, see Duis, *The Saloon*, 143–57, 160–71; Rosenzweig, *Eight Hours for What We Will*, 49–53, 55; Noel, *The City and the Saloon*, 9, 19–21; and William Kornblum, *Blue Collar Community* (Chicago, 1974), 77–79. The relationship between African Americans and their urban saloons is discussed in Duis, 157–60.

5. Royal L. Melendy, "The Saloon in Chicago: Part I," *American Journal of Sociology* 6 (November 1900): 298, 299, 303–4; Dorothy Richardson, "The Long Day: The Story of a New York Working Girl (1905)," in *Women at Work*, ed. William L. O'Neill (Chicago, 1972), 257–59, 287; Kathy Peiss, *Cheap Amusements: Working Women and Leisure in Turn-of-the-Century New York* (Philadelphia, 1986), 90–93; "The Experience and Observations of a New York Saloon-Keeper as Told by Himself," *McClure's Magazine* 32 (January 1909): 311; Calkins, *Substitutes for the Saloon*, 15. For my assessment of the few scattered references I have found regarding women in saloons, see Madelon Powers, "Rooftop Parties and Backroom Trysts: Women, Public Drinking, and Working-Class Saloons, 1890–1920" (unpublished paper, 1993).

6. Hutchins Hapgood, "McSorley's Saloon," *Harper's Weekly* (October 25, 1913): 15; Ade, *Old-Time Saloon*, 101; E. C. Moore, "The Social Value of the Saloon," *American Journal of Sociology* 3 (July 1897): 4–5.

7. Rosenzweig, *Eight Hours for What We Will*, 40–45; Kornblum, *Blue Collar Community*, 76.

8. "The roots of the [treating] custom can be traced as far back as the wassail bowl and loving cup of the fifth-century Saxons, and beyond them to practices of the Egyptians and Assyrians," according to West, *Saloon on the Rocky Mountain Mining Frontier*, 93–94. See also, Frederick W. Hackwood, *Inns, Ales, and Drinking Customs of Old England* (New York, 1909), 141–52. For a comprehensive account of taverns and drinking customs in cultures worldwide over the centuries, see Robert E. Popham, "The Social History of the Tavern," in *Research Advances in Alcohol and Drug Problems*, vol. 4, ed. Yedy Israel et al. (New York, 1978), 225–302.

9. London, *John Barleycorn*, 122–23. For a discussion of the tavernkeeper's traditional role as a hospitable and knowledgeable host, see Popham, "Social History of the Tavern," 261–63, 271–74, 284–86.

10. London, *John Barleycorn*, 184.

11. Ade, *Old-Time Saloon*, 96–97; George Washington Plunkitt, quoted in William L. Riordon, *Plunkitt of Tammany Hall* (1905; reprint, New York, 1963), 77–78; "Experience and Observations of a New York Saloon-Keeper," 304.

12. M. E. Ravage, *An American in the Making: The Life Story of an Immigrant* (New York, 1917), 125–27.

13. Ade, *Old-Time Saloon*, 95. Frontier bartenders who appeared to keep up with their customers drink for drink "perhaps were employing a familiar deception by drawing upon a bottle of colored water," according to West, *Saloon on the Rocky Mountain Mining Frontier*, 61.

14. Ade, *Old Time Saloon*, 96; George Hand and M. E. Joyce, quoted in West, *Saloon on the Rocky Mountain Mining Frontier*, 60–61.

15. Robert Bagnell, *Economic and Moral Aspects of the Liquor Business* (New York, 1911), 22.

16. For an analysis of machine politicians' methods, see Harold Zink, *City Bosses in the United States: A Study of Twenty Municipal Bosses* (Durham, N.C., 1930), 194–201. Also informative is William L. Riordon, "When Tammany Was Supreme," introduction to Riordon, *Plunkitt of Tammany Hall*, vii–xxii.

17. Lloyd Wendt and Herman Kogan, *Bosses of Lusty Chicago: The Story of Bathhouse John and Hinky Dink* (Bloomington, 1967), v–xiv. This work was originally published in 1943

as *Lords of the Levée*. Michael Kenna acquired the nickname "Hinky Dink" because of his diminutive size; John Joseph Coughlin was known as "Bathhouse John" because he started out as a Chicago bathhouse "rubber" and later acquired a string of his own establishments. For a photograph of Kenna's saloon, the Workingmen's Exchange, see George Kibbe Turner, "The City of Chicago: A Study of the Great Immoralities," *McClure's Magazine* 28 (April 1907): 577. For statistics on the deep involvement of saloonkeepers and saloons in urban politics, see Odegard, *Pressure Politics*, 248.

18. William A. Bullough, *The Blind Boss and His City: Christopher Augustine Buckley and Nineteenth-Century San Francisco* (Berkeley, 1979), 139–40; Calkins, *Substitutes for the Saloon*, 11, 371–72.

19. "To the slum dweller and especially to the recent immigrant, machine politicians often seemed the only persons in the community who took a positive interest in their plight. . . . Perhaps most important of all, they gave the slum dweller a certain sense of power, the dignity of knowing that he counted, that at least his vote was worth something." John A. Garraty, *The New Commonwealth, 1877–1890* (New York, 1968), 218.

20. For more information on the free lunch, see Calkins, *Substitutes for the Saloon*, 15–19; Duis, *The Saloon*, 52–56; Richardson, "The Long Day," 257–59; Ade, *Old-Time Saloon*, 34–38.

21. Calkins, *Substitutes for the Saloon*, 16–17; Ade, *Old-Time Saloon*, 36–37.

22. Melendy, "Saloon in Chicago," 297. For more on the reaction of reformers to the free lunch and their efforts (mostly failures) to establish "tea saloons" to replace the food-dispensing role of barrooms, see Calkins, *Substitutes for the Saloon*, 15, 221–24.

23. Odegard, *Pressure Politics*, 45; Garraty, *New Commonwealth*, 202; Peter Roberts, *Anthracite Coal Communities* (New York, 1904), 236; Kornblum, *Blue Collar Community*, 75; Peiss, *Cheap Amusements*, 23; Margaret F. Byington, *Homestead: The Households of a Mill Town* (1910; reprint, Pittsburgh, 1974), 154–55.

24. Roberts, *Anthracite Coal Communities*, 236; Calkins, *Substitutes for the Saloon*, 11; Moore, "Social Value of the Saloon," 8.

25. London, *John Barleycorn*, 206–17; Melendy, "Saloon in Chicago," 297.

26. Moody Morton, "Man's Inhumanity to Man Makes Countless Thousands Mourn," *The Trestle Board* 11 (April 1897): 180; "Experience and Observations of a New York Saloon-Keeper," 310.

27. Calkins, *Substitutes for the Saloon*, 46–47.

28. Melendy, "Saloon in Chicago," 295; Calkins, *Substitutes for the Saloon*, 62; Thomas I. Kidd, quoted in Edward W. Bemis, "Attitude of the Trade Unions Toward the Saloon," in Calkins, Appendix I, 312.

29. Melendy, "Saloon in Chicago," 295; Calkins, *Substitutes for the Saloon*, 55–56, 62.

30. Thomas J. Morgan, quoted in Royal L. Melendy, "The Saloon in Chicago: Part II," *American Journal of Sociology* 6 (January 1901): 438.

31. Duis, *The Saloon*, 73–76; "Jerry," a New York bartender, quoted in Frederick C. Howe, *The Confessions of a Reformer* (1925; reprint, New York, 1974), 51–52.

32. The percentage of single men fifteen years of age and older decreased from 40.2 percent in 1900 to 38.7 percent in 1910 and then to 35.1 percent in 1920. U.S. Bureau of the Census, *Population, 1920*, vol. 2 (Washington, D.C., 1922), 387. For a discussion of improvements in tenement housing, public parks, and other urban facilities, see Paul Boyer, *Urban Masses and Moral Order in America, 1820–1920* (Cambridge, Mass., 1978), 233–51. Regarding the competition that saloons faced from movies, see Robert Sklar, *Movie-Made America: A Social History of American Movies* (New York, 1975), 3–17; from stadiums and playgrounds, see Gunther Barth, *City People: The Rise of Modern City Culture in Nineteenth-Century America* (New York, 1980), 148–91. The growth of lodges and social clubs offering financial assistance to members is discussed in Mark C. Carnes, *Secret Ritual and Manhood in Victorian America* (New Haven, 1989), 8–9.

33. The prosecution of Boss Abraham Ruef and revelations about his betrayal of laborers' interests are detailed in Walton Bean, *Boss Ruef's San Francisco: The Story of the Union Labor Party, Big Business, and the Graft Prosecution* (Berkeley, 1952), 256–60. For more discussion of organized labor's problems with saloons and saloon-keepers, see David Brundage, "The Producing Classes and the Saloon: Denver in the 1880s," *Labor History* 26 (Winter 1985): 44–47; Timberlake, *Prohibition and the Progressive Movement*, 83–84; Calkins, *Substitutes for the Saloon*, 56–63.

34. For an analysis of the labor movement's support for temperance, though not necessarily abstinence or prohibition, see Ronald Morris Benson, "American Workers and Temperance Reform, 1866–1933" (Ph.D. diss., University of Notre Dame, 1974). Regarding the trend toward establishing independent union halls, see Bemis, "Attitude of the Trade Unions Toward the Saloon," 303–13.

35. "Experience and Observations of a New York Saloon-Keeper," 310.

# Leisure and Labor

*Kathy Peiss*

After ten or twelve hours a day bending over a sewing machine, standing at a sales counter, or waiting on tables, what energy could a turn-of-the-century working woman muster to attend a dance hall or amusement park? Quite a lot, according to the testimony of employers, journalists, and the wage-earners themselves. "Blue Monday" plagued employers. The head of a dressmaking shop, for example, observed that her employees "all took Sunday for a gala day and not as a day of rest. They worked so hard having a good time all day, and late into the evening, that they were 'worn to a frazzle' when Monday morning came." On week nights, working women hurriedly changed from work clothes to evening finery. Said one saleswoman, "You see some of those who have complained about standing spend most of the evening in dancing." The training supervisor at Macy's agreed, noting in exasperation, "We see that all the time in New York—many of the employees having recreation at night that unfits them for work the next day."[1]

Young, unmarried working-class women, foreign-born or daughters of immigrant parents, dominated the female labor force in the period from 1880 to 1920. In 1900, four-fifths of the 343,000 wage-earning women in New York were single, and almost one-third were aged sixteen to twenty. Whether supporting themselves or, more usually, contributing to the family economy, most girls expected to work at some time in their teens. Nearly 60 percent of all women in New York aged sixteen to twenty worked in the early 1900s. For many young women, wage earning became an integral part of the transition from school to marriage.[2]

Women labored for wages throughout the nineteenth century, but by the 1890s, the context in which they worked differed from that of the Victorian era. New jobs in department stores, large factories, and offices provided alternatives to domestic service, household production,

*Kathy Peiss is professor of history at the University of Massachusetts at Amherst. Reprinted from Kathy Peiss,* Cheap Amusements: Working Women and Leisure in Turn-of-the-Century New York *(Temple University Press, 1986), 34–55. Copyright 1986 by Temple University Press. Reprinted by permission of Temple University Press.*

and sweated labor in small shops, which had dominated women's work earlier. These employment opportunities, the changing organization of work, and the declining hours of labor altered the relationship between work and leisure, shaping the way in which leisure time was structured and experienced. The perception of leisure as a separate sphere of independence, youthful pleasure, and mixed-sex fun, in opposition to the world of obligation and toil, was supported by women's experience in the workplace. Far from inculcating good business habits, discipline, and a desire for quiet evenings at home, the workplace reinforced the wage-earner's interest in having a good time. Earning a living, an economic necessity for most young working-class women, was also a cultural experience organizing and defining their leisure activities.

## Women's Work in the Victorian City

In the late nineteenth century, New York's economic landscape was crowded with flourishing commercial enterprises, a thriving port, manufacturing lofts, and workshops. New York achieved prominence early in the century as the leading mercantile city in the United States, ensuring its primacy in commerce, shipping, and finance by dominating the Atlantic trade and developing transportation links to the hinterlands. By the Civil War, New York led the country in manufacturing, its strength lying in the garment trades, tobacco-processing and cigar-making, printing and publishing, metal-working, and furniture- and piano-making. Manufacturing was spurred by commercial trade, with merchant capitalists developing products such as ready-made clothing for the national market. Other types of business were developed to answer the clamor for goods and services arising from the city's burgeoning population. Unlike many American cities, where the age of industry was characterized by huge, mechanized factories, the city's high rental costs, cheap immigrant labor supply, and lack of a good energy source led to a myriad of small, highly specialized shops.[3]

This expanding mercantile and manufacturing economy brought many young women into the labor force after 1840, but not primarily as "mill girls" or factory hands, as was the case in cities where capital-intensive industries flourished. The majority of women workers in Victorian New York labored as domestic servants, needlewomen, laundresses, and in other employments seemingly marginal to an industrial economy.[4] As late as 1880, 40 percent of all New York working women were in domestic service, an experience particularly common among adolescent Irish and German girls. Home-based occupations and street trades, such as keeping boarders, washing laundry, cleaning, ragpicking, and peddling, provided necessary income for poor working-class wives and widows. In manufacturing, New York women were concentrated in the needle trades, with over one-fifth working as dressmakers, tailors, and milliners in 1880. In these years, garments were produced in small workshops or in the home. Even after the introduction of the sewing machine, much of the clothing trade was contracted to tenement sweatshops, often conducted as a family-based enterprise. A similar scale of production characterized cigar-making, a common employment among women.[5] Relatively few women, married or single, were engaged in the type of large-scale, mechanized factory production considered the vanguard of an industrial society.

Much of women's wage work was centered in the home and followed household routines, or fitted into them without serious difficulty. This was especially true for married women, whose productive labor was often ignored by census enumerators. Keeping boarders, for example, a common occupation of working-class wives, involved the same tasks of cooking, washing, and cleaning that women performed for their families. Sewing and other forms of industrial homework, which endured among southern and eastern European immigrants well into the twentieth century, filled the days of mothers already occupied with child care and housework. As the daughter of an Italian homeworker observed in 1913, "My mother works all the time—all day, Sundays and holidays, except when she is cooking or washing. She never has time to go out or she would get behind in her work."[6] The task-oriented rhythms of such work, its lack of clear-cut boundaries, and the sheer burden of the "double day" left little time for leisure.

With greater job opportunities and limited household concerns, single women had fewer restrictions on their time than did working mothers. Indeed, by the mid-nineteenth century, some young working girls achieved notoriety in the city as pleasure seekers. While their mothers turned increasingly toward domestic pursuits, young factory hands, domestic servants, and prostitutes sought a life of finery, frolics, and entertainment. Industrial workers in particular found possibilities for leisure, sociability, and fun affirmed in the workplace. These Victorian "rowdy girls"—controversial figures within working-class communities— prefigure the broader trend toward a pleasure-oriented culture that swept working women's lives at the turn of the century.[7]

At the same time, women's access to a world of leisure at midcentury was limited by their work situations, as well as by poverty and social disapprobation. Single women who labored as domestic servants found that middle-class mistresses encroached upon their opportunities for leisure. Servants' desire to wear fine clothes and attend entertainments collided with employers' edicts limiting their time off. Maids were often on call twelve or thirteen hours a day and generally had only one afternoon and evening a week free.[8] Similarly, the exploitative conditions in the dominant manufacturing industries often permitted little free time. Grueling hours of labor for small wages in sweatshops and tenements characterized the work of seamstresses and needlewomen, cigar-makers, and others. Many of them labored fifteen to eighteen hours daily, working by gaslight late into the evening to earn enough for food and rent. Fatigue and poor health were more often their lot than finery and entertainment.[9]

Periods of sociability and amusement were often snatched within the rhythms of work. Domestic servants, for example, would meet together in the street or park to gossip and socialize while tending their mistresses' children. Yet for many, the relatively isolated nature of their labor, its long hours, and task-oriented rhythms did not reinforce a concept of leisure as a separate sphere of social life. One important exception to this pattern lay in the experience of female factory workers, whose work involved the segmentation of time and sociability among peers. By the end of the century, the distinction between household-based work and new forms of labor located in centralized production widened. While married women continued to do home-based work, single women increasingly entered an array of jobs not only in factories but in department stores, restaurants, and offices.

## Changes in Women's Labor

By 1900, important changes in the social organization of labor and expanding job opportunities in New York created new work experiences for women. Small shops, lofts, and trading companies still crowded lower Manhattan, but the city's economic landscape was rapidly changing. The wards at the southern tip of Manhattan were increasingly given over to corporate headquarters, banking and investment firms, and specialized business offices. Towering skyscrapers and the canyons of Wall Street symbolized New York's transformation from a mercantile city to the nation's center for corporate industry. This expanding office complex created a demand for workers increasingly filled by female clerks, "typewriters," secretaries, and telephone operators. The explosive growth of the white-collar sector in the twentieth century, and women's participation in it, was anticipated in New York a decade before it affected the rest of the country. A negligible number of New York's clerks, typists, and bookkeepers were female in 1880; in 1900, 7 percent of all New York working women were filling such positions; and by 1920, this number had increased to 22 percent. These were native-born women who had received a public school education, primarily daughters of American, German, and Irish parents.[10]

Women's opportunities for jobs in trade and services expanded as consumers, travellers, and businesses demanded a range of urban amenities. Retail trade grew substantially, symbolized by the emergence of such large department stores as Macy's, Bloomingdale's, and Lord and Taylor's. The center for retail business moved upward, near Fifth Avenue, Broadway, and 34th Street, close to an emerging commercial center, railroad connections, and middle-class residents. This expansion coincided with a shift in the sex-typing of store work. Retail sales had been a predominantly male occupation as late as the 1880s, when only 12 percent of clerks and salespersons in New York stores were women. By 1900, the saleslady had become a fixture of the retail emporium, a much coveted position for young working women. Working as a saleswoman or store clerk was the second most common occupation of native-born single wage-earners, whether "American girls" or daughters of immigrants.[11] Other businesses catered to the work routines and pleasures of a mobile, hectic population. Restaurants and lunchrooms, laundries, hotels, beauty parlors, drugstores, and theaters offered young women desirable alternatives to domestic service.

Although small workshops and households continued to play an important role in manufacturing, the production process increasingly turned toward larger factories. In the complex world of garment-making, conditions varied in the different branches of the industry. Generally, however, production shifted from isolated homework toward small sweatshops housed in tenements by the 1880s; by 1910, as the demand for ready-made clothing grew and further mechanization of the industry occurred, it was increasingly based in large-scale factories. John Commons estimated that while 90 percent of ready-made garments had been produced in sweatshops in 1890, 75 percent were made in factories after 1900. While the clothing trades dominated New York industry, women also found work in a variety of light assembling and operative jobs producing consumer goods. Artificial flower-making, box-making, confectionary dipping, jewelry work, and bookbinding were typical female occupations.[12]

These new patterns of labor fostered differing work expectations across generations, expectations that particularly affected the American-born daughters of immigrant parents. Although domestic service remained the foremost occupation of single women, the daughters of immigrants increasingly refused to don the maid's uniform. In her 1914 study of 370 working mothers, Katharine Anthony found that almost half had been employed in domestic service and one-third in manufacturing before marriage; as working mothers, 70 percent of them labored in domestic and personal service. In contrast, most of their daughters worked in stores, offices, and factories, with only a small fraction going into service. "The German-American child wants a position in an office," noted anthropologist Elsa Herzfeld. "The daughter refuses to go into domestic service although her mother had formerly taken a 'position.' "[13] New immigrant groups from southern and eastern Europe repeated this pattern. As Thomas Kessner has shown for the years between 1880 and 1905, Italian and Jewish wives rarely worked outside the home, but depended on homework to supplement the family income. Their daughters' work patterns changed significantly in the twenty-five-year period. Italian girls' occupations shifted from unskilled labor and street trades to factory work. Jewish girls throughout the period worked in the small shops of the garment industry, but by 1905 were also finding positions in schools, offices, and department stores.[14]

Women flocked to these jobs in part because they allowed more free time and autonomy, splitting the realms of work and leisure more clearly than household-based labor. A bitter complaint about domestic service was its lack of leisure time. One woman, for example, who had turned to service after working in manufacturing asserted, "as long as I had a trade I was certain of my evenings an' my Sundays. Now I'm never certain of anything." An investigation into the "servant question" agreed with this assessment: "Especially is objection made to the fact that her evenings are not her own, so that she may go out at will with her friends or may attend places of amusement."[15]

Among working women, leisure came to be seen as a separate sphere of life to be consciously protected. Whether their employer was exploitative or well-intentioned, women resented interference with their "own" time. Nonunionized bindery workers, for example, tried to protest overtime work that kept them on the job through Christmas Eve. Shopgirls, too, who had been urged at a public hearing to state their grievances over working conditions, complained chiefly about not getting out of work on time. "Make them close at 6 o'clock," one exclaimed, testifying that her employer rang the closing bell late, causing store workers to labor an extra fifteen to thirty minutes: "Q. And that really has the result of depriving you of your evenings—of getting to places of entertainment in time, does it not? A. Yes, sir; that is right." Another store clerk observed that all the workers took turns closing up the department, so that each night one could leave early at 5:45 P.M.[16]

Those who could—predominantly the young, unmarried, and American-born—rejected the household-based, task-oriented employments that had traditionally been women's work. They preferred to labor in stores and factories, where they sold their labor and submitted to employers' work discipline for a specified portion of time. The remainder of the day, while often limited by exhaustion and household obligations, they could call their own. This distinctive sphere of leisure, demarcated in new forms of wage-earning, grew as the hours of labor decreased from 1880 to 1920.

## The Declining Hours of Labor

The actual time working women had for relaxation and amusement is difficult to assess, since women's occupations rarely conformed to a single standard. Variations in the size and scale of industries, the seasonable nature of many jobs, differences between piecework and hourly wages, and low levels of unionization contributed to the nonuniformity of women's workdays. The New York State Bureau of Labor Statistics in 1885, for example, in cataloguing hundreds of industrial concerns, found that women's working days ranged from eight to seventeen hours. Even within a single industry, vast differences among workers are apparent. In the cigar industry, for example, some cigar-makers, presumably unionized, worked only eight hours, while bunch-makers regularly worked fifteen to seventeen hours daily. Moreover, women doing piecework often felt compelled to labor extra hours in the factory or at home in the evening.[17]

For many, the seasonal demand for consumer goods and services created an alternating pattern of intense labor and slack work. Garment manufacturers made heavy demands on employees in the fall and spring, but laid off workers in the dull seasons after Christmas and in the summer. The work history of one milliner typifies the casual employment many women faced: from February to May she had steady work; she was then laid off and hunted for a job in June and July; from August to December, she worked a total of fourteen weeks at four different establishments. During intermittent layoffs and the month-long slack period after Christmas, she sold candy. Cigarette-makers, carpet weavers, candy-makers, and bookbinders all experienced the seasonal rush to produce goods, and department store clerks put in ten- to sixteen-hour stints during the Christmas and Easter holidays. While posted hours in New York City factories were usually less than those upstate, many women regularly worked overtime as many as three or four nights a week during the busy season.[18] These spells allowed little time for leisure, while the slack season left women with time on their hands. Many looked for employment and filled in at other jobs, but others "took it easy" during the layoffs and, like Maria Cichetti, spent their hard-earned money going to vaudeville shows and movies.[19]

The contracting of jobs in some trades created a peculiar weekly rhythm of heavy labor and slack work. In many small task shops, garment-makers worked a fourteen-hour stretch for three days and then were idle the rest of the week. Similarly, laundries often had little work on Saturdays and Mondays, but might keep their employees at labor sixteen or seventeen hours on other days. In some jobs, labor intensity varied widely during the day. Waitresses, for example, often worked "split tricks"—on duty during the busy hours of lunch and dinner, relieved in the afternoon, hardly the best time for social engagements.[20]

Despite the irregularity of women's labor, the general trend of the period from 1880 to 1920 was toward shorter working days for female wage-earners in factories and stores. In 1885, women's workday ranged from ten to seventeen hours, but by the 1910s the long stints were much less common. Millinery workers, for example, who typically worked fourteen hours in 1885, put in only nine to ten hours in 1914. Similarly, a 1911 study of workers in lower Manhattan found that almost two-thirds of the female wage-earners worked less than ten hours daily. In addition, growing numbers of businesses closed early on Saturdays, particularly in the slow summer months, to give their workers a half-holiday.[21] The movement for protective legislation, greater union activity among working women, the increased rationalization of production, and changing attitudes toward workers' leisure contributed to this overall decline.

Protective legislation to lower women's work hours was pushed by middle-class reformers seeking to safeguard women's health and reproductive capacities, and by craft unions anxious about women's growing role in the workforce. Under pressure from these groups, New York's state legislature enacted a series of laws limiting the hours of labor, beginning in 1886 with the restriction of minors and women under twenty-one from working in manufacturing more than ten hours a day or sixty hours a week. This ceiling was extended to all female factory workers in 1899. In 1912, a revised statute curtailed the working day for women in manufacturing to nine hours, and two years later, this limit covered women's work in the city's mercantile stores. The nine-hour day and fifty-four hour week continued to be the legal standard in New York well into the 1920s.[22]

Generous loopholes and ineffective enforcement limited the efficacy of these laws, however. The legislation failed to cover women who did not work in factories and stores. It also permitted mercantile and industrial employers to demand irregular hours and overtime on a daily basis, as long as they obeyed the weekly limit. Enforcement was hampered by the hostility of employers, the limited number of factory inspectors, and the perfunctory penalties for violations. Mary Van Kleeck echoed the criticism of many reformers in observing that "the limit of the law is exceeded in numerous instances and in many trades—so that it is by no means uncommon to find young girls in the factories of New York working twelve, thirteen, even fourteen hours in a day." Despite these limitations, protective legislation contributed to the gradual decline in hours by setting legal limits and popularizing the notion of the "right to leisure." Major employers of women, including large clothing manufacturers and department stores, generally adhered to the labor laws.[23]

For some women, the labor movement's demand for the eight-hour day held the most promise of greater leisure. Although the vast majority of working women were not organized in this period, the union movement made important inroads after 1905 in industries with high female employment, such as garment-making and bookbinding. Bookbinders successfully struck for the eight-hour day in 1907, while waist-makers and other clothing workers achieved shorter hours in the settlements following the famous garment strikes of the 1910s.[24] Workers in unionized shops experienced a dramatic increase in their leisure time, as this young woman attested:

> The shorter work day brought me my first idea of there being such a thing as pleasure. It was quite wonderful to get home before it was pitch dark at night, and a real joy to ride on the cars and look out the windows and see something. Before this time it was just sleep and eat and hurry off to work. . . . I was twenty-one before I went to a theater and then I went with a crowd of union girls to a Saturday matinee performance. I was twenty-three before I saw a dance and that was a union dance too.[25]

Changes in the scale and organization of industry also hastened the decline in hours. As they achieved greater worker productivity through scientific management and mechanization, many major employers yielded to the shorter workday. Thus the trend in New York City toward larger mercantile establishments and factories had a salutary effect on lowering working hours. The reorganization of the garment trades, for example, sharply reduced hours. When the industry was dominated by home-sewing, there were no limits placed on the hours women might work. Workers in small task shops continued to be plagued with irregular employment and fourteen-hour workdays, while large clothing factories offered more steady work and a ten- to eleven-hour day. These establishments stopped work at 6:00 p.m., giving workers their evenings for rest and recreation. Similarly, the large department stores required only nine hours of labor except in the pre-Christmas season, in contrast to smaller neighborhood stores, which kept late hours to serve the working-class trade.[26]

Finally, liberalized attitudes toward workers' leisure began to take hold by the 1910s. The philanthropic bent of some large industrialists and retail merchants, joined with their desire to forestall unionization drives, led to welfare programs and practices designed to improve workers' health and well-being, in part by reducing hours. Josephine Goldmark's influential study of workers and efficiency, Louis Brandeis's brief on the hazards of long hours and night work for women, and the publicity campaigns of the Consumers' League contributed to the growing cultural legitimacy of the short day for women.[27]

By 1920, the hours of labor had declined sharply for many urban working women. In 1923, three-quarters of the women surveyed by the New York State Department of Labor worked only forty-eight hours or less in New York City, in contrast to their upstate sisters, of whom fewer than one-third worked such a short week. The memories of Nathan Cohen and Ruth Kaminsky, brother and sister, suggest the dimensions of change in the hours of labor. Nathan, a Russian immigrant who arrived in the United States in 1912, remembers doing little at night other than working, but his sister Ruth, who came to this country in 1921, had time to go to night school: "When I came over, they didn't work ten, twelve hours a day anymore. Tops was eight, nine, unless it was a small business, or some factories." Although she worked nine hours daily with a Saturday half-holiday in the 1910s, observed another immigrant women, "at that time, we didn't consider it long."[28]

## Work Cultures and Women's Leisure

While the shortened workday allowed more leisure time, women's experiences in the workplace reinforced the appeal of pleasure-oriented recreation in the public sphere. On one level, the desire for frivolous amusement was a reaction against the discipline, drudgery, and exploitative conditions of labor. A woman could forget rattling machinery or irritating customers in the nervous energy and freedom of the grizzly bear and turkey trot, or escape the rigors of the workplace altogether by finding a husband in the city's night spots. "You never rest until you die," observed one young box-maker, "but I will get out by marrying somebody." Indeed, factory investigators recorded the "widespread belief of the girls that marriage is relief from the trouble and toil of wage labor."[29]

At the same time, women's notions of leisure were reaffirmed through their positive social interactions within the workplace. In factories, stores, and offices, women socialized with other women and informally cooperated to affect working conditions. Their experience of work in a group context differed sharply from the home-bound, task-oriented, and isolated situation of domestic servants, outworkers, and housewives. There developed in this setting a shared and public culture, which legitimized the desires and behaviors expressed in young women's leisure.

Like other work groups, women workers developed degrees of autonomy and control in their relationship to managers and the work

process by enforcing informal work rules and production quotas, socializing new employees into these patterns of behavior, and protecting their
job skills from the bosses' encroachment. Given their status as low-skilled
and easily replaced workers, wage-earning women rarely commanded
the control over the work process that men in the skilled trades could
exert, but neither were they merely victims of capitalist discipline.[30]
Department store saleswomen, for example, used their selling skills to
manipulate managers, supervisors, and customers, enforcing work rules
among the women to sell only so many goods each day and employing
code words to warn coworkers of recalcitrant customers. Bookbinders
too employed the notion of a "fair day's work," controlling the output
during each stint, while other factory hands orchestrated work stoppages and job actions over such issues as sexual harassment and pay
cuts. Even waitresses worked out their resentment toward employers
by pilfering pins and small objects, supplying themselves liberally
with ice water and towels, and eating desserts ordered for imaginary
customers.[31]

In mediating the relationship between the wage-earner and the labor process, work cultures involved not only informal efforts to control
work but also the daily interactions that helped pass the long hours.
While women characterized the workplace as tedious and demanding, a
necessity to be endured, most tried to create places of sociability and
support on the shop floor. Women sang songs, recited the plots of novels,
argued politics, and gossiped about social life to counteract the monotony
and routine of the workday. One feather-maker, for example, described
her coworkers' conversations: "We have such a good time. We talk about
books that we read, . . . the theatres, and newspapers, and the things
that go on about town." Pieceworkers, who had more control over their
time than hourly hands, could follow their own rhythms of intense work
mixed with periods of sociability. "When I was a pieceworker," recalled
one garment worker, "I would sing, I would fool around, say jokes, talk
with the girls."[32] Singing helped pace the work, as in one box-maker's
shop where songs would rise and fall while the workers sped through
their tasks:

> Three o'clock, a quarter after, half-past! The terrific tension had all but
> reached the breaking point. Then there rose a trembling, palpitating
> sigh that seemed to come from a hundred throats, and blended in a
> universal expression of relief. In her clear, high treble Angelina began
> the everlasting "Fatal Wedding." That piece of false sentiment had now
> a new significance. It became a song of deliverance, and as the workers
> swelled the chorus, one by one, it meant that the end of the day's toil
> was in sight.[33]

Even in factories with loud machinery, women would try to converse
above the noise, while lunch hours and the after-work walk home also
afforded time to socialize with workmates. At Macy's, employees were
"fond of sitting down in a corner and eating a pickle and pastry and a
cup of tea; they can do that very quickly and can then visit for quite a
long time during the rest of the noon hour."[34]

Women's work cultures varied according to type of employment, ethnic and religious affiliation, and larger cultural traditions. American-born union women, believing in self-education and uplift, often mirrored their male counterparts' behavior in the shop. In one New York cigar factory, for example, female trade unionists would pay one of their members to read aloud while they worked: "First the newspaper is read, then some literary work, such as for instance Morley's 'Life of Gladstone.' "[35] Even among nonunionized workers, the rituals, rules, and interactions governing work in stores and restaurants, where interpersonal skills were utilized, differed from semiskilled production, where machinery dominated the shop floor. The women themselves had a firm understanding of the occupational hierarchy indicated by language, mores, and "tone." The saleslady's patina of style and refinement differentiated her from the rougher manner of many tobacco or garment workers. Within a single industry, ethnic patterns also shaped different work cultures; cultural and political traditions, for example, contributed to the Jewish waist-makers' readiness to organize and strike, unlike their more hesitant Italian workmates.[36] Despite these distinctive differences, we can discern important commonalities in the work cultures of women that shaped and defined their attitudes toward leisure.

In the workplace, young women marked out a cultural terrain distinct from familial traditions and the customary practices of their ethnic groups, signifying a new identity as wage-earners, through language, clothing, and social rituals. "Learners" might adopt new names from storybook romances when they entered a workplace for the first time, and greenhorns shed their Old World names for Anglicized ones. Fads, modish attire, and a distinctive personal style were also encouraged, as wage-earners discussed the latest fashions, learned new hairstyles, and tried out cosmetics and cigarettes. Indeed, employers often found it necessary to proscribe the unseemly behavior of working women: "At Koch's there is a splendid system of rules prohibiting the chewing of gum, rougeing and excessively using face powder."[37]

For factory hands, talking and socializing forged links between the world of labor and the pleasures of leisure. Some working girls, noted Lillian Betts, "dance[d] on the street at lunch-time, in front of their factory, singing their own dance music."[38] Part of the enjoyment inherent in the evening's entertainment lay in recounting the triumphs of the ball or party to one's workmates. Moreover, coworkers became a circle of friends apart from neighborhood or ethnic group ties. One Jewish garment worker observed, for example, that "while working, [I] used to have friends—Gentile girls. Sometimes we used to go out, we used to attend weddings, [I] was in their homes a few times."[39] Others formed social clubs comprised of coworkers and school friends.

Department store workers also were irrepressible in integrating work and social life through their use of language, special events, and organizations. When extra employees were laid off at the end of the holiday season, for example, they referred to the mass exodus as the "cakewalk," after the popular Afro-American dance and strut. Holidays and engagements were constant excuses for parties, suppers, and celebrations. A popular ritual involved cutting a Halloween cake, wherein one lucky saleswoman found a ring, forecasting marriage, while an unfortunate coworker discovered a button or thimble, threatening spinsterhood. Numerous social clubs formalized the relationship between work and leisure. At the Siegel-Cooper department store, the workers banded together by department, forming, for example, the Foot Mould Social Club, comprised of women in the shoe department, and the Bachelor Girls Social Club, organized by the mail order clerks. These associations of women workers typically sponsored dances, entertainments, and excursions to Coney Island.[40]

In the workplace, women's conversations, stories, and songs often gravitated to the subject of dating and romantic entanglements with men, a discourse that accentuated the mixed-sex character of their leisure. During free moments, waitresses relished gossip about "the ubiquitous 'gentleman friend,' the only topic of conversation outside of the dining room interests." Women's socialization into a new workplace might involve a ritualistic exchange over "gentlemen friends." In one steam laundry, for example, an investigator repeatedly heard this conversation:

> 'Say, you got a feller?'
> 'Sure. Ain't you got one?'
> 'Sure.'[41]

One Jewish garment worker recalled daydreaming about love and marriage in the shops: "We used to even sing the songs . . . Yiddish naturally, singing the dream songs, the love songs, and this is how we dreamed away our youth and go out gay and happy."[42]

In department stores, the mixed-sex workplace became a setting for romance, trysts, and discussion of male-female relations. *Thought and Work*, the in-house magazine of the Siegel-Cooper department store, which was written by workers, evinced little interest in selling skills and business news, but resonated with gossip about eligible bachelors, intra-store courtships, wedding notices, and entertainments about town. Personal popularity, beauty, hair styles, clothing, and dancing ability were newsworthy items. Cultural practices among department store workers emerge from the breathless commentary of the newsletter: the saleslady who changes her hair color because, the gossip speculates, she "wants a man"; the competition between departments for the most engagements and marriages; the delivery of roses and mash notes to young women; the debates among idle saleswomen on such topics as kissing mustachioed men. Some department managers were portrayed more as popular matchmakers than enforcers of work discipline. "Mr. Eckle is a past master at securing husbands for the young ladies in his department," noted *Thought and Work*. "He'd rather do that than sign time cards."[43] While doubtlessly the magazine embellished the business of romance at the store, management eventually reined in its editors, ordering less copy on personal life and more articles on the business of selling.[44]

Bound to the language of romance was the frank discussion of sexuality among laboring women, a practice in the workplace that mirrored that of popular amusements. Risqué jokes, swearing, and sexual advice were a common part of the work environment in restaurants, laundries, factories, and department stores. Waitresses bandied obscenities and engaged in explicit discussion of lovers and husbands before work and during breaks. As one surprised middle-class observer described the scene in a restaurant: "They were putting on their aprons, combing their hair, powdering their noses, . . . all the while tossing back and forth to each other, apparently in a spirit of good-natured comradeship, the most vile epithets that I had ever heard emerge from the lips of a human being."[45] Despite their image of gentility and upward mobility, department store workers relished a similar freedom in language and behavior. At Macy's, a store that sought to maintain strict standards of employee respectability, investigators found "salacious cards, poems, etc., copied with avidity and passed from one to another, not only between girls and girls, but from girls to men." While many workers remained aloof from such vulgarities, there was "more smutty talk in one particular department than in a dance hall."[46]

Sexual knowledge was communicated between married and single women, between the experienced and the naive. A YWCA study of the woman worker observed that "the 'older hands' initiate her early through the unwholesome story or innuendo. She is forced to think of sex matters in relation to herself by the suggestions made to her of what she may expect from suitors or find in marriage." Examples of such initiation abound in the reports of middle-class investigators and reformers. In one department at Macy's dominated by married women, for example, "there was enough indecent talk to ruin any girl in her teens who might be put at work on that floor."[47] Stripped of their moralistic overtones, such observations reveal the workplace as an arena in which women wage-earners articulated their sexual feelings and shared their acquired wisdom about negotiating the attentions of men, both on the job and in their leisure time.

It was also an arena in which they experienced sexual vulnerability, a world of harassment as well as the give-and-take of humor and conversation. Then as now, sexual harassment limited women's position in the workforce and maintained male privilege and control. Wage-earning women were perceived by bosses and male workers alike to be outside the realm of parental or community protection. As one cigarmaker observed, behavior that in another context would not be tolerated was given free rein on the shop floor:

> Many men who are respected—when I say respected and respectable, I mean who walk the streets and are respected as working men, and who would not, under any circumstances, offer the slightest insult or disrespectful remark or glance to a female in the streets, . . . in the shops, will whoop and give expressions to "cat calls" and a peculiar noise made with their lips, which is supposed to be an endearing salutation.[48]

Women learned to tread a fine line between participating in acceptable workplace practices and guarding their integrity and respectability. Macy's clerks, who could trade obscenities and *double entendres* with the salesmen, knew "just how to be very friendly, without permitting the least familiarity," when conversing with male customers. As one factory investigator observed, "such women learn to defend themselves and to take care of themselves."[49] This sexual knowledge gained in the workplace informed women's relations with men in the world of leisure.

## Women's Wages and Treating

The work culture of women encouraged an ideology of romance that resonated with explicit heterosexual pleasures and perils at the same time that it affirmed the value of leisure. Still, working women's lack of financial resources posed a problem to their participation in an active social life, particularly in the world of commercial amusements. On the surface, low wages and little spending money would seem to have limited women's access to leisure, thus undercutting the heterosocial, pleasure-oriented culture of the workplace. Paradoxically, the material conditions of their lives at work and at home served instead to strengthen that culture.

Working women in New York typically earned below the "living wage," estimated by economists to be nine or ten dollars a week in 1910. Employers and workingmen alike justified women's low wages and their exclusion from higher-paying skilled trades by claiming that women were temporary wage-earners who worked only until marriage. Occupational segregation of the labor market was deeply entrenched, and women were concentrated in semi-skilled, seasonal employment. As cashgirls and salesclerks, assemblers and machine-tenders, waitresses and servants, their average earnings were one-half of those received by men in their employments. In New York factories in the early 1910s, 56 percent of the female labor force earned under $8.00 a week. Despite their higher social status, the majority of women in retail stores earned under $7.50, although the large emporia offered higher wages than neighborhood stores and five-and-tens. Deductions for tardiness, poor workmanship, and other violations further depleted wage-earners' already meager earnings.[50]

Relatively few women were able to live alone in comfort. Among the large industrial cities of the United States, New York had one of the highest percentages of wage-earning women residing with parents or relatives, from 80 to 90 percent. Self-supporting workers lodging in boardinghouses or renting rooms tended to be older, native-born women who earned higher wages than those living at home.[51] Most found, nevertheless, that their earnings were consumed by the cost of room, board, and clothing, leaving little for recreation.

To make ends meet, self-supporting women would scrimp on essential items in their weekly budgets. Going without meals was a common strategy, as was sleeping three to a bed to reduce the rent. "Some never boarded a street car for an evening's ride without planning days ahead how they could spare the nickel from their lunch or clothes money," noted reformer Esther Packard, describing women who lived on six dollars a week.[52] After work, the self-supporting woman sewed and washed her own clothing, cooked meals, and prepared for the next workday. Such scheduling and scrimping often left little time or money for evening amusements: "When the women or girls were visited at night, they were more likely to be found at home busy at the wash tub or ironing board than out at a dance or the theater." A movie and occasional ball were their only forms of leisure.[53]

By scrimping and making do, young women could provide some recreation for themselves. Yeddie Bruker, a factory worker earning seven dollars a week, spent almost two dollars of that on clothing and four dollars on room and board. A union member, she spent sixteen cents weekly for union dues and a benefit association, while for recreation she allocated ten cents a week for theatre tickets. Katia Markelov, a corset maker earning ten dollars, saved thirty dollars yearly for outings, while Rita Karpovna's low wages, six to seven dollars weekly, forced her to sacrifice essential items for union dues and the "Woman's Self-Education Society": "The Union and this club meant more to Rita than the breakfasts and luncheons she dispensed with, and more, apparently, than dress, for which she spent only $20 in a year and a half."[54]

For women living at home, recreation was limited not so much by the size of their income as by access to it. In exchange for their wages, most parents gave their daughters small sums of spending money, averaging twenty-five to fifty cents each week, in addition to lunch money and carfare. Like self-supporting women, those who lived at home necessarily scrimped and depended on others for recreation. They commonly saved their allowances for lunch by eating the free food served in saloons or skipping the meal altogether. Many, like Maria Cichetti, saved carfare by walking to or from work. Maria received ten cents for the roundtrip trolley ride to her shop; by walking home with friends at night, she could save a nickel for the movies. As one investigator of West Side girls observed, "A carfare saved by walking to work is a carfare earned for a trip to a dance hall 'away out in the Bronx.' "[55]

Women also relied on coworkers and female friends to help them out with food, clothing, and recreation. The low-wage cashgirl or salesclerk was "helped by those about her in the store with gifts of clothing or even with money," observed one salesgirl. In factories, older wage-earners would aid the youngest by paying her a dime to fetch tea or lunch. A tradition of mutual aid and support can be seen in the frequency of raffles and events to raise money for less fortunate workmates.[56]

Typically, however, young women looked to men for financial assistance and gifts. "If they didn't take me, how could I ever go out?" observed a young department store worker. Treating was a widely accepted practice, especially if the woman had a fiancé, or "steady," from which she could accept food, clothing, and recreation without compromising her reputation. One woman, for example, counted on her steady for Sunday meals, exclaiming, "Why, if I had to buy all of my meals I'd never get along." Unable to save a penny of her seven-dollar weekly wage, Clara X. depended on her beau, who earned more than twice her income, to occasionally purchase her clothes and take her on vacation.[57] Rose Pasternak paid for an overcoat on installments until she was "keeping company": "I paid and paid and paid, till I got with the company with my fella. He paid eight dollars. After I was a long time married, he used to throw it in my face, 'you made so much money that I had to pay for the plush coat.' "[58] Other self-supporting women had no qualms about accepting treats from unknown men or chance acquaintances. As one observer concluded, "the acceptance on the part of the girl of almost any invitation needs little explanation when one realizes that she often goes pleasureless unless she does accept 'free treats.' "[59]

The culture of treating was reinforced in the workplace through women's interactions with employers, male workmates, and customers, particularly in service and sales jobs. In department stores, managers were said to advise shopgirls to find gentleman friends who could buy them the clothing and trinkets that their salaries could not cover. At a government hearing, one saleswoman testified: "One of the employers has told me, on a $6.50 wage, he don't care where I get my clothes from as long as I have them, to be dressed to suit him."[60] Some investigators denied the accuracy of these reports, but their widespread currency among saleswomen suggests the tacit legitimacy of treating as a means of gaining access to the world of amusements. Waitresses knew that suggestive familiarity with male customers often brought good tips, and some used their skills and opportunities to engage in an active social life with chance acquaintances. "Most of the girls quite frankly admit making 'dates' with strange men," observed a Consumers' League study. "These 'dates' are made with no thought on the part of the girl beyond getting the good time which she cannot afford herself."[61] These working women sought a way to negotiate dependency and claim some choice, autonomy, and pleasure in otherwise dreary lives. They understood, albeit hazily, that leisure was the realm in which that quest could most easily be achieved.

NOTES

1. [Siegel-Cooper Department Store], *Thought and Work*, Dec. 1904, p. 15; "A Salesgirl's Story," *Independent* 54 (31 July 1902): 1821; Harry B. Taplin, "Training for Store Efficiency," 17 March 1915, p. 2, Box 118, Welfare Department Subject File, National Civic Federation Papers, Rare Books and Manuscripts Division, New York Public Library, Astor, Lenox and Tilden Foundation.

2. U.S. Bureau of the Census, *Statistics of Women at Work* (Washington, D.C., 1907), pp. 270–271, 148–151; New York State Factory Investigating Commission, *Fourth Report Transmitted to Legislature, Feb. 15, 1915* (S. Doc. no. 43; Albany, N.Y., 1915), vol. 1, p. 37, and vol. 4, p. 1478–1489. See also U.S. Bureau of the Census, *Women in Gainful Occupations, 1870–1920*, by Joseph A. Hill (Washington, D.C., 1929). Women's role in the labor force is surveyed in Leslie Woodcock Tentler, *Wage-Earning Women: Industrial Work and Family Life in the United States, 1900–1930* (New York, 1979); Alice Kessler-Harris, *Out to Work* (New York, 1982); Susan Estabrook Kennedy, *If All We Did Was to Weep at Home: A History of White Working-Class Women in America* (Bloomington, Ind., 1979); Miriam Cohen, "Italian-American Women in New York City, 1900–1950: Work and School," in *Class, Sex, and the Woman Worker*, ed. Milton Cantor and Bruce Laurie (Westport, Conn., 1977), pp. 120–143.

3. David C. Hammack, *Power and Society: Greater New York at the Turn of the Century* (New York, 1982), pp. 31–58; Sean Wilentz, *Chants Democratic: New York City and the Rise of the American Working Class, 1788–1850* (New York, 1984), especially pp. 107–142; Bayrd Still, *Mirror for Gotham* (New York, 1956).

4. Mary Christine Stansell, "Women of the Laboring Poor in New York City, 1820–1860" (Ph.D. diss., Yale University, 1979); Amy Srebnick, "True Womanhood and Hard Times: Women and Early New York Industrialization, 1840–1860" (Ph.D. diss., State University of New York at Stony Brook, 1979); Carol Groneman, " 'She Earns as a Child, She Pays as a Man': Women Workers in a Mid-Nineteenth-Century New York City Community," in *Class, Sex, and the Woman Worker*, ed. Cantor and Laurie, pp. 83–100; U.S. Senate, *Report on the Condition of Woman and Child Wage-Earners in the United States, Vol. 9: History of Women in Industry in the United States* (S. 645, 61st Cong., 2d sess.; Washington, D.C., 1910), pp. 115–155.

5. U.S. Bureau of the Census, *Statistics of the Population at the Tenth Census, 1880,* vol. 1 (Washington, D.C., 1883), p. 892; U.S. Bureau of the Census, *Social Statistics of Cities, 1880* (Washington, D.C., 1883), pp. 594–596; Christine Stansell, "The Origins of the Sweatshop: Women and Early Industrialization in New York City," in *Working-Class America,* ed. Michael H. Frisch and Daniel J. Walkowitz (Urbana, Ill., 1983), pp. 78–103.

6. Mary Van Kleeck, *Artificial Flower-Makers* (New York, 1913), p. 235. On the prevalence of homework in New York, see Thomas Kessner, *The Golden Door: Italian and Jewish Immigrant Mobility in New York City, 1880–1915* (New York, 1977), pp. 72–77; Mabel Hurd Willett, *The Employment of Women in the Clothing Trades* (Studies in History, Economics and Public Law, vol. 16, no. 2; New York, 1902), pp. 102, 108; New York State Legislature, Special Committee of the Assembly Appointed to Investigate the Conditions of Female Labor in the City of New York, *Report and Testimony* (Albany, N.Y., 1896), vol. 1, pp. 17–19, and vol. 2, pp. 1024–1025. See also John Modell and Tamara K. Hareven, "Urbanization and the Malleable Household: An Examination of Boarding and Lodging in American Families," *Journal of Marriage and the Family* 35 (Aug. 1973): 467–479; Joan M. Jensen, "Cloth, Butter and Boarders: Women's Household Production for the Market," *Review of Radical Political Economics* 12, no. 2 (Summer 1980): 14–24; Margaret F. Byington, *Homestead: The Households of a Mill Town* (1910; rpt. Pittsburgh, 1974), pp. 138–157.

7. Stansell, "Women of the Laboring Poor," pp. 105–108, 204.

8. *Ibid.,* pp. 139–159; David M. Katzman, *Seven Days a Week: Women and Domestic Service in Industrializing America* (Urbana, Ill., 1981).

9. Stansell, "Women of the Laboring Poor," p. 73; James McCabe, *Lights and Shadows of New York Life* (Philadelphia, 1872), p. 822.

10. Percentage changes in women's employment are derived from U.S. Bureau of the Census, *Tenth Census, 1880,* vol. 1, p. 892; U.S. Bureau of the Census, *Statistics of Women at Work,* pp. 270–271; U.S. Bureau of the Census, *Women in Gainful Occupations,* pp. 204, 206. The demand for women clerical workers is discussed in Margery Davies, *Woman's Place Is at the Typewriter: Office Work and Office Workers, 1870–1930* (Philadelphia, 1982). New York's economy in the early twentieth century is discussed in Hammack, *Power and Society,* pp. 39–51.

11. See note 10, and Susan Porter Benson, " 'The Customers Ain't God': The Work Culture of Department-Store Saleswomen, 1890–1940," in *Working-Class America,* ed. Frisch and Walkowitz, pp. 185–211.

12. John Commons quoted in U.S. Senate, *Woman and Child Wage Earners,* vol. 9, p. 143; see also Willett, *Women in the Clothing Trades.* Women's industrial jobs underwent extensive examination by New York reformers and social workers; see especially Annie M. MacLean, *Wage-Earning Women* (New York, 1910); Louise C. Odencrantz, *Italian Women in Industry: A Study of Conditions in New York City* (New York, 1919); Mary Van Kleeck, *Artificial Flower-Makers*; Mary Van Kleeck, *A Seasonal Industry: A Study of the Millinery Trade in New York* (New York, 1917); idem, *Women in the Bookbinding Trade* (New York, 1913).

13. Elsa G. Herzfeld, *Family Monographs: The History of Twenty-four Families Living in the Middle West Side of New York City* (New York, 1905), p. 12; Katharine Anthony, *Mothers Who Must Earn* (New York, 1914), pp. 49, 59, 62.

14. Kessner, *Golden Door,* pp. 71–99.

15. Helen S. Campbell, *Prisoners of Poverty: Women Wage-Earners, Their Trades and Their Lives* (1887; rpt. Westport, Conn., 1970), p. 148; Gail Laughlin, "Domestic Service," in U.S. Industrial Commission, *Report of the Industrial Commission on the Relations and Conditions of Capital and Labor Employed in Manufacturing and General Business,* vol. 14 (Washington, D.C., 1901), pp. 758, 756–757. See also Katzman, *Seven Days a Week,* pp. 236–243.

16. Special Committee to Investigate Female Labor, *Report and Testimony,* vol. 2, pp. 989–990, 994, 1083; Van Kleeck, *Women in the Bookbinding Trade,* p. 173.

17. New York State Bureau of Labor Statistics, *Third Annual Report* (Albany, N.Y., 1885), pp. 32–59, 169, and *Fourteenth Annual Report* (Albany, N.Y., 1896), pp. 918–919.

18. Alice P. Barrows, "The Training of Millinery Workers," in *Proceedings of the Academy of Political Science in the City of New York*, vol. 1 (Oct. 1910): 43–44. Testimony on irregular working hours by reformers and working women is extensive; see in particular New York Bureau of Labor Statistics, "Unorganized Workingwomen," *Fourteenth Annual Report* (1896); New York State Factory Investigating Commission, *Preliminary Report Transmitted to Legislature, March 1, 1912* (Albany, N.Y., 1912), vol. 1, p. 296, and *Fourth Report*, vol. 2, pp. 252, 516–517, 592–595; and studies cited in note 12.

19. Tapes I–116 (side A) and II–30 (side B), New York City Immigrant Labor History Collection of the City College Oral History Project, Robert F. Wagner Archives, Tamiment Institute Library, New York University.

20. Consumers' League of New York City, *Behind the Scenes in a Restaurant: A Study of 1017 Women Restaurant Employees* (n.p., 1916), p. 15; Willett, *Women in the Clothing Trades*, p. 74; Sue Ainslie Clark and Edith Wyatt, *Making Both Ends Meet: The Income and Outlay of New York Working Girls* (New York, 1911), p. 190.

21. Cf. New York Bureau of Labor Statistics, *Third Annual Report* (1885), pp. 32–59, and New York Factory Investigating Commission, *Fourth Report*, vol. 2, pp. 424–425, 209–210, 320; Edward Ewing Pratt, *Industrial Causes of Congestion of Population in New York City* (Studies in History, Economics and Public Law, vol. 43, no. 1; New York, 1911), p. 124. The growing acceptance of the half-holiday may be followed in New York State Bureau of Labor Statistics, *Fifth Annual Report* (Albany, N.Y., 1887), p. 555; New York State Bureau of Labor Statistics, *Eighth Annual Report* (Albany, N.Y., 1890), pt. 1, p. 448; New York Bureau of Labor Statistics, *Fourteenth Annual Report* (1896), p. 935; New York Factory Investigating Commission, *Fourth Report*, vol. 2, p. 88.

22. Elizabeth Faulkner Baker, *Protective Labor Legislation* (Studies in History, Economics and Public Law, vol. 116, no. 2; New York, 1925), pp. 113–114, 133–138.

23. Mary Van Kleeck, "Working Hours of Women in Factories," *Charities and the Commons* 17 (6 Oct. 1906): 13; Baker, *Protective Labor Legislation*, pp. 151, 309–313. For an example of employers' maneuvers around the law, see Van Kleeck, *Women in the Bookbinding Trade*, pp. 134, 144–145. Oral testimony of working women confirms large employers' observance of the law, particularly with respect to minors; see, for example, tape II–30 (side A), Immigrant Labor History Collection.

24. Van Kleeck, *Women in the Bookbinding Trade*, pp. 177–181. On unionization in the garment industry, see Nancy Schrom Dye, *As Equals and as Sisters: Feminism, the Labor Movement and the Women's Trade Union League of New York* (Columbia, Mo. and London, 1980); Meredith Tax, *The Rising of the Women* (New York 1980), pp. 205–240.

25. "Making Ends Meet on the Minimum Wage," *Life and Labor* 3 (Oct. 1913): 302. See also tape I–105, Immigrant Labor History Collection.

26. Kessler-Harris, *Out to Work*, pp. 180–202; Baker, *Protective Labor Legislation*, p. 331; New York Factory Investigating Commission, *Fourth Report*, vol. 2, pp. 123; New York State Department of Labor, *Hours and Earnings of Women in Five Industries* (Special Bulletin no. 121; Albany, N.Y., Nov. 1923), p. 13; Willett, *Women in Clothing Trades*, p. 74; New York Bureau of Labor Statistics, *Third Annual Report* (1885), p. 169; New York Special Committee to Investigate Female Labor, *Report and Testimony*, vol. 1, pp. 60, 86–87; Irving Howe, *World of Our Fathers* (New York, 1976), p. 82.

27. Daniel T. Rodgers, *The Work Ethic in Industrial America, 1850–1920* (Chicago and London, 1974); Alice Kessler-Harris, *Out to Work*, pp. 200–201; Florence Kelley, "Right to Leisure," *Charities* 14 (2 Sept. 1905): 1055–1062.

28. Tapes I–51 (side B) and I–21 (transcript), Immigrant Labor History Collection; New York Department of Labor, *Women in Five Industries*, p. 13.

29. New York Factory Investigating Commission, *Fourth Report*, vol. 4, pp. 1577–1578; Frances R. Donovan, *The Woman Who Waits* (1920; rpt. New York, 1974), p. 50. For an elaboration of this argument, see Tentler, *Wage-Earning Women*.

30. Pathbreaking studies of work cultures include David Montgomery, *Workers' Control in America* (Cambridge, Eng., 1979); Susan Porter Benson, "The Customers Ain't God"; Barbara Melosh, *'The Physicians' Hand': Work Culture and Conflict in American Nursing* (Philadelphia, 1982). See also Karen Brodkin Sacks and Dorothy Remy, eds., *My Troubles Are Going to Have Trouble with Me* (New Brunswick, N.J., 1984), pp. 193–263.

31. Benson, "The Customers Ain't God"; Mary Bularzik, "Sexual Harassment at the Workplace, Historical Notes," in *Workers' Struggles, Past and Present*, ed. James Green (Philadelphia, 1983), pp. 117–135; Amy E. Tanner, "Glimpses at the Mind of a Waitress," *American Journal of Sociology* 13 (July 1907): 50; Van Kleeck, *Women in the Bookbinding Trade*, p. 83.

32. Mary Gay Humphreys, "The New York Working Girl," *Scribner's* 20 (Oct. 1896): 505; tape II–30, Immigrant Labor History Collection.

33. Dorothy Richardson, *The Long Day: The Story of a New York Working Girl* (1905) in *Women at Work*, ed. William L. O'Neill (New York, 1972), pp. 105–106. Although colored by

middle-class moralisms, Dorothy Richardson's autobiographical novel gives a particularly rich portrait of young, unskilled female wage-earners' interactions in the workplace.

34. Taplin, "Training for Store Efficiency," p. 2; MacLean, *Wage-Earning Women*, p. 35; Bessie and Marie Van Vorst, *The Woman Who Toils* (New York, 1903), p. 25.

35. Conference on Welfare Work at Chicago Commons, Minutes of Seventh Meeting, 15 May 1906, p. 3, Box 121, Welfare Conferences, National Civic Federation Papers.

36. New York Factory Investigating Commission, *Fourth Report*, vol. 4, p. 1588; Anthony, *Mothers Who Must Earn*, p. 51.

37. Department Store Study, *Civic Federation Review*, galley 20B, box 116, Department Store Subject File, National Civic Federation Papers; Clark and Wyatt, *Making Both Ends Meet*, p. 184; Richardson, *Long Day*, pp. 96–97.

38. Lillian W. Betts, "Tenement-House Life and Recreation," *Outlook* 61 (11 Feb. 1899): 365.

39. Tapes I–51 (side B) and I–132 (side A), Immigrant Labor History Collection.

40. *Thought and Work*, Dec. 1903, p. 9; Jan. 1904, pp. 10, 15; and Jan. 1905, pp. 1, 3; Department Store Study, draft typescript, p. 38, box 116, Department Store Subject File, National Civic Federation Papers.

41. Tanner, "Glimpses," p. 52; Clark and Wyatt, *Making Both Ends Meet*, pp. 187–188; See also Richardson, *Long Day*, pp. 94–95.

42. Tape I–59 (side A), Immigrant Labor History Collection.

43. *Thought and Work*, June 1903, p. 7; Sept. 1904, p. 5; Jan. 1904, pp. 10, 15; 15 April 1904, p. 6; Nov. 1904, p. 5; April 1905, p. 11; and Jan. 1905, p. 11.

44. *Thought and Work*, Feb. 1905, p. 1.

45. Donovan, *Woman Who Waits*, pp. 20, 26, 80–81; Clark and Wyatt, *Making Both Ends Meet*, p. 188.

46. Committee of Fourteen in New York City, *Department Store Investigation: Report of the Sub-committee* (New York, 1915), p. 10. See also Committee of Fourteen in New York City, *Annual Report* (New York, 1914), p. 40.

47. "Report of the Commission on Social Morality from the Christian Standpoint, Made to the Fourth Biennial Convention of the Young Women's Christian Associations of the U.S.A., 1913," Pamphlets on Marriage and Family Relations, Archives of the National Board of the Young Women's Christian Association of the U.S.A., New York City; Committee of Fourteen, *Department Store Investigation*, p. 10. Cf. Sharon Hartman Strom, "Italian American Women and Their Daughters in Rhode Island: The Adolescence of Two Generations, 1900–1950," in *The Italian Immigrant Woman in North America*, ed. Betty Boyd Caroli et al. (Toronto, 1978), p. 194, in which one informant explained: "You found out about sex through the shop where you worked. The mother don't tell you nothing. The married women would put us wise."

48. New York State Bureau of Labor Statistics, *Second Annual Report* (Albany, N.Y., 1884), pp. 153, 158. Examples of sexual harassment abound; see, New York Bureau of Labor Statistics, *Third Annual Report* (1885), pp. 150–151; Clara E. Laughlin, *The Work-a-Day Girl: A Study of Some Present-day Conditions* (New York, 1913), p. 112; Richardson, *Long Day*, p. 260; U.S. Industrial Commission, *Report of the Industrial Commission on the Relations and Conditions of Capital and Labor Employed in Manufacturing and General Business*, vol. 7 (Washington, D.C., 1901), pp. 389–390. See also Bularzik, "Sexual Harassment."

49. Committee of Fourteen in New York City, *Department Store Investigation*, p. 10; U.S. Industrial Commission, *Report*, vol. 7, p. 59.

50. Wage differentials in New York City according to sex may be seen in U.S. Bureau of the Census, *Report on Manufacturing Industries in the U.S. at the Eleventh Census* (Washington, D.C., 1895), pp. 390–407, 708–710; New York Factory Investigating Commission, *Fourth Report*, vol. 4, pp. 1507–1511, 1081, and vol. 1, pp. 35–36. Estimates for the living wage of self-supporting girls varied; see, for example, Clark and Wyatt, *Making Both Ends Meet*, p. 8.

51. The exact percentage of women living alone varies in different reports. U.S. Senate, *Report on the Condition of Woman and Child Wage-Earners in the United States, Vol. 5: Wage-Earning Women in Stores and Factories* (S. 645, 61st Cong., 2d sess.; Washington, D.C., 1910), p. 15, indicates that 87 percent of factory workers and 92 percent of retail clerks lived at home. Cf. New York Factory Investigating Commission, *Fourth Report*, vol. 5, p. 2561, which stated that 85 percent of women wage-earners lived with families, friends, or relatives. For testimony on women's inability to live alone on low wages, see New York Bureau of Labor Statistics, *Fourteenth Annual Report* (1896), pp. 913–945. For a fictional account of the controversy surrounding a young woman who chooses to live alone, see Anzia Yezierska, *Bread Givers* (1925; rpt. New York, 1975).

52. New York Factory Investigating Commission, *Fourth Report*, vol. 4, p. 1685. For an excellent discussion of the survival strategies of self-supporting women, see Joanne J. Meyerowitz, "Holding Their Own: Working Women Apart from Family in Chicago, 1880–1930" (Ph.D. diss., Stanford University, 1983).

53. Odencrantz, *Italian Women in Industry*, p. 235; Lillian D. Wald, *The House on Henry Street* (1915; rpt. New York, 1971), p. 211; New York Factory Investigating Commission, *Fourth Report*, vol. 4, pp. 1675–1692; Clark and Wyatt, *Making Both Ends Meet*, p. 10.

54. Clark and Wyatt, *Making Both Ends Meet*, pp. 97, 103–104, 108.

55. Ruth S. True, *The Neglected Girl* (New York, 1914), p. 59; New York Factory Investigating Commission, *Fourth Report*, vol. 4, pp. 1512–1513; tape II–30 (side A), Immigrant Labor History Collection.

56. Salesgirl's Story," p. 1818; New York Factory Investigating Commission, *Fourth Report*, vol. 4, p. 1576, 1585; Clark and Wyatt, *Making Both Ends Meet*, p. 189.

57. New York Factory Investigating Commission, *Fourth Report*, vol. 4, pp. 1698, 1678 (quotations), 1577, 1675–1678, 1695–1714.

58. Tape I–132, Immigrant Labor History Collection.

59. New York Factory Investigating Commission, *Fourth Report*, vol. 4, pp. 1685–1686.

60. New York Factory Investigating Commission, *Fourth Report*, vol. 5, p. 2809; U.S. Industrial Commission, *Report*, vol. 7, p. 59; Laughlin, *Work-a-Day Girl*, pp. 60–61; "Salesgirl's Story," p. 1821; Clark and Wyatt, *Making Both Ends Meet*, p. 28.

61. Consumers' League, *Behind the Scenes*, p. 24; Donovan, *Woman Who Waits*, p. 42.

# Chicago's 1919 Race Riot: Ethnicity, Class, and Urban Violence*

*Dominic A. Pacyga*

In 1919, Chicago was a city long shaped by mass migrations. Just nine years earlier immigrants and their children made up nearly 80 percent of its population. It was a city of vast ethnic differences. In addition, the period from 1915 to 1920 witnessed the Great Migration. Some 50,000 southern African Americans made their way to Chicago, doubling the city's black population. Not only the huge wartime industries but also the promises of freedom and individual mobility that the North seemed to offer attracted these long-exploited southerners. They joined immense numbers of white ethnic Chicagoans who already inhabited the grimy industrial neighborhoods of the city's South and West Sides.[1]

Immigration, migration, and residential mobility were then already major forces in the history of Chicago. So, too, was the tradition of ethnic conflict, whether at the ballot box, in the church, or on the neighborhood street. Conflicts between white ethnic groups were frequent and legendary. The Irish and Germans of Bridgeport battled violently early in that neighborhood's history. Germans and Poles clashed on the North Side. Anti-Catholicism and anti-Semitism often raised their ugly heads in the city. First Catholic Germans and later Poles struggled against Irish-American domination of the Roman Catholic Church. The nature of Chicago's politics promoted ethnic and racial divisions. Divisiveness seemed to power the very engine that made Chicago grow as an industrial capitalist city.[2]

The particulars of the riot that broke out on that hot Sunday of July 27, 1919, are well known. The riot began after the killing of Eugene Williams, a young black boy, in Lake Michigan off the "white" beach at 29th Street. This event unlocked the racial rage and conflict that had been pent up for most of World War I. The riot resulted from the competition between whites and blacks over housing and jobs in the city. Both of these commodities seemed scarce in the aftermath of the war. The emergence of organized labor also presented a point of conflict. There is

*Dominic A. Pacyga is history program coordinator in the Liberal Education Department at Columbia College, Chicago. Original essay printed by permission of author.*

187

a good deal of evidence that the management of various enterprises, in particular the meatpackers, manipulated ethnic and racial differences between workers in order to destroy the labor movement emerging in Chicago's mass production industries.

The Chicago Commission on Race Relations published a long and detailed account of the riot in the early 1920s. In 1972, William M. Tuttle, Jr., gave a detailed account of the riot and its causes.[3] Various studies that deal with related subjects have also explored the racial clash. All of these have pointed the finger of blame for the active rioting—though not for the causes—at the immigrant neighborhoods west of Wentworth Avenue. The historical literature often refers to these areas as Irish and Polish or simply as "white working class" in nature. To an extent, the investigators simply accepted the stereotype that everyone west of the racial dividing line belonged to a mostly homogeneous group. In fact, in making that judgment the various investigators ignored their own evidence.[4]

The European ethnic mix west of Wentworth Avenue was great and confusing. None of the white areas in Back of the Yards, Canaryville, Bridgeport, McKinley Park, or Englewood was totally occupied by any one ethnic group. It was far easier to call everyone west of Wentworth Avenue white. The reality, however, was that the white ethnic neighborhoods to the west of the Black Belt, and indeed to the south and east of the ghetto, were very mixed—and that not all groups shared in all of the institutions.[5]

There are various conflicting claims as to the ethnicity of the white rioters. The investigators simply called them white or hostile Polish and Irish Stock Yard District residents. At least one on-the-scene observer, however, Mary McDowell of the University of Chicago Settlement House, called them Americans and not immigrants. This was an interesting statement considering the large immigrant populations of the neighborhoods surrounding the stockyards.[6]

The question of exactly who the rioters were is a complex one. Of course, the members of a mob rarely leave memoirs or sign petitions. The anonymity of the urban crowd presents a difficult problem for both contemporary investigators as well as historians. The key to understanding who did and who did not participate in the riot, however, lies within the social and economic map of the city at the time. Geography, ethnicity, and class played equal roles in creating the white rioters in Chicago in July and early August 1919.

The human geography of the South Side is crucial for understanding the city's history. In a city that by World War I was predominantly Roman Catholic, parish boundaries also proved crucial for understanding urban society. Add to this a web of ethnicity and class, and Chicago's human geography seemed formidable to the outsider. To the Chicago native, however, ethnicity was easily discernible along the streets and alleys of a familiar world. Map 1 places the Irish and Polish Catholic parishes of the city's South Side in their relationship to each other, the Black Belt, and the Union Stock Yards. The map covers the area south of 26th Street to 79th Street from Lake Michigan to California Avenue.

It therefore includes the major area of rioting in 1919 and the area where, up to 1930, racial clashes most often occurred.

Six Polish Roman Catholic parishes stood in this district. They are marked on the map by the letters *A* through *F*. Together they form a crescent-shaped area in which the majority of Polish South Siders lived in 1919. This Polish crescent stretched from an area to the north of the stockyards to one just to the south along the industry's western flank. No Polish churches existed east of Halsted Street, although without a doubt some Poles lived east of that major Chicago artery.

The Irish parish system that emerges by tracing the English-speaking territorial parishes is much more complex but nevertheless readily discernible. These parishes are marked by numbers on the map. Seven Irish ones circled the stockyards. An eighth, St. John the Baptist (5), while serving French Canadians, was nevertheless heavily attended by Irish-American families. This Irish "wheel" overlapped the Polish crescent in various spots. By 1919, however, these Irish parishes were, with the exception of those to the south and east of the yards, already in decline as Poles and other "new" immigrants occupied the neighborhoods to the north and southwest of the stockyards.

Another group of Irish parishes stood farther south, southwest, and to the east of the packing plants. These Catholic parishes reflected upward mobility for the South Side Irish. They ranged from Holy Angels (10) and St. Elizabeth's (11) on the east to St. Theodore's (19) and St. Justin Martyr (18) to the southwest. The core of Englewood and Washington Park parishes was extremely important for this grouping. Several parishes such as Visitation and St. Basil's seem to have played an intermediary role in providing a socioeconomic link from the stockyards to the more prosperous sections of Englewood and Washington Park. This Irish middle-class crescent touched, and in some cases crossed, the emerging Black Belt in 1919. Several of these parishes witnessed racial change during and after World War I.

The events of July and August 1919 occurred in various sections of the city. They centered, however, on the South Side, home to Chicago's largest African-American population and to vast European ethnic enclaves as well as to large lakefront white middle-class neighborhoods. Seventy-five percent of the more than five hundred Chicagoans hurt were injured in the area covered by Map 1. Thirty-eight male Chicagoans died during the racial fighting. Twenty-three of these were black and fifteen white. While rioters injured ten women in the fighting, none died according to the official count. Thirty-three of the thirty-eight deaths, or 89 percent, occurred in the area covered by the map.[7] Since it would be impossible to detail the ethnicity and place of injury of all those hurt in the riot, this paper will focus on the fatalities.

Map 2 plots out the thirty-three deaths that took place on the South Side during the riot. These are placed in relation to the Irish and Polish neighborhoods in that section of the city. A casual look at the map suggests that riot-related deaths occurred primarily to the east of the Union Stock Yards. This fact is not surprising because of the geographic location of the Black Belt to the east of Wentworth Avenue.

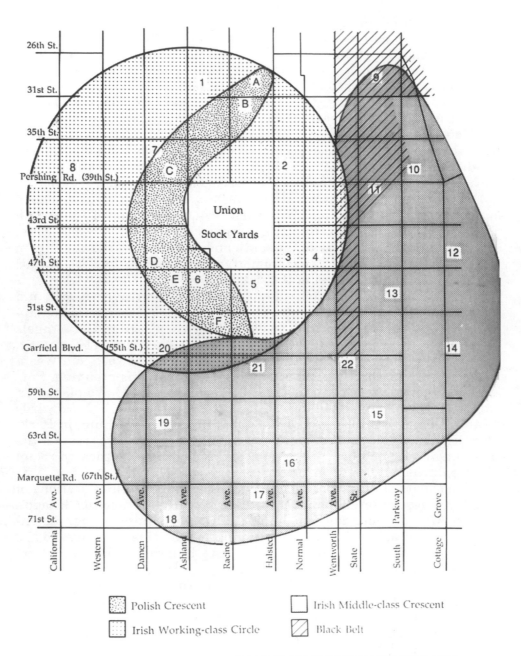

Map 1      PARISH/RESIDENTIAL AREAS IN CHICAGO'S SOUTH SIDE, 1919

MAP 1.  PARISH/RESIDENTIAL AREAS IN CHICAGO'S SOUTH SIDE, 1919

### Polish Crescent: Polish Roman Catholic
### South Side Parishes, 1919*

A.  St. Barbara, 2859 S. Throop St. (Bridgeport)
B.  St. Mary of Perpetual Help, 1039 W. 32d St. (Bridgeport)
C.  SS. Peter and Paul, 3745 S. Paulina St. (McKinley Park)
D.  Sacred Heart, 4602 S. Honore St. (Back of the Yards)
E.  St. Joseph, 4821 S. Hermitage St. (Back of the Yards)
F.  St. John of God, 1234 W. 52d St. (Back of the Yards)

### Irish Working-class Circle: English-Speaking (Irish)
### Roman Catholic South Side Parishes, 1919*

1.  St. Bridget, 2928 S. Archer Ave. (Bridgeport)
2.  Nativity of Our Lord, 653 W. 37th St. (Bridgeport)
3.  St. Gabriel, 4522 S. Wallace Ave. (Canaryville)
4.  St. Cecilia, 4515 S. Wells St. (Fuller Park)
5.  St. John the Baptist, 911 W. 50th Pl. (Back of the Yards)†
6.  St. Rose of Lima, 4747 S. Ashland Ave. (Back of the Yards)
7.  Our Lady of Good Counsel, 3528 S. Hermitage St. (McKinley Park)
8.  St. Agnes, 2648 W. Pershing Road (Brighton Park)

### Irish Middle-class Crescent: English-Speaking (Irish)
### Roman Catholic South Side Parishes, 1919

 9.  St. James, 2942 S. Wabash Ave. (Near South Side)
10.  Holy Angels, 607 Oakwood Blvd. (Oakland)
11.  St. Elizabeth, 4049 S. Wabash Ave. (Grand Boulevard)
12.  St. Ambrose, 1012 E. 47th St. (Kenwood)
13.  Corpus Christi, 4920 South Parkway (Grand Boulevard)
14.  St. Thomas the Apostle, 5472 S. Kimbark Ave. (Hyde Park)
15.  St. Anselm, 6045 S. Michigan Ave. (Washington Park)
16.  St. Bernard, 340 W. 66th St. (Englewood)
17.  St. Brendan, 6714 S. Racine Ave. (Englewood)
18.  St. Justin Martyr, 1818 W. 71st St. (West Englewood)
19.  St. Theodore, 1650 W. 62d St. (West Englewood)
20.  St. Basil, 1850 W. Garfield Blvd. (Back of the Yards/Englewood)
21.  Visitation, 843 W. Garfield Blvd. (Back of the Yards/Englewood)
22.  St. Anne, 153 W. Garfield Blvd. (Washington Park/Englewood)

Other South Side Irish parishes were located farther south, southwest, and southeast

**Source**: The map and list are based on the Rev. John McMahon, S.T.D., *City of Chicago Catholic Map Directory* (Chicago, 1954).
*The address listed is that of the parish rectory.
†A French-Canadian parish, it had a large Irish-American population.

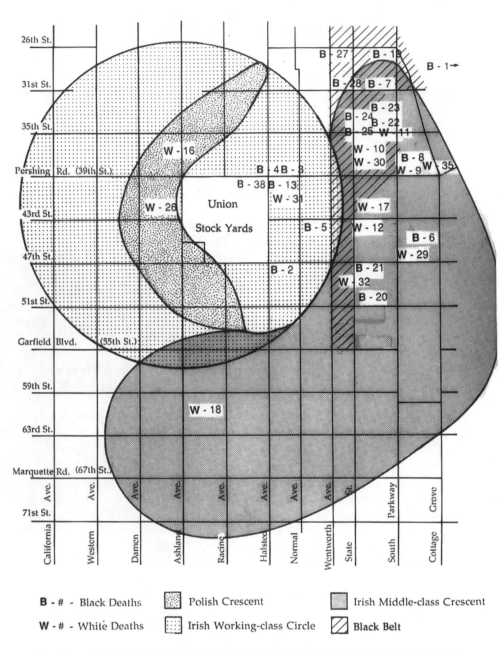

Map 2     BLACK AND WHITE RIOT DEATHS/ETHNIC RESIDENTIAL AREAS
          IN CHICAGO'S SOUTH SIDE, 1919

MAP 2.  BLACK AND WHITE RIOT DEATHS/ETHNIC RESIDENTIAL AREAS
IN CHICAGO'S SOUTH SIDE, 1919 (Name/Race/Date/Location)

1. Eugene Williams  B  7/27  Lake Michigan at 29th St.
2. John Mills  B  7/28  Normal Avenue, 150 ft. south of 47th St.
3. Oscar Dozier  B  7/28  39th St. and Wallace Ave.
4. Henry Goodman  B  7/28  39th and Union Ave.
5. Louis Taylor  B  7/28  Root St. and Wentworth Ave.
6. B. F. Hardy  B  7/28  46th and Cottage Grove Ave.
7. John Simpson  B  7/28  31st St. between Wabash Ave. and the El
8. Henry Baker  B  7/28  544 E. 37th St.
9. David Marcus  W  7/28  511 E. 37th St.
10. Eugene Temple  W  7/28  3642 S. State St.
11. William J. Otterson  W  7/28  35th and Wabash Ave.
12. Stefan Horvath  W  7/28  Root and State St.
13. Edward W. Jackson  B  7/29  40th and Halsted
14. Samuel Bass*  B  7/29  22d and Halsted or Union Ave.
15. Joseph Lovings*  B  7/29  839 Lytle St.
16. Nicholas Kleinmark  W  7/28  38th and Ashland Ave.
17. Clarence Metz  W  7/28  43d St. between Forrestville and
    Vincennes Ave.
18. Berger Odman  W  7/29  60th and Ada St.
19. James Crawford  B  7/27  29th and Cottage Grove Ave.
20. Thomas Joshua  B  7/29  51st and Wabash Ave.
21. Ira Henry  B  7/30  4957 S. State St.
22. Joseph Sanford  B  7/28  35th and Wabash Ave.
23. Hymes Taylor  B  7/28  35th and Wabash Ave.
24. John Walter Humphrey  B  7/28  35th between Wabash and the El
25. Edward Lee  B  7/28  35th and State St.
26. Joseph Schoff  W  7/30  4228 S. Ashland Ave.
27. Samuel Banks  B  7/30  2729 Dearborn St.
28. Theodore Copling  B  7/30  2934 S. State
29. George Flemming  W  8/5  549 E. 47th St.
30. Casmere Lazzeroni  W  7/28  3618 S. State
31. Joseph Powers  W  7/29  Root and Emerald Streets
32. Walter Parejko  W  7/29  51st near Dearborn St.
33. Morris I. Perel  W  7/29  51st and Dearborn St.
34. Harold Brignadello*  W  7/29  1021 S. State St.
35. George L. Wilkins  W  7/30  3825 S. Rhodes St.
36. Paul Hardwick*  B  7/29  Wabash Ave. and Adams St.
37. Robert Williams*  B  7/29  State and Van Buren St.
38. William Dozier  B  7/31  Union Stock Yards, Sheep Pens, Exchange
    Avenue near Cook Street

**Source**: The map and list are based on the Chicago Commission on Race
Relations, *The Negro in Chicago: A Study of Race Relations and a Race
Riot* (Chicago: University of Chicago Press, 1922).
*Not marked on map.

The table below gives the breakdown of deaths by race in relationship to the ethnic parish locations. Of the nineteen South Side black deaths, none occurred north or west of the stockyards or in that part of the Polish crescent south of the packinghouses. Two killings took place in these areas, and they were both white males. These two deaths occurred near the Irish parishes of St. Rose of Lima and Our Lady of Good Counsel in that part of the Stock Yard District where the Irish working-class circle and the Polish crescent intersected. Meanwhile, of the twenty-three African-American deaths citywide, five occurred in the working-class neighborhoods between Halsted and Wentworth Avenues in Irish-dominated Canaryville and Fuller Park. One African-American victim also died in the stockyards, which the map treats as neutral territory. Four more blacks and seven whites died in the middle-class Irish crescent farther to the south and east of the stockyards. These died at least a mile from any Polish Catholic parish, but all were within close proximity of an Irish church. Thus, twenty deaths occurred within the Irish working-class and middle-class zones pictured on the maps. This accounts for more than 50 percent of the riot-related deaths. Eleven additional deaths took place within the Black Belt or in areas adjacent to it. Eugene Williams died in Lake Michigan, which the map also treats as neutral territory.

**Distribution of South Side Race Riot-Related Deaths, 1919**

|  | Polish Crescent Deaths | Irish Working-Class Circle Deaths | Irish Middle-Class Crescent Deaths | Black Belt Deaths | Other | South Side Total | City Total |
|---|---|---|---|---|---|---|---|
| Black deaths | 0 | 5 | 4 | 8 | 2 | 19 | 23 |
| White deaths | 2* | 3* | 8 | 3 | 0 | 14 | 15 |

Source: Chicago Commission on Race Relations, *The Negro in Chicago: A Study of Race Relations and a Race Riot* (Chicago: University of Chicago Press, 1922).
*Two deaths counted in Polish Crescent also counted in Irish Working-Class Circle

A closer look at both maps reveals an interesting relationship between the Irish middle-class crescent and the Black Belt. A cluster of four black and one of the white deaths occurred at the intersection of 35th Street and Wabash Avenue in the Irish parish of St. James. The Catholic boys' high school, De La Salle, was also located at this intersection across the street from the Angelus House, the site of a major confrontation between Chicago police and a mob of blacks. The Angelus House was basically an Irish boardinghouse left over from the era when the Irish dominated the neighborhood. De La Salle, sometimes referred to as the "poor boy's college," served both the Irish working-class and middle-class neighborhoods of the South Side.[8] Two other whites died just south of 35th Street on State Street, one an Italian peddler, the other a white laundry owner of unknown ethnicity. Farther south another cluster of deaths took place in the Washington Park neighborhood near 51st and Wabash. This area lay within the boundaries of Corpus Christi Parish, yet another Irish middle-class parish threatened by racial change. A group of deaths also centered around Holy Angels Church just south of 39th Street. Here, too, African Americans were moving into still another Irish middle-class neighborhood. The linkage of thirty-one riot deaths to the Irish districts or to areas of the city once part of it, and by 1919 in the Black Belt, points to the ethnic and socioeconomic focus of the riot. This relationship may even point to the very nature of the riot itself.

A look at the backgrounds of those whites who died in the fighting is of some help in tracing the socioeconomic basis of the riots. Some of the whites were innocent victims killed during the most violent phases of the riots. Several of these were middle-class South Side residents. Morris I. Perel, a Jewish small businessman who lived on the 5200 block of South Indiana, died not far from his home. A mob murdered David Marcus, a sixty-year-old Jewish shoemaker, next door to his place of business on East 37th Street. Eugene Temple, a thirty-five-year-old white laundry owner of unknown ethnicity, and Casmere Lazzeroni, a sixty-year-old Italian peddler, both died on the 3600 block of South State Street on the second day of the rioting. George L. Wilkins, a Metropolitan Life Insurance agent, died while visiting black customers at 3825 South Rhodes. Wilkins lived at 5010 South Calumet Avenue. Among white working-class victims, Stefan Horvath and Walter Parejko both died while working in the Black Belt. William J. Otterson, a plasterer, died while driving past the corner of 35th and Wabash, the site of the Angelus House riot. These eight casualties do not seem to have been actively involved in the rioting. That leaves seven other white fatalities.[9]

The striking characteristics of those active participants who died, and for whom information can be found, are their age, socioeconomic background, and mixed ethnicity. The rioters were a group of young men from lower middle-class backgrounds and old immigrant stock. Twenty-year-old Nicholas Kleinmark, who died in a streetcar attack and lived at 3449 South Ashland Avenue in the McKinley Park neighborhood, appears to have been the lone working-class fatality. The two Kleinmarks listed in the prewar Chicago directories at that address both had working-class jobs. The McKinley Park area contained large Irish and German populations as well as many Poles. Kleinmark's wake was held at Hickey's Funeral Parlor in the neighborhood.

Berger Odman, an Englewood resident probably of Swedish descent, died while participating in an attack on African-American homes in Englewood. The twenty-one-year-old Odman lived at 5737 South Morgan and worked for the telephone company, a job considered lower middle class in 1919. The three Odmans listed in the 1917 directories at the Morgan Street address worked in white-collar positions. The directory listed Gustave Odman as an inspector, Arthur Odman as a clerk at Swift & Company, and Ethel Odman as a clerk at a business on 59th and Halsted.

Joseph Powers was the oldest of this group of riot victims. The twenty-nine-year-old streetcar conductor died in an attack on a black man in the Canaryville neighborhood. The newspapers listed Powers's address both as 525 West 42d Street and 3571 South Archer Avenue. In either case, Powers's position as a streetcar conductor shows that he was not a stockyard worker, thereby adding to the evidence that lower middle-class Chicagoans were very active in the riot.

Clarence Metz, a seventeen-year-old youth, also died in the fighting. Metz lived at 5201 South Ingleside in the middle-class Washington Park neighborhood. His wake was held at Sullivan's Funeral Parlor at 425 East 61st Street. A thirty-five-year-old Rock Island, Illinois, resident, Harry Brignadello, died in the South Loop north of the South Side. Nothing could be found on Joseph Schoff, while George Flemming died in a conflict with the militia. The backgrounds of Metz, Odman, and Powers combined with the sites of the killings point to the lower middle-class and northwestern European ethnic nature—that is, "old immigrants"—of the riot.[10]

Contemporaries blamed the white gangs of the Stock Yard District for much of the trouble. Emily Frankenstein, the daughter of a South Side doctor, remarked in her diary that "it was mostly the unruly element of the employees of the stockyards; the colored people who had been brought up north recently, and overstepped their freedom and privileges and rights, and thought they were better than white folkse [sic]. And some of the rowdy whites, etc. took it upon themselves to seek vengeance on the innocent of the colored."[11] While there is no doubt that the gangs played a central role in the fighting, the social, ethnic, and geographic definition of these gangs must be looked into more closely. They do not seem to be simply stockyard workers.

Sterling Morton, who served in the Illinois Reserve Militia during 1919, remarked years later that African Americans only acted in self-defense. Morton also pointed to "young toughs who would dash about in cars shooting and sometimes pillaging." He further discussed the presence of the athletic clubs and the fact that they were sponsored and protected by local politicians. He mentioned in particular Ragen's Colts, the Hamburgs, and the Lorraine Club. All of these had their headquarters in the Irish sections of the South Side.[12]

Gang activity during the riot seemed to center in the Irish-dominated districts of the South Side. Wentworth Avenue in 1919 passed through or close to various Irish-dominated districts such as Bridgeport, Canaryville, Fuller Park, Washington Park, and Englewood. Wentworth was a major thoroughfare at the time; it connected these districts along with Halsted Street to the west and the great boulevards of the South Side to the east. Ragen's Colts and its affiliates ran white gang activity on the street. The Colts were also known in other parts of the South Side as far west as Ashland Avenue and as far east as Cottage Grove. By no means were the Colts and their allies exclusively Irish-American organizations, but, as their sponsor's name testifies, the Irish predominated. Other members were usually second-generation Americans of mixed ethnic origin. The Colts had some 2,000 members who paid two dollars in annual dues in 1919. Their headquarters were at the intersection of 52d and Halsted in an area where two parishes were located, Visitation, an Irish church, and St. John the Baptist, a French-Canadian parish with a large Irish membership. Their extensive headquarters occupied several floors of the building. The organization fitted out the clubhouse with a considerable amount of athletic equipment. It also contained various "parlors," an assembly hall, and a pool and billiard room. Jimmie O'Brien served as the organization's president in 1919. Frank Ragen, a South Side politician and member of the Board of County Commissioners, sponsored the so-called athletic club. His political connections were often used to protect members of the club who came into conflict with the police. The Colts had long been identified with lawlessness and racial clashes even before the riot. According to O'Brien, members had to be at least eighteen years of age. The president claimed that the Colts had not taken part in the riot and that they had gotten a bad reputation because some five hundred new members had been recruited during World War I to make up for those who had left to serve in the armed forces. It was these members who caused the trouble. O'Brien claimed that the club had expelled the younger recruits, and that the Colts now enforced the minimum-age-of-eighteen rule.[13]

Mary McDowell, of the University of Chicago Settlement House, testifying before the Chicago Commission on Race Relations, said that politicians had extended their patronage to gangs of boys as young as thirteen and fourteen in order to exploit them. McDowell claimed that the athletic clubs provided one of the most dangerous problems that the city faced. Certainly, Frank Ragen was not the only politician supporting a club. Alderman Joseph McDonough of Bridgeport backed the Hamburg Athletic Club, which counted the young Richard J. Daley, the future mayor of Chicago, among its members.[14]

According to the Chicago Commission on Race Relations, these white gangs became bolder in the spring of 1919. The Commission pointed out various clashes in the Washington Park and Englewood areas. Once again these clashes occurred within the boundaries of the Irish middle-class crescent. As a result of the inability of the police to find witnesses, or the perceived intervention of politicians on behalf of the athletic clubs, African Americans had little faith in the Chicago police or the judicial system in the summer of 1919.[15]

The police came under suspicion from the beginning of the racial conflict. They arrested African Americans in large numbers and killed seven blacks during the riot but no whites. George Flemming, the lone white killed by a law enforcement officer, was bayonetted, along with another white named Fennesey, by a militiaman. In contrast to the Chicago police, the militia proved to be a well-trained and disciplined force that quickly cracked down on the athletic clubs.[16]

The presence of the militia after July 30 proved crucial to the restoration of order. While many of the troops originally thought that they would be fighting blacks, they quickly changed their opinions once in the field. The militia soon identified the white athletic clubs as the major problem. The troops were not tainted by any personal or political connection with the white athletic clubs. They moved especially hard against these groups. Gang members, in turn, showed a good deal of contempt for the militia. The troops, however, remained well disciplined and quelled the riot.[17]

The use of automobiles and trucks in raids in the Black Belt also is of interest in tracking down the gangs. The police definitely tied the automobiles to the athletic clubs. In the investigation after the riot, witnesses told the police that the gangs met in club headquarters and were furnished "auto trucks" to speed through the Black Belt to throw what the police called "grenade torches"—bricks that were tightly wrapped in wastepaper and saturated with oil. They could be easily thrown through a window to cause a conflagration. The police noted that the gangs also used stolen railroad gasoline torches to start the fires. Many of those involved in the firebombings were under the age of twenty. On August 14 the police arrested fifteen-year-old Matthew Walsh and eighteen-year-old Joseph Touhy, both of 59th and La Salle in the Washington Park neighborhood, for their involvement in the firebombings.[18]

The automobile gave a good deal of geographic mobility to the rioters. At first consideration, the use of cars would imply that whites driving through the Black Belt could come from any place in the city. The automobile attacks would seem to cloud the identity of the assailants. Yet, looked at in another way, the use of cars points once again to the middle- and lower middle-class origins of the gangs. In 1919 the automobile was still a middle-class luxury. Widespread use of cars and trucks by gang members indicated that these were not the children of newer immigrants but of older, more established groups. This conclusion fits well with the outbreak of violence in the zone distinguished by middle- and lower middle-class Irish parishes.

By the end of World War I, Irish Americans had started to experience upward mobility. Most still lived in a working-class world, but they had begun to move into the higher strata of that world and out of it into the middle class. Their aspirations were high, and the prosperity of the war years gave them a taste of a better future. It was here that their clash with the city's expanding black community would occur. African Americans, too, had witnessed at least the promise of prosperity. The geographic and economic history of the city put these two groups on a collision course.[19]

Polish Americans, on the other hand, were still settling in Chicago and becoming acculturated into American society. In 1919 the Polish community remained firmly entrenched in the lower levels of the working class. Most labored as unskilled or semiskilled workers. They made up a large number of the membership of the emerging unions in the steel and meatpacking industries. Poles had learned the importance of class and communal solidarity in Poland. That appreciation became intensified in industrial Chicago.[20]

Much has been said concerning the clash between white and black workers over the issue of organized labor in the stockyards. Many African Americans harbored negative views of the unions. Black leaders often spoke out against the folly of joining the "white" union. Job competition was a major source of conflict as the country attempted to adjust to peace. If the Poles and blacks were to clash in 1919, it would be over this subject. After all, few middle-class African Americans looked to the Polish tenement district in Back of the Yards for relief from the ghetto. Also, few Poles thought of moving into Washington Park, Englewood, or Hyde Park far from the communal institutions they had established in Back of the Yards, Western Bridgeport, McKinley Park, or the steel mill district in South Chicago. Unlike the Irish, the Poles had not yet made a commitment to moving out of the working-class neighborhoods. They were still in the process of making these districts their own.[21]

Since before the turn of the century blacks and whites had clashed over labor issues. Black strikebreakers arrived in the stockyards in 1894. They reappeared ten years later. The 1905 teamsters' strike resulted in twenty deaths and over four hundred injuries. The strike had turned into a race riot before it ended. All African Americans on the street became targets of mobs. In turn, blacks began to defend themselves. The 1905 strike in many ways presaged the 1919 conflict. There was plenty of historical fuel to stoke the fires after World War I.[22]

It is interesting, therefore, to note the reaction of the Polish community to the outbreak of the riot. On July 28, 1919, the *Dziennik Związkowy*, Chicago's leading Polish newspaper, ignored the riot. The first news of the racial conflict appeared the next day in a short article discussing the tumult and offering a short history of the African-American experience in the United States. It ended with the question, "Is it not right that they should hate the whites?"[23] As the riot raged on, the *Dziennik Związkowy* continued to cover the fighting. Until August 2 the paper generally took a neutral, if not pro-black, stance. By that date, however, it began to identify black interests with those of the meat-packers. The paper claimed that the packers planned to use the riot to crush the union in the stockyards.[24]

The *Dziennik Chicagoski*, the city's other leading Polish newspaper, with a point of view considerably to the right of the *Dziennik Związkowy*, covered the riot extensively from the beginning. The newspaper blamed Mayor William H. Thompson for the riot. In an editorial the paper accused Thompson of favoring African Americans over whites and of making an error in not calling out the militia earlier. The *Dziennik Chicagoski*'s editorial cartoons criticized America for its racial problems.[25]

The *Naród Polski*, the official organ of the Polish Roman Catholic Union, took the most violent stand on the race riots. The newspaper compared East European pogroms to America's race riots and took a much more anti-Semitic and antiblack stand. The newspaper wrote that both groups deserved the treatment they received. The *Naród Polski* went on to claim that both blacks and Jews were controlled by Germans and Bolsheviks. After this, like the other Polish newspapers, the *Naród Polski* warned the Polish community to remain calm.[26]

While the Polish newspapers encouraged the community to be quiet and stay out of the fighting, events continued to run their course. The calling out of the militia seemed to quell the fighting until another tragic episode took place, one that directly involved the Polish and Lithuanian community in Back of the Yards. On Saturday morning, August 2, a fire broke out in the Polish and Lithuanian neighborhoods just west of the stockyards. Forty-nine tenements eventually burned in the Polish parish of the Sacred Heart and the neighboring Lithuanian parish of the Holy Cross. These fires are crucial for understanding the role played by the Polish community in the riot. The Polish press again gives insight into the reaction of the immigrant community to the fires. The civil authorities never established the blame for the fires. Later the grand jury investigation made the argument that the white athletic clubs started the fires in an attempt to incite the East Europeans against the blacks. The Polish community did not have to deliberate. It quickly made up its mind as to who the perpetrators were. The Rev. Louis Grudzinski of St. John of God Parish in Back of the Yards openly blamed the Irish.[27]

The Poles were still a new immigrant group. They looked at American events through European eyes. Spokesmen referred to whites as a separate group from the Poles. This peculiar usage implied that Poles and whites were two different and distinct groups, that whites were Americans. When Polish leaders spoke about blacks and whites not getting along together or of the correctness of black feelings toward whites, they did not see their own group as included. Poles viewed themselves as still outside the web of race relations in American society.

Others agreed. Mary McDowell claimed that the Polish immigrants did not take part in the riot. The chief offenders were Ragen's Colts and the other athletic clubs who attacked black workers outside the stockyards and throughout the South Side. McDowell further claimed that skin color did not concern foreign-born Chicagoans as much as it did native whites. The assertion that the Polish community took no part in the riot is probably not completely true. Still, the evidence of their participation in the fighting is not overwhelming. This lack may primarily be a result of geography. The Poles in general did not live next to large black populations. Streetcar attacks did take place in Polish neighborhoods, but these were ethnically mixed areas and were also within the boundaries of Irish working-class parishes. Among those listed as either killed or as perpetrators of these assaults, no distinctly Polish names appear. There are, however, a few Slavic names, and these may have been Poles. Two of these died on their way to work in the Black Belt, and two others attacked a black man in the livestock-pen riot on the Thursday after the fighting peaked, and just before the fires in Back of the Yards. That some Poles hated blacks goes without question. Police arrested a local resident, John Lendki of 4640 South Lincoln, along with W. E. Jones, who lived in Englewood, for trying to incite a riot after the Back of the Yards fires. They both attempted to address a crowd of victims of the Saturday morning fires. Lendki and Jones harangued the crowd telling them that African Americans wanted to take their jobs and that blacks had set their homes on fire.[28]

The fires of August 2 actually give credence to the view that the East European community had generally stayed out of the fighting. If the grand jury and the Polish leadership were correct, the gangs set the homes on fire to arouse the Poles and Lithuanians against blacks. The ploy did not work. Also, while the *Dziennik Związkowy* should not be taken as the sole voice of the Polish community, the paper reflected much weaker antiblack sentiment than might have been expected. Certainly its attitude was very different from the major English-language newspapers. Perhaps Polish Chicagoans in 1919 had not yet been acculturated into the American tradition of racism.

The question of why the Irish participated in the riots in large numbers and the Poles did not has to be asked. Was it simply a result of geography, or were there other socioeconomic factors? A closer look at the riot in terms of its nature and of the Irish-American community may give some answers.

Chicago's race riot can be broadly defined as a "collective action"— that is, an action by a number of persons with a set of specific goals in mind. Samuel Clark in his study of the Irish Land War points out that participants in such an action might be voluntary or involuntary, so long as the set of goals remains constant.[29] As studies of urban crowds have shown, European crowds acted with specific goals in mind. The definition of the 1919 race riot as a collective action, following Clark's model, leads to the question of the social relationships that created the riot, which in turn leads to the question of goals. How did individuals become involved in the riot? What institution made that participation possible?

The institution that readily comes to mind is obviously the athletic clubs, which were really gangs. The clubs, however, were not the only unifying factor in the white neighborhoods. Various "integrating" factors existed, to use once again a term of Clark's. Included were Catholicism, level of and type of education, familiarity with the city and its local institutions, socioeconomic status, and level of acculturation. All of these factors provided a sense of unity for white Chicagoans. Fragmentation resulted from various "cleavage" factors, which included religious differences, ethnicity, language, and length of stay in Chicago and therefore acculturation. It is a combination of integrating and cleavage factors that point to the division between Polish and Irish South Siders and explain their different responses to the riot.[30]

Here, once again, arises the problem of the ethnic and class complexity of the city. Integrating factors are based, according to Clark and others, on both communal and associational structures. Although Catholicism predominated among both the Irish and the Poles, they lived very separate religious lives. Although the two groups could be called co-religionists, this hardly provided a unifying factor between them. In 1919 religion and ethnicity went hand in hand.

Still, it cannot be claimed that Poles remained totally isolated from the Irish and other groups. Integrating factors that were associational in nature brought these groups together at least in a superficial manner. These links could hardly be otherwise in an intensely multiethnic city such as Chicago. In 1919 organized labor provided the associational structure that predominated on the South Side and brought various ethnic groups together. The Poles enthusiastically supported the labor unions. In many ways their militancy outshone even that of the Irish, who had a longer relationship with the union movement in the United States. One historian has pointed to the very important Americanizing role that unions, especially those in meatpacking, played on the South Side.[31]

Cleavage factors can also be defined as being of two types. There are those that arise out of isolation and those that come from opposition.[32] While integrating factors between Chicago's Polish and Irish communities were few, cleavage factors based on opposition were many. These differences revolved around Catholic hierarchical rivalries, local party politics, and socioeconomic competition. The absence of frequent social interaction also compounded the division between the two groups. It is obvious that one group's internal integrating factor acted as a cleavage factor between the two. It is not surprising, then, that the Poles and Irish did not act in concert in 1919.

The question of the relationship between Polish-, Irish-, and African-American communities then becomes central to understanding the riot. What cleavage factors were most intense between the three groups to lead to violence? If these cleavage factors can be identified, the nature of the riot can be found. Except at the workplace, Poles and African Americans remained basically isolated from each other. The question of organized labor did divide the two groups, but in early 1919 this did not yet seem to be an insurmountable problem. In fact, black union membership had been growing. Indeed, the argument could be made that it was the riot itself that made organizing among African Americans impossible. The Irish and black communities, on the other hand, faced off against each other on various levels that included cleavage factors rooted both in opposition and isolation.

The Irish-American community, though based on the Catholic parish system, tended to be more diffuse than that of the Poles. The Irish were more integrated into the larger society as the result not only of a common language but also of historical chance.[33] The Irish had arrived in Chicago very early in the city's history. In a very real way the Irish community and the city grew up together. By 1919, Irish Americans could be found throughout the city's various neighborhoods. Their length of stay in the United States was much longer than that of the Poles and other new immigrant groups. Therefore, they were more acculturated into both life in industrial cities and American culture.

As is obvious from Map 1, the Irish no longer lived simply in a working-class ghetto. In many ways they had already "arrived" in American society. One is reminded of James T. Farrell's fictional Lonigan family. Mr. Lonigan had worked his way out of the Stock Yard District and into Washington Park's middle class. By the World War I era, the Irish had moved up the ladder of mobility. As sociologists and historians have pointed out, expectations are a key toward social attitudes. Discontent is often based on a group's expectations for the future rather than on the current situation. The Irish, who already dominated the American Catholic Church and who were powerful in American urban politics, expected continued success in the United States. African Americans posed a possible threat to this success, at least insofar as the way in which the Irish middle and lower middle classes perceived that success. James Davies's well-known "J-curve" is important here. Davies argued that revolutions were most likely to occur when socioeconomic advances were followed by a sharp reversal—that is, when expectations were frustrated.[34] The World War I period can be interpreted as such a period for Chicago's Irish. In fact, this era is also a period of tribulation for the growing African-American community in the city. The postwar economic collapse threatened the expectations of both groups who now faced each other on the streets of the South Side. The riot saw those expectations clash in a time-honored American orgy of racism.

The Irish- and African-American communities had clashed before. Even before the Civil War the Irish saw blacks as economic competitors. During the sectional conflict, New York City's Irish engaged in the Draft Riots of 1863, which turned quickly into a race riot in which working-class and middle-class white New Yorkers pursued African Americans through the streets. The Irish played a major role in this conflict. In his study of the riot, Adrian Cook pointed out the helplessness of local authorities to act against the mobs that roamed the city. One persistent motive of the draft rioters was a deep-seated hatred for blacks. Cook asserted that the Irish had a tradition of violence and that many saw violence as the only means of asserting their rights. The local government in New York did not command respect. All of these factors were also present in Chicago in 1919. Even streetcar attacks and the burning and looting of black homes presaged the Chicago experience nearly sixty years later. Another historian of New York's Irish has also pointed out that they often found themselves in conflict with other ethnic groups.[35]

Certainly there was a precedent for the violence of 1919 in Irish history. Ireland had a tradition of local magistrates patronizing gangs for political purposes, much like the patronage of Frank Ragen and Joseph McDonough in Chicago. Much of the agrarian protest in Ireland in the nineteenth century was of a defensive nature—that is, in defense of perceived rights and economic relationships. Irish historians often speak of the inseparable link between collective action and peasant society. Once again the roles of personalism, political families, and patron-client ties remain important. Irish mobs followed particular aims and resorted to violence in order to secure them. Obviously, Irish and Irish-American society had a rich tradition of protest, violence, and collective action from which to draw in 1919.[36]

The riot's typology further explains the reaction of both the Irish and Polish communities to the events of the summer of 1919. What kind of riot was the race riot? Some have called it a communal or ideal-type riot. William Tuttle pointed out that it was hardly a pogrom as some claimed; rather, it was a pitched battle. Over the last decade or so there has been a good deal of study concerning European forms of collective action. Charles Tilly discussed European violence over the last three hundred years in terms of three broad categories: primitive violence, reactionary violence, and modern collective violence. The first two of these tend to be communally based and are resistant to change. The third promotes change. It seems obvious that the 1919 rioters resisted change. The very nature of the institution involved, the social athletic clubs, also spoke to its communal nature. This kind of reactionary violence, localized and communally based, remained important in Ireland itself early into the twentieth century, which, of course, could be said for any place going through traumatic change. It certainly was true for Chicago at the end of World War I.[37]

Both Charles Tilly and George Rudé have discussed the nature of crowds. Rudé made a distinction between backward- and forward-looking groups. Tilly reformulated these terms as proactive and reactive forms of collective action. In 1919 the white rioters responded to what they saw as a threat to their economic well-being.[38]

The Chicago housing market provided a major source of conflict. Violence here was not essentially working-class in nature. Before the riot some twenty-four racially motivated bombings took place in the middle-class wards of the city. During the riot, whites attacked African Americans wherever they lived outside of the Black Belt. White Chicagoans saw the expansion of the Black Belt as aggressive behavior aimed at their economic investments—a type of land-grabbing by blacks and those whites who profited from Chicago's tense racial housing market. The bombings were often aimed at real estate agents and landlords, both black and white, who dealt in racially changing neighborhoods. Of course, assailants also attacked tenants.[39]

Chicago's Irish had the most to lose from an expanding Black Belt. In fact, blacks threatened the city's Irish on three basic fronts. First, housing competition was most acute for these two groups. This fact is obvious from the sections of the city where the two groups overlapped each other. Housing competition was particularly severe in the middle- and lower middle-class neighborhoods of Washington Park and Englewood. Second, with the emergence of the Republican organization of Mayor Thompson, in which African Americans played an important role, blacks threatened Irish domination of the city's political structure. Finally, competition for employment threatened the older and economically less successful Irish neighborhoods such as Canaryville and Fuller Park, out of which the middle- and lower middle-class Irish Americans had already emerged and where they feared they might be driven back.

Poles and blacks, however, did not compete on these three fronts. The Poles generally did not look to the areas east of the Polish crescent for housing. They themselves had more to fear from the Irish politically than from African Americans. It was only in the packinghouses and steel mills that competition between blacks and Poles seemed obvious. The Poles called for unionization as a solution to this problem. Labor leader John Kikulski directed many of his speeches toward this end. He spoke of interracial cooperation, as did Father Grudzinski. These leaders had a class-based appeal that did not reach the Irish. In fact, shortly after the riot, Irish union leader Dennis Lane accused Kikulski and other non-Irish labor leaders, including blacks, of being demagogues. Later, Kikulski supported the Irish, but this was after the demise of the union movement in the ashes of the race riot. It was obvious to all involved that the riot could not help the labor movement.[40]

The Polish response to the African-American community remained class based. The Irish response was also class based. However, it was founded on middle-class expectations and fears of economic slippage. The Irish, and their allied older immigrant groups, thought that they might slip downward on the economic ladder as black neighbors brought perceived economic devaluations of their investments in real estate and helped to dismantle their political and organized labor machines. The Irish middle-class goal was the removal of African Americans from their neighborhoods. While the Irish sought the removal of blacks, Polish workers wanted to bring them into the unions. The Poles knew the riot could not accomplish that.

In order to understand the riot, it is not enough to look for typologies based on the European model. The realities of American immigrant and migrant society have to be investigated. The dominant culture in the United States in 1919 was racist. The question of what it meant to be assimilated, or at least acculturated, into that society is important. To be acculturated meant to accept the dominant theme of racism. By 1919 the Irish-American community had become American. The Irish, along with other older ethnic groups, had accepted basic middle-class American values. The dead and the wounded among the active white rioters seemed to have shared membership in older ethnic groups. The interaction of middle-class expectations and racism proved to be deadly in the summer of 1919. In many ways the riot was not a working-class confrontation, as implied by various studies, but rather a middle- and lower middle-class conflict.

The Poles and other newer ethnic groups quickly became assimilated into the web of middle-class expectations and race. The riot of that summer became an acculturating event for the Polish community. Combined with the packinghouse strike of the winter of 1921–22, it solidified, if not formed, Polish opinions toward African Americans. Not surprisingly, the black community did not support the largely Polish and Lithuanian strike, whose failure ended the role of organized labor in the stockyards for nearly twenty years. In fact, the Chicago Urban League provided African-American strikebreakers during that industrial conflict. By 1928 the Poles of Back of the Yards took part in a meeting of the 14th Ward Citizens Club held at Pulaski Hall at 4831 South Throop Street, in the parish of St. John of God. The club called the meeting to discuss the gradual arrival of "other" races in the district and their negative impact on real estate values.[41]

Despite the fact that Polish and Irish Chicagoans pursued fundamentally different goals at the time of the riot, that event subsequently shaped the relationship between African and Polish Americans on much the same basis as Irish and black relations. Poles became acculturated into the dominant middle-class racist ideology. The riot then should be seen within the dynamics not simply of black-white relations but also within the historical context of the particular ethnic groups involved.

The riot and the later strike were major factors in the acculturation of East Europeans on the South Side.

The black-white dichotomy is useful only to a point. In a pluralistic society, investigators must look beyond it to understand more deeply ethnicity and acculturation and their role in the history of conflict in the United States. Subtle shadings of gray can help historians to understand more clearly the tragic history of race relations in the United States. Acculturation did not bring the Poles and Irish closer, but, unfortunately, it did provide them with a common enemy.

NOTES

*Earlier versions of this article were presented at the Modes of Inquiry for American City History Conference, Chicago, October 25–28, 1990, the University of Chicago Social History Seminar, January 1991, and the Sixteenth Annual North American Labor History Conference, Detroit, October 27–29, 1994. I wish to thank Kathleen Alaimo, Ellen Skerrett, Michael Ebner, Arnold Hirsch, Raymond Mohl, and Kathleen Neils Conzen for their comments and suggestions.

1. Department of Development and Planning, City of Chicago, *The People of Chicago: Who We Are and Who We Have Been* (Chicago: City of Chicago, 1976); James R. Grossman, *Land of Hope: Chicago, Black Southerners, and the Great Migration* (Chicago: University of Chicago Press, 1989).

2. Dominic A. Pacyga and Ellen Skerrett, *Chicago: City of Neighborhoods* (Chicago: Loyola University Press, 1986), 458; Rev. Msgr. Harry C. Koenig, S.T.D., ed., *A History of the Parishes of the Archdiocese of Chicago*, 2 vols. (Chicago: Archdiocese of Chicago, 1980), 1:135; Joseph John Parot, *Polish Catholics in Chicago, 1850–1920* (Dekalb, IL: Northern Illinois University Press, 1981), 133–60; Victor Greene, *For God and Country: The Rise of Polish and Lithuanian Ethnic Consciousness in America, 1860–1910* (Madison: State Historical Society of Wisconsin, 1975), 133–42.

3. William M. Tuttle, Jr., *Race Riot: Chicago in the Red Summer of 1919* (New York: Atheneum, 1972) offers the best overview of the riot.

4. Chicago Commission on Race Relations, *The Negro in Chicago: A Study of Race Relations and a Race Riot* (Chicago: University of Chicago Press, 1922), 5–6, 8; Tuttle, *Race Riot*, 35.

5. Grossman, *Land of Hope*, 164, 178. For a discussion of the ethnic development of the Stock Yard District, see Pacyga and Skerrett, *Chicago: City of Neighborhoods*, chap. 13; and James R. Barrett, *Work and Community in the Jungle: Chicago's Packinghouse Workers, 1894–1922* (Urbana: University of Illinois Press, 1987), chap. 2, which deals with the ethnicity of Chicago's packinghouse workers.

6. Mary E. McDowell, "Prejudice," in Caroline M. Hill, ed., *Mary McDowell and Municipal Housekeeping: A Symposium* (Chicago: Millar Publishing Company, n.d.), 27–32.

7. Chicago Commission on Race Relations, *Negro in Chicago*, 7, 27.

8. Koenig, ed., *History of the Parishes*, 1:454–61; Koenig, ed., *Caritas Christi Urget Nos: A History of the Offices, Agencies, and Institutions of the Archdiocese of Chicago*, 2 vols. (Chicago: Archdiocese of Chicago, 1981) 1:450.

9. Chicago Commission on Race Relations, *Negro in Chicago*, 656–62; *Chicago Daily News*, July 29, 30, 1919; *Chicago Tribune*, July 31, 1919.

10. Chicago Commission on Race Relations, *Negro in Chicago*, 656–62; *Chicago Daily News*, July 29, 30, 1919, August 5, 1919; *Lakeside Directory of the City of Chicago* (Chicago: Chicago Directory Company, 1917).

11. "Emily Frankenstein Diary, 1918–1920." Special Collections, Chicago Historical Society.

12. Sterling Morton, "The Illinois Reserve Militia during World War One and After," Special Collections, Chicago Historical Society.

13. *Chicago Daily News*, August 2, 1919; Chicago Commission on Race Relations, *Negro in Chicago*, 12–15.

14. Chicago Commission on Race Relations, *Negro in Chicago*, 55.

15. Ibid., 53–57.

16. Tuttle, *Race Riot*, 10; Chicago Commission on Race Relations, *Negro in Chicago*, 42.

17. Testimony of Henry McName, Illinois State Militiaman, before the Chicago Commission on Race Relations Meeting, February 25, 1920, Minutes, Microfilm Rolls 30–78, Chicago Commission on Race Relations Papers, Illinois State Archives, Springfield, Illinois; Chicago Commission on Race Relations, *Negro in Chicago*, 42–43.

18. *Chicago Daily News*, August 14, 1919.

19. James T. Farrell, *Studs Lonigan* (New York: Avon Books, 1977). For a discussion of the accuracy of Farrell's novels concerning the South Side Irish, see Charles Fanning and Ellen Skerrett, "James T. Farrell and Washington Park: The Novel as Social History," *Chicago History* 8, no. 2 (Summer 1979): 80–91.

20. *Chicago Daily News*, August 5, 1919. For a discussion of the contribution of Polish workers to organized labor in Chicago, see Dominic A. Pacyga, *Polish Immigrants and Industrial Chicago: The Back of the Yards and South Chicago, 1880–1922* (Columbus: Ohio State University Press, 1991).

21. Grossman, *Land of Hope*, 210–22.

22. Tuttle, *Race Riot*, 109–19.

23. *Dziennik Związkowy*, July 29, 1919.

24. Ibid., August 2, 1919.

25. *Dziennik Chicagoski*, August 1, 1919.

26. *Naród Polski*, August 6, 1919.

27. *Dziennik Związkowy*, August 5, 1919.

28. *Chicago Daily News*, August 2, 1919.

29. Samuel Clark, *Social Origins of the Irish Land War* (Princeton: Princeton University Press, 1979), 4.

30. Ibid., 7.

31. Edward R. Kantowicz, "Polish Chicago: Survival through Solidarity," in Melvin G. Holli and Peter d'A. Jones, eds., *Ethnic Chicago* (Grand Rapids, MI: Eerdmans Publishing Company, 1984), 214–38. For Polish participation in labor unions, see Pacyga, *Polish Immigrants and Industrial Chicago*; and Barrett, *Work and Community*, chap. 4.

32. Clark, *Irish Land War*, 9.

33. Michael F. Funchion, "Irish Chicago: Church, Homeland, Politics, and Class: The Shaping of an Ethnic Group, 1870–1900," in Holli and Jones, *Ethnic Chicago*, 17.

34. Clark, *Irish Land War*, 12.

35. Adrian Cook, *The Armies of the Streets: The New York City Draft Riots of 1863* (Lexington: University of Kentucky Press, 1974), 30, 77, 82; Ronald H. Bayor, *Neighbors in Conflict: The Irish, Germans, Jews, and Italians of New York City, 1929–1941* (Baltimore: Johns Hopkins University Press, 1979), 1.

36. S. J. Connolly, "Violence and Order in the Eighteenth Century," in Patrick O'Flanagan, Paul Ferguson, and Kevin Whelan, eds., *Rural Ireland, 1600–1900: Modernization and Change* (Cork: Cork University Press, 1987), 48, 53; Samuel Clark and James S. Donnelley, Jr., eds., *Irish Peasants: Violence and Political Unrest, 1780–1914* (Madison: University of Wisconsin Press, 1983), 25, 421–27.

37. Tuttle, *Race Riot*, 65; Connolly, "Violence and Order," 58.

38. George Rudé, *The Crowd in History: A Study of Popular Disturbances in France and England, 1730–1848* (New York: Wiley and Company, 1964), 48–55; Clark, *Irish Land War*, 353.

39. Chicago Commission on Race Relations, *The Negro in Chicago*, 3.

40. *Butcher Workman*, November 1919.

41. Grossman, *Land of Hope*, 239; *Dziennik Chicagoski*, January 7, 1928.

# Part Three

# The Twentieth-Century City

# Introduction

The patterns of American urbanization and urban life shifted, often dramatically, after 1920. As in the industrial era, dynamic growth remained a constant feature of the urban landscape. By the end of the twentieth century, massive central cities had come to anchor sprawling metropolitan areas. However, suburbia dominated the nation's residential pattern. Almost 115 million Americans, or over 46 percent of the population, resided in the suburbs by 1990—a larger proportion than for those who lived in central cities or rural areas. But in many ways municipal boundaries had become blurred as city and suburban populations pushed the residential periphery far beyond anything imagined in the nineteenth century. By 1990 some thirty-nine metropolitan areas in the United States each had more than one million residents. Giant "supercities" were created as the spreading population filled in empty spaces between existing cities and metropolitan areas.

Vast metropolitan areas thus came to characterize urban America by the 1990s. The New York City metropolitan region, for instance, contained more than 18 million people spread over 3,600 square miles, while the Los Angeles urbanized area of about 2,200 square miles was home to almost 15 million. A densely settled urbanized area of almost 5 million people has emerged along the southeast coast of Florida, an elongated metropolis situated between the Atlantic Ocean and the Everglades and stretching about 100 miles from south of Miami north to Fort Pierce. According to one study, the urbanized northeastern seaboard of the United States—or "megalopolis," as it has been called—will contain about 80 million people, or one-fourth of the nation's population, by the year 2000. These statistics barely begin to suggest the consequences of several decades of volatile demographic, economic, social, and political change.

Huge population shifts within metropolitan regions have become commonplace in the United States since about 1940. The older cities of the Northeast and Midwest—cities that experienced the industrial revolution of the late nineteenth century—have been losing substantial numbers of residents to suburban regions. The classic example is St. Louis, which suffered a 54 percent population loss between 1950 and 1990, leaving the city with less population than it had a century earlier in 1890. Similarly, by 1990, Detroit had lost almost one-half of its 1950 population of about 1.8 million. Both Pittsburgh and Cleveland lost 45 percent between 1950 and 1990. Most of the big "rustbelt" or "snowbelt" cities experienced similar population declines (see Table 1).

**Table 1. Representative Snowbelt Cities, 1950-1990**

| City and Year | Central City Population | Metropolitan Area Population | Percentage Metro Population in Central City | Percentage City Black | Percentage City Hispanic | Percentage City Foreign-Born |
|---|---|---|---|---|---|---|
| Baltimore | | | | | | |
| 1950 | 949,708 | 1,337,373 | 71.01 | 23.70 | N/A | 5.40 |
| 1980 | 786,775 | 2,174,023 | 36.19 | 54.80 | 1.00 | 3.10 |
| 1990 | 736,014 | 2,382,172 | 30.90 | 59.20 | 1.00 | 3.20 |
| Boston | | | | | | |
| 1950 | 801,444 | 2,369,986 | 33.82 | 5.00 | N/A | 18.00 |
| 1980 | 562,994 | 2,763,357 | 20.37 | 22.50 | 6.50 | 15.50 |
| 1990 | 574,283 | 2,870,669 | 20.01 | 25.60 | 10.80 | 20.00 |
| Chicago | | | | | | |
| 1950 | 3,620,962 | 5,495,364 | 65.89 | 13.60 | N/A | 14.50 |
| 1980 | 3,005,078 | 7,103,624 | 42.30 | 39.80 | 14.10 | 14.50 |
| 1990 | 2,783,726 | 6,069,974 | 45.86 | 39.10 | 19.60 | 16.90 |
| Cleveland | | | | | | |
| 1950 | 914,808 | 1,465,511 | 62.42 | 16.20 | N/A | 14.50 |
| 1980 | 573,822 | 1,898,825 | 30.22 | 43.80 | 3.10 | 5.80 |
| 1990 | 505,616 | 1,831,122 | 27.61 | 46.60 | 4.60 | 4.10 |
| Detroit | | | | | | |
| 1950 | 1,849,568 | 3,016,197 | 61.32 | 16.30 | N/A | 14.90 |
| 1980 | 1,203,339 | 4,353,413 | 27.64 | 63.00 | 2.40 | 5.70 |
| 1990 | 1,027,974 | 4,382,299 | 23.46 | 75.70 | 2.80 | 3.40 |

| | | | | | |
|---|---|---|---|---|---|
| New York | | | | | |
| 1950 | 7,891,957 | 12,911,994 | 61.12 | 9.50 | N/A | 22.60 |
| 1980 | 7,071,639 | 16,121,278 | 43.87 | 25.30 | 19.90 | 23.60 |
| 1990 | 7,322,564 | 18,087,251 | 40.48 | 28.70 | 24.40 | 28.40 |
| Philadelphia | | | | | |
| 1950 | 2,071,605 | 3,671,048 | 56.43 | 18.20 | N/A | 11.20 |
| 1980 | 1,688,210 | 4,716,818 | 35.79 | 37.80 | 3.80 | 6.40 |
| 1990 | 1,585,577 | 4,856,881 | 32.65 | 39.90 | 5.60 | 6.60 |
| Pittsburgh | | | | | |
| 1950 | 676,806 | 2,213,236 | 30.58 | 12.20 | N/A | 9.60 |
| 1980 | 423,938 | 2,263,894 | 18.73 | 24.00 | 0.80 | 5.20 |
| 1990 | 369,879 | 2,242,798 | 16.49 | 25.80 | 0.90 | 4.60 |
| St. Louis | | | | | |
| 1950 | 856,796 | 1,681,281 | 50.96 | 18.00 | N/A | 4.90 |
| 1980 | 453,085 | 2,356,460 | 19.23 | 45.40 | 1.20 | 2.60 |
| 1990 | 396,685 | 2,444,099 | 16.23 | 47.50 | 1.30 | 2.50 |

**Sources**: U.S. Census, 1950, 1980, and 1990. For 1950, all metropolitan area population statistics are for Standard Metropolitan Area. For 1980, all metropolitan area population statistics except New York are for Standard Metropolitan Statistical Area; New York statistics are for Standard Consolidated Statistical Area. For 1990, all metropolitan area population statistics except New York are for Metropolitan Statistical Area or Primary Metropolitan Statistical Area; New York statistics are for Consolidated Statistical Area.

Boston lost 28 percent of its population between 1950 and 1990, while Baltimore dropped by about 23 percent, Philadelphia by 24 percent, and Chicago by 23 percent. For smaller cities, the trend of central city population decline was much the same: Buffalo, Providence, Minneapolis, Rochester, Newark, and Jersey City all lost between 23 and 43 percent of their 1950 population by 1990. As Henry Cisneros, secretary of the Department of Housing and Urban Development (HUD), noted in a 1995 report, "Since 1950 the metropolitan population of the United States has almost doubled, but the population density of the country's 522 central cities has been halved."

Several consequences flowed from these metropolitan population shifts. Beginning in the immediate postwar era, most of those fleeing the cities were middle-class and working-class whites who found in the suburbs a more pleasant life-style and an opportunity to demonstrate their upward economic mobility. The suburbs were appealing as well because they offered racial homogeneity and social exclusivity—a means of escaping the increasing poverty and racial diversity of the central cities. Thus, while the central cities suffered the consequences of a declining population base, the suburban rings surrounding the cities were expanding at an enormous rate, even as early as midcentury. Central city populations were on the downswing, but virtually every major industrial city witnessed large population increases in its metropolitan areas between 1950 and 1970. The trend began reversing slightly in a few northeastern and midwestern metropolises between 1970 and 1980. During that decade, seven of the thirty-nine largest metropolitan areas contracted in population: New York, Philadelphia, St. Louis, Pittsburgh, Cleveland, Milwaukee, and Buffalo. During the 1980s, the picture was mixed, with some of the above cities showing additional declines, while metropolitan New York and Detroit began increasing again. For the entire period from 1950 to 1990, the general trend of metropolitan population was upward, with a slowing of growth toward the end of the century (see Table 1).

As the urban whites fled to the suburban frontier, the shrinking central cities came to be more heavily populated by poor and low-income people, blacks, Hispanics, and other new immigrant groups. Clearly, the rapid turnover of urban population left the cities with a declining population base often characterized by more precarious economic circumstances. A 1979 study by investigative journalist Ken Auletta demonstrated, for example, that almost 2 million middle-income people abandoned New York City between 1945 and 1980, while at least that many low-income people moved in. Those moving out were mostly white, while those moving in were mostly black and Hispanic. As a result, Auletta suggested, New York City "has developed a permanent underclass."[1] As the population turned over and the cities aged, housing stock and infrastructure deteriorated, human problems and social conflicts intensified. Every major U.S city faces serious problems of homelessness and welfare dependency. A dramatic pattern of economic deindustrialization was occurring at the same time, as factories shut down or moved away. The combination of a declining tax base and higher welfare and service costs pushed some cities such as New York and Cleveland to the brink of bankruptcy in the 1970s; still others experienced serious fiscal dangers in the 1980s.

Since midcentury, U.S. central cities have become home to heavy concentrations of African Americans. A great black migration from the rural and urban South to the urban North began during and after World War I. The human flow from the South slowed during the depression era of the 1930s but surged forward again after 1940. About 1.5 million blacks migrated from the South to the North and West each decade between 1940 and 1970. As the whites moved to the expanding suburbs after World War II, aided by favorable federal housing, mortgage, tax, and highway programs, the newly arriving blacks moved into aging, formerly white, inner-city neighborhoods. This process of population displacement—the creation of what urban historians have called the "second ghetto"—has dramatically altered the demographic character of the modern American city. Black population majorities or near majorities now prevail in such northern cities as Detroit, Baltimore, Washington, Cleveland, St. Louis, Newark, and Gary. In Chicago and Philadelphia, the proportion of African Americans has reached about 40 percent of the total population. Blacks also became numerically dominant in many southern cities, including Atlanta, Birmingham, Richmond, and New Orleans. In 1890 about 90 percent of black Americans lived in the South, but by 1970 less than half of the black population remained in the region. Similarly, early in the twentieth century, blacks were heavily rural, but by the 1980s they had become the most urbanized of all racial groups in the United States.

The twentieth-century American city has other newcomers, too. An enormous Hispanic migration to the urban Southwest and to selected other cities has added to the ethnic, linguistic, and political complexity of urban America. By 1990 almost 1 million Hispanics lived in the Miami metropolitan area, about half of the entire population. The arrival of massive waves of Cubans after the success of Fidel Castro's revolution in 1959 initiated a virtual demographic revolution in south Florida, a process that intensified in more recent years with the emergence of large communities of Nicaraguans, Colombians, and others from south of the border. Hispanics made up almost 25 percent of New York City's population in 1990; Puerto Ricans began coming to New York in sizable numbers by midcentury, and in more recent years they have been joined by hundreds of thousands of Colombians, Dominicans, and other Latin newcomers. In Los Angeles, the Hispanics—largely Mexican and Mexican American—totaled about 40 percent of the city's entire population in 1990. In Houston, Dallas, San Antonio, El Paso, Albuquerque, Phoenix, San Diego, and other southwestern cities, the proportion of Hispanic residents is rising rapidly. Even in Chicago, in the center of the industrial snowbelt, Mexican, Cuban, and Puerto Rican newcomers pushed the Hispanic population to about 20 percent in 1990 (see Tables 1 and 2). Most demographers agree that Hispanics will surpass blacks as the nation's largest minority group soon after the turn of the twenty-first century.

**Table 2. Representative Sunbelt Cities, 1950-1990**

| City and Year | Central City Population | Metropolitan Area Population | Percentage Metro Population in Central City | Percentage City Black | Percentage City Hispanic | Percentage City Foreign-Born |
|---|---|---|---|---|---|---|
| Albuquerque | | | | | | |
| 1950 | 98,815 | 145,673 | 67.83 | 1.20 | N/A | 2.60 |
| 1980 | 331,767 | 454,499 | 73.00 | 2.30 | 33.80 | 4.50 |
| 1990 | 384,736 | 480,577 | 80.06 | 3.00 | 34.50 | 5.50 |
| Atlanta | | | | | | |
| 1950 | 331,314 | 671,797 | 49.32 | 36.60 | N/A | 1.30 |
| 1980 | 425,022 | 2,029,710 | 20.94 | 66.60 | 1.40 | 2.30 |
| 1990 | 394,017 | 2,833,511 | 13.91 | 67.10 | 1.90 | 3.40 |
| Dallas | | | | | | |
| 1950 | 434,462 | 614,799 | 70.67 | 13.10 | N/A | 1.90 |
| 1980 | 904,074 | 2,974,805 | 30.39 | 29.30 | 12.20 | 6.10 |
| 1990 | 1,006,877 | 3,885,415 | 25.91 | 29.50 | 20.90 | 12.50 |
| Houston | | | | | | |
| 1950 | 596,163 | 806,701 | 73.90 | 20.90 | N/A | 2.90 |
| 1980 | 1,595,167 | 2,905,353 | 54.90 | 27.60 | 17.60 | 9.80 |
| 1990 | 1,630,553 | 3,711,043 | 43.94 | 28.10 | 27.60 | 17.80 |
| Los Angeles | | | | | | |
| 1950 | 1,970,358 | 4,367,911 | 45.11 | 8.70 | N/A | 12.50 |
| 1980 | 2,966,850 | 11,497,568 | 25.80 | 17.00 | 27.50 | 27.10 |
| 1990 | 3,485,398 | 14,531,529 | 23.99 | 14.00 | 39.90 | 38.40 |

| | | | | | | |
|---|---|---|---|---|---|---|
| **Miami** | | | | | | |
| 1950 | 249,276 | 495,084 | 50.35 | 16.20 | N/A | 10.80 |
| 1980 | 346,865 | 1,625,781 | 21.34 | 25.10 | 56.00 | 53.70 |
| 1990 | 358,548 | 1,937,094 | 18.51 | 27.40 | 62.50 | 59.70 |
| **Phoenix** | | | | | | |
| 1950 | 106,818 | 331,770 | 32.20 | 4.90 | N/A | 6.70 |
| 1980 | 789,704 | 1,509,052 | 52.33 | 4.80 | 14.80 | 5.70 |
| 1990 | 983,403 | 2,122,101 | 46.34 | 5.20 | 19.70 | 8.60 |
| **San Antonio** | | | | | | |
| 1950 | 408,442 | 500,460 | 81.61 | 7.00 | N/A | 8.00 |
| 1980 | 785,809 | 1,071,954 | 73.31 | 7.30 | 53.70 | 8.30 |
| 1990 | 935,933 | 1,302,099 | 71.88 | 7.00 | 55.60 | 9.40 |
| **San Diego** | | | | | | |
| 1950 | 334,387 | 556,808 | 60.05 | 4.50 | N/A | 7.00 |
| 1980 | 875,538 | 1,861,846 | 47.03 | 8.90 | 14.80 | 15.00 |
| 1990 | 1,110,549 | 2,498,016 | 44.46 | 9.40 | 20.70 | 20.90 |

**Sources**: U.S. Census, 1950, 1980, and 1990. For 1950, all metropolitan area population statistics are for Standard Metropolitan Area. For 1980, all metropolitan area population statistics are for Standard Metropolitan Statistical Area; Los Angeles statistics are for Standard Consolidated Statistical Area. For 1990, all metropolitan area population statistics except Dallas, Houston, and Los Angeles are for Metropolitan Statistical Area; population statistics for Dallas, Houston, and Los Angeles are for Consolidated Statistical Area.

The modern American city, like its industrial era counterpart, has also exercised a magnetic attraction for millions of new immigrants. European immigrants supplied the manpower to propel the industrial revolution in nineteenth-century America, but now the newcomers are arriving from all over the globe, and especially from Third World nations. From Central America, South America, Asia and the Pacific region, the Caribbean, and the Middle East, immigrants have been pouring into the United States driven by war, revolution, oppression, famine, or economic aspiration. As in the past, the city has provided the widest range of opportunities for social adjustment and economic advancement. Typically, the largest ethnic/immigrant groups in Los Angeles, in addition to Mexicans, are Iranians, Salvadorans, Japanese, Chinese, Filipinos, Koreans, Vietnamese, Palestinians, Israelis, Colombians, Hondurans, Guatemalans, Cubans, East Indians, Pakistanis, and Samoans and other Pacific Islanders. Los Angeles has become an ethnic and cultural borderland standing "on a frontier between Europe and Asia and between Anglo and Hispanic cultures."[2] The foreign-born population of Los Angeles in 1990 stood at 38.4 percent of the total. Much of urban America now shares at least some of the ethnic and cultural complexity of Los Angeles. Among the major cities, Miami, New York, San Diego, Boston, Houston, and Chicago all had foreign-born populations above 15 percent in 1990 (see Tables 1 and 2).

The central cities have become new melting pots, and even some older, inner suburbs have received an infusion of black, Hispanic, and new immigrant populations, especially Asians. But most of the suburban periphery continues to be overwhelmingly white and mostly middle class. The suburban phenomenon dates back to the middle years of the nineteenth century, when new transit technology permitted a more widespread spatial distribution of urban population. Simultaneously, changing conceptions of the role of family and home emphasized the salutary effect of domesticity and private residential space, while romanticized views of nature encouraged Americans to distance themselves from the congestion, commercialism, and other problems of the rapidly growing cities. Also, the introduction in the midnineteenth century of a cheap, new building technology—the "balloon-frame" house—transformed home building into a profitable industry for land speculators and suburban developers.

The suburban pattern intensified in the twentieth century. The automobile displaced city mass transit systems and opened up distant fringe areas for suburban development. The real estate industry played a major role as well, mass producing houses in look-alike communities from New York to California, typified by the well-known Levittowns in New York, New Jersey, and Pennsylvania. Also important in the twentieth-century development of suburbia, however, was the shaping role of the federal government after the mid-1930s. Federal highway, housing, mortgage, and tax policies all helped to promote the dispersal of the urban population, particularly the white population, in the years after World War II.

The poor, the blacks, and other minorities remained behind in the deteriorating central cities. However, in recent years, the suburbs have been experiencing many of the problems that their new residents hoped to leave behind in the cities. A 1995 special report in *Newsweek* entitled "Bye-Bye, Suburban Dream" highlighted the components of this new suburban dilemma: crime, drugs, traffic congestion, overcrowded schools, poor planning, environmental damage, declining governmental revenues, and rising expenses for social programs, among other problems. Ultimately, *Newsweek* seemed to suggest, suburbia offered no panacea for those seeking to escape big-city life.[3]

Suburbia has grown tremendously since 1950, but demographers have also noted the more recent growth of rural and nonmetropolitan areas, now labeled by some as "exurbia." During the 1970s, rural and small-town America grew faster than urban and suburban regions. A 1983 demographic analysis in *Scientific American* reported that the level of urbanization began slowing during that decade. While urban populations were still growing, the proportion of the American population in urbanized areas was no longer increasing. Much of this nonmetropolitan growth stemmed from industrial or business relocation; one recent study reported that between 1963 and 1987, three out of five newly created jobs were located in exurbia. However, some nonmetropolitan growth reflected life-style choices among more affluent or retired Americans who could afford to move to Colorado, Idaho, Utah, or Nevada. Of the twenty-five fastest growing counties in the United States between 1990 and 1995, thirteen were located in those four states. There was a perception that the fast-growing mountain and northwestern states did not share the problems of urban-centered life in California or New York. Yet, as the *Scientific American* study suggested, these new population clusters "represent small centers of urban culture transplanted to the countryside and enabled to survive by recent advances in communications, transportation, and methods of industrial production."[4]

The rise of nonmetropolitan America reflected the shifting character of the nation's urban and industrial economy. The manufacturing economies of the cities of the industrial heartland have experienced dramatic transformation, even significant decline, in many cases. Not only has production been shifted to nonmetropolitan areas but to less developed nations as well. Multinational corporations have shut down factories in the old industrial belt and transferred production to South Korea, China, Taiwan, Mexico, and Third World nations. High labor costs in the United States, stiff foreign competition, higher energy costs, corporate mergers and buyouts, and extensive employee "downsizing" all resulted in a massive reorganization of the American economy over the past two decades. A renewed drive for productivity and profit prompted corporate decision making that led to factory closings, heavy blue-collar unemployment, middle-management layoffs, and troubled times in such basic industries as textiles, automobiles, and steel. Large cities with diverse economies have adjusted to change, but many single-industry cities, such as steel-producing Gary and Youngstown or rubber-tire-city

Akron, have withered economically. As early as the 1980s, some observers began postulating the obsolescence of the nation's aging industrial cities—prophecies that have yet to be fulfilled.

As more traditional forms of manufacturing and production declined, a postindustrial and service-oriented economy arose to take its place. This process of economic transformation was well under way in the aftermath of World War II. In fact, as early as 1955, blue-collar manufacturing laborers were outnumbered by service and professional workers. The industrial sector employed less than half as many workers as the growing service economy by the 1980s. Over the past thirty to forty years, the American economy has experienced a sort of "deindustrialization" in which basic industry and its workforce have suffered a dramatic reversal.

During that same period, however, the economy has been propelled by tremendous expansion in the postindustrial service sector. Between the 1960s and the 1980s, over 38 million new service jobs were created in the United States. Many of these service jobs are now held by women, who entered the labor force in large numbers in the postwar era. The service economy now employs over 75 million workers, about 70 percent of the entire workforce. Central to the rapidly growing service economy has been expansion in governmental services, education, medical care, computer technology, information and data processing, business services, recreational activities, shopping malls, fast-food and motel chains, airline travel, and the like. Such new service industries have become essential parts of the new American economy. The provision of government services has become especially important in the new scheme of things. By the 1980s government at all levels in the United States employed more than 16 million civilian workers.

The fortunes of the modern American city have been bound up in the structural transformation of the nation's economy. One consequence of this economic change can be seen in the declining populations of the older, heavily industrial cities of the Northeast and Midwest. Central city employment has suffered, too, because the low-skill newcomers —the blacks, Hispanics, and other new immigrants—often lack the training or skills required for most "high-tech" jobs in the information-processing sector. The low-skill service jobs that are available are also low-paying ones, leaving the aging central cities with chronic problems of underemployment, unemployment, poverty, and social welfare. The city, in short, has been unable to avoid the human and social consequences of the postindustrial economic transformation.

Linked also to the shifting American economy is the dramatic rise of the "sunbelt" cities of the South and Southwest. In 1920 nine of the ten largest cities were located in the Northeast and Midwest. The same was true in 1950. Only Los Angeles was able to break into the top ten in population during that period. With a little over 600,000 people in 1950, Minneapolis was larger than Atlanta, Dallas, Houston, Phoenix, San Antonio, or San Diego. But thirty years of shifting economic and demographic activity have made a big difference in the regional distribution of urban and metropolitan population. By 1990 six of the ten largest cities were located in the Southwest: Los Angeles, Houston, Dallas, Phoenix, San Diego, and San Antonio. Among metropolitan areas in 1990, five of the ten largest were in the sunbelt: Los Angeles, Dallas, Houston, Atlanta, and San Diego (see Tables 1 and 2).

These sunbelt cities and metro areas never experienced the nineteenth-century industrial revolution; they are twentieth-century automobile cities, less densely settled and more widely extended over the urban and suburban landscape. Aided by midtwentieth-century highway building and widespread automobile ownership in the postwar era, sunbelt city populations pushed out the urban and metropolitan periphery to an extent unimagined in the industrial era. Annexation of surrounding territory, which had virtually ceased for older cities by the early twentieth century, became a way of life in the urban Southwest. Between 1950 and 1980, for instance, Houston grew from 160 to 556 square miles, and Oklahoma City from 51 to 603 square miles. By 1994, Phoenix had expanded to 450 square miles from 17 in 1950. By contrast, Philadelphia has remained stable at 130 square miles since the 1850s, and New York City's 299 square miles of territory has remained unchanged since 1898. In several ways, however, these newer sunbelt cities are similar to the older northern ones. During the 1980s, for example, almost two dozen major southern cities lost population to surrounding suburbs, including Atlanta, New Orleans, Birmingham, and Memphis. Similarly, despite massive central-city annexations, the peripheral suburban regions of the metropolitan sunbelt are growing more rapidly than the central city areas. Among the sunbelt cities listed in Table 2, only Albuquerque showed a different pattern.

The explosive urban development of the sunbelt South and Southwest stemmed largely from the deep structural changes in the American economy and consequent new migration flows. With little inherited from the industrial era, the sunbelt cities have grown along with the new service economy. Actually, urban growth in the sunshine regions began in earnest during World War II, when the federal government built dozens of new air bases, naval bases, and military training facilities in the southern and western states. This vast federal investment persisted into the Cold War era, and heavy military and defense spending has continued to sustain prosperity and urban growth in the region. From San Francisco, Los Angeles, and San Diego on the West Coast to Pensacola, Tampa, Miami, and Jacksonville in Florida, the sunbelt cities have profited from the federal military connection. Military airfields surrounded San Antonio, aircraft production boosted Seattle and Los Angeles, the aerospace industry propelled Houston's post-1950 expansion, and big U.S. Navy facilities fueled growth and prosperity in San Diego and Jacksonville.

At the same time, the emerging sunbelt cities were benefiting from the changing nature of the modern American economy. High-tech industries such as electronics and computers, along with energy development in the southwestern "oil patch," gave important stimuli to urbanization. As postwar prosperity roared ahead after 1950, the amenities factor came into play. Americans with more leisure time and higher disposable

incomes avidly began to pursue recreational interests. Almost every child
wanted a trip to Disneyland in California or Disney World in Florida.
The completion of the federal interstate highway system permitted even
working-class Americans to become winter vacationers in the sunshine
regions of the country. And as people lived longer and retired earlier,
the elderly began a migration of their own to Florida, Arizona, and other
retirement havens in the urban sunbelt. For whatever reason, 5.5 million Americans migrated from the Northeast and Midwest to the sunbelt
regions during the 1970s.

A major impetus for sunbelt city growth, it should be clear, has been
the shifting pattern of the American economy. In the postindustrial era,
the looming, almost interchangeable skyscrapers of Atlanta, Miami,
Houston, Dallas, and Los Angeles suggest the power and the persistence
of the information age. There have been some setbacks, to be sure, as
reflected in the impact of the "oil bust" on the economic vitality of such
Gulf Coast cities as Houston and New Orleans. Generally, however, the
new urban America of the South and Southwest has benefited enormously
from the growth of the service economy. Some of the older northern cities with diverse economies have adjusted to economic change; Chicago,
New York, Boston, and Minneapolis remain booming business centers,
even as their peripheral areas—now known as the "outer city"—surge
ahead as well. Some older industrial-era cities have been completely
transformed in the postindustrial age: Pittsburgh and Birmingham, once
grimy steel-producing centers, are now known primarily for new information and service industries, especially in higher education and medicine. The sunbelt migrants have been pursuing new avenues of economic
opportunity. As urban historian James F. Richardson has observed, "Now,
and for the foreseeable future, it looks as if those cities that people want
to live in will be those that generate the greatest employment opportunities."[5] The shifting urban pattern, in short, reflects both the changing
American economy and consequent migration tendencies.

Urban demographic and economic changes have been paralleled by
important transformations in the political life of urban America. Beginning in the New Deal era of the 1930s, the federal government initiated
for the first time a political partnership with the cities. President
Franklin D. Roosevelt built a new Democratic party coalition, relying
heavily on the urban electorate for his political success. As federal intervention, initiative, and activism became the order of the day, social
legislation and public works programs flowed out of New Deal Washington, much of it aimed at city people and urban problems. Since the age
of Roosevelt, the cities have sought out and become reliant on the federal connection. Public housing, urban renewal, mass transit, highway
and public works construction, and public welfare were all funded with
massive infusions of federal dollars. When President Lyndon B. Johnson
revived the New Deal spirit with his Great Society initiatives, the War
on Poverty, community development efforts, the Model Cities program,
and the civil rights crusade all had their roots in the cities. At about the
same time, an "urban crisis" was discovered by social scientists and the

media in the 1960s, especially when explosions of racial violence rocked cities across the nation, from Harlem to Watts, from Chicago and Detroit to Newark and Washington.

The burned-out ghettoes of the late 1960s suggested to many the failure of federal urban policy. In fact, the federal programs that shaped urban America after the mid-1930s did not always have positive effects. A national transportation policy emphasizing highways and the automobile ultimately siphoned population and economic activities away from the central city and toward the periphery. Urban expressways tore through existing neighborhoods, destroyed housing, and left huge empty spaces. Federal mortgage policies, especially FHA and VA, made it possible for working-class urbanites to buy their dream house in the suburbs. A residential appraisal system initiated by the Home Owners Loan Corporation, another New Deal agency, resulted in the redlining and ultimate physical decay of many inner-city neighborhoods. Federal public housing programs promoted residential segregation of the races and encouraged the image of suburbia as a haven from the problems of the city. The high-rise public housing projects that went up in many cities in the 1950s quickly became unlivable vertical ghettoes, and many such buildings have been dynamited to the ground in recent years. Thus, a new era of federal-local cooperation emerged by the midtwentieth century, but unanticipated consequences flowed from the implementation of the new federal programs.

On the other hand, heightened federal activism beginning in the 1930s brought many positive advances for American cities. New Deal agencies not only put millions of unemployed people to work but also financed the construction of needed airports, bridges, subway systems, modern water and sewer systems, parks and recreational facilities, and, according to one recent estimate, over 500,000 miles of streets and 110,000 public buildings such as schools and post offices. To get access to federal funding, city governments had to modernize their operations and develop planning procedures and more efficient management practices. In the 1960s, although President Johnson's urban policies were plagued by mismanagement and political infighting, the War on Poverty succeeded in raising 15 million American families above the official poverty line by 1968.

The difficulties of urban policymaking, along with a changing national political climate, brought a dramatic reversal of public policy and federal activism in the urban arena by the mid-1970s. The shift began in the Nixon-Ford-Carter administrations. In the 1980s the Reagan era witnessed massive federal cutbacks in the public works and social programs that had moved the cities forward in the 1960s. Seeking to turn back the governmental intervention that marked the New Deal and the Great Society, Presidents Ronald Reagan and George Bush, along with their conservative Republican supporters, attempted to restore social policy to the marketplace. Reagan's idea of urban policy was to urge the unemployed in declining cities to vote with their feet and seek new jobs in regions of the country with thriving economies.[6] Thus, tens of thousands of unemployed Michigan autoworkers migrated to Texas cities, where the "blue platers" (a reference to Michigan's blue auto license plate) arrived just in time for the big oil bust of the 1980s.

The policy dilemmas of the Reagan era have persisted into the 1990s. In the Clinton-Gore era, with even fewer financial resources and greater responsibilities, the cities are once more approaching crisis stage, especially in the provision of human and social services. As Secretary Cisneros of HUD noted in 1993, American cities are worse off in the 1990s than they were in the 1960s, when the famed Kerner Commission first declared an urban crisis. But by 1996, Cisneros optimistically noted that substantial progress had been made during the first Clinton administration in reversing the downward slide and that "cities are recovering and climbing back."[7]

Changes in urban policy have paralleled major transformations in the urban political pattern. The shifting racial demography of the cities increasingly was reflected in the local political structure. As the black population of the central cities surged, blacks came to dominate urban politics in many cities, large and small. Beginning in 1967, when black mayors were first elected in Cleveland and Gary, blacks succeeded to the mayoralty in New York, Detroit, Philadelphia, Chicago, Baltimore, Newark, New Orleans, Los Angeles, Atlanta, Richmond, Birmingham, Memphis, Charlotte, Hartford, and Washington, to name only a few major cities. Even those with relatively small black populations, such as Denver, Seattle, and Minneapolis, have elected black mayors in recent years. In Miami, Albuquerque, San Antonio, and Denver, Hispanic politicians rose to the mayoralty. And by the 1990s, reflecting changing patterns of gender relations and the power of the women's movement, women had been elected as mayors in San Francisco, Pittsburgh, Houston, Dallas, San Diego, Minneapolis, Portland, San Jose, Tulsa, Fort Worth, and Washington.

It seemed clear by the 1980s that the old political machines that dominated such cities as Chicago and Detroit had fallen into disarray, at least for a time, as black political leaders built new coalitions with Hispanic voters and white liberals. For instance, the old Chicago Democratic machine that kept Mayor Richard J. Daley in office for twenty years collapsed in the early 1980s, thereby permitting a black former congressman, Harold Washington, to rise to the mayoralty. However, urban politics had become much more complex by the 1990s. Minority political power in the cities seemed on the wane in some places, as white politicians regained power in Chicago, Philadelphia, New York, and Los Angeles.[8] Even in Gary, where the minority population surpassed 86 percent in 1990, voters sent a white candidate to the mayor's office in 1995. In Miami, after twenty years of Hispanic mayors, an "Anglo" politician was swept back into office in 1993. However, when Miami's Steve Clark died in office in 1996, he was succeeded by Cuban-born Joe Corollo.

As mayoral elections have suggested, sweeping political transformations affected late twentieth-century sunbelt cities, too. Lacking powerful ethnic voting blocs and a machine tradition, these cities mostly had been controlled politically by local business and professional elites. Motivated by the booster mentality, the urban elites sought to govern in the interests of the central city business community, at least until the 1960s. The rapid growth of suburbia, however, resulted in newer forms of political conflict in which city and suburb struggled for dominance and control. Many of the issues were spatial or territorial, such as where highways or public housing would be located, or what areas would be annexed, or which schools integrated by busing. Some places resolved these conflicts with experiments in new governmental structures: the creation of a powerful metropolitan government for Miami-Dade County in 1957, the establishment of a metropolitan services district with wide-ranging regional power in Portland, Oregon, in 1992, and city-county consolidations in Nashville, Jacksonville, Indianapolis, Lexington, and Anchorage in the 1960s and 1970s. Other cities, such as Memphis and Charlotte, have sought city-suburban consolidations, although unsuccessfully.

The vast demographic transformations of the cities since the 1960s have now pushed urban politics into a new and more participatory phase. City-suburban battles have long since been supplanted by issues revolving around race, ethnicity, and neighborhood. Neighborhoods and local communities, urban historian Carl Abbott has written, have now "become focal points for political action."[9] In Miami, for instance, with its "tri-ethnic" population of whites, blacks, and Hispanics, virtually every local political issue is perceived in terms of race and ethnicity. As the newcomers to the cities—the peoples from Asia and Latin America, from the Caribbean and the Pacific Basin—become citizens and voters, this new pattern of pluralistic urban politics will certainly intensify in the future. But as David Rusk, former mayor of Albuquerque, has pointed out, only area-wide metropolitan government will enable cities and suburbs to confront their common problems effectively.[10]

As in the industrial era, the twentieth-century American city has served as a center of growth, diversity, and dynamic change. Despite evidence of decline in some areas, the city has demonstrated a capacity for adaptation to new circumstances. While many central cities are troubled, a new urban vitality can be found in the "outer city" on the fringes of the metropolitan areas. Although fragmented socially, the city seems to be periodically regenerated as new population groups come to make their home there. As the traditional industrial economy faded, newer forms of economic activity appropriate to the service economy took the place of older patterns of production. The changing urban political structure has reflected the dramatic demographic and economic shifts of recent decades, and new issues emerged as new political players came to center stage. The progressives of the early twentieth century thought of the American city as "the hope of the future." As the history of the twentieth-century city suggests, tension existed between the utopian vision and the urban reality. It is quite likely that, although the details will surely be different, the twenty-first-century American city will continue to offer the nation a threshold for change, growth, and renewal.

In the following essays, urban historians pursue some of the diverse strands of twentieth-century city life in the United States. Recent historians have offered new interpretations of immigrant and ethnic group life in urban America. Earlier views portrayed the immigrants as uprooted peasants whose traditional cultures were undermined and extinguished during the assimilation process. GEORGE J. SÁNCHEZ gives an alternative analysis in his study of Mexican immigrant life in early twentieth-century Los Angeles. In a neat blending of cultural history, ethnic history, and urban history, he demonstrates the ways in which new leisure-time pursuits and new cultural practices sustained Mexican immigrants in the American city, encouraging the maintenance of their traditional culture and values. Los Angeles was home to almost 100,000 Mexicans by 1930, thus providing a substantial new ethnic market for new cultural forms and leisure-time pursuits. During the 1920s, Chicano entrepreneurs stepped in to serve that market with ethnic foods, restaurants, dance halls, pool halls, theaters, silent films, music, phonograph records, and radio programing. Particularly important, according to Sánchez's analysis, was the musical style known as the *corrido* (popular songs derived from a storytelling folk culture adapted to the American urban environment). *Corridos* not only served to emphasize Mexican national identity but also helped to explain something about the new world in which the immigrants found themselves. As Sánchez notes, the *corrido* composers and musicians acted as "social interpreters who translated and reflected the cultural adaptations that were taking place among the Mexican immigrant population as a whole."[11] In fact, Los Angeles experienced a "Mexican cultural renaissance" during the 1920s, similar in some ways to the better known Harlem Renaissance among black artists, musicians, and writers in New York City. Thus, the first generation of Mexican immigrants in Los Angeles was able to retain much of the traditional culture of the homeland. By the 1930s, however, younger second-generation Mexicans were assimilating to new cross-cultural entertainment forms: talking movies in the English language, dance music and dancing clubs, and English-language music. Immigrant adaptation to urban America was a complex process, but one that was facilitated by a rich and vibrant cultural life.

The Great Depression of the 1930s brought serious problems of unemployment and relief to cities throughout the United States. Most interpretations of President Roosevelt's New Deal program build on the proposition that urban America benefited enormously from an energetic and expansive federal government. That may have been true for cities in the Northeast and Midwest, but ROGER BILES demonstrates that the situation was considerably different in the South. In his article on the New Deal in Dallas, he challenges the now dominant view that FDR's new federal programs brought significant modernization and reform to the urban South. In Dallas, an autonomous local business elite, shaped by a conservative political culture, generally ignored the human and social consequences of the depression. City welfare expenditures were sharply cut back despite rising unemployment. Few gains were made by organized labor, as the Dallas business community supported the anti-union open shop movement. Little was accomplished in the way of new infrastructure and public works projects. Existing Jim Crow racial customs persisted, and African Americans suffered high rates of joblessness, political exclusion, and segregated housing. Moreover, New Deal agencies in Washington condoned racial segregation in Dallas and elsewhere in the South. In the final analysis, Biles contends, the New Deal had a strikingly minimal impact on Dallas. Local business elites demonstrated little support for new federal innovations, and the weight of traditional social customs such as racial segregation remained unchallenged. Most New Deal programs depended on local implementation, but where local officials were hostile to federal intrusion into local affairs, little could be accomplished. New Deal activism has often been portrayed as beneficial to urban America, but this Dallas case study suggests a more complex alternative interpretation.

Post-World War II demographic changes ultimately transformed big-city politics in the United States. By the 1960s, as blacks migrated to the cities and as whites moved to the sprawling new suburbs, urban political power began shifting to African-American voters. In his essay on black urban politics, ARNOLD R. HIRSCH offers a case study of two black mayors—Ernest "Dutch" Morial of New Orleans and Harold Washington of Chicago—and compares their rise to prominence, their electoral success, their exercise of power, and the consequences of their respective mayoralties. There are fascinating parallels in the political careers of the two men as well as major differences between the political structures and practices of the two cities. In New Orleans, blacks had been excluded from a major political role until the civil rights movement. Morial served his political apprenticeship in the National Association for the Advancement of Colored People (NAACP), which provided his political power base. In Chicago, Washington slowly climbed the ladder of the city's Democratic political machine and built a base of African-American electoral support in the city's South Side wards. Both were elected with the overwhelming support of black voters, but in both cases it was division among white opponents that made their election possible. Once in power, each faced new problems in governing, in challenging old power structures, and in carrying out reforms. Expectations for positive change were high among black citizens in both cities, but political realities made reform difficult to achieve, especially in such important areas as housing and schooling.

Hirsch's comparison continues through the issue of succession, as in each city a second black mayor came to power. But the politics were different. In New Orleans, Morial's successor had little commitment to reform and little support among black voters. In Chicago, white machine politicians expediently, and temporarily, supported an African American as Washington's replacement. And things continued to change in succeeding years: in 1989, Chicagoans elected as mayor Richard M. Daley, son of the legendary five-term mayor Richard J. Daley; and in New Orleans in 1994, voters chose Marc Morial, son of Dutch Morial, in a bitterly contested election.

My own article documents the startling new pattern of multi-culturalism evident in many late twentieth-century American cities. In the past thirty years the United States once again has become a nation of immigrants. Nowhere is that fact more observable than in Miami, Florida. Once a glamorous, seaside tourist resort, Miami has become a new immigrant city of tremendous diversity. The process of change began with Fidel Castro's revolution of 1959, which unleashed a massive flow of Cubans to south Florida. In recent years, Miami's exiled Cubans have been joined by other newcomers from Haiti, Nicaragua, Colombia, Jamaica, and elsewhere in the Caribbean basin. The new waves of immigrants since the 1960s have posed special problems for Miami's African-American community. The arrival of the Cubans, in particular, set off thirty years of economic competition, ethnic conflict, and political controversy. A vast array of governmental aid and resettlement programs helped them tremendously, but Miami's blacks resented the favoritism shown to the Cuban exiles. The Cubans have prospered economically and asserted their collective power politically, but the blacks have not fared as well. Miami's numerous racial disturbances since the 1960s reflect its racial division and ethnic polarization. The city provides a classic case study of ethnic and racial conflict in the emerging multicultural America. The Miami story also provides a concrete example of the economic impact of immigrants, a subject of considerable contemporary attention.

Late twentieth-century America has become a nation of suburbs. Decentralization of population and economic activities is high on the list of the major forces transforming the modern American city. Growth of the suburbs began in earnest in the 1920s with the widespread popularity of the automobile among urban businessmen and the middle class. But it was in the decades after World War II that the suburban fringe experienced its most dramatic expansion. To a certain extent, new federal mortgage, tax, and highway policies stimulated the massive postwar suburban migration, but, as WILLIAM SHARPE and LEONARD WALLOCK suggest, the suburbs had many other attractions, not the least of which were the racial homogeneity and social exclusivity of most middle-class suburban communities. They place their discussion within the context of changing interpretations of the suburban experience. A considerable social science literature since the 1970s has portrayed the modern suburb as a new form of city—"outer cities" or "edge cities" complete with office buildings, shopping malls, and high-tech industry as well as residential neighborhoods. Sharpe and Wallock challenge this new suburban conceptualization on a variety of grounds. They demonstrate that the suburbs continue to be segregated by class and race, that they lack the public culture and social diversity of the central cities, and that they remain subservient to the larger metropolitan economy. Moreover, television, film, and other forms of mass culture perpetuate older suburban stereotypes, suggesting the continuity and vitality of traditional forms of suburbia.

The essays gathered in Part Three exemplify recent historical scholarship on the twentieth-century American city. They touch upon impor-

tant interpretive issues and identify some of the powerful forces and
shaping influences that have brought urban America to its present condition. They also suggest directions for the reader seeking a more detailed exploration of twentieth-century urban development and change.


NOTES

1. Ken Auletta, *The Streets Were Paved with Gold: The Decline of New York, An American Tragedy* (New York: Random House, 1979), 12. Auletta expanded on this theme in a later book, *The Underclass* (New York: Random House, 1982). However, it was the work of sociologist William Julius Wilson that popularized the term "underclass." See, for example, William J. Wilson, *The Truly Disadvantaged: The Inner City, the Underclass, and Public Policy* (Chicago: University of Chicago Press, 1987); and William J. Wilson, *When Work Disappears: The World of the New Urban Poor* (New York: Knopf, 1996).

2. David L. Clark, "Improbable Los Angeles," in Richard M. Bernard and Bradley R. Rice, eds., *Sunbelt Cities: Politics and Growth since World War II* (Austin: University of Texas Press, 1983), 269.

3. Jerry Adler, "Bye-Bye, Suburban Dream," *Newsweek* (May 15, 1995): 40–53.

4. Larry Long and Diana DeAre, "The Slowing of Urbanization in the U.S.," *Scientific American* 249 (July 1983): 33–41, quotation on p. 36.

5. James F. Richardson, "The Evolving Dynamics of American Urban Development," in Gary Gappart and Richard V. Knight, eds., *Cities in the 21st Century* (Beverly Hills, CA: Sage Publications, 1982), 44.

6. President's Commission for a National Agenda for the Eighties, *Urban America in the Eighties: Perspectives and Prospects* (Washington, DC: Government Printing Office, 1980); U.S. Department of Housing and Urban Development, *The President's National Urban Policy Report, 1982* (Washington, DC: Government Printing Office, 1982). See also Thomas Bender, "A Nation of Immigrants to the Sun Belt," *The Nation* 232 (March 28, 1981): 359–61.

7. "HUD Chief: Cities Worse Off than in 1968," *Miami Herald*, December 27, 1993; Henry G. Cisneros, *A Report on the State of America's Communities* (Washington, DC: Department of Housing and Urban Development, 1996), 1.

8. On this point, see Jim Sleeper, "The End of the Rainbow," *New Republic* (November 1, 1993): 20–25.

9. Carl Abbott, *The New Urban America: Growth and Politics in Sunbelt Cities* (Chapel Hill: University of North Carolina Press, 1981), 211.

10. David Rusk, *Cities without Suburbs*, 2d. ed. (Washington, DC: Woodrow Wilson Center Press, 1995).

11. George J. Sánchez, *Becoming Mexican American: Ethnicity, Culture, and Identity in Chicano Los Angeles, 1900–1945* (New York: Oxford University Press, 1993), 180.

# Music and Mass Culture in Mexican-American Los Angeles

*George J. Sánchez*

Just south of Los Angeles's central Plaza lay the area known throughout the city as the main arena for activities of leisure in the Mexican community of the 1920s. Sundays were not only a big day for religious practice; they also were big business days for the area's movie theatres, gambling dens, and pool halls—all of which dominated the streets to the south. The constant sound of Mexican music—music that ranged from traditional Mexican ballads to newly recorded *corridos* depicting life in Los Angeles—was everywhere. A burgeoning Mexican music industry flourished in the central and eastern sections of the city during the 1920s, largely hidden from the Anglo majority.

The diminished role of organized religion in the day-to-day life of Mexican immigrants was coupled with increased participation in secular activities. In Mexico, most public events in rural villages were organized by the Catholic Church, with few other opportunities outside the family for diversion. Los Angeles, however, offered abundant entertainment of all sorts. These amusements were generally part of a rapidly growing market in leisure which targeted working-class families during the 1920s. Money spent on leisure-time activities easily outstripped donations to the Church, revealing much about the cultural changes occurring in the Mexican immigrant community.[1] Chicano entrepreneurs responded to the emerging ethnic mass market in cultural forms, even though that market was often dominated by outside advertising and controlled primarily by non-Mexicans. Still, the presence of a growing ethnic market in Los Angeles provided room for many traditional practices to continue, some flourishing in the new environment, but most being transformed in the process.

This chapter will explore the intersection between the growing mass market in cultural forms found in Los Angeles and the leisure-time activities of Mexican immigrants. The various actors who helped shape

*George J. Sánchez is associate professor of history and American culture at the University of Michigan. Reprinted from George J. Sánchez,* Becoming Mexican American: Ethnicity, Culture, and Identity in Chicano Los Angeles, 1900–1945 *(Oxford University Press, 1993), 171–87, 307–11. Reprinted by permission of Oxford University Press.*

the creation of a market aimed at providing Mexican immigrants with products, services, and activities that somehow connected with the ethnic self-identification and collective culture will be identified. The complicated nature of this exchange can best be described, however, by looking at one particular arena of cultural interaction. Music, specifically the creation of a Spanish-language music industry and market in Los Angeles, provides one of the best windows for viewing this nexus of cultural transformation in detail.

*L.A.'s plaza*

The Plaza itself continued to cater to single males, offering pool halls, dance rooms, bars, and a small red-light district. Protestant reformers, therefore, consistently viewed Plaza residents as prime targets for moral rejuvenation. In addition, many small, immigrant-owned eateries were located in the area which catered to a male clientele often unable or unwilling to cook for themselves.

*club life*

A description of a dancing club frequented by single males during this period indicates the extent of the intermingling between sexes and nationalities in the Plaza, a situation which concerned reformers. Located on Main Street, the club "Latino" was open every night except Sunday from 7:30 P.M. to 1 A.M., although it did most of its business on Saturday night. Inside and out, the hall was illuminated by red, white, and green lights, the colors of the Mexican flag. Entrance to the club cost 25 cents, and tickets were 10 cents apiece to dance with women. The female employees were mostly immigrant Mexicans or Mexican Americans, although Anglo American, Italian, Filipino, Chinese, and Japanese women also were available. The band, however, was made up of black musicians and played only American pieces. Mexican immigrant men, dressed in working-class garb, danced "Mexican style" to the American songs; a ticket was required for every dance; and the women partners earned 5 cents per dance. In one corner of the dance floor a Mexican woman sold sandwiches, tacos, pastries, and coffee.[2]

*entertainment*

As Los Angeles Mexicans moved away from the Plaza and the community became more familial in structure, different diversions predominated. Some customs were carried over to marriage from single life. For example, a federal survey reported that three-quarters of Mexican families in Los Angeles continued to spend an average of $14 a year for tobacco. Almost two-thirds read the newspaper on a regular basis. Increasingly, Mexican families began to purchase other forms of entertainment which could be enjoyed by all ages and in the confines of one's home. Over one-third of the families in the Los Angeles study owned radios, often buying the equipment "on time" for an average of $27 a year. A smaller number (3%) owned phonographs, and only 4 percent owned musical instruments. Expenditures for vacations, social entertainment (other than movies), and hobbies were rare.[3]

*Spanish language advertising*

During the 1920s, many American manufacturers and retailers discovered a fairly lucrative market in the local Mexican immigrant community. Despite the clamor for Mexican immigration restrictions, these producers understood that Los Angeles contained a large and growing population of Spanish-speaking immigrants. By 1930, some national products were advertised in the Spanish-language press, and increasingly large distributors sponsored programs in Spanish on the radio.[4] Among products heavily advertised in *La Opinión* during this period were cigarettes, medicinal remedies, and recordings to help immigrants learn the English language.

Even more widespread were appeals to Mexican shoppers by certain downtown department stores. In 1929, for example, the Third Street Store advertised in *La Opinión* by asking, "Why are we the store for Mexicans?" The answer stressed the appeal of special merchandise, prices, and service. Located near the Plaza, offering generous credit, the store had apparently already become a favorite in the Mexican community.[5] This kind of ethnic appeal fostered competition among some of downtown Los Angeles's largest retailers. Another department store even offered free "Cinco de Mayo" pennants to any Mexican who purchased its merchandise.[6]

Many of the mass-produced consumer goods in the 1920s were specifically marketed with an appeal to youth. This appeal had profound consequences for Mexican immigrant families. Older children who entered the work force often earned enough to become more autonomous. Adolescents and young adults were often the first to introduce a Mexican family to certain foods, clothing, or activities that were incompatible with traditional Mexican customs. For example, younger Mexican women began to use cosmetics and wear nylon stockings. Young men were more likely to seek out new leisure-time activities, such as American sports or the movie houses. Second-generation youth were often the first in their families to see a motion picture. At times, experimentation led to intergenerational conflict, with much tension revolving around consumer purchases and the control of earned income.

Despite some initial reservations, most Mexican parents joined other Americans in the 1920s in a love affair with motion pictures. Ninety percent of all families in the Los Angeles survey spent money on the movies, averaging $22 a year per family. In San Diego, a government committee investigating local economic conditions observed that "as in American families, movie tickets were an essential feature of these Mexican families' spending ways except under pressure of a special need for economy." In addition, the committee presumed that some working children retained a portion of their wages to spend on movie tickets.[7]

The movie industry in Los Angeles aided Mexicans in retaining old values, but it also played a role in cultural change. On the one hand, films produced in Mexico made their way into the many theatres in the downtown area in the late 1920s catering to the Mexican immigrant population. These supplemented American- and European-made silent films which were aimed by their promoters at an often illiterate immigrant population. Sound was not introduced until 1929, so that throughout the decade of the 1920s, movies stressed visual images and presented few language barriers for the non-English speaker.

Since their inception in the nickelodeons of eastern seaboard cities, American films consistently contained storylines intentionally made for the immigrant masses.[8] Messages tended to be largely populist and democratic in tone. Plots stressed the commonality of all Americans.

The children of Mexican immigrants were especially intrigued by the open sexuality depicted on the screen. The experience of sitting alone in a darkened theatre and identifying with screen characters, as Lary May has argued, could feel quite liberating.[9]

What made American-made films even more appealing was the appearance of actors and actresses who were Mexican by nationality. Although Ramón Navarro and Lupe Vélez were introduced to audiences in the early twenties, the arrival of Dolores del Río in 1925 brought Mexican immigrants flocking to the box office. The attraction was not simply the desire to support a compatriot; it was also generated by the close proximity of the movie industry. *La Opinión*, for example, the city's leading Spanish-language periodical, regularly followed the Hollywood scene, paying particular attention to the city's rising Latin stars. As citizens of Mexico themselves, the newspaper's editors were quick to condemn stars who distanced themselves from their national origins, while praising others, like del Río, who showed interest in preserving their Mexican identity.[10]

While the motion-picture industry displayed one aspect of the impact of consumerism on immigrant cultural adaptation, opportunities for other entrepreneurs to make an ethnic appeal emerged during this period. Ethnic marketing, usually considered a recent phenomena, in fact has long-standing roots in this era. While huge American corporations consolidated their hold on a national mass market of goods during the 1920s, much room was left for local entrepreneurs to seek submarkets that catered to the interests and desires of particular groups. In many ways, the standardization of messages brought about by large-scale advertising created new avenues for ethnic entrepreneurs. Since few national advertising agencies were located in Los Angeles or in the American Southwest, little attention was paid by national corporations to distinctly regional appeals. This void was filled by Mexican and non-Mexican entrepreneurs who realized that money could be made by servicing the large and growing Mexican population in the city.

As early as 1916, small Mexican-owned businesses advertised in Spanish-language newspapers.[11] These establishments were generally store-front operations which allegedly provided items that were "typically Mexican." El Progreso Restaurant on North Main Street, for example, claimed that it cooked food in the "truly Mexican style." Similar restaurants were frequented by the large Mexican male population around the Plaza. Other businesses attempted to bring Mexican products into the Los Angeles market directly. La Tienda Mexicana, on San Fernando Street, carried herbs and cooking supplies which were generally unavailable elsewhere. Down the street, a clothing store, the Sastrería Mexicana, was less successful in its appeal to ethnic taste in dress.[12] It was one thing to continue to put Mexican food in your stomach and quite another to continue to dress in "traditional" Mexican garb on the streets of Los Angeles.

By 1920, large, well-financed operations dominated the Mexican retail business. Their advertisements regularly appeared in the city's Spanish-language periodicals for the next two decades. Farmacia Hidalgo, run by G. Salazar and located at 362 North Main Street, declared that it was the only store "positively of the Mexican community." Farmacia Ruiz was founded by an influential Mexican expatriate and quickly gained much status in the immigrant community. Over the next ten years, it was frequented by several candidates for the Mexican presidency, most notably José Vasconcelos.[13] Mauricio Calderón, another emigrant from Mexico, would soon dominate the Spanish-language music industry in Los Angeles. During this decade he established the Repertorio Musical Mexicana, an outlet for phonographs and Spanish-language records, which he claimed was "the only Mexican house of Mexican music for Mexicans." Finally, two theatres, the Teatro Novel and the Teatro Hidalgo, located on Spring and Main streets respectively, were already in operation in 1920, offering both silent films imported from Mexico as well as live entertainment.

A host of rival Mexican-owned firms gave these early businesses much competition. Advertisements usually stressed that their particular establishment was the most "genuinely Mexican" of the group. The Farmacia Hidalgo went so far as to place an Aztec eagle on some of its products to insure "authenticity." A new and important enterprise was the Librería Lozano, providing Spanish-language books to the literate Mexican community and owned by Ignacio Lozano, the editor of *La Opinión*. Not surprisingly, Lozano heavily advertised in his own paper.

In addition, the 1920s witnessed the emergence of Mexican professionals who also targeted their fellow countrymen for patronage. A small, but significant group of doctors, dentists, and lawyers from Mexico set up shop in Los Angeles, and their advertisements stressed that their training had been conducted in the finest Mexican universities.[14]

Mexican entrepreneurs, however, were not the only individuals in Los Angeles who appealed to the Mexican consumer; non-Mexicans also tried to capitalize on the growing ethnic clientele. Leading this effort was the medical profession, particularly women doctors and physicians from other ethnic groups not likely to develop a following within a highly male-dominated, Anglo Protestant profession.[15] Most of these physicians were located near the Plaza area, particularly along Main Street, an area which provided direct access to the immigrant population. Female physicians held special appeal as specialists for women, capitalizing on the sense of propriety among immigrant women. "Doctora" Augusta Stone, for example, advertised as a specialist for "las señoras," and she was among the first to use the phrase "Habla Español" in her advertisements. Dr. Luigi Gardini, an Italian American physician, also advertised in Spanish-language newspapers in 1916. Asian American physicians, however, were the largest group of non-Mexican professionals to appeal to Mexican immigrants, largely stressing their training in herbal medicine, an area not unfamiliar to rural Mexicans. Among them was Dr. Chee, who characterized himself as "Doctor Chino" in 1920, and Dr. Y. Kim, who boasted the combination of a Yale degree and a specialty in Oriental herbal treatments.

The growth and increasing economic stability of the Mexican immigrant community in Los Angeles made these appeals profitable. While

*community stability*

*music*

the Mexican middle class remained small and relatively insignificant, the large working-class community was quickly developing east of the Los Angeles River. Lack of capital and professional training in the Mexican community made it difficult for most Mexicans to take direct economic advantage of this growth. Yet their cumulative purchasing power did allow for the growth of certain enterprises which catered to the unique backgrounds of Mexican immigrants, while creating new modes of ethnic expression.

One of the most important of these enterprises was music. Although the musical legacies of different regions in Mexico were significant, traditions were both reinforced and transformed in the environment of Los Angeles. As a diverse collection of immigrant musicians arrived from central and northern Mexico, often via south Texas, they stimulated the growth of a recording industry and burgeoning radio network that offered fertile ground for musical innovation.

Of 1,746 Mexican immigrants who began the naturalization procedure, 110 were musicians (6.3% of the total), making them the second largest occupational group in the sample, well behind the category of "common laborer."[16] Although 80 percent of the musicians did not complete the process, their ample presence among those who initiated the naturalization process indicates their willingness to remain in the United States. Unlike working-class musicians of Mexican descent in Texas, it appears that many Los Angeles-based musicians were willing to consider changing their citizenship.[17] If, as Manuel Peña has claimed, musicians do function as "organic intellectuals" for the working class, challenging American cultural hegemony while expressing the frustrations and hopes of their social group, then the experiences of Los Angeles musicians indicate a complex, if not contradictory, relationship with American cultural values.[18]

Compared with the larger sample of Mexican immigrants, musicians were more likely to have been born in the larger cities of the central plateau in Mexico, particularly Guadalajara and Mexico City. Over 25 percent of Mexican musicians in Los Angeles came from these two cities alone, compared with 10 percent of the entire sample. Other towns in central Mexico, such as Zacatecas, Guanajuato, Puebla, and San Luis Potosí, were also well represented in the musical community. Unlike the larger sample, northern states were generally underrepresented among musicians, except for the state of Sonora, which accounted for 9 percent of the performers. In central Mexico, the states of Jalisco and Guanajuato and the Federal District alone produced over 41 percent of all Mexican musicians in Los Angeles.[19]

The musical traditions brought to the United States from these locales were varied. The mobility within Mexico caused by economic upheaval and violence related to the revolution had pushed many rural residents, including folk musicians, to seek shelter in towns and cities. There, previously isolated folk music traditions from various locations were brought together, and musicians also encountered the more European musical tastes of the urban upper classes. One study of street musicians in Mexico City during the 1920s, for example, found twelve different regional styles performing simultaneously on the corners and in the marketplaces of the capital. One could hear mariachis from Jalisco, *canciones norteñas* from Chihuahua, troubadors from Yucatán, *bandas jarochas* from Veracruz, and marimba groups from Chiapas and Oaxaca.[20]

If there was one particular musical style which stood out from the rest in popularity during this period, it was certainly the *corrido*. A prominent student of this genre has called the *corrido* "an integral part of Mexican life" and the creative period after 1910 its "most glorious epoch."[21] During the Mexican Revolution, almost every important event, and most political leaders and rebels, became the subjects of one or more *corridos*. Pedro J. González, who later emerged as the most well-known Mexican musician in Los Angeles, remembered composing *corridos* with seven other soldiers fighting with Pancho Villa in secluded mountain hideouts during lulls between battles. None was a trained musician, but each used the opportunity to criticize each other jokingly for past misfortunes or to immortalize some heroic deed through song.[22] As these *corridos* made their way into Mexico's urban centers, they were codified and transformed from folk expression to popular songs.[23]

The *corrido*'s continued popularity during the 1920s in areas far away from its folk origins can be explained by particular characteristics of its style which made it appealing as an urban art form. First, the urban *corrido*, like the *canción ranchera*, embodied what was a traditional music style from the countryside, while adapting it to a more commercially oriented atmosphere. It reminded those who had migrated from rural areas of their provincial roots, and gave urban dwellers a connection to the agrarian ideal which was seen as typically Mexican.[24] Second, most *corridos* appealed to a Mexican's nationalist fervor at a time when the pride of Mexican people, places, and events was flourishing. Several observers have identified the period between 1910 and 1940 as one of "national romanticism" in Mexican cultural affairs, extending beyond music to literature and mural painting. *Corridos* produced in the United States often exalted "Mexicanism" at the expense of American culture, but even those composed within Mexico paid inordinate attention to promoting Mexican cultural identity.[25]

Finally, the *corrido* was an exceptionally flexible musical genre which encouraged adapting composition to new situations and surroundings. Melodies, for the most part, were standardized or based on traditional patterns, while text was expected to be continuously improvised. A vehicle for narration, the *corrido* always intended to tell a story to its listeners, one that would not necessarily be news but rather would "interpret, celebrate, and ultimately dignify events already thoroughly familiar to the *corrido* audience."[26] As such, *corrido* musicians were expected to decipher the new surroundings in which Mexican immigrants found themselves while living in Los Angeles. Its relation to the working-class Mexican immigrant audience in Los Angeles was therefore critical to its continued popularity. As one L.A.-based composer explained, "The *corrido* is a narrative viewed through the eyes of the people—its subject almost always follows the truth."[27] This adaptive style was particularly well suited for the rapidly expanding Los Angeles

Mexican community of the 1920s and the ever-complex nature of inter-cultural exchange in the city.

The first commercial recording of a *corrido* in the United States was "El Lavaplatos." Performed in Los Angeles on May 11, 1926, by Los Hermanos Bañuelos as a duet with guitar accompaniment, the song was apparently originally written by Pedro J. González.[28] The *corrido* describes a Mexican immigrant who dreams of making a fortune in the United States but, instead, is beset with economic misfortune. Finally, after being forced to take a job as a dishwasher, the narrator bemoans: "Goodbye dreams of my life, goodbye movie stars, I am going back to my beloved homeland, much poorer than when I came."[29]

Most Mexican composers and musicians had firsthand knowledge of working-class life in Los Angeles; not only were they products of working-class homes, but most continued in some form of blue-collar occupation while struggling to survive as musicians. Pedro J. González, for example, worked as a longshoreman on the San Pedro docks before being "discovered," and the two musicians who played with him, Victor and Jesus Sánchez, were farmworkers.[30] The vast majority of Mexican musicians never were able to support themselves as full-time artists. One composer of *corridos*, for example, worked in a cement plant, a lumber yard, an oil refinery, the railroad, the telephone company, agricultural fields, and at the Biltmore Hotel while composing songs during the 1920s and 1930s.[31] Several who applied for American citizenship listed additional occupations with authorities.[32] A similar situation existed among Texas conjunto musicians. According to Manuel Peña, they "played and earned just enough to satisfy a few—not all—of their economic needs. There simply were not enough dances during a week for full-time employment: Saturday and Sunday were practically the only days for celebrating."[33]

Los Angeles during the 1920s, however, presented more possibilities for earning a livelihood as a musician than any other location outside of Mexico City, or perhaps San Antonio. To begin with, the Los Angeles metropolitan area contained a huge Spanish-speaking population, second only to Mexico City itself. By 1930 the Chicano population in the city of Los Angeles was larger than any other in the United States. The potential audience for Mexican music was enormous. Since most of these residents were recent migrants from Mexico, they often longed for tunes from their homeland. Others had come from south Texas, where the Spanish-language musical tradition was strong and widespread.[34] In fact, one writer claimed in 1932 that more Mexican music had been composed in the United States than in Mexico.[35]

One stimulus to the Mexican music industry was the explosion of Chicano theatre in Los Angeles during the 1920s. Over thirty Chicano playwrights moved to the city during the decade, producing shows ranging from melodrama to vaudeville. The Spanish-speaking population of the region was able to support five major theatre houses from 1918 until the early 1930s: Teatro Hidalgo, Teatro México, Teatro Capitol, Teatro Zendejas (later Novel), and Teatro Principal. In addition to these five which featured programs that changed daily, at least seventeen other theatres housed Spanish-speaking professional companies on a more irregular basis.[36]

Many of these theatres alternated vaudevillian-style shows with Mexican- or Hollywood-made silent films (three shows a day, four on weekends) during the 1920s. Both live performances and silent movies required musical accompaniment. Theatres, therefore, provided relatively stable employment to a diverse collection of musicians throughout the 1920s. The lack of formal training among many of the musicians did not necessarily hamper them, since playing on the streets often helped them prepare for the spontaneity and improvisation required for this type of performance.

The presence of a large number of middle-class Mexican expatriates also created a market for formally trained musicians who could read music. They performed for a type of theater which featured drama from Spain with orchestral accompaniment, similar to the more refined entertainment among the middle-classes in Mexico City. While never enjoying the mass appeal of movies and vaudeville, this European-style performance did provide employment for other musicians from Mexico.[37]

A more disparate, yet still lucrative market for Mexican musicians existed among the streets and informal gatherings of Los Angeles. During Mexican patriotic festivals and the Christmas season, musicians had larger audiences, more exposure, and greater potential for earnings. From these "auditions," Mexican groups were often recruited to play for weddings and other ethnic festivities. Moreover, a market for "traditional" Mexican music also existed among some Anglo residents of Los Angeles, often to provide a nostalgic backdrop to the distinctive "Spanish" past of the city. Pedro J. González, for example, often entertained at parties conducted by city officials and the police department.[38] Another *corrido* composer, Jesus Osorio, was able to make a living as a singer combining work in Olvera Street booths, private gatherings, and in the small theatres and cabarets along Main Street.[39]

The emergence of Hollywood as the leading movie-making capital in the United States during the 1920s stimulated a flourishing recording industry in the city that began to rival New York's. Both these developments boded well for Mexican musicians in Los Angeles, although prejudice, union discrimination, and the lack of formal training kept many out of regular employment in the entertainment industries in the western part of town. Still, by providing the music in English-speaking theatres or working as studio musicians, some were able to break into the larger music business in Los Angeles.[40] Even the possibility of such employment—"the dream of a life in Hollywood"—was enough to attract some performers from south of the border.

Thus musicians from Mexico flocked to Los Angeles during the 1920s, becoming a significant segment of the Mexican cultural renaissance of that decade. Unlike the Harlem Renaissance, where black writers and entertainers were often sponsored by white patrons, this Chicano/Mexicano renaissance was largely supported by Mexican immigrants themselves and existed far out of the sight of the majority of Angelinos. The presence of large numbers of Mexican musicians in the city not only

preserved the sights and sounds familiar to Mexican immigrants; it also
created an environment of cultural experimentation where traditional
music was blended with new methods. In short, musicians often served
as social interpreters who translated and reflected the cultural adaptations that were taking place among the Mexican immigrant population
as a whole.[41] In fact, one astute observer of *corridos* in Los Angeles recognized that this music often served to "sing what they cannot say":

> Mexicans are so intimidated by the government officials, even by social
> workers, and so timid on account of the language difficulty that it is
> almost unheard of for a Mexican to express his opinion to an American.
> Here, however, he is speaking to his own group and an emotional outlet
> is offered in the writing of *corridos* on the subject so well known to
> every Mexican. He is reasonably sure that only Mexicans will ever hear
> his *corrido*.[42]

Despite their economic and cultural connection to the greater immigrant population, Mexican musicians displayed different patterns of
migration and settlement. As a group, they were among the first of the
migrants to see the advantages of settling in Los Angeles, with many
arriving in the city around World War I or in the early 1920s. Moreover,
they usually arrived as adults, crossing the border at an average age of
twenty-four years during the 1910s and an average of thirty-two years
during the 1920s. The profession was also dominated traditionally by
men. Only four of the 110 musicians in my sample were women, and two
of these listed their occupation as singers. One study conducted in 1939,
for example, found no *corrido* written by a woman in the music shops of
Los Angeles.[43] Few avenues of opportunity were available to women in
the Spanish-language music industry in Los Angeles, although several
women—including the singer Lydia Mendoza—did make names for themselves during the 1930s.

By necessity, most Mexican musicians lived west of the river, even
after many of their people began to venture into East Los Angeles. The
recording and film industry was located in the western part of the city,
and Mexican cultural life continued to be centered around the Plaza
and downtown areas of the city until the 1940s. Most Spanish-language
theatres were located on Main Street, and opportunities for steady income depended on the patronage of the audiences that gathered around
the Placita or in downtown restaurants. During the 1930s when so-called
"Latin" music clubs were established, they too were located in the downtown area until after World War II. Lalo Guerrero, who arrived in Los
Angeles in 1937, remembered that not until economic opportunities
around the Plaza declined did many Mexican musicians decide to move
to East Los Angeles:

> Since the clubs in the westside started dying off . . . the musicians that
> had not wanted to come to East L.A., because they thought it was a
> step down, . . . were practically forced to come back because there was
> not too much happening on the westside, 'cause the latin scene had
> passed.[44]

The data confirm this pattern of residence for musicians: 60 percent in the naturalization sample lived around the downtown area, including 20 percent that resided near the Plaza. This compares with less than 39 percent of the overall sample who lived downtown, and 9 percent whose residence was located in the Plaza area.[45] Steady income and the opening up of the electric railway into East Los Angeles gave some musicians the opportunity to move to Belvedere or some of the other communities east of the river. Pedro J. González, for example, moved to Belvedere after residing close to the Plaza.[46]

This residential pattern is an indication that life as a musician did not usually provide the glamour and security which many associated with the entertainment field. Even the advent in the 1920s of an ethnic mass market centered in Los Angeles, which prompted American recording companies and local entrepreneurs to search for Mexican musical talent, meant only short-lived economic returns. Rapid exploitation of the talents of musicians brought quick profits to upstart recording companies but left most Chicano performers—even those who developed a loyal following—with limited resources to show for their newfound fame.

When Los Hermanos Bañuelos first recorded "El Lavaplatos," they ushered in the commercial recording of Mexican music. Already, several large American recording companies such as Vocalion, Okeh (a subsidiary of Columbia), Decca, and Bluebird (RCA) had begun to produce "race" records, featuring black folk music. These companies now realized the potential ethnic market among Mexicans and sought out Chicano musicians and singers from Texas to California. Many of the early recording sessions took place in temporary studios located in Los Angeles hotels, where a steady stream of performers were expected to produce a finished product in one or two "takes."[47]

To most musicians, the $15 or $20 they earned per record seemed substantial for a few hours' work, especially when compared with the wages they earned as laborers or the limited income from playing on the streets. Yet these tiny sums were a pittance relative to the hundreds or thousands of dollars any single recording could earn, even with records selling for 35 cents apiece. Musicians rarely earned sufficient income to feel secure as recording artists. Offering only "contracts" that were usually verbal agreements consisting of no royalties or other subsidiary rights, the recording companies profited handsomely from this enterprise.[48] Similar contractual agreements were made with Chicano artists as late as the 1940s, even though the pay scale had moved up to $50 a side or $100 per record.[49]

Local ethnic middlemen played an important role in identifying talented musicians and putting them in contact with recording companies. In Los Angeles, one important liaison was Mauricio Calderón, owner of the music store Repertorio Musical Mexicana, established on Main Street around 1920 to feature records and phonographs produced by Columbia Records. According to Pedro J. González, Calderón was in charge of everything in Los Angeles that related to Mexican music. He recruited talented musicians by advertising in the Spanish-language press and

kept an ear out for the latest musical trends among the city's performers and audiences. Not only did Calderón make money by serving as a
go-between between American companies and the Mexican artists, but
he also held a monopoly on the area-wide distribution of these recordings through his store. A standard practice of the time for such businesses was to sell phonographs as well as records, and stores such as
Calderón's profited as well from these items. In fact, Calderón's store,
located at 418 North Main Street near the Plaza, regularly promoted
itself by using a loudspeaker mounted in front of the store playing the
latest *corrido*. A small group of men regularly stood in front of the store,
listening intently and enjoying the music. Another popular promotion
tactic was to give away records with the purchase of a Victrola.[50]

American laws prohibited the importation of records from Mexico, a
fact which greatly stimulated the recording industry in Los Angeles. In
addition, Mexican companies were not allowed to record in the United
States. These restrictions severely crippled the music industry in Mexico,
while creating a vast economic opportunity for American companies and
ethnic entrepreneurs. When Mexican recordings were finally admitted
during the 1950s, interest in immigrant and native-born Spanish-
language talent evaporated quickly, and many Chicano musicians were
left without an outlet in the recording world. In fact, some labels which
had showcased Mexican artists, such as Imperial, began concentrating
on black rhythm and blues artists, such as Fats Domino and T-Bone
Walker.[51]

During the 1920s and 1930s, however, a vibrant environment for
Mexican music existed in Los Angeles. Another factor in creating this
cultural explosion was the advent of the radio. During the 1920s, commercial radio was still in an experimental era where corporate sponsors
and station managers tried to discover how best to make radio broadcasting profitable and enlightening. For most of the decade, the radio
was seen as a way of uplifting the masses, of bringing elite American
culture into the homes of common laborers.[52] By the end of the decade,
however, advertising and corporate economic interests dominated the
airwaves. This transformation created a market for Spanish-language
broadcasts. Although many Anglo Americans continued to believe that
only English should be heard on the nation's airwaves, the goal of reaching Spanish-speaking consumers silenced their opposition.

American radio programmers scheduled Spanish-language broadcasts during "dead" airtime—early morning, late night, or weekend
periods which had proven to be unprofitable for English programs.
Pedro J. González remembers first broadcasting from 4 to 6 A.M. on Station KELW out of Burbank. He often scheduled live music, including
many amateur musicians and singers from the community.[53] While Anglo
Americans were rarely listening at this hour, many Mexican immigrants
tuned into González's broadcasts while they prepared for early morning
work shifts. González's daily shows provided day laborers important
information about jobs as well as cherished enjoyment to workers who
toiled all day.[54]

Corporate radio sponsors in the mid-1920s were quick to understand the profitability of ethnic programs. Large advertisers such as Folgers Coffee used airtime to push their products in the Spanish-speaking market. More often, local businesses appealed to Mexican immigrants to frequent their establishments. In Los Angeles, radio broadcasting soon became a highly competitive industry. By selling blocks of airtime to foreign-language brokers, marginally profitable stations could capture a ready-made market. During the late 1920s, the hours dedicated to Spanish-language broadcasts multiplied. González's program was expanded until 7 A.M., and additional hours were added at lunchtime and in the early evening. Chicano brokers such as Mauricio Calderón profited handsomely as they negotiated with stations, paying them a flat rate during cheap broadcasting time, which they then sold to businesses for advertisements.[55]

Key to the success of Spanish-language broadcasting was its appeal to the thousands of working-class Mexican immigrants within the reach of a station's radio signal. Radio, unlike *La Opinión* and other periodicals, reached Mexican immigrants whether or not they could read. In addition, the content of radio programming focused less on the tastes of the expatriate middle class and more on those of the masses. A 1941 analysis of Spanish-language programming found that over 88 percent of on-air time (outside of advertisements) was dedicated to music, with only 4 percent used for news.[56] Programming was dominated by "traditional" music from the Mexican countryside, rather than the orchestral, more "refined" sounds of the Mexican capital and other large urban centers. "The corrido, the shouts, and all that stuff was popular" with working people, remembered González. Although some bemoaned the commercialization of the *corrido* tradition and its removal from its "folk tradition," most Mexican immigrants found this transformation to their liking because it fit well with their own adaptations to urban living.[57]

The potential power generated by this mass appeal was so substantial that it not only threatened the cultural hegemony of the Mexican middle class in Los Angeles but also worried local Anglo American officials. González himself was the target of District Attorney Buron Fitts, who in 1934 had the musician arrested on trumped-up charges. Earlier, Fitts had attempted to force González off the air by getting federal authorities to rescind his broadcasting license. Along with other government authorities, Fitts believed that only English should be heard on the radio and that only American citizens should have the right to broadcast. As a result, many radio stations curtailed their Spanish-language programs during the early 1930s, often because of the continued harassment directed at ethnic broadcasters and the imposition of more stringent rules for radio licensing.[58]

These restrictions in the United States encouraged the growth of Spanish-language broadcasting in Mexico. Although many American stations continued to reserve Spanish-language blocks, entrepreneurs based just across the border capitalized on the potential market on both sides by constructing powerful radio towers capable of reaching far-flung audiences. Increasingly, individuals unable to be heard on American-based stations moved their operations to Mexico. It proved much harder for American authorities to control the airwaves than the recording industry. Mexican immigrants could now listen to radio programming from Mexico itself, ironically often featuring music performed by U.S.-based Mexicans.[59]

The economic crisis of the 1930s curtailed much of Mexican cultural activity in Los Angeles. First, deportation and repatriation campaigns pushed almost one-third of the Mexican community back to Mexico, effectively restricting the market for Spanish-language advertising campaigns. Second, the enthusiasm of American companies for investing in "experimental" markets that did not insure a steady flow of income understandably cooled. The Mexican immigrant community itself had fewer resources to support cultural activities, given its precarious economic situation. Since expenditures on leisure-time activities were the first to be reduced during times of need, many families cut back drastically on attendance at musical events or the purchase of radios and phonographs. Many theatres in the community shut down during the Great Depression.[60]

Movies and other forms of cheap, cross-cultural entertainment continued to thrive in Depression-era Los Angeles. Simply because of the economics of scale, Hollywood was able to continue to produce entertainment accessible to families at every economic level. In addition, the introduction of sound to motion pictures made it more difficult to sustain a steady Spanish-language audience with Mexican imports, since the Mexican film industry had difficulty throughout the transition of the 1930s.[61] English talking-pictures, on the other hand, had a wider, and therefore more secure audience. The advent of sound coincided with the rise of the second generation of Mexicans in this country, more likely to be as fluent in English as in Spanish. Increasingly, changing demographics and limited economic resources stunted the growth of the ethnic market. A new era in Mexican/Chicano cultural activity began.

Although commercial activity slowed during the Depression, Mexican cultural life did not die out in Los Angeles. Indeed, aspects of cultural life were altered dramatically, reflecting the changing composition and nature of the Mexican/Chicano community. Musical activity, for example, became less dependent on *corrido* story-telling (which required the ability to understand Spanish lyrics) and more concentrated in dance clubs. La Bamba night club, at Macy and Spring streets, and La Casa Olvera, adjacent to Olvera Street, were only two of many small clubs which opened during the decade. Dancing, of course, did not require a working knowledge of Spanish and had appeal well beyond the Mexican immigrant population.[62]

Second-generation youth, in particular, flooded the dance clubs during the 1930s. Social commentators of the period commented on the "dance craze" that had seemingly overtaken adolescents and young adults in Mexican-American families. One such nineteen-year-old, known only as Alfredo to his interviewer, boastfully explained this "craze":

I love to dance better than anything else in the world. It is something that gets in your blood. Lots of boys are that way. I go to five dances a week. I can't wait for Saturday night because all the time I am thinking of the dance. It is in my system. I could get a job playing my trumpet in an orchestra but then I couldn't dance. I quit school because I got plenty of everything they teach, but dancing.[63]

This new "dance craze" did not often sit well with Mexican immigrant parents. Even when participation was closely chaperoned in school clubs and community centers, public dancing seemed to offend the sensibilities of decency among older Mexicans. Increasingly, however, it became difficult for parents to withstand the effect of peer pressure on their children, as evidenced by the words of one mother in the early 1930s:

Juanita has joined a club and now she wants to learn to dance. That is what comes of these clubs. It is wrong to dance and my Juanita wants to do it because the others do. Because everybody does it does not make it right. I know the things I was taught as a girl and right and wrong cannot change.[64]

Although the vast majority of musicians and clientele in each of these establishments were Mexican, the music demonstrated a wide variety of American and Latin American styles. Cuban music was especially popular in the latter half of the decade, with many orchestras specializing in the mambo. The Cuban style was popular throughout Latin America, and this trend filtered into Los Angeles through traveling bands and musicians. Regular groups that played in these clubs all included Mexican songs in their repertoire.[65] In addition, English-language music increasingly became popular among American-born youth. Many Mexican immigrants bemoaned this turn of events, as evidenced by the comments of one unnamed señora:

The old Spanish songs are sung only by the old people. The young ones can sing the "Boop-da-oop" like you hear on the radio but they can't sing more than one verse of *La Cruz*. Do you know *La Cruz*? It is very beautiful. It is about our Lord carrying the cross. It is sad. In Mexico we would all sing for hours while someone played a guitar. But here, there are the drums and the saxophones.[66]

Undoubtedly, a more eclectic and diverse musical life than in former decades emerged among the Mexican/Chicano community in Los Angeles. In fact, Los Angeles probably offered a richer environment for such leisure-time activity than any other city in the American Southwest.

This diversity of choice in musical styles and taste not only created a more experimental environment for musicians themselves but also reflected developments in Chicano culture as a whole. Clearly, the control of the individual over his or her own cultural choices paralleled the growth of an ethnic consumer market. In a consumer society, each Mexican immigrant alone, or in conjunction with family, embraced cultural change—consciously or unconsciously—through the purchase of material goods or by participation in certain functions. Neither the Mexican elite nor the Anglo American reformers intent on Americanization could completely determine the character of these private decisions. Instead, an unsteady relationship between American corporations, local businesses, Mexican entrepreneurs, and the largely working-class community itself influenced the range of cultural practices and consumer items available in the Spanish-language market. If appeals to Mexican nationalism could be used to sell a product, then so be it. Although barriers to the ethnic market were constructed by local officials, particularly during the Great Depression, change in economic circumstances and in cultural tastes of the population had the most important impact.

Appeal to the tastes of youth also created subtle power shifts within the Chicano community. In Mexico, few outlets were available to young people for influencing cultural practices in an individual village or even one's own family. The American metropolis, on the other hand, gave Mexican youth an opportunity to exercise more cultural prerogatives merely by purchasing certain products or going to the movies. Rebellion against family often went hand in hand with a shift toward more American habits. This pattern was stimulated by the extent to which adolescents and unmarried sons and daughters worked and retained some of their own income. As the second generation came to dominate the Chicano population by the late 1930s, their tastes redefined the community's cultural practices and future directions of cultural adaptation.

Behind the vast American commercial network lay an enterprising group of ethnic entrepreneurs who served as conduits between the Mexican immigrant population and the corporate world. These individuals were often the first to recognize cultural changes and spending patterns among the immigrant population. Individuals such as Mauricio Calderón and Pedro J. González were able to promote Mexican music in entirely new forms in Los Angeles because they had daily contact with ordinary members of the Los Angeles Mexican community. Although they found tangible financial rewards in their efforts, they also served an important role in redefining Mexican culture in an American urban environment.

NOTES

1. The Heller Committee for Research in Social Economics of the University of California and Constantine Panunzio, *How Mexicans Earn and Live: A Study of the Incomes and Expenditures of One Hundred Mexican Families in San Diego, California*, Cost of Living Studies, 5 (Berkeley: Univ. of California Press, 1933), 49–52, 63–64.

2. "Observaciones—Los Salones de Baile," Observations of Luis Felipe Recinos, Los Angeles, Calif., 15 April 1927, Manuel Gamio collection, Bancroft Library, University of California, Berkeley.

3. U.S. Department of Labor, Bureau of Labor Statistics, "Mexican Families in Los Angeles," *Money Disbursements of Wage Earners and Clerical Workers in Five Cities in the Pacific Region, 1934–36*, Bulletin 639 (Washington, D.C.: GPO, 1939), 108–9, 231. For similar figures from San Diego, see Heller Committee and Panunzio, *Earn and Live*, 50–52.

4. See *Ballad of an Unsung Hero*, Cinewest/KPBS, 1983.

5. *La Opinión*, 10 May 1929.

6. *La Opinión*, 3 May 1927.

7. U.S. Department of Labor, *Money Disbursements*, 231; Heller Committee and Panunzio, *Earn and Live*, 50, 71.

8. See Lary May, *Screening Out the Past: The Birth of Mass Culture and the Motion Picture Industry* (Chicago: Univ. of Chicago Press, 1980), and Kathy Peiss, *Cheap Amusements: Working Women and Leisure in Turn-of-the-Century New York* (Philadelphia: Temple Univ. Press, 1986), 139–62.

9. May, *Screening*, 152–58.

10. Larry Carr, *More Fabulous Faces: The Evolution and Metamorphosis of Dolores Del Río, Myrna Loy, Carole Lombard, Bette Davis, and Katharine Hepburn* (Garden City, N.Y.: Doubleday, 1979), 1–51; De Witt Bodeen, "Dolores Del Río: Was the First Mexican of Family to Act in Hollywood," *Films in Review* 18 (1967), 266–83; José Gómez-Sicre, "Dolores Del Río," *Américas* 19 (1967), 8–17.

11. From content analysis of advertisements in Spanish-language newspapers in Los Angeles from 1916 to 1935. *El Heraldo de México*, 3 May 1916, 2 May 1920, and 13 Sept. 1925, and *La Opinión*, 6 April 1930 and 5 May 1935.

12. *El Heraldo de México*, 3 May 1916.

13. See "Juan B. Ruiz," interview by Eustace L. Williams, 6 May 1937, Racial Minorities Survey, Federal Writers Project collection, University of California, Los Angeles.

14. *La Opinión*, 6 April 1930 and 5 May 1935.

15. See Regina Markell Morantz-Sanchez, *Sympathy and Science: Women Physicians in American Medicine* (New York: Oxford Univ. Press, 1985); Mary Roth Walsh, *"Doctors Wanted: No Women Need Apply": Sexual Barriers in the Medical Profession, 1835–1975* (New Haven: Yale Univ. Press, 1977); and Gloria Melnick Moldow, *Women Doctors in Gilded-Age Washington: Race, Gender, and Professionalization* (Urbana: Univ. of Illinois Press, 1987).

16. From Naturalization documents, National Archives, Laguna Niguel, California.

17. Take for example the words of conjunto musician Narciso Martínez, who explained: "No puedo ser americano, porque mi papá y mamá eran mexicanos" ("I cannot consider myself American, because my father and mother were Mexicans"). Manuel Peña, *The Texas-Mexican Conjunto: History of a Working-Class Music* (Austin: Univ. of Texas Press, 1985), 54–55.

18. Peña, *Conjunto*, 146–48; Tim Patterson, "Notes on the Historical Application of Marxist Cultural Theory," *Science & Society* 39 (1975), 257–91. The notion of "organic intellectuals" comes from Antonio Gramsci's theory of cultural hegemony, which can be found in *Selections from the Prison Notebooks*, Quintin Hoare and Geoffrey Newell Smith, eds. and trans. (New York: International, 1971).

19. Analysis of Naturalization documents, National Archives, Laguna Niguel, California.

20. Daniel Castañeda, "La música y la revolución mexicana," *Boletín Latín-Americano de Música* 5 (1941), 447–48; Claes af Geijerstam, *Popular Music in Mexico* (Albuquerque: Univ. of New Mexico Press, 1976), 88–91.

21. Merle E. Simmons, *The Mexican Corrido as a Source for Interpretive Study of Modern Mexico (1870–1950)* (Bloomington: Indiana Univ. Press, 1957), 7, 34. See also Vicente T. Mendoza, *El corrido mexicano* (México, D.F.: Fondo de Cultura Economíca, 1974), xv, who calls the years between 1910 and 1929 the "Golden Age" of the corrido.

22. Pedro J. González, *Translated Transcripts* (Cinewest/KPBS, 1983), 75–77.

23. Geijerstam, *Popular Music*, 49–58. For traditional songs from one particular region in central Mexico, see Juan Diego Razo Oliva, *Rebeldes populares del Bajío (Hazanas, tragedias y corridos, 1910–1927)* (Mexico City: Editorial Katun, S.A., 1983).

24. Geijerstam, *Popular Music*, 68–69.

25. Ibid., 83–88; Américo Paredes, "The Ancestry of Mexico's Corridos: A Matter of Definitions," *Journal of American Folklore* 76 (1963), 233. For a collection of folk songs composed by Mexicans in conflict with Anglo Texans, see Américo Paredes, *A Texas-Mexican Cancionero: Folksongs of the Lower Border* (Urbana: Univ. of Illinois Press, 1976), particularly part II.

26. John Holmes McDowell, "The Corrido of Greater Mexico as Discourse, Music and Event," in *"And Other Neighborly Names": Social Process and Cultural Image in Texas Folklore*, Richard Bauman and Roger D. Abrahams, eds. (Austin: Univ. of Texas Press, 1981), 47, 73; Geijerstam, 52–53, 56; Merle E. Simmons, "The Ancestry of Mexico Corridos," *Journal of American Folklore* 76 (1963), 3.

27. Quoted in Nellie Foster, "The *Corrido*: A Mexican Culture Trait Persisting in Southern California" (Master's thesis, University of Southern California, 1939), 7.

28. Peña, *Conjunto*, 40, according to Library of Congress informant Richard Spottswood; Pedro J. González, videocassette tape interviews for *Ballad of an Unsung Hero* (San Diego: Cinewest/KPBS, 1983), 2:12 to 2:19. There is some dispute over whether this recording was indeed the first, since Pedro González remembers recording sessions he participated in as early as 1924. See González, *Transcripts*, 72–74. There is also a dispute over whether, indeed, González was the original composer. In 1939, a recording of "El Lavaplatos" was discovered

in Los Angeles which claimed that the music and words had been written by Jesus Ororio. See Foster, *"Corrido,"* 24.

29. "El Lavaplatos" (The Dishwasher) from Philip Sonnichsen, *Texas-Mexican Border Music, Vols. 2 & 3: Corridos Parts 1 & 2* (Arhoolie Records, 1975), 9.

30. González, *Transcripts*, 82–85, 96–98, 217–19, 227–30.

31. Foster, *"Corrido,"* 30.

32. Naturalization documents, National Archives, Laguna Niguel, California.

33. Peña, *Conjunto*, 58.

34. See ibid., esp. chap. 1.

35. J. Xavier Mondragón, "El Desarrollo de la Canción Mexicana en Estados Unidos," *La Opinión*, 27 March 1932.

36. Nicolás Kanellos, "An Overview of Hispanic Theatre in the United States," in *Hispanic Theatre in the United States*, Nicolás Kanellos, ed. (Houston: Arte Público Press, 1984), 9; Nicolás Kanellos, "Two Centuries of Hispanic Theatre in the Southwest," *Revista Chicano-Riqueña* 11 (1983), 27–35; Tomás Ybarra-Frausto, "I Can Still Hear the Applause: La Farándula Chicana: Carpas y Tandas de Variedad," in *Hispanic Theatre*, 56.

37. González, *Transcripts*, 221.

38. Ibid., 246–49.

39. Foster, *"Corrido,"* 26.

40. Pedro J. González remembers being asked to play for the studios in *Transcripts*, 96–98.

41. In this fashion, Chicano musicians in Los Angeles resembled their counterparts in Texas. See Peña, *Conjunto*, 146–48.

42. Ibid., 49–50.

43. Foster, *Corrido*, 19.

44. Quoted in Stephen Joseph Loza, "The Musical Life of the Mexican/Chicano People in Los Angeles, 1945–1985: A Study in Maintenance, Change, and Adaptation" (Ph.D. diss., University of California, Los Angeles, 1985), 110–11.

45. Analysis of Naturalization documents, National Archives, Laguna Niguel, California.

46. González, *Transcripts*, 124–25.

47. Peña, *Conjunto*, 39–41.

48. Ibid., 42; exceedingly rare was González's claim that he made $50 a recording and began receiving royalties in the 1930s. Since he was considered the top Mexican artist by 1930, this claim is understandable. González, *Transcripts*, 118, 234, 240.

49. According to Lalo Guerrero, in Loza, "Musical Life," 118.

50. González, *Transcripts*, 74; Foster, *"Corrido,"* 22–23. The only other musical outlet I have discovered that advertised in the Spanish-language press was La Platt Music Company. For go-betweens in San Antonio, see Peña, *Conjunto*, 40.

51. Loza, "Musical Life," 105, 117–20.

52. Roland Marchand, *Advertising the American Dream: Making Way for Modernity, 1920–1940* (Berkeley: Univ. of California Press, 1985), 89–94.

53. González, *Transcripts*, 99; Félix F. Gutiérrez and Jorge Reina Schement, *Spanish-Language Radio in the Southwestern United States* (Austin: Center for Mexican American Studies, Univ. of Texas, 1979), 5.

54. González, *Transcripts*, 102–6.

55. Gutiérrez and Schement, *Spanish-Language Radio*, 5–7; González, *Transcripts*, 98–99.

56. Gutiérrez and Schement, *Spanish-Language Radio*, 7.

57. Foster, *"Corrido,"* 20–22; González, *Transcripts*, 114–15; see also 249–51 for a description of rural jestering with pig.

58. González, *Transcripts*, 101–9, 119–37; Gene Fowler and Bill Crawford, *Border Radio* (Austin: Texas Monthly Press, 1987), 207–8.

59. See Fowler and Crawford, *Border Radio*, esp. 162, 247.

60. Kanellos, "Overview," 10, and "Two Centuries," 36.

61. See Carl J. Mora, *Mexican Cinema: Reflections of a Society, 1896–1980* (Berkeley: Univ. of California Press, 1982), 25–51, for a description of this period of transition in the Mexican film industry.

62. Loza, "Musical Life," 102–4.

63. Mary Lanigan, "Second Generation Mexicans in Belvedere" (Master's thesis, University of Southern California, 1932), 58.

64. Ibid., 62.

65. Ibid., 103–5.

66. Ibid., 22.

# The New Deal in Dallas

*Roger Biles*

Historians continue to analyze the New Deal and its impact on U.S. history. Did Franklin D. Roosevelt's innovative responses to hard times constitute a watershed in the nation's past? How new, in other words, was the New Deal? William E. Leuchtenburg stated the case for change, arguing in his seminal *Franklin D. Roosevelt and the New Deal*: "The New Deal, however conservative it was in some respects and however much it owed to the past, marked a radically new departure." Similarly, Carl Degler called the New Deal "a revolutionary response to a revolutionary situation." Especially since the mid-1960s, however, historians have begun to focus on the lack of reform achieved in the 1930s. New Left historians like Barton Bernstein and Paul Conkin emphasized the degree to which the New Deal overlooked the plight of the downtrodden in its desire to preserve capitalism. Although many scholars stopped short of characterizing Roosevelt's presidency as counterrevolutionary, most acknowledged the shortcomings of the New Deal in effecting meaningful economic and social reform. Clearly not a radical bent on the destruction of free enterprise capitalism, they believed, Roosevelt naturally sought limited reform within the American political consensus. The New Deal could accomplish only so much because of conservative forces in Congress and the courts. Further, James T. Patterson added, the American system of federalism bolstered the states at the expense of the national government, and the New Deal made few inroads against states' rights and strict constructionism.[1]

Historians have also noted the limited impact of the New Deal in cities. In Pittsburgh, Bruce Stave concluded, the New Deal relieved unemployment and improved the housing situation somewhat, but had little effect on the more lasting problems of economic stagnation and physical decay. A number of studies suggest that, rather than undermine the strength of big city political machines, Roosevelt supported those bosses loyal to national Democratic platforms and policies. Charles H. Trout

*Roger Biles is professor of history and chairman of the department at East Carolina University. Reprinted from* Southwestern Historical Quarterly *95 (July 1991): 1–19. Reprinted by permission of the Texas State Historical Association.*

found that "during the entire New Deal policies from Washington altered Boston, but just as surely Boston modified federal programs." Or, as Zane Miller summarized: "The federal response to depression in the cities was conservative. The New Deal's urban policy neither envisaged nor produced a radical transformation of metropolitan form and structure."[2]

In recent years, however, some historians concerned with the exceptionalism of southern cities have designated the 1930s as the time when sweeping changes engendered by the New Deal began to narrow the gap between urban Dixie and northern municipalities. Although emphasizing the distinctiveness of southern cities overall, David R. Goldfield conceded that the pace of change accelerated rapidly in the twentieth century. The watershed, he contended, was the New Deal, since "the federal government paid for the capital facilities in southern cities that northern cities had paid for themselves in earlier decades and on which they were still paying off the debt. The almost-free modernization received by southern cities would prove to be an important economic advantage in subsequent decades." In *The New Deal in the Urban South*, Douglas L. Smith looked at four southern cities—Atlanta, Birmingham, Memphis, and New Orleans—and suggested that the involvement of the federal government in local affairs during the 1930s resulted in significant changes. He concluded that public works and housing initiatives altered southern cityscapes, New Deal relief agencies paved the way for the establishment for the first time of social welfare agencies, organized labor established new footholds, and black communities mobilized to make possible significant breakthroughs in later years. Moreover, according to Smith, the New Deal helped sever the ties to the Old South and develop among southerners an urban consciousness.[3]

An earlier study of Memphis, Tennessee, during the 1930s saw little evidence of sweeping change or, for that matter, of substantial preparation for later departures. This study of Dallas, Texas, looking at local government, relief, labor, and race relations, similarly finds minimal impact by the New Deal. In Dallas the federal government worked through city hall but exerted no influence over who made policy there, and the rise of the Citizens' Council made the control of the city's corporate regency explicit and unmistakable. No appreciable increase in social welfare activity ensued to reflect an expanded commitment to relief. To a great extent, management successfully preserved the open shop and regional wage differentials, two ingredients local businessmen viewed as essential for industry to compete effectively with northern concerns. Black residents of Dallas survived the depression in somewhat better fashion because of federal aid, but their status remained largely unchanged. In short, New Deal largess provided welcome assistance but did not alter appreciably the traditional way of life.[4]

In Dallas the business community brought local government more firmly under its control in the 1930s. Agitation for political reform dated back to the first decade of the twentieth century with the founding of the nonpartisan Citizens Association. Interest flagged, however, and by the 1920s the association was dormant. In 1927 the Dallas *News* published a series of muckraking articles exposing inefficiency in city government and proposing the city manager plan as an alternative. In 1929 over thirty men ran for mayor, nine of whom constituted one-man "parties." The eventual winner, self-styled populist J. Waddy Tate, lambasted the wealthy, removed all "keep off the grass" signs from city parks, and promised to allow "plain folks" to camp there. Largely because of Tate's eccentric behavior, Dallasites began to consider seriously the *News*'s arguments for change. The remnants of the old Citizens Association formed the Citizens Charter Association (CCA) in 1930 and joined in the battle for new municipal government. Tate delayed and dissembled, but finally presented the question of charter amendments to the people in a 1930 referendum. By a two-to-one margin, the voters jettisoned the mayor-commission government for council-city manager rule. Under the new system, the nine-member council (six chosen from districts and three elected at-large) chose a mayor from its own ranks and appointed a city manager.[5]

In 1933 the CCA's slate of candidates ran unopposed, but resistance quickly formed among the ranks of the suddenly deposed politicians. They accused the CCA of being "organized . . . financed and controlled by Wall Street trusts," and unsuccessfully sought the recall of the new council. In 1935 an opposition faction composed of seasoned pols, known as the Catfish Club, bested the CCA's candidates to gain control of the city council. A haphazardly planned counteroffensive by the CCA never got off the ground in 1937, and the brief reign of the business elite seemed finished. At that time, however, two hundred of the city's corporate presidents and chief executive officers formed the Dallas Citizens' Council to breathe new life into the dying CCA. In 1939 the candidates of the fledgling Citizens' Council parlayed rumors of graft in Mayor George Sprague's parks department into a resounding victory. The council's 1941 slate won without opposition, and its dominance of local government continued into the 1970s.[6]

The Dallas Citizens' Council sprang from the imagination of Robert Lee Thornton. A former tenant farmer who mismanaged several businesses into bankruptcy, Thornton finally struck it rich as a banker. Thornton was a maverick in the local financial community; while other banks avoided risky ventures, he had the prescience to invest in the automobile industry and gave hotel tycoon Conrad Hilton his first loan. He became one of the city's most visible and esteemed philanthropists and in later years a four-time mayor who refused to keep a desk in city hall, continuing to operate from his desk at the Mercantile Bank. By the mid-1930s he had grown tired of the ineffectiveness of local government and resolved to seize authority for the city's "natural leadership." In 1936 Thornton helped persuade the Texas Centennial Commission to hold the celebration in Dallas and then served as a member of the executive committee that planned and conducted the gala. Serving on that committee convinced him that only a small, manageable group of the city's best people could effectively make decisions about such a massive undertaking as the Texas Centennial—or for that matter, he concluded, govern the city. Therefore, Thornton set out to make the emerging Citizens' Council in the form best suited to get things done.[7]

Thornton wanted to call the Citizens' Council the "Yes or No Council," but others thought the title a bit unseemly and overruled him. Thornton did prevail on a number of other matters, however, including his insistence that membership be limited to chief executive officers of major corporations—no doctors, lawyers, educators, clergymen, or intellectuals who might temporize when hasty action was needed. Similarly, Thornton's no-nonsense attitude predominated with the exclusion of proxy voting. "If you don't come," the rough-hewn banker said, "you ain't there." The Citizens' Council, sometimes called "Thornton's oligarchy," centralized power in an open and complete fashion. A local newspaper observed: "In many cities, power descends from a small group of influential businessmen to the city council. What distinguishes the Dallas power group from others is that it is organized, it has a name, it is not articulately opposed and it was highly publicized." If anything, local autonomy, concentrated in the hands of a relatively few influential citizens, increased during the depression decade; the bureaucracy-laden state and federal governments held no truck with the "yes or no" men of Dallas. Other southern city halls showed equally sparse evidence of federal presence. President Roosevelt made no effort to unseat political machines in Memphis or New Orleans, and local elites continued to predominate in countless other southern communities. In Houston, for example, four-time mayor Oscar Holcombe faithfully acted upon the concerns of the business community as represented by New Dealer and financial tycoon Jesse Jones. Just as Roosevelt kept hands off the steel barons who wielded such influence in Birmingham and the commercial elite in Atlanta, he declined to support or oppose the ascendance of the Citizens' Council in Dallas.[8]

In the months following the Stock Market Crash, no widespread panic ensued in Dallas. The Dallas *Morning News* dismissed the significance of the stock market collapse, noting: "Many individuals, undoubtedly have suffered a loss far heavier than they could afford. Yet economic conditions in general are sound . . . and, after the storm, the sun of prosperity will again shine on thrift, hard work and efficient effort." Nor did city officials appreciate discouraging talk of economic setbacks; when a local lawyer spoke on a radio broadcast about rising unemployment, the city commission enacted a statute requiring that any such negative remarks be submitted in advance for approval. In fact, hard times were not all that hard in Dallas for the first year of the depression. According to 1930 data, the city's jobless rate stood at only 4.7 percent. The merger of North Texas Bank with Republic National Bank and Trust Company constituted the largest merger of financial institutions in the state's history. Also, thanks in large part to the booster efforts of Industrial Dallas, Incorporated, a total of 802 new businesses located in the city in 1929, and some 600 more followed suit during the first nine months of 1930.[9]

Dallas seemed to suffer less than many other cities due to the discovery of oil in East Texas at the outset of the decade. In October 1930 wildcatter Columbus M. Joiner found two hundred square miles of land floating on a veritable lake of oil about 120 miles southeast of Dallas. By 1933 over nine thousand producing oil wells operated in that field. Almost immediately Dallas profited from the newfound economic opportunity a major oil strike provided. Industrial Dallas, Incorporated, launched a promotional campaign to portray the city as headquarters of the new oil field by printing advertisements in *Oil Weekly* and *Oil and Gas Journal* and mailing over five thousand reprints to oil companies. The city quickly installed telephone and telegraph service to Tyler, Kilgore, Gladewater, Longview, and the other fledgling communities of the oil field. Several Dallas banks, most notably the First National, introduced new methods of oil financing such as production loans made against oil still in the ground. As a result of these efforts, hundreds of petroleum-related businesses came to Dallas, including several oil companies that located their executive headquarters or southwest branch offices there. Several local firms, such as the Magnolia and Sun Oil Companies, and individuals, like H. L. Hunt and Clint W. Murchison, prospered from the beginning. In short order, Dallas established itself as the financial and service center for the greatest oil strike since the legendary Spindletop strike of 1901.[10]

Although the fortuitous oil discovery no doubt mitigated the economic crisis of the early depression years, Dallas did not escape hard times altogether. Unemployment became a grave problem; more than 18,500 jobless men and women applied for relief at city hall by the end of 1931. Employers discharged married female employees, and retail stores cut back to five-day work weeks. Ironically, the federal government reported in 1931 that the most serious unemployment problem in the state existed in the East Texas oil fields, where an estimated ten thousand of the many thousands who arrived from around the country to get work found none. As the federal government noted, the care of these new arrivals fell on local communities, including nearby Dallas.[11]

Other economic indicators reflected the city's troubles. Dallas building permits for 1931 totaled only $7.5 million, down from $11 million the year before. By 1933 the slowdown in construction led the Dallas Carpenters' Union to offer a 50 percent reduction on all repair and remodeling work. Dallas boasted of being the merchandising capital of the South and, therefore, suffered severely when net retail sales plummeted from $189 million in 1929 to $130 million 1935. Wholesale business in 1929 totaled $729 million but only $48 million a decade later. A persistent decline in bank deposits and loans led to frequent reorganizations and mergers. In the most notable case the city's three largest banks pooled their resources to save a smaller state bank from closing. Clearly, Dallas suffered from the weight of the Great Depression.[12]

Faced with unprecedented demands on local resources, the city responded minimally. Burdened by reduced tax collections, Dallas cut expenditures—including relief—to keep from going heavily in the red. In 1931 the city stood over $32.5 million in arrears. After its initial year the newly instituted city manager government trimmed the overdraft by more than $400,000. In its second year city hall refunded the remainder of the deficit, and the budget maintained a cash surplus for the duration of the decade. By and large, this owed to the cutting of municipal workers' salaries from 5 percent to 20 percent and the release of hundreds of employees. New city manager John Edy refused to allocate funds for street paving or building a levee sewer along the Trinity River downtown—despite significant pressure from the business community. Teachers received their monthly paychecks without interruption, but the sums decreased; in the 1931–1932 school year, for example, teacher salaries averaged $1,669 and in the 1932–1933 year only $1,463. The Board of Education reduced the number of faculty by demanding the automatic resignation of married women employees.[13]

As the monthly case load of the city welfare department rose to an average of 2,800 in 1931, city officials instituted a plan whereby the unemployed labored one day per week on public works projects and were paid in groceries bought by the city wholesale. After a prolonged campaign the Laboring Men's Relief Association persuaded the welfare department to issue some cash payments in addition to food, but the city continued to focus its efforts on encouraging self-sufficiency by subsidizing the planting of four hundred acres of vegetable gardens and distributing over one thousand packages of seeds to the unemployed. The welfare department also operated a cannery so that vegetables could be preserved for winter consumption. Noting that the thirty cents an hour it currently paid day laborers "cost the city about 40 percent more than if the work were done by private contract," the municipal government cut the pay to eighteen cents an hour, to be discharged in groceries. As in other southern cities, economy continued to be the first priority.[14] (Table 1 compares Dallas, the fourth largest southern city in 1930, with the other largest cities with respect to sources of relief funding.)

**Table 1. Relief Expenditures by Government and Private Organizations, January 1 to March 31, 1931**

| City | Municipal ($) | % | Private ($) | % | Total ($) |
|------|--------------:|----:|------------:|------:|----------:|
| Atlanta | 20,493 | 26.7 | 56,183 | 73.2 | 76,676 |
| Birmingham | 74,544 | 50.4 | 73,326 | 49.6 | 147,870 |
| Dallas | 34,622 | 48.3 | 37,109 | 51.7 | 71,731 |
| Houston | 12,329 | 20.4 | 48,224 | 79.6 | 60,553 |
| Memphis | 11,190 | 8.8 | 115,317 | 91.2 | 126,507 |
| New Orleans | 0 | 0.0 | 27,103 | 100.0 | 27,103 |
| Total | 153,178 | 30.0 | 357,262 | 70.0 | 510,440 |

Source: U.S. Bureau of the Census, *Relief Expenditures by Government and Private Organizations, 1929 and 1931* (Washington, D.C.: Government Printing Office, 1932), 6, 32–33. *Note:* Nationwide, local governments provided 60.4% and private sources, 39.6%.

With an enervated municipal government, local social welfare institutions were called on to provide relief. Their resources disappeared rapidly, however, and philanthropic activity lagged as well. An American Public Welfare Association survey concluded that "analysis of Community Chest giving in Dallas . . . indicates an unusually small proportion, both in number and amount, of gifts, by individuals as com-

pared with business firms and corporations. . . . This is not to indicate
that business firms and corporations in Dallas give too much to the Community Chest. Some should give much more." The Dallas *Morning News*
editorialized: "The richest of the rich in Dallas have fallen down on the
task. They have shirked in the face of the winter's desperate need."[15]

With city halls closely cleaving to a policy of low taxes and limited
expenditures, private giving insufficient, and state government bereft
of resources, the federal government became the last resort. In the early
days of the depression, the Dallas *Morning News* rejected the idea of
federal relief, saying: "The News has steadfastly set its face against tin-
cup-and-blue-goggles trips to Washington for 'relief' for Texans." But
the prospect of desperately needed aid proved too attractive to spurn.
The Dallas *Morning News* supported the National Recovery Administration, and the Chamber of Commerce responded so quickly and energetically that NRA chief Hugh Johnson singled out the organization for
commendation. Similarly, the paper encouraged compliance with the
Agricultural Adjustment Act, a reflection of the community's concern
with deflated cotton prices.[16]

Of most immediate concern to Dallas, to be sure, was unemployment
and the resultant relief crisis. In May 1933, Congress created the Federal Emergency Relief Administration (FERA), authorizing it to distribute $500 million for direct and work relief as well as transient care.
The federal government provided funds for distribution by state and
local governments, with emphasis on decentralization. In spring 1933
the state legislature created the Texas Rehabilitation and Relief Commission to distribute the largess through county agencies. From its inception in July 1933 to 1935, when the federal government turned
unemployment relief over to state and local authorities, FERA general
relief aided thousands of jobless in Dallas. At its peak the agency dispensed relief to 14,125 city residents monthly. Workers paved roads,
dug ditches, and performed hundreds of other tasks that improved the
city's appearance. And the federal government paid for over 80 percent
of the relief appropriations.[17]

The Public Works Administration (PWA) opened its offices in Dallas
in 1933. Unlike the other New Deal agencies concerned with unemployment, which concentrated on short-term, low-cost projects, the PWA
awarded grants to cities for large-scale efforts. (The cities had to aug-
ment these grants with sizable contributions of their own.) In PWA
projects, about 70 percent of funds went for materials and the remaining 30 percent for wages. Since "make work" was never the primary goal,
the agency directly employed relatively few men; moreover, PWA hired
indiscriminately, not just from the relief rolls, so it had only an inciden-
tal impact on gross unemployment figures. In Dallas the PWA built the
Museum of Natural History and added 130 beds to city-owned Parkland
Hospital. In 1939 the city completed negotiations with the U.S. Housing
Authority (negotiations originating with PWA) for its first slum clear-
ance project, providing shelter for 626 black families.[18] .

Such programs as FERA and PWA provided some succor for Dallas's
destitute, but by 1935 the relief crisis remained just as critical. That

year President Roosevelt created the Works Progress Administration
(WPA) to employ men in greater numbers and at a wage higher than the
relief rate. Recognizing that "make work" often had little intrinsic value,
he nonetheless favored it to the dole. (At the same time the federal government created WPA, it turned unemployment relief back over to state
and local governments.) Unlike the PWA, the WPA focused its resources
on smaller scale jobs with little cost for materials so that most of the
funds could be spent paying wages.[19]

By 1938 when Congress mandated draconian cuts in relief appropriations, WPA had spent thousands of dollars in Dallas, a substantial
contribution but somewhat less than might have been possible. Several
reasons accounted for WPA's limited success. Small payments to reliefers
underscored community values. The federal government divided the
nation into four regions to establish variable pay rates, and laborers in
the Southwest division (which included Dallas) received the second lowest wages. Certainly relief stipends fell short of desirable levels nationwide, but workers in southern cities suffered most, receiving from 33 to
65 percent of the national average emergency standard of living expense
identified by federal authorities. In 1939 in Dallas 8,939 persons received certification for relief employment, but only 4,973 actually obtained assignments. A local social worker observed that, as a result, "a
large though undetermined number of individuals in varying degrees of
need were thus left unprovided for by any existing agency, public or
private." Without federal funds after 1935, relief virtually vanished altogether; in 1935 Dallas spent approximately $350,000 to augment fed-
eral money but in 1936 appropriated nothing. Like other southern cities
Dallas increasingly relied upon external sources for care of its depen-
dents.[20] (See Tables 2 and 3.)

Indeed, substandard pay rates, paltry contributions to public relief,
and the virtually total reliance on federal funds indicate a minimal commitment to social welfare by the community. The Dallas *Morning News*
called WPA "evil but necessary," a succinct statement of how the agency
fared in the public's esteem. The acceptance of New Deal funds provided
a way to preserve traditional customs related to relief while temporarily
expanding coverage to meet an emergency. Far from being infused with
any new spirit of social welfare, Dallas seems not to have altered its
policies on indigent care at all during the Great Depression.[21]

In Dallas resistance to labor emanated from respectable, influential
businessmen's groups committed to the preservation of open shops. The
Chamber of Commerce boasted that Dallas was one of the first open-
shop cities in the country and advertised nationally the virtues of the
city's docile labor force. The chamber's Open Shop Bureau took an active role in politics, supporting candidates of antiunion persuasion. The
Dallas Open Shop Association, formed in 1919 by a coterie of local businessmen, guaranteed the solvency of all its members in case of work-
stopping strikes through the use of its rumored $2 million to $3 million
reserve fund. Further, it subjected any member who knowingly hired
union workers to a $3,000 fine. The success of the business community
in safeguarding the open shop resulted in total capitulation by the local

**Table 2. Sources of Funding for Relief Programs, 1935–1936**

| City and Year | | Total Spent on Relief ($) | Federal Dollars Spent on Relief ($) | Percent of Total from Federal Sources |
|---|---|---|---|---|
| Atlanta | 1935 | 5,910,810 | 5,051,153 | 86 |
|  | 1936 | 0 | 0 | 0 |
| Birmingham | 1935 | 5,452,319 | 5,072,506 | 93 |
|  | 1936 | 140,209 | 51,996 | 37 |
| Dallas | 1935 | 1,776,400 | 1,429,494 | 81 |
|  | 1936 | 0 | 0 | 0 |
| Houston | 1935 | 2,422,159 | 1,931,037 | 80 |
|  | 1936 | 0 | 0 | 0 |
| Memphis | 1935 | 2,280,031 | 2,123,861 | 93 |
|  | 1936 | 0 | 0 | 0 |
| New Orleans | 1935 | 9,241,949 | 8,973,956 | 97 |
|  | 1936 | 0 | 0 | 0 |

**Source**: United States Federal Emergency Relief Administration, *Final Statistical Report of the Federal Emergency Relief Administration, prepared under the direction of Theodore E. Whiting, Work Projects Administration* (Washington, D.C.: Government Printing Office, 1942), 327, 335, 343, 374, 376, 377.

AFL leadership, as witnessed by the Central Labor Council offering to help the Chamber of Commerce keep the CIO out of the community.[22]

The Dallas *Morning News* consistently took a hostile position toward labor unionization, opposing the National Labor Relations Act and the Fair Labor Standards Act. Moreover, it flaunted compliance of New Deal

**Table 3. Emergency Relief by Sources of Funds, July 1933–December 1935**

| City | Total ($) | Federal Funds ($) | Total (%) |
|---|---|---|---|
| Atlanta | 12,955,483 | 11,138,002 | 86.0 |
| Birmingham | 11,486,481 | 10,915,435 | 95.0 |
| Dallas | 4,733,623 | 3,814,125 | 80.6 |
| Houston | 5,742,238 | 4,490,605 | 78.2 |
| Memphis | 4,119,607 | 3,963,437 | 96.2 |
| New Orleans | 17,422,059 | 16,990,480 | 97.5 |
| Total | 56,459,491 | 51,312,084 | 90.9 |

| City | State Funds ($) | Total (%) | Local Funds ($) | Total (%) |
|---|---|---|---|---|
| Atlanta | 0 | 0.0 | 1,817,481 | 14.0 |
| Birmingham | 64,898 | 0.6 | 506,148 | 4.4 |
| Dallas | 891,230 | 18.8 | 28,268 | 0.6 |
| Houston | 1,241,315 | 21.6 | 10,318 | 0.2 |
| Memphis | 0 | 0.0 | 156,170 | 3.8 |
| New Orleans | 0 | 0.0 | 431,579 | 2.5 |
| Total | 2,197,443 | 3.9 | 2,949,964 | 5.2 |

**Source**: Arthur E. Burns, "Federal Emergency Relief Administration," in Clarence E. Ridley and Orin F. Nolting (eds.), *The Municipal Year Book, 1937* (Chicago: The International City Managers' Association, 1937), 413–414.

labor laws in its own business affairs, refusing to pay its employees an hourly wage with time-and-a-half for overtime. In short, the newspaper continued to treat its workers in the frankly paternalistic way it always had. It guaranteed employees a certain wage in its contracts with them and disregarded federal requirements for minimum pay levels. Nobody at the *News* ever punched a time clock, federal strictures notwithstanding. The company felt so strongly about management's right to deal freely with its own workers that it successfully withstood legal challenges by the U.S. government, first in the Fifth Circuit Court of Appeals and finally in the U.S. Supreme Court. As the most influential newspaper in Dallas, its victory lent special authority to its regular anti-labor fulminations.[23]

As in other southern cities violence against union organizers in Dallas was frequent, brutal, and shockingly open. In 1937 the United Auto Workers (UAW) initiated a campaign to organize a local Ford plant. Several union members, labor lawyers, and sympathizers suffered beatings near the automobile factory and downtown in broad daylight. Socialist Herbert Harris was knocked out, stripped, tarred and feathered, and deposited on a downtown street. A few days later several men took a UAW attorney from a downtown drugstore and beat him severely. Police did nothing. In 1939 and 1940 the UAW filed unfair labor practice charges against Ford with the National Labor Relations Board, which accused company officials in Dallas with "brutality unknown in the history of the Board." Brutal, but effective—the 1930s ended with Ford still free of UAW representation.[24]

Similar violence developed when textile unions sought to penetrate the substantial Dallas clothing industry. Hat, Cap, and Millinery Workers vice president George Baer lost sight in one eye when three men wielding blackjacks waylayed him on a busy downtown street. Baer identified his attackers, but police took no action. Sporadic violence interrupted an ILGWU strike in which hooligans stripped ten women before a crowd of hundreds in the central business district. The bitter strike dragged on for over eight months before collapsing in defeat. By 1940 several hundred garment workers belonged to two ILGWU locals, representing the signal accomplishment of labor in the city. "Nevertheless," writes labor historian George Green, "the union rated Dallas as the only Southwestern city with a considerable dress production market that was still unorganized."[25]

Both the AFL and the CIO won significant victories in the 1930s, though primarily in the smokestack cities of the Northeast and Midwest. In the tradition-laden South success came more grudgingly. Major breakthroughs, achieved earlier in other parts of the nation, were forestalled by the opposition of local authorities like Memphis's Boss Crump and organizations like the Dallas Open Shop Association. The drive to unionize the South persisted for decades; in 1946 the CIO's Operation Dixie, a comprehensive drive for closed shops from the Piedmont to Texas, commenced with great fanfare. In 1953 it ceased operation, conceding defeat. Only 14.4 percent of the region's nonagricultural workers belonged to unions as late as the mid-1960s (compared to 29.5 percent nationally). The situation in Dallas confirmed historian George Tindall's conclusion that despite nominal gains in membership and the laying of a foundation for future success, "the South remained predominantly nonunion and largely antiunion."[26]

Dallas blacks suffered severely from the economy's collapse in the 1930s. Traditionally "last hired and first fired" and confined to the lowest paying jobs, they constituted fully one-half of the city's unemployed by 1932. The few black-owned businesses faced extinction; no banks and one black insurance company (Excelsior Mutual) survived by 1937. Residential segregation continued to be the rule, despite court rulings outlawing discriminatory municipal ordinances. Expanding black communities in "Oak Cliff" and "Elm Thicket" were situated in the least desirable areas of the city, inching across the landscape only as bordering white residents surrendered their homes. But racial turnover occurred very slowly and construction nearly ceased in the Depression years, so inadequate housing remained a serious problem. Whites also used violence to keep blacks from occupying homes in white neighborhoods. The Dallas *Express* reported a dozen bombings during the winter of 1940–1941 and criticized Mayor Woodall Rodgers, who blamed blacks for inciting violence by not accepting residential segregation. A 1938 Dallas housing survey reported 86 percent of black homes substandard. Given the squalor in which so many blacks lived, the fact that in 1930 black mortality rates more than doubled those of whites is not surprising.[27]

The drive for equal rights and improved living conditions met formidable opposition in the courts. In Texas the white primary formed the major obstacle to black voting. In 1923 the state legislature revised the election laws to prohibit explicitly black participation in Democratic primaries. When the U.S. Supreme Court ruled the statute a violation of the Fourteenth Amendment's equal protection clause in *Nixon v. Herndon*, the state legislature rewrote the law deleting references to blacks and empowering the State Democratic Executive Committee to approve voting qualifications. In 1935 the nation's highest court approved the revision in *Grovey v. Townsend*, arrogating disfranchisement to the political party by virtue of its being a nongovernmental voluntary association.[28]

In 1936 a group of the state's most influential blacks, including Antonio Maceo Smith and Maynard H. Jackson of Dallas and Clifford Jackson and Richard Grovey of Houston, reorganized the defunct Independent Voters League as the Progressive Voters League to continue the battle against white primaries. In 1938 several blacks filed a class action suit in U.S. District Court seeking an injunction against the Houston Democratic Executive Committee to prevent the exclusion of black voters in that year's primary election. The court refused to grant the injunction; the black petitioners considered an appeal but finally did nothing. Not until 1944 did the U.S. Supreme Court rule the white primary unconstitutional in the landmark *Smith v. Allright* decision. In the 1930s black efforts at contesting the Democratic party's exclusive policies fell consistently short.[29]

The inability to participate in Democratic primaries severely limited the political role played by Texas blacks in the 1930s. The Dallas Progressive Voters League remained active, registering black voters and endorsing the white candidates who seemed least objectionable. Nonetheless, few blacks voted or even paid their poll taxes—only 3,400 in Dallas and just 400 in Houston in 1935. Since neither city possessed a political machine that relied on black patronage for continued electoral success, local Democratic leaders had no reason to liberalize their voting requirements. Few blacks bothered to seek elective office. In 1935 A. S. Wells did in Dallas, in a special election to fill a vacancy in the state legislature. He placed fifth with 1,001 votes as many black registered voters stayed home, allegedly in response to the Ku Klux Klan's campaign of intimidation. In 1939 black businessman James B. Grigsby ran for election to the Houston school board but received only 689 votes. In an electorate dominated by whites, blacks' efforts consistently failed to alter election outcomes.[30]

Dallas had a black chamber of commerce, an NAACP chapter, and other voluntary associations that sought to improve conditions of their constituents. Generally, their impact was unremarkable, their achievements few. Limited local resources and the overwhelming bulwark of custom, coupled with community demoralization, meant that any attempt to improve conditions for blacks would be an uphill struggle. Most blacks had only the New Deal's relief and recovery programs to fall back on. Unfortunately, in the tradition-laden southern cities the New Deal made few inroads. Nor did southern-based federal bureaucrats launch unpopular reform campaigns. Southerners feared the New Deal's reputation as liberal on the issue of race, even though Roosevelt initiated few efforts designed specifically to aid blacks, and his administration's celebrity can best be attributed to the unofficial efforts of a few activists such as Harold Ickes, Aubrey Williams, and Eleanor Roosevelt. And as in politics, local administrators exercised considerable autonomy in the application of New Deal programs and policies.[31]

Segregation also proved unassailable by New Deal agencies. Many programs enforced separation, as did the WPA in its sewing rooms and the Civilian Conservation Corps in its camps. The inchoate public housing program preserved racial segregation, first under the aegis of the PWA and subsequently, the U.S. Housing Authority. Under the PWA's Harold Ickes, about half the federal housing projects in the South went to blacks, and PWA housing contracts required the hiring of black workers. Dallas began construction of public housing projects during the 1930s, designating most of them for black occupation. No question ever arose about the suitability of segregated housing units—no one, black or white, called for integrated projects—but implementation of the program aroused considerable controversy nevertheless. Construction delays developed when black projects fell too near white neighborhoods, and despite PWA and USHA housing contract stipulations that blacks be employed in construction, local authorities often failed to do so.[32]

The New Deal provided new housing, jobs, and relief for many destitute blacks in Dallas but always under the vigilant control of local authorities. Municipal officials set guidelines and implemented policies to reinforce existing racial norms—with little or no federal incursions. Even the blacks helped by New Deal programs lived in a community where segregation and second-class citizenship went largely unquestioned. In Dallas, as throughout the South, few blacks voted and none held elective office. The assault on Jim Crowism and political disfranchisement, a post-World War II movement, received little impetus from the New Deal.

The Great Depression struck hard in Dallas. Although the city fared better than some others because of the oil bonanza, problems arose to tax local resources. Businesses shut down, workers lost jobs, productivity declined, trade ebbed, and the demands for relief skyrocketed. Reduced tax collections, no heritage of social welfare, and city government's insistence upon fiscal "responsibility" combined to curtail the amount of relief offered the needy in Dallas and other southern cities. The New Deal provided some aid but, even when most generously funded, only for a fraction of the needy and at wage levels below the standards in other regions. New Deal alphabet agencies allowed Dallas to minimize its welfare contributions, not expand them. City leadership rested more firmly than ever in the city's business elite by the end of the decade. The defenders of the status quo preserved the community's independence from union influence, at least for the immediate future. New Deal programs never excluded blacks from benefits, and occasionally explicitly included them—on paper, anyway. But the Roosevelt administration had neither the desire nor the capacity to challenge the South's rock-ribbed racial mores. The federal government's impact on Dallas in the 1930s favored continuity; resistance to change resulted from the influence of powerful elites, unvarnished fealty to long-standing values and institutions, the political powerlessness of the have-nots, and the New Deal's admittedly modest reform agenda. Comparisons with other large southern cities call into question the significance of the New Deal's impact. The forces of conservatism in Dallas and its sister cities in the South appear to have resisted—or at least slowed—the dissolution of traditional political, social, and economic customs.

## NOTES

1. William E. Leuchtenburg, *Franklin D. Roosevelt and the New Deal, 1932–1940* (New York: Harper and Row, 1963), 336 (1st quotation); Carl N. Degler, *Out of Our Past: The Forces That Shaped Modern America* (New York: Harper and Brothers, 1959), 416 (2nd quotation); James T. Patterson, *The New Deal and the States: Federalism in Transition* (Princeton: Princeton University Press, 1969), 206–207. Also see Barton J. Bernstein, "The New Deal: The Conservative Achievements of Liberal Reform" in Barton J. Bernstein (ed.), *Towards a New Past: Dissenting Essays in American History* (New York: Pantheon Books, 1968), 263–288; Paul K. Conkin, *The New Deal* (Arlington Heights, Ill.: Harlan Davidson, Inc., 1967); Barry D. Karl, *The Uneasy State: The United States from 1915 to 1945* (Chicago: University of Chicago Press, 1983); and Robert S. McElvaine, *The Great Depression: America 1929–1941* (New York: Times Books, 1984). On New Deal historiography, see Richard S. Kirkendall, "The New Deal as Watershed: The Recent Literature," *Journal of American History*, LIV (Mar., 1968), 839–852; Jerold S. Auerbach, "New Deal, Old Deal, or Raw Deal: Some Thoughts on New Left Historiography," *Journal of Southern History*, XXXV (Feb., 1969), 18–30; Alonzo L. Hamby (ed.), *The New Deal: Analysis and Interpretation* (New York: Longman, 1981); and

Harvard Sitkoff (ed.), *Fifty Years Later: The New Deal Evaluated* (New York: Alfred A. Knopf, 1985).

2. Bruce M. Stave, "Pittsburgh and the New Deal," in John Braeman, Robert H. Bremner, and David Brody (eds.), *The New Deal: The State and Local Levels* (Columbus, Ohio: Ohio State University Press, 1975), 376–402; Lyle W. Dorsett, "Kansas City and the New Deal," in Braeman, Bremner, and Brody (eds.), *The New Deal*, 407–418; Roger Biles, *Big City Boss in Depression and War: Mayor Edward J. Kelly of Chicago* (DeKalb: Northern Illinois University Press, 1984); Charles Hathaway Trout, *Boston, the Great Depression, and the New Deal* (New York: Oxford University Press, 1977), 315 (1st quotation); Zane L. Miller, *The Urbanization of Modern America: A Brief History* (New York: Harcourt Brace Jovanovich, 1973), 168–169 (2nd quotation).

3. David R. Goldfield, *Cotton Fields and Skyscrapers: Southern City and Region, 1607–1980* (Baton Rouge: Louisiana State University Press, 1982), 181–182 (quotation); Douglas L. Smith, *The New Deal in the Urban South* (Baton Rouge: Louisiana State University Press, 1988). Also see David R. Goldfield, "The Urban South: A Regional Framework," *American Historical Review*, LXXXVI (Dec., 1981), 1009–1034.

4. Roger Biles, *Memphis in the Great Depression* (Knoxville: University of Tennessee Press, 1986).

5. Dallas *Morning News*, Jan. 26, 1967; Ann P. Hollingsworth, "Reform Government in Dallas, 1927–1940" (M.A. thesis, North Texas State University, 1971), 10–16; New York *Times*, Oct. 19, 1930; Roscoe C. Martin, "Dallas Makes the Manager Plan Work," *The Annals of the American Academy of Political and Social Science*, CXCIX (Sept., 1938), 64; Louis P. Head, "Dallas Joins Ranks of Manager Cities," *National Municipal Review*, XIX (Dec., 1930), 806–809; W. D. Jones, "Dallas Wins a Place in the Sun," *National Municipal Review*, XXIV (Jan., 1935), 11–14; Work Projects Administration Writers' Project, *Dallas Guide and History* (Dallas: n.p., 1940), 193–194, 202–203; New York *Times*, Apr. 12, 1931.

6. Dallas *Morning News*, Mar. 23, 27, 1967; "'N.M.L.' Charged With Traitorous Propaganda to Install Imperialistic Government," *National Municipal Review*, XXI (Mar., 1932), 140 (quotation); Robert B. Fairbanks, "The Good Government Machine: The Citizens Charter Association and Dallas Politics, 1930–1960," in *Essays on Sunbelt Cities and Recent Urban America*, No. 23, Walter Prescott Webb Memorial Lectures, ed. Robert B. Fairbanks and Kathleen Underwood (College Station: Texas A&M University Press, 1990), 127–132.

7. Michael C. D. Macdonald, *America's Cities: A Report on the Myth of Urban Renaissance* (New York: Simon and Schuster, 1984), 114; Transcript of interview with R. L. Thornton, Jr., Nov. 8, 1980 (quotation), Dallas Mayors Oral History Project, Dallas Public Library; Stanley Walker, *The Dallas Story* (Dallas: Dallas Times Herald, 1956), 33–35.

8. Warren Leslie, *Dallas, Public and Private* (New York: Grossman Publishers, 1964), 64 (2nd quotation), 69, 84 (1st quotation); Lyle W. Dorsett, *Franklin D. Roosevelt and the City Bosses* (Port Washington, N.Y.: National University Publications, Kennikat Press, 1977). Dallas remains the largest city in the nation with a city-manager form of government. Stephen L. Elkin, "State and Market in City Politics: Or, the 'Real' Dallas," in Clarence N. Stone and Heywood T. Sanders (eds.), *The Politics of Urban Development* (Lawrence: University Press of Kansas, 1987), 50n; Biles, *Memphis in the Great Depression*, especially chap. 4; T. Harry Williams, *Huey Long* (New York: Alfred A. Knopf, 1969), 425–427, 675, 849–853; Betty Marie Field, "The Politics of the New Deal in Louisiana, 1933–1939" (Ph.D. diss., Tulane University, 1973), 83–85, 109–112, 286–287; Edward Shannon LaMonte, "Politics and Welfare in Birmingham, Alabama: 1900–1975" (Ph.D. diss., University of Chicago, 1976), 135–136; Douglas L. Fleming, "Atlanta, the Depression, and the New Deal" (Ph.D. diss., Emory University, 1984).

9. Dallas *Morning News*, Nov. 13, 1929 (quotation), June 23, 1930; Bureau of the Census, *Fifteenth Census of the United States: 1930. Unemployment* (Washington, D.C.: Government Printing Office, 1932), II, 135; Dallas *Morning News*, Oct. 13, 1929, Oct. 12, 1930.

10. James Howard, *Big D Is For Dallas: Chapters in the Twentieth-Century History of Dallas* (Austin: University Cooperative Society, 1957), 43, 89; Dorothy De Moss, "Resourcefulness in the Financial Capital: Dallas, 1929–1933," in Robert C. Cotner et al., *Texas Cities and the Great Depression* (Austin: Texas Memorial Museum, 1973), 119–121; Dallas Chamber of Commerce, "Report of Industrial Dallas, Inc., 1928–1929–1930," Dallas Public Library (Dallas: n.p., 1931).

11. Dallas *Morning News*, Dec. 11, 1931; Work Projects Administration Writers' Project, *Dallas Guide and History*, 195; J. F. Lucey to Walter S. Gifford, telegram, Oct. 27, 1931, State File: Texas, President's Organization For Unemployment Relief, Record Group 73 (National Archives).

12. Dorothy Dell De Moss, "Dallas, Texas, During the Early Depression: The Hoover Years, 1929–1933" (M.A. thesis, University of Texas, 1966), 70–81; Dallas *Morning News*, Jan. 5, 1933; Howard, *Big D Is For Dallas*, 15–16.

13. Roscoe C. Martin, "Dallas Makes the Manager Plan Work," *The Annals of the American Academy of Political and Social Science*, CXCIX (Sept., 1938), 65; Dallas *Morning News*, Apr. 28, 1932; Fairbanks, "The Good Government Machine," 127–128; De Moss, "Dallas, Texas, During the Early Depression," 119–122.

14. De Moss, "Resourcefulness in the Financial Capital," 124, 125 (quotation), 126; Dallas *Morning News*, Apr. 12, 1932. See also American Public Welfare Association, "Dallas Welfare Survey," Southern Methodist University Library, Dallas, Texas (n.p., 1938).

15. American Public Welfare Assocation, "Dallas Welfare Survey," 84 (1st quotation); Dallas *Morning News*, Dec. 4, 1931 (2nd quotation).

16. Donald W. Whisenhunt, *The Depression in Texas: The Hoover Years* (New York: Garland Publishing, 1983), 9 (quotation); Dallas *Morning News*, July 23, Aug. 11, 1933; Dallas Chamber of Commerce, "Departmental Reports for 1933," *Dallas*, XII (Dec., 1933), 6.

17. Lionel V. Patenaude, *Texans, Politics, and the New Deal* (New York: Garland Publishing, 1983), 88; United States Federal Emergency Relief Administration, *Final Statistical Report on the Federal Emergency Relief Administration*, prepared under the direction of Theodore E. Whiting, Work Projects Administration (Washington, D.C.: Government Printing Office, 1942), 177–192; Arthur E. Burns, "Federal Emergency Relief Administration," in Clarence E. Ridley and Orin F. Nolting (eds.), *The Municipal Year Book, 1937* (Chicago: The International City Managers' Association, 1937), 413–414.

18. Otis L. Graham, Jr., and Meghan Robinson Wander (eds.), *Franklin D. Roosevelt, His Life and Times: An Encyclopedic View* (Boston: G. K. Hall, 1985), 336–337; Work Projects Administration Division of Information, "Texas," Appraisal Report File, County Reports D–E, Record Group 69 (National Archives); Work Projects Administration Writers' Project, *Dallas Guide and History*, 508.

19. Graham and Wander (eds.), *Franklin D. Roosevelt, His Life and Times*, 461–464.

20. Donald S. Howard, *The WPA and Federal Relief Policy* (New York: Russell Sage Foundation, 1943), 84, 95, 178; Work Projects Administration Writers' Project, *Dallas Guide and History*, 494, 495 (quotation); *Final Statistical Report of the Federal Emergency Relief Administration*, 343. The city did employ 8,000 men in construction and landscaping work on the Texas Centennial Exposition. Work Projects Administration Writers' Project, *Dallas Guide and History*, 199.

21. Dallas *Morning News*, Mar. 30, 1935.

22. New York *Times*, Jan. 5, 1930; George Lambert, "Dallas Tries Terror," *The Nation*, CXLV (Oct. 9, 1937), 377. *The Craftsman*, local AFL organ, protested the Chamber of Commerce's depiction of a pliable labor force. *The Craftsman* (Dallas), Mar. 28, 1930.

23. Stanley Walker, "The Dallas *Morning News*," *American Mercury*, LXV (Dec., 1947), 708–711. Also see Ernest Sharpe, *G. B. Dealey of the Dallas News* (New York: Henry Holt & Co., 1955).

24. Work Projects Administration Writers' Project, *Dallas Guide and History*, 283–284; John J. Granberry, "Civil Liberties in Texas," *Christian Century*, LIV (Oct. 27, 1937), 1326–1327; Lambert, "Dallas Tries Terror," 376–378; F. Ray Marshall, *Labor in the South* (Cambridge, Mass.: Harvard University Press, 1967), 191 (quotation).

25. *The Craftsman* (Dallas), Feb. 22, Mar. 8, 1935; Work Projects Administration Writers' Project, *Dallas Guide and History*, 284; John J. Granberry, "Civil Liberties in Texas," 1327; George N. Green, "The ILGWU in Texas, 1930–1970," *Journal of Mexican American History*, I (Spring, 1971), 154 (quotation). Also see George N. Green, "Discord in Dallas: Auto Workers, City Fathers, and the Ford Motor Company, 1937–1941," *Labor's Heritage*, I (July, 1980), 20–33.

26. Billy Hall Wyche, "Southern Attitudes Toward Industrial Unions, 1933–1941" (Ph.D. diss., University of Georgia, 1969), 167; George Brown Tindall, *The Emergence of the New South, 1913–1945* (Baton Rouge: Louisiana State University Press, 1967), 515, 522 (quotation). On unionization efforts since World War II, see Robert Emil Botsch, *We Shall Not Overcome: Populism and Southern Blue Collar Workers* (Chapel Hill: University of North Carolina Press, 1980); Marshall, *Labor in the South*; and Merl E. Reed, Leslie S. Hough, and Gary M. Fink (eds.), *Southern Workers and Their Unions, 1880–1975: Selected Papers/The Second Labor History Conference, 1978* (Westport, Conn.: Greenwood Press, 1981). Outlining the failures of the CIO in the immediate post-World War II period is Barbara S. Griffith, *The Crisis of American Labor: Operation Dixie and the Defeat of the CIO* (Philadelphia: Temple University Press, 1988).

27. Bureau of the Census, *Fifteenth Census of the United States: 1930. Unemployment* (Washington, D.C.: Government Printing Office, 1931), I, 952–953; "Minutes of the Annual Meeting, Texas Commission on Interracial Cooperation," Dec. 6, 7, 1940, Houston Metropolitan Research Center, Houston Public Library; Alwyn Barr, *Black Texans: A History of Negroes in Texas, 1528–1971* (Austin: Jenkins Publishing Co., Pemberton Press, 1973), 154–155; Work

Projects Administration Writers' Project, *Dallas Guide and History*, 507, 517; Dallas *Express*, Jan. 18, Mar. 1, 1941.

28. Robert Haynes, "Black Houstonians and the White Democratic Primary, 1920–1945," in Francisco A. Rosales and Barry J. Kaplan (eds.), *Houston: A Twentieth Century Urban Frontier* (Port Washington, N.Y.: Associated Faculty Press, 1983), 122–137; James Martin SoRelle, "The Darker Side of 'Heaven': The Black Community in Houston, Texas, 1917–1945" (Ph.D. diss., Kent State University, 1980), 172–196.

29. Barr, *Black Texans*, 136; SoRelle, "The Darker Side of 'Heaven,'" 203–205. Also see Darlene Clark Hine, *Black Victory: The Rise and Fall of the White Primary in Texas* (Millwood, N.Y.: KTO Press, 1979).

30. Fairbanks, "The Good Government Machine," 130–133; Ralph J. Bunche, *The Political Status of the Negro in the Age of FDR*, ed. Dewey W. Grantham (Chicago: University of Chicago Press, 1973), 95, 466, 557; SoRelle, "The Darker Side of 'Heaven,'" 302–303.

31. Tempie Virginia Strange, "The Dallas Negro Chamber of Commerce: A Study of a Negro Institution" (M.A. thesis, Southern Methodist University, 1945); Barr, *Black Texans*, 147; Leedell W. Neyland, "The Negro in Louisiana Since 1900: An Economic and Social Study" (Ph.D. diss., New York University, 1958), 66.

32. Tindall, *The Emergence of the New South, 1913–1945*, 546; Charles S. Johnson, *Patterns of Negro Segregation* (New York: Harper and Brothers, 1943), 37.

# Harold and Dutch: A Comparative Look at the First Black Mayors of Chicago and New Orleans

*Arnold R. Hirsch*

Since the 1967 elections of Richard Hatcher in Gary, Indiana, and Carl Stokes in Cleveland, Ohio, the emergence of black mayors in major American cities has been one of the distinguishing characteristics of local politics in the United States. Since then, African Americans have been elected as chief executives in every corner of the nation. In the industrial Northeast and Midwest, blacks presently occupy, or in the recent past have occupied, city halls in New York, Chicago, Detroit, Cleveland, Philadelphia, and Newark. In the South, they have run Washington, Baltimore, Richmond, Atlanta, New Orleans, and Birmingham, among others—places where elected black officials would have been unthinkable even a single generation before. Even in the Far West where African Americans proportionately have settled more sparsely, Los Angeles and Seattle have had black mayors representing overwhelmingly white cities. Such staggering change would seem to herald the ultimate success of the civil rights revolution. Was this not, after all, what it was all about?

It is clear, however, that if the pattern of municipal officeholding has undergone a dramatic shift, the conditions that initially sparked black protest and political mobilization remain stubbornly persistent. Certainly, rates of unemployment for African Americans living in the urban core have not dropped below those of the Vietnam era. And compared to the so-called pathologies of contemporary inner-city life—such as rates of crime, illegitimacy, illiteracy, and single-parent households—the violent 1960s look almost like a "golden age" whose problems seem manageable. While there is no denying the mushrooming growth of an expansive black middle class, the emergence of a seemingly chronically dependent urban black "underclass" (as it came to be called in the 1980s) seems equally undeniable.

The black community, in short, is more complex and diverse today than it was a generation earlier. If the ghetto has been gilded for some

*Arnold R. Hirsch is professor of history at the University of New Orleans. Original essay printed by permission of author.*

and escaped by others, it now presents the dual problems of race and poverty in a new and concentrated form. If there is legitimate concern over the implicit political and ideological content of the concept of the underclass, the term's popularity stems, at least in part, from its descriptive utility. The elevation of a new class of African-American officeholders has not, in short, substantially altered the social structure of urban America.

This essay will offer a brief examination of two black mayors—Ernest Nathan "Dutch" Morial of New Orleans and Harold Washington of Chicago—in an effort to shed some light on the problems and forces they confronted. Certainly it is helpful to scrutinize African-American administrations in a northern city and a southern one to see if any regional differences come into play, but there should be no easy supposition that the individuals at the focus of this chapter are necessarily representative of black mayors as a class. If anything, Dutch Morial and Harold Washington were among the toughest and smartest of those municipal executives dedicated to attacking the status quo; each was concerned more with pursuing and exercising power than accumulating mere honors. In sum, if individual, local officeholders could shape their immediate environments, these two would be likely candidates for producing visible results.

There are three points at which the careers of each of these figures might be usefully examined. First, there is the acquisition of power. In looking at Morial's rise to the mayor's chair in 1978 and Washington's in 1983, one first sees that each reached that pinnacle at a time when blacks represented both population and voting minorities in New Orleans and Chicago. That simple fact, ultimately, had serious implications for their ability to govern. Second, there is the actual exercise of power. How did each of them govern? What obstacles did they confront and how successful were they in overcoming them? Finally, the succession of power might be revealing if scrutinized. Morial left City Hall in 1986, turned out of office after two consecutive terms by a city charter term limitation that he tried and failed to repeal. Washington, having been reelected to a second term in a city that honored a tradition of extended, multiple terms for its mayors, died, suddenly, in his office in 1987. How permanent were the advances made during their administrations? Could those advances dictate the direction of change once Morial and Washington were out of office? Had they, in other words, set their respective cities on new courses?

The rise of Dutch Morial and Harold Washington must be understood within their local political contexts. There is a tendency in the study of American race relations to homogenize everything into simple matters of black and white. A study of African-American mayors, however, reveals that within the framework provided by the American racial dichotomy, an understanding of local cultures is critical to an understanding of the individuals themselves.

Atlanta's Andrew Young, for example, entered City Hall through the ministry, and Coleman Young became industrial Detroit's chief executive officer following an extended stint as a labor radical and organizer for the United Auto Workers. The first black mayors of New Orleans and Chicago similarly launched their early careers in the most powerful local black institutions available. Local variables conditioned, if they did not dictate, the channels through which talented and ambitious African-American leaders developed their skills and became prominent figures.

In New Orleans and Chicago, those institutions were neither the black church, although it was not without influence, nor the labor movement. For Morial that central institution was the National Association for the Advancement of Colored People (NAACP). Not only was it the most important vehicle for protest and the civil rights movement in New Orleans, but it also was the institutional home for the remnants of a radical black Creole community that provided much of the city's leadership during the era of Reconstruction and kept alive a tradition of resistance to the color line since the dawning of the Jim Crow era. Personified by Homer Plessy's moral and legal challenge at the end of the nineteenth century, that Creole radicalism survived in New Orleans to tie the first and second Reconstructions together.[1]

Morial was born and raised in New Orleans's Seventh Ward, the very epicenter of the downtown Creole community. He was an integral part of it and assumed the presidency of the local branch of the NAACP during the height of the civil rights agitation of the early 1960s. The New Orleans chapter of the NAACP, created in 1915, was one of the first branches established in the Deep South and displayed roots similar to Morial's. Its chief legal counsel, through the middle of the twentieth century, was A. P. Tureaud, another Seventh Ward Creole and Morial's senior partner and mentor.

Tureaud and Morial, more than any other individuals in the Crescent City, became identified with the dismantling of the legalized system of segregation. It was a fitting role for Morial, who was himself a walking civil rights revolution. The first black to graduate from the Louisiana State University Law School, in 1952, he went on to accumulate an impressive array of other "firsts": he was the first black assistant U.S. attorney in New Orleans (1965), the first elected to the state legislature in the modern era (1967), the first named to the Juvenile Court bench (1970), the first to serve on the state's Fourth Circuit Court of Appeals (1974), and, ultimately, the first elected mayor. In short, Dutch Morial made his career by opposing, as Rodolphe Desdunes, another black Creole, put it, the "fanaticism of caste." More than a vehicle for the legal assault on Jim Crow, the local branch of the NAACP also carried out, under Morial's direction, voter registration campaigns that proved instrumental in the successful launching of his political career. Initially locked out of the system, Morial mounted an assault from outside, demolishing racial barriers while building an institutional base within the black community.[2]

In Chicago the NAACP was incapable of performing similar services. When, early in the civil rights era, it had threatened to become an activist protest organization, black political boss William Levi Dawson simply had his precinct captains infiltrate the organization as new voting members. A moderating change in leadership followed. That episode, however, gave a clue as to where the path to political power could be found in Chicago—it was in the Cook County Democratic Organization, the famed Chicago "machine" itself.

Indeed, Harold Washington had been raised in the very bosom of the organization that he would later defeat. The Democratic political machine in Chicago, and its subordinate black branch, provided a wealth of opportunity for those who could gather concentrated black votes in the city's highly segregated neighborhoods. Demography, geography, and the peculiar features of its political landscape made that arena an attractive one for skilled and ambitious players. Chicago's South Side Black Belt proved a veritable political hothouse, developing a sophisticated cadre of movers and shakers by the turn of the twentieth century. Indeed, it was that scarred battleground on the South Side, not larger New York, that produced, by 1928, the first black representative to the U.S. Congress elected from a northern district.[3]

Harold Washington's father, Roy Washington, was an attorney, an African Methodist Episcopal preacher, a dabbler in real estate, and a precinct captain in the Democratic organization. Active at the beginning of the 1930s, he was one of the earliest black Democratic stalwarts. Politics formed the core of the dinner table discussions that Harold Washington recalled from his childhood. And Harold did more than absorb stories about the machine. He watched it operate at close hand as when, in 1947, his father strapped a gun on his hip and went looking for the Democratic ward committeeman who had covertly undermined his campaign for the city council.[4]

If Harold Washington was never quite an unthinking machine loyalist (he characterized himself, at one point, as an "independent machine politician"), he paid it enough obeisance early in his career to emerge as one of its most promising stars. He had taken over the South Side Third Ward precinct worked by his father and filled the elder Washington's slot in the corporation counsel's office following his death in 1953 (Harold Washington's law degree came from Northwestern University in 1952). Though considerably younger than the Third Ward's Democratic committeeman (committeemen were the key political officers in each ward), former Olympic star and rising machine politician Ralph Metcalfe, Washington possessed political skills that were more finely honed, and it is not entirely clear who, exactly, was mentoring whom.

Finally rewarded with a seat in the state legislature, Washington became something of a renegade after his posting to Springfield (first in the state House of Representatives and, later, in the Senate) in 1964. Confronting Mayor Richard J. Daley directly on the issue of police brutality and wandering away from the party line on a host of lesser concerns, Washington soon found himself beyond Metcalfe's protective mantle and on his own. He made a longshot's futile run for City Hall in 1977 following Daley's death and fought off the organization's subsequent attempted purge. In the party primary the following year he had to survive an election in which the organization slated three opponents—two of them named Washington—against him. The attempt to confuse

Washington's electoral base into submission fell barely 200 votes short of success. Washington then confirmed his independence by successfully challenging the machine-slated nominee for the U.S. House of Representatives in his district in 1980. Displaying the power to outdraw the machine in his home district, he became a vocal critic of the Reagan administration, further ingratiating himself with his South Side constituency.

Both Dutch Morial and Harold Washington, consequently, succeeded in building solid black political bases. In Morial's case it was rooted in the downtown Creole community but extended uptown into the old "American" sector of the city. As attorney and legislative candidate, he mined those neighborhoods for supporters in both the NAACP's civil rights crusades and in his race for the state House of Representatives. For Washington, home was Chicago's massive South Side Black Belt, particularly those growing middle-class wards that were proving less than reliable for the machine. That provided the base from which he could reach out to whites (he ultimately settled in the integrated Hyde Park community that surrounded the University of Chicago) and to the newer, growing ghetto on the West Side. It is important to note also that neither Morial nor Washington emerged overnight. In both cases long years of service and an extended political apprenticeship forged an organic unity between the community and the candidates. The extraordinarily high levels of black voter turnout and solidarity that they enjoyed in their surprising initial victories were testimonies, ultimately, to their long-established credibility as well as to the magic of their respective moments.

In each case, the assertiveness of the black candidates and their ability to forge solid African-American electoral bases allowed them to surprise divided white communities that did not take them seriously as political threats. In dissecting their winning coalitions, however, analysts have divided over the relative significance of the solid black base as opposed to the essential white fragment that provided, in theory, their margins of victory. Often rooted in political or racial interests, at least some of this attention is misplaced. The key factor, it seems, is the black base in combination with the ignorance and arrogance that led to the underestimation of the African-American candidates in the white community and the internal white divisions that opened the door for seemingly quixotic challenges.

In New Orleans, in 1977, Morial faced three major white opponents that sharply divided the white vote in an "open" (nonpartisan) primary that would pit the top two finishers against one another if no one earned a majority of the ballots cast. Morial was seen as nothing more than a "spoiler" at the outset, and his relative lack of financial resources and grass-roots campaign in the black community led mainstream analysts to dismiss his prospects in a city in which black registrants amounted to no more than 43 percent of the vote. His impact on the campaign was discussed primarily in terms of how he would affect the tallies of Nat Kiefer and Toni Morrison, the "serious" white candidates who were actively courting black supporters. The fourth candidate, Joseph DiRosa, ran a white populist campaign that made no pretense of seeking black votes.[5]

In the end, the traditional paternalistic ties that linked white political elites to African-American "leaders" and voters were no match for the communal ties forged by Morial over his long career. Morial's base returned a sizable majority of the black vote in the primary, eviscerating the campaigns of both Kiefer and Morrison. Having split the white vote with DiRosa, they were left dueling over a small slice of the minority pie. Morial thus squeezed into the runoff with DiRosa, a candidate who had thoroughly alienated the business community and carried his own ethnic baggage. In the final showdown, Morial swept 97 percent of an exceptionally high black turnout and just enough whites, about 20 percent, to enable him to win a close contest.[6]

Similarly, Washington was given no chance to win when he announced his candidacy in the 1983 mayoralty. After all, he had won only 11 percent of the vote in his 1977 warm-up, and blacks still represented less than 40 percent of Chicago's electorate. The "real" race would be in the Democratic primary between the incumbent, Jane Byrne, and her major white challenger, Richard M. Daley, the present mayor of the city and the son of Chicago's legendary Richard J. Daley. Washington, until the final days of the primary campaign, enjoyed nearly a free ride. The mainstream white press virtually ignored his prospects while concentrating its closest scrutiny on Byrne and Daley. For their part, the mayor and her Irish challenger similarly refrained from attacking Washington. Seeking some portion of the black vote for themselves in the primary, they certainly did not wish to alienate that constituency and hoped to pick it back up in the general election. Only in the closing days of the campaign did it become clear that, indeed, it was Washington, not Daley, who was Byrne's most threatening opponent. That turn of events prompted Democratic party chairman Ed Vrdolyak's now famous dictum that the election had become a "racial thing." Calling on whites to desert Daley in defense of racial interests, his raw appeal backfired. With Byrne and Daley neatly dividing the white ballots almost in half, Washington won the Democratic nomination for mayor with only 36 percent of the total primary vote. His showing in the black community—he had won 85 percent of a 70 percent turnout there following a massive increase in voter registration—carried the day. Part political campaign, part religious crusade, the Washington movement capitalized on a long series of racial provocations by Mayor Byrne and Ronald Reagan that had energized black Chicagoans.[7]

Historically, the Democratic nomination for mayor in Chicago was tantamount to election. No Republican had been elected mayor since 1927, and their numbers were so few that Democrats often were pressed into service as nominally "Republican" election judges so that the precincts might be properly staffed. Washington's seizure of the Democratic nomination, however, suddenly reinvigorated the city's Republicanism. The national Republican party raised hundreds of thousands of dollars for the campaign, provided media expertise, and furnished advice on how to run a racially divisive campaign without mentioning race—all of this to secure the election of the man who won his party's nomination with only 11,000 votes (in contrast, Washington's 424,131 outpolled Byrne's 387,986 and Daley's 344,590). More important, of the fifty Democratic ward committeemen, more endorsed Washington's opponent in the general election, Bernard Epton, than supported the nominee of their own party; and even those nominally in Washington's corner often provided Epton with covert assistance in the attempt to undermine Washington. Still, in a bitter, racially charged campaign, Washington took just under 52 percent of the vote, winning by less than 50,000 out of nearly 1.3 million ballots cast. He managed to eke out about 12 percent of the white vote and 62 percent of the city's growing Hispanic vote (if Hispanics are counted as "whites," Washington's "white" vote increased to 16 to 18 percent). That support supplemented the 97 to 99 percent of the black voters who backed Washington with an astounding 85 percent turnout. He won every black vote in the city, as one Epton supporter put it, "except for the accidents."[8] If Morial's victory seemed characteristic of an "outsider's" ferocious storming of dearly protected battlements, Washington's rise seemed more like an "insider's" palace coup.

Whites in New Orleans and Chicago, who had initially taken neither the Morial nor the Washington campaign seriously and were hardly prepared even to share power, now found that they had actually lost control of City Hall to aggressive black challengers. A great deal of fear, uncertainty, and resentment were, consequently, primary political realities facing the victors. Having mobilized little more than one in ten, or, at best, less than one in five white voters on their behalf, Washington and Morial faced white communities seemingly unprepared to deal with powerful black political figures. Moreover, those whites who supported their campaigns often viewed themselves as "kingmakers" and were not well prepared for the independence displayed by the new mayors or their determination to address the needs of their "base."

Once in office, both Morial and Washington also had to deal with certain structural political realities that prevented them from having free hands with which to retool their cities. Morial had to confront not only the atavistic racial attitudes still characteristic of a majority of the white population in his southern city but also a fragmented governmental structure designed precisely to keep mayors weak and the public sector under the control of a conservative economic and social elite.

Beginning nearly one century before, in the late nineteenth century, the pillars of the New Orleans commercial community began to pull key powers out of City Hall as the ethnic Irish were coming to control the electoral arena and flexing their political muscle. No longer in control of the local ballot box, the Crescent City's economic and social elite sought alternatives given the emergence of the Regular Democratic Organization (RDO), one of the few big-city machines to appear in the South. They succeeded in making a series of end runs to the governor and state legislature and, largely through the use of those vehicles, succeeded in creating a network of appointed, nonelected boards and commissions from which they could effectively protect their interests. Controlling key city functions such as tax rates, riverfront development, and drainage, they could still dictate the pace and nature of urban development from perches on the Board of Liquidation, City Debt (created in 1880), the Sewerage and Water Board (created in 1900), and the Board of Commissioners of the Port of New Orleans (created in 1896 and known simply as the "Dock Board"), among others. When coupled with a later city charter provision that limited the mayor to two terms, such structures placed the city's elected chief executive at a considerable disadvantage. The attempt to defuse one ethnic challenge from below at the end of the nineteenth century produced a governmental structure that impeded another one a hundred years later.[9]

In Chicago, Washington's chief obstacle was not the formal structures of government but the informal political structure of the city. It was the Democratic machine, the Cook County Democratic Organization, that controlled the city council and virtually every other city agency that confronted the new black mayor. Washington's entire first term, therefore, was taken up with political battles and the struggle for control of the city's government and its budget. This was the era of Chicago's stalemated "Council Wars" that matched an antagonistic white city council (it controlled twenty-nine of the council's fifty votes, enough to frustrate mayoral initiatives but not sufficient to overcome executive vetoes) under the leadership of "Darth" Vrdolyak against Harold "Skywalker," his largely black supporters, and a handful of "reform" representatives. The white majority controlled the powerful and patronage-rich council committees and refused to approve hundreds of Washington appointments that would have threatened the status quo in other city agencies. The factionalism and infighting became so intense that the *Wall Street Journal* branded Chicago "Beirut on the Lake."[10]

It is crucial to understand that these political difficulties meant that both Morial and Washington confronted deep structural problems that transcended narrow or immediate issues of race and that their attempts at reform, even absent the race issue, would have provoked tenacious resistance. The race issue greatly added to their burdens, of course, and provided cynical political manipulators with a powerful club that they did not hesitate to employ. It also meant that both mayors had to work hard at democratizing their cities and that they each necessarily referred frequently to the need to "open" the political and economic structures of their respective towns.

In Morial's case the concept of an "open" New Orleans included a redefinition of the mayor's role that was sharply at odds with traditional practice. In asserting a primary role in urban governance for the city's democratically elected chief executive, Morial's race—or at least the public's fascination with it—obscured the real dynamics of a fundamental political challenge to the social and economic oligarchy that dominated public affairs from their seats of social privilege on those primarily nonelected boards and commissions. Indeed, in a speech before the Metropolitan Area Committee, Morial let the city know what was coming. He made pointed reference to Tulane University political scientist Charles Chai's 1971 study, "Who Rules New Orleans?" and informed his audience that he was "astounded" that the mayor was not included among the list of "influentials" compiled after discussions with community leaders. It was inconceivable to him that "a majority of the people [consulted] failed to even mention the mayor as a man essential to the communal equation." He added diplomatically that he "would like to think that that perception has changed." What he meant, of course, was that it would be changed. No longer of that class, nor willing to serve its narrow ends, a democratically responsive, independent chief executive represented a real threat to the traditional elite's interests; it was a challenge that would have set off a political firestorm for any mayor, black or white, who dared to stake out such a position.[11]

Indeed, Morial's long-standing efforts to democratize New Orleans's government—his support for a 1975 lawsuit challenging the exclusive composition of the Board of Liquidation, City Debt antedated his election as mayor—continued once he attained office. Believing a revitalized system of public education held the key to economic growth, he attacked the city's Board of Education and the "anachronism" that "separate[d] the schools from the public consensus as expressed in the powers and person of the office of mayor." Similarly, the deteriorating position of the Port of New Orleans led him to go after the Dock Board as well, and he raised "the serious question as to whether this management, set so distinctly apart from the public consensus, will not eventually bear the same bitter fruit as the antiquity of our school board policy." Although the lawsuit against the Board of Liquidation ultimately proved successful, efforts to extend mayoral influence over the Board of Education (Morial sought to add two mayoral appointees to an otherwise elected board) and Dock Board were distinctly less so. Combined with a long, acrimonious public dispute with the Sewerage and Water Board over affirmative action access to its jobs and contracts (a bitter struggle in which Morial eventually prevailed), the mayor's efforts produced mixed results.[12]

The tenor of the times, however, is perhaps best revealed by the fact that Morial also found himself forced to play defense. Using the powers of the state to attack the office of the mayor and the city of New Orleans was a well-worn strategy in Louisiana that constituted the primary thrust of earlier Progressive-era "reforms" as well as both Huey and Earl Long's bids to dominate the state. Whether legislative initiatives advanced by ostensible "good government" forces or brutal frontal assaults launched by ambitious governors, they were all self-serving power grabs that threatened the city's independence. In the early 1980s, Morial had to fight off attempts to remove the mayor as president of the Sewerage and Water Board and an effort to strip the city's authority over the metropolitan airport and Aviation Board. Successful in these defensive battles, he also fought off multiple attempts by the uptown social elite to wrest Audubon Park out of the city's hands. Morial's city attorney, Sal Anzelmo, bluntly linked this last dispute to changing demographic realities and a broader pattern of conduct when he stated that

the State takeover is an effort by those in the Uptown establishment to keep blacks from getting control of the Zoo Commission. . . . They want

> to keep it under white control. They don't want blacks to sit on the Zoo Commission, the Aviation Board, . . . the Sewerage and Water Board or anything. They say they want to "regionalize" everything. Well, that just means they want a controlling majority of whites who aren't even from Orleans Parish.[13]

Unable to extend his authority to areas he deemed vital, Morial had to expend considerable time and energy fighting to retain what powers he had.

In Chicago, Washington defeated the Cook County Democratic Organization by energizing an unprecedentedly large black base and by plugging into a long-standing stream of antimachine reform politics that brought a significant number of white voters to his coalition. Jane Byrne had done much the same four years before but returned to the machine fold as she pondered the difficulty of transforming an electoral majority into a governing one. Indeed, the organization's success in recapturing Byrne led several of the ward leaders to hope that the same could be done with Washington. It was Washington's resistance to this scenario— "I'm not going to pull a Byrne," he declared at one point—that precipitated the showdown with the machine's leadership. His continued attacks on patronage led one organization stalwart, Northwest Side alderman Roman Pucinski, to claim that he could support a machine-oriented African American for mayor but that Washington's desire to dismantle the organization asked too much. "Why should I give him the guillotine with which to cut off my head?" Pucinski asked. Finally, when Washington moved against party chairman Vrdolyak by attempting to oust him from his powerful leadership post on the zoning committee, Vrdolyak solidified the twenty-nine council members in opposition. There is no doubt that he and his retinue would have done the same to Byrne had she had the courage of her stated convictions, or that they would have been able to "play ball" with a more compliant and subservient Washington.[14]

Stalemated legislatively, Washington took a number of executive actions that placed him firmly in the "reform" camp. He cut his own salary by 20 percent and mothballed the limousine traditionally placed at the mayor's disposal. He also issued a "freedom of information" executive order that opened the city's records to public scrutiny, held budget hearings in the neighborhoods, and signed the Shakman decree that prohibited the hiring or firing of city employees for political reasons. He also announced a self-imposed cap of $1,500 on campaign contributions by companies doing business with the city and cut the payroll by 700 employees in an attempt to resolve the city's fiscal crisis.[15]

In the end, Washington's antimachine crusade was given an incomparable boost by the federal courts. Finding that the city council's ward reapportionment under Byrne was an outrageous racial gerrymander that discriminated against blacks and Hispanics, the courts ordered a new map and special elections in seven wards in 1986. The machine threw everything it had into these contests, but it could not prevent Washington from garnering four new supporters. The city council was now divided 25 to 25, with Mayor Washington casting all tie-breaking votes; he had pieced together his governing majority on his own terms.[16]

Changes followed rapidly. The mayor either stripped the machine's ward barons of their leadership posts in the council or diluted their authority and then watched as the council passed a new ethics ordinance and a tenants' bill of rights, amended taxi regulations to break up an existing near monopoly, and approved his executive appointments that had literally been held hostage for years. This last development was of the utmost importance, for it finally gave Washington control of such agencies as the Chicago Park District, a quasi-independent power base and source of patronage for machine opponent Edmund Kelly. Soon stripped of his powers, Kelly resigned.[17]

As was the case in New Orleans, Chicago's black mayor also had to play defense. As was the case with Dutch Morial, Harold Washington proved largely successful in this endeavor. Hostile interests introduced measures in the state legislature that would strip the city of its control over the Park District, the McCormick Place convention centers, Navy Pier, and the Port Authority. Another proposal called for the creation of a regional airport authority (taking O'Hare and Midway airports away from the city), and the opposition-controlled Finance Committee in the city council tried to arrogate unto itself the right to approve all city contracts. There was even a sudden, expressed desire for an elected school board.[18] Even as Dutch Morial struggled, unsuccessfully, to put a couple of mayoral appointees on New Orleans's elected board, Harold Washington's presence led some Chicagoans to question the merit of their mayorally appointed body.

The most telling episode, however, involved the effort, inspired by mayoral hopeful Richard M. Daley, to institute an "open," nonpartisan primary that would be followed by a runoff, given the likelihood that no candidate would win an outright majority in the next election. Stung by the charge that he had been the white "spoiler" who paved the way for Washington's victory, Daley wanted to make certain that the strongest white candidate in 1987 would be able to face Washington one-on-one. Petitions circulated throughout the city as sponsors of the measure hoped to get enough signatures to place it quickly before the people in a referendum. The Washington forces in the city council countered by placing three other innocuous referenda on the ballot before the nonpartisan primary petitions could be collected and validated. Under an obscure Illinois law, no more than three such propositions could be considered by a city at one time; Washington's council majority had preempted the ballot and blocked the attempt to change the rules in the middle of the game. Even his enemies grudgingly admired his deft political touch and the act of parliamentary legerdemain that left them standing in the dust. He had learned his lessons well.[19]

Washington's coup set the stage for his reelection in 1987 and a second term that promised, finally, substantive accomplishments. Having watched his first term consumed by endless political wrangling, Washington ultimately consolidated his position and prepared to move forward. It was in this realm, however, in the symmetry between their first and second terms, that the experiences of Dutch Morial and Harold Washington sharply diverged.

Morial's most notable achievements were primarily confined to his first term. The short-lived oil boom of the early 1980s and the Morial administration's management skills kept the city afloat despite underlying weaknesses and the beginning of federal retrenchment; a burst of new downtown construction and the steady growth of tourism contributed to the early sense of well-being. The mayor clearly recognized that the city's long-term health demanded greater economic diversification and fiscal reform, and he tried to nudge it in that direction. The optimism of the moment, however, and the political ethos of the city and the state proved impossible to overcome, and the city's fortunes declined radically in the mid-1980s. Still, his successful handling of a police strike, the streamlining of government, and a record of scandal-free, sound administration all graced his first term.

It was during his second term that Morial found himself constrained. The two-term limit placed on mayors by the city charter made him a "lame duck" as soon as he was reelected. Furthermore, the incoming city council included what Morial later called the Gang of Five. In the New Orleans seven-member city council (five elected by districts, two at large), the five representatives that rose in opposition could not only blunt his initiatives but override his vetoes as well. Consisting of three whites elected from districts and two black opponents (one of whom was elected at large), Morial's antagonists harassed him at every turn. When combined with the full weight of Ronald Reagan's budget cuts, Morial's second term was characterized more by stagnation than progress. Unseemly controversies regarding a pay raise for the mayor, a shopping mall near the Superdome, and, particularly, Morial's unsuccessful efforts to remove the two-term limitation from the city charter provided less than edifying public theater.[20]

The trajectory of Washington's reign was exactly the opposite. Beset with difficulties in the beginning, he enjoyed more freedom toward the end of his administration. Having gained control of the city council, he made particular strides in retiring the city debt through a combination of payroll reductions and new taxes and succeeded in restoring Chicago's favorable credit rating. Equally significant, feeling politically secure, the mayor extended an olive branch to his adversaries, endorsing candidates Richard M. Daley and Aurelia Pucinski (Roman Pucinski's daughter) for high county offices and retaining eight former Vrdolyak supporters as council committee chairs. Former adversaries, believing Washington when he claimed that he would occupy City Hall longer than Daley, began to move into his orbit following his reelection early in 1987; the most recalcitrant, such as Vrdolyak, simply left the Democratic party altogether. Preparing to move forward in building a genuine biracial coalition, Washington then died on the day before Thanksgiving, little more than a half-year after his second victorious campaign.[21]

Politically unassailable within their respective communities, Morial and Washington nonetheless endured significant undercurrents of black opposition that proved of great importance for their successions. Some of the opposition had to be due, at least in part, to the impossibility of meeting inflated expectations and the enormous difficulty in dealing with deep-seated urban problems and institutions. Few areas were of greater concern to New Orleans's and Chicago's African Americans, for example, than housing, particularly public housing, and education. Yet it was precisely in these areas that Morial and Washington proved unable or unwilling to stimulate progressive change. The political resistance that manifested itself when Morial tried to tinker with the Crescent City's school board apparently convinced him that the risks were not worth a bitter battle with uncertain outcomes; he quickly backed off and did not pick up the issue again.

In dealing with the Chicago Housing Authority, however, Washington inherited a political wasteland that, for the previous generation, served as little more than a dumping ground for the black poor and a patronage trough for the machine. It clearly demanded more attention and resources than he was willing to commit.[22] Less than forceful leadership thus combined with the inertia of these large bureaucracies and a deteriorating economic climate beyond mayoral control—longstanding trends toward deindustrialization in Chicago and the oil bust in New Orleans (not to mention federal cutbacks that impacted both)—to increase poverty and the demands placed on already inadequate and dysfunctional systems of public service.[23] Problems in these areas, if anything, got worse rather than better. Still, the overwhelming popularity of both Morial and Washington with the poor and public housing residents meant that their opposition was rooted in more than their inability to address successfully long-standing urban ills.

In each city, machine or "machine-style" patronage politicians within the black community existed in an uncomfortable relationship with Morial and Washington, as did those who might be considered racial nationalists or ethnic chauvinists. In New Orleans, Morial's predecessor, Moon Landrieu, had cultivated his own coterie of black officials, and Morial found them already in place on the public payroll and with strong ties to city government. They certainly expected to be treated no less well by the city's first black mayor and, in fact, were stunned and embittered when Morial staffed his administration with blacks and whites from private business, academia, and the professions. Conducting a minipurge, Morial even discharged large numbers of those who had entered public employment under the aegis of their former white patron. They were confused by the radical Creole who stressed "merit" and tried to transcend traditional racial divisions; and they accused the mayor of only hiring "superblacks" who had been held to unrealistically high standards.[24]

Washington similarly had to deal with a number of black ward committeemen and members of the city council who found themselves tied to his cause by an aroused constituency but who felt distinctly ill at ease with the mayor's reform posture. Creatures of the Democratic machine for most of their careers, they saw no reason to eschew "spoils" politics at the very moment that one of their own earned the keys to the city vault. Unable to oppose Washington openly—to do so would have been racial treason, as defined by the nationalists, and political suicide—they bided their time as nominal converts to a crusade in which they had no faith.[25]

The New Orleans and Chicago experiences differ at this point to the extent that a segment of the black political machinists in the southern metropolis embodied the rhetoric and goals of racial nationalism in their thirst for the emoluments of office—the novelty of the black presence in New Orleans's political life meant that the patronage seeker's racial "militance" could hold the ring of plausibility. In Chicago, however, the African-American machine politicians had been affiliated so long with Daley's organization that they could not credibly rattle the racial sabre. Instead, Chicago displayed a larger, more institutionalized, more vocal nationalist community that had played its own distinct role in Washington's initial campaign and placed its own demands on his administration. No less distressed than the machinists (albeit for quite different reasons) by Washington's transition team, cabinet of advisers, patronage policies, political priorities, and campaign endorsements, they increasingly found themselves distanced from his administration.[26] That the mayor's "Dream Slate" for county elections in 1988 included names such as Daley and Pucinski bespoke the grave differences in their agendas.

Indeed, the democratization of Chicago and New Orleans, pursued ardently by both Washington and Morial, offered something less to those seeking favor due to an "insider's" positioning—whether defined politically or racially—than either the machinists or the nationalists wanted. As far as conventionally, and more narrowly, defined racial interests were concerned, however, both mayors apparently made an impact in moderating the behavior of their respective police departments (long a primary irritant in the relations between black communities and successive municipal administrations and an achievement not to be underestimated) and in vigorously pursuing affirmative action initiatives in the granting of public jobs and contracts. If their efforts in the latter instance were denounced by their white opponents as mere patronage in disguise and by black dissenters as meager and insufficient, their attempt to open up the municipal polity and bring African Americans into the "mainstream" apparently had the approval of the vast majority of black voters who swept each of them into a second term.

Finally, the sheer strength of their personalities, their combative, aggressive, "tell-it-like-it-is" styles of governance and politics undoubtedly provided an enormous psychological boost to communities that identified closely with their travails and, apparently, values. In Chicago, those pursuing a chauvinistic black agenda found themselves further hemmed in by their own success in making support for Washington a litmus test for "blackness" during his first campaign; they could hardly oppose him later without appearing to undermine their community's "champion."

The chaos surrounding Washington's succession and the more deliberate, systematic procedures that orchestrated Dutch Morial's illustrate one last dimension of the racial struggle for political power in urban America. In each case, white opponents of the first black mayors demonstrated the resourcefulness and resolve to catapult themselves back into control by dominating the processes through which Chicago and New Orleans selected their second black mayors. And the African-American communities of the two cities, fearful and fragmented following the deaths of their most historic political figures (Morial passed away in December 1989, in the midst of his successor's reelection campaign), retreated to a narrower brand of racial politics that left them more isolated from power than before.

In Chicago, the white ethnic bloc on the city council won over a handful of former black allies who had been tied to the machine but could not openly oppose Washington while he lived. After failing to negotiate the recapture of City Hall for themselves, they threw their support to a compliant black machine operative who accepted their backing in a raucous city council meeting that ran past four A.M. With blacks and whites gathered in the streets in the predawn hours outside City Hall chanting "No deals," waving dollar bills, and throwing coins at him, a majority vote of the city council anointed Eugene Sawyer Chicago's second black mayor.[27] Shamelessly donning blackface to salvage its fortunes, what remained of the machine selected a candidate who became immediately and irredeemably tainted in the eyes of the black community. Unable to survive politically, His Conveniency's administration separated nationalists from machinists and both of those from the reform heirs of the Washington legacy. In a city where black voters still constitute a minority, Daley reclaimed the office on the fifth floor of City Hall in 1989.

In New Orleans, regular electoral procedures made Sidney Barthelemy, another Creole of color, mayor after Dutch Morial failed in his attempts to change the city charter. Barthelemy, a leading opponent of Morial's campaign for unlimited terms as well as his second effort to permit "Just 3," represented a strong assimilationist tendency among some New Orleans Creoles and was the antithesis to the fading Creole radicalism personified by Morial. A Moon Landrieu protégé, he had strong ties to the local Urban League and enjoyed close contact with the white civic and economic leadership. Running against another black candidate in what had become, during the Morial era, a majority black city, Barthelemy turned Morial's winning electoral coalition inside out. Where Morial had been elected with solid and massive black support combined with a liberal fragment of white backing, Barthelemy went into office with 85 percent of the white vote and the support of barely one in four black voters. Morial's progressive biracial coalition had been transformed into a conservative one that knit together whites and a patronage-oriented black leadership that had no agenda beyond its own perpetuation. White New Orleans had found itself a black mayor it could live with—one that would protect, rather than challenge, the status quo.[28]

Ironically, when Barthelemy ran for reelection in 1990, he campaigned, this time, as the hope of the black community. In facing a white candidate with a good civil rights record, Barthelemy ran (in the weeks immediately following Morial's unexpected death) as a racial champion.

As was the case with Sawyer, another emergent black politician who had left no tracks in the snow of the civil rights revolution, Barthelemy's campaign exploited symbolic racial issues and fears. But unlike Sawyer, he ran in what was now a majority black city and won. His second winning coalition appeared, then, as an unlikely combination that mixed reactionary whites at the top of his campaign structure with a mass of black voters at the bottom. It was a shotgun marriage of the rankest sort, and one bound to leave its partners unfulfilled.

It would, however, be a mistake to think that nothing had changed as a result of the Morial and Washington administrations. Black access to city jobs and services certainly improved, as did relations with local police departments that had earlier earned reputations for brutality within their respective black communities, although this relationship could easily slide back to that of an earlier age. Opportunities for individual African Americans within the political system also improved dramatically. But fundamental change proved more elusive. Changes in the global economy, as well as the federal government's retreat from urban affairs, obviously made purely local responses to challenges experienced on the municipal level problematic at best. To the extent that such solutions might have an ameliorative impact, it is apparent that they must await new strategies for forging governing coalitions in a multiethnic society.

## NOTES

1. For an introduction to the concept of Creole radicalism, see Arnold R. Hirsch and Joseph Logsdon, eds., *Creole New Orleans: Race and Americanization* (Baton Rouge: Louisiana State University Press, 1992), esp. 189–319.

2. A somewhat more detailed look at Dutch Morial's political career is offered in Arnold R. Hirsch, "Race and Politics in Modern New Orleans: The Mayoralty of Dutch Morial," *Amerikastudien / American Studies* 35 (December 1991): 461–84.

3. For early black politics in Chicago, see Charles Branham, "Black Chicago: Accommodationist Politics before the Great Migration," in Melvin G. Holli and Peter d'A. Jones, eds., *The Ethnic Frontier: Essays in the History of Group Survival in Chicago and the Midwest* (Grand Rapids: William B. Eerdmans Publishing Co., 1977), 211–62; see also Branham's dissertation, "A Transformation of Black Political Leadership in Chicago, 1864–1942" (Ph.D. dissertation, University of Chicago, 1981). Other important works are St. Clair Drake and Horace Cayton, *Black Metropolis: A Study of Negro Life in a Northern City* (New York: Harper and Row, 1945, 1962, 1970); Harold F. Gosnell, *Negro Politicians: The Rise of Negro Politics in Chicago* (Chicago: University of Chicago Press, 1935, 1967); Allan H. Spear, *Black Chicago: The Making of a Negro Ghetto, 1890–1920* (Chicago: University of Chicago Press, 1967); William M. Tuttle, Jr., *Race Riot: Chicago in the Red Summer of 1919* (New York: Atheneum, 1970); and John M. Allswang, *A House for All Peoples: Ethnic Politics in Chicago, 1890–1936* (Lexington: University Press of Kentucky, 1971).

4. For Washington's early life and career, see Florence Hamlish Levinsohn, *Harold Washington: A Political Biography* (Chicago: Chicago Review Press, 1983); Gary Rivlin, *Fire on the Prairie: Chicago's Harold Washington and the Politics of Race* (New York: Henry Holt and Company, 1992); Robert McClory, "Up from Obscurity: Harold Washington," in Melvin G. Holli and Paul M. Green, eds., *The Making of the Mayor: Chicago, 1983* (Grand Rapids: William B. Eerdmans Publishing Co., 1984), 3–16; William J. Grimshaw, *Bitter Fruit: Black Politics and the Chicago Machine, 1931–1991* (Chicago: University of Chicago Press, 1992); and Dempsey Travis, *An Autobiography of Black Politics* (Chicago: Urban Research Press, 1987).

5. For the primary election, see Hirsch, "Race and Politics in Modern New Orleans," 465–68; for a broader context and essential background, see also Hirsch, "Simply a Matter of Black and White: The Transformation of Race and Politics in Twentieth-Century New Or-

leans," in *Creole New Orleans*, 262–319; and "New Orleans: Sunbelt in the Swamp," in Richard M. Bernard and Bradley R. Rice, eds., *Sunbelt Cities: Politics and Growth Since World War II* (Austin: University of Texas Press, 1983), 100–137; see also Edward M. Haas, *DeLesseps S. Morrison and the Image of Reform: New Orleans Politics, 1946–1961* (Baton Rouge: Louisiana State University Press, 1974).

6. New Orleans *Times-Picayune*, October 3, November 13, 14, 1977; *Figaro*, May 4, August 3, October 5, 12, 19, November 16, 1977; *Louisiana Weekly*, November 12, 1977.

7. For Washington's first mayoral triumph, see Grimshaw, *Bitter Fruit*, 167–96; Holli and Green, *Making of the Mayor*; Levinsohn, *Harold Washington*, 189–300; Travis, *Autobiography of Black Politics*, 528–610; and Paul Kleppner, *Chicago Divided: The Making of a Black Mayor* (DeKalb: Northern Illinois University Press, 1985).

8. Rivlin, *Fire on the Prairie*, 196.

9. Joy J. Jackson, *New Orleans in the Gilded Age: Politics and Urban Progress, 1880–1896* (Baton Rouge: Louisiana State University Press, 1969); Peirce F. Lewis, *New Orleans: The Making of an Urban Landscape* (Cambridge: Ballinger Publishing Co., 1976).

10. For Chicago's "Council Wars," see Grimshaw, *Bitter Fruit*, 184–86, 189, 191, 213; Rivlin, *Fire on the Prairie*, 205–344; and Melvin G. Holli and Paul M. Green, *Bashing Chicago Traditions: Harold Washington's Last Campaign* (Grand Rapids: William B. Eerdmans Publishing Co., 1989), 166.

11. Morial's speech is reprinted in its entirety in *Figaro*, January 25, 1978; Charles Y. W. Chai, "Who Rules New Orleans?" *Louisiana Business Survey* 2 (October 1971): 2–7.

12. Hirsch, "Race and Politics in Modern New Orleans," 469–70, 472, 473, and passim.

13. *Louisiana Weekly*, September 18, 1982; July 23, 1983.

14. Rivlin, *Fire on the Prairie*, 187, 222.

15. Ibid., 235–36.

16. Grimshaw, *Bitter Fruit*, 189–90; Kleppner, *Chicago Divided*, 140; Rivlin, *Fire on the Prairie*, 348–58.

17. Rivlin, *Fire on the Prairie*, 357–61; Holli and Green, *Bashing Chicago Traditions*, 35–36.

18. Rivlin, *Fire on the Prairie*, 400–401.

19. Alderman Ed Burke, a bitter Washington foe, denounced the derailment of the nonpartisan primary proposition as a political "ploy." With knowing appreciation, however, he added that he had to "compliment whoever thought of it." See Holli and Green, *Bashing Chicago Traditions*, 36–43.

20. A more detailed summary of Morial's two terms can be found in Hirsch, "Race and Politics in Modern New Orleans," 461–84.

21. Holli and Green, *Bashing Chicago Traditions*, 170, 187–88; Rivlin, *Fire on the Prairie*, 400.

22. Hirsch, "Race and Politics in Modern New Orleans," 473; Rivlin, *Fire on the Prairie*, 384–90.

23. The social and economic trends for Chicago are closely examined in Gregory D. Squires, Larry Bennett, Kathleen McCourt, and Philip Nyden, *Chicago: Race, Class and the Response to Urban Decline* (Philadelphia: Temple University Press, 1987).

24. Hirsch, "Simply a Matter of Black and White," 310–16.

25. Grimshaw, *Bitter Fruit*, 133–36; Rivlin, *Fire on the Prairie*, 403–20.

26. The black nationalists' role in Washington's campaigns, his administration, and their growing sense of estrangement is handled in depth and throughout Rivlin, *Fire on the Prairie*. See also Abdul Alkalimat and Doug Gills, *Harold Washington and the Crisis of Black Power in Chicago* (Chicago: Twenty-First Century Books, 1989); and Dianne M. Pinderhughes, *Race and Ethnicity in Chicago Politics* (Urbana: University of Illinois Press, 1987).

27. For some background and context, see Hirsch, "Chicago: The Cook County Democratic Organization and the Dilemma of Race, 1931–1987," in Richard M. Bernard, ed., *Snowbelt Cities: Metropolitan Politics in the Northeast and Midwest Since World War II* (Bloomington: Indiana University Press, 1987), 63–90. For Sawyer's rise (and fall), see Grimshaw, *Bitter Fruit*, 197–224; and Rivlin, *Fire on the Prairie*, 403–20.

28. Hirsch, "Simply a Matter of Black and White," 317–18.

# Blacks and Hispanics in Multicultural America: A Miami Case Study

*Raymond A. Mohl*

T hirty years of new immigration have begun to transform the demographic, economic, and cultural landscape of some American states
and cities. In particular, New York, Los Angeles, and Miami have emerged
as new immigrant cities rivaling the big immigrant centers of the turn-
of-the-century industrial era. According to the 1990 census, the foreign-
born make up about one-third of the adult population in New York City,
44 percent in Los Angeles, and a staggering 70 percent in Miami. These
three cities have come to exemplify the ethnic transformations that have
begun reshaping segments of modern America into a vastly diverse
multicultural society.[1]

Major urban centers in California, New York, and Florida have also
experienced pronounced Hispanic immigration for several decades. Consequently, much of urban America has been Latinized over several generations. Mexicans and Mexican Americans have become the largest and
most conspicuous Hispanic element in the ethnic mix of Los Angeles,
although hundreds of thousands of Salvadorans, Guatemalans, and other
Central Americans have also migrated to the city in recent years. Puerto
Ricans have been migrating in massive numbers to New York since the
1940s, and they are now joined by huge communities of Colombians,
Dominicans, and others. Since 1960, almost a million Cuban exiles have
made Miami a new home, along with more recent exiles from Nicaragua. By 1990, Hispanics comprised about 25 percent of metropolitan
New York City's 7.3 million people, 38 percent of metropolitan Los
Angeles's 8.8 million residents, and 49 percent of metropolitan Miami's
1.9 million people. By the year 2010, Hispanics will surpass African
Americans as the largest minority group in the U.S.[2]

The magnitude and intensity of this new immigration has created
political controversy and social tensions in contemporary America. A

*Raymond A. Mohl is professor of history and chairman of the depart-
ment at the University of Alabama at Birmingham. Reprinted from*
Amerikastudien/American Studies *40 (1995): 389–413. Reprinted by
permission.*

vigorous debate has been under way since the early 1980s over the need for new and stricter immigration controls. The new immigrants, it is argued by some, place heavy demands on social services, public schools, prisons, and medical institutions. State and city officials in places like Florida and California have demanded more federal financial assistance, especially to cover the costs of providing for illegal immigrants and refugees.[3] At the same time, an extensive academic and policy literature has emerged suggesting that immigration has positive economic benefits for the nation generally. Some newcomers, it is contended, bring to America entrepreneurial energy, technical skills, high educational aspirations, and a strong work ethic, and over time such immigrants stimulate economic growth and contribute more in taxes than they demand in social and governmental services. Other new immigrants, particularly those from poorer nations such as Mexico who enter illegally, work at low-wage, unpleasant, sometimes dangerous jobs in garment sweatshops, in restaurant kitchens, or as migrant farm workers—jobs where demand is high but the supply of native-born American workers is low. Moreover, because they are illegals, they tend to avoid governmental agencies and seek few services.[4] Behind the political and academic debate about the positive or negative consequences of immigration lies a more general and widespread unease over immigration and its consequences. Much of mainstream America seems uncomfortable with the idea of a multicultural future. Consequently, recent immigration has spawned a modern restrictionist movement, a new "immigration scare" that bears some comparison to the early twentieth-century movement that led to immigration restriction in the 1920s.[5]

Beyond the political and policy debates, the new immigration has been accompanied by rising levels of social tension and ethnic conflict in the big immigrant cities. Newcomers seeking jobs and housing often compete with one another and with working-class Americans, particularly African Americans. Public schools and the local political system provide other arenas of ethnic conflict. Language and cultural differences create hostilities, especially among the younger generation as they engage one another in the public schools. Lack of control of community economies—the groceries, convenience stores, liquor stores, laundries, and other neighborhood shops that people patronize daily—has roused racial animosities in black communities throughout the nation. Police confrontations in African-American neighborhoods often ignite urban rebellions, as in the recent case of Los Angeles, but ethnic tensions have usually been simmering below the surface for some time. Analysts of the 1992 Los Angeles riots now suggest the importance of several layers of ethnic tension and antagonism—black versus white, black versus Latino, and black versus Asian. As one California writer put it, "the Rodney King riots were appropriately multiracial in this multicultural capital of America." Similarly, in recent years New York City has experienced community conflict and street-level violence between blacks and Koreans, blacks and Italians, and blacks and Jews. Los Angeles and New York are huge multicultural cities, so it should not be surprising that both places have experienced proportionately high levels of ethnic conflict.[6]

Ethnic antagonisms have also punctuated the recent social experience of many other American cities. Traditionally, young blacks, Italians, Mexicans, and Puerto Ricans in Chicago fought over pieces of urban turf, imposing their own version of social order on the city slums. African-American conflicts with Arab-American storekeepers are common in Detroit, where 70 percent of neighborhood groceries are owned by Syrians and Palestinians. In New York, Miami, Fort Lauderdale, and elsewhere, conflicts have erupted between African Americans and blacks from the Caribbean—Haitians, Jamaicans, and Dominicans. Along the Gulf Coast from Texas to the Florida Panhandle, Vietnamese fishermen have been targeted for violence by white southerners. Youth gangs based on race and ethnicity have brought a new level of violence and terror to American city streets; in Los Angeles alone, police officials reported a total of 770 youth gangs in the metropolitan area in 1989, mostly black and Latino. For the immigrant newcomers to modern America, ethnic tension, social conflict, and physical violence often seem to come with the territory.[7]

The late twentieth-century American city has been shaped by massive migrations of African Americans and new immigrants. Demographic trends since the 1940s increasingly found middle-class and working-class whites moving to the suburbs, while a great migration from the South brought about 5 million blacks to the northern and midwestern central cities. By the 1970s, black population majorities or near majorities were emerging in big cities such as Detroit, Baltimore, Washington, Cleveland, St. Louis, Philadelphia, and Chicago. New York and Los Angeles had huge black populations, although nowhere near majorities. Thus, when the post-1965 new immigrants began streaming into urban America in the 1970s and 1980s, they confronted the large African-American communities that had already staked claims to sprawling residential areas, segments of the urban labor market, and growing shares of local political power. Often poor and unskilled, the new immigrants pushed in along the margins of black residential areas in their search for low-cost housing. At the same time, they either competed directly with blacks in the low-skill, urban job market, or developed entrepreneurial styles that enabled them to dominate consumer economies in the inner cities. The contested territory of the emerging multicultural society seems to lie on the economic margins of urban America. Over time, and with naturalization, new immigrants eventually became politically active—new players in the now traditional urban game of ethnic politics. Some "rainbow coalitions," such as that led by Jesse Jackson, sought to bring African Americans together with Hispanic Americans and Asian Americans, but more often politics divided urban blacks from their new immigrant neighbors. Inevitably, given the new demographic, economic, and political realities of urban America, African Americans from Los Angeles to Miami have been pulled into the cauldron of modern American ethnic conflict.[8]

Few American cities can match Miami's trajectory of late twentieth-century change. An aging tourist city in the 1950s, Miami had a veneer of modern glitz that usually masked the rigid racial segregation that typically prevailed in most "Deep South" cities. Tourism continued and intensified as the century progressed, but Miami also emerged as a major international trade and finance center, as well as an immigrant city of immense proportions. Cuban, Haitian, Nicaraguan, and other migrations from the Caribbean and Latin America ultimately reshaped the city's demographic structure and cultural life. As sociologists Alejandro Portes and Alex Stepick have noted in their recent book *City on the Edge* (1993), the new immigrants were not assimilating as in the past; rather Miami presented a curious pattern of "acculturation in reverse—a process by which foreign customs, institutions, and language are diffused within the native population." High levels of crime, a dangerous drug trade, rampant personal violence, and periodic rioting also propelled Miami into the national and even international consciousness. As a consequence of these transforming forces, a new Miami began to emerge by the 1970s—a Miami of modernist architecture, television imagery, Latin tourists, Cuban politicians and bankers, and anti-communist guerrilla movements; the new Miami is a city of multicultural energy and excitement, but also of pervasive racial and ethnic polarization. A sign of the changing times, in the new Miami more than 53 percent of the people speak a language other than English at home. The old Miami persisted, too, with its heritage of segregation and racial division. The confrontation of the old Miami with the new immigration provides an illuminating case study of America's unsteady voyage toward a multicultural future.[9]

## Fire in the Streets of Miami

On Monday, 16 January 1989, hundreds of blacks in Miami took to the streets in angry rage for the fourth time in the 1980s. Over several days, they burned cars and buildings, pelted passers-by with rocks and bottles, and faced off with riot police in Overtown and Liberty City, Miami's two major black communities. The incident that touched off this new expression of black anger was sadly familiar. A Miami policeman had shot and killed a black man fleeing a traffic infraction on a motorcycle, while a second black man, a passenger on the motorcycle, was thrown from the vehicle and also killed. It was difficult to miss the irony in the fact that this latest Miami riot took place on the same day that African Americans in Miami celebrated the birthday of Martin Luther King, Jr., the modern apostle of nonviolence. There were other ironies as well. In this new immigrant city, it should not have been surprising that none of those involved in the riot-triggering incident was a native-born American. The police officer who fired the fatal bullet, William Lozano, had immigrated to Miami with his family from Colombia. Although few noticed at the time, the two dead black men, Allen Blanchard and Clement Lloyd, were also migrants from the Caribbean basin, from the U.S. Virgin Islands.

The three newcomers whose paths crossed on that fateful Monday evening had come to South Florida in search of the elusive American dream; what they found in Miami, ultimately, was something quite different.[10]

One can also find symbolic contradiction in the fact that the January 1989 riot in Miami came at the very time that this city of Cuban exiles was on the receiving end of a new mass immigration of Latin newcomers, this time from Nicaragua. Nicaraguan exiles began concentrating in Miami following the 1979 overthrow of the Somoza regime by the Sandinista revolutionaries. Politically comfortable with the right-wing, anti-communist Cubans, Anastasio Somoza set up an exile headquarters in the city, and many thousands of his countrymen—perhaps as many as 100,000—followed over the next decade. Worsening economic and political conditions in Nicaragua in 1988 coincided with a temporary loosening of U.S. immigration policy toward Central America, resulting in a new exodus of Nicaraguan exiles who trekked overland through Honduras, Guatemala, and Mexico to Texas, and then on to Miami by bus. By December 1988, a month before Miami exploded into violence, some 200 Nicaraguans were pouring into Miami every day, and the press was widely predicting that an estimated 100,000 additional Nicaraguans would arrive in Miami within the next year. The new Nicaraguan migration provided the backdrop for the latest violence in Overtown and Liberty City. It was hard to escape the contradictions: the blacks were burning down their neighborhoods in despair, but the thousands of newly arrived Nicaraguan refugees pinned their hopes for the future on a new life in Miami.[11]

For observers of the Miami scene, all of this was quite familiar. It had happened before, and more than once. The 1980 Liberty City riots had been touched off by a not-guilty verdict for several Miami policemen, some of whom were Hispanic, charged with beating a black motorcyclist to death. This riot, too, coincided with massive Caribbean migrations to Miami: the 1980 Mariel boatlift, which brought 125,000 new Cuban exiles to South Florida, and the simultaneous migration of upwards of 25,000 Haitian boat people in 1979 and 1980, some of whom were washing up on South Florida beaches within sight of heavy palls of smoke from the torched neighborhoods of Liberty City and Overtown. Two years later, in December 1982, a Hispanic policeman killed a black youth in an Overtown video-game parlor, setting off another wave of black ghetto rioting.[12]

There was a tragic sameness to these events. Confrontations of various sorts between African Americans and the police touched off violence each time. These encounters often involved Hispanic police officers. In two of the riots since 1980, mass migrations to Miami of Hispanic exiles and other Caribbean refugees occurred simultaneously, providing a poignant backdrop to the outbursts of violence in the city's black neighborhoods. As many observers have suggested, these events reflected much deeper social, economic, and political tensions between blacks and Hispanics in the Miami metropolitan area.

## *The Cuban Revolution and the Civil Rights Movement*

It is something of an historical accident that the Cuban Revolution and the subsequent exile migration to South Florida coincided with the Civil Rights Movement in the late 1950s and 1960s. In the Miami area, those two powerful forces for change not only coincided, but they collided with one another. The social consequences were enormous and long-lasting. The Cubans arrived—over 800,000 of them between 1959 and 1980— just as the Civil Rights Movement was opening opportunities for long-depressed and long-repressed black communities. As the old barriers of segregation crumbled throughout the South, blacks generally found new opportunities in employment, housing, schooling, government, and social services. African Americans also became empowered politically, which eventually led to a dramatic transformation of municipal politics and government as blacks rose to positions of leadership in the big cities and small towns of the South.[13]

But in Miami, things took a different course. In retrospect, it appears that the Cuban migration short-circuited the economic and political gains blacks were making elsewhere. Moreover, the exile "invasion," as it was called in the 1960s, touched off more than thirty years of competition and conflict between blacks and Hispanics over jobs, residential space, government services, and political power in the South Florida area. The widespread perception, supported by reams of economic and sociological data, that the Cubans have been exceptionally successful in the United States—and that they have, essentially, won out in the economic and political struggle in Miami—has contributed to a pervasive sense of powerlessness, resentment, and despair in black Miami. Each successive wave of newcomers in the 1970s and 1980s—the Haitians, the Nicaraguans, the Mariel Cubans—generated new expressions of concern for the consequences, and often of outrage and anger, in the black press and among those who spoke for the black community.

Tension between blacks and Hispanics in Miami was superimposed on a much longer history of racial conflict between whites and blacks that dates back to Miami's origin as a city in 1896. A study of the 1980 Liberty City riots pointed out that blacks had been "systematically excluded from the social, economic and political life of the city ever since it was founded around the turn of the century." Residentially, blacks were forced into a densely populated, unhealthy shacktown on the fringes of the business district. As in the rest of the South at the turn of the century, lynchings were not uncommon, and police repression in the black community was routine. The Ku Klux Klan acted with impunity into the 1930s; even as late as 1951, white night riders on three separate occasions dynamited a Miami apartment complex undergoing transition from white to black occupancy. The white primary system, and later other registration restrictions and voting procedures, effectively excluded blacks from the political process. The urban renewal and highway building of the 1950s and 1960s destroyed housing on a wide scale in Miami's black inner-city community, paving the way for an expansion of the central business district.[14]

Race relations had never been very good in Miami before the Civil Rights era. Even after voting rights were assured in the 1960s, African-American voting power was diluted by the at-large election system used in Miami and Dade County. Moreover, a troubled pattern of community-police relations plagued the city in the years between the two major ghetto riots of 1968 and 1980—a period during which at least thirteen "mini-riots" occurred, all stemming from police confrontations or altercations with African Americans. Despite its national image through the 1950s as a glitzy tourist town and vacation spa, Miami was still very much a Deep South city during the segregation era, with all that that implied for race relations. As writer Joan Didion recently commented, with wry understatement, Miami "was a city in which black people and white people viewed each other with some discontent."[15]

## Cuban Migration and Black Response

Race relations in Miami were complicated in unanticipated ways by the outcome of the Cuban Revolution in 1959. The migration of Cuban exiles over thirty years, and of more recent newcomers from other Latin nations, brought a veritable demographic revolution to the Miami metropolitan area. During that period, more than 800,000 Cubans left their homeland for the United States. They came in several waves, an erratic immigration flow dictated by the changing state of U.S.-Cuban relations. This relationship also dictated the form of the movement, since at various times Cubans arrived in South Florida by boatlift, by airlift, through third countries, even on makeshift rafts and inner tubes, and most recently by sailboard. Despite federal efforts to relocate the Cubans throughout the country, a large proportion of them eventually settled permanently in the Miami area.[16]

As a result of the Cuban exile and other migrations, the entire Miami metropolitan area is now considered to be not just "tri-ethnic," but genuinely multicultural in character. In 1950, prior to the Cuban exodus, Hispanics in the Miami area—mostly Puerto Ricans—totaled about 20,000, or 4 percent of the population. By 1990, after thirty years of Cuban, Nicaraguan, and other Latin migration, more than 950,000 Hispanics resided in the Miami area, and they made up about 50 percent of the metropolitan population, and 63 percent of the population of the city of Miami. By contrast, the percentage of blacks in the Miami area has remained relatively stable over many decades, ranging from 18 percent in 1940 to 20 percent in 1990. But even the black population is quite diverse, with large communities of Bahamians, Haitians, Jamaicans, black Cubans, and others.[17]

The dramatic outpouring of newcomers from Cuba and other nations of the Caribbean basin has had an enormous impact on the economic, political, and cultural life of the Miami area. For Miami's blacks, who had long been on the bottom rungs of the economic ladder and politically powerless, the Cuban migration posed special problems. It did not take long for Miami's black press and community leaders to recognize that the Cuban newcomers would be competing with African Americans for jobs and housing.

Although often penniless on arrival in Miami, the earliest Cuban exiles had education, skills, and a strong work ethic. An entire professional and business class literally was uprooted from Havana and set down in Miami. Because the Cubans initially lacked capital, English language skills, and the appropriate credentials to practice their professions in the United States, they moved at first into the low-paying service-type jobs traditionally held by blacks, particularly in tourist hotels and restaurants in Miami and Miami Beach. They also found work in downtown retail, office, and service jobs; in the expanding Miami garment industry; in building and construction; and in other blue-collar jobs, where they competed with black and white workers. The stories are legendary of Cuban bankers working as janitors, Cuban accountants washing dishes in greasy-spoon restaurants, and Cuban doctors emptying hospital bedpans.[18]

The sudden arrival of thousands of Cuban refugees had an immediate economic impact. As early as 1959, complaints from black and white citizens and from labor unions began to be heard, contending that the Cubans were taking the jobs of American citizens and undermining prevailing local wage levels. These perceptions were quite strong, and they affected the way Miamians responded to the Cuban influx of the early 1960s. In November 1960, for instance, former Miami mayor William M. Wolfarth complained to Florida's U.S. Senator George A. Smathers about the impact of the Cuban refugees on the Miami economy: "There is also a fear of cheap labor in a market that is already weak for the unskilled worker." Louis Foosaner, who owned a shop in downtown Miami, wanted government action to address the problem of "thousands of American citizens [who] have lost their jobs, have been displaced by Cubans who work for less pay." A black citizen from Liberty City had a similar complaint: "What a disgrace! Every store, hotel, club, restaurant, our unions—run by Cubans. . . . Miamians are demanding these Cubans quit landing here. . . . Florida jobs for Floridians." Female shop clerks were being replaced by Cuban women, Loretta Ginney informed Smathers: ". . . every store in the district have let all their help go and hired Cubans." One political friend of Senator Smathers, John H. Monahan, worried about the Senator's future political support in the black community, since over 10,000 African Americans, he wrote, had already been displaced by Cubans in low-wage jobs; the Miami NAACP, Monahan further noted, "has been asking discreet questions of where the Negroes' jobs have gone." Even the Miami office of the U.S. Department of Commerce confirmed that the Cubans were "willing to work for much smaller wages than the local people," thus creating higher unemployment for Americans in the Miami area.[19]

Concern about the economic impact of the Cuban refugees can also be found in the correspondence of Farris Bryant, Florida's governor during the early 1960s. R. H. Bennett of the Negro Citizens Service League

in Miami wrote in 1963 to complain about "the discarding of Miami laborers in favor of Cuban refugees." E. Harry Denny, a shopkeeper in
Liberty City, wrote on behalf of black merhants and tradesmen "whose
income has declined sharply due to the great amount of unemployment
caused by the influx of Cuban refugees." Another Liberty City resident,
Altie Sizemore, wrote in 1963 to complain about "all the Cuban people
coming in here and taking all our jobs." A representative of the Iron
Workers Union officially complained about "the invasion of Cuban labor
in the construction field." The substance of these and dozens of other
complaints about Cuban job displacement were seemingly officially confirmed by the 1963 report of the Florida Industrial Commission, which
noted that the "Cuban refugees had a significant effect on the rate of
unemployment in Dade County." Many Miamians, it seems clear, resented
the generous government welcome for the Cuban refugees and observed
at first hand their impact on the local job market. Although accurate or
complete statistics on job displacement were never produced, the outpouring of citizen complaints reflected the perception of a high level of
economic competition in the early 1960s.[20]

By 1963, when over 200,000 Cuban exiles had arrived, discussion of
Cuban economic competition with Miami blacks had become commonplace. In June of that year, *Ebony* magazine published an extensive article on what was already being labeled the "Cuban invasion" of South
Florida. The Cubans had injected new life and "Latin ways" into the
city, the *Ebony* piece conceded, but they "also brought in the wake of
their invasion a host of grave social and economic problems." In particular, the article pointed to the emerging competition between blacks and
Cubans over jobs, housing, schooling, and government services—a sort
of zero-sum analysis in which a limited supply of resources was now
being divided among a larger number of competing groups. "The economic penetration of the refugees is now universal," *Ebony* angrily concluded. Similarly, beginning in the early 1960s, the *Miami Times*, the
city's black weekly newspaper, regularly lamented the negative economic
impact of the Cuban influx. "The Cubans are slowly taking over the business of Dade County," the *Miami Times* typically complained in 1966.[21]

Miami's black leaders regularly conveyed their concerns about economic competition and ethnic conflict to government officials and elected
politicians, reflecting widely held views in the black community. As early
as 1961, in testimony before the U.S. Senate Subcommittee on Refugees
and Escapees, H. Daniel Lang of the Greater Miami Urban League portrayed the rising tensions and frustrations in the black community as a
consequence of the Cuban migration; African Americans, Lang reported,
were "systematically being pushed out of [jobs] to make room for Cubans." Similarly, the Miami branch of the NAACP protested in 1965 to
Florida Governor Haydon Burns over the "economic oppression" created
by the Cuban exile migration. Donald W. Jones of the NAACP also complained about job competition to Senator Smathers, hinting of "inevitable friction" between Miami blacks and the Cuban newcomers. African
Americans in Miami, Jones wrote, were tired of being the "sacrificial
lamb," offered up by the government "for the extension of freedom and

democracy to refugees from another land." In 1965, a Dade County representative to the Florida legislature warned that the continuing Cuban influx was "creating a powder keg that could blow at any moment." By the end of the 1960s, of course, Miami's black community had exploded in racial violence.[22]

Initially, the zero-sum analysis offered by *Ebony* magazine was rejected by officialdom in Miami. City and federal officials trotted out businessmen, economists, and other experts willing to argue that few blacks or whites had been displaced by the new Cuban arrivals. By the mid-sixties, however, the evidence seemed to be building that job displacement had indeed been taking place. It seemed clear that the employment gains blacks had been making elsewhere in the Civil Rights era had yet to materialize in Miami. By 1965, the city's Community Relations Board had taken up the issue at a time when it was feared that the economic competition between the two groups would spill over into violent conflict. Ironically, in view of Miami's later racial history, the city was reported by the *Wall Street Journal* in 1965 as taking "pride" in the fact that there had "never been a major race clash here." Racial violence held off until 1968, when the city exploded during the Republican national convention in Miami Beach. Cuban economic competition and governmental favoritism for the newcomers found a place among the official explanations for the 1968 Miami riot, as well as for later racial explosions. As one journalist noted in a *New York Times* article in 1974, "the role of the Cubans in the Miami job market of the early sixties contributed to a legacy of racial tension that hangs over black-Cuban relations today."[23]

## Competition for Jobs and Housing

During the 1970s and 1980s, as earlier Cubans moved upward economically and professionally, newer exiles from Cuba and elsewhere took their places in Miami's low-wage service and manufacturing economy. By the 1980s, for instance, according to the 1982 Miami report of the U.S. Civil Rights Commission, Hispanics made up two-thirds of Miami's construction labor force, and an astonishing 85 percent of the workers in Miami's extensive garment industry. By contrast, despite the area's growing economy, blacks have remained on the economic margins, with high proportions of poverty-level incomes, high levels of unemployment, and little economic opportunity. Over time, Hispanics replaced blacks in the service economy where they had formerly predominated. In the hotel industry, for example, a survey of twelve major hotels in 1981 revealed that blacks held only 9.9 percent of almost 4,300 hotel jobs. "By all social indicators," the U.S. Civil Rights Commission reported, "blacks have been excluded from the economic mainstream in Miami." Despite the gains of the Civil Rights era, the Commission contended, "generations of explicit and race-based employment discrimination have left a legacy that continues to infect the labor market." Miami was an ethnically polarized community, a Florida study commission on the 1980 riots reported, and blacks and Hispanics were "pitted against each other in a scramble for the most marginal jobs."[24]

Not only did the Cubans move into the local job market, but their collective entrepreneurialism soon had a dramatic impact on business activity in the Miami metropolitan area. By 1972, when the Hispanic population of the area was about double that of blacks, Hispanics had established more than three times as many businesses as blacks, and gross receipts surpassed those of black businesses by five times. Moreover, African-American businesses were overwhelmingly small; they were concentrated in selective services and the retail trade, they lacked access to capital, and they employed few salaried workers. Things had hardly improved by 1982, when only 1 percent of Miami's businesses were black-owned, and almost all of them—88 percent—were owner-operated with no employees. The differential business pattern had intensified by 1987, the most recent year for which U.S. census data is available. Miami Hispanics had seven times as many businesses as African Americans in 1987 (47,725 for Hispanics compared to 6,747 for blacks), while the total sales differential increased to more than thirteen times ($3.8 billion compared to $276 million).[25]

This pattern of energetic Hispanic business activity suggested to many analysts that the Cuban exiles created a self-sufficient "enclave" economy, one entirely separate from the mainstream white business community, and separate as well from the peripheral black minority economy. Some observers contend that the Cuban enclave economy has not undercut the economic standing of Miami blacks, since the Cubans carved out completely new business opportunities in ethnic goods and foods, cigar making, and international trade. Thus, say sociologists Kenneth L. Wilson and W. Allen Martin, the Cubans' extraordinary entrepreneurial success did not come at the expense of the black community.[26]

However, recent research suggests that perhaps too much has been made of the Cuban "enclave" economy in Miami, thus masking some other economic realities in the local job market. Analysis of the 1987 economic census data on minority business enterprises demonstrates that while only 14 percent of Miami's black-owned businesses had employees, the rate for Cuban-owned businesses with employees was virtually the same at 14.9 percent. Moreover, the number of workers at Cuban-owned businesses that did have employees was quite small—about 25,000. Two conclusions might be drawn from these data: first, that the number of Cubans who owned their own businesses (and were therefore entrepreneurial) was quite small—less than 10 percent of the Cuban work force in metropolitan Miami; and second, that the number of nonmanagerial or nonbusiness-owning Cubans employed in the "enclave" economy was also astonishingly small—less than 7 percent of the Cuban work force in the Miami area. The fact is that the greatest proportion of Cubans in Miami are members of the working class and not professionals or entrepreneurial businessmen. They work outside the Cuban enclave and thus compete with African Americans, whites, and other immigrants for jobs as construction workers, airplane mechanics, hotel and restaurant service workers, and unskilled laborers. The

Cuban enclave economy simply was never large enough to accommodate the masses of Hispanic immigrants over thirty years. The largest employers in the Miami area remain outside the Cuban enclave—city, county, and state government, the Dade County school system, the universities, the telephone and power companies, the airlines, the cruise and cargo ship companies, the big hotels, large finance, insurance, and real estate companies, the major retail store chains, the *Miami Herald*, and the like. Local economic power in the largest sense remains in the hands of the Anglos, while the Cubans concentrated mostly on small-scale entrepreneurialism. Neither segment of the local economy did very much over the years to advance the economic position of Miami's African-American community.[27]

Moreover, considerable evidence also suggests that even Cuban entrepreneurial success, at least to some degree, came at the expense of black-owned businesses. For example, blacks owned 25 percent of all the gasoline service stations in Dade County in 1960. By 1979, black ownership of service stations had dropped to 9 percent, but Hispanic stations numbered 48 percent of the total. Similarly, differential patterns can be found in the Miami activities of the Small Business Administration (SBA). Between 1968 and 1979, the SBA distributed about $100 million to Miami area businesses. Hispanics received 47 percent of the total over the twelve-year period, non-Hispanic whites 46.5 percent, and blacks 6.4 percent. In the year after the 1980 Liberty City riot, 90 percent of SBA loans in Miami went to Hispanics and whites. Hispanics also benefited disproportionately from the Dade County "set-aside" program for contracting with minority businesses. Over time, as writer David Rieff put it, "the blacks were frozen out" by the Cubans, who "saw no particular reason to have to assume the burden of America's historical obligation to black people."[28]

Clearly, the Cuban exiles have fared well in the United States. Numerous studies have demonstrated the rapid upward socioeconomic mobility of the early waves of Cuban exiles. Despite the leveling tendency of Cuban emigration over time, statistical evidence from the U.S. Census Bureau reveals that the Cubans have more education, better jobs, and higher incomes than the Hispanic population generally in the United States. The economic success of the Cubans, without any comparable improvement for blacks, has been a persistent source of irritation and resentment in the Miami black community. In particular, African Americans generally feel left out of the local job market, since, as one observer noted, "Miami blacks always live in danger of losing their jobs to the latest wave of immigrants off the islands prepared to work for peanuts." As the U.S. Civil Rights Commission put it in 1982, blacks were "the missing partner" in Miami's dramatic economic growth of the past several decades. This same theme was echoed six years later, in 1988, when *Newsweek* noted that "the black community has been left out of Dade County's prosperity almost entirely." The same point was emphasized once again in a 1991 Dade County study of racial discrimination and economic disparity.[29]

The Cuban influx also created a new level of competition for housing and residential space in the Miami area. Miami had always had a highly segregated residential pattern. Several sociological studies, for example, noted that of more than one hundred large American cities, Miami had the highest degree of residential segregation by race in 1940, 1950, and 1960—before the Cuban influx—a legacy of the racial zoning of the segregation era. Miami's "index of residential segregation" improved modestly after 1960 compared to other Southern cities. Nevertheless, in 1980 and again in 1990, after more than thirty years of Civil Rights activism in urban America, Miami still ranked in the high range, compared to other large metropolitan areas, in the extent of black residential segregation. Moreover, as demonstrated by sociologist Douglas S. Massey in a study of the twenty-nine largest U.S. urbanized areas, Miami had "an unusually high degree" of residential separation between blacks and Hispanics as early as 1970.[30]

At the time of the initial Cuban migration, most Miami blacks lived in Liberty City and Overtown, two large ghettoized communities north and west of the central business district, while others resided in half a dozen smaller black neighborhoods scattered throughout the metropolitan area. The urban renewal and interstate highway construction of the 1950s and 1960s, and continued downtown redevelopment activities in the 1970s and 1980s, resulted in the destruction of at least 10,000 housing units, mostly in the black, inner-city community of Overtown. At the same time, the Cubans were arriving in massive numbers and staking out their own inner-city residential space west of the central business district, in what is now known as Little Havana, and also in Hialeah in the far northwest quadrant of the metropolitan area.[31]

Blacks displaced from Overtown by urban renewal and redevelopment found their relocation choices limited. Consequently, existing black communities such as Liberty City grew in population, rising in density but also pushing out the frontiers of the ghetto into adjoining white, working-class districts such as Opa-locka and Carol City. As one social scientist noted in a 1979 study, "the Latin American community of Miami has grown so rapidly in population that it has dramatically affected the residential space of other groups within the city." Urban renewal and the Cuban influx, taken together, limited the number of housing units available to blacks, the U.S. Civil Rights Commission reported in the wake of the 1980 Liberty City riots. The conjunction of redevelopment and immigration, in the 1960s and after, contributed to excessive rents, a high level of overcrowding, a rapidly deteriorating housing stock, and worsening slum conditions in Miami's black communities.[32]

Recent federal housing policies have also had a discriminatory impact on blacks in Miami. The shift away from the construction of new public housing in the 1980s and toward government-subsidized private housing for low-income people (so-called Section-8 housing) negatively affected African-American housing choices. In Miami, 95 percent of Section-8 housing went to Hispanic residents, a reflection of the close linkages between Cuban builders and developers and federal housing officials in the Reagan-Bush administrations. At the same time, existing public housing in Miami, 95 percent of whose residents by the 1980s were African-American, became increasingly dilapidated and run down due to lack of maintenance. Policy makers came to perceive public housing as a dumping ground for the black poor, while discrimination in the Section-8 program denied alternative housing opportunities to low-income blacks. The massive Cuban migrations over many years had powerful and seemingly permanent consequences for Miami's African-American community, especially in the job and housing markets.[33]

## Government Programs for Cuban Exiles

From the early 1960s, Miami blacks were aware of the social and economic implications of the Cuban influx. Jobs and housing had always been high on the list of black grievances. But the arrival of the Cubans created a new grievance—governmental favoritism toward the newcomers. Because the Cubans were escaping communism in Cuba, they were accorded a special parolee status outside the normal immigration quota, and then given special treatment after they arrived. The Cuban Adjustment Act of 1966 regularized this procedure, granting all Cuban refugees permanent resident alien status. Initially, private voluntary and religious agencies, particularly the Catholic Church, supplied emergency assistance for the Cuban exiles. But very quickly, in December 1960, President Eisenhower created the Cuban Refugee Program (CRP) to handle the actual processing and resettlement of the Cubans in Miami.[34]

After initial security screening of the exiles by the Immigration and Naturalization Service, the CRP's Cuban Refugee Emergency Center in Miami provided them with food and clothing, housing assistance, social services, medical care, relocation assistance, educational programs, job training, and job placement. Special programs, costing $130 million in federal funds through 1972, were introduced into the Dade County public schools to aid in the adjustment and training of the newcomers and their children. Language classes, vocational training, business education, varied adult education programs, and the like proliferated to assist the Cubans. The University of Miami and other agencies were enlisted to train, "retool," and recertify Cuban professionals. As a result, thousands of Cuban physicians, nurses, lawyers, accountants, pharmacists, dentists, architects, engineers, veterinarians, and teachers were enabled to resume their professional lives in South Florida. Special federal loans were made available for Cubans wishing to attend universities. The assistance of the Small Business Administration, mentioned earlier, stimulated business start-ups among the Cuban exiles. This vast exile welfare program, according to one careful study, touched directly about 75 percent of all the Cuban arrivals before 1974. The cost was enormous: by 1973, more than $1 billion had been spent by the federal government to assist Cuban resettlement in the United States. The continuing Cuban migration, and especially the Mariel boatlift, drove federal expenses considerably higher by the 1980s. The bill for processing, settling, and detaining the Cubans from the Mariel boatlift, for example, surpassed $2 billion by 1990. Reflecting on the vast federal program for exiles, one Cuban teacher noted simply, "They have helped us a lot."[35]

There was another source of governmental support for many Cubans in Miami, as well. For years, the Central Intelligence Agency had thousands of Miami Cubans on the CIA payroll—perhaps as many as 12,000 or more at one point in the early 1960s. Under Eisenhower and Kennedy, the CIA had been authorized to recruit and train a Cuban exile guerrilla force to overthrow the Castro regime—an endeavor that ended in abject military failure at the Bay of Pigs in 1961. Later, CIA stringers from Cuban Miami surfaced during the Watergate break-in in the early 1970s, as did still others during the more recent Iran-Contra fiasco. During the 1960s, the Miami CIA station was the largest in the world outside Langley, Virginia, and the CIA may have been Miami's largest employer. The CIA established dozens of front businesses in Miami, including an airline, shipping firms, boat shops, gun shops, real estate agencies, and travel agencies. One scholarly analyst has suggested that the CIA played an important role in facilitating the early entrepreneurial success of the Cubans. In the cold war era, the hard-line, anti-communist Cuban exiles in South Florida found a ready source of financial and other support in the federal government.[36]

The vast outpouring of federal funding for the Cuban exiles had a lot to do with the quick adaptation and economic success of the newcomers from the Caribbean. Over time, blacks came to resent the preferential treatment of the Cubans by government at every level. African-American community leaders and the black press often drew comparisons between the rising condition of the Cuban refugees and the still-downtrodden situation of Miami's blacks. This issue of preferential treatment for Hispanic newcomers persisted into the 1980s and beyond. Moreover, the perception among blacks that the recent Nicaraguan exiles have been equally favored has kept this issue inflamed. The differential treatment accorded recent black immigrants from Haiti, who were for a time incarcerated in detention camps or forced back to their homeland, only served to strengthen the sense of ill treatment among Miami's blacks.[37]

## Political Conflicts

The black sense of powerlessness in Cuban Miami has been intensified by changes in the local political culture. Over time, the Cuban migration dramatically altered the political structure of the Miami area. The earliest Cuban exiles hoped to return quickly to their homeland, although the failure of the Bay of Pigs invasion in 1961 deflated some of the militant activism among the exiles. Nevertheless, for many years Castro and Cuba were more important to Miami's newcomers than local political issues. Only gradually did the Cubans come to recognize their new South Florida home as more or less permanent. But by the late 1960s, as the hope of return dimmed, most Cuban exiles began the citizenship process. Exile politics remains a powerful ingredient in Cuban Miami, strengthened by the continual replenishment of the community over several decades. But the Miami Cubans have also energized metropolitan Miami with a new brand of ethnic politics.[38]

Miami's demographic changes inevitably produced political consequences, especially as the Cubans became citizens and voters by the mid-1970s. At one time, Florida was an integral part of the solidly Democratic South. Now, the Cubans have become a major cog in Florida's conservative Republican party politics. Local elections over the past decade or more have reflected bitter ethnic divisiveness in tri-ethnic Miami. "The animosity that exists between the three communities runs deep, real deep," one political writer observed as early as 1983."[39]

Hispanic voting power led to control of city governments in Miami and Hialeah by the early 1980s. At-large elections prevented similar Hispanic gains at the county level until a court-mandated district-voting system was implemented in 1993, but Cubans now dominate the Dade County Commission as well. Both the Miami city manager and the Dade County manager are Cubans, and Hispanics make up a growing portion of city and county employees. Furthermore, ethnicity pervades most important political discussions, and the high degree of residential segregation not only lends strength to ethnic or racial voting, but intensifies certain kinds of emotional territorial issues such as zoning, or school busing, or public housing location. Even street-naming decisions generate ethnic polarization. When the Miami City Commission renamed a street in 1987 in honor of President Ronald Reagan, the wrath of the black community was poured out in a *Miami Times* editorial:

> Mr. Reagan may be a hero to the Hispanic community because of his avowed anti-communist stand, as shown in his policy toward Cuba and Nicaragua. But, to Blacks, Mr. Reagan is the person who has made life much more difficult in these United States. He has snubbed our leaders, undercut the federal institutions that have given us a chance to raise our heads high, and chopped away badly needed funds that aid us in that process. When Black folks drive down Ronald Reagan Avenue, those are the thoughts that will come to mind.

Similarly, Cuban efforts in the city commission to promote official bilingualism seemed to blacks just another step on the road to the "Cubanization" of Miami. As one recent scholarly analysis put it, "ethnic conflict in Miami shows signs of growing brittleness and intransigence in an atmosphere characterized by group polarization and zero-sum politics."[40]

The Civil Rights Movement empowered blacks politically in other southern cities, but the Cuban influx to South Florida produced a different outcome. In Atlanta, New Orleans, Richmond, Birmingham, and other southern cities, black population majorities ultimately brought political power. This has not happened in Miami, where African Americans remain a distinct minority and where at-large elections traditionally disfranchised black voters. Blacks did become a majority in Opa-locka in the 1970s, as working-class whites moved from this northwest Dade County municipality of about 15,000. However, Opa-locka's black political leaders inherited a community in decline, with an aging housing stock and serious social problems. Some black leaders in metropolitan Miami sought to overcome political weakness in the 1980s by creating a new municipality for the unincorporated Liberty City community. Black supporters of the plan viewed this so-called New City as a means of acquiring local political power, a community-controlled police force, and a higher level of services. The Dade County Commission, which has control over the incorporation of new municipalities, vetoed the New City plan numerous times. The outcome of this and other political battles suggested to some African-American leaders that "Blacks may have to fight the civil rights struggle all over again."[41]

The Cuban influx to metropolitan Miami altered the rules and the boundaries of the political game. Indeed, the Caribbean migration ultimately put a whole new team on the field, pushing the old players off to the sidelines. Black spokesmen have been alternately dismayed and infuriated by the emerging political dominance of the Cubans, or "the Cuban Takeover," as it is often referred to in the black press. As one black columnist bitterly put it in the *Miami Times* in the wake of the 1989 riots: "The reality of Miami today and in the foreseeable future, is that the Cubans are the new masters in Miami. They should not be surprised when those who feel they have nothing to lose rise up against the new rulers."[42]

The dimensions of black-Cuban political conflict were sharply etched in a bitter confrontation in 1990 over the visit of South Africa's Nelson Mandela to Miami. Although welcomed and even lionized elsewhere in the United States, in Miami both the Miami City Commission and the Dade County Commission snubbed Mandela, refusing to grant the customary welcome to visiting dignitaries. The Miami Cubans were aroused because Mandela had declared his support for Fidel Castro, but Miami's African Americans were outraged that the heroic Mandela had been treated with such official disrespect. The conflict produced reams of editorial ink, as well as a three-year black boycott of Miami convention hotels and a black demand for more jobs. A compromise settlement eventually was reached in 1993, after the Dade County Commission issued a proclamation honoring Mandela and promised economic development programs in black Miami. Black leaders, in turn, called off the three-year boycott. The entire controversy illustrated the tenuous balance of ethnic politics in multicultural Miami.[43]

## Contemporary Ethnic Relations

It should be clear, then, that ethnic relations in the Miami area are in considerable disarray. Black resentment has been festering since the 1960s over the economic success of the Cubans, their dominance of the job and housing markets, their newly developed political power, and the preferential treatment they have received from government. Other more immediate issues such as police harassment and violence, or the perception of police violence, in the ghetto have produced the racial explosions that have characterized Miami since 1968. But behind these overt incidents lies more than thirty years of economic competition and ethnic conflict between Miami's African Americans and their new Hispanic neighbors from the Caribbean basin. The issue of job displacement, in particular, has always been a prominent source of black concern. The persistent failure of the system to deliver often promised social and economic improvements—better housing, improved schools, job training, better services—contrasted with the perceived advantages and benefits received first by the Cubans, and later by the Nicaraguans, has kept black Miami on the edge of rage and despair.[44]

Objectively, it is clear that there are wide economic disparities within the Cuban community, and that not all Hispanic immigrants to South Florida have shared in the economic promise of America. The Mariel boatlift of 1980, in particular, demonstrated that there was a distinct class, and even a racial, dimension to Miami's Cuban community. Indeed, as Stephan Palmié has suggested, the increasing number of black Cubans in Miami after Mariel raised new and ambiguous questions about Cuban self-identity and interracial heritage. It is also true that, despite their vaunted economic success, the Cubans have yet to break into the upper echelons of the Miami power structure, often dominated by Anglo bankers, developers, bureaucrats, and corporate executives. Nevertheless, perceptions are important, and Miami blacks mostly see that Cubans and other Hispanics own the local businesses they patronize, control access to the local job market, dominate the local political decision-making process, limit accessibility and choice in housing, and fill increasing numbers of positions in local government and, significantly, on the police force. African Americans also share an uncomfortable sense that the Hispanic newcomers have become racists. As a black Miami architect, born in Houston, mildly suggested to a reporter recently, "too many of the Cubans . . . have adopted a Southern mentality." As social scientists have suggested, objective reality is less important than perception in shaping attitudes and determining behavior. Image-making was always important in the glitzy, glamorous tourist spa that Miami used to be, and it turns out that images and perceptions of a different kind now prevail in Miami, the new immigrant city.[45]

The 1980 Liberty City riot focused new attention on race relations in Miami. One black scholar contended that "the political economy of racism" made Liberty City and other black neighborhoods "ripe for rebellion." However, one early post-1980 riot analysis—that by journalist Bruce Porter and social psychologist Marvin Dunn—pushed the issue of Hispanic competition into the forefront of discussion. Porter and Dunn sought to explain Miami's racial explosion, at least partially, as the result of the Cuban influx into the city. In a 1981 *New York Times* article summarizing their research, Porter and Dunn noted the political and economic powerlessness of blacks in Miami. But they went on to argue that the Cuban immigration to Miami prevented blacks from making economic gains just as the Civil Rights Movement and desegregation were beginning to eliminate legal barriers. As Porter and Dunn put it, "just as blacks were groping out of their forced isolation, in came hundreds of thousands of Cubans and other Hispanic immigrants" who displaced blacks in the job market and "shouldered aside the existing black-owned businesses." The depressed economic condition of Miami's blacks, the report implied, was "the reverse side of a Hispanic economic boom."[46]

The charges that they have been somehow to blame for the economic condition of Miami's blacks and for two decades of ghetto rioting have offended the Hispanic community in South Florida. "It's not our fault," Hispanics have argued, that centuries of slavery, racism, and segregation victimized African Americans in the United States. "The centuries-old structures of racism" account for the economic condition of Miami's blacks, contended Cuban-American sociologist Lisandro Pérez, not "Miami's newly arrived Hispanic peoples, who are now being scapegoated for the consequences of those long-standing structures."[47]

Pérez has a point, to be sure, and this brings us back to the chief interpretive argument outlined at the beginning of this essay—that is, that the conjunction of the Cuban Revolution and the Civil Rights Movement moved Miami onto an alternative path in race relations. "The Cuban Revolution," one writer has noted, "was as much a pivotal event in Miami's modern history as it was in Cuba's."[48] While other cities, north and south, sought to address the burning issues dividing blacks and whites, Miami was much more preoccupied with receiving and accommodating the Cuban exiles, pushing civil rights and social reform issues into the background. The Cubans and other Hispanics from the South seized opportunities as they found them, and then created new opportunities for themselves in an amenable economic and political environment. But African Americans have not fared as well, and generally believe that they have been "displaced from mainstream opportunities by the newly arrived immigrants." The legal barriers of the segregation era are gone, but Miami blacks have "remained economically and politically invisible, especially between riots."[49]

The failure of urban policy in the Reagan-Bush era intensified Miami's problems, as was the case elsewhere in urban America. There is considerable irony, as well, in the fact that the conservative, right-wing Cubans who benefited so extensively from government welfare in their early years in the United States adamantly oppose the kinds of social investment that Miami's black community needs. Each of the riots since 1980 has produced an outpouring of verbiage on the necessity for better understanding and improved ethnic relations. But even the city's Community Relations Board, as one observer wrote, "is a power struggle between blacks and Hispanics—with the Anglos watching expectantly and playing as the occasional referee." Indeed, as one scholar has suggested, given the widely held perceptions in the black community about the "Cuban takeover," Anglo leaders now have been able "to deflect to an outside group [the Cubans] much of the black anger and frustration which had historically been directed at a political and economic system dominated by an Anglo power-elite." Miami remains a city on the edge, an ethnic cauldron that often boils over—no melting pot here. Racial division and ethnic polarization will not be easily dissipated in this new immigrant city in what was once the Deep South.[50]

As the foregoing pages have suggested, the experience of late twentieth-century Miami is unique in several ways. The arrival of massive waves of political exiles—Cubans, Haitians, Nicaraguans—has come to seem commonplace in Miami but has few parallels elsewhere. The exceptionally heavy concentration of one group—the Cubans—in one city is also unusual. The favored treatment the Cubans received from the federal government is remarkably different from the experience of other immigrant groups. But in most other respects, the Miami pattern of multicultural urban life, with all of its diversity, tension, and change, is not so untypical of the rest of modern urban America. The new immigration is remaking the economic, political, and cultural life of the United States. With its emphasis on respect for ethnic and racial diversity, the emerging multiculturalism movement represents a continuation and extension of the midtwentieth-century Civil Rights campaign. Thus, multiculturalism is not a new challenge, but one that Americans confronted with some success in the past. The ethnic and racial conflicts of the recent past, however, suggest that the road to democratic diversity is a difficult one.

NOTES

1. Douglas S. Massey, "Dimensions of the New Immigration to the United States and the Prospects for Assimilation," *Annual Review of Sociology* 7 (1981): 57–85; Michael J. Mandel and Christopher Farrell, "The Immigrants," *Business Week* 13 July 1992: 114–22; and, for a full statistical portrait of the new immigration, U.S. Bureau of the Census, *1990 Census of Population: The Foreign-Born Population in the United States*, 1990 CP-3–1 (Washington, DC: U.S. Government Printing Office, 1993). For scholarly overviews of the new immigration, see David M. Reimers, *Still the Golden Door: The Third World Comes to America*, 2nd ed. (New York: Columbia UP, 1992), and Reed Ueda, *Postwar Immigrant America: A Social History* (Boston: Bedford Books, 1994).

2. For general information on the new immigration to Los Angeles, New York, and Miami, see Thomas Muller, *The Fourth Wave: California's Newest Immigrants* (Washington, DC: Urban Institute Press, 1984); Alejandro Portes and Robert L. Bach, *Latin Journey: Cuban and Mexican Immigrants in the United States* (Berkeley: U of California P, 1985); Elliott Barkan, "Immigration through the Port of Los Angeles," *Forgotten Doors: The Other Ports of Entry to the United States*, ed. M. Mark Stolarik (Philadelphia: Balch Institute Press, 1988) 161–91; Nancy Foner, ed., *New Immigrants in New York* (New York: Columbia UP, 1987); William Pencak, et al., eds., *Immigration to New York* (Cranbury, NJ: Associated University Presses, 1991); Raymond A. Mohl, "Miami: New Immigrant City," *Searching for the Sunbelt: Historical Perspectives on a Region*, ed. Raymond A. Mohl (Knoxville: U of Tennessee P, 1990) 149–75; Raymond A. Mohl, "Florida's Changing Demography: Population Growth, Urbanization, and Latinization," *Environmental and Urban Issues* 17 (Winter 1990): 22–30. On Hispanics generally, see Douglas S. Massey and Kathleen M. Schnabel, "Recent Trends in Hispanic Immigration to the United States," *International Migration Review* 17 (Summer 1983): 212–44; Rafael Valdivieso and Cary Davis, *U.S. Hispanics: Challenging Issues for the 1990s* (Washington, DC: Population Reference Bureau, 1988); and U.S. Bureau of the Census, *1990 Census of Population: Persons of Hispanic Origin in the United States*, 1990 CP-3–3 (Washington, DC: U.S. Government Printing Office, 1993). For Hispanic population projections into the twenty-first century, see Thomas Exter, "How Many Hispanics?" *American Demographics* 9 (May 1987): 36–39, 67; U.S. Bureau of the Census, *Population Projections of the United States, by Age, Sex, Race, and Hispanic Origin: 1993 to 2050*, Current Population Reports, P25-1104 (Washington, DC: U.S. Government Printing Office, 1993), especially p. vii.

3. In 1994, both California and Florida threatened to take the federal government to court to recover the costs of immigrant-related governmental services. See Larry Rohter, "Revisiting Immigration and the Open-Door Policy," *New York Times* 19 September 1993: 4 E; Lawton Chiles, "Who Will Pay for all These Immigrants?" *USA Today* 2 March 1994: 11 A; Mark Silva, "Florida's Big Tab for Immigration," *Miami Herald* 13 March 1994: 1 A, 20 A; Mark Silva, "Immigration Suit Seeks $1 Billion," *Miami Herald* 10 April 1994: 1 A, 18 A.

4. Julian L. Simon, *The Economic Consequences of Immigration* (Oxford: Basil Blackwell, 1989); George J. Borjas, *Friends or Strangers: The Impact of Immigrants on the U.S. Economy* (New York: Basic Books, 1990); Dan Lacey, *The Essential Immigrant* (New York: Hippocrene Books, 1990); Thomas Muller, "Exploring the Facts About Immigration," *Chronicle of Higher Education* 9 February 1994: B1–B2; John J. Miller, "Immigrant-Bashing's Latest Falsehood," *Wall Street Journal* 8 March 1994: A 16.

5. Peter D. Salins, "Take a Ticket," *New Republic* 27 December 1993: 13–15; Nathan Glazer, "The Closing Door," *New Republic* 27 December 1993: 15–20; Richard D. Lamm and Gary Imhoff, *The Immigration Time Bomb: The Fragmenting of America* (New York: E. P. Dutton, 1985); Arthur M. Schlesinger, Jr., *The Disuniting of America: Reflections on a Multicultural Society* (New York: Norton, 1992); Nicolaus Mills, ed., *Arguing Immigration: The Debate Over the Changing Face of America* (New York: Simon and Schuster, 1994); Nathan Glazer, "Immigration and the American Future," *The Public Interest* 118 (Winter 1995): 45–60; Peter Brimelow, *Alien Nation: Common Sense About America's Immigration Disaster* (New York: Random House, 1995).

6. Ronald Takaki, *A Different Mirror: A History of Multicultural America* (Boston: Little, Brown, 1993) 423; Jack Miles, "Blacks vs. Browns," *The Atlantic* 270 (October 1992): 41–68; Felix Jimenez, "Dangerous Liaisons," *Hispanic* (April 1991): 13–18; Edward T. Chang, "Jewish and Korean Merchants in African American Neighborhoods: A Comparative Perspective," *Amerasia Review* 19.2 (1993): 5–21; Jonathan Rieder, *Canarsie: The Jews and Italians of Brooklyn against Liberalism* (Cambridge, MA: Harvard UP, 1985); Jim Sleeper, *The Closest of Strangers: Liberalism and the Politics of Race in New York* (New York: Norton, 1990).

7. Gerald D. Suttles, *The Social Order of the Slum: Ethnicity and Territory in the Inner City* (Chicago: U of Chicago P, 1968); Ze'ev Chafets, *Devil's Night and Other True Tales of Detroit* (New York: Random House, 1990) 31–39; Jeffrey Schmalz, "Miami's New Ethnic Conflict: Haitians vs. American Blacks," *New York Times* 19 February 1989: 1, 20; Nancy E. Roman, "Black vs. Black," *XS Magazine* [Fort Lauderdale] 18 March 1992: 12–14; Deborah P. Work, "One Color, Two Cultures," *Sun-Sentinel* [Fort Lauderdale] 3 April 1994: 1 E, 4 E; Paul D. Starr, "Troubled Waters: Vietnamese Fisherfolk on America's Gulf Coast," *International Migration Review* 15 (Spring-Summer 1981): 226–38; Joan Moore and James Diego Vigil, "Barrios in Transition," *In the Barrios: Latinos and the Underclass Debate*, ed. Joan Moore and Raquel Pinderhughes (New York: Russell Sage Foundation, 1993) 42–45; Ronald H. Bayor, "Historical Encounters: Intergroup Relations in a 'Nation of Nations,'" *Annals of the American Academy of Political and Social Science* 530 (November 1993): 14–27.

8. On post-war urban change, see Raymond A. Mohl, "The Transformation of Urban America Since the Second World War," *Amerikastudien / American Studies* 33.1 (1988): 53–71; Raymond A. Mohl, "Shifting Patterns of American Urban Policy Since 1900," *Urban Policy in Twentieth-Century America*, ed. Arnold R. Hirsch and Raymond A. Mohl (New Brunswick, NJ: Rutgers UP, 1993), 1–45; and, on the black migration to urban America, Nicholas Lemann, *The Promised Land: The Great Black Migration and How It Changed America* (New York: Knopf, 1991). On ethnic and "rainbow" politics, see Rufus P. Browning et al., *Protest Is Not Enough: The Struggle of Blacks and Hispanics for Equality in Urban Politics* (Berkeley: U of California P, 1984); F. Chris Garcia, *Latinos and the Political System* (Notre Dame, IN: U of Notre Dame P, 1988); John Mollenkopf, *A Phoenix in the Ashes: The Rise and Fall of the Koch Coalition in New York City Politics* (Princeton, NJ: Princeton UP, 1992); Chris McNickle, *To Be Mayor of New York: Ethnic Politics in the City* (New York: Columbia UP, 1992); Raphael J. Sonenshein, *Politics in Black and White: Race and Power in Los Angeles* (Princeton, NJ: Princeton UP, 1993); Gary Rivlin, *Fire on the Prairie: Chicago's Harold Washington and the Politics of Race* (New York: Henry Holt and Co., 1992); Rufus P. Browning et al., eds., *Racial Politics in American Cities* (New York: Longman, 1990); Jim Sleeper, "The End of the Rainbow," *New Republic* 1 (November 1993): 20–25.

9. Alejandro Portes and Alex Stepick, *City on the Edge: The Transformation of Miami* (Berkeley: U of California P, 1993) 8. For overviews of urban change in late twentieth-century Miami, see David B. Longbrake and Woodrow W. Nichols, Jr., *Sunshine and Shadows in Metropolitan Miami* (Cambridge, MA: Ballinger, 1976); Raymond A. Mohl, "Miami: The Ethnic Cauldron," *Sunbelt Cities: Politics and Growth Since World War II*, ed. Richard M. Bernard and Bradley R. Rice (Austin: U of Texas P, 1983) 58–99; Raymond A. Mohl, "Ethnic Transformations in Late Twentieth-Century Florida," *Journal of American Ethnic History* 15 (Winter

1996): 60–78. For percent of Miamians speaking a language other than English, see U.S. Bureau of the Census, *1990 Census of Population and Housing: Summary Social, Economic, and Housing Characteristics: Florida*, 1990 CPH-5-11 (Washington, DC: U.S. Government Printing Office, 1992) 4.

10. *Miami Herald*, 17, 18, 19, 22 January, 10 December 1989; *Miami Times* 19, 26 January 1989; *New York Times* 18, 22 January 1989; *Los Angeles Times* 17, 19, 20 January 1989; Jacob V. Lamar, "A Brightly Colored Tinderbox," *Time* (30 January 1989): 28–29; George Hackett, "All of Us Are in Trouble," *Newsweek* (30 January 1989): 36–37; Joel Achenbach, "Short Fuse," *Miami Herald, Tropic Magazine* (7 May 1989): 10–27.

11. The new Nicaraguan exile migration has been covered extensively by journalists. See Dave Von Drehle, "Nicaraguan Refugees Flock into Miami," *Miami Herald* 13 January 1989: 1 A, 18 A; Liz Balmaseda, "East Little Havana: A New Nicaragua," *Miami Herald* 5 February 1989: 1 G, 4 G; Christopher Marquis, "Nicaraguan Exiles Changed Miami's Face," *Miami Herald* 16 July 1989: 1 A, 10 A. See also Melinda Beck, "Exodus of the 'Feet People,'" *Newsweek* 14 November 1988: 37; Barry Bearak, "Miami Reacts with Charity and Anxiety to Latest Refugee Influx from Nicaragua," *Los Angeles Times* 17 January 1989: 1, 4; Paul Adams, "Next Stop, Miami," *Sun-Sentinel, Sunshine Magazine* [Fort Lauderdale] 5 March 1989: 24–30; Brad Edmondson, "In Little Managua," *American Demographics* 11 (August 1989): 53–55; Anne Moncreiff Arrarte, "The Contras and Miami: How Do You Resettle an Unemployed Army," *South Florida* 42 (August 1989): 64–67, 133–34; and Arturo J. Cruz and Jaime Suchliki, *The Impact of Nicaraguans in Miami* (Coral Gables, FL: Graduate School of International Studies, University of Miami, 1990).

12. For an analysis of the 1980 Liberty City riots, see Bruce Porter and Marvin Dunn, *The Miami Riot of 1980: Crossing the Bounds* (Lexington, MA: D.C. Heath, 1984); Thomas D. Boswell, et al., "Attitudes, Causes, and Perceptions: The 1980 Black Riot in Dade County (Miami), Florida," *The Florida Geographer* 20 (1986): 1–15. On the Mariel boatlift, see Robert L. Bach, "The New Cuban Exodus," *Caribbean Review* 11 (Winter 1982): 22–25, 58–60; Alex Larzelere, *Castro's Ploy—America's Dilemma: The 1980 Cuban Boatlift* (Washington, DC: National Defense UP, 1988). On the migration of Haitian boat people, see Alex Stepick, *Haitian Refugees in the U.S.*, Report No. 52 (London: Minority Rights Group, 1982); Jake C. Miller, *The Plight of Haitian Refugees* (New York: Praeger, 1984); Alex Stepick and Alejandro Portes, "Flight into Despair: A Profile of Recent Haitian Refugees in South Florida," *International Migration Review* 20 (Summer 1986): 329–50.

13. For analysis of the Civil Rights Movement in the urban South, see Aldon D. Morris, *The Origins of the Civil Rights Movement: Black Communities Organizing for Change* (New York: Free Press, 1984); Adam Fairclough, *To Redeem the Soul of America: The Southern Christian Leadership Conference and Martin Luther King, Jr.* (Athens: U of Georgia P, 1987); David R. Goldfield, *Black, White, and Southern: Race Relations and Southern Culture, 1940 to the Present* (Baton Rouge: Louisiana State UP, 1990).

14. Porter and Dunn, *The Miami Riot of 1980* 1. See also Paul S. George, "Colored Town: Miami's Black Community, 1896–1930," *Florida Historical Quarterly* 56 (April 1978): 432–47; Paul S. Geroge, "Policing Miami's Black Community, 1896–1930," *Florida Historical Quarterly* 57 (April 1979): 434–450; Raymond A. Mohl, "Trouble in Paradise: Race and Housing in Miami during the New Deal Era," *Prologue: Journal of the National Archives* 19 (Spring 1987): 7–21; Raymond A. Mohl, "The Pattern of Race Relations in Miami Since the 1920s," *The African American Heritage of Florida*, ed. David R. Colburn and Jane L. Landers (Gainesville: UP of Florida, 1995) 326–65.

15. On black politics in Florida and in Miami, see Hugh D. Price, *The Negro in Southern Politics: A Chapter of Florida History* (New York: New York UP, 1957); Clyde C. Wooten, et al., *Psycho-Social Dynamics in Miami* (Coral Gables: Center for Advanced International Studies, University of Miami, 1969) 372–406. On the "mini-riots" between 1968 and 1980, see Porter and Dunn, *The Miami Riot of 1980* 17–22. For the Didion comment, see Joan Didion, *Miami* (New York: Simon and Schuster, 1987) 39–40.

16. Portes and Bach, *Latin Journey* 84–90; Thomas D. Boswell and James R. Curtis, *The Cuban-American Experience: Culture, Images, and Perspectives* (Totowa, NJ: Rowman and Allanheld, 1984) 38–60; Raymond A. Mohl "Immigration Through the Port of Miami," *Forgotten Doors: The Other Ports of Entry to the United States*, ed. M. Mark Stolarik (Philadelphia: Balch Institute Press, 1988) 81–98; Felix Roberto Masud-Piloto, *With Open Arms: Cuban Migration to the United States* (Totowa, NJ: Rowman and Littlefield, 1988).

17. On Miami's changing demography, see William W. Jenna, *Metropolitan Miami: A Demographic Overview* (Coral Gables: U of Miami P, 1972); Raymond A. Mohl, "Miami: The Ethnic Cauldron," *Sunbelt Cities: Politics and Growth since World War II*, ed. Richard M. Bernard and Bradley R. Rice (Austin: U of Texas P, 1983) 67–72; Oliver Kerr, *Population Projections: Race and Hispanic Origins, Dade County, Florida, 1980–2000* (Miami: Metro-Dade County Planning Department, 1987); Oliver Kerr, *Population Projections: Patterns of*

*Population Change, Dade County, Florida, 1970–2010* (Miami: Metro-Dade County Planning Department, 1987). For Miami's historical pattern of black diversity, see Raymond A. Mohl, "Black Immigrants: Bahamians in Early Twentieth-Century Miami," *Florida Historical Quarterly* 65 (January 1987): 271–97.

18. Cal Brumley, "Cuban Exodus," *Wall Street Journal* 28 November 1960: 1, 16; Neil Maxwell, "Unwelcome Guests," *Wall Street Journal* 6 May 1963: 1, 16; Neil Maxwell, "New Influx of Cubans Faces Cool Reception from Many Miamians," *Wall Street Journal* 12 October 1965: 1, 18; *New York Times* 21 October 1961: 5; *New York Times* 17 October 1965: 84; Tom Alexander, "Those Amazing Cuban Refugees," *Fortune* 74 (October 1966) 144–49; Edward J. Linehan, "Cuba's Exiles Bring New Life to Miami," *National Geographic* 144 (July 1973): 63–95.

19. William M. Wolfarth to George A. Smathers, 30 November 1960, George A. Smathers Papers, Box 24; Louis Foosaner to Smathers, n.d. [November 1960], George A. Smathers Papers, Box 28; Alyene S. Brown to Smathers, n.d. [July 1961], George A. Smathers Papers, Box 29; Loretta B. Ginney to Smathers, 23 July 1961, George A. Smathers Papers, Box 29; John H. Monahan to Smathers, 18 April 1962, George A. Smathers Papers, Box 37; Marion A. Leonard to Smathers, 26 July 1961, George A. Smathers Papers, Box 30, P. K. Yonge Library, University of Florida, Gainesville.

20. R. H. Bennett to Farris Bryant, 7 January 1963, Farris Bryant Papers, Box 44; E. Harry Denny to Bryant, 3 March 1963, Farris Bryant Papers, Box 44; Altie Sizemore to Bryant, 24 March 1963, Farris Bryant Papers, Box 44; H. H. Chastain to Bryant, 21 May 1962, Farris Bryant Papers, Box 44; L. F. Shebel to A. Worley Brown, 3 July 1963, Farris Bryant Papers, Box 44; Florida Industrial Commission, *Characteristics of Cuban Refugees in Dade County, Florida* (Tallahassee: State of Florida, 1963), Farris Bryant Papers, Box 44, Florida State Archives, Tallahassee.

21. Allan Morrison, "Miami's Cuban Refugee Influx," *Ebony* 18 (June 1963): 96–104; *Miami Times* 15 July 1966: 9.

22. H. Daniel Lang, "Testimony for the Senate Subcommittee on Refugees and Escapees," 7 December 1961, typescript in National Urban League Papers, Part II, Series II, Box 15, Library of Congress, Washington, DC; Donald W. Jones to Haydon Burns, 19 October 1965, Haydon Burns Papers, Box 23; Ralph R. Poston to Haydon Burns, 20 October 1965, Haydon Burns Papers, Box 23, Florida State Archives, Tallahassee; Donald W. Jones to George A. Smathers, 13 October 1965, George A. Smathers Papers, Box 58, P. K. Yonge Library, University of Florida, Gainesville. See also Masud-Piloto, *With Open Arms* 62–64.

23. *Wall Street Journal* 6 May 1963: 1, 16; *Wall Street Journal* 12 October 1965: 18; Susan Jacoby, "Miami si, Cuba, no," *New York Times Magazine* 29 September 1974: 104. For analysis of the 1968 Miami riot, see John Boone and William Farmar, "Violence in Miami: One More Warning," *New South* 23 (Fall 1968): 28–37; Paul S. Salter and Robert C. Mings, "A Geographic Aspect of the 1968 Miami Racial Disturbance: A Preliminary Investigation," *Professional Geographer* 21 (March 1969): 79–86; National Commission on the Causes and Prevention of Violence, *Miami Report: The Report of the Miami Study Team on Civil Disturbances in Miami, Florida, during the Week of August 5, 1968* (Washington, DC: U.S. Government Printing Office, 1969).

24. U.S. Commission on Civil Rights, *Confronting Racial Isolation in Miami* (Washington, DC: U.S. Government Printing Office, 1982), 1–26, 124–90; State of Florida, *Report of the Governor's Dade County Citizens Committee* (Tallahassee: State of Florida, 1980) 14. See also Michael Hirsley, "Hispanics Overwhelm Blacks in Miami Jobs Fight," *Chicago Tribune* 18 January 1993; Harold M. Rose, "Blacks and Cubans in Metropolitan Miami's Changing Economy," *Urban Geography* 10 (1989): 464–86.

25. Andrew Neil, "America's Latin Beat: A Survey of South Florida," *The Economist* 16 October 1982: 21; *Minority-Owned Businesses, Miami, Florida* (Miami: Metro-Dade County Planning Department, 1975) 1–4, 15. For 1982 business data, see George J. Demas and Richard J. Welsh, *Profile of Black-Owned Businesses, Dade County, Florida, 1982* (Miami: Metro-Dade County Planning Department 1986); and Richard J. Welsh and Panos Efstathiou, *Profile of Hispanic Businesses, Dade County, Florida, 1982* (Miami: Metro-Dade County Planning Department, 1986). For 1987 business data, see U.S. Bureau of the Census, *1987 Economic Censuses: Survey of Minority-Owned Business Enterprises: Black* (Washington, DC: U.S. Government Printing Office, 1990) 44; U.S. Bureau of the Census, *1987 Economic Censuses: Survey of Minority-Owned Business Enterprises: Hispanic* (Washington, DC: U.S. Government Printing Office, 1991) 72.

26. Kenneth L. Wilson and W. Allen Martin, "Ethnic Enclaves: A Comparison of the Cuban and Black Economies in Miami," *American Journal of Sociology* 88 (July 1982): 135–60. Additional insight into the Cuban enclave economy can be found in Jan B. Luytjes, *Economic Impact of Refugees in Dade County* (Miami: Bureau of Business Research, Florida International University, 1982); Antonio Jorge and Raul Moncarz, *The Political Economy of Cubans in South Florida* (Coral Gables: Institute of Interamerican Studies, University of Miami,

1987); Kenneth L. Wilson and Alejandro Portes, "Immigrant Enclaves: An Analysis of the Labor Market Experience of Cubans in Miami," *American Journal of Sociology* 86 (September 1980): 295–319; Alejandro Portes, "The Social Origins of the Cuban Enclave Economy of Miami," *Sociological Perspectives* 30 (1987): 340–72.

27. Guillermo J. Grenier, "The Cuban-American Labor Movement in Dade County: An Emerging Immigrant Working Class," *Miami Now! Immigration, Ethnicity, and Social Change*, ed. Guillermo J. Grenier and Alex Stepick (Gainesville: UP of Florida, 1992) 133–59; U.S. Bureau of the Census, *1987 Economic Censuses: Black* 44; U.S. Bureau of the Census, *1987 Economic Censuses: Hispanic* 62.

28. *Miami Herald* 17 May 1981: 1 E, 4 E; Porter and Dunn, *The Miami Riot of 1980* 68–69; Gail Epstein, "Contracts Still Scarce for Blacks," *Miami Herald* 29 September 1991: 1 B, 3 B; David Rieff, *Going to Miami: Exiles, Tourists, and Refugees in the New America* (Boston: Little, Brown, 1987) 172, 174; Rose, "Blacks and Cubans," 477–84.

29. Neil, "America's Latin Beat" 21–22; Civil Rights Commission, *Confronting Racial Isolation in Miami* 79–123; Tom Morganthau, "Miami," *Newsweek* 25 January 1988: 29; Metro-Dade County, *Racial Discrimination and Disparities in the Market Place: Metropolitan Dade County, Florida: Executive Summary* (Washington, DC: Brimmer and Co., 1991). For the economic and demographic data suggesting Cuban success compared to other Hispanics, see A. J. Jaffe et al., *The Changing Demography of Spanish Americans* (New York: Academic Press, 1980) 245–78; and Frank D. Bean and Marta Tienda, *The Hispanic Population of the United States* (New York: Russell Sage Foundation, 1988).

30. Donald O. Cowgill, "Trends in Residential Segregation of Non-Whites in American Cities," *American Sociological Review* 21 (February 1956): 43–47; Karl E. Taeuber and Alma F. Taeuber, *Negroes in Cities: Residential Segregation and Neighborhood Change* (Chicago: Aldine, 1965) 39–41; Annemette Sorenson et al., "Indexes of Racial Segregation for 109 Cities in the United States, 1940–1970," *Sociological Focus* 8 (1975): 125–42; Douglas S. Massey, "Residential Segregation of Spanish Americans in United States Urbanized Areas," *Demography* 16 (November 1979): 553–63; Douglas S. Massey and Nancy A. Denton, "Trends in the Residential Segregation of Blacks, Hispanics, and Asians: 1970–1980," *American Sociological Review* 52 (December 1987): 802–25; Douglas S. Massey and Nancy A. Denton, *American Apartheid: Segregation and the Making of the Underclass* (Cambridge, MA: Harvard UP, 1993), 63–66, 86–87; Thomas D. Boswell, *Ethnic Segregation in Greater Miami, 1980–1990* (Miami: Cuban American National Council, 1992); *Miami Herald* 30 December 1987.

31. Harold M. Rose, "Metropolitan Miami's Changing Negro Population, 1950–1960," *Economic Geography* 40 (July 1964): 221–38; Raymond A. Mohl, "Race and Space in the Modern City: Interstate-95 and the Black Community in Miami," *Urban Policy in Twentieth-Century America*, ed. Hirsch and Mohl 100–58; Raymond A. Mohl, "Building the Second Ghetto in Metropolitan Miami, 1940–1960," *Journal of Urban History* 21 (May 1995): 395–427; F. P. Eichelberger, "The Cubans in Miami: Residential Movements and Ethnic Differentiation," M.A. Thesis, University of Cincinnati, 1974.

32. Morton D. Winsberg, "Housing Segregation of a Predominantly Middle-Class Population: Residential Patterns Developed by the Cuban Immigration into Miami, 1950–74," *American Journal of Economics and Sociology* 38 (October 1979): 403–18. See also Kerr, *Population Projections: Race and Hispanic Origin*; Morton D. Winsberg, "Ethnic Competition for Residential Space in Miami, Florida, 1970–1980," *American Journal of Economics and Sociology* 42 (July 1983): 305–14; B. E. Aguirre et al., "The Residential Patterning of Latin American and Other Ethnic Populations in Metropolitan Miami," *Latin American Research Review* 15.2 (1980): 35–63.

33. On public housing and Section-8 housing in Miami, see *Miami Herald* 16 August 1987; 3, 5, 13 May 1989; 25 September 1993; *Florida Times-Union* [Jacksonville] 17 August 1989; John Dorschner, "The Poisoned Garden," *Miami Herald, Tropic Magazine* 27 March 1988: 8–17, 23; and more generally, Irving Welfeld, *HUD Scandals: Howling Headlines and Silent Fiascos* (New Brunswick, NJ: Transaction Publishers, 1992).

34. Reimers, *Still the Golden Door* 163–65, 174–75; Masud-Piloto, *With Open Arms* 32–43; Michael J. McNally, *Catholicism in South Florida, 1868–1968* (Gainesville: University Presses of Florida, 1984) 127–66.

35. Silvia Pedraza-Bailey, *Political and Economic Migrants in America: Cubans and Mexicans* (Austin: U of Texas P, 1985) 40–52; James LeMoyne, "Most Who Left Mariel Sailed to New Life, a Few to Limbo," *New York Times* 15 April 1990: I 1. On the varied programs to resettle Cubans, see John F. Thomas, "Cuban Refugee Program," *Welfare in Review* 1 (September 1963): 1–20; John F. Thomas, "Cuban Refugees in the United States," *International Migration Review* 1 (Spring 1967): 46–57; Raul Moncarz, "Professional Adaptation of Cuban Physicians in the United States, 1959–1969," *International Migration Review* 4 (Spring 1970): 80–86; Raul Moncarz, "A Model of Professional Adaptation of Refugees: The Cuban Case in the U.S., 1959–1970," *International Migration* 11 (1973): 171–83; Joe Hall, *The Cuban Refu-*

*gee in the Public Schools of Dade County, Florida* (Miami: Dade County Board of Public Instruction, 1965).

36. For the CIA connection in Miami, see Didion, *Miami* 83–98; Rieff, *Going to Miami* 193–207; Cynthia Jo Rich, "Pondering the Future: Miami's Cubans After 15 Years," *Race Relations Reporter* 5 (November 1974): 7–9; Carlos A. Forment, "Political Practice and the Rise of an Ethnic Enclave: The Cuban-American Case, 1959–1979," *Theory and Practice* 18 (January 1989): 47–81; Warren Hinckle and William Turner, *The Fish Is Red: The Story of the Secret War Against Castro* (New York: Harper and Row, 1981). On the Bay of Pigs invasion, see Haynes Johnson, *The Bay of Pigs* (New York: Norton, 1964); Peter Wyden, *Bay of Pigs: The Untold Story* (New York: Simon and Schuster, 1979).

37. *Miami Times* 27 September 1968; 6, 27 February, 17 March, 13 August 1992; Wooten et al., *Psycho-Social Dynamics in Miami* 256–67; Herbert Burkholz, "The Latinization of Miami," *New York Times Magazine* 21 September 1980: 45–46, 84–88, 98–99. On the differential treatment of Haitian refugees, see Kevin Krajick, "Refugees Adrift: Barred from America's Shores," *Saturday Review* 27 October 1979: 17–20; Patrick Lacefield, "These Political Refugees Are from the Wrong Place," *In These Times* 7–13 November 1979: 11, 13; "Haitians, Stay Home!" *America* 16 May 1981: 398; Bill Frelick, "Haitians at Sea: Asylum Denied," *NACLA Report on the Americas* 26 (July 1992): 34–38; Lawrence H. Fuchs, "The Reactions of Black Americans to Immigration," *Immigration Reconsidered: History, Sociology, and Politics*, ed. Virginia Yans-McLaughlin (New York: Oxford UP, 1990) 293–314.

38. For Miami's Cuban exile politics, see Bill Baggs, "The Other Miami—City of Intrigue," *New York Times Magazine* 13 March 1960: 25, 84–87; Tad Szulc, "*Guerra!* Still the Word in Miami," *New York Times Magazine* 5 July 1964: 9, 14–15; Al Burt, "Cuban Exiles: The Mirage of Havana," *The Nation* 25 January 1965: 76–79; Horace Sutton, "The Curious Intrigues of Cuban Miami," *Saturday Review* 11 September 1973: 24–31; Lourdes Arguelles, "Cuban Miami: The Roots, Development, and Everyday Life of an Emigré Enclave in the U.S. National Security State," *Contemporary Marxism* 5 (Summer 1982): 27–43. On the shift to ethnic politics in Miami, see Paul D. Salter and Robert C. Mings, "The Projected Impact of Cuban Settlement on Voting Patterns in Metropolitan Miami, Florida," *Professional Geographer* 24 (May 1972): 123–32; Gerald R. Webster, "Factors in the Growth of Republican Voting in the Miami-Dade County SMSA," *Southeastern Geographer* 27 (May 1987): 1–17; Gerald R. Webster and Roberta Haven Webster, "Ethnicity and Voting in the Miami-Dade County SMSA," *Urban Geography* 8 (January-February 1987): 14–30; "Miami's Cubans—Getting a Taste for Politics," *U.S. News and World Report* 5 April 1976: 29; Dan Millott, "Cuban Thrust to the GOP," *New Florida* 1 (September 1981): 70–71; Alex Stepick, "Miami: Los Cubanos Han Ganado," *NACLA Report on the Americas* 26 (September 1992): 39–47.

39. "Florida," *Southern Political Reporter* 22 November 1983: 2. See also Guarione M. Diaz, *Ethnic Bloc Voting and Polarization in Miami* (Miami: Cuban American National Council, 1991); Raymond A. Mohl, "Ethnic Politics in Miami, 1960–1986," *Shades of the Sunbelt: Essays on Ethnicity, Race, and the Urban South*, ed. Randall M. Miller and George E. Pozzetta (Westport, CT: Greenwood Press, 1988) 143–60; Raymond A. Mohl, "Maurice Ferré, Xavier Suarez, and the Ethnic Factor in Miami Politics," *Spanish Pathways in Florida*, ed. Ann L. Henderson and Gary R. Mormino (Sarasota, FL: Pineapple Press, 1991) 303–27.

40. *Miami Times* 18 June, 30 July 1987; Mohl, "Ethnic Politics in Miami," 152–53; James Crawford, *Hold Your Tongue: Bilingualism and the Politics of "English Only"* (Reading, MA: Addison-Wesley, 1992) 90–120; Christopher L. Warren et al., "Minority Mobilization in an International City: Rivalry and Conflict in Miami," *PS* 19 (Summer 1986): 626–34. See also Christopher L. Warren and John F. Stack, Jr., "Immigration and the Politics of Ethnicity and Class in Metropolitan Miami," *The Primoridal Challenge: Ethnicity in the Contemporary World*, ed. John F. Stack, Jr. (Westport, CT: Greenwood Press, 1986) 61–79.

41. *Miami Times* 30 July 1987; Raymond A. Mohl, "Miami's Metropolitan Government: Retrospect and Prospect," *Florida Historical Quarterly* 63 (July 1984): 24–50.

42. *Miami Times* 23 February, 22 June 1989.

43. *Miami Times* 26, 27, 29 June, 9 August, 30 September, 12 November, 2 December 1990; 1, 28 July 1991; 13, 16 May 1993; *Miami Times* 14, 28 June, 5 July, 16, 23 August, 20, 27 December 1990; 30 April 1992; Sean Rowe, "The Quiet Riot," *New Times* [Miami] 26 September 1990: 12–22.

44. On perceptions about job displacement and the "Cuban takeover" generally, see Sheila L. Croucher, "Contested Reality: The Discourse of Job Displacement in Miami, Florida" (paper presented at Florida International University, Miami, 19 November 1992).

45. Stephan Palmié, "Spics or Spades? Racial Classification and Ethnic Conflict in Miami," *Amerikastudien/American Studies* 34.2 (1989): 211–21. See also Larry Mahoney, "The Cubans and the Blacks," *Miami Mensual* 5 (February 1985): 24–30, 90–94; 94; Carl Goldfarb, "Prejudice Felt by Latin Blacks," *Miami Herald* 30 June 1991: 1 B, 2 B. On the class and racial dimension of Cuban Miami, see Lisandro Pérez, "Immigrant Economic Adjustment and

Family Organization: The Cuban Success Story Reexamined," *International Migration Review* 20 (Spring 1986): 4–20; Heriberto Dixon, "A Look at the Social-Economic Adaptation of the Mariel Cubans," *Unveiling Cuba* 4 (July 1983): 4–7; Heriberto Dixon, "The Cuban-American Counterpoint: Black Cubans in the United States," *Dialectical Anthropology* 13 (1988): 227–39; Heriberto Dixon, "Variation from the Social Norm: Black Cubans in the United States, 1780–1980" (paper presented at annual meeting of the Organization of American Historians, Washington, DC, 24 March 1990). On Cubans and the local power structure, see Sylvan Meyer, "Cuban Power: Cracking the Anglo Structure," *Miami Magazine* 28 (August 1977): 22–27, 47; and the *Miami Herald*'s series, "Miami's Power Elite," *Miami Herald* 31 January, 1, 2, 3, 4, 5, 6 February 1988.

46. Bruce Porter and Marvin Dunn, "A Year After the Miami Riot, Embers Still Glow," *New York Times* 17 May 1981: E 23. On the "political economy of racism," see Manning Marable, "The Fire This Time: The Miami Rebellion, May, 1980," *The Black Scholar* 11 (July-August 1980): 2–18. See also Susan Harrigan and Charles W. Stevens, "Roots of a Riot," *Wall Street Journal* 22 May 1980: A 26.

47. Lisandro Pérez, "Where Analysts of the 1980 Miami Riot Went Astray," Letter to Editor in *New York Times* 5 June 1981: 15 A. See also Sergio Lopez-Miro, "Shattering a Few Latin-Black Myths in South Florida," *Miami Herald* 14 February 1989: 15 A; Anthony Ramirez, "Making It," *Wall Street Journal* 20 May 1980: 1, 35.

48. Barry B. Levine, "Miami: The Capital of Latin America," *The Wilson Quarterly* 9 (Winter 1985): 46–73.

49. Frank Soler, "Thoughts from a Wounded Heart," *Miami Mensual* 5 (August 1985): 11; Robert Joffe, "Riot Politics: The Tokenism Aftermath," *South Florida* 42 (May 1989): 32.

50. Irwin S. Morse, Letter to the Editor, *Miami Herald* 24 July 1989: 14 A; Croucher, "Contested Reality" 22.

America has created a new form of urban settlement. It is higher, bolder, and richer than anything man has yet called city.

. . . Most Americans still speak of suburbs. But a city's suburbs are no longer just bedrooms. They are no longer mere orbital satellites. They are no longer *sub*.

—JACK ROSENTHAL, "The Outer City: U.S. in Suburban Turmoil," *New York Times*

Postsuburban regions have become the most common form of metropolitan development in this country. And this emergence has undeniably transformed our lives.

—KLING, OLIN, AND POSTER, eds., *Postsuburban California*

# Bold New City or Built-up 'Burb? Redefining Contemporary Suburbia

*William Sharpe and Leonard Wallock*

In the last few decades, the United States has become a suburban nation. Between 1950 and 1980 the number of people living in suburbia nearly tripled, soaring from 35.2 to 101.5 million. By 1990, almost half of all Americans called suburbia home.[1] But whereas the typical commuter suburbs of the 1950s were almost entirely residential, today's suburbs feature corporate headquarters, high-tech industries, and superregional malls. Consequently, about twice as many people now commute to work within suburbs as commute between them and cities.[2] Rapidly expanding suburbs contain more office space than downtowns and most of the new jobs.[3] As a result, suburbs are in the forefront of American economic development and are far less dependent upon cities than before.[4]

Such explosive growth is having a profound impact on both the landscape and people's conception of suburban life. Condominium projects, office complexes, and industrial parks abound; crowded eight-lane highways lead to commercial strips and vast shopping malls; medical

*William Sharpe is associate professor of English at Barnard College. Leonard Wallock teaches in the Interdisciplinary Humanities Center at the University of California at Santa Barbara. Reprinted from* American Quarterly 46 (March 1994): 1–30. *Reprinted by permission of the Johns Hopkins University Press.*

facilities and research centers compete to develop open land. Cultural centers, sports arenas, and multiplex cinemas have proliferated across an increasingly built-up terrain. Meanwhile, the image of the suburb as a pastoral haven from the harsh realities of the city has been shattered by the spread of homelessness, drug addiction, and crime. Relentlessly, the countryside appears to be urbanizing. The city, with its attendant problems and pleasures, seems to be coming to the suburbs.

The rapid transformation of the landscape has prompted critics to redefine the very nature of suburbia and to contend that built-up areas on the urban fringe have become cities in their own right. Some have even declared that suburbia is dead. This article reviews the current literature in order to assess the accuracy of the latest representations of suburbs and to determine the degree to which the social practices and ideals of traditional suburbia still survive.

As we will show, there has been a turnabout in the way suburbs are perceived. During the last two decades, some analysts of contemporary suburbs have begun to sound like apologists. In the 1950s, 1960s, and early 1970s, critics vigorously attacked suburbia for its racial discrimination, patriarchal familism, political separatism, and geographical sprawl and earnestly proposed solutions to overcome these ills. Such influential works as Betty Friedan's *The Feminine Mystique* (1963), Anthony Downs's *Opening Up the Suburbs* (1973), Richard Babcock and Fred Bosselman's *Exclusionary Zoning* (1973), and Michael Danielson's *The Politics of Exclusion* (1976) measured the social costs of suburban life. Many accounts stressed the disastrous consequences of suburban development for both the inner city and the nearby countryside.

By contrast, in the 1980s and early 1990s, critics recognized that the problems caused by suburbanization remained unsolved, but they implicitly accepted, and in some cases enthusiastically embraced, suburbia on its own terms. Indeed, the willingness even to consider the "new city" as a utopia in the making—albeit a "bourgeois utopia"—implies that a truly searching critique of it is unnecessary.[5] Margaret Marsh has defined the best postwar studies of suburbia as those that "attempt to understand suburban communities from the point of view of the suburbanites."[6] Yet such sympathetic treatments, accepting suburban ideology at face value, may sacrifice their own critical distance. This is to a large extent what has happened with the current generation of critics; their conceptualization of the "new city" has been influenced by their own suburbanophilia.

As we will argue, the current literature reflects a skewed perception of city and suburb alike. Section one of our essay outlines the evolution, since the 1970s, of the idea that suburbs have become cities. Section two challenges that claim by pointing to the continuing social segregation within suburbs, a pattern that contemporary critics tend to minimize because they employ functional criteria—such as the increase in office space and retail trade—to measure suburban development. Although suburbs have assumed many of the functions of traditional cities, they are not fully comparable to cities. Nor have they become independent entities. In our view, equating suburbs with cities implies that suburbs possess a diversity, cosmopolitanism, political culture, and public life that most of them still lack and that most cities still afford.

Section three of this essay maintains that recent analysts have misrepresented the actual character of suburbia because they have too readily accepted certain mainstays of suburban ideology. They perpetuate the myths of suburbia's accessibility to all Americans, its suitability for women, and its harmony with nature, despite evidence that it excludes "undesirables," offers inadequate opportunities for women, and has a destructive impact on the environment.

Responding to the claim that "suburbia is dead," section four employs cultural rather than functional criteria to illustrate the tenacity of traditional suburban values. Just as the social exclusivity of suburbia has survived, so too have the fundamental attitudes associated with the "classic" American suburb of the 1950s. One indication of how suburban ideals persist can be found in prime-time television shows and Hollywood films; despite the increasing variety and complexity of their characters, they frequently promote the stereotyped gender roles and social hierarchies of the early postwar years. Only by considering the cultural and social context in which functional changes occur can scholars hope to assess the status of suburbia today.

## The Name Game

Over the last twenty years, journalists and scholars have coined a new set of terms to redefine the changing American suburb. In the early 1970s, as concern about the inner-city crisis waned and the decentralization of the metropolis reached new proportions, "the urbanization of the suburbs" suddenly became a topic of national interest.[7] The ensuing flurry of articles and books[8] introduced neologisms such as "outer city," "satellite sprawl," "new city," "suburban 'city,'" "urban fringe," and "neocity" to describe this phenomenon.[9]

If, two decades ago, commentators were taken with the novelty of urbanized suburbs, currently they are stressing the urbanized character of entire regions and their multinucleated form. This shift in emphasis was prompted by the unprecedented scope and pace of suburbanization itself, which called into question the urban-centered models of metropolitan development.[10] By 1991, Mark Gottdiener and George Kephart were using the phrase "multinucleated metropolitan regions" to describe "fully urbanized and independent spaces that are not dominated by any central city."[11]

Whether they focus on particular suburban towns or entire metropolitan regions, observers are unanimous in their belief that suburbs are becoming cities—though of a new sort. This is especially evident in the literature announcing the birth of the "new city." In 1981, Peter Muller called suburbia "the essence of the late twentieth century American city," and found that its "burgeoning new centers" have further transformed it "into an increasingly independent and dominant *outer city*." This transformation, he asserted, "represents . . . a wholly new metropolitan reality."[12] In 1986, Christopher B. Leinberger and Charles Lockwood argued that suburban "focal points," such as Century City in Los Angeles, constitute "urban village" cores "amid a low-density cityscape."[13] For them, each core represents "a kind of new downtown— where the buildings are tallest, the daytime population largest, and the traffic congestion most severe."[14] Similarly, in 1987, architectural critic Paul Goldberger maintained that suburban centers are "outlying versions of downtown that have sprung up outside urban cores."[15] Declaring that "the major urban form of our age" is "the outtown," he described it as an automobile-oriented, "new-style commercial center" located in places such as Post Oak near Houston and White Plains near New York.

The most sustained arguments for the urban character of suburbia have been provided by Robert Fishman and Joel Garreau. In *Bourgeois Utopias*, Fishman uses examples such as Route 128 outside of Boston and the Route 1 corridor between Princeton and New Brunswick in New Jersey to contend that

> the most important feature of postwar American development has been the almost simultaneous decentralization of housing, industry, specialized services, and office jobs; the consequent breakaway of the urban periphery from a central city it no longer needs; and the creation of a decentralized environment that nevertheless possesses all the economic and technological dynamism we associate with the city. This phenomenon, as remarkable as it is unique, is not suburbanization but a *new city*.[16]

For Fishman, suburbs become self-sufficient cities when they achieve a "critical mass" of population, industry, construction, and services. Although they lack the "dominant single core and definable boundaries"[17] that distinguish traditional downtowns, their "real structure is aptly expressed by the circular superhighways or beltways" that encircle them.[18] These beltways link various parts of the urban periphery "without passing through the central city at all."[19] Because the economy of such vast peripheral zones thrives on high-tech industry and operates via highway growth corridors and electronic networks, Fishman calls them "technoburbs."[20] As a result of being bypassed both physically and electronically, "the old central cities have become increasingly marginal, while the technoburb has emerged as the focus of American life."[21]

Building on Fishman's work, Garreau's *Edge City: Life on the New Frontier* is the first book devoted to the cultural significance of the new urban-style developments on the periphery of metropolitan America.[22] Among his prime examples are the Camelback Corridor north of Phoenix, the Perimeter Center north of Atlanta, and the Bridgewater Mall area at the junction of Interstates 287 and 78 in New Jersey. He calls these settlements "edge cities" because they are burgeoning on the "frontiers" of the urban landscape, and they contain "all of the functions a city ever has, albeit in a spread-out form."[23] According to Garreau, this "vigorous world of pioneers and immigrants, rising far from the old downtowns," has emerged "where little save villages or farmland lay only thirty years before." Like Fishman, Garreau views his emerging "city" as a manifestation of the long-standing American desire, best expressed by Frank Lloyd Wright, to integrate work, residence, and leisure within the natural environment. This "new, restorative synthesis," Garreau maintains, has "smashed the very idea behind suburbia" as "a place apart."[24] Thus, Garreau's view that peripheral development reunites the workplaces and homes of the middle class extends Fishman's claim that "in this transformed urban ecology the history of suburbia comes to an end."[25]

## Have Suburbs Become Cities?

What are the implications of claiming that suburbs have now assumed an urban identity? Most importantly, the competition to baptize the "new city" deflects attention from the enduring social realities behind the ephemeral nomenclature. Designations such as Goldberger's "outtowns" and Leinberger and Lockwood's "urban villages," while implying the independence of suburbs from cities, tell nothing about the social, cultural, and political identity of these settlements. Their coiners are curiously silent about some of the most pronounced features of the contemporary suburb. By focusing on morphology and aesthetics, they play down suburban parochialism and separatism. In the process, they lose sight of the fact that, historically, suburbs have sought to preserve social homogeneity and masculine authority. And, in defining the "new city," critics misrepresent what by implication is the "old" one; they forget that it possesses social and cultural heterogeneity still absent from much of suburbia. This section challenges the "urbanity" that has been claimed for built-up 'burbs by looking at their racial and class segregation. As we will demonstrate, the functional criteria used by those who regard suburbs as cities lead them to understate the social exclusivity of suburbs, while overstating their cultural variety.

Advocates of the "new cities"—such as Muller, Fishman, and Garreau—contend that suburbs have broken away from the older central cities that spawned them. But the relation between the contemporary suburbs and the central cities is one of continued *inter*dependence. In *The New Suburbanization*, Thomas M. Stanback, Jr., illustrates how even today "city and suburb, linked in a symbiotic yet competitive relationship, together constitute an economic system—the metropolitan economy."[26] The central city depends heavily on the suburban workforce, while at the same time it sends a considerable number of its own residents to jobs in outlying areas. The urban and suburban sectors of the metropolitan economy constantly exchange goods and services; for example, branch stores and back offices on the periphery are linked to retail and corporate headquarters based downtown. The greatest proof of their interdependence can be found in the location of the "new cities"; they flourish on the outskirts of established urban centers.[27] As Jean Gottmann observes, "these 'emerging cities' in suburban areas" are "really satellites of major central cities."[28] For all the fanfare, suburbs have not achieved full autonomy.

Furthermore, the socioeconomic character of suburbs has not changed fundamentally. In the past few decades, the suburbs have grown markedly more diverse, but overall they remain heavily segregated by race and class. The traditional bedroom suburb of the 1950s was the home of young, white, middle-class families. By the 1970s, however, a single suburban type no longer predominated. Instead, as Muller shows, there was a wide range of community types: upper-income suburbs, middle-class suburbs, working-class suburbs, suburban cosmopolitan centers, and even black suburbs.[29] Yet, despite such diversification, suburbia has remained an essentially exclusive domain. For example, in 1980, blacks constituted just 6.1 percent of suburbanites, as compared to 23.4 percent of city dwellers. That same year, only 8.2 percent of suburbanites reported incomes below the federal poverty line, as compared to 17.2 percent of city residents. Minorities and the poor are still excluded from most suburbs; even when they do relocate to suburbia, they usually settle in heavily segregated areas. "Whether for reasons of race, insufficient income, or both," Muller says, "these populations are widely refused access to the voluntary congregations of mainstream suburbia and are compelled to cluster behind powerful social barriers in the least desirable living environments of the outer city."[30]

Neither the mere presence nor the growing proportion of minority groups and poor people within suburbs should necessarily be taken as evidence of "urbanization."[31] Aggregate population figures provide few clues to the pattern—let alone the extent—of social interaction occurring within a community.[32] In their introduction to *Postsuburban California*, Rob Kling, Spencer Olin, and Mark Poster make much of the Hispanic and Asian presence in Orange County and its role in bringing about a "shift from provincialism to cosmopolitanism." Yet, in 1980, the population of Orange County was 87.2 percent white, its poverty level was a mere 5.2 percent, and its minority groups were residing in distinct concentrations: Hispanics in Santa Ana, Asians in Westminster and Garden Grove. As Gottdiener and Kephart point out, "this type of [population] distribution contrasts markedly with that in traditional urban centers, which are more racially heterogeneous, even if they are in many cases fragmented into segregated areas."[33] Moreover, the traditional centers—with their compact downtowns, public spaces, social institutions, and mass transportation—still generate a greater intermingling of diverse groups than occurs in multicentered, automobile-oriented "new cities." Eric E. Lampard captured how segregation persists in contemporary suburban America when he wrote in 1983 that "the population was relentlessly spreading out *via* superhighways and freeways into 'defensible,' low density, residential space . . . graded by socioeconomic class, age, and affinity."[34]

The increasing movement of minorities out of the cities has not substantially diminished racial segregation in suburbs, particularly between blacks and whites. The migration of blacks to the suburbs began to pick up in the late 1960s and accelerated rapidly during the next decade. Between 1970 and 1980, the number of black suburbanites rose an average of 4 percent annually. In comparison, the population of white suburbanites grew at a rate of only 1.5 percent. Consequently, the proportion of all suburbanites who were black climbed from 4.8 percent in 1970 to 6.1 percent in 1980.[35] At the same time, the proportion of all blacks residing in suburbs jumped from 16 to 21 percent. Yet when John Logan and Mark Schneider examined data on over 1,600 incorporated suburbs in forty-four metropolitan regions for 1970 and 1980, they found that black suburbanization had "followed well-established patterns of segregation."[36] Commenting on this phenomenon, Douglas Massey and Nancy Denton noted in 1988 that "once a suburb acquires a visible black presence, it tends to attract more blacks than whites, which leads to neighborhood secession and the emergence of a black enclave."[37] Citing a half-dozen studies conducted between the mid-seventies and mid-eighties, they concluded that "suburban secession and segregation" were still being "generated through a variety of individual and institutional mechanisms, including redlining, restrictive zoning, organized resistance to black entry, and racial steering."[38]

The growing presence of poor people beyond the city limits has not reduced suburban class segregation. The migration outward of the urban poor began in the 1960s.[39] Suburbanites living below the poverty line amounted to 5,199,000 (or 7.1 percent) by 1970 and rose to 7,377,000 (or 8.2 percent) by 1980. The uneven distribution of poor people among suburbs is indicated by the large differential in per-capita income between suburbs. A Rand Corporation study noted that

> the ten suburbs with the richest residents, including Grosse Point Farms (MI), Beverly Hills (CA), and Scarsdale (NY), had average per-capita incomes of over $15,000 in 1977, but the ten places with the poorest populations—East St. Louis (MO), Mission (Hidalgo County, TX), and Compton (CA), among others—showed [incomes of] less than $4,000 per capita.[40]

By 1989, the differences in per-capita income between suburbs had grown much larger and the number of suburbanites earning incomes below the poverty line had risen to 9.5 million. Summing up these trends, *Newsweek* declared that "whites still constitute a majority of poor suburbanites. But minorities—25 percent of all black suburbanites and 22 percent of Hispanics—are the most severely affected: they are increasingly clustered in heavily segregated suburbs. . . ."[41]

What accounts for these segregated patterns and exclusionary practices? "White flight" has contributed heavily to the mushrooming growth of the suburbs. The reasons why white middle-class Americans have left the cities in large numbers since the Second World War are familiar: the desire to flee crime, drugs, poor schools, expensive housing, and high taxes, as well as the quest for better jobs, home ownership, clean air, recreational space, and a safer place to raise children. That suburbanites effectively wall out those unlike themselves after arriving, however, suggests that a major force driving their migration is the wish to escape racial and class intermingling.[42] In the United States, upward mobility and social status are predicated on living apart from racial and economic groups considered inferior. As Michael N. Danielson remarks in *The Politics of Exclusion*, "most Americans . . . are convinced that a decent home, nice neighborhood, and good schools depend heavily on the absence of lower-income and minority groups."[43] Thus it is not simply the racism of individuals but also the collectively perceived threat that race and class differences pose to home ownership and social standing that drives suburbanites to keep their territory segregated.[44]

Recent observers understate the significance of suburbia's segregation because they conceptualize the so-called "new city" in largely physical and technological terms. Their chief measures are the extent of its housing, jobs, office space, and shopping. For Leinberger and Lockwood, "high-rise office buildings and hotels, increasingly sophisticated shopping, and high-density housing" signal the presence of "urban-village cores."[45] Similarly, for Goldberger the "outtown" is defined by "strange clusters of office towers and shopping malls and hotels and condominiums that are away from downtowns."[46] Garreau also uses criteria that are "above all else meant to be functional" when he defines his "edge city"; it must have at least five million square feet of leasable office space, at least 600,000 square feet of leasable retail space, and more jobs than bedrooms. In addition, it must "be perceived by the population as one place . . . that 'has it all,' from jobs, to shopping, to entertainment."[47]

At least five writers—Muller, Leinberger and Lockwood, Fishman, and Garreau—also argue that a "critical mass" of such attributes transforms a suburb into a city. "The complex economy of the former suburbs has now reached a critical mass," Fishman writes. "These multifunctional late-20th-century 'suburbs' . . . have become a new kind of city."[48] This line of thought suggests that a certain quantitative change in the economy and built environment—the sheer agglomeration of services, jobs, and buildings—has generated a qualitative transformation that yields the "new city." This is the suburb as nuclear reactor, complete with "core" and "critical mass."[49]

The nuclear metaphor points to the technocratic fallacy operating in these accounts. By stressing the infrastructure rather than the human element in defining cities, these writers minimize the social interaction and cultural variety that are a crucial part of urban life. Like "critical mass," Fishman's neologism "technoburb" focuses on the high-tech economies of industrialized suburban areas, as well as on the transportation and communication networks that make it possible for them to exist apart from cities. Implying that advances in science and engineering make deconcentration inevitable, the term "technoburb" conceals the purposefully segregated arangement of this brave new world. For, as Andrea Oppenheimer Dean and others have pointed out, "the new suburban cities" possess "one thing in common: they are growing in white, upper-middle-class areas."[50]

The preoccupation with functional rather than social measures of urbanity extends even to matters of culture, which those who argue for the "new city" define in terms of consumption. In *Postsuburban California*, Kling, Olin, and Poster describe Orange County as having a well-developed "cosmopolitan culture," which turns out to be based on the existence of

> a ready clientele for ethnic restaurants, European and Japanese cars, a wide variety of imported goods, and cultural events such as modern theater, foreign films, and classical music. Not satisfied with mainstream goods and services that were available in their neighborhood shopping centers, these residents were willing to patronize establishments virtually anywhere in the county that catered to their tastes.[51]

The presence of words like "clientele," "shopping," "patronize," and "cater" reveals that this culture is fully commodified, and the sequence in which the consumables are presented suggests that restaurants and cars have more cachet than the arts. The suspicion that fine dining and consumption have become the indispensable marks of urban culture is confirmed when Fishman proclaims that "the new city is a city *à la carte*."[52]

Far from promoting cosmopolitanism, the culture of consumption merely reinforces the homogeneity it supposedly erodes. Consumer culture is built to conformist standards because it must appeal to many people to achieve commercial success. At the same time that it solidifies group identity, however, status-conscious consumerism also magnifies the social distinctions that mark off one group from another. Ultimately, such "cosmopolitanism" contributes to the conformity and exclusivity that typify contemporary suburbs. As Goldberger complains about Orange County, this is "community as product more than community as place."[53]

Just as suburban consumption is equated with cosmopolitan culture, so too private malls dedicated to profit are likened to downtown public space.[54] "Superregional malls are the suburban counterparts of Main Street," writes Muller.[55] They constitute "a virtual one-stop culture," notes William S. Kowinski, "providing a cornucopia of products nestled in an ecology of community, entertainment, and societal identity."[56] In the mall, a palace of consumption takes on the appearance of a civic arena. With fountains and benches, healthmobiles and community information booths, malls convey the impression that they are enclosed versions of town squares. But the mall is not a new downtown; it is private property masquerading as public space. In this policed enclosure, where spending is the only alternative to loitering, the rights of assembly and free speech are not guaranteed as they would be in a city park or square. With its travertine "boulevards" that serve as sanitized streets, the mall is a controlled, artificial environment that screens out undesirable persons and weather and even the passage of time.[57] However much it may assume the guise of a public forum or community center, the entire enterprise is fundamentally dedicated to promoting consumption.

The ability of malls to keep out "undesirables" extends to suburbia as a whole. Because incorporated suburbs have their own governments and services, they bear a superficial likeness to cities. But one of the underlying reasons why suburbanites sought to establish their political independence in the first place was to pass laws to restrict access to outsiders and to preserve a low-density landscape. As Jon C. Teaford remarks, "through the exercise of municipal zoning powers, each of these newly-incorporated communities could exclude whatever seemed obnoxious or threatening."[58] Over the years, the suburbs have devised an array of defensive zoning measures, from the regulation of building lot sizes and construction procedures to prohibitions on multiple dwellings. "Restrictive techniques of land-use control are both innumerable and interchangeable," Richard F. Babcock and Fred P. Bosselman explained in the 1970s. "If a particular device is invalidated it is often easy for the town to substitute a different device that has the same depressing effect."[59] The still widespread stipulation that new housing take the form of single-family homes on large lots pushes up prices and effectively keeps out lower-income groups, in which racial minorities are disproportionately represented. Once established, this socioeconomic uniformity is self-perpetuating. What Danielson found in the 1970s remains true today: "Most suburban jurisdictions are small and have relatively homogeneous populations, which makes it easier to secure consensus on exclusionary policies than is commonly the case in larger and more heterogeneous cities."[60] Thus, for all the claims of "outer city" cosmopolitanism, suburban social engineering succeeds precisely because suburbs continue to lack—and actively resist—the varied populations and interests that distinguish urban centers.

## Suburbanophilia

Evidence that the "old" suburbia still flourishes can be found in the way its ideals tacitly inform discussion of the "new city." Believing that the suburban way of life holds promise and hoping that the problems of the old suburbia will disappear in the new, recent critics sometimes sound like boosters. For example, although they acknowledge the barriers that restrict entry into suburbs, some authors discuss housing, commuting, and "lifestyle" options available to many suburbanites as though these choices were open to all. The notion that choice is now a key ingredient of suburbia has been developed most fully by Fishman, who contends that in the technoburbs, "families create their own 'cities' out of the destinations they can reach (usually travelling by car) in a reasonable length of time."[61] Only traffic congestion, he argues, can deny "the ready access that is a hallmark of the new city."[62] Ready access for whom? The rhetoric of free choice negates—but in no way alters—the segregated reality of suburban life.

Kling, Olin, and Poster also disguise the barriers to access within suburbs. They imply the absence of racial and class segregation in Orange County when they mention the minorities living there only as an example of the county's cosmopolitanism. For them, the tightly clustered ethnic enclaves of Garden Grove, Westminster, and Santa Ana exist by virtue of free choice rather than socioeconomic constraint; these communities are regarded as significant only because of their abundance of ethnic restaurants and cafés. Defining cosmopolitanism in terms of cuisine, they maintain that poor Mexicans and Vietnamese who eat their native food at home enjoy a "more genuine . . . cosmopolitan consumption" than is "accessible to a white diner."[63] Thus, by reducing minority cultures to a matter of culinary expertise and by overlooking the unequal status of minorities in other respects, Kling, Olin, and Poster manage to suggest that the only people without full access in Orange County are members of the white, privileged classes.[64] The euphemisms they employ to conclude their analysis—such as "segmentation" for segregation and "tensions" for social conflict—betray their awareness of the county's divided character.[65] Nevertheless, they treat racial and class fragmentation as though it were evidence of Orange County's "impressive mingling of diverse cultures."[66]

Another example of the tendency among critics to make the best of suburbia lies in their belief that, by its very nature, the "new city" liberates suburban women from the domestic servitude of the past. Since the late 1950s, a sharply rising proportion of married women has been employed outside the home, especially in retail trade and back-office jobs. According to Fishman, the increased availability of jobs close to home that offer decent pay and permit flexible schedules has been "responsible for the remarkable influx of married women into the work force." He believes that the "new city . . . decisively breaks with the older suburban pattern that restricted married middle-class women with children to a life of neighborhood-oriented domesticity." For this reason, Fishman concludes, "the economic and spatial structure of the new city tends to equalize gender roles."[67] Garreau goes even further to claim that his "Edge City" represents "the empowerment of women."[68]

But, while women may appear to be freer in the "new city," the fact of their paid employment does not guarantee an end to their exploitation. Given the continuing expectation that they will do most of the housework and provide most of the child care—not to mention chauffeuring the children—their opportunity to labor outside the home carries with it an invitation to perform double duty.[69] Moreover, the jobs they usually fill—whether in retail sales or electronic sweatshops—offer low pay, few benefits, inadequate day care, and little security or chance of promotion to managerial positions.[70] Even worse, the word- and data-processing jobs that constitute the mainstay of today's "information factories" are hazardous to health: "Women complain of physical problems such as eye strain, fatigue, even radiation exposure,"[71] in addition to new levels of stress brought on by computer monitoring of their performance.[72] It is true that married middle-class suburban women are no longer restricted to being homebound caretakers of house, children, and commuting husband. Yet, even if the "imposed domesticity of the 50s" is disappearing, the expanding role of middle-class suburban women in the labor force has not rescued them from their subordinate status.[73]

Some observers also paint a deceptively rosy picture of suburbia when they portray it in temporal, not spatial, terms. Garreau writes that "Edge Cities are not created in units of distance, but in units of time."[74] Similarly, Fishman contends that "the essential element in the structure of the new city" is that it is "a megalopolis based on *time* rather than space."[75] This formulation uses driving time as the main measure of distances that are too large to cover on foot. By transferring attention from the geographical extent of the built environment to the length of time required to traverse it by car, these critics gloss over the physical vastness of the new conurbations. Yet, given the complex patterns of commuting, shopping, and socializing engaged in by suburbanites and the considerable distances that they travel, space has become all the more important as a measure of suburban sprawl. As Gottdiener notes, "with the . . . increase in spatial scale interjecting itself in economic, political and cultural activities," the only way to comprehend these "massive multi-centered regions" is by focusing on spatial relations.[76] Maps and aerial views clearly show that contemporary stretch suburbs are consuming ever-greater quantities of once-open land.

Minimizing the suburban hunger for space also helps to sustain the myth that suburbs are ecologically balanced environments. Fishman envisions the "new city" as forming "a marriage of town and country, a reconciliation of nature and the man-made world."[77] Garreau likewise imagines "a newfound union of nature and art" enjoying marital bliss along the interstate. But he claims even more for Edge City, describing it as "the most purposeful attempt Americans have made since the days of the Founding Fathers . . . to create something like a new Eden."[78] Yet there is a snake in this garden, one brought in by the gardeners themselves. Their Wrightian celebration of wide-open green spaces cannot hide the fact that suburbanization is an ecologically devastating mode of life, one that savages the nature in which it nests. Bulldozing open acres in the name of a spurious balance between human beings and nature, developers gobble up land, carving deeper and deeper into the countryside. Each new suburb is built to reclaim the green tranquillity that the overbuilding of the last suburb has already destroyed.[79] Wanting to believe that suburban growth will lead us "back to the garden," post-Woodstock critics fail to expose the peculiar logic of suburbanization: that leapfrogging suburbs recreate the very conditions that suburbanites flee.

What critics in the 1970s were unable to do, and those in the 1980s and 1990s seem unwilling to attempt, is to *desuburbanize* their thinking: to transcend the traditional American mindset that regards moving ever outward—from cities to suburbs, to exurbs and beyond—as the final answer to any problem, from urban decline to peripheral congestion.[80] Rather than accept continued suburbanization and its destructive consequences as inevitable, and rather than treat as natural the subordination of one part of the metropolis to another, critics need to think in regional terms.

Critics in the 1960s were quasi-regionalist in approach; they treated the suburbs as dependent upon the city and thus necessarily focused on the interaction between the two. Yet most of them did not have a vision of the role that outlying rural land would play—both for development and refuge from it—as suburbanization continued. Responding to the unprecedented growth of suburbs since then, recent analysts, with their urban-based neologisms and assertions of suburban autonomy, have tended to regard the suburbs as a bold new world no longer connected to the city and free to encroach on the exurbs. In order to reach a more balanced and accurate understanding of today's cities and suburbs— where conditions are very different from those of the immediate postwar period—we need to devise a new paradigm that brings their interactive relation back into focus while also considering the part played by vulnerable exurbs. Currently, critics overlook the one-sidedness of their analysis; they discuss access without mentioning restriction, time without considering space, women's opportunities without comparing them to men's, the planting of gardens without the razing of forests. They forget that suburbia does not constitute a world unto itself but a particular place and set of attitudes created in response to the *overall* metropolitan context.

This compartmentalizing of life in suburbia, setting it apart from the metropolitan region as a whole, mirrors the segregated character of the suburbs themselves.[81] Fishman, Garreau, and others regard the "new city" not as an *underlying cause* but as the *ultimate solution* to the problems plaguing urbanized regions. Thus they reverse the way scholars and journalists viewed suburbs in the 1950s and 1960s. This reversal is due not only to the conservative course that national politics took during the 1980s and the continuing suburbanization of the United States but also to the life experiences of the critics themselves, many of whom were born, raised, or now reside in suburbia.[82] Having given up on the "old city" as a place where social equity and ecological balance may be achieved, they have extolled a verdant "new city"—rather like the emerald one in *The Wizard of Oz*—where their dreams of an ideal society may be realized. Their search for redemption through nature and salvation on the frontier places them within a long American cultural tradition. But as Dorothy and Toto discovered, there is a lot more show than substance to the Emerald City.

## Is Suburban Ideology Dead?

Because critics rely on functional rather than cultural criteria to proclaim the birth of the "new city," they forget that the "old" suburbia represented something more than a bedroom community. Focusing on changes in the suburban infrastructure enables Fishman to declare that "suburbia in its traditional sense now belongs to the past."[83] Similarly, Marsh's emphasis on new patterns in suburban family life—especially "wives holding jobs outside the home"—permits her to assert that "the suburban domestic ideal . . . no longer holds sway."[84] Both conclusions assume that functional and behavioral changes rapidly ensure liberating ideological ones. The patterns of employment and commuting that defined "classic suburbia"—where the white middle-class housewife and mother was sequestered at home while her husband worked in the city— may have evolved. But the fundamental attitudes underlying this way of life remain potent.[85] They include belief in female subordination, class

stratification, and racial segregation, all wrapped up in a pastoral my-
thology. Nearly two hundred years in the making, suburban ideals are
still widespread.[86] They continue to influence social behavior, particularly through mass culture media, and must be taken into account when
analyzing the status of the suburbs today. As this section will demonstrate, television and film have helped keep the "old" suburbia alive.

Representations that reinforce suburban ideals abound both on television and in the movies. Televised images of suburbia are so prevalent
that they now operate simultaneously on many levels. Programs affec-
tionately recalling earlier eras—such as "The Wonder Years" (1988–1993),
a sitcom which portrays the white-bread homogeneity of a boy's suburban schooldays in the 1960s—coexist with reruns of the original 1950s
celebrations of suburban life—such as "Leave It to Beaver" (1957–1963)
and "Father Knows Best" (1954–1962), where dads dispense sage advice to compliant wives and children. These visions of suburban yester-
year are complemented by programs that depict white middle-class life
today. Among them are "Growing Pains" (1985–1992), which has been
called a "Father Knows Best" for the 1980s, and "Family Ties" (1982–
1989), a role-reversal comedy featuring a teenage son who worships
William F. Buckley, Jr., espouses Reaganomics, and strives to bring his
ex-hippie parents more in line with conventional suburban values. Finally, shows such as "Married . . . with Children" (1987– ), "The
Simpsons" (1990– ), and "Dinosaurs" (1992– ) parody the now-classic
suburban sitcoms of the 1950s only to recreate in detail for new audiences the very conventions of suburban life they ostensibly subvert.

Cinematic treatments of suburbia offer a similar assortment of takes
on a patriarchal world. In the nostalgic *Peggy Sue Got Married* (1986),
an unhappily wed suburban mother of the 1980s magically returns to
her youth, where she passively reenters the relationship that will en-
trap her. Films dating from the "golden age" of suburbia, such as *Mr.
Blandings Builds His Dream House* (1948) and *The Man in the Gray
Flannel Suit* (1956), focus sympathetically on the struggle of commuting husbands to maintain their wives and children in pastoral splendor.
Contemporary comedies of domestic crisis, such as *Home Alone* (1991)
and *Suburban Commando* (1991), shore up the embattled patriarchy by
relying on stand-in fathers, whether from grammar school or outer space,
to protect the home and community against outsiders. Golden-age suburbia has also been the subject of film parodies like *Edward Scissorhands*
(1990), which, in the midst of recounting a cruel fairy tale of suburban
ostracism, still fondly reimagines the quaint conformity and rigid gender roles of tract-house life.

Television has played an especially decisive part in the social construction of suburbia. Television came of age during the suburban boom
of the 1950s, and, as a home-based form of entertainment, it soon
emerged as the perfect vehicle to sell the suburban lifestyle—with its
fixation on good housekeeping, the newest appliances, and a late-model
car—to a national audience.[87] Television shows and advertisements offered consumer items and behavioral models designed to be attractive
to all members of the family. Erasing time as easily as space, television

represented consumer-oriented suburbia, with its housebound mothers and commuting fathers, as both perennial and universal; in the early 1960s, the cartoon series "The Flintstones" (1960–1966) and "The Jetsons" (1962–1963) imagined gadget-conscious suburban life as the ultimate human condition, from the stone age to the space age.

To be sure, the effect of television as a socializing agent is much disputed by theoreticians of mass media. While earlier analysts regarded consumers as passive recipients of capitalist brainwashing, more recently, proponents of the "uses and gratifications" approach have contended that television viewers are "actively judging and deciding subjects," who manipulate visual images rather than being manipulated by them.[88] But both of these positions overstate the case. The crux of the matter is, as Stephen Heath points out, that experience and reality "are not separate from but are also determined by television which is a fundamental part of them. . . . [They] are complexly defined, mediated, [and] realized in new ways in which the power of the media is crucial."[89] Thus, rather than regarding the viewer as incapable of resisting or interpreting images, it makes more sense to view television reception as a partly determined, partly determinative process. As Ella Taylor puts it, television images "both echo and participate in the shaping of cultural trends."[90]

Representations of suburban life on television help hold social practices in place by sanctioning classic suburban patterns of consumption, social exclusivity, and familial relations. In the 1990s, many television programs continue to reinforce the myth of suburbia as a haven in which white middle-class families live sheltered from the ills of the city.[91] Not only are suburban-based series overwhelmingly populated by well-to-do whites,[92] but when urban outsiders do appear, their working-class behavior makes them objects of humor and suspicion.[93] Set in Connecticut, "Who's the Boss" (1984–1992) focuses on the class tension between a female advertising executive who works in Manhattan and her live-in male housekeeper from Brooklyn. On the West Coast, "The Fresh Prince of Bel-Air" (1990– ) explores a similar situation; a streetwise black teenager from West Philadelphia creates havoc when he goes to live with his rich relatives in an elite suburban-style enclave in Los Angeles. The newcomer's embarrassing presence also signals to viewers how out of place black families seem in this rarified milieu. These series build upon the prime-time tradition that usually restricts minorities and members of the working class to cities: "The Jeffersons" (1975–1985) and "Diff'rent Strokes" (1978–1985) are set in Manhattan; "Amen" (1986–1991) in Philadelphia; "All in the Family [Archie Bunker's Place]" (1971–1983) in Queens; "Laverne and Shirley" (1976–1983) in Milwaukee; and "Roc" (1991– ) in Baltimore. Even the black, dual-career professional family depicted on "The Cosby Show" (1984–1992) resides in Brooklyn, when in reality they would have been more likely to live in the suburbs. Thus, television segregates its imaginary suburbs to an even greater degree than suburbs are segregated in real life.[94]

Television's penchant for suburban sameness is coupled with its preference for traditional male-female roles.[95] In particular the suburban middle-class housewife has been stereotyped as consumer, home manager, and sexual object.[96] The "ideal" role of the suburban woman was most thoroughly charted in the situation comedies that originated in the 1950s, such as "The Donna Reed Show" (1958–1966) and "The Adventures of Ozzie and Harriet" (1952–1966). These series provided a "natural" environment in which docile homemakers acted out prescribed rituals of social interaction and material consumption. As Mary Beth Haralovich writes, "the suburban family sitcom indicates the degree of institutional as well as popular support for ideologies which naturalize class and gender identities."[97]

But if in the 1950s television focused on minor family crises which momentarily disrupted the placid domesticity of suburbia, programming in the 1980s explored the threat to familial harmony posed by working women[98] and reiterated the message that they belonged at home. In her 1989 study of "prime-time families," Ella Taylor concludes that many contemporary television shows provide "at best a rehearsal of the costs of careerism for women, at worst an outright reproof for women who seek challenging work."[99] Susan Faludi extensively documents in *Backlash* that "in the mid-'80s, [television] reconstructed a 'traditional' female hierarchy, placing suburban homemakers on the top, career women on the lower rungs, and single women at the very bottom."[100] With a few exceptions, such as "L.A. Law" (1986– ) and "Murphy Brown" (1988– ), network television featured women like Hope Murdoch in "thirtysomething" (1987–1991), who gave up her career to stay home with the kids, or Elizabeth Lubbock in "Just the Ten of Us" (1988–1990), an outspoken antifeminist who proved her womanhood as a homemaker while her gym-teacher husband struggled to make ends meet.

Many Hollywood films also bolster the idea that women must stay at home to preserve suburban domesticity. Sometimes they elaborate a related theme: that women may need to combat outsiders who menace the security of suburban neighborhoods. Two of the most notorious affirmations of the classic female sequestration pattern are *Fatal Attraction* (1987) and *Presumed Innocent* (1990).[101] In *Fatal Attraction*, a husband's efforts to end a brief affair with a career woman he meets at work in the city lead her to attack his family and home in the suburbs. The spurned woman is presented amid trappings of the horror genre—lurid sunsets, oil-barrel fires outside her apartment—and she brings urban evil into the suburban backyard, schoolground, and colonial-style home. She can only be stopped by a bullet, and only the beleaguered wife is able to pull the trigger, thereby rescuing the nuclear family and shoring up patriarchy.[102] In *Presumed Innocent*, a suburban homemaker makes a preemptive strike; she murders her husband's lawyer mistress and conceals the crime so well that her husband is almost convicted of it. Both films portray wives fighting the dangerous power that urban career women exert over their husbands. What seems at first to be a feminist twist—the wives, not the husbands, seize the initiative and intervene—in fact reinforces the notion that suburban women are vitally needed in the home to defend their marriages and families against other women who have none. The film critic Kathi Maio neatly sums up

Hollywood's "anti-feminist punch": "the good/chaste/suburban/wife/home-maker must fend off the attack of the evil/sexy/urban/slut/career woman. When the Mother and the Whore do battle, can the victor be in doubt?"[103]

Films in which women battle to save home, husband, and children belong to a larger, "home-in-danger" genre that exploits suburbanite fears that their way of life is imperiled by the breakdown of exclusivity, the traditional family, and cultural homogeneity. The genre is predicated on the nineteenth-century realization—explored by Poe, Dickens, and others—that since the bourgeois household appears to be the last refuge from social disruption, nothing will be more terrifying than threats to the safety of the family in its own home.[104] *The 'Burbs* (1989), one of the best recent examples, is a comic analysis of suburban paranoia in which bickering neighbors unite to spy on peculiar new residents with foreign accents, whom they suspect of being body snatchers. Patient, detached wives mother their inept husbands through futile raids on the newcomers' house. Momentary doubts prompt the protagonist to shout, "so they're different—they didn't do anything to us," but his plea for tolerance loses all credibility when he discovers that the trunk of the strangers' car is full of human bones. The film ends with the most aggressive of the vigilantes shouting to television cameras, "I think the message to psychos, fanatics, murderers, nutcases all over the world is: do not mess with suburbanites, because we're just not going to take it anymore." Despite its self-mocking tone, the film vocalizes and validates suburban fears of the immigrant Other.

In films focusing on children and teenagers, the streets and backyards of suburbia belong to kids, who create a microcosmic version of their parents' world. Among the most-watched films of all time, suburban classics such as *E.T. The Extra-Terrestrial* (1982) and *Back to the Future* (I, II, and III) (1985–1990) follow a "kids save the day" plot in which adults are hopeless bumblers or symbols of sinister self-interest.[105] Only the children, by practicing self-reliance and ingenuity, can eventually restore the social order that their parents taught them and thus maintain its gender and class structures. In *E.T.*, children in a tract-house settlement in California befriend a childlike extraterrestrial whose only aim is to "go home." While their sister trails behind, boys on their bikes succeed in foiling representatives of the adult world (the U.S. government and the police) so that domestic harmony can be restored.

The *Back to the Future* trilogy uses its complex chronology to convey a similar message: young males must temporarily assume adult responsibility to protect their suburban world from outsiders. With the aid of a father figure, Doc Brown, a teenager named Marty McFly alters history to provide a better life for his family in their suburban California town, "Hill Valley." In the first film, Marty returns to the 1950s to redirect the course of his parents' relationship by standing up, in the place of his father, to the local bully, Biff. The second film, set in the near future, echoes Frank Capra's *It's a Wonderful Life* (1946) by showing the urban nightmare that would have befallen Hill Valley if Biff's son had succeeded in turning the town over to developers and to organized crime.

As in Capra's film, the hero realizes that he can save his town only by remaining in it as a loyal citizen and by raising his children there. The third episode of *Back to the Future* journeys to the Wild West period of the town's history, when Biff's ancestors were also determined to foment crime and vice. Foiling his enemies one last time, Marty returns to the present and rejoins his passive girlfriend, who has slept through most of the story. He reassumes the conventional role of boyfriend and husband-to-be in a now-stable suburb in the 1980s, the best of all possible worlds.[106]

Thus, despite the growth of the "new city," the suburbs are still frequently represented as the same old neighborhood, though now they are besieged by grave new threats—sexual, social, supernatural—that require ever more extreme responses. As these examples indicate, women's opportunity to work in high-rise office parks down the interstate has not brought about the "end of suburbia." Amid a changing landscape, the "suburbanization" of a new generation continues, aided by the long-lived relics of the 1950s suburb. From detergent commercials on daytime television to comic strips such as "The Family Circus," "Blondie," and "Dennis the Menace," the middle-class housewife still stands at the stove while commuting husband and rambunctious kids dominate the action and create piles of laundry around her.[107] In many representations, children assume parental roles and reestablish domestic order so as to preserve a suburban way of life. Through such *rites de passage*, children are taught to defend and practice the same values as their parents, for the video image performs the same work of socialization on its young audience that it depicts happening to the children on-screen. Thus it comes as no surprise that in 1986 *Newsweek* ran an article on suburbia subtitled "Boomers Are Behaving Like Their Parents" or that in 1987 a suburban rock group's anthem to teen-age alienation concluded:

And the kids in the basement will carry on the family name
And the kids in the basement will turn out just the same
And the kids in the basement will have more kids to blame.[108]

Far from expiring, the ideology of suburbia—as embodied in film, television, and other forms of mass culture—still aggressively perpetuates the stereotypes upon which the traditional suburb was built.

Thus, while some scholars and journalists have declared that suburbia is now "over," its vitality—whether defined in physical, social, or cultural terms—remains undiminished. Indeed, the forces driving suburbanization have grown even stronger in the last few decades. Since World War II, suburban America has changed in substantial and even profound ways. But the rush to identify its new features has obscured something equally important—the underlying continuity in its character. Prematurely declaring the death of traditional suburbia, observers overlook the persistence of its essential features: a continuing resistance to heterogeneity and a desire to remain apart. Even as suburbia evolves, its ethos is likely to endure. Rather than having come to an end, the history of suburbia is still in the making.

NOTES

1. Census figures indicate that by 1990 about 46 percent of the American population re-
sided in suburbs. See Frank Clifford and Anne C. Roark, "Big Cities Hit by Census Data
Showing Declining Role," *Los Angeles Times*, 24 Jan. 1991; and Robert Reinhold, "Chasing
Votes from Big Cities to the Suburbs," *New York Times*, 1 June 1992.

2. Mark Baldassare, *Trouble in Paradise: The Suburban Transformation in America* (New
York, 1986), 7.

3. William K. Stevens, "Beyond the Mall: Suburbs Evolving into 'Outer City,'" *New York
Times*, 8 Nov. 1987.

4. This trend became apparent in the early 1970s: see Paul Gapp, Richard Phillips, and
James Elsener, "Meet the 'New America,' " *Chicago Tribune*, 4 Feb. 1973.

5. Baldassare defines the "utopian view" as one of the three major perspectives on the
future of the suburbs (*Trouble in Paradise*, 1–2, 207).

6. Margaret Marsh, *Suburban Lives* (New Brunswick, N.J., 1990), 220, n. 1.

7. Louis H. Masotti and Jeffrey K. Hadden, eds., *The Urbanization of the Suburbs*, Urban
Affairs Annual Reviews (Beverly Hills, Calif., 1973), 8, 16–17.

8. Among them were Masotti and Hadden's *The Urbanization of the Suburbs*; "Suburbia:
The New American Plurality," *Time*, 15 Mar. 1971, 14–20; "The Battle of the Suburbs,"
*Newsweek*, 15 Nov. 1971, 61–64, 69–70; "New Role of the Suburbs," *U.S. News & World Report*, 7 Aug. 1972, 52–56; Gurney Breckenfeld, "'Downtown' Has Fled to the Suburbs," *Fortune*, Oct. 1972, 80–87, 156, 158, 162.

9. For "outer city," see Jack Rosenthal, "The Outer City: U.S. in Suburban Turmoil," *New
York Times*, 30 May 1971; for "satellite sprawl," see Anthony Downs, "Alternative Forms of
Future Urban Growth in the United States," *Journal of the American Institute of Planners* 36
(Jan. 1970): 11; for "new city," see Louis H. Masotti, "Prologue: Suburbia Reconsidered—
Myth and Counter-Myth," in Masotti and Hadden, *Urbanization of the Suburbs*, 21; for "sub-
urban 'city,'" see Jack Rosenthal, "Suburban Land Development: Towards Suburban
Independence," in *Suburbia in Transition*, ed. Louis H. Masotti and Jeffrey K. Hadden (New
York, 1974), 298; for "urban fringe" and "neocity," see Masotti, "Prologue," in Masotti and
Hadden, *Urbanization of the Suburbs*, 15.

10. Even in the 1970s geographers such as James E. Vance, Jr., Brian J. L. Berry, and Peter
O. Muller began to reject the core-periphery model of metropolitan form in favor of a
multicentered one. See Peter O. Muller, *Contemporary Suburban America* (Englewood Cliffs,
N.J., 1981), 7–9; Brian J. L. Berry and Yehoshua S. Cohen, "Decentralization of Commerce
and Industry: The Restructuring of Metropolitan America," in Masotti and Hadden, *Urbanization of the Suburbs*, 453; and Peter O. Muller, *The Outer City: Geographical Consequences
of the Urbanization of the Suburbs* (Washington, D.C., 1976).

11. Mark Gottdiener and George Kephart, "The Multinucleated Metropolitan Region: A
Comparative Analysis," in *Postsuburban California: The Transformation of Orange County
since World War II*, ed. Rob Kling, Spencer Olin, and Mark Poster (Berkeley, 1991), 34.

12. Muller, *Contemporary Suburban America*, x.

13. Christopher B. Leinberger and Charles Lockwood, "How Busines Is Reshaping America,"
*The Atlantic* (Oct. 1986): 43–52.

14. Ibid., 43.

15. Paul Goldberger, "When Suburban Sprawl Meets Upward Mobility," *The New York Times*,
26 July 1987. Other recent terms for the urbanizing suburbs are: "growth corridors," used by
George Sternlieb and Alex Schwartz, *New Jersey Growth Corridors* (New Brunswick, N.J.,
1986); "dispersed urban regions," used by Sam Bass Warner, Jr., *The Private City: Philadel-
phia in Three Periods of Its Growth*, rev. ed. (Philadelphia, 1987), xiv; "DISURBs" (Dense,
Industrial, Self-contained Urban Regions), used by Mark Baldassare, quoted in Ellen J.
Bartlett, "America's Cities: Revival and Despair," Part 5, "Emerging City Fits a Different
Way of Life," *The Boston Globe*, 28 Jan. 1988; and "shock suburbs," used by Michael H. Ebner,
"Shock Suburbs: Growth in the Exploding American Metropolis since 1945" (unpublished
manuscript). For a discussion of the various terms that have been used to describe suburban
downtowns, see Thomas J. Baerwald, "The Evolution of Suburban Downtowns in Midwestern
Metropolises," in *Suburbia Re-examined*, ed. Barbara M. Kelly (Westport, Conn., 1989), 45.

16. Robert Fishman, *Bourgeois Utopias: The Rise and Fall of Suburbia* (New York, 1987),
184.

17. Robert Fishman, "Megalopolis Unbound," *Wilson Quarterly* 14 (Winter 1990): 28.

18. Fishman, *Bourgeois Utopias*, 185.

19. Ibid.

20. For a detailed local study of this phenomenon, see Michael H. Ebner, "Technoburb,"
*Inland Architect* 37 (Jan.-Feb., 1993): 54–59.

21. Fishman, *Bourgeois Utopias*, 185–86.

22. For a fuller evaluation of cultural assumptions embedded in Joel Garreau's *Edge City: Life on the New Frontier* (New York, 1991), see William Sharpe and Leonard Wallock, "The Edge of a New Frontier?" *Journal of the American Planning Association* 58 (Summer 1992): 391–93.

23. Garreau, *Edge City*, 4.

24. Ibid., 14, 397–98.

25. Fishman, *Bourgeois Utopias*, 186.

26. Thomas M. Stanback, Jr., *The New Suburbanization: Challenge to the Central City* (Boulder, Colo., 1991), 1.

27. For an extensive listing of new "edge cities," organized by the metropolitan areas to which they belong, see Garreau, *Edge City*, 426–39.

28. Jean Gottmann and Robert A. Harper, *Since Megalopolis: The Urban Writings of Jean Gottmann* (Baltimore, 1990), 8–9.

29. Muller, *Contemporary Suburban America*, 71–89.

30. Ibid., 82. That blacks and Hispanics continue to face discrimination in the housing market was recently confirmed by an Urban Institute Study conducted for the Department of Housing and Urban Development. See Timothy Noah, "Housing Report Says Racial Bias Remains Prevalent," *Wall Street Journal*, 30 Aug. 1991.

31. As defined by Louis Wirth, "a city is a large dense settlement of socially heterogeneous individuals" ("Urbanism as a Way of Life," *American Journal of Sociology* 44 [July 1938], reprinted in *Classic Essays on the Culture of Cities*, ed. Richard Sennett [Englewood Cliffs, N.J., 1969], 143–65).

32. See William W. Pendleton, "Blacks in Suburbs," in Masotti and Hadden, *Urbanization of the Suburbs*. "Blacks appear to participate in the demographic dimensions [of suburbanization], but not in the social dimensions. Black suburbanization is not unequivocally an indicator of social integration" (184).

33. Gottdiener and Kephart, "Multinucleated Metropolitan Region," 42–43.

34. Eric E. Lampard, "The Nature of Urbanization," in *Visions of the Modern City: Essays in History, Art, and Literature*, ed. William Sharpe and Leonard Wallock (Baltimore, 1987), 82.

35. Reynolds Farley, *Blacks and Whites: Narrowing the Gap?* (Cambridge, Mass., 1984), 33.

36. John R. Logan and Mark Schneider, "Racial Segregation and Racial Change in American Suburbs, 1970–1980," *American Journal of Sociology* 89 (Jan. 1984): 874. See Carol A. O'Connor, "The Suburban Mosaic: Patterns of Land Use, Class, and Culture," in *American Urbanism: A Historiographical Review*, ed. Howard Gillette, Jr., and Zane L. Miller (Westport, Conn., 1987). "Despite the existence of laws barring discrimination in the sale of real estate, blacks . . . number only 2 per cent or less in 70 per cent of the nation's suburbs" (252).

37. Douglas S. Massey and Nancy A. Denton, "Suburbanization and Segregation in U.S. Metropolitan Areas," *American Journal of Sociology* 94 (Nov. 1988): 593.

38. Black suburbanites also live in neighborhoods which are of lower quality than those inhabited by whites. According to Massey and Denton, the "suburbs that attract black residents tend to be older areas with relatively low socioeconomic statuses." Typically they are "near the central city and relatively unattractive to white renters and home buyers." In addition, they are often "older, manufacturing suburbs characterized by weak tax bases, poor municipal services, and high degrees of debt. In a less extreme fashion . . . black suburbs replicate the conditions of inner cities." Massey and Denton, "Suburbanization and Segregation," 593–94. Winning a settlement in 1992 against a suburban beach club in Westchester County that had locked her out, a black woman told reporters that she "doubted it would alter deep patterns of discrimination. 'It's a way of life,' she said." "Beach Club Settles Suit on Race Bias," *The New York Times*, 4 Apr. 1992.

39. Blumenthal, "The Suburban Poor," in Masotti and Hadden, *Suburbia in Transition*, 212.

40. Judith Fernandez and John Pincus, *Troubled Suburbs: An Exploratory Study*, with the assistance of Jane Peterson, The Rand Corporation (Santa Monica, Calif., 1982), 42.

41. John McCormick and Peter McKillop, "The Other Suburbia," *Newsweek*, 26 June 1989, 22–24.

42. "Whites are leaving many big cities in massive numbers, Hispanics are entering in large numbers, and the number of blacks already there is expanding through high birth rates. This transformation is occurring in part because of the white majority's deliberate policy of segregating itself from both poor and non-poor minority group members. Such segregation is most evident in housing and schools, where it operates by excluding nearly all poor and most minority households from new suburban areas." Anthony Downs, "The Future of Industrial Cities," in *The New Urban Reality*, ed. Paul E. Peterson (Washington, D.C., 1985), 285.

43. Michael N. Danielson, *The Politics of Exclusion* (New York, 1976), 356.

44. See Danielson, *Politics of Exclusion*: "most of those moving outward have been seeking social separation from the lower classes as well as better housing and more spacious surroundings. Middle-class families commonly equate personal security, good schools, maintenance of property values, and the general desirability of a residential area with the absence of lower-income groups" (6).

45. Leinberger and Lockwood, "How Business Is Reshaping America," 46.

46. Goldberger, "When Suburban Sprawl Meets Upward Mobility," 30.

47. Garreau, *Edge City*, 6–7. See also Garreau's earlier formulation, "From Suburbs, Cities Are Springing Up in Our Back Yards," *The Washington Post*, 8 Mar. 1987; and the related guide (developed with the help of Leinberger, a real estate consultant) on "How to Pinpoint a City: Five-Part Definition Applied in Suburbs," *The Washington Post*, 8 Mar. 1987.

48. Fishman, "Megalopolis Unbound," 27. See also Leinberger and Lockwood, "How Business Is Reshaping America," 45; Muller, *Contemporary Suburban America*, 6; and Garreau, *Edge City*, 31.

49. The nuclear analogy carries negative as well as positive implications; if in physics the hazardous process of bringing an atom to critical mass releases a powerful yet potentially destructive energy, so in suburbia it unleashes the power to develop and consume, to build and pollute.

50. Andrea Oppenheimer Dean, "The State of the Cities: Paradox," *Architecture* 77 (Dec. 1988): 72. See also Leinberger and Lockwood, "How Business Is Reshaping America," 49.

51. Kling, Olin, and Poster, *Postsuburban California*, 21.

52. Fishman, "Megalopolis Unbound," 38.

53. Paul Goldberger, "Orange County: Tomorrowland—Wall to Wall," *New York Times*, 11 Dec. 1988.

54. William S. Kowinski, *The Malling of America: An Inside Look at the Great Consumer Paradise* (New York, 1985), 64–68.

55. Muller, *Contemporary Suburban America*, 126–27.

56. William S. Kowinski, quoted in Muller, *Contemporary Suburban America*, 125.

57. Kowinski, *Malling of America*, 60–61; Mark Gottdiener, "Recapturing the Center: A Semiotic Analysis of Shopping Malls," in *The City and the Sign: An Introduction to Urban Semiotics*, ed. Mark Gottdiener and Alexandros Ph. Lagopoulos (New York, 1986), 288–301.

58. Jon C. Teaford, *The Twentieth-Century American City: Problem, Promise, and Reality* (Baltimore, 1986), 108. For the reasons behind suburban incorporation, see Kenneth T. Jackson, *Crabgrass Frontier: The Suburbanization of the United States* (New York, 1985), 150–55.

59. Richard F. Babcock and Fred P. Bosselman, *Exclusionary Zoning: Land Use Regulation and Housing in the 1970s* (New York, 1973), 7.

60. Danielson, *Politics of Exclusion*, 4.

61. Fishman, "Megalopolis Unbound," 38. Choice is also a major theme of Garreau's work. See also Leinberger and Lockwood ("How Business is Reshaping America," 52), who speak of "easy access" and the "opportunity for all kinds of Americans to live, work, shop, and play in the same geographic area."

62. Fishman, "Megalopolis Unbound," 39. But this is a significant obstacle. By 1980, traffic congestion in suburbia had increased to the point that the average journey to work within suburbia was no faster than that between suburbs and cities. See Robert Cervero, *Suburban Gridlock* (New Brunswick, N.J., 1986), 34.

63. Kling, Olin, and Poster, *Postsuburban California*, 18.

64. Ibid., 17, 18.

65. Ibid., 23.

66. Ibid., 21.

67. Fishman, "Megalopolis Unbound," 41.

68. Garreau, *Edge City*, 111.

69. On how the suburban dream home is "the least suitable housing imaginable for employed wives and mothers," see Dolores Hayden, *Redesigning the American Dream: The Future of Housing, Work, and Family Life* (New York, 1984), 50. The car that supposedly liberates women from the home also confines them behind the wheel for hours at a time as they run errands and drive children between school and various activities. See Mary Cahill, *Carpool: A Novel of Suburban Frustration* (New York, 1991).

70. Roslyn L. Feldberg and Evelyn Nakano Glenn, "Technology and Work Degradation: Effects of Office Automation on Women Clerical Workers," in *Machina Ex Dea: Feminist Perspectives on Technology*, ed. Joan Rothschild (New York, 1983), 59–78; and Heidi H. Hartmann, ed., *Computer Chips and Paper Clips: Technology and Women's Employment*, vol. 2 (Washington, D.C., 1986).

71. Linda M. Blum, *Between Feminism and Labor: The Significance of the Comparable Worth Movement* (Berkeley, 1991), 148. On "information factories," see Thomas J. Lueck, "New

York Back-Office Job Surge Has Pitfalls," *New York Times*, 5 July 1987.

72. Barbara Baran and Suzanne Teegarden, "Women's Labor in the Office of the Future: A Case Study of the Insurance Industry," in *Women, Households, and the Economy*, ed. Lourdes Beneria and Catherine R. Stimpson (New Brunswick, N.J., 1987), 220.

73. Alice Kessler-Harris and Karen Brodkin Sacks, "The Demise of Domesticity," in Beneria and Stimpson, *Women, Households, and the Economy*, 73.

74. Garreau, *Edge City*, 111.

75. Fishman, "Megalopolis Unbound," 38.

76. Gottdiener, "Space, Social Theory, and the Urban Metaphor," 309.

77. Fishman, *Bourgeois Utopias*, 206.

78. Garreau, *Edge City*, 14. Here Garreau not only glosses over the extensive history of American utopian communities from Shaker villages to 1960s communes, but he also forgets that he has described "Edge City" as antithetical to planning and therefore anything but "purposeful."

79. See Marion Clawson, "Land-Use Trends," in *Nonmetropolitan America in Transition*, ed. Amos H. Hawley and Sara Mills Mazie (Chapel Hill, N.C., 1981), 645–67.

80. As Kenneth T. Jackson writes, "unfortunately, the edge city phenomenon represents more an escape than a solution," one which uses "the beltways and interstates to keep one jump ahead of the huddled masses" ("The View from the Periphery," *New York Times Book Review*, 22 Sept. 1991, 11). Or, as Clawson notes, "in the United States the problem of re-building older urban areas still tends to be solved by running away from them" ("Land-Use Trends," in Hawley and Mazie, *Nonmetropolitan America in Transition*, 648).

81. Ann Snitow, "Suburban on the Rocks: Waking up from the American Dream," *Voice Literary Supplement* (Mar. 1988), 21.

82. Stuart M. Blumin, "The Center Cannot Hold: Historians and the Suburbs," *Journal of Policy History*, vol. 2, no. 1 (1990): 119.

83. Fishman, *Bourgeois Utopias*, 205.

84. Marsh, *Suburban Lives*, 187.

85. In 1976, Barry Schwartz argued that the urbanization of the suburbs was not likely to alter their essential character. The "superimposition in the suburbs of drastic population and economic growth upon a stubbornly permanent sociopolitical base," he found, meant that "the 'face' of the suburb is changing" but its "underlying structure—its 'soul,' so to speak—is not." "Images of Suburbia: Some Revisionist Commentary and Conclusions," in *The Changing Face of the Suburbs*, ed. Barry Schwartz (Chicago, 1976), 339.

86. As Mary Corbin Sies writes, the "suburban ideal—the assumption that the proper resi-dential environment was one in which every family resided in a one-family home with plenty of yard within a locally controlled, homogeneous community—is still embraced by many Ameri-cans today, having been incorporated into our common understanding of the American dream itself." See "The City Transformed: Nature, Technology, and the Suburban Ideal, 1877–1917," *Journal of Urban History* 14 (Nov. 1987): 83.

87. See Mary Beth Haralovich, "Sitcoms and Suburbs: Positioning the 1950s Homemaker," *Quarterly Review of Film and Video* 11 (1989): 61–83.

88. See Stephen Heath, "Representing Television," in *Logics of Television: Essays in Cul-tural Criticism*, ed. Patricia Mellencamp (Bloomington, Ind., 1990), 284.

89. Ibid., 289–90.

90. See Ella Taylor, *Prime-Time Families: Television Culture in Postwar America* (Berke-ley, 1989), 4. See also Lynn Spigel, "Television in the Family Circle: The Popular Reception of a New Medium," in Patricia Mellencamp, ed., *Logics of Television: Essays in Cultural Criti-cism* (Bloomington, Ind., 1990), 73–97.

91. Police shows set in the city contribute to this picture by sensationalizing urban crime and violence: cf. *Miami Vice* (1984–1989), *Hill Street Blues* (1981–1987), *Kojak* (1973–1978), *The Equalizer* (1985–1989), and *NYPD Blue* (1993– ). On the "antiseptic model of space" pro-posed by television's rendition of suburbia, see Lynn Spigel, "The Suburban Home Compan-ion: Television and the Neighborhood Ideal in Postwar America," in *Sexuality and Space*, ed. Beatriz Colomina (New York, 1992), 185–217.

92. Among the prime-time shows set in affluent white suburbs and having few or no black or working-class characters are: *Dallas* (1978–1991); *Family Ties* (1982–1989); *The Golden Girls* (1985–1993); *Alf* (1986–1990); *Parker Lewis Can't Lose* (1990–1993).

93. Urbanites do not necessarily have to be visible to provoke displays of suburban antipa-thy. In a September 1991 episode of *Growing Pains*, a Long Island schoolteacher who has taken in a homeless boy named Luke rejects the application of would-be foster parents from the city: "forget about that couple from Brooklyn—I don't want Luke being raised by people who drag their knuckles on the ground."

94. As Mark Crispin Miller argues, prime-time segregation "betrays the very fears that it denies. In thousands of high-security buildings, and in suburbs reassuringly remote from the

cities' 'bad neighborhoods,' whites may, unconsciously, be further reassured by watching not just Cosby, but a whole set of TV shows that negate the possibility of black violence with lunatic fantasies of containment." "Cosby Knows Best," *Boxed In: The Culture of TV* (Evanston, Ill., 1988), 74.

95. For an analysis of television's persistent gender stereotyping since the 1950s, see Susan Faludi, *Backlash* (New York, 1991), 140–68.

96. See Elaine Tyler May, *Homeward Bound: American Families in the Cold War Era* (New York, 1988); and Haralovich, "Sitcoms and Suburbs," 61–83.

97. Haralovich, "Sitcoms and Suburbs," 81.

98. Literary views of the suburbs during the 1950s, as exemplified by the works of John Cheever and John Updike, were far more critical of the constricting roles that men and women were expected to play. In the 1980s, such authors as Don Delillo, Gloria Naylor, and Frederick Barthelme continued to emphasize suburban status-consciousness, sexual anomie, and racial and social stratification.

99. Taylor, *Prime-Time Families*, 159.

100. Faludi, *Backlash*, 148.

101. Other recent Hollywood movies suggesting that women belong in the home, caring for their children, are *Someone to Watch over Me* (1987) and *Baby Boom* (1987).

102. For an extended discussion of the filmmakers' antifeminist intent, see Faludi, *Backlash*, 112–26.

103. Kathi Maio, *Feminist in the Dark: Reviewing the Movies* (Freedom, Calif., 1988), 218.

104. Some examples of the suburban horror genre include *The Amityville Horror* (1979), *Friday the 13th* (1980), *A Nightmare on Elm Street* (1984), and their various sequels.

105. The darker side of this genre is represented by films such as *Over the Edge* (1979), in which alienated suburban kids living in still unfinished tract housing are so disgusted with their environment that they lock their parents in the local school and go on an apocalyptic rampage. An outsider explains to the parents, "you all were in such a hopped up hurry to get out of the city that you turned your kids into exactly what you were trying to get away from."

106. See Maio's incisive analysis of the difference between male and female time-travel in the suburbs: "*Back to the Future* allows a teenage boy, Marty McFly, to go back and change life for the better. He is able to bring his parents together, improve the lives and lifestyle of his entire family, *and* save the life of his friend and mentor, Doc Brown. . . . It is an *empowering* vision of what a young man can do." But in *Peggy Sue Got Married*, where a mother returns to her high-school days in 1960, "a grown woman . . . is totally unable to change even the course of her own life. . . . In a world of happy and successful male time travelers, the female time-traveler is passive in and little enriched by her re-exploration of the past" (*Feminist in the Dark*, 192–93).

107. Although Blondie now has a paying job, Dagwood has yet to assume many of her domestic chores.

108. Raymond Jalbert, quoted in Donna Gaines, *Teenage Wasteland: Suburbia's Dead End Kids* (New York, 1991), 16.

*Part Four*

# *The Historiography of Urban America*

# New Perspectives on American Urban History

*Raymond A. Mohl*

T he writing of American history has been transformed dramatically over the past two decades. In particular, a new interest in social history has energized the field and substantially altered the way historians research, conceptualize, and interpret the past. In the field of urban history, a subdivision of the larger province of social history, scholars have brought exciting new perspectives to the study of the American city. New methods, new approaches, and new interpretations have illumined dim corners of the urban past and pushed back the frontiers of historical understanding.

The rise of the American industrial city came to be one of the dominant characteristics of the late nineteenth century. Since the turn of the twentieth century, the city in its various permutations has continued to reflect or to shape modern social, economic, and political life. Yet American historians, Richard C. Wade has suggested, "arrived at the study of the city by slow freight."[1] The historians lagged far behind scholars in other disciplines, who by 1900 had begun to apply the tools of the social sciences to the examination of urban America and its problems. Indeed, American urban history as a distinctive field of scholarly inquiry does not date much earlier than 1940, when Arthur M. Schlesinger published his landmark article on "The City in American History."[2] But interest in the field grew rather slowly, and by the mid-1950s only a half-dozen or so universities offered courses on the subject. Progress in urban history research was also less than dynamic, the chief accomplishments being several fine urban biographies and a handful of monographs. Among the best were the works of Carl Bridenbaugh on the colonial seaport towns, Oscar Handlin's study of Boston's immigrants, and Wade's book, *The Urban Frontier* (1959).[3]

The decade of the 1960s, however, brought powerful changes to the historical profession—changes that affected research and writing in urban history in significant ways. The mainstream consensus history that grew out of the conditions of the Great Depression, the Second World War, and the Cold War peaked in the Eisenhower era of the 1950s but

*Raymond A. Mohl is professor of history and chairman of the department at the University of Alabama at Birmingham.*

began to crack amid the social strains and political conflicts of the 1960s. The ghetto riots of the 1960s and the social-crusading spirit of the Kennedy-Johnson years riveted attention on the American city and its discontents. The writing of history generally reflects the climate of opinion at any particular moment in time, and certainly this was the case in the 1960s. Traditional interest in political and diplomatic history—a sort of elitist history concerned with the ideas and activities of decision-makers, opinion-shapers, and power-wielders—gave way to a new and invigorated commitment to social history broadly considered. American historians began to examine with new interest such subjects as race, ethnicity, and class and the ways in which people ordered their lives in the family, at work, and in various group and community settings; they began to look into the social values, behaviors, and processes that shaped the lives of people; and they began to pay attention to the local as well as the national level, and to the people at the bottom of the social and economic heirarchy as well as at the top. As social historian Olivier Zunz has suggested, the appearance of this newer form of social history "generated great excitement in the progressive and eclectic intellectual atmosphere of the sixties."[4]

These shifts in historiographical tradition coincided with two other powerful changes in 1960s America. First, the computer revolution made possible a more careful and exact social science history based on analysis of massive amounts of information collected, stored, sorted, and manipulated by computer. Second, the arrival of the baby boom generation at the college gate spurred an explosion of graduate education, generating in turn a substantial amount of new research as young historians wrote dissertations, articles, and books. By the end of the 1960s, the historiographical landscape had been altered considerably from the mid-1950s, the heyday of the consensus historians.[5]

Urban history, in particular, was energized by the convergence of these changing social patterns and historiographical trends. The ferment of scholarly innovation and shifting interests pushed urban history in at least two new directions in the early 1960s. Each new path was illuminated by an important and innovative book—one path by Sam Bass Warner's *Streetcar Suburbs: The Process of Growth in Boston, 1870–1900* (1962), and the other by Stephan Thernstrom's *Poverty and Progress: Social Mobility in a Nineteenth-Century City* (1964).

Sam Warner's work had an ecological slant, focusing on the process of urbanization and population redistribution in the Boston metropolitan area in response both to technological innovation in urban transit and to the rural appeal of suburbia. Warner also used an inventive methodology. The examination of some 23,000 building permits for three Boston suburbs enabled him to make certain judgments about construction patterns, architectural and building styles, and the class structure underlying neighborhood formation. The result was a book that leaped beyond the established perimeters of urban history and provided powerful insights into the growth of the American industrial city.[6]

In *Streetcar Suburbs* and in some of his other work, Warner essentially dealt with the processes of urban growth. In rejecting more traditional approaches to urban history, such as biography or the study of social problems or political movements within an urban context, he demonstrated the ways in which fresh thinking can be historiographically liberating. Warner was not entirely alone in this emphasis on urbanization in the early 1960s. Eric Lampard, who published a number of suggestive articles over thirty years, was also an early advocate of the study of urbanization as a "societal process." Studying urbanization from this perspective, Lampard argued, required urban historians to examine such "interacting elements" as population, topography, economy, social organization, political process, civic leadership, and urban imagery.[7] In a similar vein, Roy Lubove suggested the utility of the "city-building process" as a conceptual framework for analyzing decision making, social organization, and urban change. Lubove illustrated this methodology in a little-heralded but nevertheless important book, *Twentieth-Century Pittsburgh: Government, Business, and Environmental Change* (1969).[8]

The work of Stephan Thernstrom staked out a second new path in American urban history in the 1960s. In *Poverty and Progress*, he tested the widely asserted conception of nineteenth-century America as a land of opportunity for the urban working class. Drawing samples from manuscript census schedules for Newburyport, Massachusetts, between 1850 and 1880, Thernstrom pioneered in the use of new kinds of sources and in quantitative analysis, although he did not ignore more traditional literary sources. His chief concern was the relatively narrow question of social mobility rather than the larger process of urbanization or city-building. Nevertheless, Thernstrom's approach was widely imitated and came to be associated with a "new urban history."[9]

Younger historians began pumping out a stream of books and articles replicating Thernstrom's work for other cities. By the early 1970s, the new urban history had been taken over by the quantifiers in the Thernstrom tradition who were mostly studying mobility and related issues.[10] Indeed, when Thernstrom catalogued the achievements of the new urban history in a 1971 article, he wrote primarily of findings about mobility. These included tremendously high rates of urban population turnover, positive correlations between economic failure and spatial mobility, and a general fluidity in rates of occupational and social mobility, although rates varied for different economic classes and ethnic groups, and blacks had considerably fewer opportunities.[11]

Thernstrom's approach rather than Warner's came to dominate among practitioners of the new urban history by the early 1970s. Michael Frisch has suggested that the popularity and influence of Thernstrom's *Poverty and Progress* "stemmed less from the book's substance than from the way it brought together a number of diverse concerns central to the historiographical moment." These included a methodology conducive to quantification at the beginning of the computer age, a model that could be applied easily to other communities, and, finally, a concern for nonelitist history, or history from the bottom up, at the height of the political radicalism of the 1960s. As Frisch put it, "quantification, as applied by Thernstrom, . . . came to be invested with an aura of social and political relevance," making this particular approach appealing to a younger generation of urban historians.[12]

Thus, the new urban history came to be perceived as a special sort of quantitative history. Yet, ironically, at about the same time that he was carrying his quantitative methodology to a new level of sophistication in his prize-winning book, *The Other Bostonians* (1973), Thernstrom had begun having second thoughts about the term "new" urban history. Indeed, as he confessed in an interview in the *Journal of Urban History* in 1975, he had not only given up the term but he also had even stopped labeling himself as an urban historian. Rather, Thernstrom contended that urban historians were really engaged in social history, that "the modern city [was] so intimately linked to the society around it, and [was] so important a part of the entire social order that few of its aspects [could] safely be examined in isolation."[13]

Always difficult to categorize, Warner, too, rejected the emerging notion of a new urban history. In a 1977 article, he labeled the narrow mobility studies "a bare-boned empiricism" and "a quantitative anti-quarianism," the purpose behind such studies "lost in technique." Nothing, he suggested, was "more likely to put a researcher on a false track than the advertisement: new urban history." Building on his earlier emphasis on the process of urbanization, Warner asserted that the central focus of urban history should be the spatial distribution of population, institutions, activities, and artifacts—the basic elements in all human communities that are continuously evolving in relation to each other over time.[14] By the mid-1970s, therefore, the two chief pioneers of new ways of doing urban history had abandoned or rejected the notion altogether.

The new urban history made one last gasp, however. Theodore Hershberg and others associated with the Philadelphia Social History Project promoted the continued viability of a new, quantified urban history. In an important article in 1978 and in the introduction to a collection of essays on Philadelphia, Hershberg provided yet another prescriptive statement about urban history. For him, the essential distinction between the old and the new urban history was one between the city as site and the city as process. By site, he meant "the conceptual treatment of the city as a passive backdrop to whatever else [was] the subject of central concern." By contrast, he wrote, "urban as process should be thought of as the dynamic modelling of the interrelationships among environment, behavior, and group experience—three basic components in the larger urban system." Such an approach, Hershberg contended, would explain what was distinctively different about life and change in the city. By Hershberg's account, neither Warner nor Thernstrom had been pursuing a new urban history; they were simply working within the older tradition of urban as site rather than urban as process.[15] Interestingly, at about the same time that Warner and Thernstrom were abandoning the idea of a new urban history as unsatisfying and incomplete, a new band of purists was tossing the pioneers off the team, consigning their work to the historiographical scrap heap.

Through the 1970s, then, debates over the new urban history held center stage within the discipline. This apparent absorbing interest, however, tended to mask the fact that an extensive urban history literature was pouring from the university presses and filling the scholarly journals—a literature that often paid little attention to the new urban history controversy.[16] Indeed, for some areas of urban history the new quantitative or social science approaches had little relevance or application. The sort of microlevel analysis of work, residence, family, and group experience typical of the Hershberg school is important and informative, but many dimensions of the urban experience cannot be addressed in exactly that way. The new urban history has been particularly unhelpful in suggesting alternative ways of approaching the twentieth-century American city. The Hershberg book, for instance, concentrates almost exclusively on the years 1850 to 1880, and only one of its fourteen chapters even ventures into the twentieth century. This concentration on the nineteenth century clearly reflected the reliance of the new urban history on manuscript census data, which only recently became available for early years of the twentieth century.

The now perceived weaknesses of an exclusively quantitative approach to urban history research have liberated urban historians to pursue many diverse paths of the urban experience, to follow their instincts and their interests. The results have been fruitful and stimulating. Historians of the American city have begun to carve out a variety of new and exciting areas of urban research. Meanwhile, suggested Bruce M. Stave, the heavy emphasis on quantification diminished considerably by the early 1980s. Students and scholars, Stave wrote in 1983, "will be less overtly confronted by the numbers as historians increasingly recognize the problems of sometimes imprecise data and flawed methodology. Qualitative rather than quantitative analysis will be the historian's prime goal."[17]

Stave's epitaph for the new urban history sparked surprisingly little comment, which suggests that his observation was right on target.[18] But if the now old, quantitative urban history is dead or dying, the larger field itself is brimming with new approaches, new interpretations, and new ideas. The remainder of this essay will survey briefly a dozen or so of these new perspectives on American urban history.

*Urban Political History.* Studies of urban political history traditionally focused on the political machines that emerged in the late nineteenth century and on the reformers and reform organizations that challenged the city bosses. The traditional view was highly moralistic; the bosses and machines were corrupt and venal, while the reformers upheld the democratic ideal. In the 1950s and 1960s sociologists and historians reversed these widely accepted stereotypes, suggesting instead that the bosses extended democratic politics down to the neighborhood level, provided needed services, supported urban growth and development, and centralized power and decision making at a time of rapid urbanization and social change. As one of these bosses, George B.

Cox of Cincinnati, had argued in 1892, the boss was "not necessarily a public enemy."[19]

The defense of the machine reached its epitome in Leo Hershkowitz's study of Boss William Tweed of New York City. Often singled out as the most notorious of the bosses, Tweed became in Hershkowitz's account "a pioneer spokesman for an emerging New York" and "a progressive force in shaping the interests and destiny of a great city and its people."[20] Few historians carried the revisionist argument that far. More recent studies of the urban political machine and its origins have made fewer expansive claims for the city boss, seeking instead to locate the machine within the broader pattern of American political and social processes.[21]

Meanwhile, historians were revising the traditional picture of the urban reformer. Increasingly, urban reform was perceived as badly splintered, a congeries of separate little movements devoted to single issues like the saloon or playgrounds or civil service reform. The general thrust of recent research suggests that urban reform was a complex, constantly shifting, multidimensional movement. Reformers, it seems, came from all social and economic classes, and they supported a diversity of often conflicting reform legislation, programs, and causes. Some reformers, it now appears, took extremely elitist and undemocratic positions in their attack on the electoral base of the machine. At the same time, other reformers supported social causes dear to the heart of the bosses; indeed, some reformers were bosses and vice versa. As a result of this research, the traditional practice of portraying urban politics simply as a sharply defined struggle between bosses and reformers seems less useful now than it did in the 1960s.[22]

The acknowledged weaknesses of the boss-reformer interpretive model forced urban historians to pose new questions and view the evidence in alternative ways. The work of Samuel P. Hays, in particular, shifted the focus away from the boss-reformer debate toward the "social analysis" of urban political history. In a series of important articles beginning in the 1960s, Hays moved beyond the study of political institutions and policies toward the study of underlying structural and socioeconomic forces that produced political change. In the industrial city, he argued, the shaping political struggle was not between machine and reform but between "forces making for decentralization and forces making for centralization." The old decentralized ward system worked in favor of the immigrant working class, while schemes for citywide centralization, such as the city commission or city manager system, concentrated political power in the hands of urban elites.[23]

Some recent historical work has begun to challenge the functional view of the boss as a provider of positive government. More research is needed, Jon C. Teaford has written, to determine "to what degree the boss actually bossed." Teaford's important book, *The Unheralded Triumph: City Government in America* (1984), demonstrated the powerful and decisive role of urban professionals and experts in running the industrial city. More important than bosses or reformers, Teaford contended, the growing army of bureaucrats and technicians may have been the real shapers of the city. Public policymaking depended on what was technically or financially feasible. Thus, the politicians came to rely on the experts, who by the twentieth century staffed the administrative departments in city government. They were municipal engineers, landscape architects, city planners, public health officials, accountants, attorneys, educators, even librarians. Neither the bosses nor the reformers, this new interpretation suggests, had as much power or influence as historians once believed.[24] Similarly, in a number of studies, Terrence J. McDonald has demonstrated that urban politicians were sharply limited by fiscal constraints and paid more attention to property-owning taxpayers than to immigrant voting blocs.[25]

Other historians have begun addressing the issue of urban political power, particularly its distribution and uses. Established political science models advocate either elitist or pluralist positions regarding the distribution of power—political power is either concentrated among the wealthy or widely dispersed among competing social groups. Recent historical research offers some alternatives to these political science models while illuminating new dimensions of the American urban experience.

In *Political Power in Birmingham, 1871–1921* (1977), for instance, Carl V. Harris focused on two interrelated aspects of political power, office holding and governmental decision making. He concluded that the elitist model did fit electoral patterns in Birmingham, where officeholding was concentrated heavily among the richest 20 percent of the city's population. But these officeholding patterns did not always dictate public policy outcomes. Indeed, decision-making power in Birmingham was distributed in complex ways. Depending on the policy issue involved, the city's politics were complicated by shifting alliances among and within economic groups, and by religious, ethnic, and racial influences. Neither the power-elite thesis nor the pluralist interpretation matched perfectly the political reality in this growing industrial city of the New South. Nevertheless, by abandoning the boss-reformer framework and by posing new questions, Harris was able to bring a fresh perspective to urban political history.[26]

Similar conclusions were reached by David C. Hammack in his important study, *Power and Society: Greater New York at the Turn of the Century* (1982). Hammack examined both the pattern of mayoral politics and the conflicts surrounding three big public policy issues: the consolidation of greater New York City in 1898, the building of the first subway, and the centralization of the public school system. The city's increasing ethnic and economic heterogeneity, he argued, stimulated a shift from elitist politics "to a politics of competing elite and nonelite economic, social, and cultural interest groups mediated and managed by specialized professional politicians."[27]

Several forces coalesced in Hammack's New York to undermine the earlier dominance of power elites. First, the elites were divided among themselves, which was also the case in Harris's Birmingham. They often had different economic interests and competing political ambitions. Second, as the city's population grew through immigration and economic diversification, varied nonelite groups (ethnic communities, small business interests, labor unions, and so on) developed into active pressure groups. The community-based political parties that represented these interest groups siphoned off power from the elites. Finally, as the political arena became a place where different interests were compromised and mediated, technical experts, professionals, and bureaucrats came to exercise a great degree of governmental power and authority. The chief interpretive thrust of these new studies is that political decision making reflected the economic, ethnic, and cultural complexity of the cities. The new city of the industrial era, according to this argument, was shaped by the continual political interaction of competing elites, pluralistic interest groups, and urban technicians.

Discussion of the political urban machine has also been revived in the past decade. The work of political scientists Amy Bridges, Martin Shefter, and Ira Katznelson—mostly on New York City—has been especially important in developing a more theoretically based discussion of the urban political machine. Bridges, in *A City in the Republic* (1984), advanced a class analysis of the growth of New York City's Tammany machine. Mass immigration in the pre-Civil War era coincided with the extension of the vote to the working class, effectively excluding the formerly dominant elites from political power. At the same time, industrialization brought social and economic issues into the political arena, providing the nascent machine the means for political mobilization of the working class. Focusing on a later era in his book *Political Parties and the State: The American Historical Experience* (1994), Shefter sought to revive the centrality of the "machine/reform dialectic" in urban political history. In *Urban Trenches* (1981), Katznelson applied class analysis to late twentieth-century New York City machine politics.[28]

A still newer urban political history has been advanced by Philip Ethington in *The Public City: The Political Construction of Urban Life in San Francisco, 1850–1900* (1994). Moving beyond an ethnocultural or class-based political model, Ethington drew on Jürgen Habermas's theories about the "public sphere" in offering new ways of "reconstructing" urban political history. He was particularly interested in exploring an expansive conception of urban politics—one that focused primarily on public discussion and political communication rather than on the more narrow and traditional issue of government policy and administration. Thus, he found that women, although excluded from voting, entered the public sphere, challenged male political dominance, organized a myriad of voluntary associations, and actively engaged in political discourse. A "maternalist" ideology shaped women's political activity in the nineteenth century, leading to many of the Progressive-era social reforms of the early twentieth century. The growth of mass journalism and other new forms of communication at the end of the nineteenth century made possible an extraordinary expansion of popular political participation. In the "public city," a new political culture emerged that transformed American political and social life.[29] The scholarly output of the past decade or so, especially the work of Teaford, Hammack, McDonald, Bridges, Shefter, and Ethington, suggests many new lines of analysis for urban political history.

*Suburbanization.* Recent historians of the American city have demonstrated great interest in suburbanization. Census statistics have revealed that more Americans now live in the suburban rings surrounding the big cities than in the central cities themselves. Thus, it is appropriate that the historical process that created this demographic reality has been brought under scholarly examination. Warner initiated this sort of study more than thirty years ago in *Streetcar Suburbs*, but few followed his lead at that time. However, the subject has been revitalized in the past decade with the publication of a number of new books and articles on the history of suburbanization.

The most important of these studies is Kenneth T. Jackson's *Crabgrass Frontier: The Suburbanization of the United States* (1985), a synthesis of two centuries of the suburbanization process. It began with the preindustrial "walking city" of the eighteenth and early nineteenth centuries, a residential pattern gradually altered by new transit provisions and the romantic lure of suburbia. By the 1850s and after, revolutionary transit technology—first the horsecar, later the electric trolley—encouraged the deconcentration of population to the urban periphery. There was a political dimension to the process as well, as cities sought to recapture lost population through the annexation of the suburbs. Much of the municipal political history of the late nineteenth century reflected the conflict between the center and the periphery. For the twentieth century, Jackson focused on the impact of the automobile and on the role of the federal government. Since the 1930s, especially, the suburbanization process has been shaped by federal policymaking. Government highway construction, federal housing programs, and federal mortgage and tax policies all propelled the suburban drift of population and economic activities. Jackson's study is the most sophisticated and thorough account of these subjects. However, some critics have suggested that he has overly emphasized the federal role in suburbanization while ignoring the racial and class dimensions of suburban growth.[30]

Jackson's *Crabgrass Frontier* has been joined by a number of more specific studies of suburbs and the suburbanization process. Henry C. Binford's *The First Suburbs: Residential Communities on the Boston Periphery, 1815–1860* (1985) pushed suburbanization back well before the development of mass transit at midcentury. This study of Cambridge and Somerville saw the suburbanization process stemming from a variety of "fringe" economic activities, an emerging sense of middle-class domesticity, and the rise of new commuter patterns.[31] In *Borderland: Origins of the American Suburb, 1820–1939* (1988), landscape historian John R. Stilgoe offered a richly descriptive account of the presumed Edenic attractions of the suburban "borderlands." Distant from the cities but still within commuting range, the nineteenth-century suburban village offered an escape from the evils of the city, but by midtwentieth century such places increasingly were being swallowed up by a seemingly unstoppable urban sprawl.[32] In *City and Suburb* (1979), Jon C. Teaford provided the first sustained historical analysis of the politics of metropolitan deconcentration, governmental fragmentation, annexation, and consolidation. With a wealth of detail on city-suburban political conflicts from 1850 to 1970, Teaford's book opened up some new territory for urban historians.[33] Margaret Marsh's *Suburban Lives* (1990) explored the nineteenth-century merger of the suburban ideal with the new ideology of domesticity. Her book charted the changing meanings of suburban life for families and for women as the domestic ideal experienced transformation over time.[34] Not to be overlooked are studies of planned suburban communities such as Radburn, New Jersey and Forest Park, Ohio, and of such classic suburbs as Scarsdale, New York, Chestnut Hill near Philadelphia, the Country Club District of Kansas City, and the North Shore towns near Chicago.[35] In addition, recent works have explored the activities of suburban builders, subdividers, and developers, providing new perspectives on the explosive development of the suburban fringe.[36]

Debate among suburban historians has been stimulated by two recent books, Robert Fishman's *Bourgeois Utopias* (1987) and Joel Garreau's *Edge City* (1991). Fishman's book offered a quick, comparative study of Anglo-American suburbanization, from London in the eighteenth century to Los Angeles in the twentieth. The classic suburb represented the expression of deeply embedded middle-class values, such as homeownership, family life, communion with nature, and isolation from the urban-industrial world. New suburban forms themselves became an "active force in urban history," providing models for builders and homeowners that eventually transformed the metropolitan landscape. But in the past half century, a still newer suburban form—what Fishman called the "technoburb"—has taken shape, created as a consequence of the movement of industry and commerce to new "perimeter cities" on the outskirts of the old urban cores. As Fishman put it, "urban functions disperse across a decentralized landscape that is neither urban nor rural nor suburban in the traditional sense." Old residential suburbs, in short, have begun taking on many of the functions of the cities, dramatically altering their character in the process.[37]

Fishman's basic thesis has been developed at length by Garreau in *Edge City*, which demonstrated the spread of multiple-nuclei urban centers distant from old downtowns. Usually growing up around shopping malls at the intersections of interstate highways, these edge cities expanded still farther with the addition of hotels, industrial parks, office buildings, additional retail centers, and eventually massive new residential housing. Often a regional airport is not far away, and in some cases, as in Chicago, Washington, or Miami, the edge cities grow up around an airport. Most American cities have such new "outer cities," but Garreau focused on particularly pertinent examples in Washington, Atlanta, Phoenix, Boston, San Francisco, and a few other places. For Garreau, the edge city increasingly represented the dominant urban form of the present and the future.[38]

Not all urban historians agree with the Fishman-Garreau prognosis. In their chapter in this book, "Bold New City or Built-up 'Burb," William Sharpe and Leonard Wallock reject the new conceptualization of suburbia, showing that in most important ways the suburbs remain subservient to and dependent on the central city.[39] Historiographical essays on suburbia by Michael H. Ebner and Margaret Marsh provide a good introduction to the suburban literature and the key interpretive issues.[40]

*City and Region*. Increasingly, some urban historians have sought to link the American city to its hinterland, to the surrounding region of which it is a part. As historian David R. Goldfield has suggested, by the 1970s some historians in the United States and elsewhere had begun to pursue urban research within a regional framework. The regionalist idea in the United States derived largely from the work of sociologist Howard W. Odom, who argued in the 1930s that "cultures evolve and can be understood only through the study of regional areas." As Goldfield put it, regionalist research was based on a convergence of geography and history, and it hoped to discover links between environment and culture. For urban historians, the regional approach promised to broaden the study of the city to the wider region to which it was linked geographically, economically, and culturally. By this method, it has been argued, the processes of urbanization might be more precisely examined and defined.[41]

Goldfield himself has provided an excellent example of how the regionalist approach can invigorate the writing of urban history. His *Cotton Fields and Skyscrapers: Southern City and Region, 1607–1980* (1982) analyzed southern urbanization within the context of southern history and culture.[42] Goldfield challenged earlier views that the pattern of southern urban development was similar to the national urban experience— a position that he himself had once taken.[43] As Goldfield put it, "the southern city is different because the South is different"; the southern city "is much closer to the plantation than it is to Chicago and New York." More specifically, he argued that three distinctive aspects of regional history and culture have shaped southern urbanization. These are, first, a rural life-style in which the cities maintained a symbiotic relationship with staple agriculture, cotton especially; second, the importance of race and the reality of a biracial society; and third, a colonial economy in which southern cities remained "in economic servitude to the North not only for manufactured products but for all of the financial, credit, legal, accounting, and factoring services that attend a national economy." The application of this regionalist model of explanation resulted in a stimulating reinterpretation of southern urban history.[44]

A second major study that explored the links between city and region is William Cronon's magisterial *Nature's Metropolis: Chicago and the Great West* (1991). Primarily known as an environmental historian, Cronon demonstrated that late nineteenth-century Chicago was at the center of a vast economic ecosystem that stretched from the Ohio Valley to the Pacific Coast. The Midwest metropolis, he contended, was built not so much by the work of individual entrepreneurs but by the functioning of impersonal economic forces, especially the enormous flows of raw materials and commodities such as meat, timber, and grain. The city became a major processing center, with great grain elevators, immense stockyards for cattle and hogs, and numerous timber yards, sawmills, and furniture factories. New technology and machinery, as well as the creation of a commodities futures market, made Chicago's rural-based industries possible and profitable. The commodity flows, for instance, were facilitated by a complex railroad transportation system, which inextricably linked the city and the hinterland. The relationship between city and farm was a symbiotic one: as commodities flowed into Chicago, outward-bound trains carried farm machinery, processed meat, and mail-order catalog items. Showing his environmentalist inclinations, Cronon also made clear that the economic exploitation of the natural environment produced a host of negative consequences—the degradation of the forests, the plowing of the tall-grass prairies, the slaughtering of the bison herds. As a consequence of farming, grazing, and lumbering, the natural ecosystem of the "Great West" was eventually destroyed, replaced by new and more wide-ranging economic relationships between city and region. Indeed, the linkage between Chicago and its hinterland ultimately pulled the Great West into the orbit of the world capitalist system, with powerful modernizing influences. Urban and rural history are blended together in this original study that demonstrates the value of a regionalist perspective for urban history.[45]

Cronon and Goldfield have presented the most fully developed regional interpretations of U.S. urban history. A number of other recent studies, when taken together, also suggest the utility of such a regional research strategy. These include Jeffrey S. Adler's book on the economic role of St. Louis in the antebellum West, Timothy R. Mahoney's study of the urbanization in the upper Mississippi River valley region, books on the rise and fall of the industrial Midwest by Jon C. Teaford and Anthony M. Orum, Diane Lindstrom's analysis of economic change in the Philadelphia region between 1810 and 1850, and books on the urban South by Blaine A. Brownell, David R. Goldfield, Don H. Doyle, and Douglas L. Smith.[46] John M. Findlay in *Magic Lands* (1992) and Carl Abbott in *The Metropolitan Frontier* (1993) surveyed the urban West in the rapid growth years after 1940, while Bradford Luckingham's *The Urban Southwest* (1982) examined the common patterns in the growth and development of Albuquerque, El Paso, Phoenix, and Tucson.[47] Some other new or recent studies of urban development in various regions, while not specifically regionalist in the Goldfield or Cronon tradition, nevertheless supply more grist for the interpretive mill. These include studies of the urban South by Lawrence H. Larsen and James C. Cobb, and books on the urban West by Larsen, Gunther Barth, and Gerald D. Nash.[48]

*Sunbelt Cities.* One of the most dramatic demographic and structural shifts in American history has occurred in the years since 1940 with the growth of the so-called sunbelt cities. Carl Abbott's *The New Urban America* (1981; rev. ed., 1987) presented the first full-scale historical analysis of sunbelt city growth. Abbott identified two distinct growth regions—a seven-state sunbelt Southeast, and a ten-state sunbelt West. Since 1950, these regions experienced population increases, urban and metropolitan growth, and expansion in government employment and per capita income. These growth patterns, Abbott suggested, began during World War II, when the federal government built military bases and training facilities in the South and Southwest. Defense industries such as shipbuilding and aircraft manufacture were concentrated in those regions as well. Wartime migration and new federal contracts made boomtowns of Atlantic, Gulf, and Pacific coastal cities. By 1980, five of the nation's ten largest cities—Houston, Dallas, Phoenix, San Diego, and Los Angeles—were located in the Southwest.[49]

The post-World War II sunbelt boom was characterized by sustained economic growth, particularly in defense and high-technology industries as well as in tourism, recreation, and retirement activities. In the automobile era, speedy population dispersal from the central city was commonplace, often following new highway construction and the decentralization of economic activities. Suburban growth accompanied the rise of the sunbelt cities, as the social ecology of the central cities was reproduced at the metropolitan periphery. Population growth and dispersal eventually led the sunbelt cities to active programs of annexation, often on a massive scale. Between 1950 and 1980, typically, Houston grew in area from 160 to 556 square miles, while Oklahoma City expanded from 51 to 603 square miles. Rapid growth created urban-management problems and occasionally led to governmental experimentation, such as in the implementation of metropolitan government in Miami-Dade County in 1957 and city-county consolidations in Nashville, Jacksonville, Indianapolis, and elsewhere in the 1960s and 1970s. Relaxed state-annexation laws, a tradition of single-party politics in the South, and the fear of a growing black or Hispanic vote in the central cities all speeded up the annexation and consolidation process in the sunbelt in the 1950s and 1960s.

In an innovative section on sunbelt city politics, Abbott identified three successive stages in postwar political development. In the immediate postwar era, the urban boosters and Chamber of Commerce reformers who controlled city governments sought to manage physical and economic growth so as to benefit central city business interests. A new political pattern began to emerge by the 1950s, as vigorous suburban politicians and interest groups fought central city establishments on various issues. More recently, urban politics in the sunbelt has been characterized by neighborhood and ethnic conflict in which local communities have become "focal points for political action." Metropolitan politics in the sunbelt, Abbott argued, reflected urban spatial and territorial realities. Indeed, the crucial issues of local politics—growth policies, annexation, consolidation, school integration, urban renewal, public housing location, highway planning, environmental protection, taxes, and services—are all at least partly spatial issues, and local political actors perceive them in terms of their spatial consequences. These are only some of the conclusions drawn in this pioneering study of the sunbelt cities.

If there are common patterns among sunbelt cities, however, the differences among them may be as great as those between sunbelt and frostbelt. This point certainly emerged in a collection of original essays edited by Richard M. Bernard and Bradley R. Rice, *Sunbelt Cities: Politics and Growth since World War II* (1983). Examining twelve sunbelt cities, ranging from Miami and Tampa in the East to Los Angeles and San Diego in the West, the Bernard-Rice volume demonstrated the incredible variety in the demographic, cultural, economic, and political patterns in the sunbelt. The same conclusion might be drawn from several other sunbelt anthologies, some of which challenged the utility of sunbelt conceptualization: Raymond A. Mohl, ed., *Searching for the Sunbelt* (1990); Randall M. Miller and George E. Pozzetta, eds., *Shades of the Sunbelt* (1988); and Robert B. Fairbanks and Kathleen Underwood, eds., *Essays on Sunbelt Cities and Recent Urban America* (1990).[50] Numerous studies have focused on specific sunbelt cities, suburbs, or states, providing additional perspectives on modern southern and western urban growth.[51]

*Technology and the City.* From the midnineteenth century, technological innovation has been one of the chief stimulants to urban growth and change. New transit technology encouraged the outward movement of population; new or improved municipal utilities and services made urban life safer and more pleasant; and new building technologies permitted the rise of the skyscraper. A number of recent books have elaborated on these aspects of urban history. For example, Charles W. Cheape's *Moving the Masses: Urban Public Transit in New York, Boston, and Philadelphia, 1880–1912* (1980) gave an excellent analysis of the financial, political, and technological context of the building of city transit systems.[52] In *722 Miles* (1993), Clifton Hood demonstrated the ways in which the construction of the world's largest subway system transformed New York City after it opened in 1904.[53] The dramatic modernizing impact of electricity on urban life is documented in Harold L. Platt's *The Electric City* (1991) and in David E. Nye's *Electrifying America* (1990).[54] Mark H. Rose's *Cities of Light and Heat* (1995) offered an innovative analysis of the domestication of gas and electricity in Kansas City and Denver.[55] Martin V. Melosi's collaborative work, *Pollution and Reform in American Cities, 1870–1930* (1980), carved out some new research areas for urban historians. Covering various types of pollution (water, air, noise), the individual essays emphasized the role of technological innovation and of municipal engineers in developing new systems of sewage disposal, water purification, and environmental change. Melosi's *Garbage in the Cities* (1981) analyzed changing patterns of solid waste disposal, a rather unappealing but nevertheless ubiquitous urban problem.[56]

Technology revolutionized not only urban transit but also many other types of urban systems. Essays in Joel A. Tarr and Gabriel Dupuy's edited collection, *Technology and the Rise of the Networked City in Europe and America* (1988), explored varied dimensions of urban infrastructures (sewers, water lines, transit, and power and communications systems), particularly the speed at which these new systems became available in the late nineteenth century and the impact of such innovations on the modernizing city.[57] New industrial-era communications systems such as the telegraph and the telephone played an important role in reorganizing urban life, as suggested in studies by Joel A. Tarr, Edwin Gabler, and Claude S. Fischer.[58] Other important works examining aspects of improving technology and municipal service delivery include Tarr's study of transportation patterns in Pittsburgh, Harold L. Platt's book on public utilities in Houston, Judith Walzer Leavitt's treatment of public health in Milwaukee, Louis P. Cain's analysis of water supply and sanitation in Chicago, and Andrew Hurley's study linking class, race, and industrial pollution in Gary, Indiana.[59]

The electric streetcar was the technological innovation of the late nineteenth century that most stimulated the physical growth of the American city; in the twentieth century, the automobile served that function. In *From Streetcar to Superhighway* (1981), Mark S. Foster studied the role of city planners in urban transportation between 1900 and 1940. Foster attributed the decline of mass transit to the perceived flexibility and economy of the automobile.[60] Clay McShane advanced a slightly different interpretation of the auto's rise to dominance in *Down the Asphalt Path: The Automobile and the American City* (1994). For McShane, changing patterns of American culture, especially new conceptions of city streets as "trafficways" rather than as open public spaces, paved the way for acceptance of the automobile.[61] Case studies of Chicago by Paul Barrett, of Atlanta by Howard L. Preston, and of Los Angeles by Scott L. Bottles also explored the decline of streetcar systems and the rise of the automobile after 1900.[62] In *Interstate: Express Highway Politics, 1941–1956* (1979; 2d. ed., 1990), Mark H. Rose shifted from the municipal to the national level, where public policies affecting the automobile and the city also were being made. It should be no surprise that the 1956 legislation creating the interstate highway system, supported by massive federal subsidies, had a tremendous impact on urban-suburban America. Rose detailed the postwar, interest-group politics behind the highway program.[63] The central achievement of these varied recent works has been to demonstrate the important link between technological systems and urban growth and change—a point made in several important historiographical surveys of the literature.[64]

*Planning and Housing.* Technology is related closely to the ways in which Americans planned and built their cities. Technological innovations established the parameters of what was possible and feasible in the built environment. Studies of planning history published in the 1960s and 1970s focused inordinately on the nineteenth-century roots of city planning. These works emphasized the landscape architecture tradition, in which Frederick Law Olmsted played such a major role, and the emergence of the "city beautiful" movement under the leadership of such Chicago figures as architect and planner Daniel Burnham and architect Louis Sullivan.[65] These nineteenth-century traditions and Olmsted's work, especially, continue to attract scholarly interest.[66]

However, planning history in the 1980s pushed into the twentieth century. Abandoning the "great planner" tradition, such works

concentrated on the practical and utilitarian side—the efficient implementation of zoning policies, urban transit, highway building, public
utilities, and central-city development and redevelopment. Moreover,
most recent writing in planning history tends strongly toward placing
planning decisions into a wider political and social context. This is particularly true of planning histories by Sylvia D. Fries on American colonial cities, Judd Kahn on San Francisco, Christopher Silver on Richmond,
and Carl Abbott on Portland.[67] Four recent books have analyzed the rebuilding of cities after great fires, such as the disastrous Chicago Fire of
1873.[68] The most important and comprehensive recent book is *Planning
the Twentieth-Century American City* (1996), edited by Mary Corbin Sies
and Christopher Silver, a wide-ranging collection of essays on the
subject.[69]

Several other recent works have provided specific analytical focus
on American urban planning as well. For instance, David Schuyler's *The
New Urban Landscape* (1986) offered a detailed examination of the reception of city planning in the nineteenth century. In *The City Beautiful
Movement* (1989), William H. Wilson gave the most detailed study of
that turn-of-the-century campaign to beautify urban America; case studies of Kansas City, Seattle, Denver, and Dallas shifted the focus away
from the more heavily studied eastern cities and demonstrated that the
movement depended on wide popular support and that it had appeal
throughout the United States. Stanley Buder's *Visionaries and Planners* (1990) presented a comparative study of the "garden city movement" in Great Britain and the United States, suggesting the continuing
influence of such planning ideals in the contemporary "new towns" on
both sides of the Atlantic. Stanley K. Schultz's *Constructing Urban Culture* (1989) linked city planning with new technological innovations that
made the modernized city possible. In *The Mysteries of the Great City*
(1993), a study of New York, Chicago, and Cincinnati, John D. Fairfield
emphasized the connections between urban political power and new
patterns of urban design. Finally, in *The Park and the People* (1992),
Roy Rosenzweig and Elizabeth Blackmar wrote a masterful social history of New York City's pioneering planning endeavor, Central Park.[70]

Twentieth-century planning has been centrally related to the expansion of modern government. Governmental decision making in this area
often stemmed from motives other than those originally conceived by
planners—making cities more rational, more pleasant, more liveable.
Recent planning histories have emphasized the government's role in urban planning, and they demonstrate the often negative consequences of
its actions—that is, highway construction that helped destroy central
city areas, or urban renewal programs that leveled vibrant inner-city
neighborhoods. A full-scale critique of the role and function of planners
can be found in M. Christine Boyer's *Dreaming the Rational City* (1983)
and in Richard E. Fogelsong's *Planning the Capitalist City* (1986). Both
books argued that city planning served the interests of the dominant
capitalist economy and sought to impose order and control on the urban
masses.[71]

One aspect of urban planning that generally received short shrift in the United States was housing. In European nations, from the late nineteenth century the provision of housing was linked integrally to all other facets of planning.[72] Not so in the United States, where housing reform was generally a matter for private action. Elizabeth Blackmar's *Manhattan for Rent, 1750–1850* (1989) pushed housing history back to the early nineteenth century, demonstrating the linkage between the urban housing market and the emerging capitalist economy.[73] The Progressive era did see some housing reform legislation, but the prevailing view was that the private building market was responsible for the provision of decent housing. Good accounts of Progressive-era housing reform can be found in Thomas L. Phillpott's *The Slum and the Ghetto* (1978), a study of Chicago, and in Robert B. Fairbanks's *Making Better Citizens* (1988), a study of Cincinnati.[74] Carrying the story beyond the Progressive period, Gail Radford's *Modern Housing for America* (1996) analyzed New Deal housing programs, suggesting the ultimate failure of innovative federal housing policies. Gwendolyn Wright placed housing history in the broad context of modern urban and suburban development in *Building the Dream: A Social History of Housing in America* (1981).[75] More specific studies by Arnold R. Hirsch and Dominic J. Capeci traced the agonizing question of housing for blacks in Chicago and Detroit since 1940. In both cities, racial conflict and violence accompanied black efforts to widen their housing opportunities. John F. Bauman's recent book on the history of housing in Philadelphia, *Public Housing, Race, and Renewal* (1987), explored another important dimension of this subject.[76] The best of these histories go beyond the purely physical aspect of housing provision and focus on the political, social, and racial context within which housing decisions were made by governments, by citizen groups, and by individuals.

*The Urban Working Class.* Building on the insights of the British historian E. P. Thompson, students of the American working class have been revamping our understanding of workers and of class relations in the city. Herbert Gutman's important study, *Work, Culture, and Society in Industrializing America* (1976), led the way. His research on the first generation of industrial workers in America demonstrated the surprising strength and persistence of the communal, preindustrial work pattern, even in the midst of the drive toward industrialization. The chief thrust of Gutman's work has been that workers exercised some control over their lives and over the workplace.[77]

Other historians have pushed the rise of working-class activism back into the preindustrial era. In *The Urban Crucible* (1979), colonial historian Gary Nash concluded that social and economic distinctions developed very early in New York, Philadelphia, and Boston. During the economic dislocations of the mideighteenth century, Nash contended, the urban working class developed an increasingly radical and participatory politics; as a sense of class consciousness emerged, the urban working class began to take charge of their lives in new and dramatic ways. Crowd action in the cities, for instance, became an instrument of collective power, the means by which cohesive colonial communities protected their perceived interests. The American Revolution, Nash asserted, was one result. [78]

Several other recent studies have fleshed out our knowledge of preindustrial working-class history. For instance, Sean Wilentz, in a detailed and important study of the New York City working class, *Chants Democratic* (1984), carried the class analysis into the early nineteenth century. Adhering fiercely to an egalitarian ideology, the urban artisans emerged after the American Revolution as a powerful anticapitalist force with a strong sense of working-class consciousness. In *New York City Cartmen, 1667–1850* (1986), Graham R. Hodges explored the dynamics of working-class culture among a highly politicized group of unskilled urban workers. Ronald Schultz and David A. Zonderman documented the workers' difficult transition from artisanal life to industrial capitalism in Philadelphia and New England, respectively. David R. Roediger in *The Wages of Whiteness* (1991) and Eric Lott in *Love and Theft* (1995) explored the emergence of racism among white workers in industrializing America. Peter Way, in *Common Labour* (1993), detailed the difficult experiences of Irish immigrant canal workers prior to 1860.[79] The rise of urban rioting and popular disorder is analyzed in books by Paul Gilje and Iver Bernstein.[80]

During the industrialization process, urban artisans became factory workers; skilled craftsmen suffered loss of status and economic position as the production process was mechanized and skill became less important. A number of studies have focused on the ways in which the urban working class resisted, protested, and adapted to the changes brought about by industrialization. In *Worker City, Company Town* (1978), Daniel J. Walkowitz traced the divergent patterns in Troy and Cohoes, New York. Alan Dawley and Paul G. Faler analyzed the workers' response to industrialization in Lynn, Massachusetts. Other studies have examined the process and its impact on the working class in Newark, Philadelphia, Pittsburgh, Cincinnati, Detroit, Albany, and Chicago. The general thrust of this work is that workers did not accept industrialization passively, that they resisted the new work disciplines of the industrial era, that preindustrial values and traditions persisted, and that workers exerted some control over their own lives.[81] As Daniel Rogers suggested in *The Work Ethic in Industrial America, 1850–1920* (1978), "there is ample evidence that large numbers of industrial workers failed to internalize the faith of the factory masters." Closely allied to this position is David Montgomery's argument in *Workers' Control in America* (1979) that trade unions ultimately became the mechanism for maintaining craft-worker autonomy and for enforcing work rules.[82]

Working-class history has traditionally focused on male workers, but some newly published research has demonstrated that women workers played an increasingly important role in the urban economy. In the late nineteenth century, for instance, women entered the urban workforce on a large scale, taking jobs in offices, as telephone operators, and as department store clerks; simultaneously, the proportion of women in factory and domestic service jobs began to decline. Lisa M. Fine's *The Souls of the Skyscraper* (1990), a study of Chicago, documented the gender shift from male to female in clerical jobs. In separate books, Sharon H. Strom and Margery W. Davies linked the "feminization" of office work to the implementation of principles of scientific management. Stephen H. Norwood's *Labor's Flaming Youth* (1990) discovered a pattern of militancy among telephone operators, while Susan P. Benson's *Counter Cultures* (1986) analyzed the world of women with jobs in the new department stores in the late nineteenth century. But women continued to work in the home as well, a subject documented in great detail in Eileen Boris's *Home to Work* (1994). Joanne J. Meyerowitz explored the role of single women workers in Chicago in *Women Adrift* (1988), while S. J. Kleinberg researched the impact of industrialization on families in Pittsburgh in *The Shadow of the Mills* (1989).[83] Women workers became active in labor unions, as a number of recent books have demonstrated.[84] All of these volumes on women in the workplace suggest that urban history cannot be entirely disconnected from labor history and, more generally, from social history.

*Immigration and Ethnicity*. Recent historians have altered dramatically the portrait of immigrants and ethnic groups in the American city. The traditional view had been summarized ably in Oscar Handlin's *The Uprooted* (1951), a prize-winning book that first brought social science conceptualization to the study of immigration history. Handlin depicted the immigrants as a displaced peasantry wrenched from the communal past and thrust into the industrial city in a harsh, foreign land. In the urban ghettos of industrial America, the newcomers suffered the destruction of their traditional cultures, social breakdown and disorganization, and eventual assimilation. Virtually every aspect of Handlin's "ghetto hypothesis" of immigrant adjustment now has been rewritten by recent historians.[85]

The historical scholarship of the past two decades has given new perspectives on the migration process, the creation of the ethnic village in the American city, and the development of immigrant institutional life. Historians have discovered the importance of "chain migration"— the family and community-based process that brought most immigrants to America.[86] Once in the new land, the immigrant family structure remained a powerful determinant of life and culture. For Italians, Germans, Poles, French Canadians, the Irish, Jews, and most others, the family bolstered ethnic culture and aided in the adaptation to industrial work. Old Country cultural, religious, and folk patterns did not disappear but persisted as vital ingredients of the ethnic community.[87]

Rather than weakening under the strains of migration and urban life, recent historians have concluded, the ties of family, kinship, and community remained strong in the American industrial city. Ethnic churches, parochial schools, and a bewildering variety of cultural and fraternal groups kept ethnicity alive despite the powerful forces of assimilation. Drawing on the strength of their Old County culture, the newcomers sought both to preserve their traditions and to adapt to the new urban environment.[88]

Moreover, as historian Rudolph J. Vecoli has argued, the immigrants demonstrated "a powerful tendency to reconstitute community in accordance with Old World origins." Thus, Chicago's "Little Italies" were in reality dozens of Old Country village groups reorganized and reconstituted in the new land. Similarly, in his study *Ethnics and Enclaves: Boston's Italian North End* (1981), historian William DeMarco noted the importance of Old Country village and regional loyalties and concluded that "in terms of subcultural neighborhoods, the North End resembled the Italian countryside by 1920." Among the Poles in Philadelphia, Caroline Golab wrote in *Immigrant Destinations* (1977), settlement and work patterns "strongly reflected their feudal past and peasant culture."[89]

Many of the new immigrant histories focus on a single group in a single community, microstudies that provide detail and insight into the larger processes of migration, adjustment, and change. Several recent studies of immigrant labor history have followed this model, most demonstrating immigrant commitment to union activism; one study, however, David M. Emmons's *The Butte Irish* (1990), revealed a different pattern, as the Irish in Butte, Montana, displayed a striking degree of indifference to union militancy and working-class radicalism.[90] A number of important books have explored the shaping role of immigrant women in the family and community—a subject most recently discussed in Donna Gabaccia's broadly interpretive *From the Other Side* (1994).[91] Pushing the immigrant saga back into the colonial period, Joyce D. Goodfriend's *Before the Melting Pot* (1992) revealed the startling degree of ethnic diversity in colonial New York City.[92] Reflecting the considerable recent interest in "whiteness" in American history, Noel Ignatiev's *How the Irish Became White* (1995) showed how midnineteenth-century Irish immigrants speeded up their assimilation by embracing white supremacy.[93] The unique ethnic and racial amalgam of New Orleans, beginning with its early colonial Franco-African culture, is explored in *Creole New Orleans* (1992), edited by Arnold R. Hirsch and Joseph Logsdon.[94] Several immigration historians have examined Hispanic, Asian, and Afro-Caribbean immigrants, and a considerable body of literature has documented the late twentieth-century Third World immigration to the United States.[95]

Such research has uncovered important dimensions of the immigrant experience. Portraying dynamic and vibrant ethnic communities in the industrial city, this new work effectively demolished the traditional immigration model put forth by Handlin. The most sophisticated summary of the new immigration history model is found in John Bodnar's *The Transplanted: A History of Immigrants in Urban America* (1985), which pulled together in a seamless account the many and varied strands of immigrant history research.[96]

*African-American Urban History*. African-American urban history has experienced a dramatic shift of focus in the past decade. Many early studies of blacks in the city emphasized the physical and institutional structure of black communities—this was the "ghetto synthesis model" used by Gilbert Osofsky and Allan H. Spear in their studies of New York City and Chicago.[97] By contrast, the major thrust of recent work in the field has adopted an "agency model," demonstrating the extent to which African Americans in slavery and freedom shaped and controlled their own destinies. This newer work also has emphasized an internal focus on kinship and communal networks, class and culture, and the diversity and complexity of black communities. These new directions are most fully articulated in *The New African-American Urban History* (1996), edited by Kenneth W. Goings and Raymond A. Mohl.[98]

The beginnings of a new approach to African-American urban history can be found in the mid-1970s. Challenging a contemporary social science literature, Herbert Gutman, in *The Black Family in Slavery and Freedom, 1750–1925* (1976), contended that the black family had a long history as a strong and vital institution. Similarly, studies of Boston and Cleveland revealed that southern blacks in northern cities maintained stable, two-parent families supported by extended-kin networks. In his innovative study, *Alley Life in Washington* (1980), James Borchert found a remarkable persistence of black folklife in the capital. Blacks retained their old cultural patterns and "were able to maintain stability through their primary groups of family, kinship, neighborhood, community, and religion." These cultural patterns, Borchert maintained, helped black migrants in their "adjustment to a harsh and difficult urban experience."[99]

By the mid-1980s, most new work in black urban history pursued the agency model. The new African-American urban history conveys a sense of active involvement, of people empowered, engaged in struggle, living their lives in dignity, and shaping their own futures. For instance, Gary B. Nash's *Forging Freedom* (1988) portrayed blacks in Revolution-era Philadelphia as actively creating community and institutions, building political consciousness, and energetically advocating the abolition of slavery. Shane White made a similar argument in *Somewhat More Independent* (1991), a study of New York City. Numerous African-American community studies of later periods advanced similar interpretations.[100] In studies of the late nineteenth and early twentieth centuries, Robin Kelley, Kenneth W. Goings, and Gerald L. Smith have documented new patterns of black resistance to white racism in Birmingham and Memphis. In *Race Rebels* (1994), Kelley described a tradition of "infrapolitics"—a pattern of daily behavior, an oppositional culture, in which African Americans demanded recognition and respect in daily encounters in the streets, on streetcars, on the job, in the courts, and elsewhere. Goings and Smith, in their work on Memphis, revealed a record of violent encounters as blacks resisted white supremacy.[101]

The new African-American urban history has pursued several other lines of investigation. An earlier emphasis on black elites has been abandoned, as scholars have focused instead on a more diverse community with sharply etched divisions of class and culture. This newer work has provided a deeper and more textured sense of the black working class —of its transformation from southern agricultural roots to urban

industrial labor, from peasantry to proletariat.[102] Similarly, recent
work has emerged on black people in labor and radical movements, on
African-American sports, and on black festival behavior and the use of
streets and public spaces.[103] New studies of the migrations of southern
blacks, such as James R. Grossman's *Land of Hope* (1989), have been
written from the perspective of the migrants themselves.[104] New research
on twentieth-century urban uprisings (or race riots) now focuses more
centrally on the working-class African Americans who participated or
were victimized.[105] Important work on black churches and black women
has drawn a fuller picture of African-American institutional life.[106] A
new history of the civil rights movement has also emerged in recent
years—one that challenges earlier top-down histories that focused almost exclusively on elite national leaders and organizations. The emerging new interpretation contends that the freedom struggle at the
community level took place independently of national activities in response to local conditions, suggesting many different civil rights *movements* rather than a single unified movement dominated by a few elite
leaders. Such a community-oriented interpretation shows a new appreciation of the role of individual struggle in achieving civil rights.[107]

The ongoing scholarly debate over the "underclass" also has broad
implications for African-American urban history. Although widely used
in the 1980s as a journalistic shorthand for the high levels of crime,
poverty, and social disorganization in the mostly black central cities,
the conception of an urban underclass was given scholarly credence by
William Julius Wilson. In his influential *The Truly Disadvantaged* (1987),
he explained the emergence of the black underclass as a consequence of
deep structural shifts in the American economy since about 1970—
namely, the decline of industrial employment and the rise of a bifurcated postindustrial job market. Blacks were unprepared and untrained
for the high-skill, high-tech economy but could never get ahead by relying only on the low-skill, low-pay service economy. Wilson has elaborated and refined this argument in his latest book, *When Work Disappears*
(1996), but the economic explanation for the emergence of the underclass
remains dominant. Wilson's thesis, however, has been challenged by sociologists Douglas S. Massey and Nancy A. Denton, whose *American
Apartheid: Segregation and the Making of the Underclass* (1993) strongly
argued that the persistence of racism and racial segregation were to
blame for the continuing plight of the inner cities.[108]

African-American urban history, in short, has been completely
reconceptualized since the early 1980s. The new historical research depicts a group of urban Americans who rejected passivity in the face of
powerful forces of opposition, who sought to shape their own lives despite pressures of the city, the factory, and the reality of white racism.
As with the white immigrants, for African Americans human agency
made possible a new life in the city.

*Urban Policy History.* As urban history has begun to focus on the
twentieth century, the increasingly powerful role of the federal government in urban policymaking has come under study. Two books in the

mid-1970s initiated research on this subject—Mark Gelfand's *A Nation of Cities: The Federal Government and Urban America, 1933–1965* (1975) and Philip Funigiello's *The Challenge to Urban Liberalism: Federal-City Relations during World War II* (1978). Both volumes demonstrated the hesitant effort of the federal government to grapple with urban issues during the economic disaster of the 1930s and the wartime emergency of the early 1940s. While the government did embark on a range of new programs for relief, employment, and wartime planning—programs especially welcomed in America's big cities—what is remarkable is the lack of any coherent national urban policy. Indeed, government initiatives usually were undermined by the enduring strength of a localist tradition, the power of entrepreneurialism and privatism, and destructive competition among various interest groups for governmental favoritism.[109]

In the 1980s urban scholars developed some of these themes more fully. Roger W. Lotchin's edited collection, *The Martial Metropolis* (1984), explored the connection between federal military spending and urban development. In what is now referred to as the Lotchin thesis, the city and the sword are seen as inseparably linked in such cities as Norfolk, San Francisco, San Antonio, Los Angeles, Seattle, and Portland. Lotchin's *Fortress California* (1992) offered a massively detailed analysis of the metropolitan-military complex in the nation's largest state.[110] John Mollenkopf's *The Contested City* (1983) provided an ambitious overview of the development of urban public policy since the New Deal era. Mollenkopf argued that the Democratic party put together a national progrowth coalition that altered the urban environment and, not incidentally, kept the party in power throughout much of the period between the 1930s and 1980. Mollenkopf also demonstrated that the Democrats' urban liberalism often made conditions worse for inner-city residents while stimulating conservative countermovements. Despite some weaknesses, the book gave a powerful account of federal interventionism since the 1930s.[111] However, a second book on the same subject rejected the interpretation that politics motivated public policymaking. In *Metropolitan America: Urban Life and Urban Policy in the United States, 1940–1980* (1986), Kenneth Fox contended that social science research, government data, and rational argument have had a greater impact in shaping urban public policy. Despite their varied interpretations, all of the authors cited here would agree to the basic premise that federal decision making has shaped urban America over the past sixty years.[112]

In the past decade, the focus of scholarship on urban policy history has shifted from the national to the local level. Numerous case studies have provided detailed information and analysis on the implementation and consequences of policy decisions. For instance, Joel Schwartz's *The New York Approach* (1993) attributed the devastating consequences of post-World War II urban renewal in New York City not only to policy czar Robert Moses but also to various liberal groups willing to sacrifice the interests of working-class neighborhoods. Robert Fitch added new dimensions to the story in his book, *The Assassination of New York* (1993), which placed much of the blame for the city's decline on New York's financial and real estate interests.[113] Howard Gillette's *Between Justice and Beauty* (1995) reported a similar record of urban policy failures in Washington. Policies designed to make the nation's capital more beautiful and efficient were usually at odds with programs to improve housing, welfare, and social conditions. Consequently, many of the city's neighborhoods began to undergo physical and social decay, despite many programs for public works and redevelopment.[114] In *Race and the Shaping of Twentieth-Century Atlanta* (1996), Ronald H. Bayor demonstrated the crucial role of race in the making of urban policy decisions on such issues as highways, housing, development, and employment. Thomas J. Sugrue's *The Origins of the Urban Crisis* (1996) offered a similar perspective on Detroit.[115]

The evolution of urban policy has also been reevaluated in a new round of more general and comparative scholarly works. Jon C. Teaford's *The Rough Road to Renaissance* (1990) systematically explored the efforts of twelve northeastern and midwestern cities to revitalize their downtowns in the decades after 1940. Teaford noted that urban renewal programs began in the 1950s with great optimism but that these hopes for better cities were dashed by the late 1960s in the midst of the so-called urban crisis of the time. By the 1980s, mayors and planners once again began talking about the possibility of an urban renaissance, but economic and demographic decentralization was still draining the life out of many central cities.[116] The essays in *Urban Policy in Twentieth-Century America* (1993), edited by Arnold R. Hirsch and Raymond A. Mohl, turn attention to urban policies relating to housing segregation, highway building, social welfare, political representation, and the environment.[117] Robert Halpern's *Rebuilding the Inner City* (1995) effectively analyzed the history of public housing, urban renewal, and economic development initiatives, especially the War on Poverty.[118] An extensive social science and urban policy literature has addressed virtually every facet of the modern American city; Robert A. Beauregard's *Voices of Decline: The Postwar Fate of U.S. Cities* (1993) gave a good introduction to the issues and the literature.[119]

*Urban Culture.* Some scholars of the city have turned their attention to various dimensions of urban cultural history, to the popular institutions, ideas, and behaviors that characterized the city. The intellectual historian Warren I. Susman conceptualized this approach in an essay, "The City in American Culture," published in his *Culture as History* (1984). Susman suggested the emergence of a new urban culture in the late nineteenth century—a common culture based on new methods of communication, new organizational structures in American life, and new forms of interpersonal relationships demanded by modern urban society. Cultural processes were at work creating a greater degree of social homogeneity, Susman argued. By the turn of the twentieth century, modernity had arrived for urban Americans.[120]

Among urban historians, the view that the city encouraged cultural homogeneity was most fully expressed by Gunther Barth in *City People: The Rise of Modern City Culture in Nineteenth-Century America* (1980).

In this somewhat eclectic book, Barth contended that out of diversity and heterogeneity American urbanites created a modern city culture oriented around common institutions and forms. These common cultural patterns, Barth argued, helped people of vastly different backgrounds "cope with the complex demands of a strange cityscape." The book concentrated on five new elements that contributed to this common urban culture—the apartment house, the metropolitan newspaper, the department store, the ballpark, and the vaudeville house. These new institutions "came into existence with the modern city." Moreover, Barth wrote, they "contributed more directly and extensively to the emergence of modern city culture than did the factory and the political machine." This interpretation is asserted rather than proven, but the argument provided a fascinating new perspective on the rise of the industrial city.[121] In a similar vein, Neil Harris, in *Cultural Excursions* (1990), suggested the important roles played by great American fairs, by museums and libraries, by popular literature and music, and eventually by movies and other forms of cultural production in developing social cohesion in the midst of rapid urban change.[122]

Some cultural historians have discovered another powerful homogenizing force in the modern city—the culture of consumption. Initially ignited and sustained by advertising and mass magazines in the late nineteenth century, the culture of consumption was promoted by dominant elites and corporate bureaucracies. Ordinary Americans, especially city folk, so the argument goes, were pulled into the marketplace and encouraged to believe that their goals and dreams could be achieved through consumption. Roland Marchand in *Advertising the American Dream* (1985), Jackson Lears in *Fables of Abundance* (1994), and William Leach in *Land of Desire* (1993) have presented this argument effectively.[123] Several specialized studies have provided additional evidence for the power of commercial culture. For instance, Elaine S. Abelson's *When Ladies Go A-Thieving* (1989) demonstrated not only that department store shopping had come to be associated with pleasure and personal freedom but also that middle-class women often became shoplifters to realize their consumer dreams.[124] In *Adapting to Abundance* (1990), Andrew R. Heinze explored the relationship of the consumption habits of New York City's East European immigrant Jews to their patterns of cultural assimilation.[125] William R. Taylor's *In Pursuit of Gotham* (1992) revealed the national impact of cultural forms produced in New York City; Times Square, for instance, shifted in the early twentieth century "from its earlier role as a hub of New York's commercial culture to become a national cultural marketplace."[126] The general interpretive thrust of this body of scholarship is that the industrial revolution and the communication revolution of the late nineteenth century dramatically reshaped consumption patterns in urban America.

If the emergence of mass culture and consumerism reflected a homogenizing trend, considerable evidence suggests the persistence of pluralism and diversity in American cultural life as well. For instance, Jackson Lears's *No Place of Grace* (1981) uncovered a powerful antimodernist culture between 1880 and 1920, an intellectual and social tradition that rejected or resisted modernizing change.[127] In *Rudeness and Civility* (1990), John F. Kasson analyzed the emergence by the late nineteenth century of a middle-class urban culture of civility and manners, a social trend promoted by the popularity of etiquette books that discussed proper ways of behaving in public. But it is clear that public behavior in the big city was a matter of contestation, as reflected in rude and raucous working-class behavior in theaters and other public venues.[128] While bourgeois folk were refining their manners, working-class urbanites were enjoying parades and street festivals, burlesque, vaudeville, and ethnic theater, jazz music, dance halls, and other forms of public culture and amusement—activities that had not yet been conquered or appropriated by mass culture.[129] Even as late as the 1920s and 1930s, as Lizabeth Cohen has demonstrated in *Making a New Deal* (1990), immigrant families in Chicago avoided chain stores and their standardized products in an effort to maintain neighborhood shops and the ethnic cultures they sustained; similarly, neighborhood movie theaters and local radio catered to community tastes and interests.[130] These and other studies suggest the persistence of diversity despite the power of mass culture and consumerism.

Research on the history of sports also has begun to fill gaps in our knowledge of urban culture and the uses of leisure time. The best synthesis of urban sports history can be found in Steven A. Riess, *City Games: The Evolution of American Urban Society and the Rise of Sports* (1989), which recognized both the ways in which sports defined class boundaries (in the early nineteenth century) and promoted a mass spectator culture (beginning in the late nineteenth century).[131] Baseball, in particular, was extremely popular in the city from the late nineteenth century, but other sporting and recreational activities also caught on. Baseball, boxing, horse racing, and other sports also came to be linked to city politics and to city gambling activities.[132] Some playground reformers thought of baseball as a means of socializing and controlling urban and immigrant children, as suggested in Dominick Cavallo's *Muscles and Morals* (1981). Working from the same interpretive framework, Peter Levine's *Ellis Island to Ebbets Field* (1992) contended that sports in America, especially baseball, basketball, and boxing, helped to transform immigrant Jews into assimilated Jews.[133]

Other dimensions of urban culture also have been investigated by recent historians. Serving many functions (social, political, and economic), the street-corner saloon became a ubiquitous urban institution. David W. Conroy's *In Public Houses* (1995) pushed the scholarly study of the saloon back into the colonial period, where the shifting dynamics of tavern life and the drinking culture revealed new patterns of political power and authority.[134] Books by Roy Rosenzweig, Perry Duis, and Thomas J. Noel detailed the multifaceted roles of industrial-era saloons in Worcester, Boston, Chicago, and Denver.[135] The general thrust of these studies seems to be that working-class urban institutions had important social and other functions and that such agencies demonstrate the complexity and diversity of urban culture rather than the cultural consensus suggested by Susman and Barth. Historians have also demonstrated an interest in the history of sexuality in the city. Two important books of this genre are Timothy J. Gilfoyle's *City of Eros* (1992), a study of the commercialization of sex in New York City, and George Chauncey's *Gay New York* (1994), an investigation into the hidden gay male world between 1890 and 1940.[136]

Most of the recent research on urban culture has focused on the working class, but a few studies of other class groups have been published. Richard L. Bushman's *The Refinement of America* (1992) discovered that the quest for urban gentility began in the colonial era and spread to the middling levels of society after 1800.[137] Stuart M. Blumin's *The Emergence of the Middle Class* (1989) explored the growth of a distinctive middle-class society and life-style in the early nineteenth-century city.[138] Frederic Cople Jaher's monumental *The Urban Establishment* (1982) concentrated on the rich, the well-born, and the powerful in Boston, New York, Charleston, Chicago, and Los Angeles from the nineteenth to the twentieth century. The cities created unparalleled opportunities for the acquisition of wealth, power, and knowledge. In contrast to the studies of working-class culture, Jaher's perspective offered an alternative analysis of the dynamics of economic, political, and social change in urbanizing America.[139] One additional perspective is provided by Thomas Bender in *New York Intellect* (1987) and in several essays on professional and intellectual elites in the American city.[140] Taken together, the work of Bushman, Blumin, Jaher, and Bender shows a more complete picture of American urban society and culture.

*The Search for Synthesis.* The foregoing general topics all represent important new thrusts of urban history research in the United States. With sufficient space, attention might have been given as well to recent work on women and gender relations in the city, to studies of neighborhood and community, to work on the visual dimension of the city, to biographical studies of urban thinkers and policy makers such as Lewis Mumford or Robert Moses, to studies of urban architecture, crime, violence, and a dozen or more other subjects.[141] This essay has concentrated on books and monographs, but the reader also should be aware of an extensive article literature on all of these subjects.[142] The field, in short, has been enlivened and invigorated with an enormous amount of new research, especially in the past decade.

It is also true, however, that the outpouring of scholarship has fragmented the field and created problems of comprehension and analysis. As historian Bernard Bailyn put it in a 1985 address, "It is a confusing time in historical study, and yet a creative time—in which all sorts of new departures are being made, new materials being assembled, and new viewpoints being aired. But it calls for an occasional reassessment." Similarly, Thomas Bender has written that it is time for a new synthesis pulling together social, political, and cultural history—time to "make history whole again."[143] There have been a few attempts at synthesis in American urban history—mostly survey texts of the field by Charles N. Glaab and A. Theodore Brown, by Howard P. Chudacoff and Judith E.

Smith, by Zane L. Miller and Patricia M. Melvin, and by David R. Goldfield and Blaine A. Brownell.[144] Interpretative texts by Raymond A. Mohl,
Carl Abbott, Jon C. Teaford, and Eric Monkkonen have also sought at
least a partial synthesis of U.S. urban history.[145] More synthesis is
needed, obviously, and works of this sort will probably emerge in the
future. Meanwhile, the recent scholarship detailed in this essay should
provide a sufficiently marked pathway leading interested students,
teachers, and researchers into the exciting field of American urban
history.

NOTES

1. Richard C. Wade, "Urbanization," in C. Vann Woodward, ed., *The Comparative Approach to American History* (New York, 1968), 203.

2. Arthur M. Schlesinger, "The City in American History," *Mississippi Valley Historical Review* 27 (June 1940): 43–66. See also idem, *The Rise of the City, 1878–1898* (New York, 1933).

3. Blake McKelvey, "American Urban History Today," *American Historical Review* 57 (July 1952): 919–29; Carl Bridenbaugh, *Cities in the Wilderness* (New York, 1938); Carl Bridenbaugh, *Cities in Revolt* (New York, 1955); Oscar Handlin, *Boston's Immigrants* (Cambridge, 1941); Richard C. Wade, *The Urban Frontier: The Rise of Western Cities, 1790–1830* (Cambridge, 1959). For a model urban biography from this period see Bayrd Still, *Milwaukee: The History of a City* (Madison, 1948). For outstanding examples of the multivolume genre of urban biography see Bessie L. Pierce, *A History of Chicago*, 3 vols. (Chicago, 1937–57); and Constance McLaughlin Green, *Washington*, 2 vols. (Princeton, 1962–63).

4. Olivier Zunz, "The Synthesis of Social Change: Reflections on American Social History," in Olivier Zunz, ed., *Reliving the Past: The Worlds of Social History* (Chapel Hill, 1985), 54. See also Irwin Unger, "The 'New Left' and American History: Some Recent Trends in United States Historiography," *American Historical Review* 72 (July 1967): 1237–63; Michael Kammen, "The Historian's Vocation and the State of the Discipline in the United States," in Michael Kammen, ed., *The Past before Us: Contemporary Historical Writing in the United States* (Ithaca, 1980), 19–46.

5. W. O. Aydelotte, "Quantification in History," *American Historical Review* 71 (April 1966): 803–25; Jerome M. Clubb and Howard Allen, "Computers and Historical Studies," *Journal of American History* 54 (December 1967): 599–607; Edward Shorter, *The Historian and the Computer* (Englewood Cliffs, NJ, 1971); Allan G. Bogue, "Numerical and Formal Analysis in United States History," *Journal of Interdisciplinary History* 12 (Summer 1981): 137–75; Jerome M. Clubb, "Computer Technology and the Source Materials of Social Science History," *Social Science History* 10 (Summer 1986): 97–114; Allan G. Bogue, *Clio and the Bitch Goddess: Quantification in American Political History* (Beverly Hills, 1983). For an early critique of quantitative history see Jacques Barzun, *Clio and the Doctors* (Chicago, 1974). On the monographic explosion since the 1960s see Bernard Bailyn, "The Challenge of Modern Historiography," *American Historical Review* 87 (February 1982): 1–24.

6. Sam Bass Warner, Jr., *Streetcar Suburbs: The Process of Growth in Boston, 1870–1900* (Cambridge, 1962). See also Warner's other writings: "If All the World Were Philadelphia: A Scaffolding for Urban History, 1774–1930," *American Historical Review* 74 (October 1968): 26–43; *The Private City: Philadelphia in Three Periods of Its Growth* (Philadelphia, 1968); *The Urban Wilderness: A History of the American City* (New York, 1972); *The Way We Really Live: Social Change in Boston Since 1920* (Boston, 1977); *Province of Reason* (Cambridge, 1984); and with Sylvia Fleisch, *Measurements for Social History* (Beverly Hills, 1977).

7. Eric E. Lampard's articles include "American Historians and the Study of Urbanization," *American Historical Review* 67 (October 1961): 49–61; "Urbanization and Social Change: On Broadening the Scope and Relevance of Urban History," in Oscar Handlin and John Burchard, eds., *The Historian and the City* (Cambridge, 1963), 225–47; "Historical Aspects of Urbanization," in Philip M. Hauser and Leo F. Schnore, eds., *The Study of Urbanization* (New York, 1965), 519–54; "Historical Contours of Contemporary Urban Society: A Comparative View," *Journal of Contemporary History* 4 (July 1969): 3–25; "The Dimensions of Urban History: A Footnote to the 'Urban Crisis,' " *Pacific Historical Review* 39 (August 1970): 261–78; "The Pursuit of Happiness in the City: Changing Opportunities and Options in America," *Transactions of the Royal Historical Society* 23 (1973): 175–220; "The Urbanizing World," in

H. J. Dyos and Michael Wolff, eds., *The Victorian City*, 2 vols. (London, 1973), 1:3–57; "City Making and City Mending in the United States," in Woodrow Borah et al., *Urbanization in the Americas* (Ottawa, 1980), 105–18; and "The Nature of Urbanization," in William Sharpe and Leonard Wallock, eds., *Visions of the Modern City* (New York, 1983), 47–96. See also Bruce M. Stave, "A Conversation with Eric E. Lampard," *Journal of Urban History* 1 (August 1975): 440–72.

8. Roy Lubove, "The Urbanization Process: An Approach to Historical Research," *Journal of the American Institute of Planners* 33 (January 1967): 33–39; idem, *Twentieth-Century Pittsburgh: Government, Business, and Environmental Change* (New York, 1969); idem, *Twentieth-Century Pittsburgh: The Post-Steel Era* (Pittsburgh, 1996).

9. Stephan Thernstrom, *Poverty and Progress: Social Mobility in a Nineteenth-Century City* (Cambridge, 1964); Stephan Thernstrom and Richard Sennett, eds., *Nineteenth-Century Cities: Essays in the New Urban History* (New Haven, 1969); Leo F. Schnore, ed., *The New Urban History: Quantitative Explorations by American Historians* (Princeton, 1975). See also the extensive discussion of *Poverty and Progress* in *Social Science History* 10 (Spring 1986): 1–44.

10. For a small sampling of this mobility literature see Richard J. Hopkins, "Occupational and Geographical Mobility in Atlanta, 1870–1896," *Journal of Southern History* 34 (May 1968): 200–13; Stephan Thernstrom and Peter R. Knights, "Men in Motion: Some Data and Speculations about Urban Population Mobility in Nineteenth-Century America," *Journal of Interdisciplinary History* 1 (Autumn 1970): 7–35; Peter R. Knights, *The Plain People of Boston, 1830–1860: A Study in City Growth* (New York, 1971); Howard P. Chudacoff, *Mobile Americans: Residential and Social Mobility in Omaha, 1880–1920* (New York, 1972); Michael B. Katz, *The People of Hamilton, Canada West: Family and Class in a Mid-Nineteenth-Century City* (Cambridge, 1975); Dean R. Esslinger, *Immigrants and the City: Ethnicity and Mobility in a Nineteenth-Century Midwestern Community* (Port Washington, NY, 1975); Thomas Kessner, *The Golden Door: Italian and Jewish Mobility in New York City, 1880–1915* (New York, 1977); Gordon W. Kirk, Jr., *The Promise of American Life: Social Mobility in a Nineteenth-Century Immigrant Community, Holland, Michigan, 1847–1894* (Philadelphia, 1978); Peter R. Decker, *Fortunes and Failures: White-Collar Mobility in Nineteenth-Century San Francisco* (Cambridge, 1978); Robert G. Barrows, ' "Hurrying Hoosiers' and the American Pattern: Geographic Mobility in Urban North America," *Social Science History* 5 (Spring 1981): 197–222; Michael B. Katz et al., *The Social Organization of Early Industrial Capitalism* (Cambridge, 1982); and, most recently, Peter R. Knights, *Yankee Destinies: The Lives of Ordinary Nineteenth-Century Bostonians* (Chapel Hill, 1991).

11. Stephan Thernstrom, "Reflections on the New Urban History," *Daedalus* 100 (Spring 1971): 359–75.

12. Michael Frisch, "American Urban History as an Example of Recent Historiography," *History and Theory* 18 (1979): 350–77.

13. Stephan Thernstrom, *The Other Bostonians: Poverty and Progress in the American Metropolis, 1880–1970* (Cambridge, 1973); Bruce M. Stave, "A Conversation with Stephan Thernstrom," *Journal of Urban History* 1 (February 1975): 189–215.

14. John B. Sharpless and Sam Bass Warner, Jr., "Urban History," *American Behavioral Scientist* 21 (November–December 1977): 221–44. See also Bruce M. Stave, "A Conversation with Sam Bass Warner, Jr.," *Journal of Urban History* 1 (November 1974): 85–110; and Stave, "A Conversation with Sam Bass Warner, Jr.: Ten Years Later," *Journal of Urban History* 11 (November 1984): 83–113.

15. Theodore Hershberg, "The New Urban History: Toward an Interdisciplinary History of the City," *Journal of Urban History* 5 (November 1978): 3–40; idem, ed., *Philadelphia: Work, Space, Family and Group Experience in the Nineteenth Century* (New York, 1981), 3–35.

16. For historiographical surveys see Charles N. Glaab, "The Historian and the American City: A Bibliographic Survey," in Hauser and Schnore, eds., *The Study of Urbanization*, 53–80; Dwight W. Hoover, "The Diverging Paths of American Urban History," *American Quarterly* 20 (Summer 1968): 296–317; Dana F. White, "The Underdeveloped Discipline: Interdisciplinary Directions in American Urban History," *American Studies: An International Newsletter* 9 (Spring 1971): 3–16; Raymond A. Mohl, "The History of the American City," in William H. Cartwright and Richard L. Watson, Jr., *The Reinterpretation of American History and Culture* (Washington, 1973), 165–205; Michael H. Ebner, "Urban History: Retrospect and Prospect," *Journal of American History* 68 (June 1981): 69–84; Bruce M. Stave, "Urban History: A Tale of Many Cities," *Magazine of History* 2 (Winter 1986): 32–37; Howard Gillette, Jr., and Zane L. Miller, eds., *American Urbanism: A Historiographical Review* (Westport, CT, 1987); and Howard Gillette, Jr., "Rethinking American Urban History: New Directions for the Posturban Era," *Social Science History* 14 (Summer 1990): 203–28.

17. Bruce M. Stave, "In Pursuit of Urban History: Conversations with Myself and Others —A View from the United States," in Derek Fraser and Anthony Sutcliffe, eds., *The Pursuit*

*of Urban History* (London, 1983), 424. See also Clyde Griffin, "The United States: The 'New Urban History,'" *Urban History Yearbook* (Leicester, England, 1977), 15–23.

18. For one objection to Stave's conclusion see Terrence J. McDonald, "The Pursuit of Urban History: To the Rear March," *Historical Methods* 18 (Summer 1985): 116.

19. Zane L. Miller, *Boss Cox's Cincinnati: Urban Politics in the Progressive Era* (New York, 1968), 94. The reinterpretation of the urban political machine began with Robert K. Merton, *Social Theory and Social Structure* (New York, 1967). Other revisionist studies include Seymour J. Mandelbaum, *Boss Tweed's New York* (New York, 1965); and John M. Allswang, *Bosses, Machines, and Urban Voters: An American Symbiosis* (Port Washington, NY, 1977). Two useful collections of readings are Alexander B. Callow, Jr., ed., *The City Boss in America: An Interpretive Reader* (New York, 1976); and Bruce M. Stave and Sondra Astor Stave, eds., *Urban Bosses, Machines, and Progressive Reformers* (Malabar, FL, 1984).

20. Leo Hershkowitz, *Tweed's New York: Another Look* (Garden City, NY, 1977), 348.

21. For an interpretive overview see Bruce M. Stave et al., "A Reassessment of the Urban Political Boss: An Exchange of Views," *The History Teacher* 21 (May 1988): 293–312. For post-1980 studies of the machine see Edward K. Spann, *The New Metropolis: New York City, 1840–1857* (New York, 1981); Scott Greer, ed., *Ethnics, Machines, and the American Urban Future* (Cambridge, 1981); Roger Biles, *Big City Boss in Depression and War: Mayor Edward J. Kelly of Chicago* (DeKalb, IL, 1984); Paul Kleppner, *Chicago Divided: The Making of a Black Mayor* (DeKalb, IL, 1985); Steven P. Erie, *Rainbow's End: Irish-Americans and the Dilemmas of Urban Machine Politics, 1840–1985* (Berkeley, 1988); William J. Grimshaw, *Bitter Fruit: Black Politics and the Chicago Machine, 1931–1991* (Chicago, 1992); Chris McNickle, *To be Mayor of New York: Ethnic Politics in the City* (New York, 1993); Peter McCaffery, *When Bosses Ruled Philadelphia: The Emergence of the Republican Machine, 1867–1933* (University Park, PA, 1993); and Alan Lessoff, *The Nation and Its City: Politics, "Corruption," and Progress in Washington, D.C., 1861–1902* (Baltimore, 1994). Important urban political biographies include Thomas Kessner, *Fiorello La Guardia and the Making of Modern New York* (New York, 1989); and Jack Beatty, *The Rascal King: The Life and Times of James Michael Curley* (Reading, MA, 1992).

22. John D. Buenker, *Urban Liberalism and Progressive Reform* (New York, 1973); Michael H. Ebner and Eugene M. Tobin, eds., *The Age of Urban Reform: New Perspectives on the Progressive Era* (Port Washington, NY, 1977); Paul S. Boyer, *Urban Masses and Moral Order in America, 1820–1920* (Cambridge, 1978). For a critique of the literature see Terrence J. McDonald, "Putting Politics Back into the History of the American City," *American Quarterly* 34 (Summer 1982): 200–209; idem, "The Burdens of Urban History: The Theory of the State in Recent American Social History," *Studies in American Political Development* 3 (1989): 3–55.

23. Samuel P. Hays, "The Social Analysis of American Political History, 1880–1920," *Political Science Quarterly* 80 (September 1965): 373–94; idem, "The Changing Political Structure of the City in Industrial America," *Journal of Urban History* 1 (November 1974): 6–38; idem, *American Political History as Social Analysis* (Knoxville, 1980). See also Bradley R. Rice, *Progressive Cities: The Commission Government Movement in America, 1901–1920* (Austin, 1977); Martin J. Schiesl, *The Politics of Efficiency: Municipal Administration and Reform in America, 1880–1920* (Berkeley, 1977); and Kenneth Fox, *Better City Government: Innovation in American Urban Politics, 1850–1937* (Philadelphia, 1977).

24. Jon C. Teaford, "Finis for Tweed and Steffens: Rewriting the History of Urban Rule," *Reviews in American History* 10 (December 1982): 136; idem, *The Unheralded Triumph: City Government in America, 1870–1900* (Baltimore, 1984). See also Roger Lotchin, "Reclaiming the Reputation of the City in the Gilded Age and Progressive Era," *Continuity: A Journal of History* 20 (Spring 1996): 13–38.

25. Terrence J. McDonald, *The Parameters of Urban Fiscal Policy: Socioeconomic Change and Political Culture in San Francisco, 1860–1906* (Berkeley, 1986); idem and Sally K. Ward, eds. *The Politics of Urban Fiscal Policy* (Beverly Hills, 1984); Terrence J. McDonald, "The Problem of the Political in Recent American Urban History," *Social History* 10 (October 1985): 323–45.

26. Carl V. Harris, *Political Power in Birmingham, 1871–1921* (Knoxville, 1977). For a somewhat different approach to urban political power and officeholding, see Eugene J. Watts, *The Social Bases of City Politics: Atlanta, 1865–1903* (Westport, CT, 1978).

27. David C. Hammack, *Power and Society: Greater New York at the Turn of the Century* (New York, 1982), 180. For a different approach to the question of political power see William Issel and Robert W. Cherny, *San Francisco, 1865–1932: Politics, Power, and Urban Development* (Berkeley, 1986).

28. Amy Bridges, *A City in the Republic: Antebellum New York and the Origins of Machine Politics* (Cambridge, England, 1984); Martin Shefter, *Political Parties and the State: The American Historical Experience* (Princeton, 1994); idem, "The Electoral Foundations of the

Political Machine: New York City, 1884–1897," in Joel Silbey et al., eds. *The History of American Electoral Behavior* (Princeton, 1978), 263–98; Martin Shefter, "The Emergence of the Political Machine: An Alternative View," in Willis D. Hawley et al., eds. *Theoretical Perspectives on Urban Politics* (Englewood Cliffs, 1976), 14–44; Ira Katznelson, *Urban Trenches: Urban Politics and the Patterning of Class in the United States* (New York, 1981).

29. Philip J. Ethington, *The Public City: The Political Construction of Urban Life in San Francisco, 1850–1900* (Cambridge, England, 1994); idem, "Recasting Urban Political History: Gender, the Public, the Household, and Political Participation in Boston and San Francisco during the Progressive Era," *Social Science History* 16 (Summer 1992): 301–33.

30. Kenneth T. Jackson, *Crabgrass Frontier: The Suburbanization of the United States* (New York, 1985).

31. Henry C. Binford, *The First Suburbs: Residential Communities on the Boston Periphery, 1815–1860* (Chicago, 1985). See also Tamara Plakins Thornton, *Cultivating Gentlemen: The Meaning of Country Life among the Boston Elite, 1785–1860* (New Haven, 1989), and, for a later period, Matthew Edel, Elliott D. Sclar, and Daniel Luria, *Shaky Palaces: Homeownership and Social Mobility in Boston's Suburbanization* (New York, 1984).

32. John R. Stilgoe, *Borderland: Origins of the American Suburb, 1820–1939* (New Haven, 1988). On similar themes see Clifford Edward Clark, Jr., *The American Family Home, 1800–1960* (Chapel Hill, 1986).

33. Jon C. Teaford, *City and Suburb: The Political Fragmentation of Metropolitan America, 1850–1970* (Baltimore, 1979).

34. Margaret Marsh, *Suburban Lives* (New Brunswick, NJ, 1990). Also on the suburban ideal see Mary Corbin Sies, "The City Transformed: Nature, Technology, and the Suburban Ideal, 1877–1917," *Journal of Urban History* 14 (November 1987): 81–111.

35. Daniel Schaffer, *Garden Cities for America: The Radburn Experience* (Philadelphia, 1982); Zane L. Miller, *Suburb: Neighborhood and Community in Forest Park, Ohio, 1935–1976* (Knoxville, 1981); Carol A. O'Connor, *A Sort of Utopia: Scarsdale, 1891–1981* (Albany, 1983); David R. Contosta, *Suburb in the City: Chestnut Hill, Philadelphia, 1850–1990* (Columbus, 1992); William S. Worley, *J. C. Nichols and the Shaping of Kansas City* (Columbia, MO, 1990); Michael H. Ebner, *Creating Chicago's North Shore: A Suburban History* (Chicago, 1988).

36. Ann Durkin Keating, *Building Chicago: Suburban Developers and the Creation of a Divided Metropolis* (Columbus, 1988); Marc A. Weiss, *The Rise of the Community Builders: The American Real Estate Industry and Urban Land Planning* (New York, 1987); Barbara M. Kelly, *Expanding the American Dream: Building and Rebuilding Levittown* (Albany, 1993); Joseph L. Arnold, *The New Deal in the Suburbs: A History of the Greenbelt Town Program, 1935–1954* (Columbus, 1971); and the early chapters of Mike Davis, *City of Quartz: Excavating the Future in Los Angeles* (London, 1990).

37. Robert Fishman, *Bourgeois Utopias: The Rise and Fall of Suburbia* (New York, 1987); idem, "America's New City: Megalopolis Unbound," *The Wilson Quarterly* 14 (Winter 1990): 25–48.

38. Joel Garreau, *Edge City: Life on the New Frontier* (New York, 1991). See also Carl Abbott, "To Boldly Go Where No Data Have Gone Before," *Journal of Urban History* 19 (May 1993): 139–45. For earlier studies of the edge city phenomenon see Peter O. Muller, *The Outer City: Geographical Consequences of the Urbanization of the Suburbs* (Washington, 1976); and idem, *Contemporary Suburban America* (Englewood Cliffs, NJ, 1981).

39. William Sharpe and Leonard Wallock, "Bold New City or Built-Up 'Burb? Redefining Contemporary Suburbia," *American Quarterly* 46 (March 1994): 1–30.

40. Michael H. Ebner, "Re-reading Suburban America: Urban Population Deconcentration, 1810–1980," *American Quarterly* 37 (1985): 368–81; Margaret Marsh, "Reconsidering the Suburbs: An Exploration of Suburban Historiography," *Pennsylvania Magazine of History and Biography* 112 (October 1988): 579–605. See also Barbara M. Kelly, ed., *Suburbia Reexamined* (Westport, CT, 1989); and Daniel Schaffer, ed., "Post-Suburban America," special issue of *Built Environment* 17, nos. 3/4 (1991).

41. On the concept of regionalism see David R. Goldfield, "The New Regionalism," *Journal of Urban History* 10 (February 1984): 171–86; and idem, "The Urban South: A Regional Framework," *American Historical Review* 86 (December 1981): 1009–34.

42. Idem, *Cotton Fields and Skyscrapers: Southern City and Region, 1607–1980* (Baton Rouge, 1982). For a critique see Bradley R. Rice, "How Different Is the Southern City?" *Journal of Urban History* 11 (November 1985): 115–21.

43. See the essays in Blaine A. Brownell and David R. Goldfield, eds., *The City in Southern History: The Growth of Urban Civilization in the South* (Port Washington, NY, 1977); and Leonard P. Curry, "Urbanization and Urbanism in the Old South: A Comparative View," *Journal of Southern History* 40 (February 1974): 43–60.

44. Goldfield, *Cotton Fields and Skyscrapers*, 3, 8. See also the essays in Howard N. Rabinowitz, *Race, Ethnicity, and Urbanization* (Columbia, MO, 1994).

45. William Cronon, *Nature's Metropolis: Chicago and the Great West* (New York, 1991). Cronon's book stimulated considerable discussion and debate. See, for instance, Richard Walker, ed., "William Cronon's *Nature's Metropolis*: A Symposium," *Antipode: A Radical Journal of Geography* 26 (April 1994): 113–76; Peter A. Coclanis, "Urbs in Horto," *Reviews in American History* 20 (March 1992): 14–20; and Paul Barrett, "Chicago and Its Interpreters, 1892–1992," *Journal of Urban History* 20 (August 1994): 577–84.

46. Jeffrey S. Adler, *Yankee Merchants and the Making of the Urban West: The Rise and Fall of Antebellum St. Louis* (Cambridge, England, 1991); Timothy R. Mahoney, *River Towns in the Great West: The Structure of Provincial Urbanization in the American Midwest, 1820–1870* (Cambridge, England, 1990); Jon C. Teaford, *Cities of the Heartland: The Rise and Fall of the Industrial Midwest* (Bloomington, 1993); Anthony M. Orum, *City-Building in America* (Boulder, 1995); Diane Lindstrom, *Economic Development in the Philadelphia Region, 1810–1850* (New York, 1978); Blaine A. Brownell, *The Urban Ethos in the South, 1920–1930* (Baton Rouge, 1975); David R. Goldfield, *Urban Growth in the Age of Sectionalism: Virginia, 1847–1861* (Baton Rouge, 1977); Don H. Doyle, *New Men, New Cities, New South: Atlanta, Nashville, Charleston, Mobile, 1860–1910* (Chapel Hill, 1990); Douglas L. Smith, *The New Deal in the Urban South* (Baton Rouge, 1988).

47. John M. Findlay, *Magic Lands: Western Cityscapes and American Culture after 1940* (Berkeley, 1992); Carl Abbott, *The Metropolitan Frontier: Cities in the Modern American West* (Tucson, 1993); Bradford Luckingham, *The Urban Southwest: A Profile History of Albuquerque, El Paso, Phoenix, and Tucson* (El Paso, 1982).

48. Lawrence H. Larsen, *The Rise of the Urban South* (Lexington, 1985); idem, *The Urban South: A History* (Lexington, 1990); James C. Cobb, *Industrialization and Southern Society, 1877–1984* (Lexington, 1984); Lawrence H. Larsen, *The Urban West at the End of the Frontier* (Lawrence, 1978); Gunther Barth, *Instant Cities: Urbanization and the Rise of San Francisco and Denver* (New York, 1975); Gerald D. Nash, *The American West Transformed: The Impact of the Second World War* (Bloomington, 1985). See also Bradford Luckingham, "The Urban Dimension of Western History," in Michael Malone, ed., *The West in American Historiography* (Lincoln, NE, 1983), 323–43; Carl Abbott, "The Metropolitan Region: Western Cities in the New Urban Era," in Gerald D. Nash and Richard W. Etulain, eds., *The Twentieth–Century West: Historical Interpretations* (Albuquerque, 1989), 71–98; and Carol A. O'Connor, "A Region of Cities," in Clyde A. Milner II et al., *The Oxford History of the American West* (New York, 1994), 535–63.

49. Carl Abbott, *The New Urban America: Growth and Politics in Sunbelt Cities* (Chapel Hill, 1981; rev. ed., 1987). See also idem, *Urban America in the Modern Age, 1920 to the Present* (Arlington Heights, IL, 1987).

50. Richard M. Bernard and Bradley R. Rice, eds., *Sunbelt Cities: Politics and Growth since World War II* (Austin, 1983); Raymond A. Mohl, ed., *Searching for the Sunbelt: Historical Perspectives on a Region* (Knoxville, 1990); Randall M. Miller and George E. Pozzetta, eds., *Shades of the Sunbelt: Essays on Ethnicity, Race, and the Urban South* (Westport, CT, 1988); Robert B. Fairbanks and Kathleen Underwood, eds., *Essays on Sunbelt Cities and Recent Urban America* (College Station, TX, 1990). For an excellent counterpoint to the sunbelt city studies, see Richard M. Bernard, ed., *Snowbelt Cities: Metropolitan Politics in the Northeast and Midwest since World War II* (Bloomington, 1990).

51. Joe R. Feagin, *Free Enterprise City: Houston in Political and Economic Perspective* (New Brunswick, NJ, 1988); Bradford Luckingham, *Phoenix: The History of a Southwestern Metropolis* (Tucson, 1989); Eugene P. Moehring, *Resort City in the Sunbelt: Las Vegas, 1930–1970* (Reno, 1989); Char Miller and Heywood T. Sanders, eds., *Urban Texas: Politics and Development* (College Station, TX, 1990); Rob Kling et al., eds., *Postsuburban California: The Transformation of Orange County since World War II* (Berkeley, 1991); Norman M. Klein and Martin J. Schiesl, eds., *20th-Century Los Angeles: Power, Promotion, and Social Conflict* (Claremont, CA, 1990); Michael F. Logan, *Fighting Sprawl and City Hall: Resistance to Urban Growth in the Southwest* (Tucson, 1995); Alejandro Portes and Alex Stepick, *City on the Edge: The Transformation of Miami* (Berkeley, 1993); Raymond A. Mohl, "City Building in the Sunshine State: The Urbanization of Florida," *Locus: Regional and Local History of the Americas* 8 (Fall 1995): 1–24.

52. Charles W. Cheape, *Moving the Masses: Urban Public Transit in New York, Boston, and Philadelphia, 1880–1912* (Cambridge, 1980).

53. Clifton Hood, *722 Miles: The Building of the Subways and How They Transformed New York* (New York, 1993).

54. Harold L. Platt, *The Electric City: Energy and the Growth of the Chicago Area, 1880–1930* (Chicago, 1991); David E. Nye, *Electrifying America: Social Meanings of a New Technology* (Cambridge, 1990).

55. Mark H. Rose, *Cities of Light and Heat: The Domestication of Gas and Electricity in Urban America* (State College, PA, 1995).

56. Martin V. Melosi, ed., *Pollution and Reform in American Cities, 1870–1930* (Austin, 1980); idem, *Garbage in the Cities: Refuse, Reform, and the Environment, 1880–1980* (College Station, TX, 1981). See also idem, *Coping with Abundance: Energy and Environment in Industrial America, 1820–1980* (New York, 1984). A special issue of the *Journal of Urban History* 20 (May 1994) dealt with "The Environment and the City."

57. Joel A. Tarr and Gabriel Dupuy, eds., *Technolgy and the Rise of the Networked City in Europe and America* (Philadelphia, 1988).

58. Joel A. Tarr et al., "The City and the Telegraph: Urban Telecommunications in the Pre-Telephone Era," *Journal of Urban History* 14 (November 1987): 38–80; Edwin Gabler, *The American Telegrapher: A Social History, 1860–1900* (New Brunswick, NJ, 1988); Claude S. Fischer, *America Calling: A Social History of the Telephone to 1940* (Berkeley, 1992).

59. Joel A. Tarr, *Transportation Innovation and Changing Spatial Patterns in Pittsburgh, 1850–1934* (Chicago, 1978); Harold L. Platt, *City Building in the New South: The Growth of Public Services in Houston, Texas, 1830–1910* (Philadelphia, 1983); Judith Walzer Leavitt, *The Healthiest City: Milwaukee and the Politics of Health Reform* (Princeton, 1982); Louis P. Cain, *Sanitation Strategy for a Lakefront Metropolis: The Case of Chicago* (DeKalb, IL, 1978); Andrew Hurley, *Environmental Inequalities: Class, Race, and Industrial Pollution in Gary, Indiana, 1945–1980* (Chapel Hill, 1995). See also Ann Durkin Keating et al., *Infrastructure and Urban Growth in the Nineteenth Century* (Chicago, 1985); and idem, *Invisible Networks: Exploring the History of Local Utilities and Public Works* (Malabar, FL, 1994).

60. Mark S. Foster, *From Streetcar to Superhighway: American City Planners and Urban Transportation, 1900–1940* (Philadelphia, 1981).

61. Clay McShane, *Down the Asphalt Path: The Automobile and the American City* (New York, 1994).

62. Paul Barrett, *The Automobile and Urban Transit: The Formation of Public Policy in Chicago, 1900–1930* (Philadelphia, 1983); Howard L. Preston, *Automobile Age Atlanta: The Making of a Southern Metropolis, 1900–1935* (Athens, GA, 1979); Scott L. Bottles, *Los Angeles and the Automobile: The Making of the Modern City* (Berkeley, 1987). See also Martin Wachs and Margaret Crawford, eds., *The Car and the City: The Automobile, the Built Environment, and Daily Urban Life* (Ann Arbor, 1991).

63. Mark H. Rose, *Interstate: Express Highway Politics, 1941–1956* (Lawrence, KS, 1979; 2d. ed., Knoxville, 1990).

64. For historiographical analysis see Joel A. Tarr and Josef W. Konvitz, "Patterns in the Development of the Urban Infrastructure," in Gillette and Miller, eds., *American Urbanism*, 195–226; Mark H. Rose, "Machine Politics: The Historiography of Technology and Public Policy," *The Public Historian* 10 (Spring 1988): 27–47; Josef W. Konvitz et al., "Technology and the City," *Technology and Culture* 31 (April 1990): 284–94; and Martin V. Melosi, "Cities, Technical Systems, and the Environment," *Environmental History Review* 14 (Spring–Summer 1990): 45–64. See also special issues of the *Journal of Urban History* on "The City and Technology" (May 1979 and November 1987).

65. Albert Fein, *Frederick Law Olmsted and the American Environmental Tradition* (New York, 1972); Laura Wood Roper, *FLO: A Biography of Frederick Law Olmsted* (Baltimore, 1973); Elizabeth Stevenson, *Park Maker: A Life of Frederick Law Olmsted* (New York, 1977); Dana F. White and Victor A. Kramer, eds., *Olmsted South: Old South Critic/New South Planner* (Westport, CT, 1979); Thomas S. Hines, *Burnham of Chicago: Architect and Planner* (New York, 1974); Robert Twombly, *Louis Sullivan: His Life and Work* (Chicago, 1986).

66. Cynthia Zaitzevsky, *Frederick Law Olmsted and the Boston Park System* (Cambridge, 1982); Charles E. Beveridge and David Schuyler, eds., *Creating Central Park, 1857–1861*, vol. 3 of *The Papers of Frederick Law Olmsted* (Baltimore, 1983); Galen Cranz, *The Politics of Park Design: A History of Urban Parks in America* (Cambridge, 1982); Giorgio Ciucci et al., *The American City* (Cambridge, 1979); Irving D. Fisher, *Frederick Law Olmsted and the City Planning Movement in the United States* (Ann Arbor, 1986); David Charles Sloane, *The Last Great Necessity: Cemeteries in American History* (Baltimore, 1991); Melvin Kalfus, *Frederick Law Olmsted: The Passion of a Public Artist* (New York, 1990); David Schuyler, *Apostle of Taste: Andrew Jackson Downing, 1815–1852* (Baltimore, 1996).

67. Sylvia D. Fries, *The Urban Idea in Colonial America* (Philadelphia, 1977); Judd Kahn, *Imperial San Francisco: Politics and Planning in an American City* (Lincoln, NE, 1979); Christopher Silver, *Twentieth-Century Richmond: Planning, Politics, and Race* (Knoxville, 1984); Carl Abbott, *Portland: Planning, Politics, and Growth in a Twentieth-Century City* (Lincoln, NE, 1983).

68. Christine M. Rosen, *The Limits of Power: Great Fires and the Process of City Growth in America* (Cambridge, England, 1986); Ross Miller, *American Apocalypse: The Great Fire and the Myth of Chicago* (Chicago, 1990); Karen Sawislak, *Smoldering City: Chicagoans and the Great Fire, 1871–1874* (Chicago, 1995); Carl Smith, *Urban Disorder and the Shape of Belief* (Chicago, 1995).

368                                                                THE MAKING OF URBAN AMERICA

69. Mary Corbin Sies and Christopher Silver, eds., *Planning the Twentieth-Century American City* (Baltimore, 1996).

70. David Schuyler, *The New Urban Landscape: The Redefinition of City Form in Nineteenth-Century America* (Baltimore, 1986); William H. Wilson, *The City Beautiful Movement* (Baltimore, 1989); Stanley Buder, *Visionaries and Planners: The Garden City Movement and the Modern Community* (New York, 1990); Stanley K. Schultz, *Constructing Urban Culture: American Cities and City Planning, 1800–1920* (Philadelphia, 1989); John D. Fairfield, *The Mysteries of the Great City: The Politics of Urban Design, 1877–1937* (Columbus, 1993); Roy Rosenzweig and Elizabeth Blackmar, *The Park and the People: A History of Central Park* (Ithaca, NY, 1992). See also James Gilbert, *Perfect Cities: Chicago's Utopias of 1898* (Chicago, 1991).

71. M. Christine Boyer, *Dreaming the Rational City: The Myth of American City Planning* (Cambridge, 1983); Richard E. Fogelsong, *Planning the Capitalist City: The Colonial Era to the 1920s* (Princeton, 1986).

72. Anthony Sutcliffe, *Towards the Planned City: Germany, Britain, the United States, and France, 1780–1914* (Oxford, 1981), 88–125; Peter Marcuse, "Housing in Early City Planning," *Journal of Urban History* 6 (February 1980): 153–76.

73. Elizabeth Blackmar, *Manhattan for Rent, 1750–1850* (Ithaca, NY, 1989).

74. Thomas L. Phillpott, *The Slum and the Ghetto: Neighborhood Deterioration and Middle-Class Reform, Chicago, 1880–1930* (New York, 1978); Robert B. Fairbanks, *Making Better Citizens: Housing Reform and the Community Development Strategy in Cincinnati, 1890–1960* (Urbana, IL, 1988). For an earlier study in this tradition see Roy Lubove, *The Progressives and the Slums: Tenement House Reform in New York City, 1890–1917* (Pittsburgh, 1962).

75. Gail Radford, *Modern Housing for America: Policy Struggles in the New Deal Era* (Chicago, 1996); Gwendolyn Wright, *Building the Dream: A Social History of Housing in America* (New York, 1981). See also Larry R. Ford, *Cities and Buildings: Skyscrapers, Skid Rows, and Suburbs* (Baltimore, 1994). On New York City see Richard Plunz, *A History of Housing in New York City: Dwelling Type and Social Change in the American Metropolis* (New York, 1990); and Elizabeth C. Cromley, *Alone Together: A History of New York's Early Apartments* (Ithaca, NY, 1990). On Cleveland, see Jan Cigliano, *Showplace of America: Cleveland's Euclid Avenue, 1850–1910* (Kent, OH, 1991).

76. Arnold R. Hirsch, *Making the Second Ghetto: Race and Housing in Chicago, 1940–1960* (Cambridge, England, 1983); Dominic J. Capeci, Jr., *Race Relations in Wartime Detroit: The Sojourner Truth Housing Controversy, 1937–1942* (Philadelphia, 1984); John F. Bauman, *Public Housing, Race, and Renewal: Urban Planning in Philadelphia, 1920–1974* (Philadelphia, 1987).

77. E. P. Thompson, *The Making of the English Working Class* (New York, 1963); Herbert G. Gutman, *Work, Culture, and Society in Industrializing America* (New York, 1976); idem, *Power and Culture: Essays on the American Working Class* (New York, 1987).

78. Gary B. Nash, *The Urban Crucible: Social Change, Political Consciousness, and the Origins of the American Revolution* (Cambridge, 1979). See also Dirk Hoerder, *Crowd Action in Revolutionary Massachusetts, 1765–1780* (New York, 1977); Charles G. Steffen *The Mechanics of Baltimore: Workers and Politics in the Age of Revolution, 1763–1812* (Urbana, 1984); and Gary B. Nash, "The Social Evolution of Preindustrial American Cities, 1700–1820: Reflections and New Directions," *Journal of Urban History* 13 (February 1987): 115–45.

79. Sean Wilentz, *Chants Democratic: New York City and the Rise of the American Working Class, 1788–1850* (New York, 1984); Graham R. Hodges, *New York City Cartmen, 1667–1850* (New York, 1986); Ronald Schultz, *The Republic of Labor: Philadelphia Artisans and the Politics of Class, 1720–1830* (New York, 1993); David A. Zonderman, *Aspirations and Anxieties: New England Workers and the Mechanized Factory System, 1815–1850* (New York, 1992); David R. Roediger, *The Wages of Whiteness: Race and the Making of the American Working Class* (London, 1991); Eric Lott, *Love and Theft: Blackface Minstrelsy and the American Working Class* (New York, 1995); Peter Way, *Common Labour: Workers and the Digging of North American Canals, 1780–1860* (Cambridge, England, 1993); Amy Bridges, "Becoming American: The Working Classes in the United States before the Civil War," in Ira Katznelson and Aristede R. Zolberg, eds., *Working-Class Formation: Nineteenth-Century Patterns in Western Europe and the United States* (Princeton, 1986), 157–96.

80. Paul A. Gilje, *The Road to Mobocracy: Popular Disorder in New York City, 1763–1834* (Chapel Hill, 1987); Iver Bernstein, *The New York City Draft Riots: Their Significance for American Society and Politics in the Age of the Civil War* (New York, 1990); idem, *Rioting in America* (Bloomington, 1996). For efforts to curb massive urban violence see Robert M. Fogelson, *America's Armories: Architecture, Society, and Public Order* (Cambridge, 1989).

81. Daniel J. Walkowitz, *Worker City, Company Town: Iron and Cotton-Worker Protest in Troy and Cohoes, New York, 1855–84* (Urbana, 1978); Alan Dawley, *Class and Community: The Industrial Revolution in Lynn* (Cambridge, 1976); Paul G. Faler, *Mechanics and Manufacturers in the Early Industrial Revolution: Lynn, Massachusetts, 1780–1860* (Albany, 1981);

Susan E. Hirsch, *Roots of the American Working Class: The Industrialization of Crafts in Newark, 1800–1860* (Philadelphia, 1978); Bruce Laurie, *Working People of Philadelphia, 1800–1850* (Philadelphia, 1980); Frances G. Couvares, *The Remaking of Pittsburgh: Class and Culture in an Industrializing City, 1877–1919* (Albany, 1984); Stephen J. Ross, *Workers on the Edge: Work, Leisure, and Politics in Industrializing Cincinnati, 1788–1890* (New York, 1985); Richard Oestreicher, *Solidarity and Fragmentation: Working People and Class Consciousness in Detroit, 1875–1900* (Urbana, 1986); Brian Greenberg, *Worker and Community: Response to Industrialization in a Nineteenth-Century American City, Albany, New York, 1850–1884* (Albany, 1985); James R. Barrett, *Work and Community in the Jungle: Chicago's Packinghouse Workers, 1894–1922* (Urbana, 1987); William F. Hartford, *Working People of Holyoke: Class and Ethnicity in a Massachusetts Mill Town, 1850–1960* (New Brunswick, NJ, 1990); Gary Gerstle, *Working-Class Americanism: The Politics of Labor in a Textile City, 1914–1960* (Cambridge, England, 1989); David Brundage, *The Making of Western Labor Radicalism: Denver's Organized Workers, 1878–1905* (Urbana, 1994).

82. Daniel T. Rodgers, *The Work Ethic in Industrial America, 1850–1920* (Chicago, 1978), 155; David Montgomery, *Workers' Control in America* (Cambridge, England, 1979). See also idem, *The Fall of the House of Labor* (Cambridge, England, 1987); and idem, *Citizen Worker* (Cambridge, England, 1993).

83. Lisa M. Fine, *The Souls of the Skyscraper: Female Clerical Workers in Chicago, 1870–1930* (Philadelphia, 1990); Sharon H. Strom, *Beyond the Typewriter: Gender, Class, and the Origins of Modern American Office Work, 1900–1930* (Urbana, 1992); Margery W. Davies, *Women's Place Is at the Typewriter: Office Work and Office Workers, 1870–1930* (Philadelphia, 1982); Stephen H. Norwood, *Labor's Flaming Youth: Telephone Operators and Worker Militancy, 1878–1923* (Urbana, 1990); Susan P. Benson, *Counter Cultures: Saleswomen, Managers, and Customers in American Department Stores, 1890–1940* (Urbana, 1986); Eileen Boris, *Home to Work: Motherhood and the Politics of Industrial Homework in the United States* (Cambridge, England, 1994); Joanne J. Meyerowitz, *Women Adrift: Independent Wage Earners in Chicago, 1880–1930* (Chicago, 1988); Miriam Cohen, *Workshop to Office: Two Generations of Italian Women in New York City, 1900–1950* (Ithaca, NY, 1993). Women also found wide-ranging types of work in the industrial sector. See Thomas Dublin, *Transforming Women's Work: New England Lives in the Industrial Revolution* (Ithaca, NY, 1994); S. J. Kleinberg, *The Shadow of the Mills: Working-Class Families in Pittsburgh, 1870–1907* (Pittsburgh, 1989); Patricia A. Cooper, *Once a Cigar Maker: Men, Women, and Work Culture in American Cigar Factories, 1900–1919* (Urbana, 1987); and Ardis Cameron, *Radicals of the Worst Sort: Laboring Women in Lawrence, Massachusetts, 1860–1912* (Urbana, 1993).

84. Dana Frank, *Purchasing Power: Consumer Organizing, Gender, and the Seattle Labor Movement, 1919–1929* (Cambridge, England, 1994); Nancy F. Gabin, *Feminism in the Labor Movement: Women and the United Auto Workers, 1935–1975* (Ithaca, NY, 1990); Amy Kesselman, *Fleeting Opportunities: Women Shipyard Workers in Portland and Vancouver during World War II and Reconversion* (Albany, 1990).

85. Oscar Handlin, *The Uprooted: The Epic Story of the Great Migrations That Made the American People* (Boston, 1951); David J. Rothman, "*The Uprooted*: Thirty Years Later," *Reviews in American History* 10 (September 1982): 311–19; Peter Kvisto, "The Transplanted Then and Now: The Reorientation of Immigration Studies from the Chicago School to the New Social History," *Ethnic and Racial Studies* 13 (October 1990): 455–81; Rudolph J. Vecoli, "From *The Uprooted* to *The Transplanted*: The Writing of American Immigration History, 1951–1989," in Valeria Gennaro Lerda, *From "Melting Pot" to Multiculturalism* (Rome, 1990), 25–53.

86. On chain migration see Josef J. Barton, *Peasants and Strangers: Italians, Rumanians, and Slovaks in an American City, 1890–1950* (Cambridge, 1975); John W. Briggs, *An Italian Passage: Immigrants to Three American Cities, 1890–1930* (New Haven, 1978); Dino Cinel, *From Italy to San Francisco: The Immigrant Experience* (Stanford, 1982); Walter Kamphoefner, *The Westphalians: From Germany to Missouri* (Princeton, 1987); Donna R. Gabaccia, *Militants and Migrants: Rural Sicilians Become American Workers* (New Brunswick, NJ, 1988); Robert C. Ostergren, *A Community Transplanted: The Trans-Atlantic Experience of a Swedish Immigrant Settlement in the Upper Middle West, 1835–1915* (Madison, WI, 1988); Walter Nugent, *Crossings: The Great Transatlantic Migrations, 1870–1914* (Bloomington, 1992). Historians have also discovered very high rates of "return migration" for some groups. See Dino Cinel, *The National Integration of Italian Return Migration, 1870–1929* (Cambridge, England, 1991); Mark Wyman, *Round-Trip to America: The Immigrants Return to Europe, 1880–1930* (Ithaca, NY, 1993); and essays by Ewa Moraska and Walter Kamphoefner in Rudolph J. Vecoli and Suzanne M. Sinke, eds., *A Century of European Migrations, 1830–1930* (Urbana, 1991).

87. Virginia Yans-McLaughlin, *Family and Community: Italian Immigrants in Buffalo, 1880–1930* (Ithaca, NY, 1977); Tamara K. Hareven, *Family Time and Industrial Time: The Relationship between the Family and Work in a New England Industrial Community* (Cambridge,

England, 1982); John Bodnar et al., *Lives of Their Own: Blacks, Italians, and Poles in Pitts-burgh, 1900–1960* (Urbana, 1982); Olivier Zunz, *The Changing Face of Inequality: Urbaniza-tion, Industrial Development, and Immigrants in Detroit, 1880–1920* (Chicago, 1982); Judith E. Smith, *Family Connections: A History of Italian and Jewish Immigrant Lives in Providence, Rhode Island, 1900–1940* (Albany, 1985); Hartmut Keil, ed., *German Workers' Culture in the United States, 1850 to 1920* (Washington, 1988); Stanley Nadel, *Little Ger-many: Ethnicity, Religion, and Class in New York City, 1845–80* (Urbana, 1990).

88. Jay Dolan, *The Immigrant Church: New York's Irish and German Catholics, 1815–1865* (Baltimore, 1975); Randall M. Miller and Thomas D. Marzik, eds., *Immigrants and Religion in Urban America* (Philadelphia, 1977); June G. Alexander, *The Immigrant Church and Com-munity: Pittsburgh's Slovak Catholics and Lutherans, 1880–1915* (Pittsburgh, 1987); James W. Sanders, *The Education of an Urban Minority: Catholics in Chicago, 1833–1965* (New York, 1977); Raymond A. Mohl and Neil Betten, *Steel City: Urban and Ethnic Patterns in Gary, Indiana, 1906–1950* (New York, 1986); Scott Cummings, ed., *Self-Help in Urban America: Patterns of Minority Economic Development* (Port Washington, NY, 1979); Frede-rick M. Binder and David M. Reimers, *All the Nations under Heaven: An Ethnic and Racial History of New York City* (New York, 1995).

89. Rudolph J. Vecoli, "*Contadini* in Chicago: A Critique of *The Uprooted*," *Journal of Ameri-can History* 51 (December 1964): 404–16; idem, "The Formation of Chicago's 'Little Italies,'" *Journal of American Ethnic History* 2 (Spring 1983): 5–20; William DeMarco, *Ethnics and Enclaves: Boston's Italian North End* (Ann Arbor, 1981); Caroline Golab, *Immigrant Destina-tions* (Philadelphia, 1977).

90. Hartmut Keil and John B. Jentz, eds., *German Workers in Industrial Chicago, 1850–1910: A Comparative Perspective* (DeKalb, IL, 1983); David J. Goldberg, *A Tale of Three Cit-ies: Labor Organization and Protest in Paterson, Passaic, and Lawrence, 1916–1921* (New Brunswick, 1989); Dominic A. Pacyga, *Polish Immigrants and Industrial Chicago: Workers on the South Side, 1880–1922* (Columbus, 1991); Bruce C. Levine, *The Spirit of 1848: German Immigrants, Labor Conflict, and the Coming of the Civil War* (Urbana, 1992); David M. Emmons, *The Butte Irish: Class and Ethnicity in an American Mining Town, 1875–1925* (Urbana, 1989).

91. Hasia Diner, *Erin's Daughters in America: Irish Immigrant Women in the Nineteenth Century* (Baltimore, 1983); Elizabeth Ewen, *Immigrant Women in the Land of Dollars: Life and Culture on the Lower East Side, 1890–1925* (New York, 1985); Louise Lamphere, *From Working Daughters to Working Mothers: Immigrant Women in a New England Industrial Com-munity* (Ithaca, NY, 1987); Donna Gabaccia, *From the Other Side: Women, Gender, and Immi-grant Life in the U.S., 1820–1990* (Bloomington, 1994).

92. Joyce D. Goodfriend, *Before the Melting Pot: Society and Culture in Colonial New York City, 1664–1730* (Princeton, 1992).

93. Noel Ignatiev, *How the Irish Became White* (New York, 1995).

94. Arnold R. Hirsch and Joseph Logsdon, eds., *Creole New Orleans: Race and American-ization* (Baton Rouge, 1992).

95. On Hispanic immigrants see George J. Sánchez, *Becoming Mexican American: Ethnicity, Culture, and Identity in Chicano Los Angeles, 1900–1945* (New York, 1993); Zaragosa Vargas, *Proletarians of the North: A History of Mexican Industrial Workers in Detroit and the Mid-west, 1917–1933* (Berkeley, 1993); and María Cristina García, *Havana USA: Cuban Exiles and Cuban Americans in South Florida, 1959–1994* (Berkeley, 1996). On black immigrants see Iram Watkins-Owens, *Blood Relations: Caribbean Immigrants and the Harlem Commu-nity, 1900–1930* (Bloomington, 1996). On Asians, begin with Roger Daniels, *Asian America: Chinese and Japanese in the United States since 1850* (Seattle, 1988); and Sucheng Chan, *Asian Americans: An Interpretive History* (New York, 1991). For a comparative study see Bradford Luckingham, *Minorities in Phoenix: A Profile of Mexican-American, Chinese-American, and African-American Communities, 1860–1992* (Tucson, 1994). For an overview of Third World immigration see David Reimers, *Still the Golden Door: The Third World Comes to America* (2d ed., New York, 1992); Nancy Foner, ed., *New Immigrants in New York* (New York, 1987); and Elliott R. Barkan, *And Still They Come: Immigrants and American Society, 1920 to the 1990s* (Wheeling, IL, 1996).

96. John Bodnar, *The Transplanted: A History of Immigrants in Urban America* (Bloomington, 1985); Nora Faires et al., "John Bodnar's *The Transplanted*: A Roundtable," *Social Science History*, 12 (Fall 1988): 217–68. Recent books pursuing the interpretive lines laid out by Bodnar include Gary R. Mormino, *Immigrants on the Hill: Italian-Americans in St. Louis, 1882–1982* (Urbana, 1986); idem and George E. Pozzetta, *The Immigrant World of Ybor City: Italians and Their Latin Neighbors in Tampa, 1885–1985* (Urbana, 1987); Robert Anthony Orsi, *The Madonna of 115th Street: Faith and Community in Italian Harlem, 1880–1950* (New Haven, 1985); Ewa Morawska, *For Bread with Butter: Life-Worlds of East Central*

*Europeans in Johnstown, Pennsylvania, 1890–1940* (Cambridge, England, 1985); Robert A. Rockaway, *The Jews of Detroit: From the Beginning, 1762–1914* (Detroit, 1986).

97. Gilbert Osofsky, *Harlem: The Making of a Ghetto: Negro New York, 1890–1930* (New York, 1966); Allan H. Spear, *Black Chicago: The Making of a Negro Ghetto* (Chicago, 1967). See also Leonard P. Curry, *The Free Black in Urban America, 1800–1850: The Shadow of a Dream* (Chicago, 1981).

98. Kenneth W. Goings and Raymond A. Mohl, eds., *The New African-American Urban History* (Thousand Oaks, CA, 1996).

99. Herbert G. Gutman, *The Black Family in Slavery and Freedom, 1750–1925* (New York, 1976); Kenneth L. Kusmer, *A Ghetto Takes Shape: Black Cleveland, 1870–1930* (Urbana, 1976); Elizabeth Pleck, *Black Migration and Poverty: Boston, 1865–1900* (New York, 1979); James Borchert, *Alley Life in Washington: Family, Community, Religion, and Folklife in the City, 1850–1970* (Urbana, 1980).

100. Gary B. Nash, *Forging Freedom: The Formation of Philadelphia's Black Community, 1720–1840* (Cambridge, 1988); Shane White, *Somewhat More Independent: The End of Slavery in New York City, 1770–1810* (Athens, GA, 1991). For recent black community studies see Douglas Henry Daniels, *Pioneer Urbanites: A Social and Cultural History of Black San Francisco* (Philadelphia, 1980); George C. Wright, *Life behind a Veil: Blacks in Louisville, Kentucky, 1865–1930* (Baton Rouge, 1985); Albert S. Broussard, *Black San Francisco: The Struggle for Racial Equality in the West* (Lawrence, KS, 1993); Quintard Taylor, *The Forging of a Black Community: Seattle's Central District from 1870 through the Civil Rights Era* (Seattle, 1994); and Earl Lewis, *In Their Own Interests: Race, Class, and Power in Twentieth-Century Norfolk, Virginia* (Berkeley, 1991). For an excellent study of race relations in Chicago and other northern cities see John T. McGreevy, *Parish Boundaries: The Catholic Encounter with Race in the Twentieth-Century North* (Chicago, 1996).

101. Robin D. G. Kelley, *Race Rebels: Culture, Politics, and the Black Working Class* (New York, 1994); Kenneth W. Goings and Gerald L. Smith, " 'Unhidden' Transcripts: Memphis and African American Agency, 1862–1920," *Journal of Urban History* 21 (March 1995): 372–94.

102. Joe William Trotter, *Black Milwaukee: The Making of an Industrial Proletariat, 1915–45* (Urbana, 1985); Richard W. Thomas, *Life for Us Is What We Make It: Building Black Community in Detroit, 1915–1945* (Bloomington, 1992); Cheryl L. Greenberg, *Or Does It Explode? Black Harlem in the Great Depression* (New York, 1991).

103. On labor and radical movements see Peter Rachleff, *Black Labor in Richmond, 1865–1890* (Philadelphia, 1984); Mark Naison, *Communists in Harlem during the Depression* (Urbana, 1983); Robin D. G. Kelley, *Hammer and Hoe: Alabama Communists during the Great Depression* (Chapel Hill, 1990); Eric Arnesen, *Waterfront Workers of New Orleans: Race, Class, and Politics, 1863–1923* (New York, 1991); and Michael K. Honey, *Southern Labor and Black Civil Rights: Organizing Memphis Workers* (Urbana, 1993). On African-American sports see Rob Ruck, *Sandlot Seasons: Sport in Black Pittsburgh* (Urbana, 1987); and Jules Tygiel, *Baseball's Great Experiment: Jackie Robinson and His Legacy* (New York, 1983). On black festival behavior see William H. Wiggins, Jr., *O Freedom: Afro-American Emancipation Celebrations* (Knoxville, 1987); and Geneviève Fabre and Robert O'Meally, eds., *History and Memory in African-American Culture* (New York, 1995).

104. James R. Grossman, *Land of Hope: Chicago, Black Southerners, and the Great Migration* (Chicago, 1989); Peter Gottlieb, *Making Their Own Way: Southern Blacks' Migration to Pittsburgh, 1916–30* (Urbana, 1987); William Cohen, *At Freedom's Edge: Black Mobility and the Southern White Quest for Racial Control, 1861–1915* (Baton Rouge, 1991); Joe W. Trotter, ed., *The Great Migration in Historical Perspective: New Dimensions of Race, Class, and Gender* (Bloomington, 1991); Gretchen Lemke-Santangelo, *Abiding Courage: African American Migrant Women and the East Bay Community* (Chapel Hill, 1996); Nicholas Lemann, *The Promised Land: The Great Black Migration and How It Changed America* (New York, 1991).

105. Dominic J. Capeci, Jr., and Martha Wilkerson, *Layered Violence: The Detroit Rioters of 1943* (Jackson, MS, 1991); Roberta Senechal, *The Sociogenesis of a Race Riot: Springfield, Illinois, in 1908* (Urbana, 1990); Sidney Fine, *Violence in the Model City: The Cavanagh Administration, Race Relations, and the Detroit Riot of 1967* (Ann Arbor, 1989); Gerald Horne, *Fire This Time: The Watts Uprising and the 1960s* (Charlottesville, 1995); Mark Baldassare, ed., *The Los Angeles Riots: Lessons for the Urban Future* (Boulder, 1994).

106. Robert Gregg, *Sparks from the Anvil of Oppression: Philadelphia's African Methodists and Southern Migrants, 1890–1940* (Philadelphia, 1993); Evelyn Brooks Higginbotham, *Righteous Discontent: The Women's Movement in the Black Baptist Church, 1880–1920* (Cambridge, 1993); Vickie Crawford et al., eds., *Women in the Civil Rights Movement: Trailblazers and Torchbearers, 1941–1965* (Bloomington, 1990).

107. Aldon D. Morris, *The Origins of the Civil Rights Movement: Black Communities Organizing for Change* (New York, 1984); James R. Ralph, Jr., *Northern Protest: Martin Luther*

*King, Jr., Chicago, and the Civil Rights Movement* (Cambridge, 1993); Kim Lacy Rogers, *Righteous Lives: Narratives of the New Orleans Civil Rights Movement* (New York, 1993); Armstead L. Robinson and Patricia Sullivan, eds., *New Directions in Civil Rights Studies* (Charlottesville, 1991).

108. William Julius Wilson, *The Truly Disadvantaged: The Inner City, the Underclass, and Public Policy* (Chicago, 1987); idem, *When Work Disappears: The World of the New Urban Poor* (New York, 1996); Douglas S. Massey and Nancy A. Denton, *American Apartheid Segregation and the Making of the Underclass* (Cambridge, 1993). See also William Julius Wilson, "Another Look at *The Truly Disadvantaged*," *Political Science Quarterly* 106 (Winter 1991–92): 639–56; and Michael B. Katz, ed., *The "Underclass" Debate: Views from History* (Princeton, 1993).

109. Mark I. Gelfand, *A Nation of Cities: The Federal Government and Urban America, 1933–1965* (New York, 1975); Philip Funigiello, *The Challenge to Urban Liberalism: Federal-City Relations during World War II* (Knoxville, 1978).

110. Roger W. Lotchin, *The Martial Metropolis: U.S. Cities in War and Peace* (New York, 1984); idem, *Fortress California, 1910–1961: From Warfare to Welfare* (New York, 1992); Marilynn S. Johnson, *The Second Gold Rush: Oakland and the East Bay in World War II* (Berkeley, 1993); Roger W. Lotchin, "Fortress California at War," special issue of *Pacific Historical Review* 63 (August 1994): 277–420.

111. John Mollenkopf, *The Contested City* (Princeton, 1983).

112. Kenneth Fox, *Metropolitan America: Urban Life and Urban Policy in the United States, 1940–1980* (Jackson, MS, 1986).

113. Joel Schwartz, *The New York Approach: Robert Moses, Urban Liberals, and the Redevelopment of the Inner City* (Columbus, 1993); Robert Fitch, *The Assassination of New York* (London, 1993). See also Charles Rutheiser, *Imagineering Atlanta: The Politics of Place in the City of Dreams* (London, 1996).

114. Howard Gillette, Jr., *Between Justice and Beauty: Race, Planning, and the Failure of Urban Policy in Washington, D.C.* (Baltimore, 1995). For similar policy contradictions in other cities see Lawrence W. Kennedy, *Planning the City upon a Hill: Boston since 1630* (Amherst, MA, 1992); Thomas O'Connor, *Building a New Boston: Politics and Urban Renewal, 1950 to 1970* (Boston, 1993); and Janet R. Daley-Bednarek, *The Changing Image of the City: Planning for Downtown Omaha, 1945–1973* (Lincoln, NE, 1992).

115. Ronald H. Bayor, *Race and the Shaping of Twentieth-Century Atlanta* (Chapel Hill, 1996); Thomas J. Sugrue, *The Origins of the Urban Crisis: Race and Inequality in Postwar Detroit* (Princeton, 1996). On race and policy, see also Henry Louis Taylor, Jr., *Race and the City: Work, Community, and Protest in Cincinnati, 1820–1970* (Urbana, 1993); Christopher Silver and John V. Moeser, *The Separate City: Black Communities in the Urban South, 1940–1968* (Lexington, 1995).

116. Jon C. Teaford, *The Rough Road to Renaissance: Urban Revitalization in America, 1940–1985* (Baltimore, 1990).

117. Arnold R. Hirsch and Raymond A. Mohl, eds., *Urban Policy in Twentieth-Century America* (New Brunswick, NJ, 1993). See also Martin V. Melosi, ed., *Urban Public Policy: Historical Modes and Methods* (University Park, PA, 1994).

118. Robert Halpern, *Rebuilding the Inner City: A History of Neighborhood Initiatives to Address Poverty in the United States* (New York, 1995).

119. Robert A. Beauregard, *Voices of Decline: The Postwar Fate of U.S. Cities* (1993). See also Peter K. Eisinger, "The Search for a National Urban Policy, 1968–1980," *Journal of Urban History* 12 (November 1985): 3–23; and Raymond A. Mohl, "Shifting Patterns of American Urban Policy since 1900," in Hirsch and Mohl, eds., *Urban Policy in Twentieth-Century America*, 1–45.

120. Warren I. Susman, *Culture as History: The Transformation of American Society in the Twentieth Century* (New York, 1984). See also Stephen Kern, *The Culture of Time and Space, 1880–1918* (Cambridge, 1983); and David Ward and Olivier Zunz, "Between Rationalism and Pluralism: Creating the Modern City," in David Ward and Olivier Zunz, eds., *The Landscape of Modernity: Essays on New York City, 1900–1940* (New York, 1992), 3–15.

121. Gunther Barth, *City People: The Rise of Modern City Culture in Nineteenth-Century America* (New York, 1980), 5, 230.

122. Neil Harris, *Cultural Excursions: Marketing Appetites and Cultural Tastes in Modern America* (Chicago, 1990). See also Gregory Bush, " 'Genial Evasion' in the Big Time: Changing Norms of Respectability within an Expansive Urban Culture," *Journal of Urban History* 19 (May 1992): 121–38.

123. Roland Marchand, *Advertising the American Dream: Making Way for Modernity, 1920–1940* (Berkeley, 1985); T. J. Jackson Lears, *Fables of Abundance: A Cultural History of Advertising in America* (New York, 1994); William Leach, *Land of Desire: Merchants, Power, and the Rise of a New American Culture* (New York, 1993). See also Richard W. Fox and T. J.

Jackson Lears, eds., *The Culture of Consumption: Critical Essays in American History, 1880–1980* (New York, 1983); and idem, eds., *The Power of Culture: Critical Essays in American History* (Chicago, 1993).

124. Elaine S. Abelson, *When Ladies Go A-Thieving: Middle-Class Shoplifters in the Victorian Department Store* (New York, 1989).

125. Andrew R. Heinze, *Adapting to Abundance: Jewish Immigrants, Mass Consumption, and the Search for American Identity* (New York, 1990).

126. William R. Taylor, *In Pursuit of Gotham: Culture and Commerce in New York* (New York, 1992), xxiii; idem, ed., *Inventing Times Square: Commerce and Culture at the Crossroads of the World* (New York, 1991). For a later period see Leonard Wallock, ed., *New York: Culture Capital of the World, 1940–1965* (New York, 1988).

127. T. J. Jackson Lears, *No Place of Grace: Antimodernism and the Transformation of American Culture, 1880–1920* (New York, 1981).

128. John F. Kasson, *Rudeness and Civility: Manners in Nineteenth-Century Urban America* (New York, 1990). See also Richard Butsch, "Bowery B'hoys and Matinee Ladies: The Re-Gendering of Nineteenth-Century American Theater Audiences," *American Quarterly* 46 (September 1994): 374–405.

129. Susan G. Davis, *Parades and Power: Street Theatre in Nineteenth-Century Philadelphia* (Philadelphia, 1986); Mary P. Ryan, *Women in Public: Between Banners and Ballots, 1825–1880* (Baltimore, 1990); Robert C. Allen, *Horrible Prettiness: Burlesque and American Culture* (Chapel Hill, 1991); Robert W. Snyder, *The Voice of the City: Vaudeville and Popular Culture in New York* (New York, 1989); Kathy Peiss, *Cheap Amusements: Working Women and Leisure in Turn-of-the-Century New York* (Philadelphia, 1986); Lewis A. Erenberg, *Steppin' Out: New York Nightlife and the Transformation of American Culture, 1890–1930* (Westport, CT, 1981); Samuel Kinser, *Carnival American Style: Mardi Gras at New Orleans and Mobile* (Chicago, 1990); David Nassau, *Going Out: The Rise and Fall of Public Amusements* (New York, 1993); Burton W. Peretti, *The Creation of Jazz: Music, Race, and Culture in Urban America* (Urbana, 1992); Adrienne Siegel, *The Image of the American City in Popular Literature, 1820–1870* (Port Washington, NY, 1981); Maxine Seller, *Ethnic Theatre in the United States* (Westport, CT, 1983).

130. Lizabeth Cohen, *Making a New Deal: Industrial Workers in Chicago, 1919–1939* (Cambridge, England, 1990).

131. Steven A. Riess, *City Games: The Evolution of American Urban Society and the Rise of Sports* (Urbana, 1989).

132. Stephen Hardy, *How Boston Played: Sport, Recreation, and Community, 1865–1915* (Boston, 1982); Dale Somers, *The Rise of Sports in New Orleans, 1850–1900* (Baton Rouge, 1972); Steven A. Riess, *Touching Base: Professional Baseball and American Culture in the Progressive Era* (Westport, CT, 1980); Melvin A. Adelman, *A Sporting Time: New York City and the Rise of Modern Athletics, 1820–1870* (Urbana, 1986); Bruce Kuklick, *To Every Thing a Season: Shibe Park and Urban Philadelphia, 1909–1976* (Princeton, 1991); Elliott J. Gorn, *The Manly Art: Bare-Knuckle Prize Fighting in America* (Ithaca, NY, 1986); Jeffrey T. Sammons, *Beyond the Ring: The Role of Boxing in American Society* (Urbana, 1988); Kathryn Grover, ed., *Hard at Play: Leisure in America, 1840–1940* (Amherst, MA, 1992).

133. Dominick Cavallo, *Muscles and Morals: Organized Playgrounds and Urban Reform, 1880–1920* (Philadelphia, 1981); Peter Levine, *Ellis Island to Ebbets Field: Sport and the American Jewish Experience* (New York, 1992).

134. David W. Conroy, *In Public Houses: Drink and the Revolution of Authority in Colonial Massachusetts* (Chapel Hill, 1995).

135. Roy Rosenzweig, *Eight Hours for What We Will: Workers and Leisure in an Industrial City, 1870–1920* (Cambridge, England, 1983); Perry R. Duis, *The Saloon: Public Drinking in Chicago and Boston, 1880–1920* (Urbana, 1983); Thomas J. Noel, *The City and the Saloon: Denver, 1858–1916* (Lincoln, NE, 1982). See also Madelon Powers, "Decay from Within: The Inevitable Doom of the American Saloon," in Susanna Barrows and Robin Room, eds., *Drinking: Behavior and Belief in Modern History* (Berkeley, 1991), 112–31; and Mary Murphy, "Bootlegging Mothers and Drinking Daughters: Gender and Prohibition in Butte, Montana," *American Quarterly* 46 (June 1994): 174–94.

136. Timothy J. Gilfoyle, *City of Eros: New York City, Prostitution, and the Commercialization of Sex, 1790–1920* (New York, 1992); George Chauncey, *Gay New York: Gender, Urban Culture, and the Making of the Gay Male World, 1890–1940* (New York, 1994). See also Marilynn Wood Hill, *Their Sisters' Keepers: Prostitution in New York City, 1830–1870* (Berkeley, 1993).

137. Richard L. Bushman, *The Refinement of America: Persons, Houses, Cities* (New York, 1992).

138. Stuart M. Blumin, *The Emergence of the Middle Class: Social Experience in the American City, 1760–1900* (Cambridge, England, 1989).

139. Frederic Cople Jaher, *The Urban Establishment: Upper Strata in Boston, New York, Charleston, Chicago, and Los Angeles* (Urbana, 1982). See also Don H. Doyle, "History from the Top Down," *Journal of Urban History* 10 (November 1983): 103–14. For variations on the theme of class, culture, and power see Edward Pessen, *Riches, Class, and Power before the Civil War* (Lexington, MA, 1973); John S. Gilkeson, Jr., *Middle-Class Providence, 1820–1940* (Princeton, 1986); and William H. Pease and Jane H. Pease, *The Web of Progress: Private Values and Public Styles in Boston and Charleston, 1828–1843* (New York, 1985).

140. Thomas Bender, *New York Intellect: A History of Intellectual Life in New York City, From 1750 to the Beginnings of Our Own Time* (New York, 1987); idem, "The Cultures of Intellectual Life: The City and the Professions," in John Higham and Paul K. Conkin, eds., *New Directions in American Intellectual History* (Baltimore, 1979), 181–95; idem, "The Erosion of Public Culture: Cities, Discourses, and Professional Disciplines," in Thomas L. Haskell, ed., *The Authority of Experts: Studies in History and Theory* (Bloomington, 1984), 84–106.

141. For a sampling of this work see Christine Stansell, *City of Women: Sex and Class in New York, 1789–1860* (New York, 1986); Peter Bacon Hales, *Silver Cities: The Photography of American Urbanization, 1839–1915* (Philadelphia, 1984); Marianne Doezema, *George Bellows and Urban America* (New Haven, 1992); Robert A. M. Stern et al., *New York 1930: Architecture and Urbanism between the Two World Wars* (New York, 1987); Donald L. Miller, *Lewis Mumford: A Life* (New York, 1989); Robert A. Caro, *The Power Broker: Robert Moses and the Fall of New York* (New York, 1974); Carol Willis, *Form Follows Finance: Skyscrapers and Skylines in New York and Chicago* (New York, 1995); Mona Domash, *Invented Cities: The Creation of Landscape in Nineteenth-Century New York and Boston* (New Haven, 1996); Jenna W. Joselit, *Our Gang: Jewish Crime and the New York Jewish Community, 1900–1940* (Bloomington, 1983); M. Christine Boyer, *The City of Collective Memory: Its Historical Imagery and Architectural Entertainments* (Cambridge, 1994); Dolores Hayden, *The Power of Place: Urban Landscapes as Public History* (Cambridge, 1995); and Sidney H. Bremer, *Urban Intersections: Meetings of Life and Literature in the United States* (Urbana, 1992).

142. For guides to the scholarly journal literature see John D. Buenker, ed., *Urban History: A Guide to Information Sources* (Detroit, 1981); Neil Shumsky and Timothy Crimmins, eds., *Urban America: A Historical Bibliography* (Santa Barbara, 1983); and Dale E. Casper, ed., *Urban America Examined: A Bibliography* (New York, 1985). Also consult the key journal in the field, the *Journal of Urban History* (1974–present).

143. Bernard Bailyn, *History and the Creative Imagination* (St. Louis, 1985), 3; Thomas Bender, "Making History Whole Again," *New York Times Book Review*, October 6, 1985, 1, 42–43; idem, "Wholes and Parts: The Need for Synthesis in American History," *Journal of American History* 73 (June 1986): 120–36. But see also Eric H. Monkkonen, "The Dangers of Synthesis," *American Historical Review* 91 (December 1986): 1146–57.

144. Charles N. Glaab and A. Theodore Brown, *A History of Urban America* (3d ed., New York, 1983); Howard P. Chudacoff and Judith E. Smith, *The Evolution of American Urban Society* (4th ed., Englewood Cliffs, 1994); Zane L. Miller and Patricia M. Melvin, *The Urbanization of Modern America* (2d ed., San Diego, 1987); David R. Goldfield and Blaine A. Brownell, *Urban America: A History* (2d ed., Boston, 1990).

145. Raymond A. Mohl, *The New City: Urban America in the Industrial Age, 1860–1920* (Arlington Heights, IL, 1985); Carl Abbott, *Urban America in the Modern Age, 1920 to the Present* (Arlington Heights, IL, 1987); Jon C. Teaford, *The Twentieth-Century American City: Problem, Promise, and Reality* (2d ed., Baltimore, 1993); Eric H. Monkkonen, *America Becomes Urban: The Development of U.S. Cities and Towns, 1780–1980* (Berkeley, 1988).

# Index